MCSE/MCSA Windows® XP Professional Study Guide

(Exam 70-270)

MCSE/MCSA Windows® XP Professional Study Guide

(Exam 70-270)

Curt Simmons, MCSE, CTT

McGraw-Hill Osborne

New York Chicago San Francisco Lisbon London Madrid Mexico City Milan New Delhi San Juan Seoul Singapore Sydney Toronto

McGraw-Hill/Osborne
2600 Tenth Street
Berkeley, California 94710
U.S.A.

To arrange bulk purchase discounts for sales promotions, premiums, or fund-raisers, please contact McGraw-Hill/Osborne at the above address. For information on translations or book distributors outside the U.S.A., please see the International Contact Information page immediately following the index of this book.

MCSE/MCSA Windows® XP Professional Study Guide (Exam 70-270)

567890 DOC DOC 01987654

Book p/n 0-07-222298-0 and CD p/n 0-07-222299-9
parts of
ISBN 0-07-222297-2

Publisher
Brandon A. Nordin

Vice President & Associate Publisher
Scott Rogers

Editorial Director
Gareth Hancock

Associate Acquisitions Editor
Timothy Green

Project Editor
Jody McKenzie

Acquisitions Coordinator
Jessica Wilson

VP, Worldwide Business Development Global Knowledge
Richard Kristof

Technical Editor
Rory McCaw

Copy Editor
Carl Wikander

Indexer
Jack Lewis

Production and Editorial
Apollo Publishing Services

Series Design
Roberta Steele

Cover Design
Greg Scott

This book was published with Corel VENTURA™ Publisher.

FOREWORD

9000 Regency Parkway, Suite 500
Cary, NC 27512
1-800-COURSES
www.globalknowledge.com

From Global Knowledge

Global Knowledge supports many styles of learning. We deliver content through the written word, e-Learning, Classroom Learning, and Virtual Classroom Learning. We do this because we know our students need different training approaches to achieve success as technical professionals. This book series offers each reader a valuable tool for Microsoft certification.

Global Knowledge is the world's largest independent IT trainer. This uniquely positions us to offer these books. We have trained hundreds of thousands of students worldwide. Global Knowledge captured those years of expertise in this series. The quality of these books shows our commitment to your lifelong learning success.

For those of you who know Global Knowledge, or those of you who have just found us for the first time, our goal is to be your lifelong training partner. Global Knowledge commits itself daily to providing all learners with the very best training.

Thank you for choosing our training. We look forward to serving your needs again in the future.

Warmest regards,

Duncan Anderson
President and Chief Executive Officer, Global Knowledge

ABOUT THE CONTRIBUTORS

About the Author

Curt Simmons (B.A., M.Ed, MCSE, CTT) is a technology author, trainer, and courseware developer based in Dallas, Texas. Curt specializes in Windows operating systems and networking technologies, and he is the author of more than twenty books focusing on Windows and related networking technologies. He is also the author of *MCSE Internet Security* and *Acceleration Sever 2000 Study Guide*. When he is not writing or teaching, Curt spends his time with his wife and daughters. You can reach Curt at curt_simmons@hotmail.com.

About the Tech Editor

Rory McCaw is an independent certified technical trainer and a successful author of numerous technical books with more than five years of experience in information technology. Rory's interest in writing led him to courseware development, where he has designed courses focused on different Microsoft technologies. Rory holds numerous designations, including MCSE, MCT, and CTT. An accomplished speaker, Rory has developed and delivered presentations for Microsoft at Comdex and currently designs custom courses to meet the needs of his growing list of corporate clients.

For the last three years, Rory has been providing technical instruction to IT professionals and consulting for large organizations on enterprise implementations of IIS and Active Directory. Prior to training, Rory filled the role of Systems Administrator for an Internet start-up after graduating with a Bachelor Degree in Business Administration and a major in Management Information Systems.

ACKNOWLEDGMENTS

I would like to thank the following people:

- Richard Kristof of Global Knowledge for championing the series and providing access to some great people and information. In addition, David Marini, Duncan Anderson, Julie Ungaro, Rich Thompson, Richard Cleveland, and Ronda Swaney.
- All the incredibly hard-working folks at McGraw-Hill/Osborne: Brandon Nordin, Scott Rogers, Gareth Hancock, Tim Green, and Jessica Wilson for their help in launching a great series and being solid team players.
- Finally, special thanks to Rory McCaw for a great technical review, to Margot Maley Hutchinson, my literary agent, and to my family for their support.

CONTENTS AT A GLANCE

CONTENTS

PREFACE

Windows XP Professional is the latest iteration of the Windows product, bringing a number of new features to the Windows operating system and to the Windows 2000 networking environment. This book is designed to help you learn all about Windows XP Professional in preparation for Exam 70-270, Installing, Configuring, and Administering Windows XP Professional. The Windows XP Professional MCSE exam tests your XP knowledge when using Windows XP Professional in a Windows 2000/.NET network. Exam 70-270 explores many different installation, configuration, and administrative issues, and this book, along with your real-world experience and hands-on practice, can help you prepare for and pass the exam.

The Windows XP Professional exam counts as a core requirement in the Windows 2000 certification. The core requirements include passing scores for the Windows XP Professional *or* Windows 2000 Professional exam, the Windows 2000 Server exam, the Windows 2000 networking exam, and the Windows 2000 Active Directory exam. In keeping with Microsoft's certification tradition, the Windows XP Professional exam is challenging. You will need knowledge of Windows XP Professional both conceptually and as it functions on a Windows 2000/.NET network, and you will need hands-on experience in order to master the exam. This book is designed to help you be successful. Using the knowledge you gain from this book, the hands-on labs you perform, and the practice questions and exam, you will be ready to tackle Exam 70-270.

In This Book

This book is organized to serve as an in-depth review for the Windows XP Professional exam for both experienced Windows 2000 professionals and newcomers to Microsoft networking technologies. Each chapter covers a major aspect of the exam, with an emphasis on the "why" as well as the "how to" of working with and supporting Windows 2000 as a network administrator or engineer.

On the CD

This book includes a CD-ROM with simulation assessment and training and test preparation software, including more than one hour of instructional video, one hour of online training, and more than 50 test questions that appear only on the CD. For more information on the CD-ROM, please see Appendix A.

In Every Chapter

We've created a set of chapter components that call your attention to important items, reinforce important points, and provide helpful exam-taking hints. Take a look at what you'll find in every chapter:

- Every chapter begins with the **Certification Objectives**—what you need to know in order to pass the section of the exam dealing with the chapter topic. The Objective headings identify the objectives within the chapter, so you'll always know an objective when you see it!

- **Exam Watch** notes call attention to information about, and potential pitfalls in, the exam. These helpful hints are written by authors who have taken the exams and received their certification—who better to tell you what to worry about? They know what you're about to go through!

- **Practice Exercises** are interspersed throughout the chapters. These are step-by-step exercises that allow you to get the hands-on experience you need in order to pass the exam. They help you master skills that are likely to be an area of focus on the exam. Don't just read through the exercises; they are hands-on practice that you should be comfortable completing. Learning by doing is an effective way to increase your competency with a product. The practical exercises will be very helpful for any simulation exercises you may encounter on the MCSE Migrating from Windows NT 4.0 to Windows 2000 Exam.

- **On the Job** notes describe the issues that come up most often in real-world settings. They provide a valuable perspective on certification- and product-related topics. They point out common mistakes and address questions that have arisen from on the job discussions and experience.

- **From the Classroom** sidebars describe the issues that come up most often in the training classroom setting. These sidebars highlight some of the most common and confusing problems that students encounter when taking a live Windows 2000 training course. You can get a leg up on those difficult-to-understand subjects by focusing extra attention on these sidebars.
- **Scenario and Solution** sections lay out potential problems and solutions in a quick-to-read format:

SCENARIO & SOLUTION	
Does Windows XP Professional provide image-based installations?	Yes. Windows XP Professional supports both Remote Installation Service and System Preparation.
Can Remote Desktop be used with ICF?	Yes. You can use Remote Desktop with the Internet Connection Firewall, but you must configure ICF to allow Remote Desktop traffic.

- The **Certification Summary** is a succinct review of the chapter and a restatement of salient points regarding the exam.

- The **Two-Minute Drill** at the end of every chapter is a checklist of the main points of the chapter. It can be used for last-minute review.

- The **Self Test** offers questions similar to those found on the certification exams. The answers to these questions, as well as explanations of the answers, can be found at the end of each chapter. By taking the Self Test after completing each chapter, you'll reinforce what you've learned from that chapter while becoming familiar with the structure of the exam questions.
- The **Lab Question** at the end of the Self Test section offers a unique and challenging question that requires the reader to understand multiple chapter concepts to answer correctly. These questions are more complex and more comprehensive than the other questions, as they test your ability to take all the knowledge you have gained from reading the chapter and apply it to complicated, real-world situations. These questions are aimed to be more difficult than what you will find on the exam. If you can answer these questions, you have proven that you know the subject!

The Global Knowledge Web Site

Check out the Web site. Global Knowledge invites you to become an active member of the Access Global Web site. This site is an online mall and an information repository that you'll find invaluable. You can access many types of products to assist you in your preparation for the exam, and you'll be able to participate in forums, online discussions, and threaded discussions. No other book brings you unlimited access to such a resource. You'll find more information about this site in Appendix B.

Some Pointers

Once you've finished reading this book, set aside some time to do a thorough review. You might want to return to the book several times and make use of all the methods it offers for reviewing the material:

1. *Reread all the Two-Minute Drills*, or have someone quiz you. You also can use the drills as a way to do a quick cram before the exam. You might want to make some flash cards out of 3 × 5 index cards that have the Two-Minute Drill material on them.
2. *Reread all the Exam Watch notes.* Remember that these notes are written by authors who have taken the exam and passed. They know what you should expect—and what you should be on the lookout for.
3. *Review all the S&S sections* for quick problem solving examples.
4. *Retake the Self Tests.* Taking the tests right after you've read the chapter is a good idea, because the questions help reinforce what you've just learned. However, it's an even better idea to go back later and do all the questions in the book in one sitting. Pretend that you're taking the live exam. (When you go through the questions the first time, you should mark your answers on a separate piece of paper. That way, you can run through the questions as many times as you need to until you feel comfortable with the material.)
5. *Complete the Exercises.* Did you do the exercises when you read through each chapter? If not, do them! These exercises are designed to cover exam topics,

and there's no better way to get to know this material than by practicing. Be sure you understand why you are performing each step in each exercise. If there is something you are not clear on, reread that section in the chapter.

INTRODUCTION

Welcome to the Windows XP Professional Study Guide. This book is all you need to master the concepts that you are likely to see on Exam 70-270. This book is written so you can study each individual exam objective and then use the knowledge you gain in order to tackle those difficult and often tricky Microsoft exam questions. The Windows XP Professional exam tests your knowledge of installing, configuring, and administering Windows XP on a Windows 2000/.NET network. This book's exploration of the functionality and use of Windows XP will help you meet the exam's objectives and provide you with the knowledge that the exam expects you to have.

The Windows XP Professional exam is a core exam option for Windows 2000 MCSE certification. This means that you have the option to take the Windows XP Professional exam or the Windows 2000 Professional exam as one of your core exams. Since Windows XP is the newest Microsoft operating system exam in this track, your choice to take Exam 70-270 will show people in the industry that you have cutting edge skills with the latest Microsoft technologies. Some of you are probably new to the certification game—in fact, this may be your first exam, or you may be updating your certification to Windows 2000. Regardless of your status, this book is your best source of information, along with real-world experience and hands-on practice, for passing Exam 70-270.

MCSE Certification

This book is designed to help you pass the MCSE Windows XP Professional exam (Exam 70-270). As previously mentioned, the Windows XP Professional exam serves as a possible core requirement for MCSE certification. This means that you have the option of taking the Windows XP Professional exam *or* the Windows 2000 Professional exam. Either exam can count as the workstation core requirement.

In addition to the Windows XP Professional or Windows 2000 Professional exam, you must also pass three additional core requirement exams, one design exam, and two elective exams. The following table outlines the requirements and options for you.

The following table lists the requirements at the time of this writing. Requirements and exam availability changes from time to time, so you should get in the habit of checking *http://www.microsoft.com/traincert* ***periodically so that you are aware of any program changes that might occur.***

Windows 2000 Certification Track

Core Exams
Exam 70-270: Installing, Configuring, and Administering Microsoft Windows XP Professional, *or* **Exam 70-210:** Installing, Configuring, and Administering Microsoft Windows 2000 Professional
Exam 70-215: Installing, Configuring and Administering Microsoft® Windows® 2000 Server
Exam 70-216: Implementing and Administering a Microsoft® Windows® 2000 Network Infrastructure
Exam 70-217: Implementing and Administering a Microsoft® Windows® 2000 Directory Services Infrastructure
PLUS—All Candidates—*One of the Following Core Exams Required:*
Exam 70-219: Designing a Microsoft® Windows® 2000 Directory Services Infrastructure
Exam 70-220: Designing Security for a Microsoft® Windows® 2000 Network
Exam 70-221: Designing a Microsoft® Windows® 2000 Network Infrastructure
PLUS—All Candidates—*Two Elective Exams Required:*
Any current MCSE electives. Electives scheduled for retirement will not be considered current. Selected third-party certifications that focus on interoperability will be accepted as an alternative to one elective exam. At the time of this writing, the following exams are available as elective exams:
Exam 70-085: Implementing and Supporting Microsoft SNA Server 4.0
Exam 70-086: Implementing and Supporting Microsoft Systems Management Server 2.0
Exam 70-019: Designing and Implementing Data Warehouses with Microsoft SQL Server 7.0
Exam 70-029: Designing and Implementing Databases with Microsoft SQL Server 7.0 *or* **Exam 70-229:** Designing and Implementing Databases with Microsoft SQL Server 2000 Enterprise Edition
Exam 70-028: Administering Microsoft SQL Server 7.0 *or* **Exam 70-228:** Installing, Configuring, and Administering Microsoft SQL Server 2000 Enterprise Edition
Exam 70-056: Implementing and Supporting Web Sites Using Microsoft Site Server 3.0
Exam 70-081: Implementing and Supporting Microsoft Exchange Server 5.5 *or* **Exam 70-224:** Installing, Configuring, and Administering Microsoft Exchange 2000 Server

PLUS—All Candidates—*Two Elective Exams Required:* (cont.)
Exam 70-088: Implementing and Supporting Microsoft Proxy Server 2.0 or Installing, Configuring, and Administering Microsoft Internet Security and Acceleration (ISA) Server 2000, Enterprise Edition
Exam 70-080: Implementing and Supporting Microsoft Internet Explorer 5.0 by Using the Microsoft Internet Explorer Administration Kit
Exam 70-218: Managing a Microsoft Windows 2000 Network Environment
Exam 70-219: Designing a Microsoft Windows 2000 Directory Services Infrastructure
Exam 70-220: Designing Security for a Microsoft Windows 2000 Network
Exam 70-221: Designing a Microsoft Windows 2000 Network Infrastructure
Exam 70-222: Migrating from Microsoft Windows NT 4.0 to Microsoft Windows 2000
Exam 70-223: Installing, Configuring, and Administering Microsoft Clustering Services by Using Microsoft Windows 2000 Advanced Server
Exam 70-226: Designing Highly Available Web Solutions with Microsoft Windows 2000 Server Technologies
Exam 70-230: Designing and Implementing Solutions with Microsoft BizTalk Server 2000 Enterprise Edition
Exam 70-232: Implementing and Maintaining Highly Available Web Solutions with Microsoft Windows 2000 Server Technologies and Microsoft Application Center 2000
Exam 70-234: Designing and Implementing Solutions with Microsoft Commerce Server 2000
Exam 70-244: Supporting and Maintaining a Microsoft Windows NT Server 4.0 Network

How to Take a Microsoft Certification Exam

Microsoft certification exams are complex and difficult, in a number of ways. The exams expect you to have solid conceptual knowledge of the exam objectives, yet you must also have hands-on experience in order to master the exam questions. Put these two elements with a time limit and a lot of reading, and there is no doubt that even the most seasoned test takers—myself included!—find the Microsoft exams nerve-racking.

Yet, despite the difficultly, thousands of people have mastered these exams—and you can as well. The difficulty in the Windows 2000/.NET certification track is that exam objectives overlap. Sure, in the Windows XP Professional exam, you are primarily focused on the local operating system, but you also have to know a few things about

Windows 2000 Server, the Active Directory, and Group Policy. In other words, your real-world IT work will not function in discrete segments, but rather your knowledge must be somewhat global. The exams take this approach too. Yes, this book will help you prepare for Exam 70-270, but I'm expecting that you bring some experience and prior knowledge to the table. If you are just getting started in the IT business, you should consider studying some general Windows 2000 networking books before tackling certification—this will make your likelihood of success much higher.

The Windows XP Professional exam expects you to be a Microsoft product expert. This means that you have to know the ins and outs of Windows XP, but you must also know how to use and configure Windows XP on a Windows 2000/.NET network. In order to test your knowledge, you are likely to see the following kinds of questions:

- Conceptual questions: Conceptual questions are designed to test your knowledge. You'll be asked a question and you must provide the technically correct answer.
- Interface/Diagram questions: In order to test your real-world knowledge of Windows XP Professional, you may see questions that give you portions of the XP interface or questions that give you a network diagram. You must then examine the interface and correctly answer the question.
- Scenarios: Most all questions on the exam are scenario based. This means you will be put into a situation where an problem is at hand, and then you will be asked to solve the problem. Even when the question is a basic conceptual question, you'll find that the exam often gives a long (and often unnecessarily detailed) scenario concerning that question.

Test Structure

Like all good test takers, you want to know what the test will be like, especially if you have never taken a Microsoft exam before. If you have taken a Microsoft exam, you can expect the same kinds of questions and formats as you have seen in the past.

Question Types

Let's first consider the question types that you are likely to see on the exam. The concepts in the following sections apply to the Windows XP Professional exam, but you will also see these same formats on other exams as well.

Multiple Choice

Almost all questions on the exam are structured in a multiple choice format. This means that you will see a question and several possible answers. You must click the correct answer in order to get the question right. Some questions require two or more answers, while others say "Choose all that apply." However, the great majority of the exam questions give you a question for which there is one correct answer. For example:

> Susan is a user on your network. Susan's laptop computer was recently upgraded to Windows XP Professional. Susan travels frequently with her laptop, giving sales presentations at various client sites. Susan needs to make certain that she is able to use Windows XP's hibernation feature. However, Susan reports that hibernation is unavailable. You check Susan's computer and discover that the Advanced Power Configuration Interface (ACPI) is not supported in the current computer's BIOS. You install a new BIOS on the computer. What must you do now?
>
> A. Enable Hibernation.
>
> B. Reinstall Windows XP Professional.
>
> C. Run the File and Settings Transfer Wizard.
>
> D. Enable the L2TP protocol.
>
> As you can see, you are presented with a scenario problem and asked to choose the correct answer. By the way, the correct answer here is B. When you upgrade a computer's BIOS, you must reinstall Windows XP Professional.

Graphical Questions

Some questions will contain a screen capture of the interface or a network diagram. When you read the question on the screen, you will need to click the Exhibit button to see the picture. You must then inspect the picture and make a decision about the correct answer. The question is still a multiple choice question, but the exhibit simply helps you answer the question correctly. For example:

A user in your company travels frequently with his laptop computer. When the user is away from the office, he primarily uses battery power. During meetings, the user often accesses the laptop, and then the laptop may be idle for an hour or more. You need to configure the laptop to conserve as much power as possible while still being readily available to the user. Consider the current Power Options configuration:

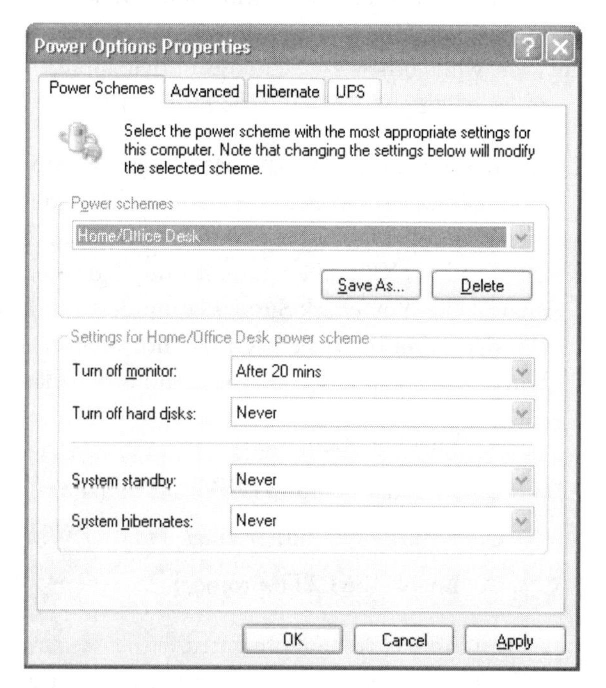

What do you need to change in order to conserve power while keeping the laptop readily available?

A. Turn the monitor off after 10 minutes of inactivity.

B. Turn on System Stand by after 10 minutes of inactivity.

C. Configure hibernation to become active after 10 minutes of inactivity.

D. Turn off the hard disk after 10 minutes of inactivity.

As you can see, you simply review the current setting and determine what needs to be changed in order to meet the needs. In this case, the best answer is B. System Standby conserves the most power without shutting down the system (which hibernation does), so that the system saves power and is readily available.

The trick with graphical questions is to keep in mind that the picture is provided to help you answer the question. Do not get so bogged down in the graphic that you lose sight of the question and what the question *really* wants you to do.

Free Response Questions

More than likely, your entire Windows XP Professional exam will be made up of multiple choice questions. However, you may encounter free response questions, which are usually configured in drag-and-drop fashion. For example, a question may ask you to provide a series of steps in order to complete some action. You'll see the steps listed, and you have to drag and drop those steps so that they appear in the correct order. Again, you may not see even a single question of this type on this exam, but don't be surprised if you do.

Knowledge-Based and Performance-Based Questions

As I have mentioned, the exam consists of knowledge-based and performance-based questions. Often, questions contain a mix of the two question types. Keep in mind that knowledge-based questions require a technical answer from memory, while performance-based questions put you in situations where you must choose the best action. The idea is that the exam tests your real-world experience along with your technical knowledge.

Let's consider a few examples. First, here is a basic knowledge-based question:

You need to configure a VPN connection with a Windows XP Professional computer and a Windows NT 4.0 RRAS Server. In order to configure the connection, which protocol should be used?

A. PPTP

B. L2TP

C. FTP

D. HTTP

This is a simple knowledge-based question. In order to answer the question correctly, you have to know that VPN connections use either the PPTP or L2TP protocols. However, Windows NT Server 4.0 supports only PPTP, so A is the correct answer. This is a simple knowledge question.

Most questions that you will see on the exam will try to combine both knowledge-based concepts and real-world experience. For example:

Your company uses a firewall in order to protect network users and sensitive information. You need to configure a Windows XP Professional computer for Remote Desktop with another Windows XP Professional computer. One computer is located at a remote office, while the second computer is located on the network. You configure the computers for Remote Desktop, but you are unable to connect to the computer on the network. What needs to be done?

A. Configure the firewall to allow Remote Desktop traffic.

B. Make the network computer a member server.

C. Configure the external computer to allow TCP port 4483.

D. Configure the internal computer's ICF.

This question combines both knowledge-based information and real-world experience. You have to know the acronyms and connection issues that come into play in order to answer the question. The correct answer is A. By default, firewalls do not automatically allow remote desktop traffic, so the firewall will have to be configured to allow the traffic to pass. The Windows XP Professional exam will not ask you specific questions about how to configure the firewall, but you have to know enough to be aware of what is causing the problem.

Study and Testing Strategies

In order to successfully pass Exam 70-270, you'll need to study hard, but you'll also need to study smartly. This means that you'll need to use this book and your time wisely. I've taken many Microsoft exams and taught many classes to students taking the exams, and the following format works best for most people:

1. Study each chapter. I recommend that you take notes when you study the chapter. Most people remember technical information more accurately if

they write the information down. Highlighting huge sections of the chapter will normally not help you, although some highlighting may be beneficial. Review the Certification summaries and Key Point Summaries at the end of the chapters.

2. Once you have studied the chapter, take the quiz and perform the lab exercise at the end of the chapter. The quiz and the lab exercise are designed to test your knowledge of the chapter's content. If you miss some questions, make sure you review the missed material before moving on.
3. Make sure you perform the hands-on lab exercises. There is no replacement for hands-on practice, so make sure you have a Windows XP Professional computer that you can practice on. Explore! Try different settings and configurations! Get your hands dirty!
4. Continue this same process until you have studied the entire book. Then, go back and review all key point summaries and all quizzes.
5. Take the practice exam on the CD-ROM. The practice exam contains questions similar in style and content to that you may see on the exam. The practice exam is a good measuring tool for determining how ready you are for the exam.

Once you have studied carefully and smartly, you are ready to take the exam. When you are taking the exam, I recommend the following strategies:

- Relax. Sure, the exam is important, but it does not define you as a person. If you fail the exam, you can always take it over again, and if you are very nervous about the exam, you probably will not do well.
- Remember that the exam is timed. This doesn't mean that you have to be in a ridiculous hurry, but you can't spend twenty minutes on a single question either.
- Rule out answers that are incorrect. If you are unsure of an answer, try ruling out answer options that you know are incorrect. This will help narrow your decision and increase the odds that you will answer the question correctly.
- Answer every question. Unanswered questions are counted as incorrect, so if you simply do not know the answer to a question, make your best guess.
- The exam contains a "mark" feature. This allows you to mark a question for review at the end of the exam so you can change your answer (if you have time).

The mark feature can be helpful, but only mark questions that you may have a reasonable chance of answering correctly. If you simply do not know the answer to the question, take a guess and move on. Spend your time on questions that you at least have a chance of answering correctly.

- Do not skip questions. If you do not know or are unsure of the answer, take a guess and move on. You may not have time to return to the question, and unanswered questions are counted as incorrect.
- Make sure you know what the question is asking. Some questions will be confusing and give you a lot of information that you really don't need. Always ask yourself "What does the question *really* want to know?"
- Use scratch paper. The testing center will provide you with as much scratch paper as you want. Use the scratch paper to help untangle complicated questions or sketch diagrams when necessary.

Signing Up

Microsoft exams are administered by Sylvan Prometric and Virtual University Enterprises (VUE). A testing center is near you, and you can find it and register for an exam by visiting one of these:

- **www.prometric.com**
- **www.vue.com**

Regardless of the testing company you choose to go with, the exam and the fee will be the same. When you sign up for a test, you'll need to provide your contact information and social security number, the exam number you are signing up for, the testing center at which you want to test, and a payment method (credit card or voucher). See Prometric's and Vue's Web sites for more details.

When You Take the Test

And finally, here's a few tips to remember on test day:

- You need two forms of ID in order to take the exam—and one of them has to be a picture ID. A driver's license and social security card work well.
- You cannot take anything into the testing center except a pen or pencil. Sorry, you can't take this book along for the ride.
- Schedule the exam during a time of the day when you are most alert. If you are a morning person, take the exam during the morning—if you are an afternoon/evening person, take the exam then. Do yourself a favor and give yourself the best edge possible.
- Don't take the exam on an empty stomach. Food fuels the brain, so eat a modest, balanced meal before the exam. Avoid excessive caffeine or alcohol before the exam—both of these drugs impair your ability to think clearly and to take the exam in a calm manner.
- If you feel yourself getting overwhelmed during the exam, pause for moment, close your eyes, and count backward from 20 to 1. This will help calm you down. You can take a break if you like, but the exam clock keeps ticking.
- Finally, keep a good perspective. You probably will not answer every question correctly, and that is okay. Just remember to work carefully and pace yourself. Apply what you know and take the exam questions for what they really are—questions to test your knowledge and skills.

1

Introduction to the Windows XP Professional Exam

CERTIFICATION OBJECTIVES

1.01	What Is Installing, Configuring, and Administering Microsoft Windows XP Professional?
1.02	Overview of Exam 70-270
1.03	What Is Covered in this Book
1.04	What You Should Already Know
✓	Two-Minute Drill
Q&A	Self Test

Welcome to Microsoft's Windows XP Professional and Exam 70-270. Exam 70-270 is one of two optional core requirements for Windows 2000 certification, which allows certification candidates to choose between Windows XP Professional and Windows 2000 Professional. As Microsoft's newest operating system at the time of this writing, Windows XP Professional brings rich functionality, as well as fun, to the Windows 2000 code.

You can think of Windows XP Professional as an operating system that has the power of Windows 2000 (if not more) and the friendliness of Windows Me. In fact, a number of Windows Me features, such as System Restore and Movie Maker, are available in Windows XP Professional. However, let there be no mistake, Windows XP Professional is a business machine that takes full advantage of the Windows 2000 code and all that Windows 2000 has to offer—with some new additions and features of its own. In short, Windows XP, both Home and Professional versions, is the new operating system of choice among home users and complex office networks where speed, friendliness, and powerful networking capabilities are a must. Wrap all of this together with a new interface, and Windows XP provides what many home and office users have been waiting for.

As an IT professional, you are expected by Microsoft to be able to install, configure, and administer Windows XP Professional, primarily in a networking environment. To test your job skills, Exam 70-270 is provided as a core requirement for Windows 2000 certification. This exam helps prove to employers that you are ready to tackle the issues and challenges that await you in an XP networking environment. Exam 70-270 is a core optional exam (with Windows 2000 Professional) for the Microsoft Certified Professional (MCP) and Microsoft Certified Systems Engineer (MCSE) certifications. Passing this exam will prove that you, as a networking professional, have the skills to implement and manage this powerful and popular new Microsoft product.

CERTIFICATION OBJECTIVE 1.01

What Is Installing, Configuring, and Administering Microsoft Windows XP Professional?

I've taken many Microsoft exams, and whenever I look at an exam title and see the words "installing, configuring, and administering," I always think to myself, "So the exam can ask virtually anything!"—and that sentiment is right. Exam 70-270 expects you to know almost everything about Windows XP Professional—from planning a deployment to solving implementation and administration problems. However, don't feel overwhelmed, because this book is designed to give you knowledge and technical skills you'll need to master Exam 70-270. In order to understand all that the exam covers, it is important to spend a few moments considering a broad overview of Windows XP Professional. The following sections explore the primary features of Windows XP Professional so you can fully understand the type of content on which the exam is likely to focus.

What Is Windows XP Professional?

Windows XP Professional is Microsoft's contribution to desktop and networking power and friendliness. It is the first true end-user system (considering the Home and Professional editions) that incorporates the power of Windows 2000 and the friendliness of Windows Me. Also, with a new interface design that is less cluttered and highly configurable, Windows XP Professional is easy for the new user to master and complex enough to interest the advanced user. In the following sections, I'll give you a brief overview of some of Windows XP Professional's features (from the perspective of the exam). This is meant to be an overview, not a comprehensive review. Of course, the best introduction to the operating system is to simply get your hands on the keyboard and explore!

New Look and Feel

Windows XP Professional, along with Windows XP Home edition, provides a new interface for users. With this interface, you'll see a simplification of Windows menus and the desktop, which is now typically clean except for the Recycle Bin. The Start

Menu, which you can see in Figure 1-1, gives you more items than previously, as well as expandable menus that you can choose to configure. By accessing the Start Menu and Taskbar properties, you can completely configure the way the system looks, and you completely customize the items you see on the Start Menu. The idea is to provide a complex operating system that does not overwhelm the user. Users can configure the items they need to see, while allowing other items to remain hidden. You can also choose to use the "classic" Start Menu view as well. The new Windows XP interface is a "theme" applied to Windows XP by default. However, you can completely remove the default Windows XP interface simply by choosing a different theme, such as the Windows Classic theme, or you can even get new themes from the Internet.

By accessing Display Properties, shown in Figure 1-2, you see that Windows XP Professional makes use of the theme concept, with "Windows XP" functioning as a theme. You can choose to return to the classic Windows settings if you like, or you can choose to use a completely different theme.

FIGURE 1-1

Windows XP Professional Start Menu

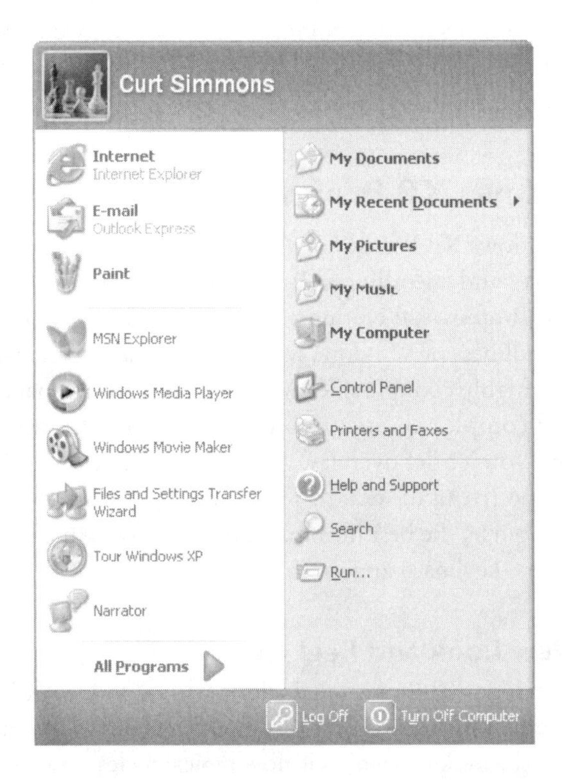

FIGURE 1-2

XP functions as a theme.

You'll also see a more graphical, streamlined view through the system. Folders are very easy to use and even suggest tasks to users. The Windows XP Professional Control Panel, shown in Figure 1-3, also hides its typical icon list and tries to help users in a task-based manner through a category view. Again, here you can also switch to classic view and use Windows XP in a way that works for you. Overall, the new XP look is easier, provides more options, and makes the operating system more interesting for end users.

Windows 2000 Tools

If you have spent any time working with Windows 2000 Professional or Windows 2000 Server, you'll quickly recognize many of the features of Windows XP Professional. Here are some examples of the features:

- Windows XP Professional is designed for the NTFS file system, which provides the greatest security and management features of any file system. Even the Home edition of Windows XP prefers NTFS.
- The Microsoft Management Console (MMC) is heavily utilized for a number of utilities and features. As with Windows 2000, you even create customized MMC consoles by adding standalone snap-ins, as shown in Figure 1-4.

FIGURE 1-3

The new Windows XP control provides a category view.

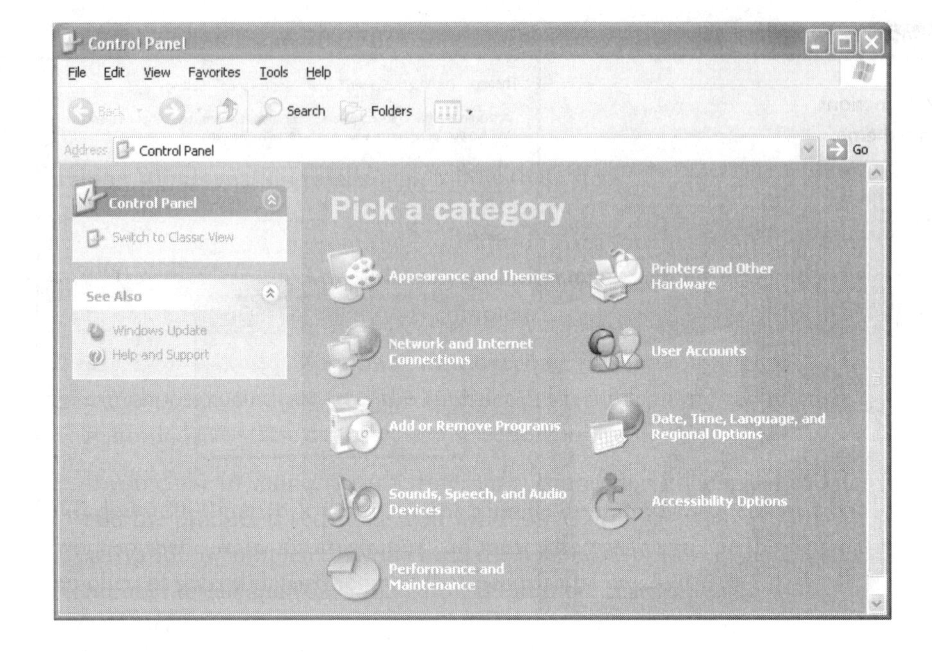

FIGURE 1-4

The MMC and Standalone Snap-ins are provided in Windows XP Professional.

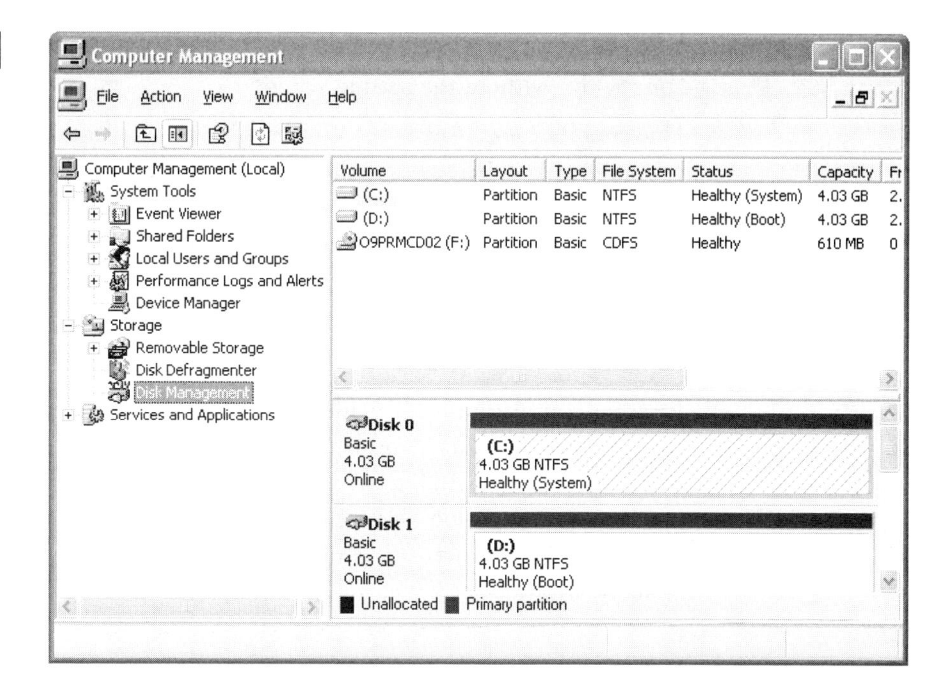

FIGURE 1-5 The Computer Management console provides a centralized location for configuration functions.

- Common management tools also appear in Windows XP Professional, including Performance and the Computer Management console, shown in Figure 1-5. Local Users and Groups, Shared Folders, Event Viewer, Device Manager, Disk Management, and a number of other tools are readily available.

Networking

Windows XP Professional is a true network operating system. It provides the features and functionality as well as the security technology to make it the operating system of choice for large Microsoft networks as well as the operating system of choice for the home or small office user. Although the exam focuses on Windows XP Professional as the operating system for larger networks, it is an operating system that can essentially function anywhere. Regardless of your networking needs, Windows XP Professional can meet the goal. Following are some examples you can use for networking:

- For the home or small office user, Windows XP Professional can automatically assign itself an IP address and auto-configure TCP/IP settings. In the domain environment, Windows XP Professional is fully compatible with Windows 2000 networking and can function with DHCP and DNS network servers.

You can make changes to Windows XP Professional's IP configuration "on the fly" without the need to reboot.

- Universal Plug and Play makes Windows XP an excellent choice for a network operating system because Windows XP can more easily detect network media and automatically install the necessary drivers to function with that media.
- Aside from local area networking, Windows XP Professional can easily function in a variety of roles. For example, Windows XP Professional can be used as a dial-up server or as a Web server, and it can be used to establish virtual private networks.
- Internet connectivity is provided via modem or broadband connectivity (or LAN connectivity), and Internet Explorer 6 is the most secure version of IE ever produced. Additionally, home and small office users can take advantage of Internet Connection Sharing, in which one computer is connected to the Internet and other network computers use the Internet via that connection. A simple wizard helps home and small office users configure these connections.

New Features

Along with the new desktop and interface design, Windows XP Professional does come with some additional new features that can be of assistance. This list does not address every addition, but here are some of the more important ones:

- **File and Settings Transfer Wizard** The new File and Settings Transfer Wizard helps you easily migrate settings and files from other XP installations or earlier versions of Windows. Using the network or removable media, you can easily move files and settings from one system to another. This feature provides you with an easy way to move files, system settings, e-mail configuration, and even e-mail itself to a new computer system. Long gone are the aggravating days of moving data from one computer to another manually—now you can do it quickly and easily with the help of a wizard.
- **Program Compatibility Wizard** The new Program Compatibility Wizard helps users maintain programs while moving to the new operating system. The Program Compatibility Wizard can "act like" a previous version of Windows so that older software can run on Windows XP. The wizard supports hundreds of older programs and can make the operating system provide the necessary

API calls and responses to older programs so that you avoid those famous "lock ups"—in theory, at least.

- **Remote Assistance/Remote Desktop** You can assist users over the Internet using Remote Assistance, and you can even run a computer remotely using Remote Desktop. These features give you the flexibility you need and greatly assist help centers in larger networking environments. Using Remote Assistance, you can accept a Remote Assistance invitation from a user and connect to that user's computer over the intranet or Internet. You can then see the user's desktop and can even take control of the computer to troubleshoot and configure it. Remote Desktop, which works with terminal services, enables you to remotely connect with another computer and use that computer. For example, Remote Desktop is highly effective in instances in which you need to connect to an office computer from home or vice versa.
- **Internet Connection Firewall (ICF)** The new firewall is designed to work with ICS and help home or small office users protect their computers and networks from Internet attacks. ICF works by keeping a table of listing the data that you have explicitly requested from Internet Explorer. For example, let's say you enter **www.microsoft.com** in your Web browser. ICF records this request in the table. When the Web page arrives from **Microsoft.com**, ICF recognizes that the data has been requested and allows it to enter the firewall. Any data that arrives at the firewall that has not been explicitly requested is dropped, which helps ward off hacker attacks.

CERTIFICATION OBJECTIVE 1.02

Overview of Exam 70-270

Exam 70-270 is designed to test your knowledge of installing, configuring, and administering Microsoft Windows XP Professional. Specifically, the exam expects you to have the installation, configuration, and administration knowledge for using Windows XP Professional in a Microsoft network environment. In other words, you can expect the exam to focus on Windows XP Professional in terms of network connectivity and functionality. Since Microsoft networking essentially defines the MCP

FROM THE CLASSROOM

All Things to All People

At first glance, it may appear that Windows XP is trying to be all things to all people. In a sense, that is true. After all, Windows XP Professional is a great home or small office system. It provides you with everything you need, including Internet connectivity, and helps you manage a small home or office network. With file sharing and NTFS permissions and easy user account setup, Windows XP Professional has everything the home user might want. On the other side of the scale, Windows XP Professional has the power and security features that enable it to participate on a large LAN or WAN. Complex networking features such as EFS, NTFS permissions, and IIS can be used to make Windows XP Professional a simple desktop operating system on the network, or it can function as a file server, print server, or Web server. Is Windows XP Professional the right thing for all people? At this point in time, it is the closest Microsoft has ever come!

SCENARIO & SOLUTION

Scenario	Solution
Can Windows XP Professional host intranet Web sites?	Yes. IIS is available in Windows XP, and since Windows XP prefers the NTFS file system, you can securely host intranet sites.
When should the automatic IP addressing feature of Windows XP Professional be used?	The automatic IP address assignment feature of Windows XP is designed for small office or home networks where there is no Windows domain. In other words, a workgroup setting is the perfect place. On a Windows domain, however, a DHCP server typically handles the IP address assignment task.
How does ICF work?	Basically, ICF keeps a table of requested information from the Internet. Information that comes back from the Internet must match a request before it is allowed into the system. Information that does not match the request or information that attempts to use an incorrect TCP port or protocol is dropped.

and MCSE certifications, you will not see many questions—if any at all—that focus on home or even small office configurations.

Exam 70-270 builds on basic Windows 2000 knowledge and assumes that you have hands-on experience working with Windows XP Professional in a Microsoft network environment. Because of the real-world experience factor, the exam does not narrowly focus on single objectives. Instead, you are likely to see questions that combine a number of objectives into a scenario. Will you see questions that seem outside of the exam scope? Probably yes. Because Microsoft expects your knowledge to be holistic, you are likely to see questions concerning installation and administration of Windows XP Professional via a Windows 2000 Server, the Active Directory, and Group Policy. In other words, Microsoft sees your education and technical knowledge as global and not specifically defined to one product. This is why you can expect the Windows XP Professional exam to overlap with other exams.

Audience Profile

As you are beginning your Exam 70-270 studies, it is important to consider the audience for which this exam was developed and to make sure you fit into that audience profile. This exam is designed for IT professionals who work in medium to very large networking environments that use Windows XP Professional as the desktop operating system. The exam assumes these network environments use Windows 2000, including all of the features of a Windows 2000 network, such as Group Policy, DNS, Active Directory, and so on. You should have a minimum of one year's experience in implementing and administering network operating systems in such an environment.

The reality, of course, is that not all of us work in environments with those kinds of specifications. So, does that mean you cannot pass the exam? No, not at all. What it does mean is that the exam was written with this audience in mind, so you'll need to take a close look at the audience profile and your own skills and then determine how you can study and practice using Windows XP Professional and, ideally, Windows 2000 Server as well. You may need to study harder and spend more time working with Windows XP and Windows 2000 Server concepts, but this book will help guide you through that study process.

SCENARIO & SOLUTION	
I have not taken any of the Windows 2000 exams, but I did pass the NT 4.0 exams. Should I take the Windows XP Professional exam now?	Yes. You can start your Windows 2000 certification with Windows XP Professional, but it wouldn't hurt for you to study for the server and Active Directory exam before taking the XP exam. Remember that exams may overlap.
Should I spend some time working with Windows 2000 Server and the Active Directory before taking the Windows XP Professional exam?	Yes. Exam content overlaps, and you should spend some time working with Windows 2000 Server's networking functionality, Group Policy, and deployment strategies.
Is the Windows XP Professional exam very different from the Windows 2000 Professional exam?	The exams' contents are very similar, and many of the objectives are the same. You can expect the XP exam to focus more on new features that XP offers.

Getting Ready

Before taking Exam 70-270, I recommend a three-part preparation process that will help you be successful on exam day:

- **Study this book and get hands-on practice.** This book is designed to be all you need to master Exam 70-270, but you need to make use of all of the book's components in order be successful. Be sure to practice and study all of the chapter content and chapter questions carefully. Then, use the book's CD-ROM to further practice and test your skills. You also need hands-on practice with Windows XP Professional. The CD-ROM in this book provides you with an evaluation version of Windows XP Professional. You may also want to install and practice using Windows 2000 Server. Downloadable trial versions of the server software are available at **www.microsoft.com/windows2000**.
- **Check for updates.** Although they rarely do, exam certification objectives *can* change from time to time. So you should get in the habit of periodically checking **http://www.microsoft.com/trainingandservices** for updates to Exam 70-270 or the MCP program in general. Also, as you are studying Windows XP Professional, keep a check on **http://www.microsoft.com/windowsxp** for late-breaking news and product updates.

- **Explore the exam format.** If you are somewhat unfamiliar with Microsoft exams or just the new Windows 2000 exams, you can download some sample versions at **http://www.microsoft.com/trainingandservices** so you can see the exam format you might have. Be advised that the exams may give you scenario-based questions or interface questions where you are required to configure portions of Windows XP Professional. Perfect practice makes perfect performance, so know what to expect before arriving at the testing center.

Exploring the Exam Objectives

You can access the Windows XP Professional exam objectives by visiting **http://www.microsoft.com/trainingandservices**. The exam objectives are the primary skills being measured on the exam. It is important that you understand the major focus of those exam objectives, and the following sections review them so you'll know what to expect.

Installing Windows XP Professional

The exam expects you to know how to prepare for a Windows XP Professional installation, install the OS, and resolve installation problems. Specifically, you can expect the exam to focus on the following topics:

- **Perform an attended installation of Windows XP Professional.** You'll need to know the process for CD or over-the-network installations of Windows XP Professional.
- **Perform an unattended installation of Windows XP Professional.** You'll need to know how to use Setup Manager to create answer files for an unattended installation and how to use Remote Installation Services. You will also need to know about the features and functionality of System Preparation.
- **Upgrade from a previous version of Windows to Windows XP Professional.** The exam will test you on upgrade strategies, issues, and support. You'll need to know how to prepare a computer to meet upgrade requirements and how to migrate existing user settings to a new installation of Windows XP Professional.

- **Perform post-installation updates and product activation.** This objective covers service packs and fixes, as well as Windows XP's new product activation feature.
- **Troubleshoot failed installations.** For the most part, Windows XP Professional installation is very easy, but you'll need to know how to resolve problems when they occur.

Implementing and Conducting Administration of Resources

Exam 70-270 expects you to be able to administer resources on a Windows XP Professional computer. Specifically, you will need to know how to do the following:

- **Monitor, manage, and troubleshoot access to files and folders.** You'll need to know about file compression, accessing shared files and folders along with NTFS permissions, and how to optimizing access to files and folders.
- **Manage and troubleshoot access to shared folders.** You will create and remove shared folders, control access to shared folders using permissions, and manage and troubleshoot Web server resources.
- **Connect to local and network print devices.** Since Windows XP Professional can be used as a print server, you will need to know how to manage printers and print jobs, how to control access to printers via permissions, how to connect to an Internet printer, and how to connect to a local print device.
- **Configure and manage file systems.** Windows XP Professional supports FAT, FAT32, and NTFS. You will need to know how to convert from one file system to another and how to configure FAT, FAT32, and NTFS.
- **Manage and troubleshoot access to and synchronization of offline files.** Offline files and resource accesses also form a portion of this exam; you must know how to manage access to offline files.
- **Configure and troubleshoot fax support.** Windows XP Professional provides a new fax console and additional support for managing faxes. You'll need to know how to configure and troubleshoot fax support for the exam.

Implementing, Managing, Monitoring, and Troubleshooting Hardware Devices and Drivers

Hardware configuration and support continues to be a focus of the Windows XP Professional exam, as it has been in the past. You'll need to know how to do the following:

- **Implement, manage, and troubleshoot disk devices.** You'll need to know how to install and configure DVD and CD-ROM devices; monitor and configure hard disks; monitor, configure, and troubleshoot volumes; and configure removable media.
- **Implement, manage, and troubleshoot display devices.** The exam expects you to know how to configure multiple display support and how to install, configure, and troubleshoot video adapters.
- **Configure Advanced Configuration Power Interface (ACPI).** For the exam, you'll need to know the issues with ACPI and how to configure it.
- **Implement, manage, and troubleshoot input and output (I/O) devices.** I/O device configuration is an important issue on this exam and applies to a wide range of products, such as printers, mouse types, keyboards, smart card readers, cameras, modems, IrDA devices, wireless devices, USB devices, and hand held devices.

exam watch

Windows XP Professional provides the best support for I/O devices of any of Microsoft's previous operating systems. You can expect to see some questions and issues concerning these products.

- **Manage and troubleshoot drivers and driver signing.** You'll need to know how to install, remove, and update device drivers and how to ensure that they come from a reliable source.
- **Monitor and configure multiprocessor computers.** Windows XP Professional can support computers with more than one processor. The exam expects to know how to configure and monitor computers equipped in this manner.

Monitoring and Optimizing System Performance and Reliability

Windows XP Professional is a robust operating system providing superior performance and reliability. The exam expects you to know how to optimize and monitor the system. You are expected to know how to do the following:

- **Monitor, optimize, and troubleshoot performance of the Windows XP Professional desktop.** This area includes the optimization and performance of memory, processor, disk, applications, and scheduled tasks.
- **Manage, monitor, and optimize system performance for mobile users.** For laptop users, you should know how to configure Windows XP Professional to take advantage of mobility while conserving system resources.
- **Restore and back up the operating system, system state data, and user data.** You'll need to know how to recover system state data and user data using Windows backup, how to troubleshoot system restoration by starting in Safe Mode, and how to recover system state data and user data by using the Recovery console.

Configuring and Troubleshooting the Desktop Environment

Windows XP Professional contains a new desktop interface that you can configure locally or via Group Policy. For the exam, you need to know how to do the following:

- **Configure and manage user profiles.** Windows XP Professional is designed as a multi-user environment, and you can still use roaming user profiles as well.
- **Configure support for multiple languages or multiple locations.** Windows XP Professional can support multiple languages and location formats at the same time, and the exam expects you to be able to configure these regional settings.
- **Manage applications by using Windows Installer Packages.** Windows Installer Packages, along with Group Policy, will make the deployment of applications quick and easy.
- **Configure and troubleshoot desktop settings.** Windows XP Professional supports a number of desktop configuration features; and, as an IT professional, you'll need to know how to support, as well as enforce them, using Group Policy.

- **Configure and troubleshoot accessibility services.** Windows XP Professional supports a number of accessibility services for users with certain disabilities. You'll need to know about these services and how to configure them.

Implementing, Managing, and Troubleshooting Network Protocols and Services

Since the Windows XP Professional exam focuses on the use of Windows XP as a desktop system in Windows networks, you are expected to know how to configure network protocols and services. You'll need to know how to do the following:

- **Configure and Troubleshoot the TCP/IP protocol.** TCP/IP is the standard protocol used in most major networks. The exam expects you to have a firm understanding of how to configure TCP/IP and troubleshoot on a Windows XP Professional computer.
- **Connect to computers by using dial-up networking.** Dial-up networking continues to be an important aspect of any computer system. For the exam, you'll need to know how to configure it. Specifically, you'll need to know how to create a VPN connection, access a remote access server, and configure Internet Connection Sharing.
- **Connect to resources using Internet Explorer.** Internet Explorer is the default browser for Windows XP Professional, and the exam expects you to know how to use to connect to resources.
- **Configure, manage, and implement Internet Information Services (IIS).** IIS is used to host Web sites or intranet sites. You can run IIS on Windows XP Professional, and the exam expects that you know how to use it.
- **Configure, manage, and troubleshoot Remote Desktop and Remote Assistance.** These two new tools enable you to remotely access a computer and offer remote assistance to users—both of which are powerful tools for the IT professional. You'll need to know all about these for the exam.
- **Configure, manage, and troubleshoot an Internet Connection Firewall.** Windows XP Professional is the first Microsoft desktop system to offer a built-in Internet Connection Firewall. Naturally, you'll need to know about this feature and how to configure, manage, and troubleshoot it for the exam.

Configuring, Managing, and Troubleshooting Security

Built on the Windows 2000 code, Windows XP Professional provides all of the bells and whistles of Windows 2000 and NTFS security, but it is now easier for users and easier for IT professionals to handle. For the exam, you'll need to know how to do the following:

- **Configure, manage, and troubleshoot Encrypting File System (EFS).** EFS provides security while allowing easy access, and you'll need to know how to manage this security feature of Windows XP Professional.
- **Configure, manage, and troubleshoot local security policy.** Windows XP Professional can be configured locally with a security policy, and the exam expects you to know how to configure, manage, and troubleshoot a local security policy.
- **Configure, manage, and troubleshoot local user and group accounts.** You'll need to know how to configure and manage local user and group accounts in Windows XP Professional, including such issues as auditing, account settings, policy, user and group rights, and cache credentials.
- **Configure, manage, and troubleshoot a security configuration.** Using Windows XP Professional security tools, you can create a security configuration for a local computer. The exam expects you to be able to configure, manage, and troubleshoot a local security configuration.
- **Configure, manage, and troubleshoot Internet Explorer security settings.** Because of online threats, Internet Explorer's security settings have been beefed up, and the exam expects you to be able to configure these settings.

CERTIFICATION OBJECTIVE 1.03

What Is Covered in this Book

This book is designed to cover every exam objective and give you the technical information and practice you need to master Exam 70-270. Although I cover every exam objective, it is important to note that Microsoft exam objectives are often not listed in a logical order. However, in this book, I have reorganized these exam objectives so you can learn all about Windows XP Professional logically and completely. The following sections give you a global overview of the chapters to come.

Chapter 2: Performing an Attended Installation of Windows XP Professional

In this chapter, you'll learn about a Windows XP Professional attended installation. An attended installation means that you physically "attend" the installation of Windows XP Professional on a particular computer. Specifically, you start the installation using the Windows XP Professional installation CD-ROM, or you start setup.exe over the network. You then answer setup prompts that are posed to you during the installation.

This chapter also explores upgrading to Windows XP Professional and the upgrade issues you are likely to face on the exam, as well as in real life. You'll also learn about how Windows XP Professional's new File and Settings Transfer wizard can easily migrate user settings and documents from one computer to another.

Chapter 3: Performing an Unattended Installation of Windows XP Professional

Aside from the basic attended installation of Windows XP Professional, you can also use several unattended or automated methods that enable the IT professional to install hundreds or even thousands of workstations at the same time. In this chapter, you'll learn about using Setup Manager to create answer files for unattended installations. You'll also learn about Windows 2000's Remote Installation Services and how to prepare a system for imaging using the System Preparation tool.

Chapter 4: Configuring and Troubleshooting the Desktop Environment

Windows XP Professional provides a new desktop environment that is typically easier for end users, but complex enough for power users. From an IT professional's perspective, Exam 70-270 expects you to be able to configure a number of different items, collectively called the desktop environment.

First, you'll learn about accessibility features and services in Windows XP Professional that enable persons with certain disabilities to more easily use the computer.

As an IT professional, you'll need to know how to configure these options. Next, this chapter explores Windows XP's desktop settings. You'll see how they are configured locally and how standardized settings can be enforced with Group Policy.

Then you'll learn about Windows XP's multiple languages and locations features in regional options and settings. You'll see how to use these features to enable multiple language and region support. After that, Windows Installer packages are explored, particularly in relation to deployment via Group Policy.

Finally, this chapter explores user profiles, as well as the configuration of roaming user profiles.

Chapter 5: Managing Windows XP Professional Hardware

As a network professional, you should have hardware configuration and troubleshooting high on your skills list. The requirement holds true for Windows XP Professional, and you'll need to know a thing or two about hardware management for the exam. In this chapter, you'll learn about configuring devices, such as CD/DVD-ROM drives, and about removable media and multiple display support. You'll also learn about video adapter configurations, ACPI, and device drivers and driver signing.

Chapter 6: Configure and Manage I/O Devices

Input/Output devices enable you to interface with the operating system or exchange different kinds of data with the operating system. I/O devices have become more numerous and more complex during the past few years—and more popular as well. In this chapter, you'll learn how to configure and manage such I/O devices as keyboards, mice, smart card readers, multimedia hardware, cameras, modems, IrDA devices, wireless devices, USB devices, and hand-held devices.

on the job

The number of users of I/O devices has dramatically increased in recent years. In the past, most users had just a keyboard, mouse, and a printer. Today, all kinds of digital cameras, PDAs, and numerous other devices are in use. Fortunately for you, the IT professional, these devices are typically easy to install and manage.

Chapter 7: Configuring Disk Drives and Disk Volumes

Windows XP Professional supports dynamic disks and volume management, which was first introduced in Windows 2000. In this chapter, you'll learn how to configure and manage Windows XP Professional disk drives and disk volumes. Specifically, you'll learn how to monitor and configure disk drives and volumes, how to convert from one file system to another, and how to configure FAT, FAT32, and NTFS.

Chapter 8: Printing and Faxing

Printing and faxing remain important configuration topics and support issues for IT professionals. Since Windows XP Professional can be used as a print/fax server, you'll want to study this chapter to learn all about Windows XP Professional's printing and faxing features.

In this chapter, you'll learn about managing printers and print jobs, how to control access to printers and faxes with permissions, how to connect to an Internet printer, how to configure a local print device, and how to configure and troubleshoot fax support. Although at first glance, the subject of printing and fax support seems simple enough, printers and printer management can easily become complex. For this reason, an entire chapter is devoted to the subject and the exam issues and problems you are likely to face.

Chapter 9: Resource Administration

When Windows XP Professional is used on a network, a number of resources for network users can be made available, and the management of those resources is an important aspect of the exam. In this chapter, you'll learn about resource administration and how to control and manage resources in Windows XP Professional.

In this chapter, you'll learn how to configure, manage, and troubleshoot file compression, control access to files and folders with permissions, create and remove shared folders, manage and troubleshoot Web server resources, manage offline files and synchronization, and manage applications.

Chapter 10: Networking

Windows XP Professional is designed to be the desktop operating system of choice in Windows 2000 networks. Windows XP Professional provides you with the tools and functionality that you need for complex networking scenarios.

In view of the exam objectives, this chapter explores the configuration of TCP/IP, dial-up networking, VPN configuration, and RAS configuration. You'll also explore network connection troubleshooting. Since the exam expects to you to support Windows XP in larger network environments, you will need to have a firm grasp of networking concepts and skills. You can read an overview of Windows 2000 networking later in this chapter, but there is no replacement for hands-on experience.

Chapter 11: Internet Usage, Support, and Security

Windows XP Professional provides a number of tools that make Internet usage and connectivity easy and safe. In this chapter, you'll learn about Internet connections, how to connect to resources using Internet Explorer, and how to configure and manage Internet Information Services. You'll also learn about Windows XP Professional's new Remote Desktop and Remote Assistance features, as well as about Internet Connection Sharing and the new Internet Connection Firewall.

Since the Remote Desktop and Remote Assistance features (along with ICS) are new features in Windows XP, you can expect a few exam questions about them. Remote Desktop and Remote Assistance provide excellent ways to connect to remote computers. With Remote Destkop, you can connect to and use a remote computer, such as accessing an office computer from your home. Remote Assistance can be a very helpful desktop support tool with which a user can connect to and use a remote computer. The user can configure the computer and make changes to it in order to fix problems. Finally, ICS, designed for home and workgroup users, provides a way to protect the network against outside attacks. Using a table method, ICS does not allow any network traffic to enter the computer that was not explicitly requested by the user.

Chapter 12: Configuring, Managing, and Troubleshooting Security

Windows XP Professional provides you with a number of security features that can make networking safe and secure. In this chapter, you'll explore these security features. Specifically, you'll learn about EFS, local security policy, user and group accounts, local security configuration, and the configuration of Internet Explorer's security features.

As networks continue to develop and expand, the security problems and issues facing networks today can be very challenging. Windows XP supports a number of important security features that can help reduce security problems. For example, at the local level, a user can easily encrypt documents and folders so that only he or she can access them. The encryption features are invisible to the user, who can continue using the documents and folders as normal. At the networking and Internet level, Windows XP supports all of the networking security features provided by Windows 2000, and Internet Explorer 6 hosts a number of additional security features that can help you manage cookies and private information exchange with Web servers.

Chapter 13: Monitoring and Optimizing System Performance and Reliability

Windows XP Professional provides you with the tools and features that enable you to monitor system performance and optimize performance for the computer. In this chapter, you'll learn about monitoring and optimization for the desktop environment and for mobile users, as well as how to back up and restore the operating system and user data. Considering the graphics-intensive nature of the Windows XP operating system and the stringent hardware requirements needed to run the system, the issues of system performance and reliability are very important. In fact, Windows XP even enables you to control the graphics intensive use of the desktop by the operating system—you can optimize the desktop for performance over appearance. Use Performance Monitor and related tools, you can easily track and manage performance on Windows XP, and in this chapter you'll learn all about these features.

CERTIFICATION OBJECTIVE 1.04

What You Should Already Know

Exam 70-270 is a demanding exam that expects prior knowledge and skills. As such, this is not a beginner's exam. Before beginning your study of Windows XP Professional

SCENARIO & SOLUTION	
I use Windows XP Professional on a small network with ICS. Will the exam cover this?	The exam focuses on the use of Windows XP Professional as the desktop system of choice in larger environments, but ICS and ICF are certainly covered on the exam.
Can Group Policy be used to standardize desktop settings for Windows XP Professional clients?	Yes. See Chapter 4 to learn more about Group Policy configuration.
Can I use Remote Installation Services to install Windows XP Professional clients?	Yes, Remote Installation Services (RIS) supports Windows 2000 Professional clients and Windows XP Professional clients. See Chapter 3 for details.

in preparation for Exam 70-270, you should consider the following sections carefully to make sure you have the required prerequisite knowledge.

Windows 2000

Windows XP Professional is designed after Windows 2000 and is intended to work on a Windows 2000 network. Because of this functionality, you are very likely to see some overlap of Windows 2000 networking technologies that are not explicitly stated as objectives for Exam 70-270. In light of this fact, you need a firm command of a few concepts, namely:

- Windows 2000 Networking
- Windows 2000 Domain Controller and Member Server Roles
- Active Directory Management
- Group Policy
- Remote Access Service
- Virtual Private Networking

Although not designed to be a comprehensive overview, the following sections review each of these issues. As you are reading, consider your own skills. If you believe you may be deficient in a particular area, you may need further study before tackling exam 70-270.

Windows 2000 Networking

Windows 2000 provides premier networking serves, functions, and features that can meet the needs of a small workgroup or a global network. In the days of Windows NT, Microsoft entered the networking arena, previously dominated by Novell and UNIX systems. However, Windows NT left a lot to be desired, was difficult to manage, and did not scale well as networks grew and changed.

The entire construct of Microsoft networking changed with the release of Windows 2000. Windows 2000/.NET networks are easier to manage, provide more services, and have essentially no practical limit in terms of scalability. There are a number of reasons of for these changes and a number of technologies behind the change.

Network Configuration In order to understand Windows 2000/.Net networking, we must first take a look at the structure of a Windows 2000 network. Windows 2000 networks are built on sites, domains, and organizational units (OUs). An understanding of these components is critical to understanding Windows 2000 networking and the management of Windows XP Professional clients.

Networks are physically divided into sites. A site is simply a physical collection of networked computers. Typically, a site denotes that the computers are located in one geographic location. For example, let's say that a company has an office in New York and an office in Houston. A network exists in each location. In terms of Windows 2000 networking, each location can function as a site. Then, using the site configuration, network administrators can determine how those two physical locations can connect to the wide area network. This connection may be a WAN link, such as a T3 connection, or in the case of small network sites, it might a modem connection or a VPN connection over the Internet. There are number of connection possibilities, all depending on the needs of the network and the cost.

So why does Windows 2000 use site configuration to group computers? There are a few different reasons that this physical configuration is important:

- Sites help Windows 2000 networking components determine what network traffic is considered "inexpensive" and local. In other words, the definition of sites helps the Windows 2000 Server know if certain computers are considered local or on a remote subnet that requires a more expensive and less reliable WAN link in order to communicate.

- Sites help Windows 2000 control replication. Replication is the process of updating the Active Directory data that resides on each Windows 2000 domain controller. Updates flow easily between domain controllers within a site, but Windows 2000 knows that replication to domain controllers out of the site can be costly and troublesome. When you define those sites, you can further define how Windows 2000 Servers can communicate with each other in remote sites. You can see that sites enable an administrator to define locations and the WAN links connecting them. Windows 2000 can then use this information to help you control replication and traffic.

While site configuration is a physical look at the geographical locations that make up local and remote network segments, Windows 2000 domains and organization units (OUs) are logical divisions of that network. A domain is a Windows 2000 grouping of users and computers for management and security purposes. The domain is not connected to the site—a domain can contain several different sites, or a site can contain several different domains. The site physically segments the network while the domain is a logical division.

Why are domains used? Consider this example: Let's say you have a network with two sites: New York and Houston. The New York site contains 2,000 users while the Houston site contains 4,000 users. Each site is managed by its own administrative team and has different security standards. In this case, two domains can be used, one at each site, so that different administrative teams can manage the sites and implement different security standards. Now let's consider this same example in a different way. What if New York and Houston were managed by the same administrative team with the same security standards? In this case, only one domain is needed. The single domain encompasses both sites and the administrative team manages both the single, logical domain.

In Windows NT, domains caused a lot of problems because Windows NT could only handle so many users and computers per domain. For large networks, the domain structure often grew ridiculously complex and earned Windows NT the reputation of not scaling well. Not so in Windows 2000 networks—Windows 2000 domains can scale to millions of objects with no complications. In many cases, a large network now needs only a single domain. Only when different administrative structures or security needs are necessary do networks need to use a multiple domain model.

However, what happens if you want to use a single domain, but enable different administrators to manage different portions of it? This is where OUs come into play.

Using an OU is a way to segment a large domain into manageable chunks. Different administrators can be delegated to have control over different OUs, and you can apply different Group Policy objects to different OUs. OUs can be used in a number of helpful administrative ways, for example:

- Different departments can be configured as OUs so that an administrator can handle the department's specific needs.
- Different divisions, such as Users, Management, and Production, can be created to manage users more easily.
- Different resources, such as Printers and Shared Folders, can even be configured into an OU structure so that different administrators can manage those resources.

As you can see, there are a number of different approaches that can be taken with OUs. The point is that a large domain can be easily segmented and controlled by different administrators without the headache and expense of creating multiple domains.

on the job

Multiple domain environments are more expensive than single domain environments, both in terms of monetary expense and time expense. Multiple domains require more server hardware and more administrative time and focus in order to manage. However, under the Windows 2000 domain model, most environments can easily function with one domain and multiple OUs to meet specific administrative needs.

Domain Name System In order for a network to scale well, it must be able to accommodate users, computers, and resources as they are acquired. In other words, the structure of the network must easily allow growth. The Windows 2000 domain structure allows growth, but its naming structure also easily allows growth as well. Domain Name System (DNS) is the name of the IP address mapping system used in Windows 2000 networks. Windows XP Professional is fully compatible with the DNS standard and is capable of functioning and communicating on a Windows 2000 network.

DNS is a naming standard that uses a series of discrete domain names in order to identify network hosts. DNS is highly scalable; in fact, every computer on the Internet is identified by a DNS name. DNS uses domain names to identify host computers. For example, **server1.osbornet.com** uniquely recognizes server1, which resides in the Osborne domain, which is located in the com domain. By resolving com, Osborne, and server1, the server's IP address, can be located so that communication can occur on the Internet.

Windows 2000 networks function using this same standard, which provides unlimited scalability and a cohesive naming strategy with the Internet. **Mycompany.com** is a Windows domain as well as an Internet site. **jwilliams@mycompany.com** is both a username and an e-mail address. The use of DNS also enables child and grandchild domains. For example, let's say you have a domain named **mycompany.com**. You want to create an additional domain that will function as a child called Production. When you create the new domain using Windows 2000 Server, the new domain will be named **Production.mycompany.com**. What if you want to further subdivide the Production domain in to North and South? Then you would have **North.production.mycompany.com** and **South.production.mycompany.com**.

If you have spent any time working with Windows NT, you may be wondering what happened to Windows Internet Naming Service (WINS). WINS provided a NetBIOS name to IP address mappings in pre–Windows 2000 networks. WINS is still supported in Windows 2000 networks for backward compatibility with older Windows systems, such as NT and 9*x*. A pure Windows 2000/XP network does not need WINS because DNS is used.

Windows 2000 Domain Controller and Member Server Roles

One of the reasons that Windows 2000 can support large domains and a flexible domain/OU structure concerns the use of domain controllers. A domain controller is a Windows 2000 Server computer that holds and manages the Active Directory database. Using the Active Directory, you can add users, manage groups and security, manage resources, and other domain specific tasks. In other words, a domain controller manages the domain, and you manage the domain through the functions that you perform on a domain controller.

Windows NT used domain controllers, but it used a master model in which there was one Primary Domain Controller (PDC) per domain and multiple Backup Domain Controllers (BDCs). The PDC contained a writeable copy, the domain database, while the BDCs contained copies. BDCs helped in load management and could be used in the event of the a PDC failure. The problem is that a single PDC per domain could not scale well and was not flexible in terms of management.

In Windows 2000, a multimaster domain controller model is used. This means that there are no PDCs or BDCs. Every domain controller maintains a copy of the Active Directory database. You can make changes to that database on any domain controller, and those changes are replicated to other domain controllers throughout the environment. Because of the multimaster model, Windows 2000 domains can scale to the millions of objects with as many domain controllers as needed. Administrators have the management flexibility they need without the configuration confusion that often came with PDCs and BDCs.

Other Windows 2000 Servers can be used in the domain without functioning as domain controllers. These servers can function as DNS servers, DHCP servers, intranet servers, print servers, and file servers. This feature enables many different servers to be used for different purposes without taxing the use of domain controllers. The end result is a network that is much easier to manage and much more flexible.

exam watch

It is important to keep in mind that the Windows XP Professional exam does not test your knowledge of Windows 2000 networking—at least, not directly. However, the exam expects you to understand how Windows XP can be used in a domain environment and how you can manage Windows XP in that environment. In order to understand those features, part of your prerequisite knowledge is to have a firm understanding of Windows 2000 networking functions and features.

Active Directory Management

The Active Directory, which was first introduced in Windows 2000, is a directory service for the network. It is a way for administrators to store user and computer accounts, network resources, and manage the network. For users, the Active Directory provides a highly searchable way to find network resources. The Active Directory stores information about resources based on attributes. For example, a shared printer might have attributes for "laser, staple, color," and other characteristics. Users can then search on those attributes, such as "laser printer," and locate a shared laser printer on the network.

In terms of administration, the Active Directory provides three tools on Windows 2000 domain controllers that enable administrators to manage the directory and the Windows 2000 network:

- **Active Directory Sites and Services** This MMC snap-in contains information about sites and site links. You can add site links here, configure costs, schedules, and manage how replication occurs over those links.

- **Active Directory Domains and Trusts** The Domains and Trust console enables you to manage Active Directory domains and trust relationships. By default, Windows 2000 domains in the same tree all share transitive trust relationships. However, you can configure one-way and two-way trusts with Windows NT domains that might still exist in the network.
- **Active Directory Users and Computers** The Users and Computers console configures and manages users, computers, resources, and even OUs. Of the three, this console is used most frequently.

A common question new Windows 2000 network enthusiasts often ask is "Where, exactly, is the Active Directory?" The Active Directory resides on each domain controller. When a domain controller is created, it receives a copy of the Active Directory database and is set up as a replication partner with another domain controller. For this reason, there is no single master copy of the Active Directory database. Rather, each domain controller in a domain contains a writeable copy of that database that can be managed by administrators. Let's say your environment has five domain controllers. You add a new user on one of them. Since this new user has to be added to all domain controllers, the replication process begins in order to replicate that data. Any time a change is made on one domain controller, replication makes certain that change occurs on all of the domain controllers. This feature assures that each domain controller has the same copy of the Active Directory database. The good news with this multimaster model, aside from ease of administration, is fault tolerance. If a domain controller goes down, the network is not affected, since other domain controllers are available and performing the same functions. In fact, every domain controller in the domain would have to fail at the same time in order for there to be domain functionality failure.

Group Policy

Group Policy is a powerful feature of Windows 2000 networks that enables administrators to finely control desktop settings, computer configurations, account policies, and even software. Implemented at the site, domain, or OU level, network use of Group Policy enables an environment to streamline user and computer configuration and enables different administrators to impose different policies.

For example, let's say that you have a basic site policy. That site policy is inherited by all domains and OUs in the environment. However, a certain domain in that environment has additional policies that it needs to invoke. Computers and users in that domain receive the site policy first and then the domain policy. However, the site policy sits at the top of the hierarchy and cannot be overwritten or contradicted by the domain policy. In other words, the domain policy can only further strengthen the site policy and provide additional restrictions or configurations—not make them easier. The same holds true for the OU policy; it can only further strengthen the site and domain policy.

Windows XP Professional also enables you to configure a local group policy that applies to local users of that computer. The Local Group Policy console, shown in Figure 1-6, provides configuration options for both computers and users, but it should be noted that site, domain, and OU policies can always override the local policy

Remote Access Service

Windows 2000 networks continue to provide support for RAS, or the Remote Access Service. RAS enables a Windows 2000 to accept logins from remote clients. For example, let's say you are traveling with your laptop computer. Using RAS, you can use a modem to dial an RAS server and gain access to the local network remotely. This feature enables users to access network resources even when they are not physically connected to the network.

FIGURE 1-6

Local Group Policy console

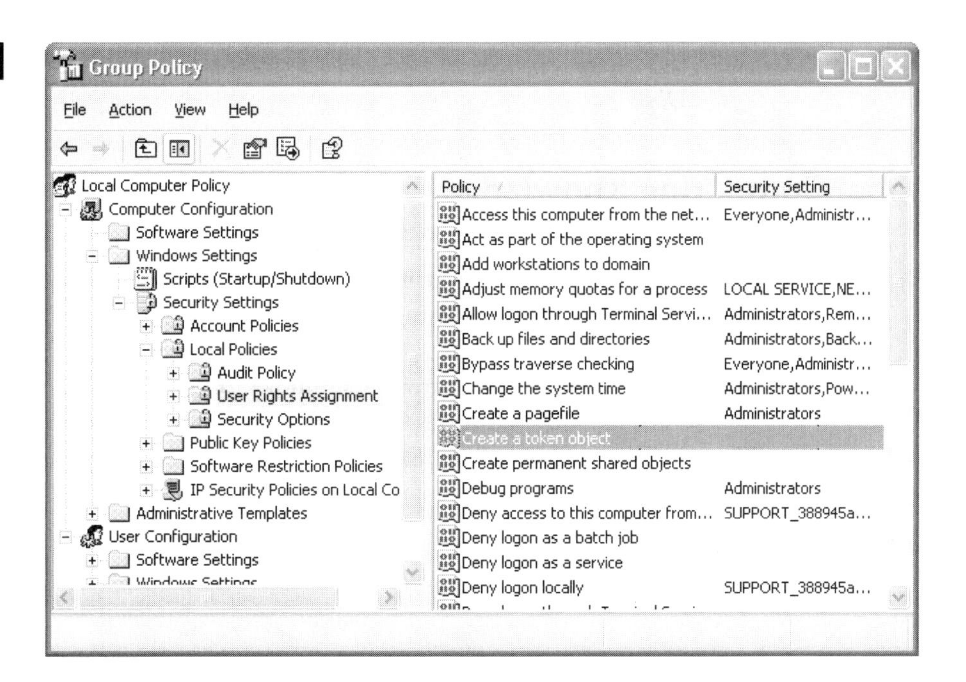

Virtual Private Networking

Virtual private networks (VPNs) enable a remote computer to connect securely to a Windows 2000/XP computer using the Point-to-Point Tunneling Protocol (PPTP) or the Layer 2 Tunneling Protocol (L2TP). This feature, which was supported back in the days of Windows NT, enables a secure tunnel over a public network, such as the Internet or intranet, so that private data can be securely passed using the public network as a WAN link.

TCP/IP Networking

Windows 2000 is built on TCP/IP networking, and Windows XP Professional is designed for TCP/IP. You don't need to be a master IP planner, but you do need to have a good handle on TCP/IP networking concepts, such as the following:

- IP addressing
- Subnet masks
- Default gateways
- Common transmission control protocols
- Common Internet protocols
- DHCP
- DNS

Global Computing Knowledge

Finally, as with any Microsoft certification exam, the more you know, the more likely you are to succeed. It's important that you have a strong background in all kinds of operating systems and networking issues. You should know a thing or two about a wide range of client computers, such as Windows, Macintosh, and perhaps Linux. You need to know your way around Windows 2000 Server and how things work on a Windows 2000 network. Armed with these tools, you are ready to tackle Windows XP Professional and Exam 70-270!

CERTIFICATION SUMMARY

This chapter gave you an overview of Windows XP Professional and explored the exam objectives. In order to be successful on this exam, you'll need to spend time studying the chapters to come and working with Windows XP Professional. As you study, keep in mind the target audience and remember that the exam will approach Windows XP Professional in terms of a LAN or WAN network desktop system.

As you study for the exam, also keep in mind that exam objectives may overlap with content from other exams. You should have a firm handle on Windows 2000 networking and Active Directory concepts, and you should spend some time with Windows 2000 Server. This cross-objective approach has been very common on the Windows 2000 exams, and you can expect the Windows XP Professional exam to follow this approach. In short, study this book carefully, but study smartly as you prepare for Exam 70-270.

TWO-MINUTE DRILL

What Is Installing, Configuring, and Administering Microsoft Windows XP Professional?

- ❑ Windows XP Professional is the operating system of choice for Windows 2000 networks. Available in both the Professional and Home versions, Windows XP Professional contains the networking and management functions necessary for small networks and large networks. Exam 70-270 will test your knowledge of Windows XP Professional in a medium size to large Windows 2000 network.
- ❑ Windows XP Professional contains the power of Windows 2000 and the friendliness of Windows Me.
- ❑ There are many new features, including the File and Settings Transfer wizard, Application Compatibility, and ICF. You'll also find familiar Windows 2000 management tools, such as the MMC and Computer Management.

Overview of Exam 70-270

- ❑ You must be able to perform an attended and unattended installation of Windows XP Professional.
- ❑ You must show your ability to implement and conduct the administration of resources.
- ❑ You will need to be able to implement, manage, monitor, and troubleshoot hardware devices and drivers.
- ❑ You must be able to monitor and optimize performance and reliability.
- ❑ You must be able to configure and troubleshoot the Windows XP Professional desktop environment.
- ❑ You must be able to implement, manage, and troubleshoot network protocols and services.
- ❑ You must be able to configure, manage, and troubleshoot security.

What Is Covered in This Book

- ❑ In Chapter 2, you will perform an attended installation of Windows XP.
- ❑ In Chapter 3, you will perform an unattended installation of Windows XP.

- ❑ In Chapter 4, you will configure the desktop environment.
- ❑ In Chapter 5, you will configure and manage hardware devices and drivers.
- ❑ In Chapter 6, you will configure and manage I/O devices.
- ❑ In Chapter 7, you will configure disk drives and disk volumes.
- ❑ In Chapter 8, you will configure printing and fax services.
- ❑ In Chapter 9, you will configure networking components.
- ❑ In Chapter 10, you will administer resources.
- ❑ In Chapter 11, you will configure Internet usage, support, and Internet security.
- ❑ In Chapter 12, you will manage and troubleshoot security.
- ❑ In Chapter 13, you will monitor and optimize Windows XP performance.

What You Should Already Know

- ❑ You should be familiar with Windows 2000 networking and Windows 2000 Server.
- ❑ You should have a global knowledge of TCP/IP networking and IP networking protocols and services.

SELF TEST

The following questions will help you measure your understanding of the material presented in this chapter. Read all of the choices carefully, as there may be more than one correct answer. Choose all correct answers for each question.

1. The Windows XP Professional exam is likely to view your role with Windows XP Professional in what type of environment?

   A. Home use

   B. Small office

   C. Windows 2000 LAN or WAN

   D. All of the above

2. Windows XP's ICF feature is designed for what user?

   A. Home

   B. Small office

   C. Windows 2000 LAN or WAN

   D. None of the above

3. You need to install Windows XP Professional on a certain computer, but you must move all of the settings and user documents from a Windows 98 computer to the new XP computer. How can you easily accomplish this?

   A. Manually move the data.

   B. Use the Files and Settings Transfer wizard.

   C. Move them via the Active Directory.

   D. You cannot perform this action.

4. What does the Application Compatibility wizard do?

   A. Makes downlevel applications compatible with Windows XP Professional.

   B. Makes Windows XP Professional compatible with downlevel applications.

   C. Creates applications that are compatible.

   D. There is no Application Compatibility wizard.

5. You want to install Windows XP Professional on 1,000 computers. What automated methods are available to you?

A. Remote Installation Services

B. Setup Manager

C. System Preparation

D. Network Share

E. E-mail server

6. What file system is the preferred file system for Windows XP Professional?

A. FAT

B. FAT32

C. DVNS

D. NTFS

7. When is Windows XP's automatic IP address feature typically used?

A. Home/Small office network

B. Windows 2000 domain

C. When a DHCP server is not available

D. When a DNS server is not available

8. Which of the following features are supported by Windows XP Professional?

A. IIS

B. VPN

C. ICS

D. TCP/IP

9. The new XP interface can be considered as which of the following?

A. HTML object

B. Theme

C. Skin

D. API

10. Which statement best describes Exam 70-270?

   A. The exam is very objective specific.

   B. The exam may include items from other exams.

   C. The exam requires subnet masking skills.

   D. None of these statements are correct.

11. Which Windows 2000 network features provides physical information about network locations?

   A. Sites

   B. Domains

   C. OUs

   D. Group Policy

12. You work in a Windows 2000 network that contains a single domain. Management wants to segment the network so that certain administrators can more effectively manage the networking needs and group policy of several departments. What needs to be created?

   A. Sites

   B. Domains

   C. OUs

   D. Group Policy

13. Which statement best describes how Windows 2000 uses domain controllers?

   A. A master model is used.

   B. A multimaster model is used.

   C. PDCs are used.

   D. BDCs are used.

14. How is WINS used in a Windows 2000 network?

   A. WINS is supported for backward compatibility.

   B. WINS is used for name resolution by all Windows 2000/XP clients.

   C. WINS is used by Windows 2000 BDCs.

   D. WINS is used to support VPNs.

15. What two protocols can be used by VPNs in Windows XP?

A. PPP

B. PPTP

C. DLC

D. L2TP

SELF TEST ANSWERS

1. ☑ C is correct. Exam 70-270 will test your knowledge of Windows XP Professional installation, configuration, and administration in a larger networking environment where Windows XP Professional is the operating system of choice.

   ☒ A, B, and D are all incorrect. Although Windows XP Professional is a great home or small office system, the exam focuses on Windows XP Professional in a domain environment.

2. ☑ A and B are correct. The Internet Connection Firewall is designed for home users or small office users.

   ☒ C and D are incorrect. ICF is not designed for the LAN or WAN.

3. ☑ B is correct. The Files and Settings Transfer wizard helps you move settings and files quickly and easily from one computer to the next.

   ☒ A, C, and D are all incorrect because these answer options either do not provide a way to migrate the data.

4. ☑ B is correct. The Application Compatibility wizard enables Windows XP Professional to act as a downlevel Windows operating system so that downlevel applications can run.

   ☒ A, C, and D are incorrect because the Application Compatibility wizard does not function in the described ways.

5. ☑ A is correct. You can use RIS and System Preparation to automatically install Windows XP Professional.

   ☒ B and D are incorrect. These methods are not automated installation methods. C is incorrect because Sysprep only prepares a system for imaging.

6. ☑ D is correct. NTFS is the file system of choice.

   ☒ A, B, and C are incorrect. FAT and FAT32 are supported, but NTFS is the preferred file system. DVNS is a not a file system

7. ☑ A is correct. Automatic IP addressing is typically used in a home or in small office networks so that users avoid the trouble of configuring TCP/IP.

   ☒ B, C, and D are incorrect. Automatic IP address assignment is designed for the home or small office and not a Windows 2000 domain. Although Windows XP Professional can assign itself an IP address in the event that a DHCP server is not available, this is not its typical use. DNS does not affect IP addressing.

8. ☑ A, B, C, and D are all correct. Windows XP Professional supports all of these features, and this question also serves as a good warning that you will need to know your acronyms!

9. ☑ B is correct. The new XP interface is a theme. You can continue to use the XP interface, change to the Classic theme, or install and apply a different theme.

   ☒ A, C, and D are incorrect because the XP interface is considered a theme.

10. ☑ B is correct. Although the exam objectives are your primary guide, the exam may include items from other exams since Microsoft expects your knowledge to be global.

    ☒ A, C, and D are incorrect. These statements do not accurately describe the exam.

11. ☑ A is correct. Windows 2000 sites determine how computers are physically located in different geographic locations and how traffic between sites should be handled..

    ☒ B, C, and D are incorrect. Domains and OUs are used to logically manage the network, so B and C are incorrect. D is incorrect because Group Policy does not affect network location structure.

12. ☑ C is correct. When you need to segment a domain for management purposes, Organizational Units can be used.

    ☒ A, B, and D are incorrect. Sites are not used to segment domains, so A is incorrect. Although additional domains could be used, there is no need for them in this case, since a different administrative or security structure is not needed. Therefore, B is also incorrect. Group Policy cannot be used to segment a domain, so D is also incorrect.

13. ☑ B is correct. A multimaster model is used. All domain controllers function as peers and all contain a copy of the Active Directory database

    ☒ A, C, and D are incorrect. Since a multi-master model is used, there is no need for PDCs or BDCs.

14. ☑ A is correct. In a true Windows 2000/XP network, only DNS is needed for name resolution. WINS is maintained for backwards compatibility with downlevel clients, such as NT and 9*x*.

    ☒ B, C, and D are incorrect. Since WINS is provided for backwards compatibility only, all of these answer options are incorrect.

15. ☑ B and D are correct. VPN networking in Windows XP can use the PPTP or L2TP protocol.

    ☒ A and C are incorrect. PPP and DLC are not used by Windows XP virtual private networks.

2

Performing an Attended Installation of Windows XP Professional

CERTIFICATION OBJECTIVES

2.01	Planning a Windows XP Professional Installation
2.02	Upgrade Considerations
2.03	Installing Windows XP Professional
2.04	Performing Post-Installation Updates and Product Activation
2.05	Migrating Existing User Environments to Windows XP
2.06	Troubleshooting Failed Installations
✓	Two-Minute Drill
Q&A	Self Test

The installation of a new operating system is always one of those tasks that leaves people holding their breath. After all, the installation of a new operating can introduce a number of problems, and in an upgrade scenario the possibility of data loss is always present. The good news is that Windows XP Professional is very easy to install, and under most circumstances, if the minimum hardware requirements are met, installation is typically problem free. As a support professional, you'll need to know the ins and outs of Windows XP Professional installation, and you can expect the exam to question you on a number of features and issues as well. In this chapter, we'll explore Windows XP Professional installation procedures, upgrade issues, the migration of existing user environments, and some typical installation pitfalls.

CERTIFICATION OBJECTIVE 2.01

Planning a Windows XP Professional Installation

An attended installation of Windows XP Professional means that you will "attend" to the computer as installation is taking place. In this situation, you can use a CD-ROM to install Windows XP, or you can install Windows XP over the network from a network share. In either case, you physically run the installation and answer installation prompts as they occur. You can also install Windows XP Professional in several "unattended" ways, which you can learn more about in Chapter 3.

As with previous versions of Windows, particularly Windows 2000 Professional, the key to a successful Windows XP Professional installation is careful planning before the installation takes place. All too often, IT professionals as well as end users are a little too eager to install a new operating system and do not take the time to plan the installation first. Through proper planning, you can avoid problems before they occur and you can make sure your computer and applications are ready to meet the demands of Windows XP Professional. Armed with the correct information, installation is typically anticlimactic because you solve potential problems before they occur. In the following sections, you'll explore the important planning steps you should take before installing Windows XP Professional.

Minimum Hardware Requirements

Sure, you've heard this before, but the simple fact remains: your computer must be able to handle the hardware demands of Windows XP, or your installation will either fail or give you a system that is so pitifully slow that it is of no practical value. Before installing Windows XP Professional, you need to check out the computer's hardware and make sure it's powerful enough to handle the demands of Windows XP. Table 2-1 gives you the minimum, as well as the recommended hardware requirements, for Windows XP. As you might expect, the base, or minimum, hardware requirements are just that—what you need to install Windows XP Professional and for it to actually run. However, if you want good performance from the machine, you should meet the recommended hardware requirements and, preferably, exceed them.

exam Watch

On the exam, most hardware requirements questions expect you to respond in light of the minimum hardware requirements. However, I recommend that you simply memorize both minimum and recommended hardware requirements so that you are ready to respond to any question of this nature.

TABLE 2-1 Windows XP Professional Installation Requirements

Component	Minimum Requirement	Recommended Requirement
Processor	233 MHz Pentium.	300 MHz or higher—the faster the processor, the better performance you are likely to see. Windows XP Professional also supports two processor systems.
RAM	64MB.	128 + MB recommended—4GB maximum.
Hard disk space	1.5GB free disk space.	4 + GB.
Monitor	VGA monitor.	VGA monitor.
Mouse	Windows compatible.	Windows compatible.
CD-ROM	Windows compatible CD or DVD-ROM drive.	Windows compatible CD or DVD-ROM drive.
Network card	Compatible network card and cable if over-the-network installation is desired.	Compatible network card and cable if over the network installation is desired.

During setup, Windows XP Professional will check the computer's hardware, as well as software applications, to determine whether there are incompatibilities. However, your best bet is to check these items first so that problems can be avoided during installation. You should also take inventory of the computer's hardware, such as the sound card, video card, modem, and related components, and check the Windows XP Hardware Compatibility List (HCL) found at **www.microsoft.com/hcl**. Hardware that is not explicitly listed on the HCL is not recognized as compatible; however, this does not mean that the hardware will not work—it just has not been tested by Microsoft. If you have some questionable hardware, you should check the hardware manufacturer's Web site for more information and possible driver updates or upgrade packs. You should acquire the new drivers or updates before starting the installation of Windows XP Professional.

Network Considerations

If your Windows XP Professional computer will be a part of a network, then you will need to gather some information from an appropriate network administrator. If the computer is not connected to a network or is not connected to a Windows domain, you can simply choose the "workgroup" option during setup. You'll need to enter the name of your workgroup (or the name of a new workgroup if you are creating one with this installation).

Let's make sure your terminology is up to speed here. A *domain* is a logical grouping of users and computers on a Microsoft network. The domain is designed to be an administrative unit that is controlled by network administrators via Windows 2000/.NET servers. The domain is an effective way to partition a large network into manageable "chunks." The domain model has been around since the days of Windows NT, but it has been greatly simplified and made less restrictive since the days of Windows 2000. The domain model is recommended (but is not required) on networks with more than ten computers.

A *workgroup*, on the other hand, is a collection of local computers that function together in order to share data. There is no domain controller, nor a computer in charge of the network, and each user typically manages his or her own computer on the network. The workgroup model does not have the overhead of a domain, but it can be more difficult to manage as it grows, since it is not centrally controlled.

In a domain environment, you should be familiar with a few different concepts and issues as you consider the functionality of Windows XP Professional in a Windows 2000/.NET domain. It is important to note here that the features you see in Windows XP are the same found in Windows 2000 Professional. So, if you have spent any time with Windows 2000 Professional in a Windows 2000 network, these features will not be foreign to you. As you study for this exam and for additional MCSE exams, keep the following Windows 2000 networking issues in mind:

- **Active Directory** Windows 2000 introduced the concept of the Active Directory, which is managed by Windows 2000/.NET domain controllers and is the core networking functionality of the network. The Active Directory contains all user and computer accounts, all network resources (such as network printers), and it provides a way for the network to grow easily while being manageable. The Active Directory manages network computers and users in terms of sites and domains and provides a number of replication and management features that make it very powerful. Windows XP Professional computers have the capability to join the network using the Active Directory and the search capabilities that allow users to search the Active Directory in order to locate network resources.
- **Dynamic Host Configuration Protocol (DHCP)** DHCP is nothing new in Windows networks, but its importance remains. DHCP's job is to automatically provide and manage unique IP addresses and subnet masks to Windows clients. In a TCP/IP network, each client must have an appropriate and unique IP address and the correct subnet mask that identifies the subnet on which the computer is located. Without this information, the computer cannot function on the network. In the past, TCP/IP was considered a "high overhead" protocol because of the addressing requirements. Manual configuration was difficult and very time consuming. With DHCP, however the process is automated. DHCP Servers are Windows 2000 domain controllers or member servers that are configured to provide a scope of IP addresses to network clients. Once the DHCP Server is configured, the IP addressing tasks are automated by the server. Network clients "lease" an IP address from the DHCP Server for a period of time and then renew that lease (or obtain a new IP address) once the lease expires.
- **Domain Name System (DNS)** Windows 2000/.NET networks are built on DNS, which is the naming standard used on the Internet. DNS functions through the use of unique domain names, such as com, net, and org. Second-level domains, such as Microsoft(.com) and Osborne(.com) provide a way to uniquely identify businesses and individuals. To provide standardization and

easy integration with the Internet, Windows 2000/.NET networks are built on the DNS standard and cannot function without it. DNS is highly scalable and provides friendly, recognizable names that can be accessed by network clients.

If the computer will become a member of a domain, Windows XP Professional can join the domain during the installation of XP, but there is some information you might need to know during setup, which is described in the following list:

- **The computer name and Windows domain name** In order to join the domain, you'll need to know the name of your computer and the name of the domain.
- **An appropriate IP address and subnet mask** In order for a computer to communicate on any TCP/IP network, the computer must be configured with an IP address and subnet mask that is appropriate for the particular subnet. In most Windows networks, this task is handled automatically by a Dynamic Host Configuration Protocol (DHCP) server. The DHCP server automatically assigns IP addresses and subnet masks to client computers, ensuing that they have both an appropriate address and one that is unique on the network. If DHCP is not used on the network, then you'll need a unique IP address and subnet mask in order for network connectivity to work. See Chapter 10 to learn more about networking.
- **Domain Controller and DNS Server** During the installation, at least one domain controller and DNS server must be online on the network for you to join the domain. The computer must have a computer account in the Active Directory (configured by a domain administrator), or your user account must have the permission to create a computer account.
- **Hardware** The computer must be outfitted with a network adapter card, and it must be physically connected to the network. See Chapter 5 to learn more about hardware.

Typically, the information just described is readily available from a network administrator (if you are network administrator, you'll need to have this information ready for the installation).

on the job

As you are installing Windows XP Professional, keep in mind that you can always join a workgroup or domain once the installation is finished, if it is more convenient for you to do so at that time. Active Directory users have the default right to add up to ten computer accounts to a domain.

Hard Disk Configuration

If you are installing Windows XP Professional on a computer that has no existing operating system, and XP is the only operating system you want to use, there is nothing you need to do. The setup routine will format the drive for you and allow you to select a file system of your choice (FAT, FAT32, or NTFS). Windows XP is optimized for the NTFS file system, which provides file-level security and a number

SCENARIO & SOLUTION	
I have a laptop computer that I want to install with Windows XP Professional. The laptop barely meets the minimum hardware requirements. What problems will I likely see?	Computers that barely meet the minimum hardware requirements are at a disadvantage because the memory and processor will have a hard time handling the load placed on them. The more you try to do with the computer, the slower it will likely work. There are a few things you can do to help reduce RAM and CPU usage (see Chapter 13). As a general rule, however, you should strongly consider hardware upgrades before installing Windows XP on a system that barely meets the requirements; the end results are usually not worth the installation trouble.
Instead of using DHCP, doesn't Windows XP support an automatic IP feature?	Windows XP supports the Automatic Private IP Addressing (APIPA) technology. This feature, used in workgroups, allows the computer to auto-configure its own IP address in a special IP address range reserved for this purpose. In short, it is provided so that TCP/IP can be used on home and small office networks without any configuration from users. It is not designed for larger networking environments, and in most all cases, larger environments will use DHCP.

of additional security features that are not available under FAT or FAT32, such as the following:

- **Encryption** NTFS drives under Windows XP support encryption. You can seamlessly encrypt user data so that only the owner can view it, but you can use that data without having to decrypt and re-encrypt every time you want to use it.
- **Compression** NTFS drives under Windows XP natively support compression. You can compress a drive or folder in order to save disk space, but you can continue to use the compressed drive normally.
- **Quotas** On NTFS drives, you can configure how much space a user is allowed to access for data storage. This feature is particularly helpful on systems that have a Windows XP Professional computer functioning as a file server.

The most important difference, however, is file and folder-level security, which is the backbone of a Windows network. Although FAT and FAT32 are useful in some respects, they do not contain the advanced management features; for this reason, Windows XP is optimized for NTFS. See Chapter 7 to learn more about Windows XP Professional file system options.

If an operating system currently exists on your computer, Windows XP can either upgrade the existing operating system or install a clean copy of Windows XP, which essentially erases the previous operating system and data, or you can install Windows XP Professional in a separate partition for a dual-boot scenario. A dual-boot scenario enables you to boot more than one operating system on the same computer. For example, you could have a system that will boot Windows 2000 Server or Windows XP Professional, or you could have a system that will boot Windows Me or Windows XP Professional. Each operating system resides in its own partition, and during boot, you are given a boot menu so that you can choose which operating system you want to boot. Across the board, dual-boot configurations are easy to configure, but it is important to keep in mind that only Windows XP, Windows 2000, and Windows NT 4.0 with service pack 4.0 and higher can read NTFS partitions. Windows 9*x*, Me, and 95 can read only FAT or FAT32 drives. So, if you want the downlevel operating system to read the Windows XP partition, you'll need to use FAT32 as the file system instead of NTFS.

exam Watch

There is no real-world benefit of using FAT or FAT32 over NTFS unless you are using a very small hard drive or you want to dual boot so that a downlevel operating system can access the Windows XP partition. Other than for these reasons, NTFS is always your best choice.

If your computer has more than one partition, or you are working with a new computer for which you want to have more than one partition, you can use Windows XP's Disk Administrator tool to create new partitions as needed. If you are working with a computer that has no current operating system, you can create partitions using FDISK or a third-party tool, such as Partition Magic. If you are partitioning a disk for installation, make sure that the partition you will use for Windows XP meets the minimum storage requirements as described in the previous section.

Though dual-boot scenarios and partitioning options are beyond the scope of the exam objectives, it is a good idea to get familiar with them, preferably by practice configurations on a test machine. You can learn more about dual booting by performing a search at **Microsoft.com** (try Knowledge Base articles Q153762 and Q306559) or any Internet search engine.

Service Packs

Microsoft makes service packs available on occasion that contain system updates and fixes to problems. Services packs are available on CD-ROM or downloadable from **Microsoft.com**. Once you install Windows XP Professional, you should also install any current service packs that may be available for the operating system.

EXERCISE 2-1

Planning a Windows XP Installation

The Scenario: You need to install Windows XP Professional on a computer with no current operating system. You know the computer's processor and RAM requirements are met, but you believe the modem may not be supported. What actions should you take?

The Solution:

1. Gather as much information about the modem as possible; then access the Windows HCL. Check the list to see if the modem is supported.
2. If the modem is not supported, visit the modem manufacturer's Web site and see if there are updated drivers for the modem or if there is any information about compatibility. If drivers are available, you can download them for later installation.
3. If no information is available, you can install the Windows XP Professional and test the modem yourself. If the modem does not work, then simply replace it with a supported modem.

SCENARIO & SOLUTION	
Do I need to partition a drive on an unformatted computer before I start installation?	If the hard drive is not currently partitioned, you can allow Windows XP setup to do it for you if you want one partition. If you want more than one partition, you need to use FDISK or some other disk management software in order to partition the drive.
I have two hard disks in my computer. I want to use the first hard disk for the installation of Windows XP with one partition only. Do I need to do anything before starting the Windows XP setup?	No. The setup program will allow you to choose the disk you want to install Windows XP on, and then it will create a single partition for you.
What is the best file system to use with Windows XP Professional?	Windows XP Professional is designed for NTFS, and this is the file system you should use. The only exception to this rule is in the case of a dual-boot scenario where a downlevel version of Windows cannot read NTFS (such as Windows Me and 9*x*).

CERTIFICATION OBJECTIVE 2.02

Upgrade Considerations

In many cases, you will want to upgrade a previous operating system to Windows XP. This feature enables you to maintain the existing settings and applications (hopefully) during the upgrade to Windows XP. As a general rule, upgrades are more troublesome than clean installations. Windows XP must deal with previous operating system files, possible incompatibilities, driver issues, and often hardware that were not designed with Windows XP in mind. Because of this, upgrades should be carefully studied before they are performed. Careful consideration will help you ensure that the upgrade will be successful.

When you begin the installation of Windows XP, the setup routine detects any previous versions of Windows that may be present, depending on the version, Windows XP can either upgrade the existing operating system or it can install a clean copy of Windows XP. The procedures are as follows:

- **Upgrade** Windows XP installs in the same folder as the previous operating system, upgrading files and drivers as needed. Your existing applications and settings are preserved.
- **Clean Install** Windows XP installs in a different folder. Once installation is complete, you must reinstall any applications that you want to use.

If you want to maintain existing settings and applications, choose the upgrade option. However, in some cases, a clean install may be desirable. For example, let's say you are upgrading Windows 98 to Windows XP. A first choice might be to perform an upgrade and keep your existing settings. However, let's say there are some problems with the Windows 98 installation that you have been unable to resolve. A better choice might be the clean installation, so that you can be sure of avoiding installation problems with Windows XP. In either case, you'll have to make a decision about what is best for your needs and the particular computer you are installing. As a general rule, upgrading to Windows XP is very easy and straightforward, but you should be certain to adhere to the guidelines set out in the following sections.

Upgrade Compatibility

All hardware requirements still apply in an upgrade scenario, so it is important to check out the computer's hardware before starting an upgrade. Also, spend a few moments checking out the applications you are installing to see if they are compatible with Windows XP. You can check the software vendors' Web sites for upgrade information.

Windows XP Professional can directly upgrade the following operating systems:

- All versions of Windows 98
- Windows Me
- Windows NT 4.0 Workstation (with service pack 6 or later)
- Windows 2000 Professional
- Windows XP Home edition

Notice that Windows 95 did not make the list; nor did any previous versions of Windows NT. If you want to upgrade these operating systems, your choices are a clean install (in which case, you lose all of your applications and settings) or an upgrade of the unsupported operating system to a supported version, followed by an upgrade to Windows XP. For example, you could upgrade Windows 95 to Windows 98 and then to Windows XP.

Running a Backup

It is easy for IT professionals to get sloppy with data backup. After all, backups take time to configure, and depending on how you are using them, they can be disruptive. However, the best action you can take before installing Windows XP Professional as an upgrade is to back up the previous operating system and all of your data. In the event that something goes wrong during installation, you can always recover from backup. Of course, if you are installing a clean copy of Windows XP Professional or installing XP on a new computer with no operating system, a backup is unnecessary. In an upgrade scenario, however, it is very important to protect your data by backing it up. Depending on the operating system you are currently using, your backup options may vary—you can even use third party backup tools, so you'll need to check your current operating system for backup instructions.

SCENARIO & SOLUTION

In an upgrade scenario, will the old applications still work?	Maybe. Applications that are maintained during an upgrade will work if they are compatible with Windows XP. Applications that are not compatible will be identified and flagged for your review during the upgrade process. Even if an application is reported as not compatible, you still may be able to use it with Windows XP, due to Windows XP's Program Compatibility wizard, which you can learn more about in Chapter 13.
I want to upgrade Windows NT 3.*x* to Windows XP. What do I need to do?	First, carefully check for hardware compatibility. If everything checks out, then you need to upgrade NT 3.*x* to NT 4.0. Next, apply service pack 6, and then run the Windows XP upgrade.
What is the biggest problem with upgrades?	The most common problem is hardware compatibility. Keep in mind that Windows XP is built on the power of Windows 2000, and the operating system expects that you have a powerful processor and enough RAM in order for it to function. Although you can directly upgrade Windows 98/Me to Windows XP, it is not unusual for these computers to not have enough RAM or processing power for XP. So, investigate hardware carefully.

Application Compatibility

Before installing Windows XP Professional, you should take a look at the applications that you want to use with the operating system. If you are moving from some earlier version of Windows, such as Windows 98, you may have applications that are not compatible with Windows XP. If you are moving from Windows 2000, you are not likely to experience any problems. The good news is that Windows XP Professional contains an application compatibility tool that will often enable you to run applications designed for previous versions of Windows. See Chapter 13 to learn more.

Finally, you need to remove any software that may interfere with installation:

- Uninstall any antivirus programs. Setup needs full access to your computer's hard drive and antivirus programs may interfere.

- You cannot install Windows XP Professional on any drives that are compressed. Decompress affected drives before running the installation.
- Remove any disk management software as these programs may interfere with installation.
- This is a good time to do housecleaning—remove any programs that you no longer use, are incompatible with Windows XP, or are outdated.

EXERCISE 2-2

Preparing for an Upgrade

The Scenario: You are currently using Windows NT 3.51 Workstation. The computer's hardware meets the compatibility requirements for Windows XP Professional. You would like to upgrade the computer to Windows XP Professional, but it is very important that you keep your existing settings. What can you do?

The Solution: You cannot directly upgrade to Windows XP Professional from Windows NT 3.51. In this situation, where you must keep the existing settings, you need to upgrade Windows NT 3.51 to Windows NT 4.0 and apply the latest service pack. Then, you can upgrade to Windows XP Professional.

CERTIFICATION OBJECTIVE 2.03

Installing Windows XP Professional

Windows XP Professional can be installed as an attended installation using the installation CD-ROM or over the network from a network share. In many network environments, the network installation option is often used to make installations easier and provide one central location for the installation files. The following sections explore both types of installations.

SCENARIO & SOLUTION	
Why do I need to reinstall my applications if I choose a clean install?	A clean installation installs Windows XP to a separate folder from your previous operating system. As a result, applications are not migrated to Windows XP, thus requiring reinstallation.
I am upgrading from Windows Me to Windows XP Professional, but I want to use the NTFS file system. What can I do?	The easiest solution is to run the installation and then convert the drive to NTFS using Windows XP's disk administrator tool. All of your data will be preserved in the conversion process. See Chapter 7 to learn more about disk configuration and file systems.
Why do I have to uninstall antivirus software?	Antivirus software typically works in the system background, constantly checking your system for viruses. It is this the antivirus software's accessing of your computer's hard drive that will interfere with installation. In order to avoid the problem, just uninstall the software and then reinstall it once the upgrade is complete (assuming your current version is compatible with Windows XP Professional).

Installing from CD-ROM

The Windows XP installation CD is bootable, and you can start installation by simply booting from the CD if your computer supports CD booting. In an upgrade or clean install scenario, just insert the CD-ROM while you are booted into your current operating system and follow the setup instructions. If your computer has no operating system and your CD-ROM drive is not bootable, you'll need to boot into DOS using a startup disk (or even a Windows 98 startup disk). You can then start the installation by accessing your CD-ROM drive and running setup.exe.

At the Welcome to Microsoft Windows XP screen, you can launch setup, or you can have setup check your system for compatibility. Setup is rather straightforward. Exercise 2-3 walks you through the installation process.

EXERCISE 2-3

Installing Windows XP Professional

To install Windows XP Professional, follow these steps:

1. Launch the CD-ROM or setup.exe, as appropriate for your particular installation.
2. Setup begins and collects information about your computer. In the Welcome to Windows Setup screen, seen in Figure 2-1, you can use the drop-down menu to select New Installation or Upgrade. Make your decision and click Next.
3. The Licensing Agreement window appears. Read the agreement, click the "I accept this agreement" radio button, and click Next.
4. The Product Key window appears. Enter the 25-character product key that is found on the yellow sticker on the back of your CD case. Enter the key, and click Next.
5. The Setup Options window appears, as shown in Figure 2-2 (if you selected the Clean Install option in Step 2). At this point, you can change the Accessibility Options and language if desired. Click the Advanced button.

FIGURE 2-1

Select an installation type and click Next.

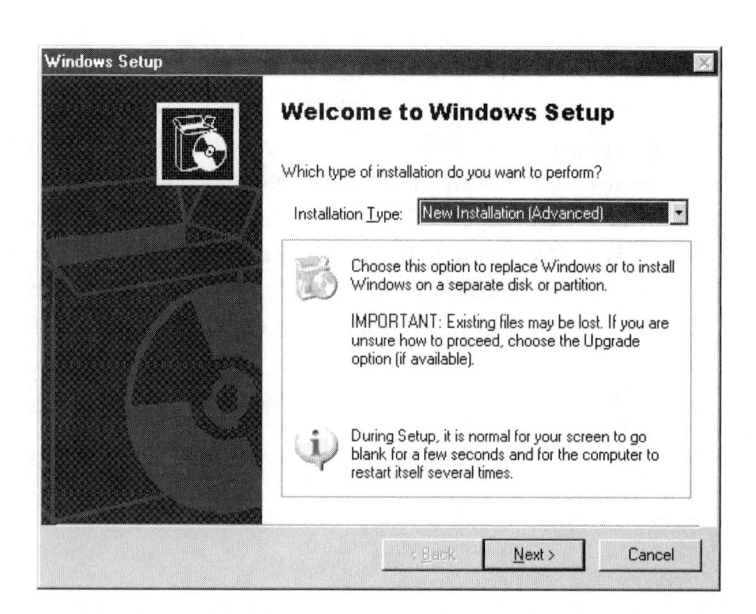

FIGURE 2-2

The Setup Options window

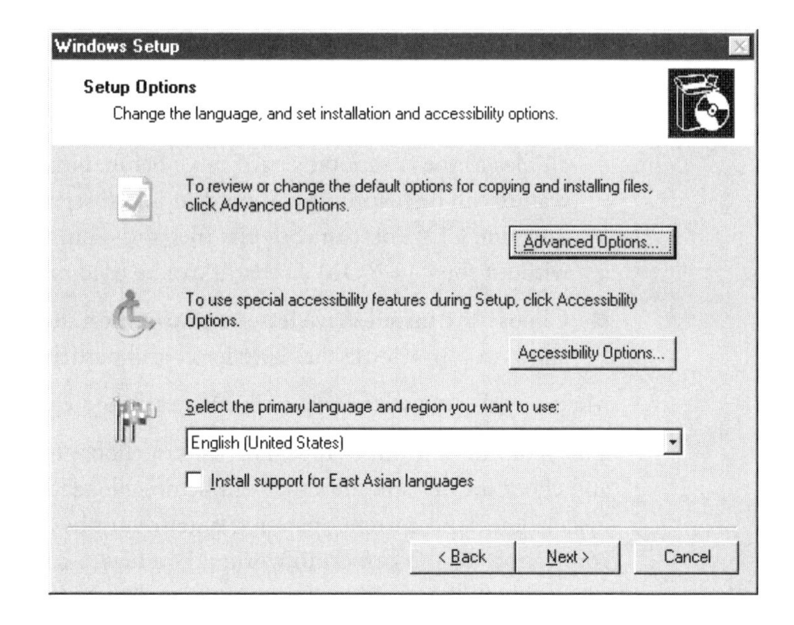

6. In the Advanced Options window, shown in Figure 2-3, you have the following options:
   - **Installation file copy** You can specify the location from which the setup files should be copied. This feature can be useful if you need to start setup from a CD but actually want the files copied from another location.

FIGURE 2-3

The Advanced Options window

Advanced Options

Customize your Windows XP installation options.

Copy installation files from this folder:

E:\i386

Browse...

To this folder on my hard drive:

\WINDOWS

Copy all installation files from the Setup CD

I want to choose the install drive letter and partition during Setup

OK

Cancel

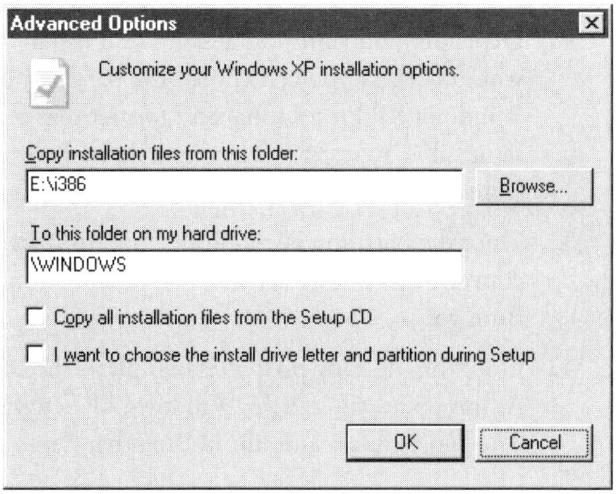

- **Folder location** You can specify the folder name to which the files should be copied. \Windows is the default and typically what you should use.
- **Copy all installation files from the Setup CD** Use this option to copy all files to the computer's hard drive before beginning installation. This feature can be helpful if you need to install several computers but have only one CD. You can copy the files and continue with the installation without the CD-ROM so that it can be used on another machine.
- **Choose the install drive letter and partition during Setup** This option allows you to choose the drive letter and partition during Setup.

Make any desired selections, click OK, and then click Next.

7. The Setup Files window appears. You can choose to connect to the Internet and check for updated files that can be downloaded and used during the installation. Your current operating system must be configured with an Internet connection for this option to work; if you have a connection, you should use the option. Choose either Yes or No and click Next.
8. At this point, the file copy process begins. The setup procedure copies necessary files to your computer's hard drive and then automatically reboots your computer. (Make sure there is no floppy disk in the disk drive.)
9. Once the computer reboots, the MS-DOS portion of setup begins. The Setup Notification window appears. Press ENTER to continue.
10. In the Welcome to Setup window, you can choose to install Windows XP Professional now by pressing ENTER, repair an existing installation by pressing R, or quit setup by pressing F3. Press ENTER to continue with Setup.
11. Depending on your upgrade or clean install choices, you may see a partition window where you can choose the partition in which you want to install Windows XP Professional and format that partition as well. Follow the setups that appear for selecting a desired partition, creating a partition from unpartitioned space, and formatting that partition.
12. Once the partition is established and formatted with a file system, the file copy process begins. This may take some time and requires no intervention from you.
13. Once the file copy process is complete, the computer automatically reboots. At this point, you see the Windows XP Setup screen and installation continues. The approximate amount of time that Setup will require is displayed here as

well. It is not unusual for the screen to flicker several times during this phase of setup.

14. During the installation of Windows XP Professional, the Regional and Language Options window appears. You can click the Customize button to choose a different language or region, or you can click the Details button to view information about your current regional configuration. Click Next to continue.
15. In the Personalize Your Software window, enter your name and organization. Click Next.
16. In the Computer Name and Administrator Password window, enter a name for the computer (or accept the default) and an administrator password. The password will be used in conjunction with the Windows XP Professional administrator account and should be kept private. Typically, for the best security, the local administrator password should be at least seven characters long and should contain both letters and numbers.
17. In the Modem Dialing information window, choose your country and enter your area code and outside line number (if necessary). This window does not appear if you do not have a modem attached to your computer. Click Next.
18. In the Date and Time Settings window, use the drop-down menus to choose the correct time, date, and time zone. Click Next.
19. Setup continues, and a Networking Settings window appears if a network adapter card is installed on the computer. You can choose Typical Settings (which installs TCP/IP), Client for Microsoft Networks, and File and Printer Sharing for Microsoft Networks. If you want to select the services and IP address you will configure, choose the Custom Settings option and click Next to complete the information.
20. The Choose Workgroup or Computer Domain window appears. Choose a desired work or domain name and click Next. If you are creating a new workgroup, enter the desired name in the provided dialog box.
21. Setup continues and may require another 30 minutes or longer before the computer reboots.
22. Once the computer reboots, Windows XP Professional boots for the first time.

Once setup completes, a few questions appear for the user to answer, such as the Internet connection configuration, the user's name, registration, and other subjects. The user can also choose to activate Windows XP Professional if an Internet connection exists. See "Activating Windows XP Professional" later in this chapter for more information about activation of the software.

Installing from a Network Share

You can easily install Windows XP on client computers via the network by using a network installation. The actual installation steps and procedures remain the same when installing over a network share, but the installation is started by connecting to the network share and launching setup.exe.

In order to install Windows XP Professional over the network, you must first set up a server that will function as a "distribution server." This server holds a shared folder that contains all of the contents of the Windows XP Professional installation CD-ROM. In actuality, the distribution server can even be another workstation—the requirement is that client computers have access to the server, whether it is an actual server or another client computer. To use a distribution server, create a shared folder on the desired computer and copy the contents from the Windows XP installation CD-ROM to this folder.

For client computers to access the shared folder, the client computer must be configured with a network card and connection cabling. In most cases, the use of a distribution server is helpful for upgrades, where IT support personnel or even end users themselves use the existing operating system to connect to the shared folder and begin installation. If a computer has no current operating system, then you need a network boot disk in order to install Windows XP in this manner.

To begin the installation, the client computer simply connects to the distribution server's shared folder and launches setup.exe. For example, if the distribution server's name is Server12 and the shared folder's name is XP, then the installation can be started by connecting to \\Server12\XP\setup.exe. When setup.exe is launched, the files are copied from the distribution server to client computer, and installation proceeds as it typically would.

Using Winnt32.exe

You can modify setup using Winnt32.exe. Winnt32.exe is a setup program used to start a Windows XP installation using a variety of setup switches. Windows XP

Professional, as with previous versions of Windows, supports Winnt32.exe, and you can use this program for an upgrade of supported version of Windows. Using the provided setup switches, you can make the installation of Windows XP easier by invoking different needs or setup options automatically. Also, if you want to use an unattended installation of Windows XP Professional, you can start the unattended installation using Winnt32.exe as well. See Chapter 3 to learn more about unattended installations. The syntax of Winnt32.exe and an explanation of the available command line switches are provided in Table 2-2.

exam Watch

You should be very familiar with these setup switches and syntax for the exam. You may be provided with a scenario question that requires a certain outcome when using Winnt32.exe. In order to choose the correct configuration, you'll need to know the syntax and switches.

```
winnt32 [/checkupgradeonly] [/cmd:command_line] [/cmdcons]
[/copydir:i386\folder_name] [/copysource:folder_name]
[/debug[level]:[filename]] [/dudisable] [/duprepare:pathname]
[/dushare:pathname] [/m:folder_name] [/makelocalsource]
[/noreboot] [/s:sourcepath] [/syspart:drive_letter]
[/tempdrive:drive_letter] [/udf:id
[,UDB_file]] [/unattend[num]:[answer_file]]
```

TABLE 2-2 Winnt32.exe Command Line Parameters

Switch	Explanation
/checkupgradeonly	Checks your computer for upgrade compatibility with Windows XP. If you use this option with /unattend, no user input is required. Otherwise, the results are displayed on the screen, and you can save them under the filename you specify. The default filename is Upgrade.txt in the systemroot folder.
/cmd:command_line	Tells Setup to carry out a specific command before the final phase of Setup. This occurs after your computer has restarted and after Setup has collected the necessary configuration information but before Setup is complete.

TABLE 2-2 Winnt32.exe Command Line Parameters *(continued)*

Switch	Explanation
/cmdcons	Installs the Recovery Console as a startup option on a functioning computer. You can only use the /cmdcons option after normal Setup is finished.
/copydir:i386\folder_name	Creates an additional folder within the folder in which the Windows XP files are installed. You can use /copydir to create as many additional folders as you want.
/copysource:folder_name	Creates a temporary additional folder within the folder in which the Windows XP files are installed. You can use /copysource to create as many additional folders as you want, but the folders /copydir creates, /copysource folders, are deleted after Setup completes.
/debug[level]:[filename]	Creates a debug log at the level specified, for example, /debug4:Debug.log. The default log file is C:\systemroot\Winnt32.log, and the default debug level is 2. The log levels are as follows: 0 represents severe errors, 1 represents errors, 2 represents warnings, 3 represents information, and 4 represents detailed information for debugging. Each level includes the levels below it.
/dudisable	Stops Dynamic Update from running. This option will disable Dynamic Update, even if you use an answer file and specify Dynamic Update options in that file.
/duprepare:pathname	Carries out preparations on an installation share so that it can be used with Dynamic Update files that you downloaded from the Windows Update Web site. This share can then be used for installing Windows XP for multiple clients.
/dushare:pathname	Specifies a share on which you previously downloaded Dynamic Update from the Windows Update Web site and on which you previously ran /duprepare:pathname. When run on a client, specifies that the client installation will make use of the updated files on the share specified in pathname.
/m:folder_name	Specifies that Setup copies replacement files from an alternative location. Instructs Setup to look in the alternate location first and, if files are present, to use them instead of the files from the default location.

TABLE 2-2 Winnt32.exe Command Line Parameters *(continued)*

Switch	Explanation
/makelocalsource	Tells Setup to copy all installation source files to the local hard disk. Use /makelocalsource when installing from a CD to provide installation files when the CD is not available later in the installation.
/noreboot	Instructs Setup to not restart the computer after the file copy phase of Setup is completed, so that you can execute another command.
/s:sourcepath	Specifies the source location of the Windows XP files. To simultaneously copy files from multiple servers, type the /s:sourcepath option multiple times (up to a maximum of eight). If you type the option multiple times, the first server specified must be available, or Setup will fail.
/syspart:drive_letter	Specifies that you can copy Setup startup files to a hard disk, mark the disk as active, and then install the disk into another computer. When you start that computer, it automatically starts with the next phase of Setup. You must always use the /tempdrive parameter with the /syspart parameter. See Chapter 3 to learn more about the System Preparation Tool.
/tempdrive:drive_letter	Directs Setup to place temporary files on the specified partition. For a new installation, Windows XP will also be installed on the specified partition. For an upgrade, the /tempdrive option affects the placement of temporary files only; the operating system will be upgraded in the partition from which you run winnt32.
/udf:id [,UDB_file]	Uses an identifier (id) for Setup to specify how a Uniqueness Database (UDB) file modifies an answer file (see the /unattend entry).
/unattend	Runs an upgrade using the previous operating system (if supported). All user settings are taken from the previous installation, so no user intervention is required during Setup.
/unattend[num]:[answer_file]	Performs a fresh installation in unattended Setup mode. The specified answer_file provides Setup with your custom specifications. num is the number of seconds between the time that Setup finishes copying the files and when it restarts your computer. You can use num on any computer running Windows 98, Windows Me, Windows NT, Windows 2000, or Windows XP.

SCENARIO & SOLUTION	
What about licensing with a distribution server?	The distribution server provides the installation files required for a Windows XP Professional installation, but the actual product numbers users can use is based on your licensing agreements with Microsoft. In order to widely distribute Windows XP Professional in a network environment via a distribution server, your company must purchase the required CALs (Client Access Licenses) so that installations are in legal compliance with Microsoft.
I need to run Setup in a way so that it asks no setup questions. How can I do that?	With an attended installation, you must reply to Setup prompts. However, you can configure an unattended installation of Windows XP in which an answer file provides the answers for you. See Chapter 3 to learn more.
I want to make sure that the Windows XP Recovery Console is installed with my XP installation. How can I configure this?	Use Winnt32.exe and use the /cmdcons switch. The Recovery Console will be installed once the XP Professional installation is complete. See Chapter 13 to learn more about the Recovery Console.

CERTIFICATION OBJECTIVE 2.04

Performing Post-Installation Updates and Product Activation

Once the installation of Windows XP Professional is complete, your final tasks as an IT professional will often include post installation updates and Windows XP Professional product activation. The following sections take a look at each of these.

Post-Installation Updates

From time to time, Microsoft releases service packs. If you have spent any time in a Windows NT or Windows 2000 environment, the concept of "service pack" is

FROM THE CLASSROOM

Network Installations in the Real World

Although the MCSE Windows XP Professional exam expects you to know the ins and outs of the attended setup, the exam is more likely to focus on issues with over the network installations and unattended installations. In network environments where hundreds or possibly thousands of XP Professional upgrades may be necessary, IT professionals typically use over-the-network installations, often using an unattended setup. Because an unattended setup uses an answer file that you create in order to answer the setup questions posed, administrators can install numerous machines at the same time in a hands-off manner—which saves a lot time and effort.

In other environments, other mass installation methods may be used, including Remote Installation Service and even image ghosting (see Chapter 3). The point is that Windows XP Professional provides a number of different setup options that can meet the installation needs of busy networks and busy IT professionals. With use of these automated methods, great numbers of computers can be installed and configured quickly and easy, which allows IT professionals to spend their time focused on more complicated tasks.

certainly nothing new. For those of you who are new to the IT world, I'll give you a brief explanation.

A *service pack* is an installation program that updates files on Windows XP Professional. Typically, these "updates" correct problems within the operating system, close security holes, and deal with other types of problems. As you are probably aware, operating systems are released to the public after extensive beta testing, but there is no way to test the operating system in every possible scenario. So, once the operating system is released, Microsoft develops service packs based on customer feedback. Customers identify problems with the operating system, and developers write code that can correct the problems. These "fixes" are collectively called service packs, and Microsoft releases them in a bundle that can be installed together, or if a fix is critical, Microsoft posts the fix on **Microsoft.com**, where it can be downloaded and installed. Service packs are free—you can download them from **Microsoft.com** or order them on CD at a minimal cost.

As an IT professional, you'll want to apply the latest service pack or any critical fixes that may exist once the installation of Windows XP Professional is complete. Service pack installation works by launching a typical setup program, which can be initiated after download, from a CD-ROM or from a network distribution server. You can also apply service packs to a distribution image through a process called *slipstreaming*. With slipstreaming, the service pack becomes integrated with the installation files and is installed at the same time so that installation of service packs is not a separate process. You can use the Update.exe file with the /slip switch in order to overwrite appropriate distribution files with the service pack files.

Aside from service packs, Windows XP Professional also includes the Automatic Updates tab of System Properties, shown in Figure 2-4. With Automatic Updates, Windows XP can automatically check **Microsoft.com** for updates to Windows XP, download those updates, and let the user know when they are ready to be installed. As you can see in Figure 2-4, you can choose to automatically download, notify before download, or turn off the automatic updates feature. Of course, this feature works best with a continuous connection to the Internet, and it can be helpful in keeping the system current. However, since updates are downloaded automatically or require an OK by the user, some end-user training may be necessary.

FIGURE 2-4

The Automatic Updates tab

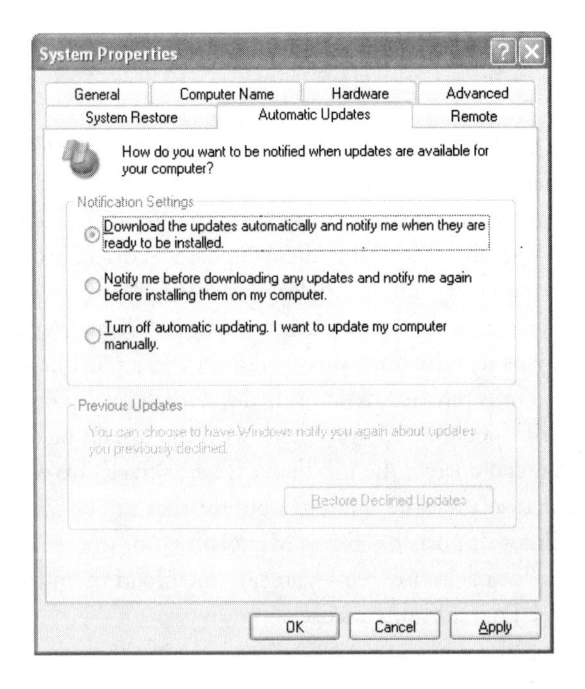

Product Activation

Windows XP Home and Professional versions use a new feature from Microsoft called Product Activation. Due to software piracy, product activation is now used to enforce the end-user license agreement in which one copy of Windows XP can be installed on one computer only. This feature prevents the copying of installation CDs, otherwise known as "softlifting."

During installation, the product key found on the back of the CD-ROM case is combined with a generated hardware identifier number, taken from information about the computer system on which the software is being installed. Taken together, the two numbers create a unique installation ID that is uploaded to Microsoft servers via the Internet or manually through a call to Microsoft customer support. Once the product is activated, the CD cannot be used to install another computer with Windows XP Professional, which enforces the end-user license agreement of one CD per one computer.

on the Job

Customers and end users are often worried that that the installation ID will use some personal information or files from the computer. This is not so. The ID does not scan the system, but uses identity numbers from the computer hardware and then combines those in a one-way hash algorithm. In short, no personal information is included in the ID, none is sent to Microsoft, and personal information is perfectly safe.

In large environments where large number of computers are configured with Windows XP Professional, activation may work differently or not be necessary at all, depending on the licensing agreement between the corporation and Microsoft.

In a typical activation scenario, the user is prompted to activate Windows XP once an installation completes, if a modem is detected on the computer. If one is not detected or a connection cannot be made, the user is prompted to contact Microsoft in order to activate the product manually. Users can skip over this step and activate Windows at a later time because there is a 30-day grace period in which to activate. From an IT professional's perspective, however, users should activate as soon as installation is completed in order to avoid further problems. If Windows XP is not activated immediately after setup, then an Activate icon appears in the Notification Area that can be clicked to start the activation process, or you can simply click Start | All Programs | Activate Windows. Activation is easy, and Exercise 2-4 walks you through this process.

EXERCISE 2-4

CertCam 2-4

Activating Windows XP Professional

To activate Windows XP Professional, follow these steps:

1. Click the Activate icon in the Notification Area, or click Start | All Programs | Activate Windows. Activation can also be launched at the prompt that appears immediately after installation is complete.
2. The "Let's activate Windows" window appears, shown in Figure 2-5. You can choose to activate over the Internet or via a telephone call or choose to reminded every few days. Make a selection and click Next.
3. If you chose to connect via the Internet, a connection is launched to Microsoft and the product is activated. You will receive a message telling you when activation is complete. If you chose the telephone option, you are given a number to call and your installation ID number that you will read to a support representative.

FIGURE 2-5

Windows activation

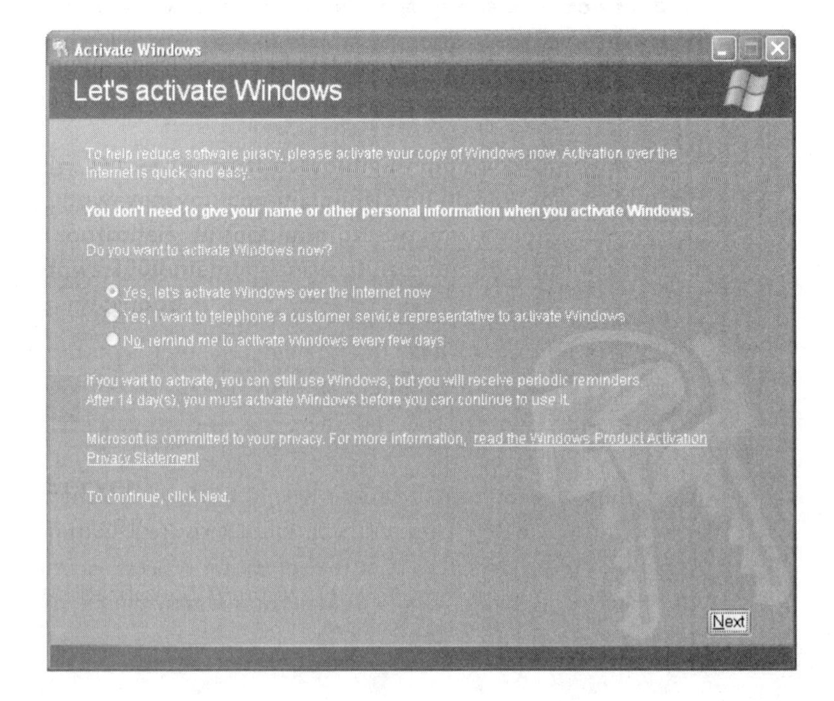

SCENARIO & SOLUTION	
How often should service packs be applied?	Service packs should be applied at the time they are released from Microsoft, and they do not need to be reapplied to Windows XP unless major configuration changes take place. In corporate cases, service packs are typically received automatically via CD, or they can be downloaded from **Microsoft.com**
What happens if a user does not activate Windows XP?	After the 30-day grace period, the user can boot Windows XP and log on, but the activation window will appear and the user must activate the operating system before anything else can be done with the computer system.

CERTIFICATION OBJECTIVE 2.05

Migrating Existing User Environments to Windows XP

One of the big problems with a implementing a new computer system involves migrating documents and settings to that new computer. As PC upgrades and changes have become more common in the ever growing hardware market, this problem has only grown—even at the home user level. Windows XP Professional addresses this problem by providing a new File and Settings Transfer wizard.

The File and Settings Transfer wizard enables you to copy files and settings from a previous version of Windows, where they are saved on some kind of removable media or network connection and then transferred to a new computer. Keep in mind that this feature works for moving data from one computer to another and is not necessary when upgrading the operating system on the same computer. For example, let's say I have an old Windows 98 computer and I purchase a new computer with Windows XP. I can use the File and Settings Transfer wizard to move all of my information and settings to the new computer quickly and easily. You can transfer files and settings from any of the following operating systems:

- Windows 95
- Windows 98
- Windows 98 SE
- Windows Me
- Windows NT 4.0
- Windows 2000
- Windows XP (32 bit only)

The File and Settings Transfer wizard can transfer settings from accessibility, Command Prompt settings, display properties, IE settings, Microsoft Messenger settings, NetMeeting settings, mouse and keyboard settings, MSN Explorer, Network printer and drivers, Outlook Express, Regional settings, sounds and multimedia, taskbar options, Windows Media Player, and Windows Movie Maker. You may also be able to transfer settings from other software, such as Microsoft Outlook. The wizard can also transfer specific folders, such as Desktop, Fonts, My Documents, My Pictures, Shared Desktop, and Shared Documents. Additionally, the wizard can transfer most other multimedia files not found in these folders.

To transfer settings from an older version of Windows, you can use the Windows XP Professional installation CD. The following exercise walks you through the process.

EXERCISE 2-5

CertCam 2-5

Transferring Settings from a Downlevel Operating System

To transfer settings from a downlevel operating system, follow these steps:

1. On the downlevel computer, insert the Windows XP Professional CD-ROM. At the Windows XP startup screen, click Perform Additional Tasks and then click Transfer Files And Settings.

2. The File and Settings transfer wizard appears. Click Next.
3. The system is scanned and the "Select a transfer method" window appears, as shown in Figure 2-6. You can choose to use a direct cable connection, network connection, removable media connection, or another type of connection (such as saving the settings to disk drive or network folder). Make your selection and click Next.
4. In the "What do you want to transfer" window, you can choose to transfer settings only, files only, or both. You can click the "Let me select. . ." check box to specifically select what you want to transfer, as shown in Figure 2-7. Make your selection and click Next.
5. If you chose the "Let me select. . ." check box option in Step 4, the custom window appears, shown in Figure 2-8. From this window, you can add/remove settings and files, file types, and folders, as desired. When you are done, click Next.
6. The wizard collects the data that you specified. This may take some time, depending on how much information you want to transfer. When the wizard is done, click Finish.

FIGURE 2-6

Choose a transfer method.

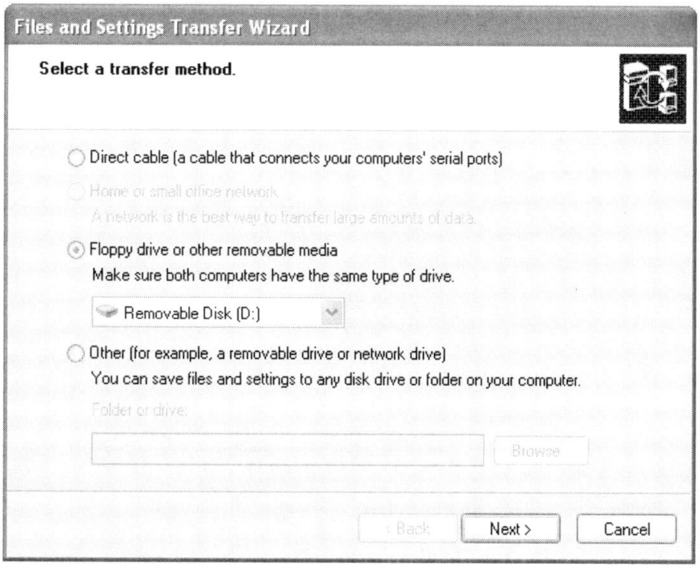

FIGURE 2-7

Choose what to transfer.

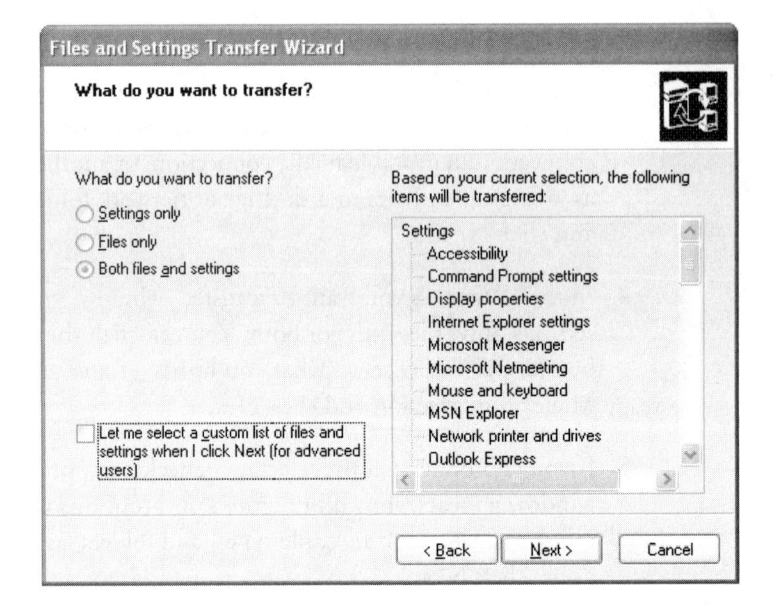

FIGURE 2-8

Choose a custom transfer selection.

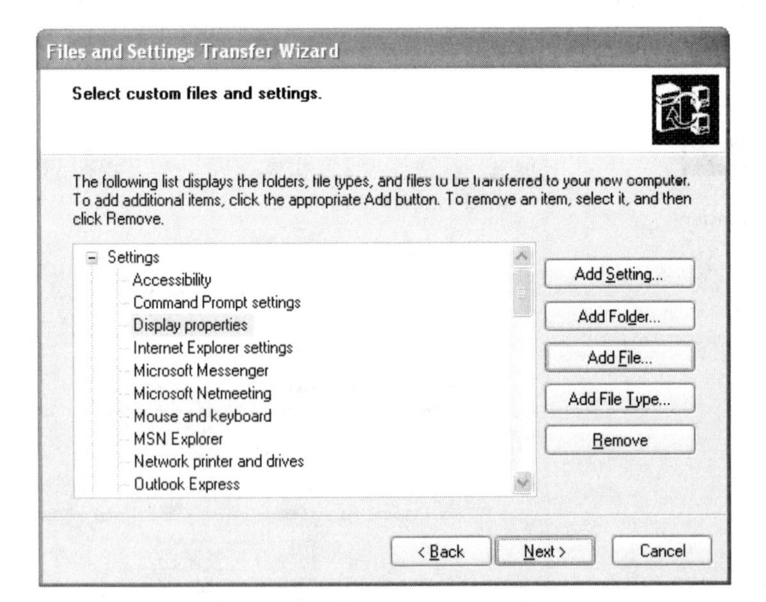

Once you have completed the collection portion of the File and Settings Transfer wizard, you can now run the wizard on your Windows XP computer so that the settings can be migrated and configured. Once again, the File and Settings Transfer wizard walks you through this process, and you can view a walkthrough in Exercise 2-6.

EXERCISE 2-6

CertCam 2-6

Migrating Settings and Files to Windows XP

To migrate the desired files and settings to Windows XP, follow these steps:

1. Click Start | All Programs | Accessories | System Tools | Files and Settings Transfer Wizard.
2. Click Next on the Welcome screen.
3. On the "Which computer is this" screen, click the New Computer radio button and click Next.
4. The wizard then provides a screen asking if you have a Windows XP CD and telling you that you need to run the wizard on the old computer. Notice here that the wizard can create a wizard disk for you if you are missing the CD-ROM. Since you have already collected your settings in the previous exercise, click the "I don't need the Wizard Disk" radio button option, shown in Figure 2-9, and then click Next.
5. Choose where the files should be collected (for instance, direct cable connection, removable media, or network folder). Make your selection and click Next.
6. The wizard locates the files and transfers them to the new computer. Click Finish. You will be prompted to log off and log back on in order for the settings to take effect.

FIGURE 2-9

Preparation screen

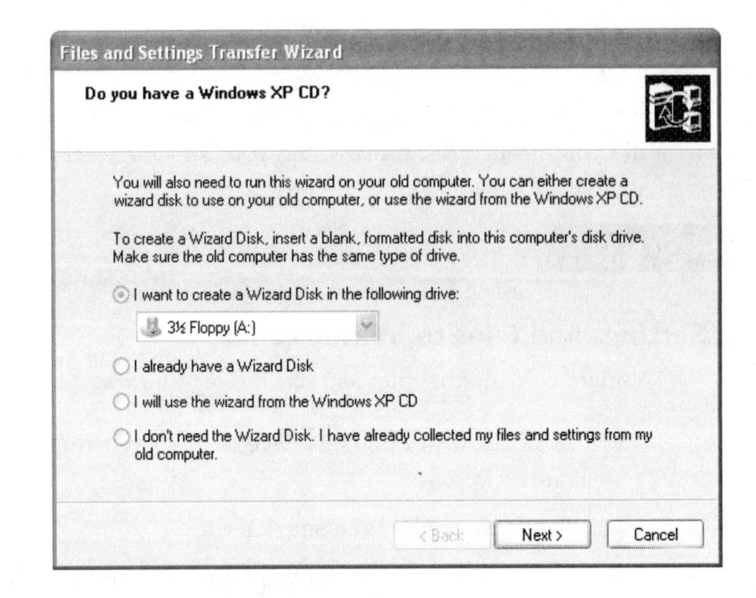

CERTIFICATION OBJECTIVE 2.06

Troubleshooting Failed Installations

Windows XP Professional is the best operating system Microsoft has ever produced, in my humble opinion. However, it is not perfect, and there is always a possibility that something may go wrong during installation. Typically, if you follow the hardware guidelines and setup procedures, you are unlikely to experience installation problems, but, as an IT professional, you should be aware of potential problems and troubleshooting areas.

In a typical Windows XP Professional installation scenario, the most common causes of installation problems or failure are these:

- Hardware incompatibilities or hardware that does not meet the minimum hardware requirements. Typically, Windows XP will tell you if the hardware in the PC is not compatible or does not meet minimum standards; however, in a failed installation, you should always start here and make sure there are no compatibility problems.

- Some CD-ROM drives, particularly older drives, may not work well with Windows XP. Make sure the CD-ROM drive is compatible. Also, make sure you do not have a faulty CD.
- During hardware detection and driver installation, your computer can lock up. Although this typically does not happen with Windows XP, you can simply restart the computer and installation should continue where it left off.
- Make sure your video card is up to date and is supported by Windows XP Professional. Installation problems can occur due to faulty video cards.

If you are having extensive problems with setup and you have checked the previous bullet points, you can also access a setup log to determine what problems may have occurred. This assumes that you can get the operating system actually installed. The log is called setupact.txt and is located in C:\Winnt (if you installed in a different drive, just substitute the correct drive letter for C). You can see a sample of Setupact.txt in Figure 2-10.

FIGURE 2-10 The Setupact.txt installation log file

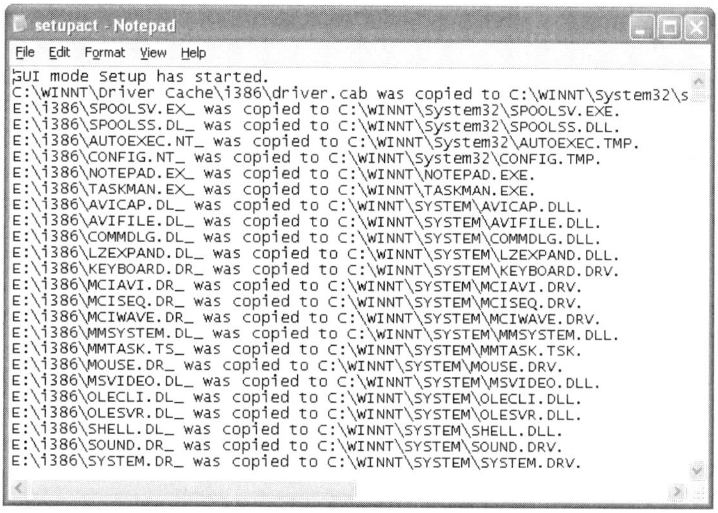

```
setupact - Notepad
File Edit Format View Help
GUI mode Setup has started.
C:\WINNT\Driver Cache\i386\driver.cab was copied to C:\WINNT\System32\s
E:\i386\SPOOLSV.EX_ was copied to C:\WINNT\System32\SPOOLSV.EXE.
E:\i386\SPOOLSS.DL_ was copied to C:\WINNT\System32\SPOOLSS.DLL.
E:\i386\AUTOEXEC.NT_ was copied to C:\WINNT\System32\AUTOEXEC.TMP.
E:\i386\CONFIG.NT_ was copied to C:\WINNT\System32\CONFIG.TMP.
E:\i386\NOTEPAD.EX_ was copied to C:\WINNT\NOTEPAD.EXE.
E:\i386\TASKMAN.EX_ was copied to C:\WINNT\TASKMAN.EXE.
E:\i386\AVICAP.DL_ was copied to C:\WINNT\SYSTEM\AVICAP.DLL.
E:\i386\AVIFILE.DL_ was copied to C:\WINNT\SYSTEM\AVIFILE.DLL.
E:\i386\COMMDLG.DL_ was copied to C:\WINNT\SYSTEM\COMMDLG.DLL.
E:\i386\LZEXPAND.DL_ was copied to C:\WINNT\SYSTEM\LZEXPAND.DLL.
E:\i386\KEYBOARD.DR_ was copied to C:\WINNT\SYSTEM\KEYBOARD.DRV.
E:\i386\MCIAVI.DR_ was copied to C:\WINNT\SYSTEM\MCIAVI.DRV.
E:\i386\MCISEQ.DR_ was copied to C:\WINNT\SYSTEM\MCISEQ.DRV.
E:\i386\MCIWAVE.DR_ was copied to C:\WINNT\SYSTEM\MCIWAVE.DRV.
E:\i386\MMSYSTEM.DL_ was copied to C:\WINNT\SYSTEM\MMSYSTEM.DLL.
E:\i386\MMTASK.TS_ was copied to C:\WINNT\SYSTEM\MMTASK.TSK.
E:\i386\MOUSE.DR_ was copied to C:\WINNT\SYSTEM\MOUSE.DRV.
E:\i386\MSVIDEO.DL_ was copied to C:\WINNT\SYSTEM\MSVIDEO.DLL.
E:\i386\OLECLI.DL_ was copied to C:\WINNT\SYSTEM\OLECLI.DLL.
E:\i386\OLESVR.DL_ was copied to C:\WINNT\SYSTEM\OLESVR.DLL.
E:\i386\SHELL.DL_ was copied to C:\WINNT\SYSTEM\SHELL.DLL.
E:\i386\SOUND.DR_ was copied to C:\WINNT\SYSTEM\SOUND.DRV.
E:\i386\SYSTEM.DR_ was copied to C:\WINNT\SYSTEM\SYSTEM.DRV.
```

CERTIFICATION SUMMARY

The MCSE Windows XP Professional exam expects you to know how to perform an attended Windows XP Professional installation. Windows XP Professional is an operating system that can be easily installed via CD-ROM or via a network share. You can choose an upgrade installation or a clean installation. Windows XP Professional can directly upgrade all versions of Windows 98, Windows Me, Windows NT 4.0 Workstation, Windows 2000 Professional, or Windows XP Home edition. A clean installation installs Windows XP Professional into a different folder, in which case all settings must be reconfigured and all applications reinstalled.

Before installing Windows XP Professional, make sure the computer meets the minimum hardware requirements, check the HCL for compatibility, and check applications for compatibility as well. The setup routine can also check these items for you as well.

Once installation is complete, apply the latest service pack and activate the software by connecting to Microsoft via the Internet or over the telephone to support personnel. Windows XP Professional can also easily transfer settings from earlier versions of Windows to Windows XP via the Files and Settings Transfer wizard.

Typically, installations are problem free, but should you experience problems, always check the hardware for compatibility and take a look at setupact.txt in C:\Winnt for clues about setup problems.

TWO-MINUTE DRILL

Planning a Windows XP Professional Installation

- Windows XP Professional's minimum hardware requirements are a 233 MHz Pentium processor or equivalent, 64 MB of RAM, 1.5 GB of hard disk space. A standard mouse, CD-ROM, and keyboard should also be used.
- You should always check the Hardware Compatibility List at **Microsoft.com** for the latest information about Windows XP Professional and hardware compatibility.
- Hardware not explicitly listed on the HCL may be compatible, but you will need to do some research on the manufacturer's Web site.
- Hard disks can be partitioned and formatted before and during an installation. Additional partitioning can also be performed after installation
- Check applications for compatibility before upgrading. You can also use the Compatibility checking tool found on the Windows XP Professional CD-ROM.

Upgrade Considerations

- You can upgrade all versions of Windows 98, Windows Me, Windows NT 4.0 Workstation, Windows 2000 Professional, or Windows XP Home edition to Windows XP Professional. All other downlevel operating system must be upgraded to one of these, or a clean installation can be used.
- You should perform a complete backup before upgrading to Windows XP Professional in the event that you need to return to the previous version of Windows.

Installing Windows XP Professional

- An attended installation can be performed by CD-ROM or over the network from a distribution server.
- You must have a valid product key in order to install Windows XP Professional.

- You can begin the installation directly from the CD or over the network by starting setup.exe.
- You can upgrade to Windows XP Professional or choose a clean installation.

Performing Post-Installation Updates and Product Activation

- Microsoft produces service packs from time to time that contains fixes for Windows XP Professional. Once installation is complete, any current service pack should be applied. Service packs are typically installed via a simple setup program and can be distributed via a network share.
- Windows XP Professional generates a unique installation ID using your CD number and numbers from your computer's hardware. This ID is used to prevent piracy and must be submitted to Microsoft via the Internet or by a phone call within 30 days of the installation.

Migrating Existing User Environments to Windows XP

- You can easily migrate user environments and files to Windows XP using the Files and Settings Transfer wizard.
- You can migrate files and settings from Windows 9*x*, Me, Windows NT 4.0, Windows 2000, and Windows XP.

Troubleshooting Failed Installations

- Failed installations typically occur because of hardware incompatibilities. Be sure the check the computer for compatibility before installation begins.
- If you have a problematic installation, check the setupact.txt log, which can give you clues and information about the setup routine.

SELF TEST

The following questions will help you measure your understanding of the material presented in this chapter. Read all of the choices carefully, as there may be more than one correct answer. Choose all correct answers for each question.

Planning a Windows XP Professional Installation

1. A user wants to install Windows XP Professional on a computer that has a 300 MHz Pentium, 128MB of RAM, and 1.2GB of hard disk space. What would you say to the user?

A. The hardware meets installation requirements.

B. The processor needs to be upgraded.

C. The computer needs more RAM.

D. The computer needs more hard disk space.

2. What is the recommended amount of RAM a computer should have installed before installing Windows XP Professional?

A. 64MB

B. 128MB

C. 256MB

D. 512MB

3. You want to install Windows XP on a particular computer, but you are not sure if the modem installed on this computer will work with Windows XP Professional. What should you do first?

A. Download new drivers.

B. Check the manufacturer's Web site for compatibility instructions.

C. Check the HCL.

D. Call the computer manufacturer.

4. In which case should NTFS not be used as the file system with Windows XP Professional?

A. When you need partitions larger than 10MB

B. When you have more than three volumes

C. In a dual-boot scenario with a Windows 9*x* computer

D. In a dual-boot scenario with Windows 2000

Upgrade Considerations

5. Which operating system cannot be directly upgraded to Windows XP Professional?

A. Windows 95

B. Windows NT 4.0 Workstation

C. Windows 2000 Professional

D. Windows XP Home

6. During an attended upgrade, you do not want any of the previous operating system's settings or applications to apply to Windows XP Professional. What installation option should you select?

A. Upgrade

B. Install

C. Clean Install

D. Custom

7. You need to upgrade a Windows NT 3.51 computer to Windows XP Professional. All of the computer's hardware meets the recommended hardware guidelines. You want to make sure that you do not lose any current settings during the upgrade. What should you do?

A. Run the upgrade directly to Windows XP Professional.

B. Save the documents and settings in a backup file, perform a clean install of Windows XP, and the restore the backup.

C. Upgrade to Windows NT 4.0 Workstation first, and then upgrade to Windows XP Professional.

D. You cannot save the settings.

8. Before performing an upgrade, which of the following actions is *not* necessary?

A. Check the system for application compatibility.

B. Uninstall any antivirus software.

C. If the drive is compressed, decompress it.

D. Remove any screen savers.

Installing Windows XP Professional

9. What are the two ways you can start an attended installation?

A. CD-ROM

B. Network distribution server

C. Answer file

D. Floppy disk

10. Which statement is true concerning Windows XP Professional in a Windows domain?

A. Windows XP Professional does not function with domains.

B. You can join a Windows domain during Windows XP Professional installation or even after installation is complete, with appropriate permissions.

C. Windows XP Professional can be a domain user but not a domain member.

D. Windows XP Professional can join a domain once installation is complete, but not during an installation.

11. You want to use Winnt32.exe to run an attended setup of Windows XP Professional. During setup, you want to automatically disable Dynamic Update from running. What switch can you use?

A. /dynamicST

B. /cmdcons

C. /dudisable

D. /dustop

12. You want to use Winnt32.exe to install Windows XP Professional. During installation, you want all of the files copied to a location on your local hard drive. What switch can you use to invoke this option?

A. /makefolderdr

B. /makelocal

C. /makelocaldr

D. /makelocalsource

Performing Post Installation Updates and Product Activation

13. What are the two primary methods used to keep Windows XP Professional updated?

A. Service packs

B. Dynamic updates

C. Automatic updates

D. Resource kits

14. What is used to create the installation ID that is used during product activation?

A. Product ID found on the CD installation case

B. User's e-mail address

C. Hardware ID information

D. Document scans

15. If a user does not activate Windows XP Professional during installation, what happens?

A. The user is locked out of the system.

B. The user is given a 30-day grace period to activate.

C. The user cannot access any Windows menus.

D. The user cannot access the Internet.

Migrating Existing User Environments to Windows XP

16. On which operating systems can you use Windows XP's Files and Settings Transfer wizard?

A. Windows XP

B. Windows 2000

C. All versions of Windows 98

D. Windows NT 4.0

E. Windows 95

17. You want to move some files and settings from a Windows 95 computer to a Windows XP Professional computer. What two ways can you use the Files and Settings Transfer wizard on Windows 95?

A. Use the Windows XP Professional installation CD to run the wizard on the Windows 95 machine.

B. Use a direct cable connection and run the program from Windows XP.

C. Run the program from **Microsoft.com**.

D. Run the Files and Settings Transfer wizard on Windows XP and create a wizard disk to use on the Windows 95 machine.

Troubleshooting Failed Installations

18. Under most circumstances, what is the most likely cause of installation failure or troublesome installations involving Windows XP Professional?

A. Hardware incompatibilities

B. DLL failure

C. File system incompatibilities

D. Upgrade incompatibilities

LAB QUESTION

A small company has hired you as a consultant. You need to install Windows XP Professional on a primary computer in a small office. Currently, all four computers in the office run Windows 95. The computer on which Windows XP Professional should be installed currently has a 400 MHz processor, 32MB of RAM, 5GB of free disk space, and standard keyboard, mouse, CD-ROM, and so on. All settings and applications currently installed on the computer must be preserved. Also, once the installation is complete, the company wants all of the e-mail and documents from one of the other computers moved to the Windows XP Professional computer. How would you handle this upgrade?

SELF TEST ANSWERS

Planning a Windows XP Professional Installation

1. ☑ D is correct. In order to install Windows XP Professional, the minimum amount of free hard disk space required is 1.5GB.

   ☒ A, B, and C are incorrect. The hard disk space requirement does not meet the recommended minimum, so A is incorrect. B and C are both incorrect because the processor and RAM meet minimum requirements.

2. ☑ B is correct. The recommended amount of RAM is 128MB.

   ☒ A, C, and D are incorrect. A is incorrect because 64MB is the minimum requirement, not the recommended requirement. C and D are also incorrect. Although higher amounts of RAM are certainly fine, they are not the published recommended amount.

3. ☑ C is correct. If a hardware device is in question, the first thing you should do is check the HCL at **Microsoft.com/hcl** to see if it is listed or not.

   ☒ A, B, and D are incorrect. Although these actions might be helpful, the first thing you should do is check the HCL. If the device is not listed on the HCL, then the manufacturer's Web site is a good place to start.

4. ☑ C is correct. Windows 95, 98, and Me cannot read NTFS, so in a dual-boot scenario, you should use the FAT or FAT32 file system in order for these downlevel operating systems to be able to access the partition that holds Windows XP Professional.

   ☒ A, B, and D are incorrect. The selection of NTFS is your best choice in terms of partition/volume management, so A and B are incorrect. D is also incorrect, since Windows 2000 can read NTFS as well.

Upgrade Considerations

5. ☑ A is correct. Windows 95 cannot be directly upgraded to Windows XP Professional.

   ☒ B, C, and D are incorrect. All of these operating systems can be directly upgraded to Windows XP Professional.

6. ☑ C is correct. When performing an upgrade, you should choose the clean install option if you do not want to preserve any settings or applications.

☒ A, B, and D are incorrect. The only options you have are to upgrade or clean install. Upgrade is incorrect in this answer, and options B and D are "distracters."

7. ☑ C is correct. If an operating system is not supported for a direct upgrade, you can upgrade to a supported system and then to Windows XP Professional in order to ensure that no settings are lost.

☒ A, B, and D are incorrect. You cannot clean install or directly upgrade in this scenario, and the only way to move the settings is to upgrade to a supported operating system and then to Windows XP Professional.

8. ☑ D is correct. Screen Saver configuration does not impact installation, so this answer option is not necessary.

☒ A, B, and C are incorrect. You should perform all of these actions. Check the system for compatibility, make sure no antivirus programs are installed, and decompress the drive if necessary. You should also uninstall any disk management tools as well.

Installing Windows XP Professional

9. ☑ A and B are correct. For an attended installation, you can run setup.exe either from the CD-ROM or from a network distribution server.

☒ C and D are incorrect. You cannot start an attended setup using an answer file or floppy disk.

10. ☑ B is correct. Windows XP Professional gives you the option to join a domain during installation. You can also join a domain once installation is complete.

☒ A, C, and D are incorrect. Windows XP Professional can be a domain member, and you can join a domain during installation if you like.

11. ☑ C is correct. Use /dudisable to stop the use Dynamic Update

☒ A, B, and D are incorrect. A and D are not real switches, and /cmdcons installs the Recovery Console.

12. ☑ D is correct. Use /makelocalsource to copy all of the installation files to the local hard disk.

☒ A, B, and C are incorrect. None of these are real Winnt32.exe switches.

Performing Post Installation Updates and Product Activation

13. ☑ A and C are correct. Current service packs should be applied to Windows XP Professional when they become available, and you can also choose to use Automatic Updates so that update files can be periodically downloaded from the Web. Automatic Updates are configured in System Properties.

☒ B and D are incorrect. Dynamic Updates occur during installation only, and Resource Kits do not provide any updates.

14. ☑ A and C are correct. The installation ID is made up of your product ID and ID information taken from your computer's hardware.

☒ B and D are incorrect. E-mail addresses or private document information is not used. No personal information is used at all, and activation with Microsoft is completely anonymous.

15. ☑ B is correct. The user is prompted to activate Windows upon the first boot of Windows XP Professional. If the user does not activate Windows, then the user has a 30-day grace period in which to activate. If the user does not activate after the 30-day grace period, the user will not be able to log on to the system, but will be prompted to activate.

☒ A, C, and D are incorrect. Activation provides a 30-day grace period before locking a user out of the system.

Migrating Existing User Environments to Windows XP

16. ☑ A, B, C, D, and E are correct. You can use the Files and Settings Transfer wizard on Windows 9*x*, Me, NT 4.0, 2000, and XP.

☒ All answers are correct.

17. ☑ A and D are correct. Use the installation CD to run the wizard, or Windows XP can create a wizard disk for you.

☒ B and C are incorrect. These are not valid options.

Troubleshooting Failed Installations

18. ☑ A is correct. The most likely cause of installation problems is typically hardware. You should carefully inspect the computer's hardware before installation begins and pay attention to any problem areas Windows XP points out when it scans your system at the beginning of the installation routine.

☒ B, C, and D are incorrect. These answer options are not likely to cause installation failures.

LAB ANSWER

In order to perform this upgrade, you need to complete the following steps:

1. Upgrade the computer's RAM to at least 128MB.
2. Check the HCL for problems with the computer's current hardware, such as the modem, sound card, video card, and so on. Make any upgrades necessary.
3. Upgrade the Windows 95 computer to Windows 98 or Me.
4. Upgrade the computer again to Windows XP Professional. Note any application compatibility issues that are reported to you.
5. Apply any current Windows XP Professional service packs.
6. Use the Files and Settings Transfer wizard to move the desired files from the other Windows 95 machine to the Windows XP Professional computer.

3

Performing an Unattended Installation of Windows XP Professional

CERTIFICATION OBJECTIVES

3.01	Installing Windows XP Professional Using Setup Manager
3.02	Installing Windows XP Professional Using Remote Installation Service
3.03	Installing Windows XP Professional Using System Preparation
✓	Two-Minute Drill
Q&A	Self Test

Like Windows 2000 Professional, Windows XP Professional provides some advanced installation tools that enable large rollouts in corporate networks. These installations, collectively called "unattended" installations, enable IT professionals to deploy Windows XP Professional on thousands of machines at time—quickly, easily, and in a hands-off manner. The benefits of unattended installations are obvious—one IT professional can install hundreds of computers in a single day, whereas an attended installation of each computer would require too much time. Also, unattended installations provide a way to streamline installs so that each computer has the same settings and configuration once the installation is complete. In short, these unattended installations save a tremendous amount of time and money.

We can globally classify Windows XP Professional's unattended installation methods in two broad categories—scripted installations and image installations. The first, scripted installations, is what is most often thought of when we say "unattended installations." An answer file is used to answer setup prompts so that once installation begins, the process is completely automated. The second category can be referred to as an imaging process. A computer with no operating system and with similar hardware receives a complete installation image that is copied to the hard drive. Remote Installation Services and System Preparation both work on an image-based install, but each is quite different As you will see in this chapter, all of these installation options have unique advantages in a number of scenarios, and we will explore them in the following sections.

CERTIFICATION OBJECTIVE 3.01

Installing Windows XP Professional Using Setup Manager

Windows XP Professional contains a program called Setup Manager that can help you generate answer files for a Windows XP Professional unattended installation. Before getting into answer file creation, let's back up a bit and talk about unattended installations and answer files. In an unattended installation, you typically start Setup with Winnt32.exe using an "unattended" option and pointing to an answer file. An answer file is simply a text file that Setup can read to find the "answers" to Setup prompts. For example, Setup always asks if you want to check for Dynamic Updates on the Web. Using the answer file, you can answer the question one time—Setup reads the file, and no input is required directly from you. The advantages are obvious—you can start the installation routine on hundreds of computers at one time and never have to return to them in order to baby-sit the setup program. You can find a sample of an answer file in the I386 folder on your Windows XP Professional CD-ROM. The file is called Unattend.txt, and as you can see in Figure 3-1, the file is a simple text file that you can read.

In the past, answer files were somewhat difficult to create because you had to write them from scratch. With Setup Manager, a wizard guides you through the process and helps you create the answer file, which makes unattended setups a lot easier.

Setup Manager and the other deployment tools explored in this chapter are not available directly from Windows XP Professional after installation, but you must copy them from a cabinet file (compressed) on the Windows XP Professional CD-ROM. Exercise 3-1 walks you through this process.

FIGURE 3-1

Unattended.txt sample answer file found in the I386 folder on the installation CD-ROM

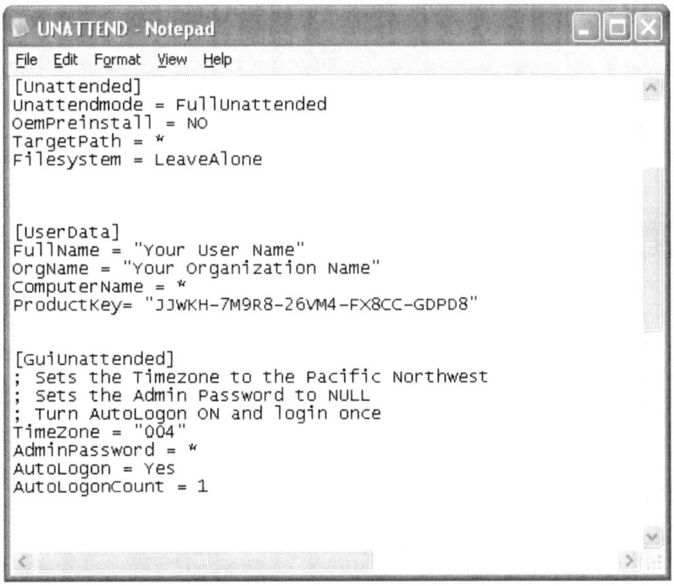

UNATTEND - Notepad

File Edit Format View Help

```
[Unattended]
Unattendmode = FullUnattended
OemPreinstall = NO
TargetPath = *
Filesystem = LeaveAlone



[UserData]
FullName = "Your User Name"
OrgName = "Your Organization Name"
ComputerName = *
ProductKey= "JJWKH-7M9R8-26VM4-FX8CC-GDPD8"


[GuiUnattended]
; Sets the Timezone to the Pacific Northwest
; Sets the Admin Password to NULL
; Turn AutoLogon ON and login once
TimeZone = "004"
AdminPassword = *
AutoLogon = Yes
AutoLogonCount = 1
```

EXERCISE 3-1

Extracting the Deploy.cab Files

To extract the Windows XP Professional deployment tools, follow these steps.

1. On the desired computer, log on as the administrator, create a folder in which to place the deployment tools, and name the folder as desired.
2. Insert the Windows XP Professional installation CD-ROM. Close the installation window that appears.
3. Open My Computer, right-click the CD-ROM drive, and click Explore.
4. Open the Support folder and then the Tools folder. You'll see the Deploy.cab file, as shown in Figure 3-2.
5. Double-click the Deploy.cab file to open it. You'll see several different tools appear, including Setup Manager (setupmgr).
6. Click Edit | Select All, right-click the files, and click Extract.
7. In the Select a Destination dialog box that appears, browse for the folder you created, select it, and then click the Extract button. The tools are copied from the CD-ROM to the desired folder.

FIGURE 3-2

Deploy.cab is found in \Support\Tools.

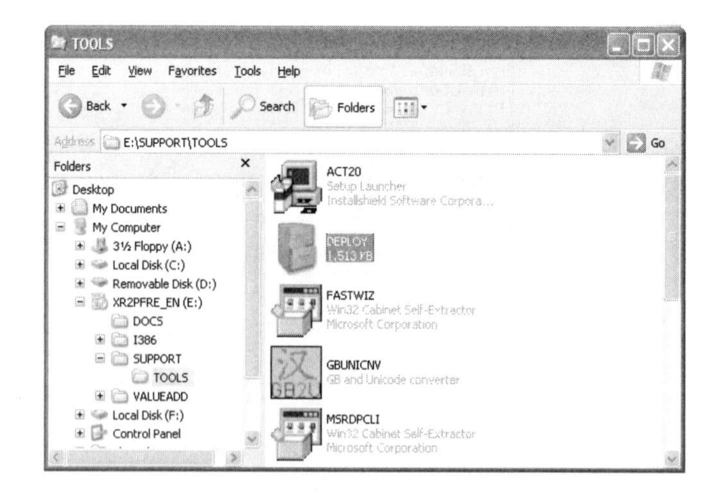

Now that the Deployment tools have been copied to the desired computer, you can create an answer file to use for an unattended installation. Remember that an answer file simply answers the questions that the setup routine typically poses to you during an attended setup. With this automated method, an IT technician can start an installation and not have to wait for each prompt the setup routine poses. Instead, the answer file contains the answers that you want, and it can even provide Setup with information about hardware, such as sound cards and modems.

exam Watch

Windows XP Professional's setup routine is designed to continue, even if certain pieces of hardware, such as modems and sound cards, do not install properly. This feature prevents Setup from stopping due to a single hardware problem.

Of course, the Windows XP Professional CD-ROM gives you unattend.txt, which you can use for unattended installations. This text file provides basic setup options, but you may need to customize your own setup file. Using Setup Manager, you can easily create this file, and Exercise 3-2 walks you through the process.

EXERCISE 3-2

CertCam 3-2

Using Setup Manager to Create an Answer File

To use Setup Manager to create an answer file, follow these steps:

1. Launch the setupmgr program in your deployment folder.
2. Click Next on the Welcome screen.
3. In the New or Existing Answer File window, you can choose to create a new answer file or to modify an existing answer file (just select the option and browse for the file if you want to modify an existing answer file), as shown in Figure 3-3. For this exercise, we are going to create a new answer file. Click the radio button for that option and then click Next.
4. In the Product to Install window, shown in Figure 3-4, you can create the answer file for a Windows Unattended Installation, a Sysprep Install, or a Remote Installation Services installation. For this exercise, we are creating an answer file for a Windows Unattended Installation (we will cover the other two options later in this chapter). Select that option and click Next.

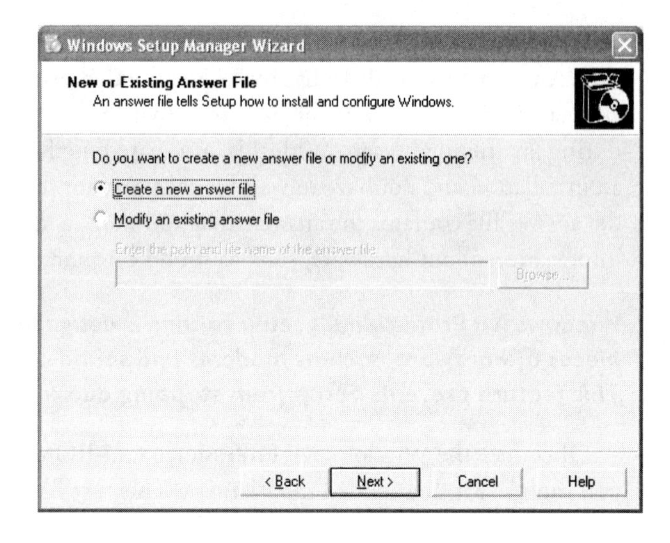

FIGURE 3-3 Create a new answer file.

5. In the "Product to Install" window, choose the Windows Unattended Installation radio button and click Next.
6. The User Interaction Level window appears, as shown in Figure 3-5. You have five different options, which are as follows:
   - **Provide Defaults** This option provides an unattended setup, in which the answers you provide are considered the defaults. When the

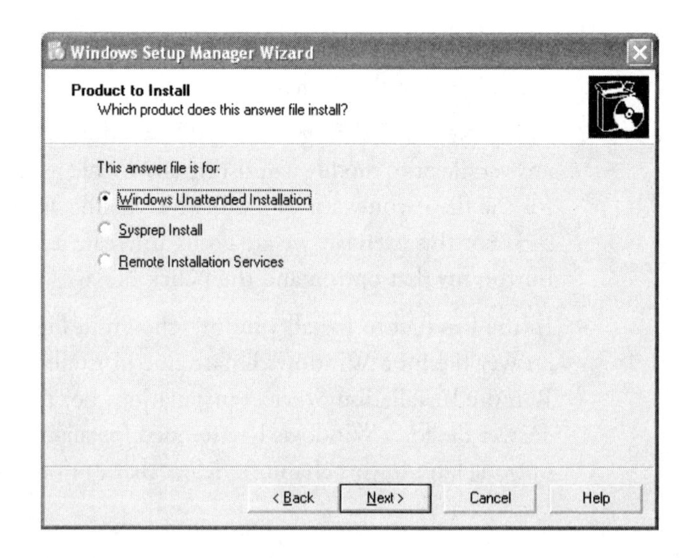

FIGURE 3-4 Select the product to install.

FIGURE 3-5

Choose a user interaction level.

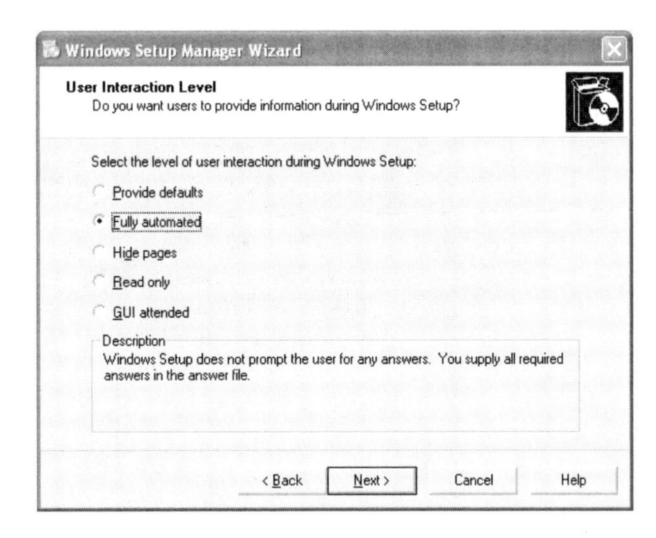

installation is run, the user can see the answer defaults and interrupt setup to change them if desired. As you can see, this option is not fully automated, but it does provide the answers up-front for review.

- **Fully Automated** Using this method, the user is never prompted to answer any questions. All answers are taken from the answer file, and the user cannot interrupt setup or change any of the options.
- **Hide Pages** If you provide all of the answers for the Windows Setup wizard page, the wizard page is hidden from the user.
- **Read Only** If the Windows Setup wizard page is not hidden from the user, you can use this option so that the page is read-only. The user can make no changes to the Setup wizard.
- **GUI Attended** Only the text-mode portion of Windows Setup is automated.

Make your selection based on the level of user input/automation that you want and click Next.

7. The Distribution Folder window appears, as shown in Figure 3-6. When using an answer file, you can choose to install Windows XP Professional from the CD or from a distribution folder. A network distribution folder holds the Windows XP Professional installation files, so you can connect to this folder over the network. In conjunction with an answer file, you can roll out any

FIGURE 3-6

The Distribution Folder window

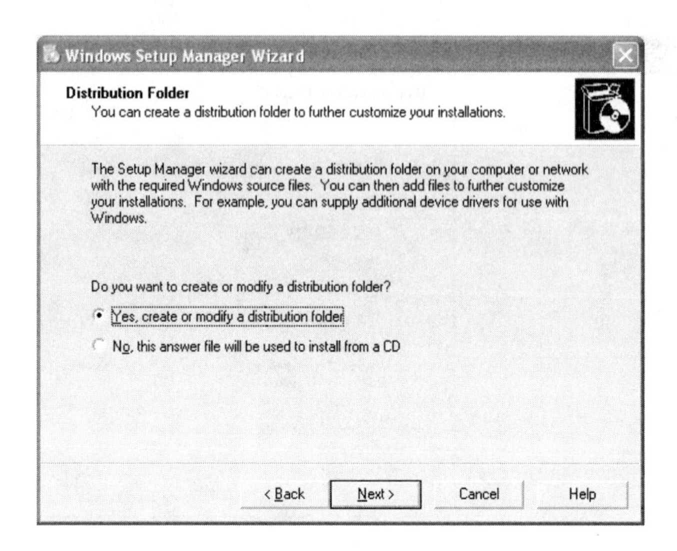

number of installations at one time. Choose the desired radio button; for this exercise, we will create a distribution folder. Click Next.

8. If you chose to create a distribution folder, you can copy the files from a CD or from another location. Make your selection and click Next.
9. In the Distribution Folder Name window, you can choose to create a new distribution folder or modify an existing one. If you choose to create a new distribution folder, select the location and the share name for the folder and click Next.
10. The License Agreement window appears. Read the basic End User License Agreement (EULA) and click the I Accept check box. Click Next.
11. The Customize window appears next, as shown in Figure 3-7. At this point, you can click through each setting in the left window and enter your answer in the right pane. Setup will use the answers provided here to configure the answer file, which automates setup. Simply respond to the answer prompts and click Next through the entire list of settings.
12. After you answer the final prompt, a dialog box appears, telling you that Setup Manager has successfully created an answer file and prompting you for the location to save the file. Choose the desired location and click OK. Click Finish when prompted.

FIGURE 3-7

Customize your answer file settings.

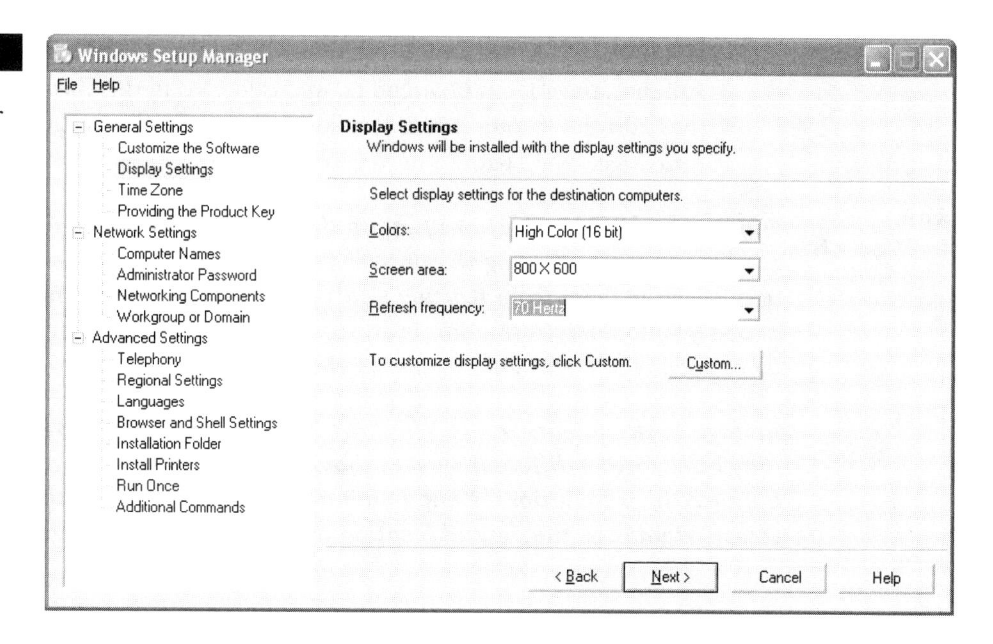

Once the answer file is created, you can begin running unattended setups with the answer file. Before doing so, however, you should open the unattended file you created and scan through it—look for any errors or other issues that might be a problem. You can directly edit the unattended text file as needed, should there be any mistakes.

Once you are ready to run setup, you can use Winnt32 to begin the unattended installation of Windows XP Professional. The syntax for running the unattended setup is shown here:

```
Winnt32 /s: d:\i386 /u:c:\unattend\unattend.txt
```

where the following is true:

- /s: d:\i386 specifies the location of the Windows XP Professional installation files—this can be your I386 folder on the CD-ROM or a network distribution folder.

- /u:c:\unattend\unattend.txt specifies that this is an unattended installation and the answer file is unattend.txt and is located in the Unattend folder on the C drive. Of course, your location will probably be different, so just enter the correct UNC path to the answer file.

exam Watch

Fully automated installations require the administrator password that you configured when creating the answer file. This security feature prevents unauthorized users from starting unattended installations. A new feature also allows you to encrypt the administrator password so that it cannot be stolen by anyone who might gain access to the setup file.

on the Job

In large environments where Windows XP Professional is being rolled out, you may have several different servers that hold distribution files in order to load-balance the installations. Keep in mind that this is not a problem, since you direct Winnt32 to the desired location of the setup files using the /s switch.

SCENARIO & SOLUTION

Scenario	Solution
Can an unattended installation be used in both clean install and upgrade scenarios?	Yes. You can run an unattended installation in either case.
Is it best to use a distribution folder?	This, of course, depends entirely on your needs. In most cases, however, large installations involving a number of computers are best served with a distribution folder that is centrally located on a computer acting as a server.
Do I have to name the answer file unattend.txt?	No. You can name the answer file any name that you like, since you use the Winnt32 syntax to point to the desired answer file. In fact, in many environments, there may be several unattended files that are named differently and can install differently, depending on the particular needs of the client.

CERTIFICATION OBJECTIVE 3.02

Installing Windows XP Professional Using Remote Installation Service

Although unattended installations can be extremely helpful in situations where numerous machines will be installed, Windows XP Professional also supports Remote Installation Services, which uses the Active Directory to automatically run setup on computers that connect to it. Remote Installation Service (RIS) is technically a service that runs on Windows 2000 Server—it is simply supported by Windows XP Professional and not something you can configure on the Professional computer. However, since the MCSE Windows XP exam expects you to be an IT professional, you'll need to know how to configure Windows 2000 Server as a Remote Installation Server in order to deploy Windows XP Professional. So, in this section, we'll move over to Windows 2000 Server in order to continue our discussion and exercises.

Remote Installation Service was first introduced with Windows 2000 as a way to roll out massive installations of Windows 2000 Professional. A former criticism of Windows workstations concerned the difficulty of mass installations. By providing Setup Manager and RIS, Microsoft has tried to make mass installations of Windows 2000 and, now, Windows XP much easier. RIS meets that challenge—to a point anyway.

RIS is a server-based networking product that is designed to use the power of the Active Directory, DHCP, and DNS to install Windows XP Professional software over the network to machines that support the Pre-Execution Environment (PXE) Rom. PXE enables a computer to boot over the network. In order to support PXE, your computer must be outfitted with a network adapter card that is PXE compliant. Windows 2000 Server supports only PCI network adapter cards that are PXE enabled. The good news is that an RIS boot disk can be used instead of the PXE network adapter card on PCs that have a certain PCI network adapter card, if your computers do not support the PXE boot ROM. Computers that meet the NetPC standard can take advantage of RIS as well.

When you start a computer using a PXE boot ROM or an RIS boot disk, the computer queries the network for a DHCP server using a BootP message. The

DHCP Server must be configured to allocate IP addresses to the BootP client. The Boot Information Negotiation Layer (BINL) extensions are used on the DHCP server to redirect the RIS client to the RIS Server so that the installation of Windows XP Professional can begin. Depending on network configuration, the user may need to log on to continue the installations. The server installation is completely automated. This type of installation is especially helpful in networks that are upgrading all computers at one time and on new networks where new machines with no operating systems awaiting installation. When installation begins, the Trivial File Transfer Protocol is used (TFTP) to transfer the image files to the RIS client. Once the transfer is completed, the client simply reboots as a normal network client.

There are several different steps you will need to follow in order to set up RIS, and you should study the following sections carefully. RIS is the preferred method of rolling out Windows XP Professional installations, so you can certainly expect exam questions on it.

Installing RIS

To use RIS, you have a number of different steps that you must complete, and for the exam, I recommend that you get some practice in using Windows 2000 Server and setting up an RIS server. The following exercise shows you how to install RIS on a Windows 2000 Server, which is your first step in this process.

The Active Directory must be configured on your network in order for RIS to work; however, you can install RIS on any Windows 2000 Server—not just domain controllers. In fact, in most circumstances, RIS Servers are installed on Windows 2000 member servers instead of domain controllers in order to reduce service load.

EXERCISE 3-3

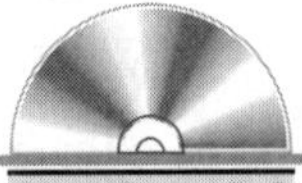

Setting up the RIS Server

To set up the RIS Server, follow these steps:

1. On the desired Windows 2000 Server, click Start | Settings | Control Panel.

FIGURE 3-8

The Windows Components window

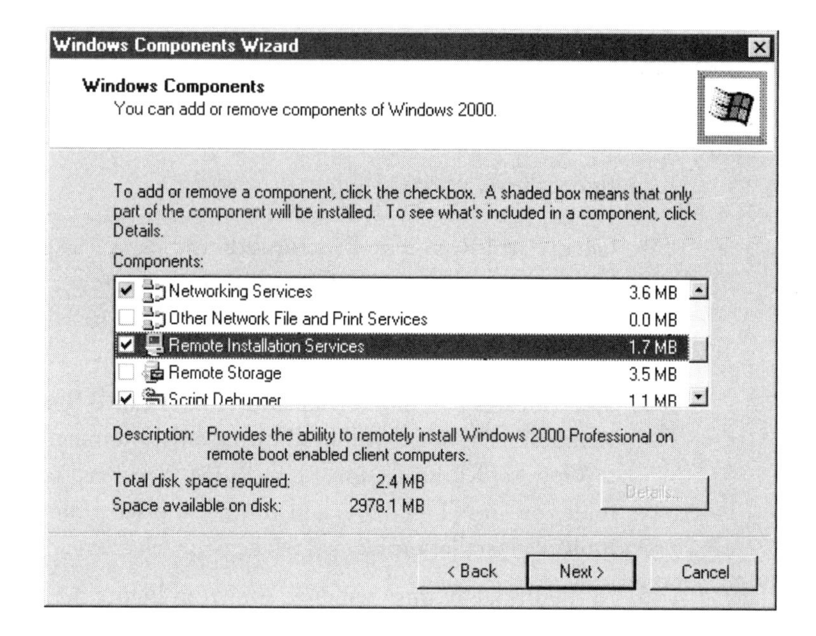

2. Double-click Add/Remove Programs and click Add/Remove Windows Components.
3. In the Windows Components window, shown in Figure 3-8, select Remote Installation Services and click Next.
4. Windows copies the necessary files and configures Remote Installation Services.
5. Click Finish. You will need to restart the server.

Configuring the RIS Server

Once you have installed the RIS, it needs to be configured on the server. Exercise 3-4 shows you how to set up and configure the RIS Server.

EXERCISE 3-4

Configuring the RIS Server

To configure the RIS Server, follow these steps:

1. Click Start | Run, type **RISetup.exe**, and press ENTER. The Remote Installation Services Setup wizard appears. Note on the Welcome screen that DHCP and DNS must be active on your network. Click Next on the Welcome screen.
2. Setup creates a Remote Installation folder called RemoteInstall. The RemoteInstall folder will hold the installation images that you will copy from a Windows XP Professional CD-ROM. You need to place the RemoteInstall folder on an NTFS drive, and you need to have enough disk space to support multiple installation images. Make your selection and click Next.
3. In the Initial Settings window, shown in Figure 3-9, you can determine whether the RIS Server should respond to client requests automatically once setup is complete. By default, the server does not respond to clients until it is configured to do so, but you can have the server begin servicing clients once

FIGURE 3-9 The Initial Settings window

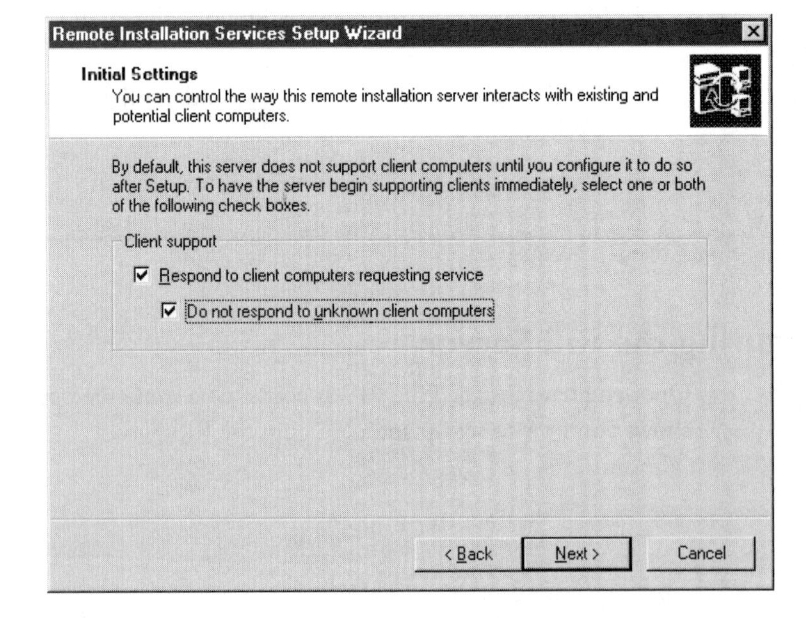

setup is complete by checking the box. Also, if you want to make sure that the RIS server does not respond to unknown clients on the network, you can check that box as well. Make your selections and click Next.

4. Choose the location of the source files, such as the CD-ROM or a network share, and click Next.
5. Enter the desired folder name in which the Windows XP files will be copied. Click Next.
6. The Friendly Description and Help Text window appears, shown in Figure 3-10. Enter a friendly description for the image (such as Windows XP Professional) and any desired help text that you want to enter.
7. Review your settings and click Finish. The file copy process begins, as you can see in Figure 3-11, and may take some time to complete. When the process is complete, click the Done button.

FIGURE 3-10

Enter the desired description and help text.

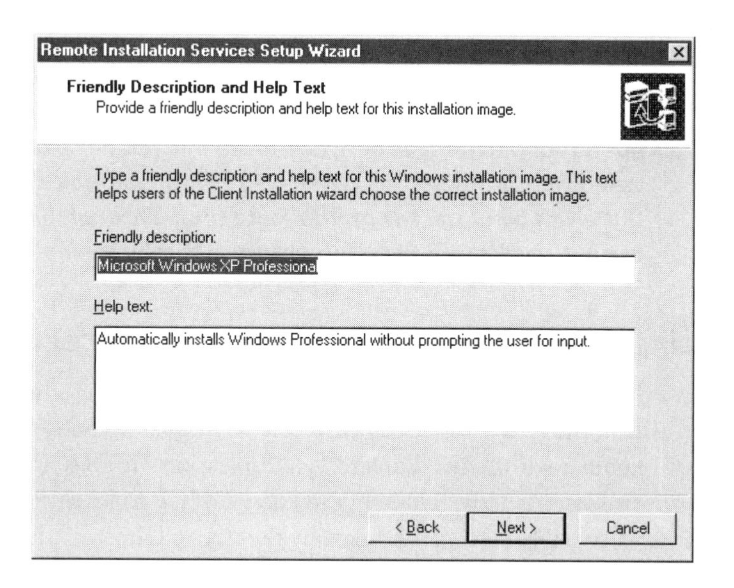

FIGURE 3-11

Configuration of RIS image

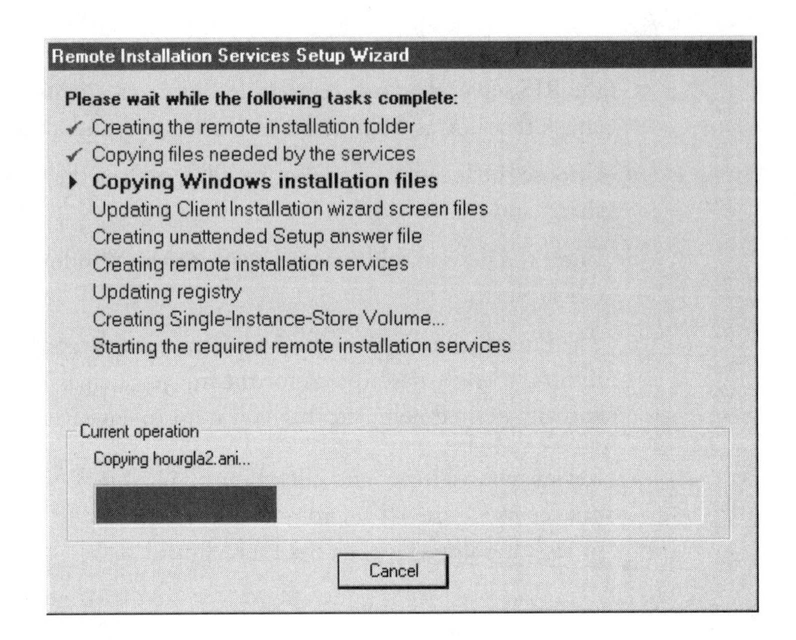

exam watch

You may notice in Figure 3-11 that a Single-Instance-Store volume is created. The Single-Instance-Store volume enables you to create several different images, but not duplicate files between those images. For example, let's say you create two different images of Windows XP Professional. Between the two images, there will be hundreds of duplicate files. Through Single-Instance-Store, files are not duplicated between images, thereby saving disk space on the server.

Authorizing the RIS Server in the Active Directory

Once the RIS Server is configured, your next step is to at to authorize the RIS Server with the Active Directory. If you have studied Windows 2000 Server, you may be familiar with Active Directory authorization for DHCP Servers. Authorization enables the Active Directory to allow DHCP to lease IP addresses to clients. Unless a DHCP Server is authorized by the Active Directory, it cannot lease IP addresses. The same is true for RIS Servers. You do not want someone creating an RIS Server and running it on the network without Active Directory authorization. Because you must have domain administrator rights in order to authorize a RIS or DHCP Server in the Active Directory, "rogue" servers are prevented as a result of the rights issue.

In a nutshell, authorization is simply a security feature of the Active Directory, but one that is required in order for the RIS Server to function. Exercise 3-5 shows you how to authorize a RIS Server in the Active Directory.

EXERCISE 3-5

Authorizing the RIS Server

To authorize the RIS Server, follow these steps:

1. Log on to a DHCP Server (or access it via the DHCP snap-in from any Windows 2000 computer with enterprise admin rights). This may or may not be the actual RIS Server, but authorization is performed through DHCP, so you'll need to log on to the DHCP Server.
2. Click Start | Programs | Administrative Tools | DHCP.
3. In the DHCP window, right-click DHCP and click Add Server, as shown in Figure 3-12. In the dialog box that appears, type the IP address of the RIS Server (or browse for it) and click OK.
4. Right-click DHCP and click Manage Authorized Servers.
5. Select the RIS Server and click Authorize. Click OK.

FIGURE 3-12

Right-click DHCP and click Add Server

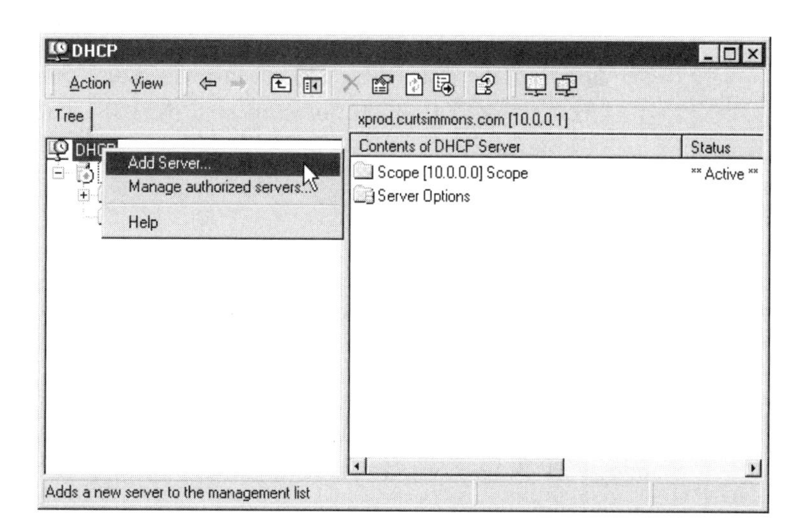

Creating an RIS Boot Disk

Remember that a client computer with a PXE-enabled network adapter card can boot from the network. Essentially, the PXE boot ROM enables the computer to look for a DHCP Server in order to lease an IP address. Then, the RIS Server can be contacted for installation service. If the client computer you are using is not PXE enabled, you can create a RIS boot disk that simulates the PXE environment. The problem with this option is that only a few PCI network adapters are supported (they are listed for you when you run the boot disk generator). So, even with a boot disk, you still may not be able to use RIS if the client's network adapter card is not supported.

In order to create a client boot disk, you run the RBFG.exe boot disk generator utility available on the RIS Server. Exercise 3-6 walks you through this process.

EXERCISE 3-6

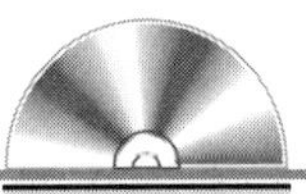

CertCam 3-6

Creating an RIS Boot Disk

To create an RIS boot disk, follow these steps:

1. On the RIS Server, log on as an administrator.
2. Click Start | Run, type **RBFG.exe**, and click OK. You can also access the utility via UNC path at *servername*\REMINST\Admin\i386\rbfg.exe
3. The Remote Boot Disk Generator window appears, shown in Figure 3-13.
4. To create the disk, insert a blank formatted disk into the disk drive and click Create Disk. To see a list of supported network adapters, click the Adapter List button.

Remote Installation Preparation Wizard

As you have seen so far, you can copy the installation files from the Windows XP Professional CD and store those files in a RemoteInstall folder. Then, clients can connect and begin an automatic installation. However, what if you want to install Windows XP Professional across 1,000 computers with the same applications and

FIGURE 3-13

Remote Boot Disk Generator

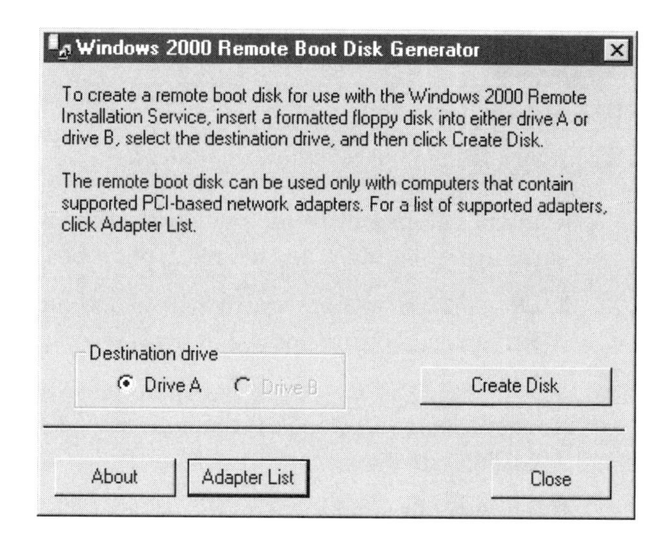

desktop configuration? You can use RIS to install these clients as well. The difference is that you create an image from a current client computer.

Let's consider an example. Let's say that you want to install 1,000 client computers using RIS, but you want to configure certain desktop settings in advance, and you want to install Microsoft Office along with the Windows XP Professional installation. You can create a setup package that installs these parameters by first installing a single Windows XP Professional computer, configuring the settings, and then installing Microsoft Office. Then, you can run the Remote Installation Preparation wizard and create an image of that installation. From the image, RIS clients can then connect to the RIS Server and have the image installed.

The Remote Installation Preparation wizard, or RIPrep, can only duplicate a single disk with a single partition; however, all client computers do not have to have identical hardware. They must have the same Hardware Abstraction Layer, but Plug and Play will handle any differences in hardware in the systems. Again, this type of installation enables you to create one image and duplicate that single image to hundreds or thousands of client computers.

You can create a RIPrep image on either Windows 2000 Professional or Windows XP Professional—only these two operating systems are currently supported. Exercise 3-7 walks you through the creation of a RIPrep image.

EXERCISE 3-7

Creating a RIPrep Image

To create a RIPrep image, follow these steps:

1. Install a desired client computer with Windows XP Professional and then configure and install any desired applications.
2. Once the system is configured as desired, connect to the RIS Server and run the RIPrep.exe program, located in the *servername**RISsharename*\Admin\I386\ folder.
3. The Remote Installation Preparation wizard's Welcome screen appears. Click Next.
4. The wizard prompts you for the name of the RIS Server on which the image will be copied. Click Next.
5. Choose the name of the folder that the image will be copied to. Click Next.
6. The Friendly Description and Help Text window appears. Choose a friendly name for the image and a description if you like. Click Next.
7. Review the summary. Click Next. The image is copied to the RIS Server, which may take several minutes to complete.

Controlling RIS Images with Group Policy

Consider the following scenario. You have five different RIS images that you have created using RIPrep.exe. One image is for Marketing, three images are for Production, and one image is for Finance. How can you make sure that the Marketing image is not installed on a computer in Finance? The answer is with Windows 2000 Group Policy.

Using Group Policy and NTFS permissions, you can control client installation options and prevent the wrong image from being installed on the desired client computer. You can do this by controlling what images clients can access. Exercise 3-8 walks you through the steps.

EXERCISE 3-8

Controlling RIS Images with Group Policy

To control RIS images with Group Policy, follow these steps.

1. Log on to the RIS Server as an enterprise administrator.
2. Click Start | Programs | Administrative Tools | Active Directory Users and Computers.
3. In the right console pane, right-click the desired domain and click Properties. Click the Group Policy tab.
4. Select the default domain policy and click the Edit button.
5. In the Group Policy window, expand User Configuration, and then expand Windows Settings. Select Remote Installation Services and double-click the Choice Options icon that appears in the right pane, shown in Figure 3-14.
6. In the Policy window, shown in Figure 3-15, you have a few different configuration options, which are listed on the following page.

FIGURE 3-14

The Choice Options icon

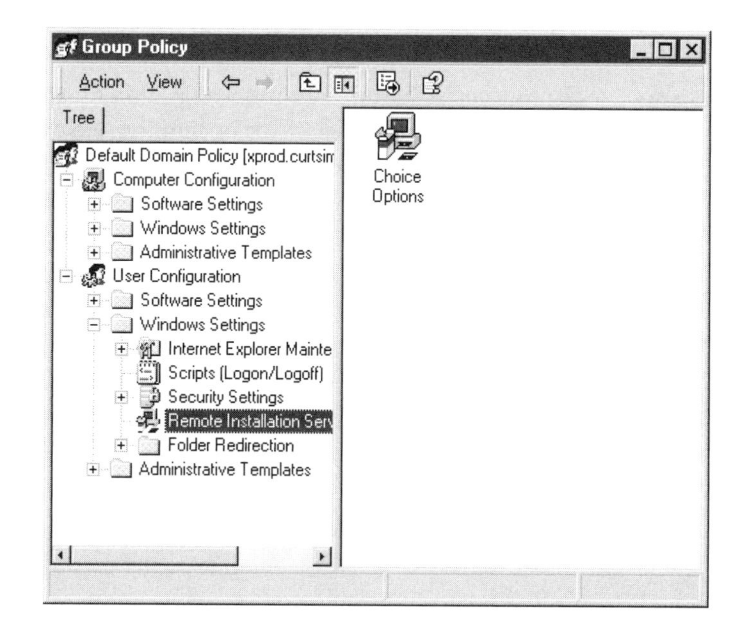

FIGURE 3-15

Choosing a control level

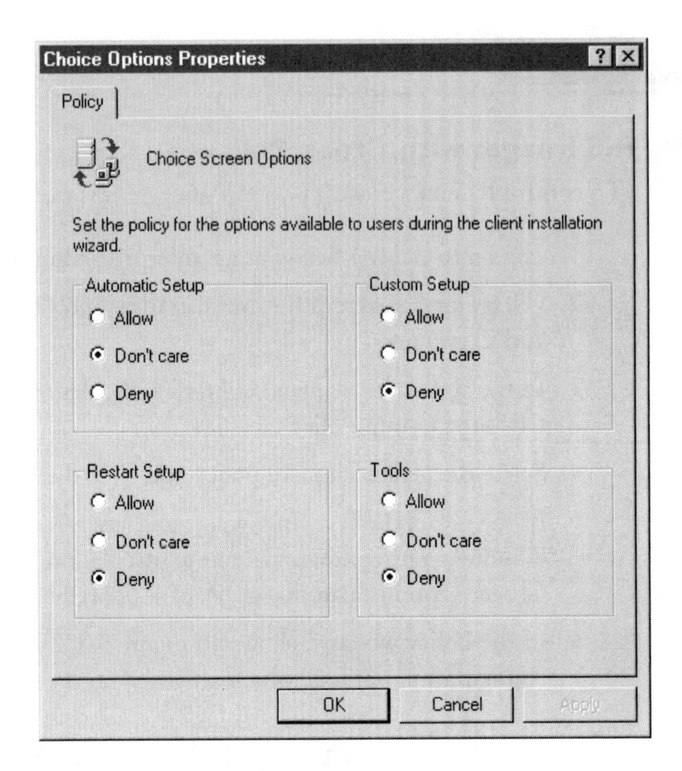

- **Automatic Setup** Configured as Don't Care by default, this option allows the user to select the operating system image; no more prompts are given to the user. Once the image is selected, the remainder of the process is automated. This assumes that the Allow permission was granted at the parent location.
- **Custom Setup** Denied by default. This option enables users to override the setup process and configure setup parameters as desired.
- **Restart a previous Setup attempt** The user can restart a failed setup attempt, but the user is not prompted for any input. This option is also denied by default.
- **Maintenance and troubleshooting Tools** This option enables you to use third-party tools before installation begins. This option is also denied by default.

Make your selections as desired and click OK.

7. Once you have configured the desired Group Policy options, you can close the Group Policy window and Active Directory Users and Computers. At this point, you need to set permissions on the image(s) as desired. If users are allowed to select the image, simply use permissions to allow or deny Read access as needed. Locate the winXP.pro/win2000.pro folder and open the i386 folder.
8. Right-click the Templates subfolder and click Properties. Click the Security tab, and you see the familiar Security tab options found in Windows 2000. Select the desired users/groups who can access the image. Repeat this step to configure permissions on other images.
9. Click OK when you are done.

---

on the job

A good way to configure image permissions is to only give permissions based on what image(s) the user might need to access. If the user should use only one image, deny access to other images, and the user will not even see a menu option to choose an image.

Using an Answer File with an RIS Image

As with Winnt32 answer files, you can create an answer file to use with an RIS installation. RIS answer files are configured with an .SIF extension and should be placed in the image folder for the answer file to work properly. Use Setup Manager to create the answer file, and choose the Remote Installation option at the beginning of the wizard. The prompts you will see are basically same as the Winnt32 answer prompts. Refer to the Setup Manger section earlier in this chapter for more information.

Solving RIS Problems

Problems with Remote Installation Services are typically not difficult to solve. Under most circumstances, the problems with RIS will involve connectivity to the RIS server and simple management of RIS images. Just keep the following points in mind:

- Connection to an RIS Server may be made only by PXE-enabled clients or those clients whose network adapter cards support the RIS boot disk. Only PCI network adapter cards are supported for this function, and there are no workarounds.

- The RIS Server must be authorized by the Active Directory before it can begin servicing clients. Authorization is performed in the DHCP console.
- You can create a custom image using RIPrep. Computers to which images are copied must have the same HAL, but can have different plug-and-play hardware. Each system can detect and install its own plug-and-play hardware.
- Make sure the DHCP Server is configured and is active on the network. RIS clients cannot access the RIS Server without an IP address lease from the DHCP Server.
- If there is a router between the RIS clients and the RIS Server, make sure the router is configured to forward BootP broadcast packets so that the RIS Server can respond to client requests.
- Use Group Policy and NTFS permissions to manage and control RIS images and which groups can access which image.

SCENARIO & SOLUTION	
Can I use RIS to deploy a collection of Windows Me computers?	No. RIS works only with the deployment of Windows 2000 Professional or Windows XP Professional computers at this time.
What can I do if my network card is not PXE compliant and is not supported by the RIS boot disk?	In order for RIS to work, the client's network adapter card must be RIS compliant, or it must have a supported network adapter card that can use the RIS boot disk. If neither of these conditions is met, you must install a supported network adapter card. There is no other workaround.
Do I have to use RIPrep?	RIPrep enables you to create an image of a Windows 2000 or XP Professional computer that is already installed and configured in a certain way. If you just want to use the CD-ROM installation and not an image from an existing client computer, then you simply use the CD option when running Remote Installation Services setup.
Why is DHCP required for RIS?	Clients who boot from the network must be able to contact a DHCP server in order to lease an IP address. Without an IP address, RIS clients would not be able to communicate on the network and, thus, would not be able to access the RIS Server.

CERTIFICATION OBJECTIVE 3.03

Installing Windows XP Professional Using System Preparation

The third and final type of disk imaging deployment that is supported by Windows XP Professional is System Preparation. System Preparation, which is also available once you copy the Deploy.cab file from the Windows XP installation CD-ROM to your hard drive, enables you to remove machine-specific information from an installation so that an image can be created with a third-party imaging tool. This image can then be used to install hundreds or thousands of computers using the third-party imaging process. System Preparation is a useful tool in organizations that are rolling out many new computers, and they want all of the computers to have the same configuration. However, as you can see, Sysprep is just that—a tool to help you prepare a system for imaging. Windows XP/2000 does not provide any software that enables you to deploy that image to other computers. That task is reserved for third-party applications, such as Symantec's Norton Ghost.

The System Preparation tool, called Sysprep, which is included in your deployment tools, is used to remove machine-specific information from a computer so that a third-party tool can use it for imaging from a desired Windows XP Professional computer. This includes all configurations and applications—everything. Basically, the computer becomes the master computer and is imaged so that other computers are exactly the same. The good news is that you can install and configure the operating system, any service packs, and any applications and then run Sysprep for image creation. This image, which contains all of the configuration and applications, can then be rolled out to thousands of other computers using a third-party imaging tool. There are some issues with using Sysprep which you should know for both the exam and real-life application:

- Sysprep images are designed to be used on computers that have the same hardware. The image is not "installed" per se, but it is burned on the computer's hard drive. Therefore, the hardware must be same. The exception is minor Plug and Play devices, such as sound cards, modems, and so forth. These can be redetected and installed, but the hard drives, controllers, and HAL must be the same.

- Sysprep is used for clean installations only—you cannot upgrade a computer using a Sysprep image.
- Sysprep creates the image only—Windows XP or Windows 2000 Server does not provide a way to burn images onto other computers. You'll need to use a third-party tool, such as Symantec's Norton Ghost or PowerQuest's DriveImage software.
- The master computer must be thoroughly tested before Sysprep is run, or any problems or errors will be copied to the image as well.
- You must be an administrator on the Windows XP computer to run Sysprep.
- You must have a volume licensing agreement with Microsoft to comply with the EULA.

Before using Sysprep, you should understand the function of the System Preparation tool and related files. First, there are four components associated with System Preparation—Sysprep.exe, Sysprep.inf, Setyupcl.exe, and a mini-setup wizard. Sysprep.exe is the application that is used to generate the image. Sysprep.inf is an answer file that you can use to automate the mini-setup portion so that that the installation process is completely "hands free." Setupcl.exe runs the mini-setup wizard and generates security IDs for both the master and destination computer. Since each computer must have a unique security ID, Setupcl.exe ensures that the ID is unique. Finally, mini-setup asks users some final questions, concerning such things as the agreement of the EULA and the product key, the domain, and the username. These can be automated using Sysprep.inf. You can use Setup Manager to create the Sysprep.inf answer file if you like. This is probably the easiest way to generate the .inf file—just run Setup Manager and choose the System Preparation wizard option at the opening wizard screen.

In order to use the System Preparation tool, simply install Windows XP Professional on the desired computer, configure the system as desired, apply any service packs, and install applications as desired. Test the system thoroughly for problems, and once you are satisfied with the configuration, run the Sysprep tool. The tool will run, then reboot your computer. Mini-setup will appear, and your computer will be given a new security ID. Then you can run the third-party imaging software. Now that you have the image, you can begin image deployment using a third-party imaging tool of your choice. Exercise 3-9 walks you through the process of running Sysprep.

exam Watch

You might wonder why the master computer is given a new security ID. Because each computer's security ID is unique, Sysprep removes the security ID before creating the image. Therefore, the image has no security ID, and when mini-setup is run, Setupcl.exe can assign the unique security ID.

FROM THE CLASSROOM

Sysprep in the Real World

Sysprep is a great tool that enables you to generate an image of a Windows XP Professional installation and then copy that complete and configured installation to other computers using a third-party imaging tool. This type of imaging is often used by Original Equipment Manufacturers (OEMs). For example, let's say that you own a small computer company. You have just sold 8000 of your new desktop computers to a startup company. All of the hardware is the same, and the operating systems are sold bundled with certain applications. You can use Sysprep to copy a configured system and then image that system to all of the other computers. You ship the computers on their way, and users then see the mini-setup program run once they boot the computer. If you have bought an OEM computer before, such as a Compaq, HP, Dell, or other popular brand, you are seeing a type of mini-setup run that completes the imaging that was done at the factory. The end result—thousands upon thousands of computers can be imaged with an operating system, configuration parameters, and applications with just a few keystrokes.

EXERCISE 3-9

Running Sysprep

To run Sysprep, follow these steps:

1. Log on to the master Windows XP Professional computer as administrator.
2. Access your deployment tools folder and launch Sysprep.exe.
3. A message appears telling you some security parameters may be modified. Click OK to continue.
4. The System Preparation tool window appears. The message tells you to finish installing and testing applications, then click the Reseal button. Notice that you also have certain check box parameters that you can invoke, which are explained in the text following this exercise.
5. Once you click Reseal, Sysprep begins copying the drive and eventually reboots your computer. At this point, mini-setup runs, and a new SID is assigned to the computer.

You can also use Sysprep.exe with a few different switches that provide you with some options. You should keep these in mind for the exam:

Sysprep.exe [/quiet] [/nosidgen] [/pnp] [/reboot]

- **/quiet** No messages are generated on the screen when run in quiet mode.
- **/nosidgen** No security ID is generated for the computer, which allows an administrator to customize the SID for that particular computer.
- **/pnp** Forces a full Plug and Play detection once imaging is complete.
- **/reboot** Forces a reboot of the master computer once imaging is complete.

SCENARIO & SOLUTION	
Can I use Sysprep to install Windows XP Professional on a small network?	You can use Sysprep as long as the computers have the same hardware configuration and as long as you have some third-party disk imaging software to use for the actual imaging process.
How do application licenses apply when using Sysprep?	Since every software vendor handles licensing in a different way, you need to check the EULA of the software to determine what you need to do to be in compliance.
Can I use Windows 2000 Server to image the Windows XP Professional Sysprep image?	No. Windows 2000 Server, or any other Windows product for that matter, does not natively provide imaging software. Sysprep "prepares the system" for imaging, but you must have a third-party product to actually image the other computers.

CERTIFICATION SUMMARY

In order to meet the deployment needs of larger installations of Windows XP Professional, Microsoft provides three different deployment options.

The first is a scripted option, called "unattended installations." Unattended installations function by using an answer file in conjunction with Winnt32. The setup routine questions that are typically posed during an installation are pre-answered using the unattended file that you can create. You can create unattended files for Winnt32, RIS, or System Preparation using the Setup Manager program, found in the Deploy.cab file on your Windows XP Professional CD-ROM.

The next two deployment options are imaging options. The first, Remote Installation Services (RIS), enables you to copy either a CD image of Windows XP Professional; with the second, you can use RIPrep.exe to create an image from a configured computer, including applications. These images can them be installed on client computers that are configured to support PXE or that have network adapter cards that support the RIS boot disk. RIS leverages the power of the Active Directory to function, and you are required to use DHCP in order for clients to contact the RIS server.

The last option, System Preparation, is a tool that prepares a Windows XP Professional computer for imaging. The image can then be deployed to other computers with the same basic hardware using a third-party imaging tool. This type of setup is a good choice when many computers need to be installed that are identical and need the same identical installation configuration.

TWO-MINUTE DRILL

Installing Windows XP Professional Using Setup Manager

- Windows XP's deployment tools are located in Deploy.cab in the Support folder on your installation CD-ROM.
- In order to perform unattended installations, you need an answer file that answers setup prompts typically posed to the user. This file can be created using the Setup Manager wizard, which walks you through the process of building the answer file.
- During the creation of an answer file for an unattended installation, you can choose the desired user interaction level; the options are Provide Defaults, Fully Automated, Hide Pages, and Read Only.
- Setup Manager can also create a distribution folder for you so that the Windows XP Professional installation files can be run from a network share.
- The correct syntax for running an unattended setup is Winnt32 /s: d:\i386 /u:c:\unattend\unattend.txt, where /s is the location of the Windows XP Professional installation files and /u is specifies an unattended setup and the location of the answer file.

Installing Windows XP Professional Using Remote Installation Service

- Remote Installation Service is run on a Windows 2000 Server. Windows XP Professional and Windows 2000 Professional support installation with RIS.
- An RIS Server must be installed on a Windows 2000 Server and must be authorized in the Active Directory. Additionally, DHCP must be available and configured on the network to support BootP broadcasts so that DHCP can allocate an IP address to RIS clients.
- RIS clients must be PXE enabled or use a PCI network adapter card that supports the RIS boot disk so that they can boot from the network.
- You can create an RIS image from the Windows XP installation CD-ROM, or you can create a custom image including system settings and applications by setting up a target computer and running RIPrep.exe to copy the image of the computer.

- An RIS Server must be authorized in the Active Directory via a DHCP Server. You must be an enterprise administrator in order to authorize an RIS Server.
- You can use the RBFG.exe utility to create an RIS Boot Disk.
- You can control what installation package clients access on your network via Group Policy and standard NTFS permissions.
- You can use Setup Manager to create an answer file that can be used with RIS.

Installing Windows XP Professional Using System Preparation

- System Preparation, or Sysprep, is a deployment tool that is used to create an image of a master computer, including settings and applications. This image can then be deployed to blank computers using a third-party imaging tool.
- In order to use Sysprep, you need to use computers with the same hardware configuration. Plug and Play can detect differences in sound cards, modems, and the like, but the HAL and hard drive configuration and controllers must be the same.
- You can also create an answer file to use with Sysprep via Setup Manager.
- Sysprep removes the SID of the master computer before the image is created, then assigns a new SID during mini-setup. This same SID assignment feature is handled as the image is used, via Setupcl.exe.

SELF TEST

The following questions will help you measure your understanding of the material presented in this chapter. Read all of the choices carefully, as there may be more than one correct answer. Choose all correct answers for each question.

Installing Windows XP Professional Using Setup Manager

1. You would like to use Setup Manager to create an answer file for an unattended installation. Where is Setup Manager located?

   A. Administrative Tools

   B. Deploy.cab

   C. Add/Remove Windows Components

   D. Control Panel

2. When an unattended installation is used, how is hardware installation handled?

   A. You must specify the hardware in the answer file.

   B. Plug and Play will detect hardware.

   C. Hardware in source and target computer must be identical.

   D. The image does not consider hardware.

3. You want to use Setup Manager to create an answer file that allows the user to see the setup pages, but does not allow the user to make any changes. What type of answer file should you create?

   A. Provide Defaults

   B. Fully Automated

   C. Hides Pages

   D. Read Only

4. Which statement is true about answer files?

   A. Answer files for unattended setups are text files that can be easily edited.

   B. Answer files for unattended setups are .scl files that can be easily edited.

   C. Answer files for unattended setups are .anc files that cannot be easily edited.

   D. You can edit unattended answer files only using Setup Manager.

5. You want to run an unattended installation. The files are located on a CD-ROM drive, which is E on your computer. The answer file is called answer.txt and is located in the Unattend folder on your C drive. What is the correct syntax to start this installation?

   A. Winnt32 /s d: /u

   B. Winnt32 /s:d:\setup.exe /u:c:\unattend

   C. Winnt32 /s:d:\i386 /u:c:\unattend\answer.txt

   D. Winnt /s:d:\setup /u/c:

6. You want to start a fully automated unattended installation on a Windows XP Professional computer, but a permissions error occurs. What permission do you need on the Windows XP Professional computer to run the fully automated unattended installation?

   A. Domain Administrator

   B. Administrator

   C. Domain Controller Administrator

   D. Power User

Installing Windows XP Professional Using Remote Installation Services

7. What must RIS clients support in order to install from an RIS Server?

   A. PXE ROM

   B. Automatic IP Addressing

   C. The RIS Boot disk

   D. DNS BootP addressing

8. When an RIS client contacts an RIS Server, what protocol is used to transfer installation files to the RIS client?

   A. FTP

   B. TFTP

   C. HTTP

   D. TCP

9. Once you install the RIS Server on the desired Windows 2000 Server, what to do you need to do to set up the server?

   A. Authorize it in the Active Directory.

   B. Run RISetup.exe.

C. Run RIPrep.exe.

D. Run RBGF.exe.

10. Which feature of RIS image storage saves space by not duplicating installation files across the images?

A. Compression.

B. Single-Instance-Store.

C. Single-File Store.

D. RIS does not save disk space in this way.

11. Consider the illustration shown here. What do you need to do in the DHCP console in order to authorize a RIS Server?

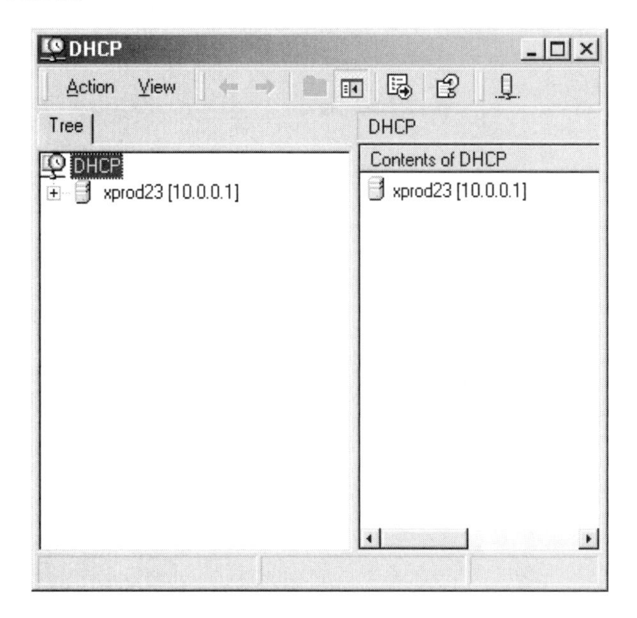

A. Right-click the server name, select the desired scope, and click Manage Authorized Server.

B. Right-click the server name, and click Authorize RIS Server.

C. Right-click DHCP and select Authorize Server.

D. Right-click DHCP and select Manage Authorized Servers. Enter the IP address of the RIS server and click Authorize.

12. You want to use a certain Windows XP Professional computer to create an image. You have configured numerous settings and installed applications. What tool can you use to create the image so that it can be deployed by RIS?

    A. RISetup.exe.
    B. RIPrep.exe.
    C. Sysprep.exe.
    D. You cannot create this image for RIS deployment.

13. Consider the illustration shown here. You want to make sure that users for whom the RIS options are configured in Group Policy can make changes to the setup routine when RIS runs it. What do you need to do on this window to configure the option?

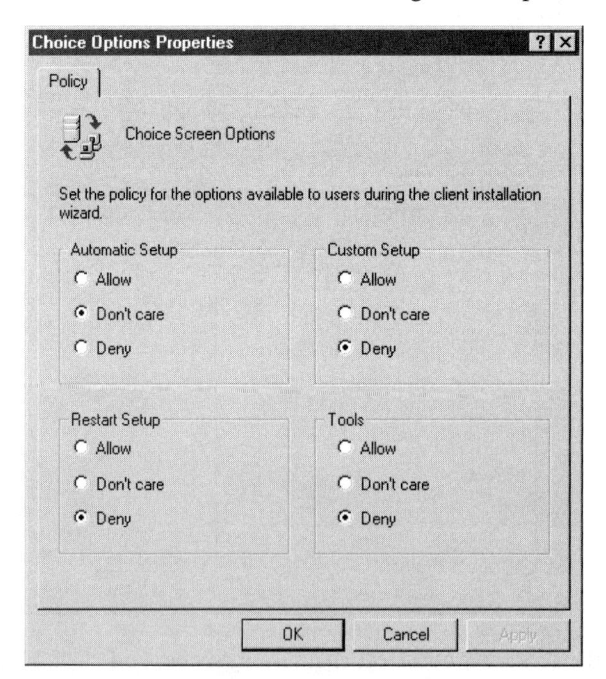

    A. Change Automatic Setup to Deny.
    B. Change Restart Setup to Don't Care.
    C. Change Custom Setup to Allow.
    D. Change Tools to Don't Care.

Installing Windows XP Professional Using System Preparation

14. Which statement is true concerning Sysprep?

A. Sysprep can be used to deploy images from a master computer.

B. Sysprep only images the operating system configuration.

C. Sysprep only images applications.

D. A third-party tool is required to create images.

15. You want to use Sysprep to upgrade 100 Windows 98 computers. How can you use the tool?

A. You cannot use Sysprep in upgrade scenarios.

B. Use Sysprep with the /noos switch.

C. Use Sysprep with the /upgrade switch.

D. Use Sysprep with the /upsid switch

16. What program is responsible for assigning a new SID to computers that are imaged with a Sysprep image?

A. Sysprep.inf

B. Setupcl.exe

C. Mini-setup

D. Sysprep.exe

17. Which file is an answer file that can be used with a Sysprep installation?

A. Unattend.txt.

B. Unattend.sif

C. Unattend.inf

D. Sysprep does not support answer files.

18. You want to use Sysprep , but you do not want a new security ID to be generated. What switch can you use?

A. /quiet

B. /nosidgen

C. /pnp

D. /reboot

LAB QUESTION

A company that wants to roll out 2000 installations of Windows XP Professional has hired you. The company has heard of Remote Installation Services, and since the company already has a Windows 2000 infrastructure, they are interested in using RIS to roll out the Windows XP Professional installation. The company asks you for your opinion. What issues would you point out so that a final decision can be made?

SELF TEST ANSWERS

Installing Windows XP Professional Using Setup Manager

1. ☑ B is correct. Setup Manager is located in Deploy.cab. You can extract the cab files, which include other deployment tools as well, to the computer's hard drive.

☒ A, C, and D are incorrect. Setup Manager is found on the installation CD-ROM and is not found on the Windows XP Professional system by default.

2. ☑ B is correct. Plug and Play detects and installs hardware as usual.

☒ A, C, and D are incorrect. Don't confuse RIS, Sysprep, and unattended installations. Plug and Play works as it typically would during an unattended installation. Hardware does not have to be the same, and there is no master computer or image with an unattended installation.

3. ☑ D is correct. If you answer all of the questions in the answer file, but you still want users to see the screen prompts, use the Read Only option when creating the answer file.

☒ A, B, and C are incorrect. The Provide Defaults option allows users to change default answers. Fully Automated does not show all interaction screens, and Hide Pages hides all installation screens from the user.

4. ☑ A is correct. You can easily edit unattended answer files with any text editor or with Setup Manager.

☒ B, C, and D are incorrect. Unattended files are not scl files or anc files, but rather text files. You can easily edit unattended answer files with any text editor.

5. ☑ C is correct. In this situation, the correct syntax is Winnt32 /s:d:\i386 /u:c:\unattend\answer.txt, which points to the location of the i386 folder on the CD-ROM and the Unattend folder for the answer.txt file.

☒ A, B, and C are incorrect. All of these syntax options are incorrect.

6. ☑ B is correct. You must be an administrator on the local machine in order to run a fully automated unattended installation.

☒ A, C, and D are incorrect. Since the installation occurs locally, you do not need network group permissions, such as domain administrator.

Installing Windows XP Professional Using Remote Installation Services

7. ☑ A and C are correct. In order for a computer to function as an RIS client, the computer's network adapter card must support PXE or be one of the few PCI network adapter cards supported for the RIS boot disk.

☒ C and D are incorrect. Automatic IP addressing is not required and there is not "DNS BootP" support.

8. ☑ B is correct. Trivial File Transfer Protocol (TFTP) is used to transfer installation files from the RIS Server to the RIS client.

☒ A, C, and D are incorrect. These protocols are not used by the RIS Server for file transfer.

9. ☑ B is correct. In order to set up the RIS Server, first run RISetup.exe.

☒ A, C, and D are incorrect. A is incorrect because authorization should not occur until RISetup.exe is run. B is incorrect because RIPrep.exe is used to make Windows XP Professional images. C is incorrect because RBFG.exe is used to make RIS boot disks.

10. ☑ B is correct. The Single-Instance-Store is used to prevent multiple copies of the same file across images. Since hundreds of files are duplicates in each image, this feature saves storage space.

☒ A, C, and D are incorrect. None of these options describes how RIS saves space through image storage.

11. ☑ D is correct. In order to authorize an RIS Server, access the DHCP Server, right-click DHCP and click Manage Authorized Servers. Then, enter the IP address of the RIS Server and click Authorize.

☒ A, B, and C are incorrect. You cannot authorize an RIS Server using any of these steps.

12. ☑ B is correct. In order to create a customized image, you use the Remote Installation Preparation wizard (RIPrep.exe).

☒ A, C, and D are incorrect. RISetup.exe is used to set up the RIS Server. Sysprep is not used with RIS, and you can only use RIS to deploy custom images with RIPrep.exe.

13. ☑ C is correct. If you want to allow users to customize setup, change the Deny setting to Allow.

☒ A, B, and D are incorrect. None of these settings will enable custom setup.

Installing Windows XP Professional Using System Preparation

14. ☑ D is correct. You must use a third-party tool to deploy Sysprep images. Sysprep only creates the image for you, but no tool is included to deploy the image.

☒ A, B, and C are incorrect. Sysprep cannot deploy images, and Sysprep can image the entire computer, including the operating system, settings, and applications.

15. ☑ A is correct. Sysprep is used to create an entire disk image. Then, you use a third-party tool to burn the image onto a new disk. Because you are imaging disks, you cannot run upgrades using this tool.

☒ B, C, and D are incorrect. None of these options are valid, and all of the switches listed here are not real switches.

16. ☑ B is correct. Setupcl.exe works with mini-setup and provides the new imaged drive a security ID (SID). Setupcl.exe ensures that all SIDs are unique.

☒ A, C, and D are incorrect. Sysprep.inf, mini-setup, and Sysprep.exe are not responsible for SID assignment.

17. ☑ C is correct. Unattend.inf is the correct answer file that can be used with a Sysprep installation. All answer files have an .inf extension when used with Sysprep, and they can be created with Setup Manager.

☒ A, B, and D are incorrect. Unattend.txt is used for unattended installations, while Unattend.sif is used for RIS installations.

18. ☑ B is correct. The /nosidgen ensures that no new SID is generated when mini-setup runs.

☒ A, C, and D are incorrect. You cannot use these switches to stop the SID generation.

LAB ANSWER

RIS is an excellent installation tool, but careful planning is required. In your discussion, you should highlight the following issues:

- Client computers must support PXE ROM, or they must have a network adapter card that supports the RIS boot disk. Currently, there are only a handful of supported PCI network adapter cards.
- The client computers should have the same HAL and disk controller/drive size configuration.

- You must configure a Windows 2000 Server to act as an RIS Server, and the service must be authorized by the Active Directory.
- DHCP has to be configured to support BootP requests from RIS clients.
- You can copy installation files from a Windows XP Professional CD-ROM, or you can create a custom image using RIPrep.exe.

4

Configuring and Troubleshooting the Desktop Environment

CERTIFICATION OBJECTIVES

4.01	Configure and Troubleshoot Accessibility Services
4.02	Configure and Troubleshoot Desktop Settings
4.03	Configure Support for Multiple Languages and Multiple Locations
4.04	Manage Applications Using Windows Installer Packages
4.05	Configure and Manage User Profiles
✓	Two-Minute Drill
Q&A	Self Test

Windows XP Professional provides the friendliness of Windows Me with the power and functionality of Windows 2000. Windows XP Professional is easy to use and typically easy for the end user to configure. From an IT management perspective, however, the numerous services and functions that are provided in Windows XP Professional give a number of configuration options and features. As for new additions, accessibility services have been beefed up, desktop settings and configuration provide more options, and there is greater support for multiple languages and multiple locations, as well as for applications and user profiles. In this chapter, we will explore all of these issues, collectively called the *Desktop Environment*. The Windows XP Professional exam expects you to have both knowledge of and hands-on experience with these configuration issues, and you will gain both in this chapter.

CERTIFICATION OBJECTIVE 4.01

Configure and Troubleshoot Accessibility Services

The issue of accessibility has become more important in Microsoft operating systems in the past few years. *Accessibility services* refers to different tools and features of Windows XP Professional that enable users with certain disabilities to use the operating system more easily. We saw accessibility options beefed up in Windows Me, and that trend continues in Windows XP Professional. Specifically, the accessibility services provided in Windows XP Professional can aid people who have hearing and vision difficulties, as well as difficulties using the keyboard or mouse. In today's diverse computer user market, the need and importance of these features cannot be overstated.

From an IT professional's perspective, you will find these tools rather easy to use and configure, but for the exam and in the real world, it is important that you spend some time configuring and working with them so you will know what is available. In many circumstances, you may encounter a user in your work environment who is having difficulty, so it is important for you to know how accessibility services can help that particular user.

If you click Start | All Programs | Accessories | Accessibility, you can see the tools that are available—the Magnifier, Narrator, On-Screen Keyboard, and Utility Manager—and an Accessibility Wizard that can help users choose what accessibility features they want to use. You can also configure some specific options under

Accessibility Options in Control Panel. The following sections explore each of these features.

Magnifier

The Magnifier is a simple tool that magnifies information the screen. It is designed to help people with slight visual problems to see small items or text that appears on the screen. Users with greater visual difficulties will find third-party solutions that meet their needs by enlarging the entire desktop area. As you can see in the following illustration, simply moving your mouse over any item or text on the desktop will cause a blown-up version of the item or text to appear in the Magnifier window.

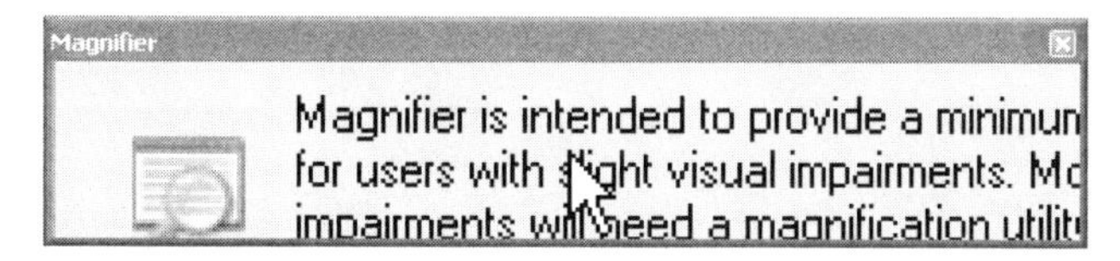

When you first start Magnifier, a Magnifier Settings window appears, shown in Figure 4-1, where you can select a few check box options. You can use the Magnification Level drop-down menu to set the desired level from 1 to 10. Level 2 is the default, and the higher the number, the greater the magnification. Under tracking, you can have the magnifier follow the mouse cursor, keyboard focus, and text editing. By default, all of these are selected. Finally, you can choose to invert colors, start the Magnifier minimized, or show the Magnifier when it is started, which is selected by default.

On-Screen Keyboard

Windows XP Professional provides an On-Screen Keyboard, shown in Figure 4-2. You use the mouse pointer to click the On-Screen Keyboard keys. As you can see, the Keyboard provides basic functionality. If you don't want to have to click the mouse, select Typing Mode in the Settings Menu and then select the "Hover to select" option within the Typing Mode dialog box. You can choose to use a joystick as well.

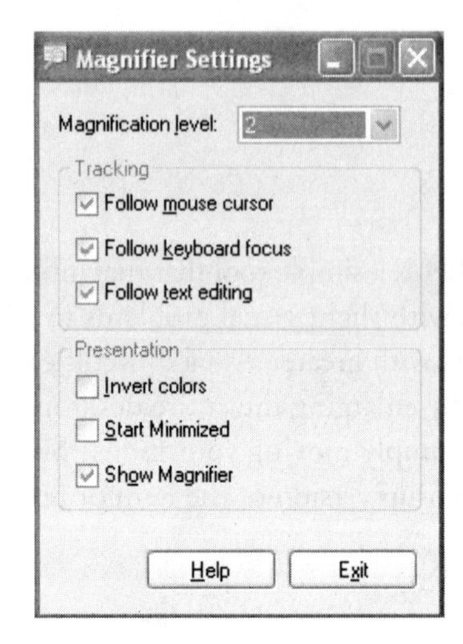

FIGURE 4-1

Magnifier Settings

Narrator

Narrator is a text-to-speech utility that can read menu commands, dialog boxes, and other options that appear on-screen. It is designed to assist people with vision problems, but you may enjoy using it even if you do not have vision problems. Narrator will not read everything that appears on your screen, and if you want a text-to-speech program for daily use, there are certainly better options out there. Still, this is a useful utility and one that may be beneficial to many people.

When you start the Narrator, a simple dialog box appears that enables you to have narrator announce events on the screen, read typed characters, move mouse pointer to the active item, and start the Narrator minimized. If you are having problems with the Narrator's voice, just click the Voice button. A second window appears where you can adjust the speed, volume, and pitch of the voice until it reads in a manner that is helpful for the user.

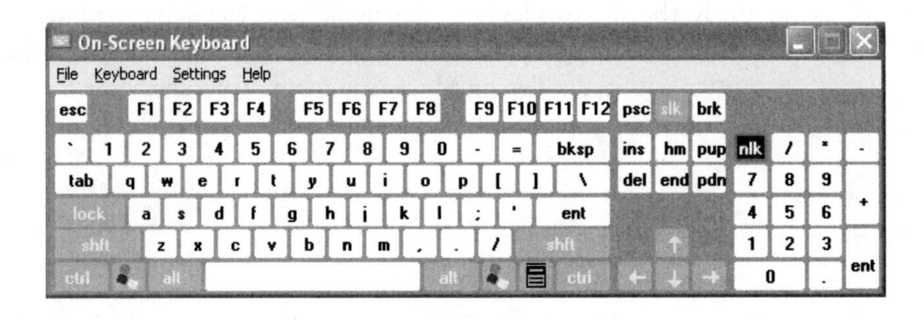

FIGURE 4-2

The On-Screen Keyboard

Accessibility Wizard

Windows XP Professional includes an Accessibility Wizard that can help you configure a computer to meet the specific accessibility needs of the user. The wizard provides a number of options, and you should spend some time working with it for your own practice. Exercise 4-1 walks you through the wizard and shows you what is available.

EXERCISE 4-1

CertCam 4-1

Running the Accessibility Wizard

To use the Accessibility Wizard, just follow these steps:

1. Click Start | All Programs | Accessories | Accessibility | Accessibility Wizard.
2. Click Next on the Welcome screen.
3. In the Text Size window, shown in the following illustration, point and click or use the keyboard to select the smallest text size that can be read. Click Next.

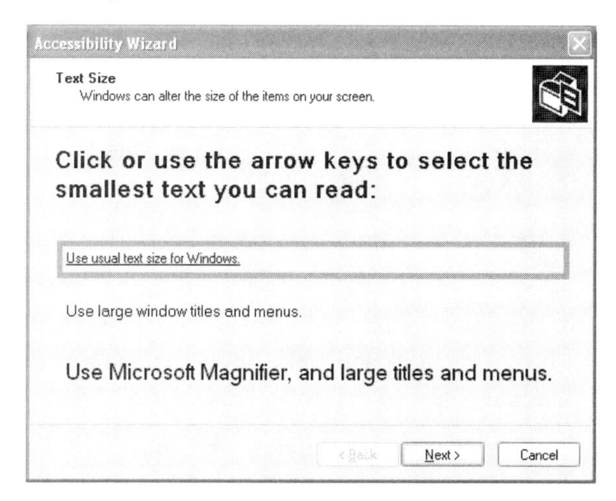

4. In the Display Settings window, you can change the font size, switch to a lower screen resolution, use Magnifier, and disable Personalized Menus. Make any desired check box selections and click Next.
5. In the Set Wizard Options window, shown in the following illustration, select the options that apply to you. Your selections determine the remaining screens

that are provided during the wizard. In order to show you all of the wizard options, I have selected all of them. Make your selections and click Next.

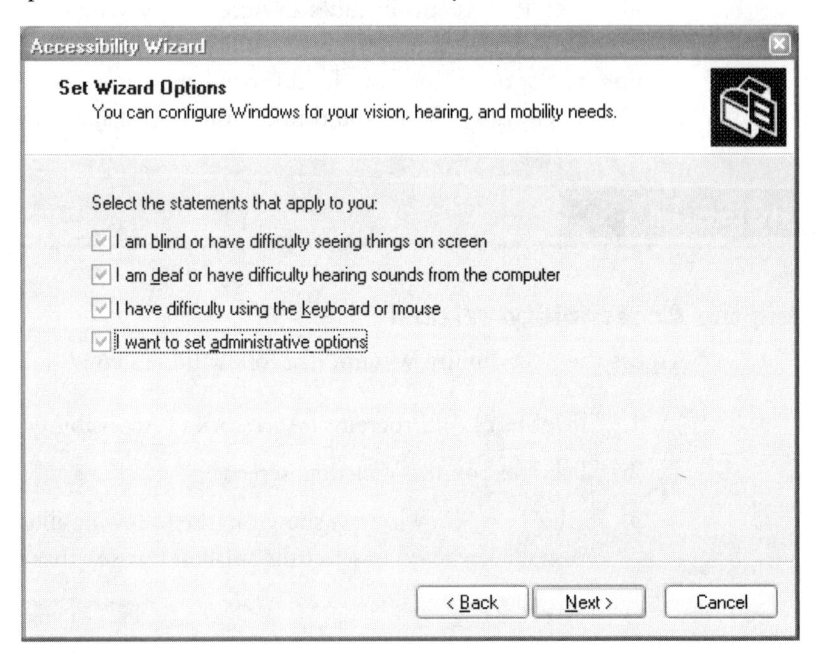

6. In the Scroll Bar And Window Border Size window, point and click or use the keyboard to select the scroll bar and window border size that is right for you. Click Next.
7. In the Icon Size window, point and click or use the keyboard to select the icon size that you want to use (small, large, or extra large). Click Next.
8. In the Display Color Settings window. You can choose a high contrast display scheme or a black and white display, which may make the screen easier to read. Select any desired option and click Next.
9. In the Mouse Cursor window, shown in the following illustration, choose the desired mouse cursor you would like to use and click Next.

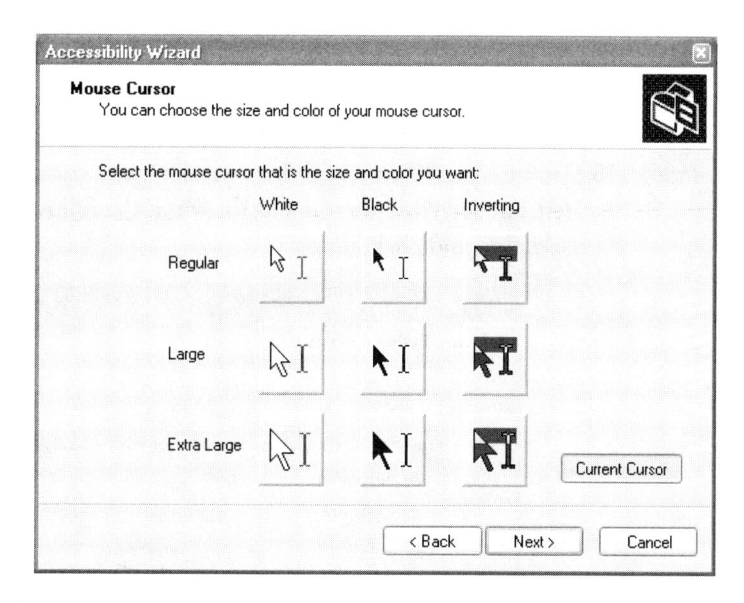

10. In the Cursor settings window, move the slider bars to choose a cursor width and blink rate. Click Next.
11. In the SoundSentry window, choose either Yes or No if you want Windows to generate a sound when a visual warning is given. Click Next.
12. In the ShowSounds window, choose either Yes or No to have programs that support ShowSounds display text when a sound event is used. Click Next.
13. In the StickyKeys window, choose whether or not to use StickyKeys by pressing Yes or No. Click Next. (You can learn more about StickyKeys in the "Accessibility Options" section later in this chapter.)
14. In the BounceKeys window, choose whether or not to use BounceKeys by pressing Yes or No. Click Next. (You can learn more about BounceKeys in the "Accessibility Options" section later in this chapter.)
15. In the ToggleKeys window, choose whether or not to use ToggleKeys by pressing Yes or No. Click Next. (You can learn more about ToggleKeys in the "Accessibility Options" section later in this chapter.)
16. In the Extra Keyboard Help window, choose whether or not use to use Extra Keyboard Help when it is available by clicking Yes or No. Click Next.

17. In the MouseKeys window, choose whether or not to use MouseKeys by clicking Yes or No. The MouseKeys feature enables you to use the numeric keypad on the keyboard instead of the mouse. Click Next.
18. In the Mouse Button Settings window, you can choose right-handed or left-handed configuration, as shown in the following illustration. Make a selection and click Next.

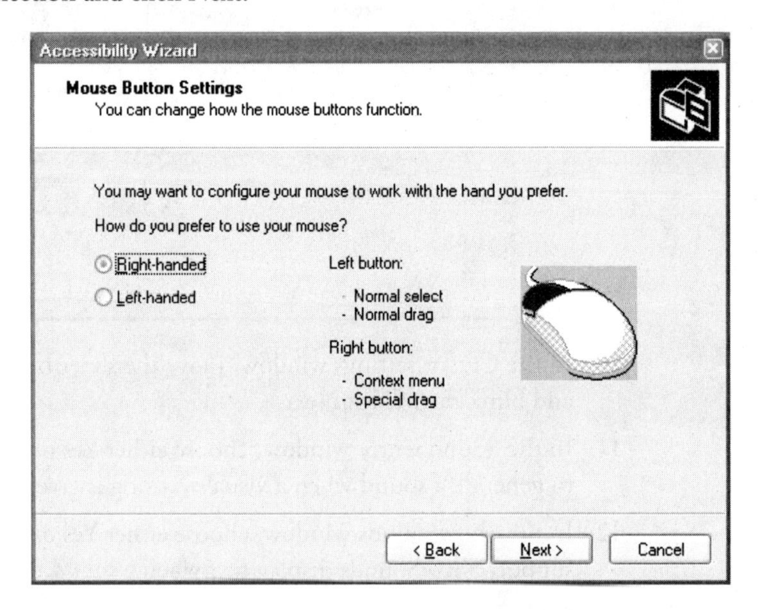

19. In the Mouse Speed window, adjust the slider bar to configure the desired mouse speed. Click Next.
20. In the Set Automatic Timeouts, you can choose to turn off StickyKeys, FilterKeys, ToggleKeys, and High Contrast when the computer has been idle for a specified number of minutes. If you want to configure a timeout value, choose the option, enter the value, and then click Next.
21. In the Default Accessibility Settings window, you can choose whether or not to make the settings you have configured in the wizard the default settings. Make your selection and click Next.
22. Click Finish to save the settings.

Utility Manager

The Utility Manager, which is located in the Accessibility Menu, is a simple utility that lets you manage Magnifier, Narrator, and the On-Screen Keyboard. Specifically, you can start or stop these utilities and set them to start automatically when you log on, when you lock the desktop, or when utility manager starts.

Accessibility Options

As I mentioned earlier, the Accessibility Options found in Control Panel is another place where you can configure some accessibility options for people who have difficulty using the display and keyboard. If you open Accessibility Options in Control Panel, you'll see right away that the tabs and features presented are the same ones found in the Accessibility Wizard—you can simply configure them here without the wizard's help. There are a number of important items to consider on each of these tabs, and the following sections explore them. Keep in mind that the exam expects you not only to understand the configuration options available, but where and how those options can be configured. For this reason, you should spend some time working with these options on a practice computer.

Keyboard

The Keyboard tab, shown in Figure 4-3 contains some options that may be useful to a number of people and that certainly make good exam fodder. You have the following options on this configuration tab:

- **StickyKeys** This option makes the keys "stick" on the keyboard. In other words, in situations where you need to press more than one key at a time, such as CTRL-ALT-DEL, StickyKeys enables you press these separately and still open the Close Program window. For users have trouble pressing key combinations, this feature is very helpful.
- **FilterKeys** This option filters out quickly repeated keystrokes. For people with poor motor control in their hands, FilterKeys can filter out keyboard punches that are not intended. You can click Settings on the Keyboard tab and customize it to meet your needs.
- **ToggleKeys** This option enables you to hear tones whenever you press CAPS LOCK, NUM LOCK, or SCROLL LOCK.

FIGURE 4-3

Keyboard tab

Sound

The Sound tab enables you to turn on the SoundSentry and/or ShowSounds. SoundSentry enables Windows to give you a visual warning on the screen when the computer makes a sound. To use it, just click the check box and choose the type of visual warning that you want from the drop-down menu.

ShowSounds is a feature that tells programs to display captions for speech and sounds that they make. Keep in mind that not all programs will work correctly under this setting, but many will and you can easily enable it by clicking the check box option on this tab.

Display

The Display tab, shown in Figure 4-4, provides you with two configuration features for the Display—High Contrast and Cursor Options. If you want to use High Contrast, click the check box option and click the Settings button. Under Settings, you can choose a high contrast appearance scheme that may make the display easier to see for some people with visual impairments.

FIGURE 4-4

Display tab

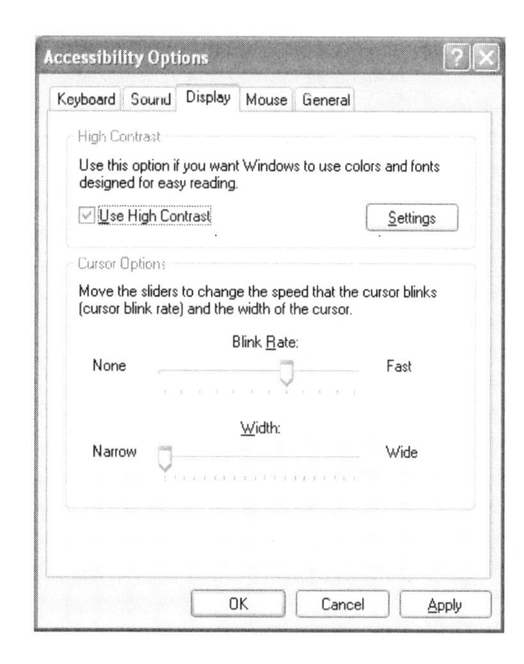

If you want to use Cursor Options, use the Narrow and None slider bars to configure the cursor blink rate and cursor width. The width feature makes the cursor easier for some users to see.

Mouse

The Mouse tab allows to use MouseKeys. MouseKeys enable the user to control mouse movements with the numeric keypad on the keyboard, which can be very helpful to users with poor motor control. If you want to use MouseKeys, click the check box option and then the Settings button. The Settings window, shown in Figure 4-5, enables you to control the pointer speed, NUM LOCK usage, and the MouseKey display on screen and shortcut.

General

The General tab gives you a number of important settings that govern the overall behavior of accessibility options, as you can see in Figure 4-6. These can be important to the operation of accessibility services and you should certainly keep them in mind for the exam.

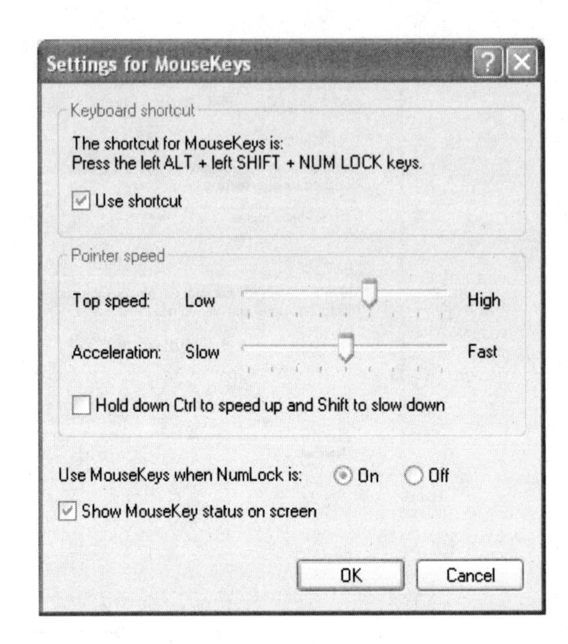

FIGURE 4-5 Settings for MouseKeys

- **Automatic Reset** You can choose to turn of accessibility features if the computer is idle for a set number of time (which you select). This setting, however, does not turn off SerialKeys. Use this setting if several different people use the computer without logging off or on.
- **Notification** The Notification section enables you to configure accessibility services to give you a warning message when you turn on a feature and to make a sound when a feature is turned on or off.
- **SerialKey Devices** If you have additional SerialKey devices, you can enable the feature here and configure settings for those additional devices.
- **Administrative Options** Under this feature, you can choose to have all accessibility settings apply to the logon desktop, and you can choose to apply all settings as defaults for new users.

FIGURE 4-6

The General tab

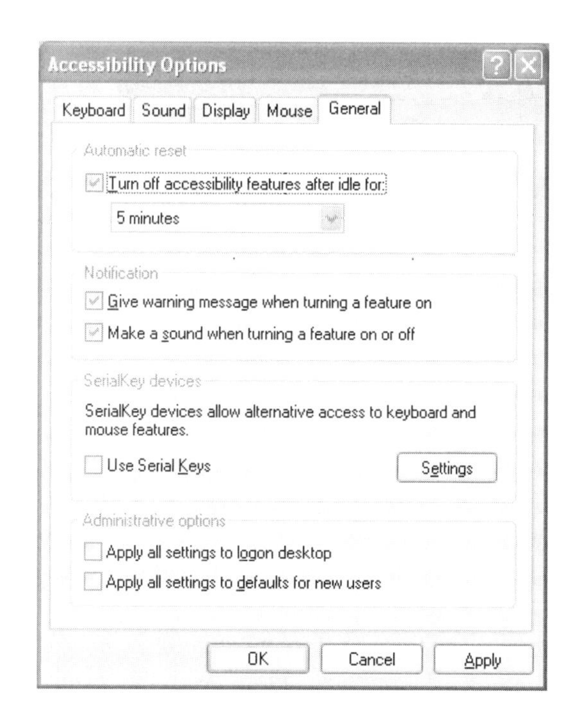

SCENARIO & SOLUTION	
Should the Accessibility Wizard or the Control Panel icon be used to configure accessibility options?	The two options are the same in that they offer the same configurations. Advanced users will probably find the Accessibility Options tabs in Control Panel faster.
How is ToggleKeys helpful?	ToggleKeys is helpful if you accidentally find yourself pressing CAPS LOCK, NUM LOCK, or SCROLL LOCK. The tones let you know if one of these keys has been pressed.
Can I make the Narrator talk faster?	Yes. Open Narrator and click the Voice button. You'll see options to speed up the voice and change the voice volume and pitch.

CERTIFICATION OBJECTIVE 4.02

Configure and Troubleshoot Desktop Settings

One of the most striking new features of Window XP Professional is the new desktop and graphics design. Windows XP Professional is certainly not a new operating system—it is built on Windows 2000 code and contains a number of the bells and whistles of Windows Me, but there's a different look and feel in the new graphics-intensive desktop and Windows XP theme. Don't be fooled, however; under the hood, you are definitely working with Windows 2000.

The Windows XP Professional exam expects you to know how to configure and troubleshoot desktop settings. However, since this exam is focused on the IT professional in a network setting, you can expect the exam to explore your relationship to Windows XP Professional in light of networking and user management. From the local computer's point of view, configuring the desktop settings is rather easy, so I'll spend only briefly point out a few things before moving to the issue of global desktop management.

Windows XP Professional installs with the default Windows XP look, which is simply a theme. If you upgrade to Windows XP, your existing theme remains the same. As you can see in Figure 4-7, Display Properties now contains a Themes tab, where the Windows XP theme is selected. You can choose to use this theme, modify it by changing the settings on the remaining tabs, or choose a different theme or create your own. The point is that *themes* drive all of the Windows settings, and you can make changes to any desired theme by simply reconfiguring settings on the other tabs as desired.

Aside from making changes to Display Properties, you can also access the Start menu and Taskbar properties sheets, where you can choose to use the Classic Windows view of the Start Menu or configure the behavior of the Windows XP Start menu. There are a number of customization options that are available for both the Start Menu and Taskbar properties. Although they are too simple to review here, you should certainly spend some time working with these settings and getting familiar with Windows XP's appearance.

From an IT professional's point of the view, the concept of managing and troubleshooting desktop settings is more likely to fall under the issue of user control. For example, let's say that your company has strict computer settings that define how

FIGURE 4-7

Display Properties

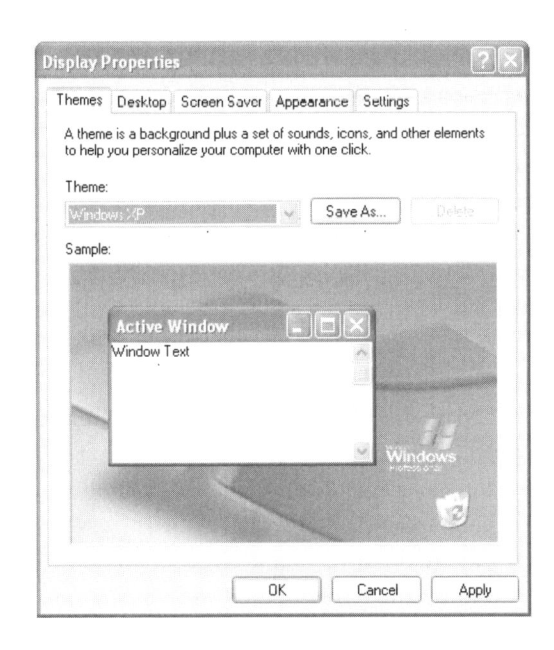

the user's computer should appear. How can you configure 1,000 computers with the same desktop settings and keep those desktop settings from changing as a result of user configuration? The answer is through *Group Policy*.

Windows 2000 Group Policy is a powerful feature designed for Windows 2000 Professional computers and, now, Windows XP Professional computers. With Group Policy, you can finely control the appearance and use of operating systems, software, and even Internet Explorer settings. In order to manage the user desktop environment, you access Group Policy for the desired site, domain, or organizational unit (OU), depending on where you want to implement the policies.

exam watch

You may be thinking, "Wait a minute—Group Policy isn't a part of the exam objectives." That is technically true, but you will see that portions of the Server exam overlap with the Windows XP Professional exam, and this is one area where that happens. In order to manage desktops, you must use Group Policy on a Windows 2000 Server.

Although it is outside of the scope of this book to provide a through tutorial on Group Policy's features, we will take a look at what is available and how you can configure desktop management in Group Policy.

As you are aware, Windows 2000 networks are divided into logical units called *domains*, and domains can be further segmented by OUs. OUs can be managed by different administrators and can provide a way to break apart large domains for management or organizational purposes. Physically, Windows 2000 networks are divided into sites, so that replication over WAN links can be controlled. Group Policy enables you to enforce settings at the site, domain, or OU level, depending on your level of permissions (enterprise administrator, domain administrator, and so on). For example, let's say that you have a group called Marketing in the Dallas domain. The Marketing group requires certain desktop settings that are uniform, but you don't care about desktop settings for the rest of the domain. How can you control Marketing's settings alone? Create a Group Policy at the Marketing OU level so that the settings are implemented only on those computers. What if you decide you want the entire domain to have the policy? Re-create the policy configurations at the domain level.

As you are thinking about Group Policy at the domain level, it is important to keep in mind that "inheritance" is in effect. Group Policy is applied at the site level first, domain level next, and OU level last. Settings are inherited from the top down, so a site level policy can override settings of an OU level policy if they happen to conflict. It is possible for administrators to block and override inheritance settings at a lower level, such as the OU level, but under most circumstances, this is not done. Rather, enterprise administrators configure site and domain policies that apply to all computers/users. OU settings are often very specific and only further strengthen the site/domain policy. If the OU policy conflicts with a site or domain policy, or if a domain policy conflicts with the site policy, the higher group policy always wins. This hierarchical structure is built in and simply a part of the management structure of Windows 2000.

However, aside from implementing Group Policy via Windows 2000 Server and the Active Directory, you can implement Group Policy at the local level as well. Windows XP Professional has the Group Policy software, so that you can configure a local policy that applies to all users who locally log on to the computer. You must have administrative rights on the Windows XP Professional computer in order to configure Group Policy. However, before going any further, let me offer a big warning for the real world and the exam. Local Group Policy is the weakest form of Group Policy. It is designed for networking with Windows XP Professional on a small network where no domain is used or where specific requirements are needed. You can implement the policy, users will log on, and everything works great. However, if the Windows XP

Professional computer is a part of a domain environment, any local policy settings will likely be overwritten by a site, domain, or even OU policy.

exam Watch

Keep in mind that the Local Group Policy is the weakest form of Group Policy, and it is typically overwritten by site, domain, or OU policy when the computer is a member of a Windows 2000 domain.

For the exam, you are likely to see questions concerning Local Group Policy. The good news is that the Group Policy console looks the same at the local level as it does at the domain level, so either way you can see how Group Policy works on your local machine.

Click Start | Run and type **gpedit.msc**. You can also open the Group Policy console by opening the MMC, choosing to add a standalone snap-in and then clicking Group Policy from the list that appears. Either way, you see that Local Group Policy is a simple MMC interface and contains settings for Computers and Users, as shown in Figure 4-8.

To configure desktop settings, access Administrative Templates under the User Configuration portion of the Group Policy console. In the right pane, you'll see a folder for Desktop. Exercise 4-2 shows you how to use the Local Group Policy console to create a local desktop Group Policy.

FIGURE 4-8

Local Group Policy console

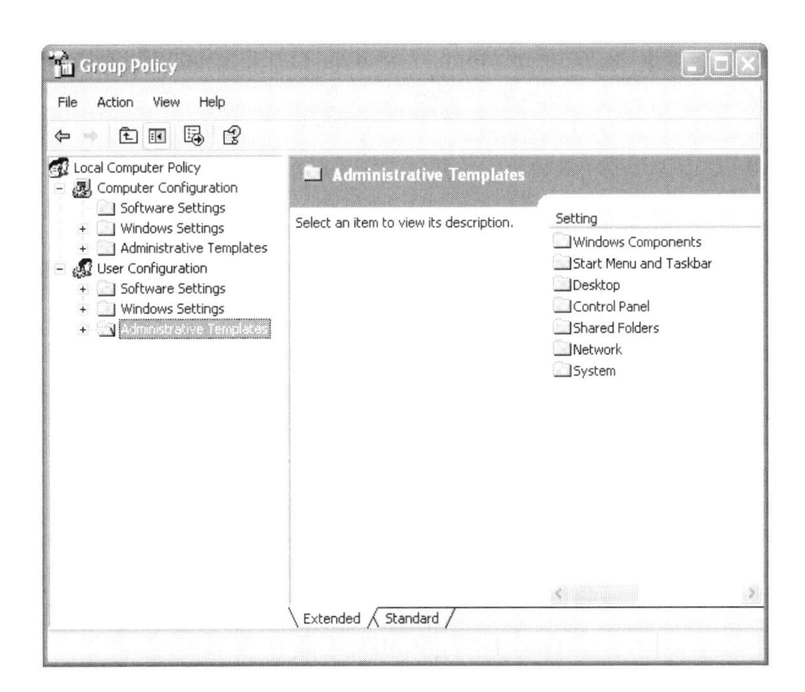

EXERCISE 4-2

Configuring a Local Group Policy

To configure a Local Group Policy, just follow these steps:

1. In the Group Policy console, expand User Configuration and select Administrative Templates.
2. In the right console pane, double-click Desktop to open the folder. You see a listing of available policies and also a folder for Active Desktop and Active Directory settings, shown in the following illustration. Notice that by default all of the settings are Not Configured. This means that none of the policies are currently being invoked on the computer.

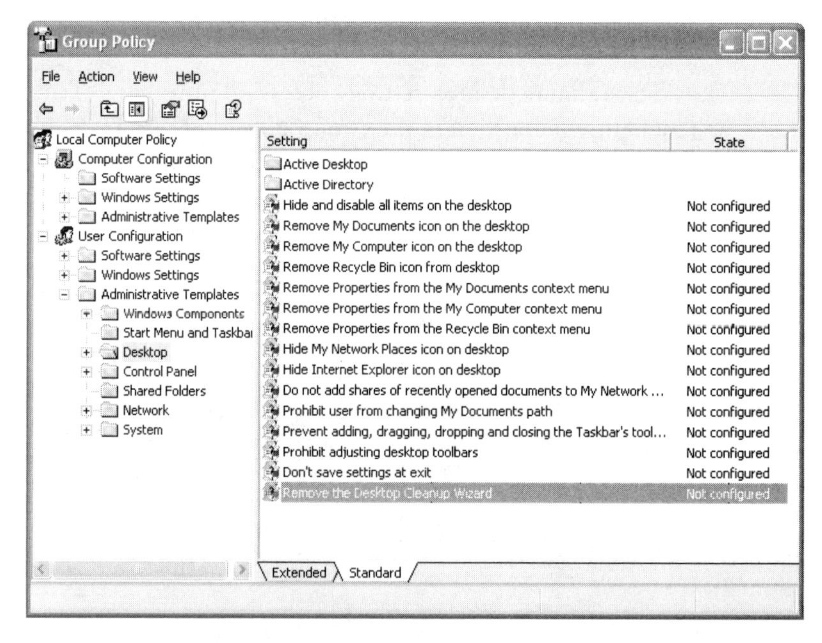

3. To configure a policy, choose one that you want to invoke and double-click it. You see the Policy Settings window, shown in the following illustration. In order to configure the settings, you have these three radio button options:

- **Not Configured** This is the default setting. Not Configured means that policy is not invoked and no registry settings are made concerning the policy. This is the default setting.

- **Enabled** The registry is written to and the policy is invoked. In the illustration, the policy is to "Remove the Desktop Cleanup Wizard." With the policy enabled, the wizard is removed and is not available to users to log on to the computer.
- **Disabled** The registry is written to and the policy is disabled. For this particular policy, the Desktop Cleanup wizard would be available under this setting. As you can see with this policy, the Disabled setting does not actually do anything, but for some policies it can be useful in disabling the feature of some policy.

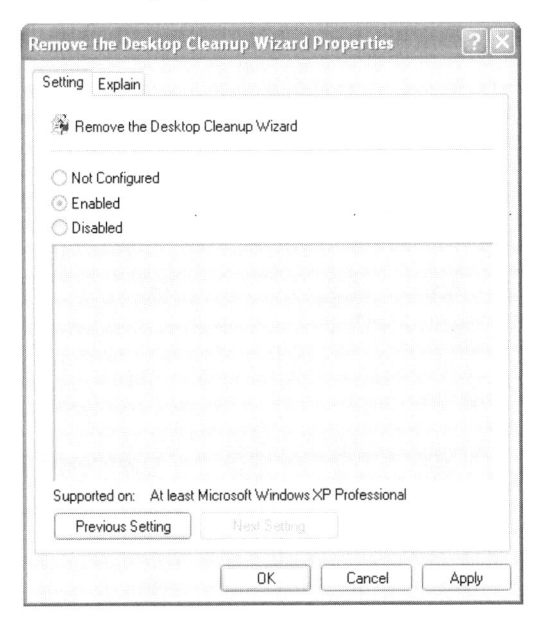

Choose a radio button selection and click OK. If you would like to read an explanation of the policy, click the Explain tab, shown in the illustration on the next page:

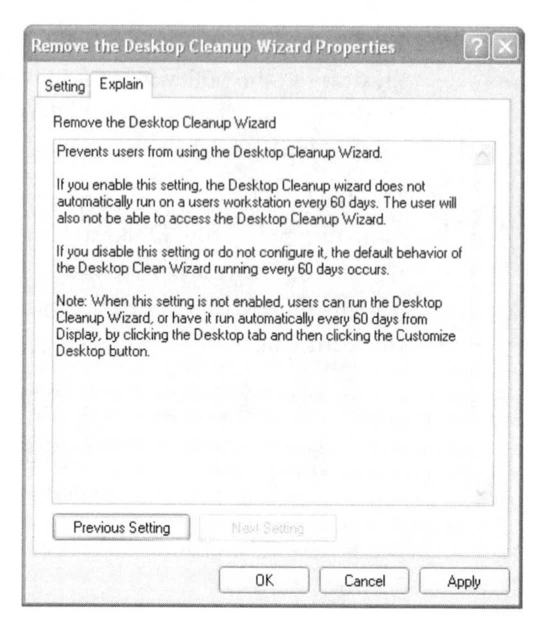

4. Once you click OK, you return to the Group Policy console. You can see that the policy you invoked is now listed as Enabled, shown in the following illustration. You can repeat this process to continue configuring policies as desired.

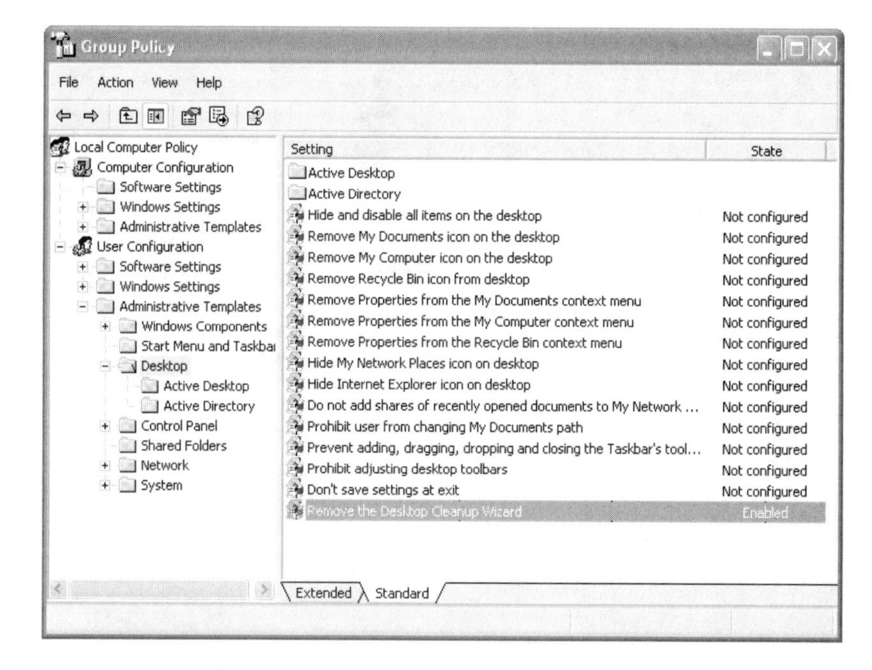

exam **Watch**

It is important to remember that the default settings for all policies is Not Configured. For policies that you do not want to use, leave the Not Configured button enabled. In other words, if you "don't care" about a policy, do not click the Disable button, because doing so creates a registry entry. Essentially, you are causing Windows XP Professional to do more work when you disable policies that should be left as Not Configured.

Aside from the Desktop folder, you'll also find a Start Menu and Taskbar folder. As you can see in Figure 4-9, there are a bunch of policies you can choose to invoke. For example, you can clear history of documents on exit, turn off personalized menus, prohibit changes to the Start Menu, lock the Taskbar, or force users to use the classic Start Menu. If you double-click these policies, you see that they have the same configuration window as the Not Configured, Enabled, and Disabled settings. You can click through these and invoke any desired settings that you like.

As you are thinking about Local Group Policy, there are a few important considerations to keep in mind at all times, and you should keep these straight in your

FIGURE 4-9

Start Menu and Taskbar policy options

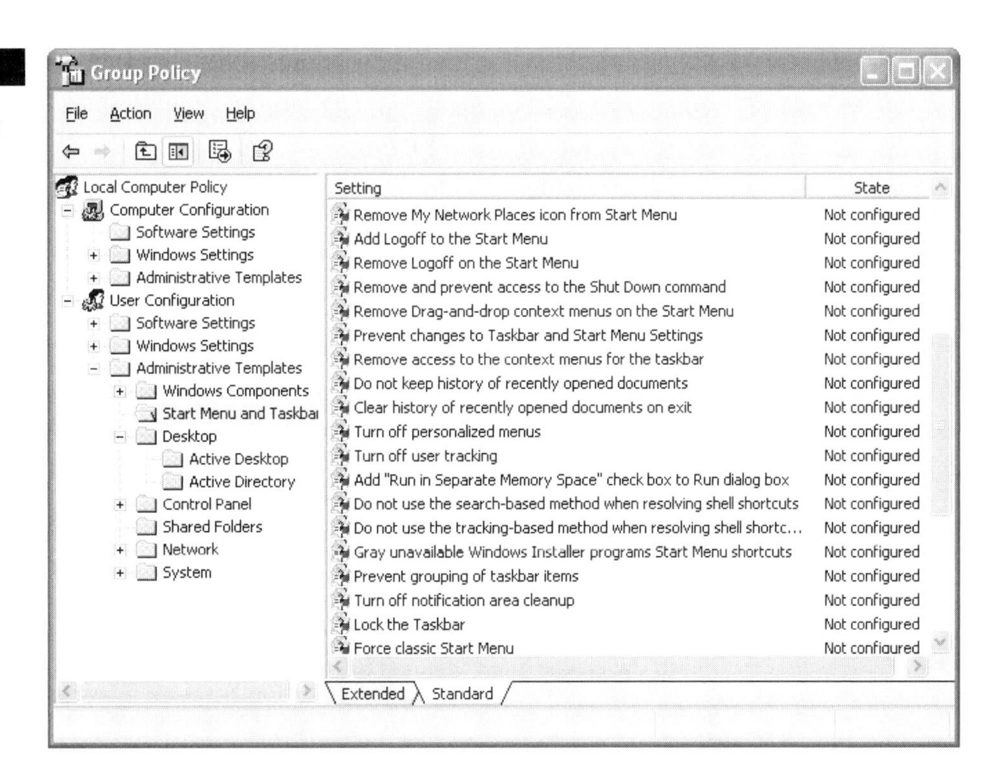

mind for the exam as well. These issues also address the bulk of the troubleshooting questions you are likely to see:

- Local Group Policy is the weakest form of Group Policy. If the Windows XP Professional computer is a domain member, the local policy will most likely be overwritten by the domain policy.
- You must be an administrator on the local Windows XP Professional computer to create a Local Group Policy. The Group Policy you create affects all users who log on to the computer—you cannot single out users and individually apply the Local Group Policy to one of them.
- Depending on your Group Policy settings, users may be able to change some settings when logged on, but those settings are not saved—once the user logs back on, the policy is invoked again. This does not mean that the policy can be "worked around"; it simply means that if a setting allows a configuration change, the change will not be saved and the policy rule is used instead.
- Use the Enable or Disable settings only on policies that you want to invoke. If you do not care about a listed policy, leave it as Not Configured. The Not Configured setting does not write information to the registry, while the Enable and Disable settings do. Enabling or Disabling all of the settings will require more time for Windows XP Professional to boot, because the registry has to process all of the settings.

Finally, I would like to make one final note about desktop settings. It is important to keep in mind that the basic Windows XP theme is rather graphics intensive and makes large demands on resources. Sure, it looks great, but if the computer you are using or the computers on your network barely meet the minimum hardware requirements, the Windows XP theme may be consuming more system resources than you like. If inadequate resources raise a performance issue, you may have to make some setting adjustments based on the current performance of the machine(s) and your needs. Here are a two important performance tips concerning the Windows XP desktop:

- Remember that you do not have to use the XP theme and XP Start Menu. If memory and processing power are an issue, choose a different theme and go to the classic Start Menu. This will tone down the graphics and give your system more processing cycles to work with. You can change these settings on the Display Properties, Themes tab, on the Start Menu, and on the Taskbar Properties, Start Menu tab.

- You can also choose how you want Windows XP to handle graphics and display features. Open System Properties in Control Panel, click the Advanced tab, and then click the Settings button under Performance. Note on the Visual Effects tab, shown in Figure 4-10, that you can adjust the visual effects for the best performance—you can choose the custom setting and select check boxes in order to reduce the visual effects impact on system performance. By default, Windows XP attempts to strike a balance between visual effects and performance, but you can override that process here and invoke the settings that you want.

FIGURE 4-10

Adjust visual effects performance on this tab.

SCENARIO & SOLUTION

Scenario	Solution
I want to invoke a Group Policy on all computers in my enterprise. How can I do that?	In order to invoke Group Policy at the Enterprise level, you must configure the policy via the Active Directory Sites and Services console for all sites. You must be an Enterprise administrator to configure site policy.
If a setting I make to a Local Group Policy and a setting in an OU policy conflict, what policy takes effect?	Domain and OU policies override Local Group Policy. If the computer is a domain member, the OU policy will overwrite the local policy.
What users can make changes to the Local Group Policy on my Windows XP computer?	Only administrators of the local computer can configure or make changes to Group Policy. If you want to ensure that no one makes changes to your settings, do not give anyone else administrative privileges.

FROM THE CLASSROOM

Local Group Policy

Keep in mind that Group Policy is a powerful tool that enables you to do everything from controlling user desktop environments to installing software on those client computers. The Local Group Policy has most of the features of the domain Group Policy found in Windows 2000 Server, but the Local Group Policy applies only to the users logged onto the local computer. The purpose of the Local Group Policy is to give an administrator control over a local machine that is used by several different people and is not connected to a Windows 2000 network. This feature enables you to invoke great control even in small workgroup environments. From a domain point of view, you would typically not use the Local Group Policy console in a domain environment because the Group Policy is configured at the site, domain, or OU level. As you are working with Windows XP Professional, a good mindset is to think of Local Group Policy as policy control for a workgroup or standalone machine, whereas domain Group Policy is the management tool for Windows XP Professional computers that are domain members.

CERTIFICATION OBJECTIVE 4.03

Configure Support for Multiple Languages and Multiple Locations

Our consideration of desktop management includes the issue of multiple language and location support and configuration. The concept of computing environments that function via a human interface is certainly nothing new—after all, with the Windows environment, you are looking at systems that use plain language and graphics in order to communicate with users. In the olden days, you had to know the computer's programming language or operating system language in order to communicate with the computer. Today, the computer's job is to communicate with us. Bridging the gap between digital data and a human interface has been a challenging task—and an important one. The concept of "human interface" in PCs continues to get attention as developers find ways to make computers talk to us and work with us naturally—through speech and even sight. The future of human interface is very exciting and almost seems a little "Star Trekish" in nature, but we can expect that operating systems will be more and more "human interface friendly" in the years to come.

In an attempt to meet some of those human interface issues today, Windows XP Professional contains support for multiple languages, currencies, locations, and related interaction features. Because all of the world does not speak English or use the American dollar, Windows XP attempts to make itself multilingual. This is a great benefit in a number of ways—even for the business traveler who can speak several languages and works in different countries. As an IT professional, you are expected by the Windows XP Professional exam to know a thing or two about configuring multiple languages and locations, and in the next sections, we'll consider these configuration issues.

Configuring Regional Options

Support for multiple languages and regions is configured in the Regional and Language Options in Control Panel. You can also configure language support when you first install Windows XP Professional. If you open Regional and Language Options in

Control Panel, the first tab you see is Regional Options. Exercise 4-3 explores the options on this tab.

EXERCISE 4-3

Regional Options

To configure the Regional Options tab, just follow these steps:

1. In the Standards And Formats section of the Regional Options tab, as you can see in the following illustration, use the drop-down menu to choose a desired language. Once you select the language, you can see the default settings for how numbers, currency, time, short date, and long date are handled in applications.

2. If you want to change how the language features are handled, click the Customize button. This opens the Customize Regional Options window, as you can see in the following illustration. Note the tabs for Numbers, Currency, Time,

and Date. See the "Configuring Locations" section later in this chapter for more information about these options.

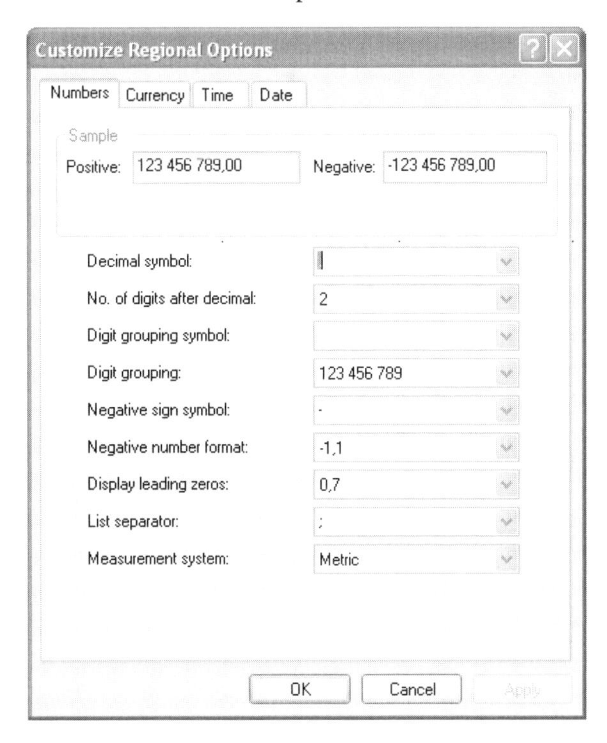

3. If you return to the Location tab, you can also use the drop-down menu to select a location so that programs and services can provide you with local information, such as news and weather.

Languages

The second tab on the Regional And Language Options properties dialog box is the Languages tab. You have two different options on this tab, which are shown in Figure 4-11. First, you can choose the Text Services and Input Languages that you wish to use to enter text. This feature affects the characters on your keyboard so that you can write documents and e-mail using different languages.

FIGURE 4-11

Languages tab

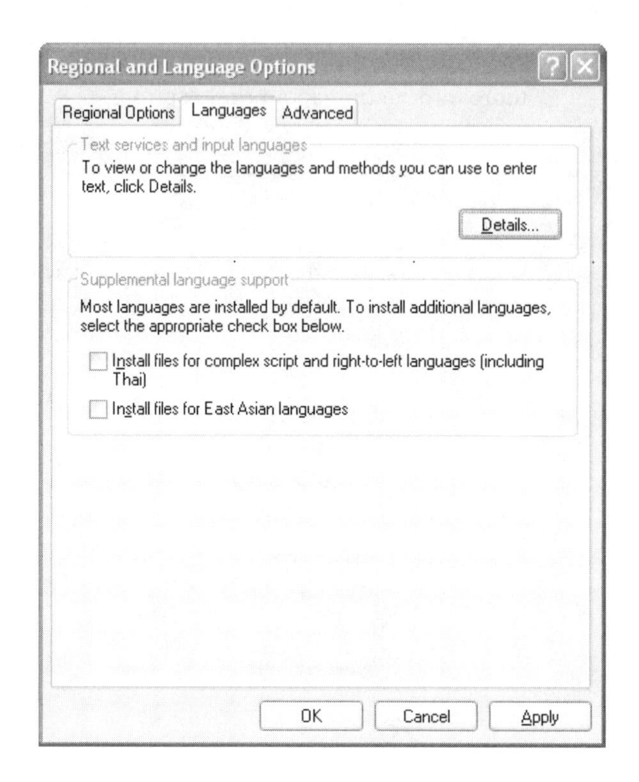

If you click the Details button, you can see the Default Input Language and the Installed Services, shown in Figure 4-12. If you want to use additional languages, click the Add button, select the language from the list, and click OK. I can then click the Language Bar and Key Settings button to configure how my keyboard uses these languages and how I can toggle between them when I am working.

exam Watch

The exam is more likely to test on configuration issues, such as getting the keyboard to work with a different language and how to toggle between languages. You should spend some time working with these windows and installing other languages as a test. There is no substitute for hands-on practice with these options.

Finally, you can also choose to install files for complex script and right-to-left languages, as well as files for East Asian languages from this tab. To install these options, click the "Install files for complex script and right-to-left languages" and

FIGURE 4-12

Text Services And Input Languages

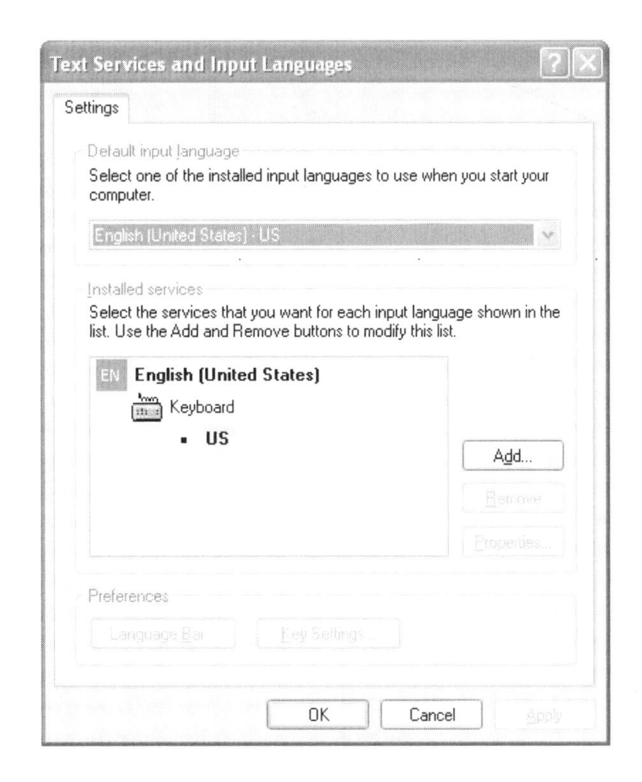

"Install files for East Asian Languages" check boxes in order to install support for these languages.

Advanced Tab

Finally, you have an Advanced tab on the Regional And Language Options properties dialog box. Windows XP Professional's default configuration for handling multiple languages occurs through Unicode. Unicode is an ISO (International Organization for Standardization) standard that combines character sets from major languages so that your computer can have multiple language support. Instead of having a different character set for each language, repeating characters are used in the set, making the use of several languages at one time possible on your computer. However, some programs may not work with Unicode, so the Advanced tab enables you to select a language version of the non-Unicode program that you want to use. As shown in Figure 4-13, you can select the language from the drop-down list and select a desired code page conversion table. Once the selections are set, you can check the box at the

FIGURE 4-13

Advanced tab

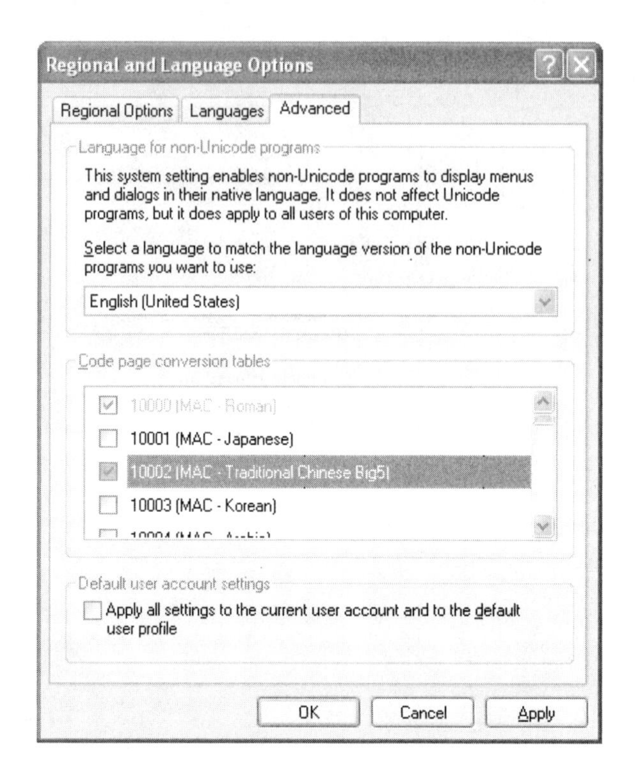

bottom of the page to have the settings apply to the default user account and default profile.

exam Watch

It is important to note that each user can set up language settings as he or she needs. Because Windows XP keeps each user's settings separate, the configuration of language options for one user does not affect the language settings of another user. If you have different users on the same computer with different language needs, do not use the default settings check box at the bottom of the Advanced tab. Instead, configure each user separately and let Windows XP keep up with the differences.

Configuring Locations

Now that you have taken a look at the basic Regional And Language Options settings, let's take a closer look at configuring multiple locations. Let's say you speak multiple languages and you travel with your laptop computer. When you are in other countries, you want to be able switch your computer over to that location easily. Before we get started, it is important to note that the concept of "Locations" includes a number of settings, such as language choice, keyboard input, money symbols, and related features. The idea is that you can travel from country to country, and Windows XP can easily adjust itself to your location.

The configuration for Locations takes place on the Regional And Language Options tab, so we will re-examine a few things here, which are items you should keep in mind for the exam.

First of all, the Regional Options window provides the current language standard your computer adheres to. You can edit the settings that are placed on that location by default when you click the Customize button. For each location you intend on using, you should select the location from the drop-down list and click the Customize button in order to see if the settings meet your needs and approval. The Customize Regional Options window, shown in Figure 4-14, gives you configuration tabs for Numbers, Currency, Time, and Date. These configuration tabs are rather self-explanatory, but you can check the options to see if they are correct for your location. As you can see in Figure 4-14, I am showing the Currency tab, which contains information about how currency is displayed and managed in this particular location.

FIGURE 4-14

Customize Regional Options

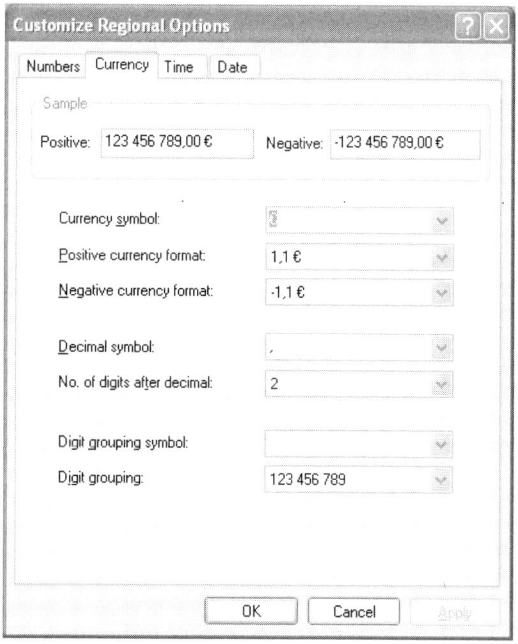

Once you have made any necessary configuration changes to the Regional Options page, you can then install and configure additional input languages. Click the Languages tab and click the Details button. You see the default input language, which you can change by making a different selection the drop-down menu. To add additional languages that you can use, click the Add button. In the Add Input Language window that appears, choose an Input Language and a Keyboard layout, as you can see in Figure 4-15.

Once you have made your selection, the new input language appears in the window, as you can see in Figure 4-16. At this point, you can then configure Language Bar Preferences and Key Settings for the input language.

If you click the Language Bar button on the Settings window, you see a number of check box options:

- Show the Language Bar on the desktop
- Show the Language Bar as transparent when inactive
- Show additional Language Bar icons in the Notification Area
- Show text labels on the Language Bar
- Turn off Advanced text services

You can select the items that you want and click OK on the dialog box. Once the Language Bar is enabled, it appears in the upper-right portion of the Windows XP Desktop. You can easily toggle between languages by simply clicking the bar and selecting the language that you want to use.

FIGURE 4-15

Add Input Language

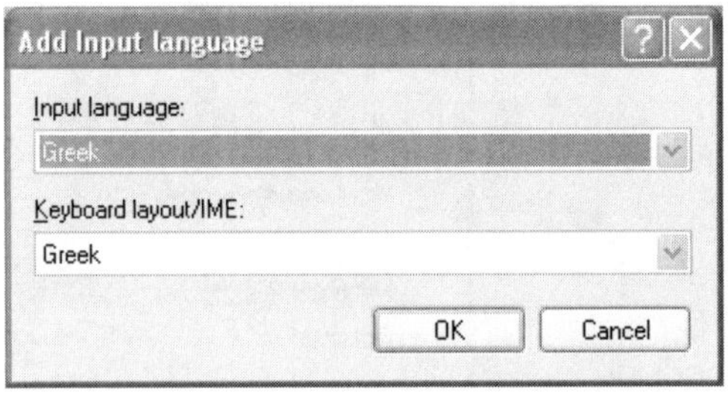

FIGURE 4-16

The new input language appears in the Settings window.

If you click the Key Settings option on the Settings tab, an Advanced Key Settings window appears, as shown in Figure 4-17. This window enables you to configure Hot Keys for input languages so that you can use the keyboard to switch between them.

FIGURE 4-17

Advanced Key Settings

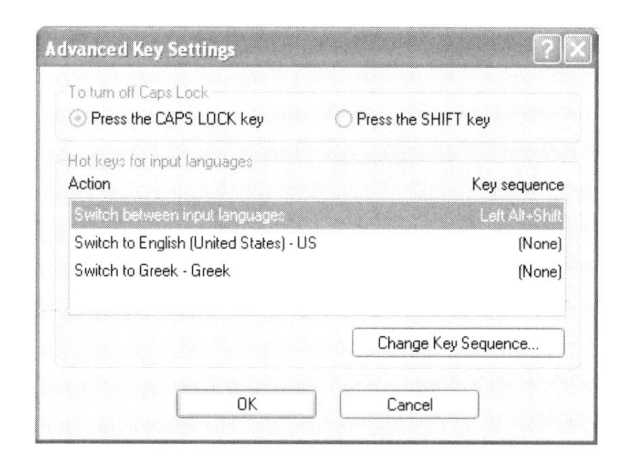

SCENARIO & SOLUTION	
I am using two languages. How can I easily switch from one to the other?	Access the Languages tab of Regional And Language Options Properties. On the Languages tab, click Details. Once you have configured the second language, you can click the Language Bar button and place an icon in your Notification area or configure a toggle key to switch back and forth.
I am using a second language, but I do not like the way Windows is handling the date. How can I change this?	On the Regional Options tab, click the Customize button. Then, click the Date button and edit the dialog boxes as needed.

CERTIFICATION OBJECTIVE 4.04

Manage Applications Using Windows Installer Packages

Software installation in Windows XP Professional works like previous versions of Windows. Users can install software using Add/Remove Programs in Control Panel, and most programs today contain their own setup routines and are very easy to install. The only problem users are likely to face is program incompatibilities with Windows XP Professional, and even then Windows XP includes a new Application Compatibility wizard that can enable Windows XP to act like a downlevel Windows operating system, such as Windows 98.

Besides testing your ability to install and manage applications "manually," the exam focuses one of its objectives on the management of Windows Installer Packages. Windows Installer Packages are single-file packages that contain all of the necessary components to install an application, such as.exe and .dll files. The package exists as a single unit, and a user need only double-click the package to start the installation. The package and setup routine handle the installation of files and the process is rather hands-off. Windows Installer Packages, which are represented with *.msi extension are rather common and are a great way to deploy software.

The creation of *.msi packages is beyond the scope of the exam, but the exam expects you to be able to manage their installation and deployment. Aside from double-clicking them to start the installation, what else is involved in the process? How can you deploy an .msi package to 1,000 computers on your network? If you guessed Group Policy, you are correct.

As I mentioned earlier in the chapter, Group Policy is a powerful Windows 2000 feature that enables you to manage user and computer configuration at the OU, domain, or site level. You can also deploy and remove .msi packages from Windows 2000 and Windows XP Professional computers that are domain members. Windows Installer packages have some great features for administrators—you can easily roll out an application via one file, completely uninstall the application, repair corrupted installations, and even script the installation so that no intervention is necessary from the user. This flexibility makes Windows Installer packages the product of choice for application rollouts via the Active Directory. As you might further guess, the deployment of .msi packages seems outside the exam scope. Remember, however, that the Windows XP Professional exam concerns the management and deployment of Windows XP, and so even though Group Policy is not explicitly stated in the exam objectives, you must know a few things about it. This overlap approach to exam objectives is quite common, and this exam is simply another example of that approach.

Software deployment using Group Policy must be configured at the site, domain, or OU level—it is not a Local Group Policy function. To install software using Group Policy, you use a Windows 2000 domain controller and run the Group Policy snap-in for the desired OU, domain, or site where the software will be deployed. Concerning software deployment, there are two deployment methods, and you need to know these for the exam:

- **Assign** The first method of software deployment is assignment. When you assign a software package, it is automatically installed on the users' computers, often during bootup without any intervention from the user. The user has no control over setup and receives no prompts. The package is assigned to the computer and automatically installed. Software can be assigned to users or computers.
- **Publish** The second method of deployment is publication. When you publish software, you make it available to the user if he or she wants to install it. This option is used with software that is optional—if the user needs it, he or she can install it. If not, the user can simply ignore it. Software is published to users.

exam Watch

You are likely to see questions that mix these concepts (assign and publish)—study them carefully!

Software can be assigned to both computers and users. For example, you can assign software to all computers in a particular site, domain, or OU so that the software is installed on each computer managed by the GPO. Likewise, you can assign software to users for automatic installation. However, you can publish software only to users. Publication gives users the option to install the software or not, depending on their needs.

Setting up a Windows Installer package for distribution in Group Policy is rather easy. Exercise 4-4 walks you through the process.

EXERCISE 4-4

Deploying Software Using Group Policy

To deploy software using Group Policy, just follow these steps:

1. In Windows 2000 Server, open Active Directory Users And Computers if you want to deploy software at the OU or domain level. Open Active Directory Sites And Services if you want to deploy software at the site level. You will need to be logged on with appropriate enterprise administrative rights for site-level configuration. You'll need to be logged on with domain administrator rights for domain and OU configuration.
2. Access the Properties of the desired site, domain, or OU, as you can see in the following illustration. On the Group Policy tab, select the desired Group Policy and click the Edit button.

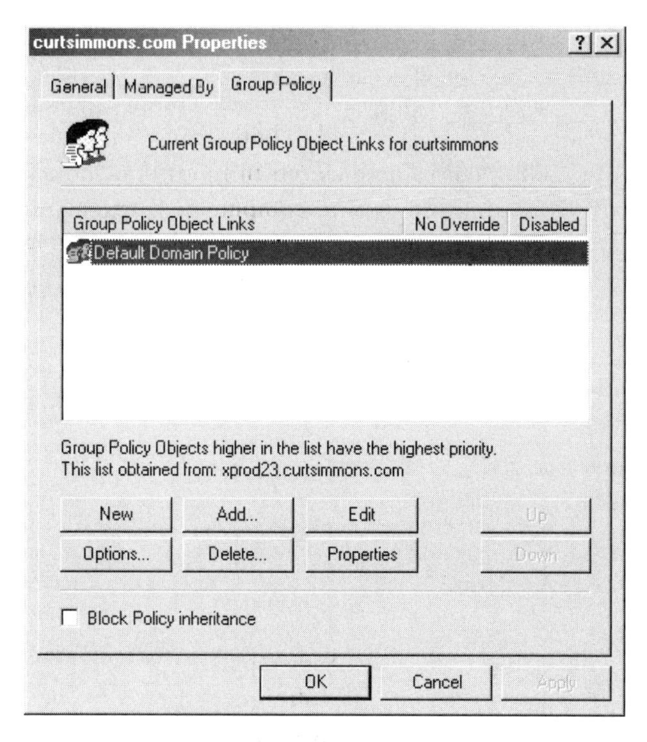

3. Under User Configuration, expand Software Settings. Right-click the Software Installation icon and click New | Package.
4. In the browse window that appears, browse for the .msi package that you want to deploy. The location that you choose must be a network share path, not a local drive path.
5. The Select Deployment method window appears, as shown in the following illustration. Choose to assign or publish the software as desired; then click OK.

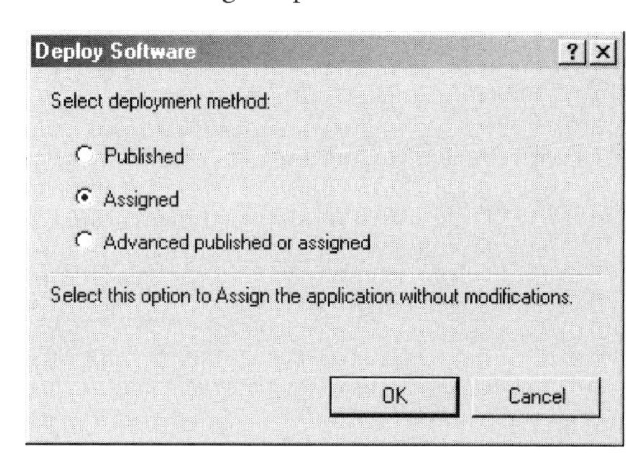

6. The software is added to the console and is ready for deployment, as you can see in the following illustration. You can also right-click the package and choose Properties to further configure deployment options.

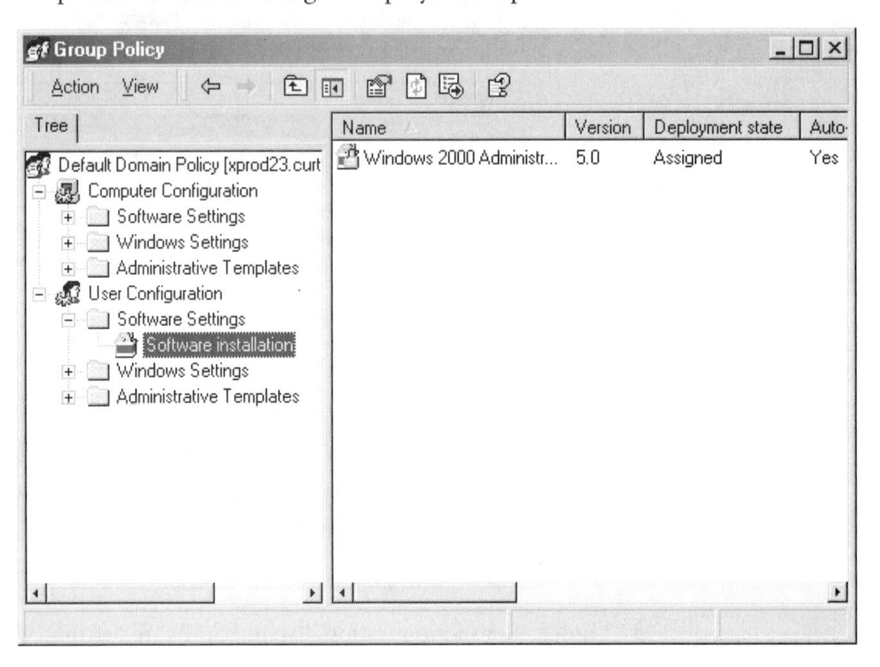

SCENARIO & SOLUTION

What happens if I deploy software using the Computer Configuration option instead of user configuration?	The process is the same, except that you can publish software only to users. You can choose to assign or publish software to users, but you can only assign software to computers.
How is a software package deployed at the domain level if there is both a site policy and a domain policy?	Policies are applied at the local computer level first, then the site level, next at the domain level, and last at the OU level. In this case, the site policy is applied as usual, but only the domain policy has the software package for deployment. So, all users in the site policy scope receive the site policy, but only users in the domain scope receive the domain policy, thus only the "domain" users receive the software package.

CERTIFICATION OBJECTIVE 4.05

Configure and Manage User Profiles

User profiles are designed so that more than one person can use a particular computer. Windows XP Professional is the best operating system that Microsoft has produced in terms of user and profile management. Any number of people can use the same Windows XP Professional computer and maintain their own settings and documents. This is a great feature because one user does not overwrite system settings or move/remove another user's files. Windows XP makes user management easy with both a graphical Control Panel tool and the Computer Management console. As we discuss user profiles and user accounts, we will approach them from a local machine point of view. Obviously, on a Windows domain, user accounts are managed on a domain controller. However, for computers not on a domain, you can manage user profiles and accounts locally.

For starters, you can create user accounts via the graphical User Accounts tool found in Control Panel, shown in Figure 4-18. From this location, you can create and delete accounts, edit accounts, and change the way users log on or off. An

FIGURE 4-18

User Accounts in Control Panel

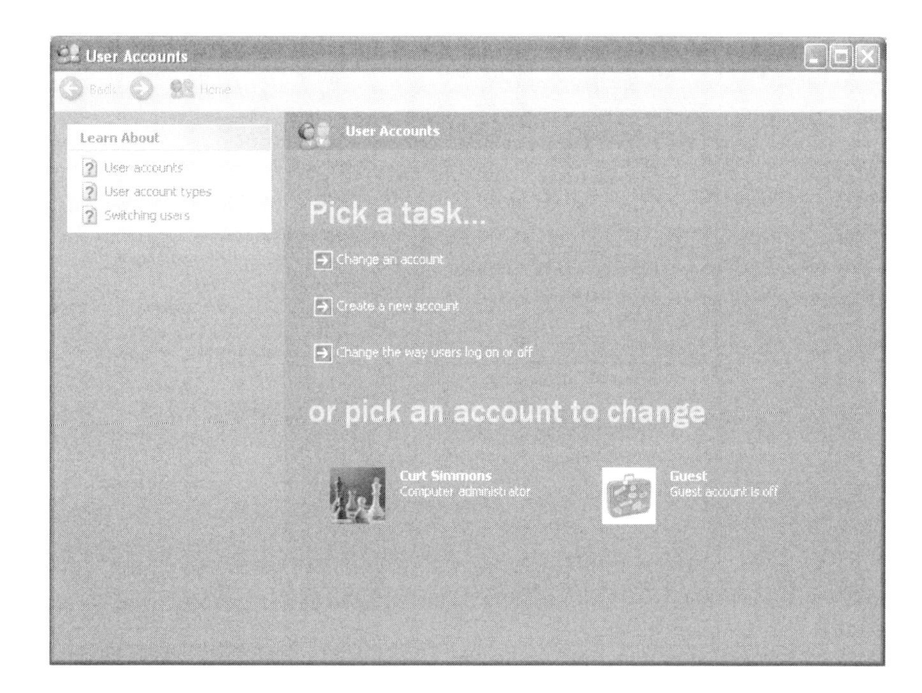

account consists of a user name and password if desired. The User Accounts feature provided here is more appropriate for end users and is in keeping with the graphical nature of Windows XP.

You can also configure and manage user accounts via the Computer Management console, found in Administrative Tools in Control Panel. Expanding local users and groups, you can create, edit, and assign user/administrative level permissions as desired, as shown in Figure 4-19. Primarily, the Users tool found in Control Panel is available for end users who share their PCs with other users. The Computer Management snap-in gives you an easier way to manage several users and configure options for them, so it is better choice for the IT professional.

Once a user account is created, a Documents and Settings folder is created where any settings configured by the user and any personal documents are stored. Users cannot access each other's folders, with the exception of the administrator, who can access any folder as needed. Once users are created, they can be grouped as needed for organizational purposes and rights assignment. Granted, most of the work you will do with users and groups will occur at the server level and not at the local level; however, the discussion here is brief and will segue into our exploration of user profiles.

FIGURE 4-19 Users in Computer Management

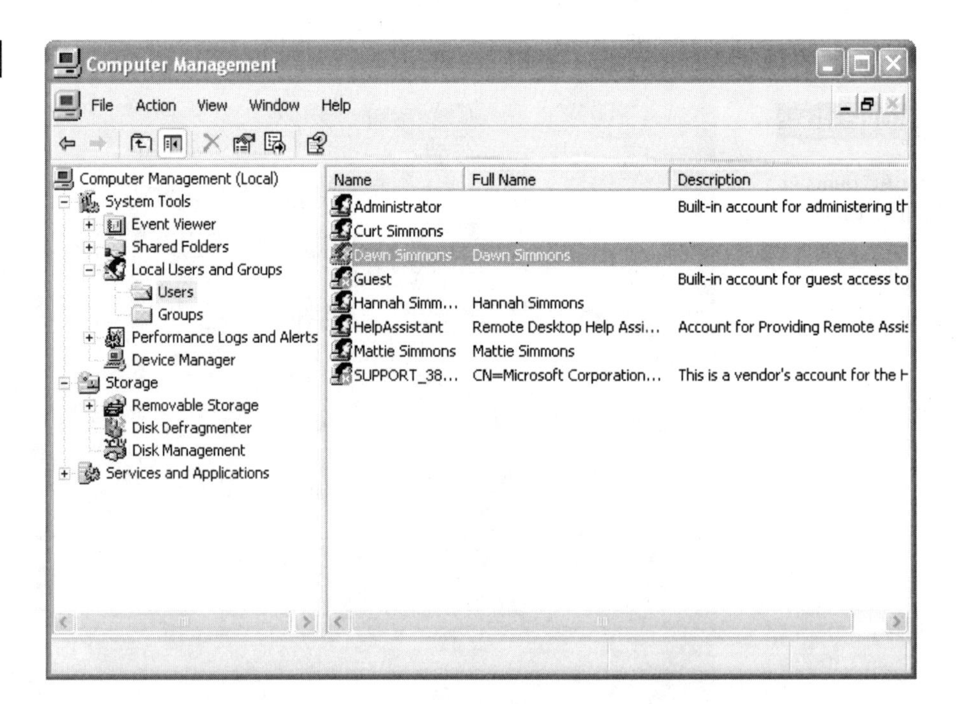

As I said, each local user account is given a folder, which is found \Documents and Settings*username.* (If the computer was upgraded to Windows XP, the user's profile could be stored in \\%windir%\profiles.) Documents and Settings is the default location where all user profiles are stored. You can change this location if you like and configure some additional profile options. In order to make changes to the default profile path, you must access the user account's properties via the Computer Management console. Expand Local Users and Groups, in the right pane right-click the desired user account, and click Properties. Click the Profile tab, as shown in Figure 4-20.

As you can see, the Profile path is empty, which means the default of \Documents and Settings*username* is being used. If you want to store the profile in a different location, just enter a new path. You may want the profile stored in a more secure location or even on a different disk. You can also choose to have the profile apply to more than one user. Let's say you log as juser, but sometimes you log on as administrator. Since each profile is different, your settings under each account will be different. However, you can redirect one of your profiles to the other profile path. For example, let's say you make a number of configuration changes and have a number of Internet Explorer favorites under juser. You can configure your administrator profile so that it uses the juser profile—this way, you are working with one profile

FIGURE 4-20

Profile tab

when you log on, regardless of the account. Regardless of your needs, just enter the new path here. If a logon script is used, you can enter the script path in the provided dialog box here as well.

The Home Folder option is used to establish a local home folder. By default, My Documents is used, but you can specify a different home folder where the user's files will be stored by entering a local path. This Home Folder configuration helps applications, such as Microsoft Word, that try to guess where you want to put documents to make the correct choice for that particular user.

You can also configure a roaming user profile here. This feature is beneficial to users who access several different computers each day, but want the same documents and settings regardless of where they log on. The profile can be configured on a server, such as in a domain environment, and then the profile path can be configured as a network address, such as \\server1\profile1. Exercise 4-5 shows you how to set up a roaming user profile.

EXERCISE 4-5

Setting Up a Roaming User Profile

To set up a roaming user profile, just follow these steps:

1. On the primary computer the user accesses, configure a shared Home folder with a desired network path. For example, let's say that a user, JohnM, has an account on a computer, XP49, and a Home folder stored in Documents and Settings\JohnM. Configure the system as desired for JohnM or create a shared folder on a server in the domain environment where the profile can be stored.
2. Go to the next machine JohnM will use and create a user account with the same name and password for the user.
3. Access the user account properties and click the Profile tab, as shown earlier in Figure 4-20. Choose a desired drive letter and then enter the UNC path to the original profile you created. In this example, the profile would be \\XP49\Documents and Settings\JohnM. The user should receive the same settings on the remote computer.

SCENARIO & SOLUTION	
Why does Windows XP provide two locations to manage user accounts?	The User Accounts icon in Control Panel provides a graphical location where end users can easily configure accounts. The Computer Management console is built for administrators so that multiple accounts can be easily managed.
Can I store my Home folder on a different computer?	You can store your home folder on a different computer. Depending on your needs, this may be OK, so just choose the Connect option and enter the UNC path to the Home folder. However, make sure you determine whether or not this configuration is really beneficial.

CERTIFICATION SUMMARY

Windows XP Professional contains a number of features that support the configuration needs of end users. As an IT professional, you'll make use of these features in a number of important managerial ways.

First, Windows XP provides rich support for accessibility services, including a number of built-in accessibility features, such as Magnifier, Speech, On-Screen Keyboard, and even an Accessibility Wizard that makes configuration easier. You can also configure a number of additional features that assist in accessibility, including several keyboard and mouse functions.

Next, Window XP Professional contains a number of desktop settings that can be configured locally or via Windows 2000 Group Policy. From an exam point of view, Group Policy is the preferred method of configuring uniform desktop settings and standards in networking environments.

Windows XP supports the use of multiple languages and locations, enabling you to configure Windows XP to use several languages at one time. You can easily toggle between languages and settings as desired.

Windows XP also makes software installation and management easy with Add/Remove Programs and Windows Installer packages. From an IT professional's perspective, you can add and remove software from users' computers via an assigned or published format through Group Policy as well. Software can be assigned or published at the site, domain, or OU level.

Finally, Windows XP Professional continues to support user profiles and the use of a home folder for users where their personal desktop settings and files are stored. You can also configure roaming user profiles so that users can log on to different network computers and receive the same settings and files.

TWO-MINUTE DRILL

Configure and Troubleshoot Accessibility Services

- Windows XP Professional includes a number of accessibility services and feature that make the computer easier to use for people with certain disabilities.
- The Magnifier can provide a dialog box that greatly magnifies different portions of the screen. You can make the Magnifier mouse and keyboard sensitive in that it will follow your mouse pointer and keystrokes.
- The On-Screen Keyboard enables you to type using your mouse. You can use a Joystick with the On-Screen Keyboard as well.
- The Narrator is a speech product that reads dialog boxes and messages that appear on your screen.
- Use the Accessibility Wizard to configure all of the accessibility services. The Accessibility Wizard is particularly helpful to end users who want to take full advantage of all that Windows XP Professional's accessibility services have to offer.
- You can manually configure all of the accessibility services via Accessibility Options in Control Panel.
- Use Utility Manager to control the On-Screen Keyboard, Magnifier, and Narrator from one place.
- To assist persons who have difficulty using a keyboard, you can configure StickyKeys, FilterKeys, and ToggleKeys.

Configure and Troubleshoot Desktop Settings

- Desktop Settings can be configured locally using Display Properties in Control Panel. Windows XP Professional uses the XP theme by default, which you can customize. You can also choose a completely different theme if you like.
- Use Group Policy to invoke standardized settings in your domain environment. Group Policy can be invoked at the site, domain, or OU level.

- Group Policy elements have Not Configured, Enabled, or Disabled radio button options. The Not Configured setting is used by default and causes no registry entry, while the Enabled and Disabled settings cause the registry to be written to.
- If the Windows XP theme and graphics are causing system performance problems, you can customize the use of graphics by accessing the Performance tab on the System Properties dialog box.

Configure Support for Multiple Languages and Multiple Locations

- Windows XP Professional supports the use of multiple languages and locations.
- Languages and locations options can be configured on the Regional Options Properties pages in Control Panel.
- You can configure your system to toggle between languages as needed.

Manage Applications Using Windows Installer Packages

- Windows Installer Packages (*.msi files) contain all of the files necessary to install an application and appear as a single icon that the user can click to start.
- You can assign or publish Windows Installer Packages at the site, domain, or OU level using Group Policy.
- In Group Policy, assigned software is configured at the Computer level or User level and is automatically installed on users' computers. You can publish software at the User level. Published software is not automatically installed, but, rather, users choose to install the software or not.

Configure and Manage User Profiles

- User Profiles enable different users to access the same computer with their own personalized settings and documents.
- Windows XP Professional stores user profiles in their own folder, which is located in \Documents and Settings*username* by default. In the case of an upgrade to Windows XP, the default location is \\\\%windir%\profiles.

- ❑ You can manage user accounts locally in Windows XP using User Accounts in Control Panel or the Computer Management console. The Computer Management console gives you the ability to manage multiple accounts easily, reset passwords, and perform other administrative tasks.
- ❑ You can configure the Home Folder to reside in a different location using the Profile tab of a user's account properties in Computer Management. You can also configure the network path for a roaming user profile here.

SELF TEST

The following questions will help you measure your understanding of the material presented in this chapter. Read all of the choices carefully, as there may be more than one correct answer. Choose all correct answers for each question.

Configure and Troubleshoot Accessibility Services

1. A particular user in your organization has problems seeing small items on the computer. What accessibility features would be particularly helpful to this user?

   A. On-Screen Keyboard

   B. Magnifier

   C. Speech

   D. StickyKeys

2. Which tool is especially helpful to end users who want to configure their own accessibility settings?

   A. Accessibility Wizard

   B. Accessibility Options

   C. Utility Manager

   D. File and Settings Transfer Wizard

3. In your environment, a particular user suffers from a condition that causes his hands to shake. Because of the problem, the user often hits keyboard keys accidentally or often hits the same key twice with a single stroke. What configuration option would be most helpful?

   A. StickyKeys

   B. FilterKeys

   C. ToggleKeys

   D. Utility Manager

Configure and Troubleshoot Desktop Settings

4. What processing order is used when several Group Policy objects are in effect in an environment?

   A. OU, domain, site

   B. Domain, site, OU

C. Site, OU, domain

D. Site, domain, OU

5. Consider the following illustration:

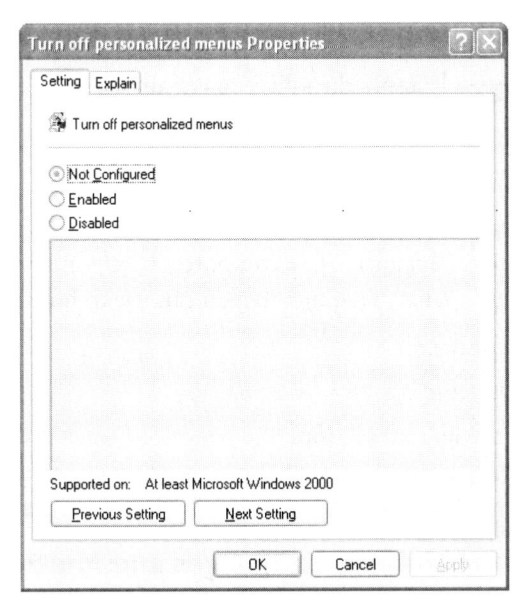

For this Group Policy setting, you want to make certain that users can access personalized menus. What setting needs to be configured here?

A. Not Configured.

B. Enabled.

C. Disabled.

D. This setting cannot be used.

6. You manage a local workstation where five other users log on to the computer. As the administrator, you configure a Local Group Policy that assigns certain Start Menu settings. However, you notice that the settings are never invoked when users log on. Your computer is a part of a Windows 2000 domain. What is the problem?

A. User permissions are overriding the administrator account.

B. You can't use a local policy in a domain.

C. A site, domain, or OU Group Policy is overwriting the local policy.

D. You didn't configure the policy correctly.

7. You are the local administrator of a Windows XP Professional computer that is used as a print server. Five other users access the computer. You create a Local Group Policy. You want to apply the policy to two of the five users. However, you cannot seem to apply the policy to the two users only. What is the problem?

   A. The users have administrative rights.

   B. You cannot selectively apply the policy to certain users.

   C. You configured the policy under Computer Configuration instead of User Configuration.

   D. You do not have administrative rights.

8. You want your users to use the XP theme and XP Start Menu. However, many users report that their systems seem "sluggish." The computers barely meet the Windows XP Professional processor requirement. What is a quick fix you can use to boost processing power?

   A. Install new processors.

   B. Remove the XP theme.

   C. Change the Start Menu to Classic.

   D. Configure the Visual Effects tab to adjust visual effects for the best performance.

Configure Support for Multiple Languages and Multiple Locations

9. When configuring regional and language ptions, you want to make sure that different Windows services can gather regional information for you, such as local information, weather, and so on. What Regional and Language Options tab allows you to configure this setting?

   A. Regional Options

   B. Languages

   C. Advanced

   D. Money

10. You need to configure settings for a user who regularly accesses three different languages. You want the user to be able to easily toggle between languages using a hot key. Where can you configure this in Regional And Language Options?

    A. Regional Options tab, Details button

    B. Regional Options tab, Toggle button

    C. Languages tab, Details button

    D. Advanced tab, Toggle button

Manage Applications with Windows Installer Packages

11. Which of the following files is a Windows Installer Package file?

A. Myapp.exe

B. Myapp.jpeg

C. Myapp.msc

D. Myapp.msi

12. You want to use Group Policy to automatically install software on users' computers in a particular OU. Considering the illustration that follows, which radio button option do you need to select?

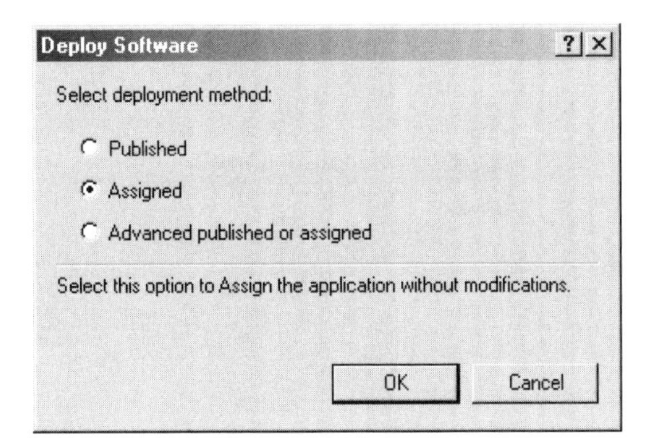

A. Assign.

B. Publish.

C. Advanced Assign or Publish.

D. You cannot automatically install software this way.

13. You want to use Group Policy to publish a software package. You access Computer Configuration and configure the package, but you see no option to publish the software. What is the problem?

A. You do not have domain administrative rights.

B. You do not have enterprise administrator rights.

C. You can't publish software via Computer Configuration.

D. The chosen package is not a Windows Installer Package.

Configure and Manage User Profiles

14. On a particular computer, there are several users. One user is named Jsmith. In Windows XP Professional, where is Jsmith's user profile stored by default if the computer running XP Professional was cleanly installed and not upgraded?

A. \My Documents\jsmith

B. \Documents and Settings\jsmith

C. \Documents and Settings\profiles\jsmith

D. *Computername*\Profiles\jsmith

15. Consider the following illustration:

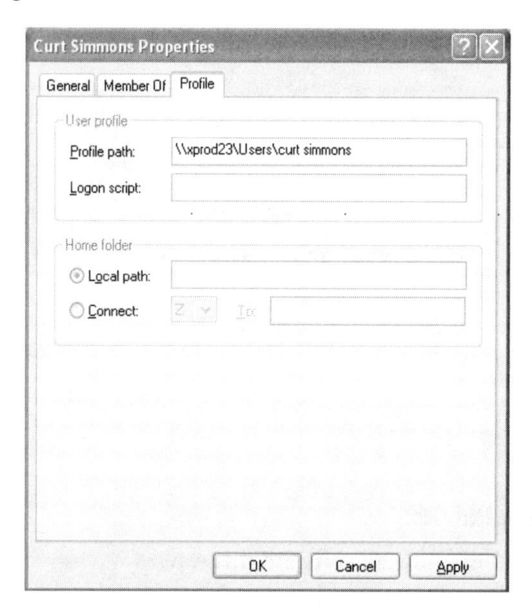

What does the Configured items on this tab tell you?

A. There is no home folder.

B. A roaming user profile is in use.

C. A local user profile is in use.

D. The default logon script is used.

LAB QUESTION

You are a domain administrator for a large company. The company would like to roll out some custom software to everyone in your particular domain. The company wants to do this without any intervention from end users and to complete the rollout as quickly and as easily as possible. What steps do you need to follow in order to accomplish this goal?

SELF TEST ANSWERS

Configure and Troubleshoot Accessibility Services

1. ☑ B and C are correct. The Magnifier will help the user see items on the screen, and Speech can read small dialog boxes to the user.

☒ A and D are incorrect. Considering that the user has problems seeing small items on the screen, the On-Screen Keyboard and StickyKeys will not be of any assistance.

2. ☑ A is correct. The Accessibility Wizard is the easiest way for end users to configure accessibility settings

☒ B, C, and D are incorrect. Although settings can be configured via Accessibility Options in Control Panel, the Accessibility Wizard is the easiest way to configure these settings, so B is incorrect. C is incorrect because the Utility Manager just lets you manage the tools, not configure them. D is incorrect because the File and Settings Transfer Wizard does not help in the configuration of accessibility features.

3. ☑ B is correct. FilterKeys filter out additional and accidental keystrokes, so this is the best choice in this situation.

☒ A, C, and D are incorrect. A is incorrect because StickyKeys causes the keys to stick, which is helpful to people who cannot press keys simultaneously. C is incorrect because ToggleKeys gives you a tone when CAPS, NUM or SCROLL LOCK is turned on, which would not help this user. Finally, D is incorrect because the Utility Manager does not help with keyboard accessibility.

Configure and Troubleshoot Desktop Settings

4. ☑ D is correct. Group Policy is processed from the top down—site, then domain, then OU.

☒ A, B, and C are incorrect. All of these order options are incorrect.

5. ☑ A is correct. In this situation, you want to make sure that personalized settings are available. Since they are available by default, you would simply leave this setting as Not Configured. This causes no registry entry to be written, while allowing personalized menus to be available to users.

☒ B, C, and D are incorrect. You would not want to enable the setting because doing so would make personalized menus unavailable, so B is incorrect. You would also not want to Disable the setting because doing this causes a registry entry to be written when Not Configured would work as well. Finally, D is incorrect, because the desired setting can be configured.

6. ☑ C is correct. A site, domain, or OU Group Policy is overwriting the local policy. Local Group Policies are the weakest policy, and in a domain environment, any site, domain, or OU level policy can overwrite the local policy.

☒ A, B, and D are incorrect. Permissions do not affect this issue, so A is incorrect. B is incorrect, because you can use a local policy, and D is also incorrect, because this is not the most likely explanation.

7. ☑ B is correct. You cannot selectively apply Local Group Policy to certain users. Once configured, it applies to all users logging onto the computer.

☒ A, C, and D are incorrect. Permissions do not affect this particular configuration, and you would not be able to configure the Group Policy at all if you were not an administrator.

8. ☑ D is correct. The easiest fix is to use the Visual Effects tab and tell Windows to adjust visual effects for the best performance.

☒ A, B, and D are incorrect. These options will not produce the desired outcome.

Configure Support for Multiple Languages and Multiple Locations

9. ☑ A is correct. Use the Locations drop-down menu on the Regional Options tab to choose a desired region.

☒ B, C, and D are incorrect. You can't configure the regional option on the Languages and Advanced tabs, and there is no Money tab.

10. ☑ C is correct. You can configure the hot keys by clicking the Details button on the Languages tab. Once you have added the languages, click the Key Settings button.

☒ A, B, and D are incorrect. None of these options will enable you to configure languages used or hot key settings.

Manage Applications with Windows Installer Packages

11. ☑ D is correct. *.msi files are Windows Installer Package files.

☒ A, B, and C are incorrect. *.exe are executable files, *.jpeg are picture files, and *.msc files are Microsoft Management Console files. Therefore, all of these answer options are incorrect.

12. ☑ A is correct. The Assign option, when assigned to the computer, installs the software automatically without any input or permission from the user. The user does not interact with the installation at all. When assigned to the user, the application is configured for installation and application shortcuts appear on the Start Menu as though it is installed, but the installation takes place at first use. The application can also be installed through document invocation.

    ☒ B, C, and D are incorrect. If you Publish the software, users can choose to install it if they wish, so B is incorrect. There is no question indicator for an advanced install or publish option, so C is also incorrect. Since you can install software using Group Policy, D is also incorrect.

13. ☑ C is correct. Software publication applies to users, while assignment applies to computers and users. You cannot publish software via Computer Configuration in Group Policy. Instead, configure publication using User Configuration.

    ☒ A, B, and D are incorrect. The problem here is not a permissions issue, so A and B are incorrect. D is incorrect because Group Policy will let you select only *.msi files.

Configure and Manage User Profiles

14. ☑ B is correct. By default, user profiles are stored in \Documents and Settings*username* in Windows XP Professional when the operating system was cleanly installed.

    ☒ A, C, and D are incorrect. None of these locations is the default storage location.

15. ☑ B is correct. A roaming user profile is in effect because the profile path points to a UNC path, which in this case is a server. If the profile path had been blank, then the default location of \Documents and Settings*username* would have been in use.

    ☒ A, C, and D are incorrect. A is incorrect because a default home folder is in use. C is incorrect because the default profile path is not in use. D is incorrect because there is no default script.

LAB ANSWER

In this situation, you want to assign the software to all computers in the domain. Follow these steps:

1. In Windows 2000 Server, open Active Directory Users and Computers. You will need to be logged on with domain administrator rights.
2. Access the Properties of the domain. Select the desired Group Policy and click the Edit button.

3. Under Computer Configuration, expand Software Settings. Right-click the Software Installation icon and click New | Package.
4. In the browse window that appears, browse for the .msi package that you want to deploy and make sure that it is located on a network share.
5. The Select Deployment method window appears. Note that only the Assign option is available, since publication only works under User Configuration. Click OK.
6. The software is added to the console and is ready for deployment. You can also right-click the package and choose Properties to further configure deployment options.

5

Managing Windows XP Hardware

CERTIFICATION OBJECTIVES

- 5.01 Install and Remove Hardware on Windows XP
- 5.02 Manage and Troubleshoot Device Drivers and Driver Signing
- 5.03 Configure Advanced Configuration Power Interface (ACPI)
- 5.04 Implement, Manage, and Troubleshoot Display Devices
- 5.05 Monitor and Configure Multi-Processor Computers
- 5.06 Implement, Manage, and Troubleshoot Disk Devices
- ✓ Two-Minute Drill
- Q&A Self Test

In the past, hardware installation, configuration, and management presented significant challenges—after all, you had to know some things about hardware interrupts, IRQ numbers, and related lower-level configuration. Since the days of plug and play, however, installing and managing hardware on Windows computers has become easier with each new operating system release, and Windows XP is no exception to that pattern. Hardware installation and management has, however, become difficult in other ways, especially since there is more hardware to choose from. In the past, hardware typically consisted of a sound card, video card, hard disk, keyboard, and mouse, along with a monitor and printer. Today, users may have multiple internal cards and multiple external devices, including cameras and handheld devices. So, while plug and play generally makes life easy for the Windows user, managing hardware can still be complex for a particular computer.

From an exam perspective, you'll need to know plenty about hardware configuration and management and the hardware management features that are found in Windows XP. In this chapter, you'll take a look at the basic hardware installation and configuration issues, and in Chapter 6, you'll learn about a number of different input/output devices that you can use with Windows XP.

CERTIFICATION OBJECTIVE 5.01

Install and Remove Hardware on Windows XP

Windows XP is a fully compliant plug and play system. This means that Windows XP can detect hardware changes and adapt to them. For example, you can install a new video card, and, upon reboot, Windows XP will detect the new hardware and attempt to automatically install it. If the installation is successful, the hardware is automatically ready for use—no wizards or installation screens—it simply appears on the system. This is a great feature that further automates hardware configuration and management for the end user.

If installation is not successful, a prompt appears for the Add Hardware wizard, so that you can attempt to manually install the hardware. Under most circumstances, up-to-date plug and play hardware can be automatically installed by Windows XP—Windows XP has the most extensive device driver database to date, and Windows can usually locate a basic driver to work with most plug and play devices. The trick is to use hardware that is compatible with Windows XP. When purchasing and installing new hardware, check for compatibility and also check the HCL for a list of compatible devices at **www.microsoft.com/hcl**.

on the Job

Just because a hardware device is not listed on the HCL does not mean that the device will not work with Windows XP—it simply means that "official" testing for that device has not been performed. You can also check the hardware vendor's Web site for more information about compatibility.

exam Watch

Keep in mind that the "official" way to install hardware is to always check for compatibility on the HCL. If you see exam questions that ask for a series of steps when installing new hardware, the HCL check is always a part of that series of steps, if provided by the answer prompts.

Manually Installing Hardware

In the event that you need to manually install a hardware device on Windows XP, you can use the Add Hardware wizard in Control Panel, which will help you install the device. Before installing a device manually, you'll probably need the driver for the device. A driver is a piece of software that allows Windows XP and the hardware device to communicate with each other. As I mentioned, Windows XP has a large database of generic drivers that will often work, but the specific driver created for the hardware device (by the hardware vendor) is often your best choice. If Windows XP is having problems installing the device automatically through plug and play, then you will probably need the device manufacturer's specific device driver. The driver often accompanies the hardware device on a floppy disk or CD-ROM, or you can usually find it on the device manufacturer's Web site.

Exercise 5-1 walks you through the process of using the Add Hardware wizard.

EXERCISE 5-1

CertCam 5-1

Using the Add Hardware Wizard

To use the Add Hardware wizard, just follow these steps:

1. Click Start | Settings | Control Panel | Add Hardware.
2. Click Next on the Welcome screen.

3. The wizard searches for any hardware that has been connected to the computer. If the hardware is not found, then a window appears, shown in the following illustration, that asks if the hardware is connected. Make the correct selection and click Next.

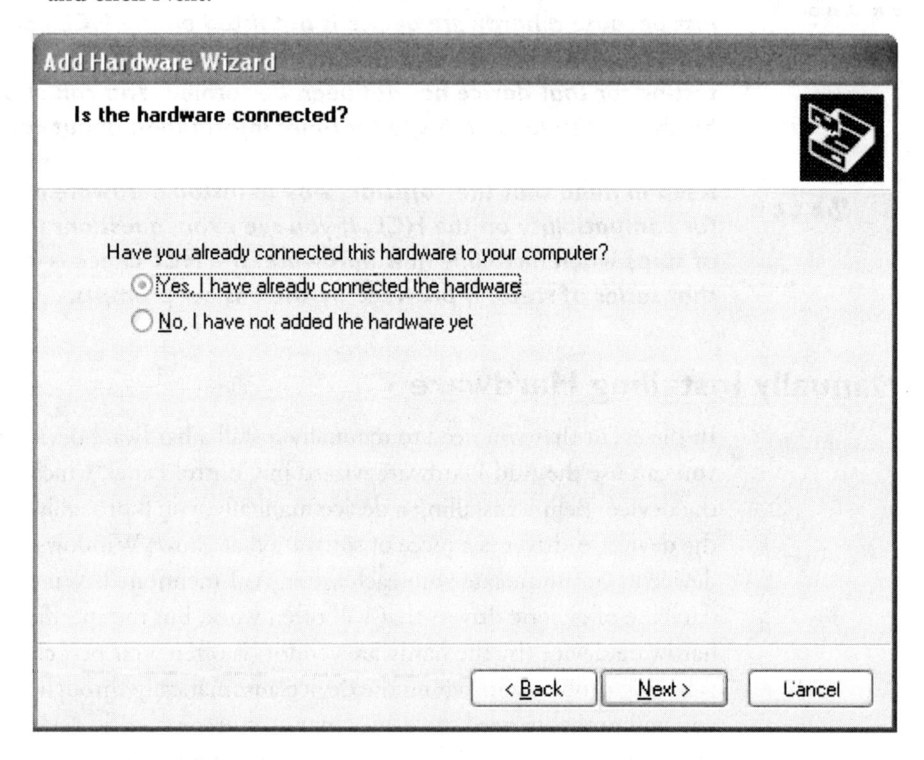

4. You can use the Add Hardware wizard to troubleshoot a device that is not working or add a new hardware device. In the provided window, shown in the following illustration, make a selection. For this exercise, I'm going to select "Add a new hardware device."

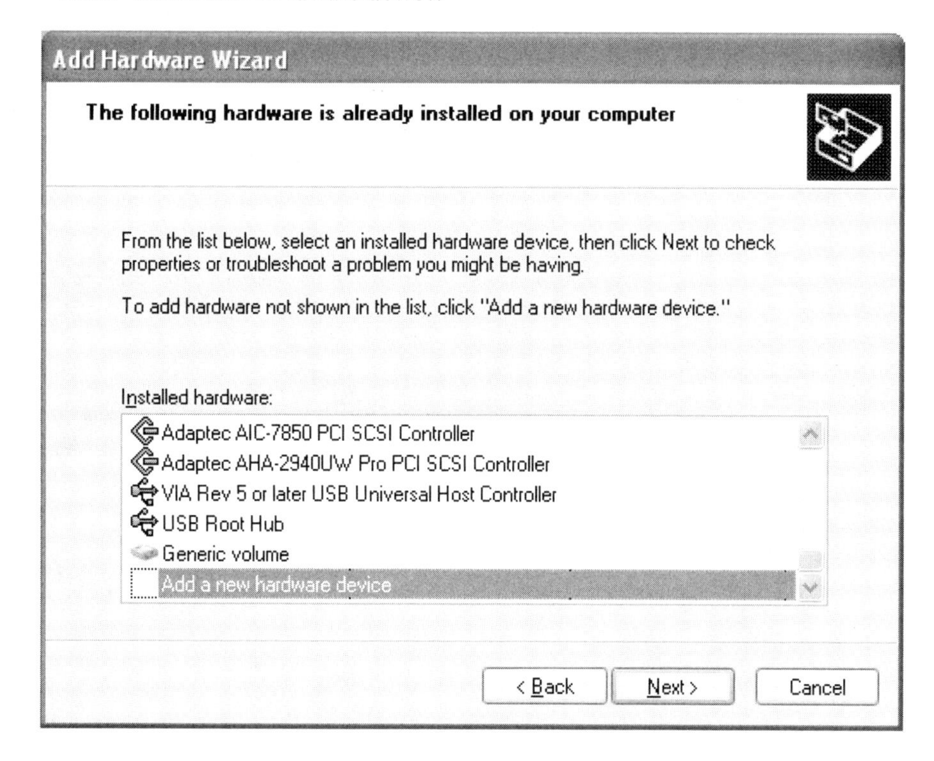

5. The wizard prompts you to either install the hardware by selecting it from a list or have windows search again. Since Windows has not been able to detect the hardware up to this point, it is usually best to choose the "Install the hardware that I manually select from a list (Advanced)" radio button, shown in the following illustration. Click Next.

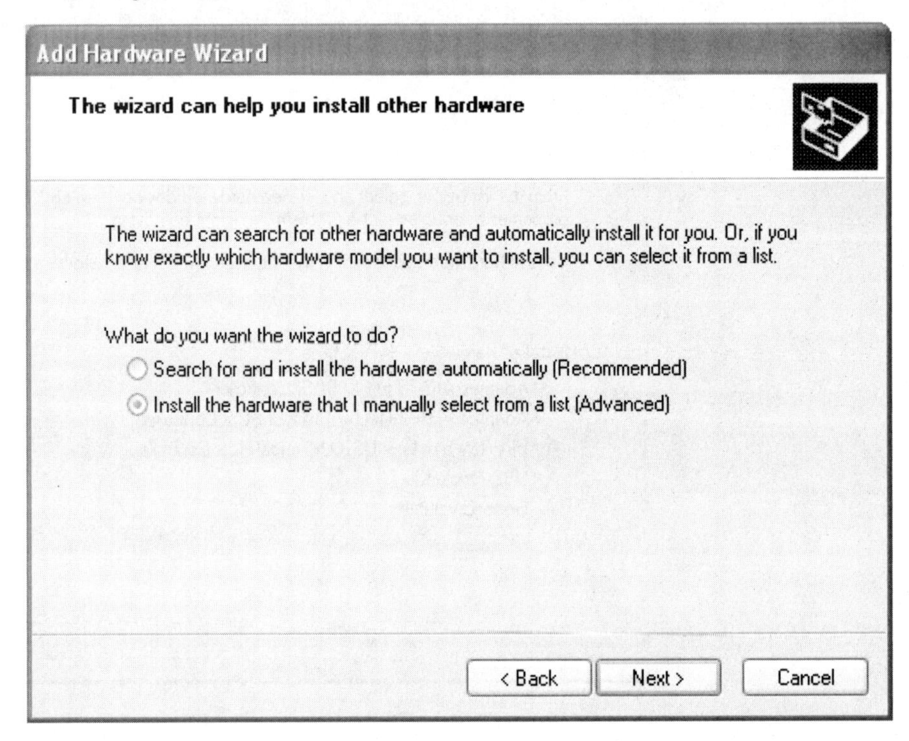

6. A hardware type window appears, shown in the following illustration, that allows you to choose the kind of hardware device that you want to install. Choose a desired category and click Next.

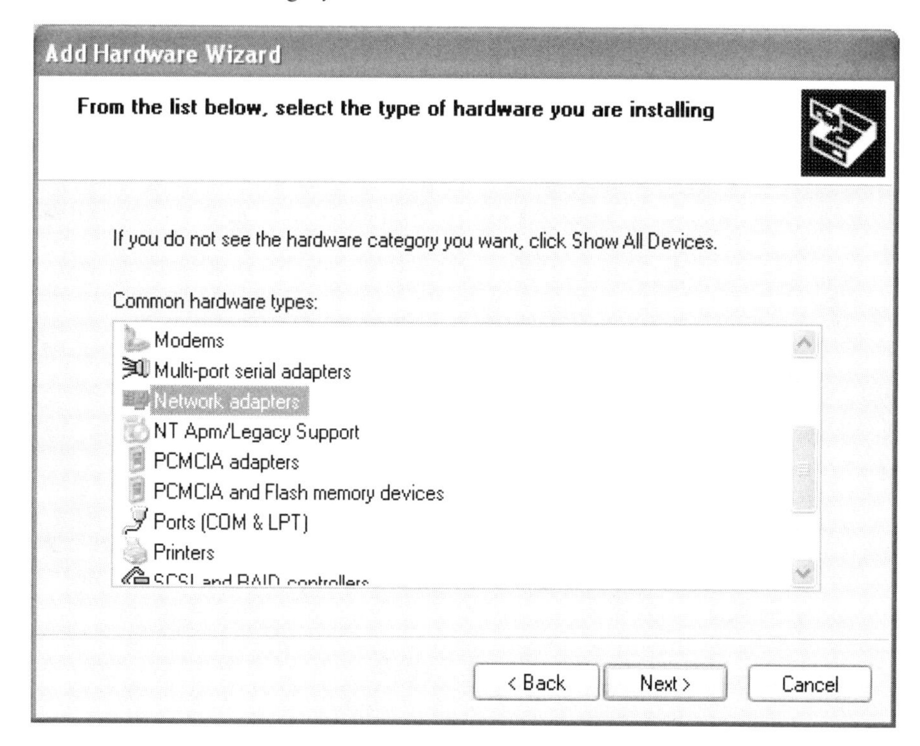

7. Windows XP generates a list of hardware from the category that you selected. In the selection window, shown in the following illustration, choose the manufacturer and the model of the hardware that you want to install. If you have an installation disk for the hardware, you can click the Have Disk button and run the hardware installation routine from the disk. Make a selection and click Next.

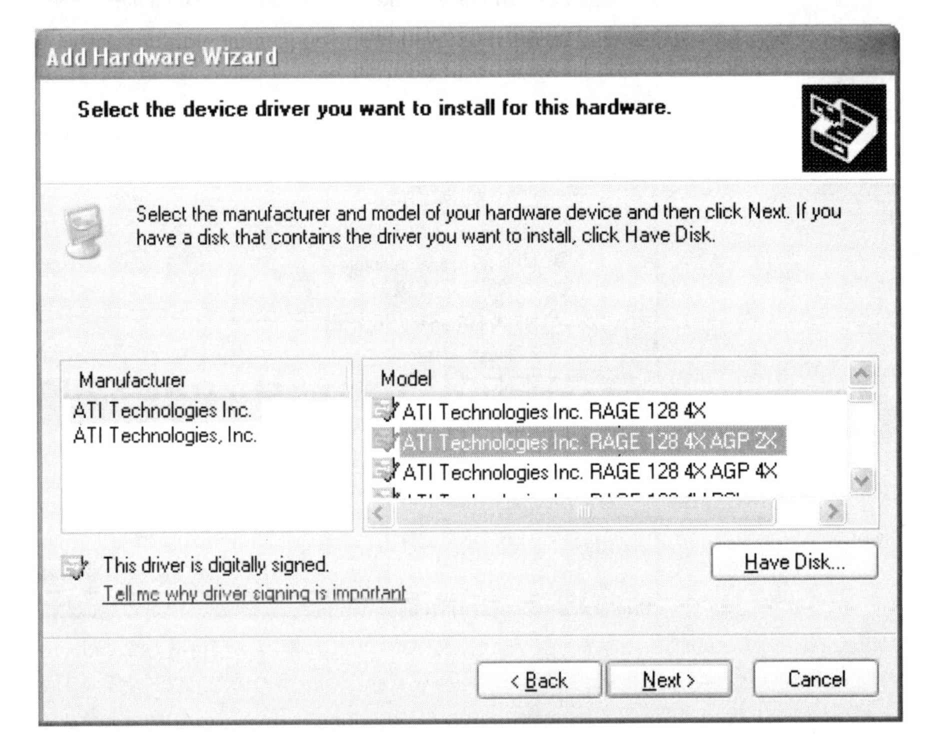

8. The hardware you want to install is listed. Click Next to continue the installation. Files are copied and the device is installed. Click Finish to complete the installation.

As mentioned in the previous exercise, you can also use the Add Hardware wizard to troubleshoot problematic devices. This option essentially provides you with a look at the device's properties and attempts to help you discover what is causing the problem so that it can be fixed. Exercise 5-2 shows you how the wizard can be used to troubleshoot a device.

EXERCISE 5-2

Using the Add Hardware Wizard to Troubleshoot a Device

To use the Add Hardware wizard to troubleshoot a device, just follow these steps:

1. Click Start | Settings | Control Panel | Add Hardware.
2. Click Next on the Welcome screen.
3. Windows XP searches for new hardware. If none is found, you'll see the list of devices currently installed on the computer. Devices that are not functioning properly appear with a exclamation point beside them (in yellow), as you can see next to the top item in the list in the following illustration. Select the problematic device and click Next.

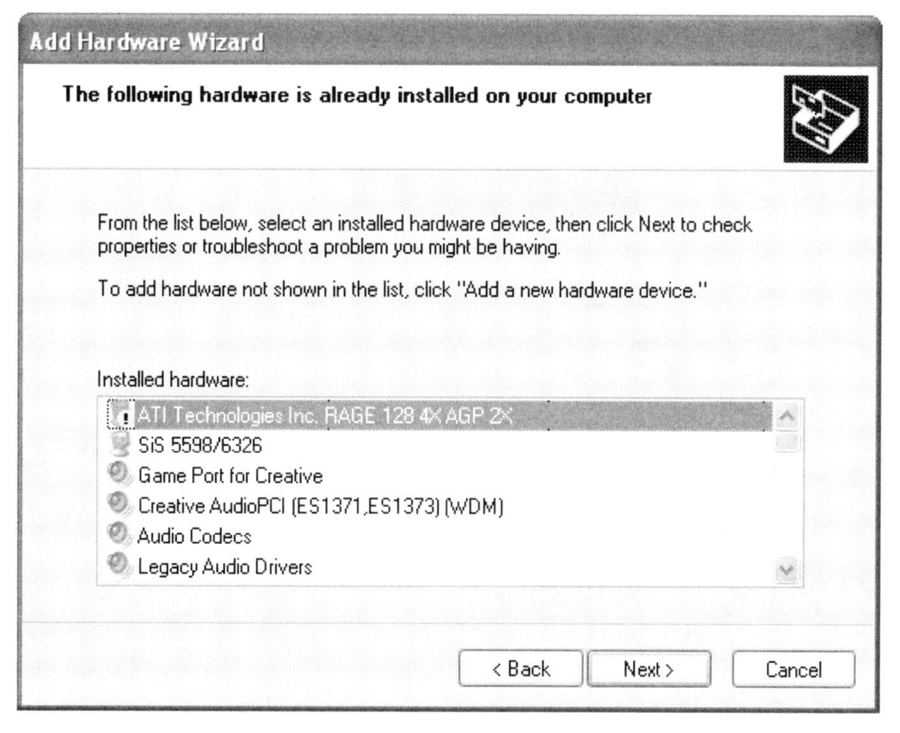

4. The final screen appears with a status message for the device. As you can see in the following illustration, the device cannot start. At this point, you can

click Finish, and the troubleshooter for the device begins. From this point, you can use the troubleshooter or attempt to solve the problem on your own.

on the job

The troubleshooting feature of the Add Hardware wizard is helpful, but you can easily gain the same information using Device Manager, which is explored in the next section.

Using Device Manager

A helpful tool that you can use to explore the configuration of hardware devices and make changes to that configuration is Device Manager. Device Manager has been around for several iterations of Windows, and its importance in Windows XP continues. You can access Device Manager via the Computer Management console, or you can simply click the Device Manager option on the Hardware tab of System Properties.

Computer Management can also be accessed from the desktop, if you are using Classic Start Menu, by right-clicking My Computer and clicking Manage.

Either way, the Device Manager interface, shown in Figure 5-1, gives you a listing of hardware categories. If you expand a category, you can see the hardware devices installed under that category. Notice in Figure 5-1 that any hardware that is not functioning correctly appears with a yellow exclamation point. Using Device Manager, you can easily scan hardware categories and the hardware installed. If you right-click a hardware device, you can update the driver, disable the device, uninstall it, scan for hardware changes, or access the device's properties.

on the job

If you click the View menu, you'll see some options to view devices by type (default) and connection, or you can view resources by type and connection. Simply changing views may make hardware information easier to view and explore when using Device Manager.

If you right-click the desired device and click Properties, you'll see a few different tabs. It is standard for most devices to have a General, Driver, and Resources tab. Some devices may have additional tabs specific to those devices. For example, Mouse properties will usually have an Advanced Settings tab where you can configure how the wheel operates.

FIGURE 5-1

Device Manager

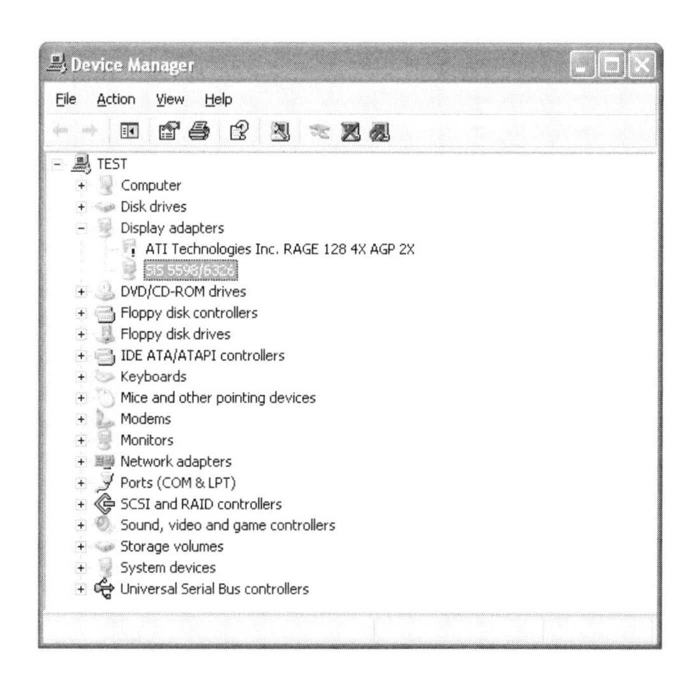

Since the General, Driver, and Resources tabs are available on most devices, let's consider the available options on each.

exam Watch

Although memorizing properties tabs may seem unnecessary, the exam could throw tab-specific questions at you and ask where you change the configuration of some item. (For example: Where can you disable a device using the properties pages? Answer: The General tab.) Make sure you get some hands-on practice using Device Manager and that you become familiar with the tab location of standard configuration items.

On the General tab, shown in Figure 5-2, you have a few basic items. First, you see the device's name, type, manufacturer, and physical location on the system. In the Device Status window, you can see any error messages or problems that apply to the device. If there are problems, you can start the hardware troubleshooter by clicking the Troubleshoot button. In the Device usage drop-down menu, you have the enable or disable device options. To disable the device, simple choose the Disable device option from the drop-down menu.

FIGURE 5-2

The General tab for device properties

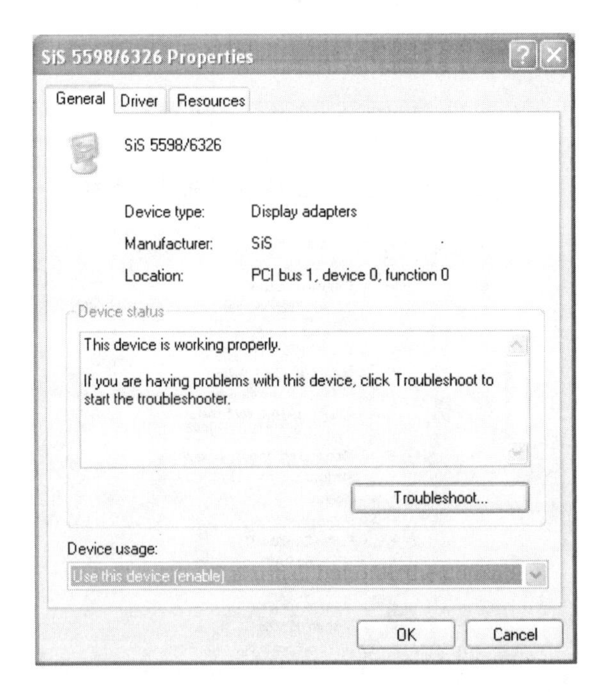

on the job

When you disable a device, the device cannot work on the system—however, the device's driver and related software are not uninstalled. At any time, you can return to this tab and enable the device again. The "on the fly" enable and disable feature can be very helpful when troubleshooting hardware problems.

The Driver tab provides you with an easy way to manage a device driver. Since driver management is a big part of hardware management and great exam fodder, we will devote more time to device drivers and the information on this tab in the next section.

On the Resources tab, shown in Figure 5-3, you'll see the memory ranges, I/O range, IRQ setting, and related hardware resource settings that have been configured automatically by Windows XP. Note that the settings cannot be changed unless there is a conflict. If there is a conflict, the conflicting device will be listed in the dialog box and the option to manually change the setting will not be grayed out. You can then try to adjust the resource settings so that the devices do not conflict with each other.

FIGURE 5-3

The Resources tab for device properties

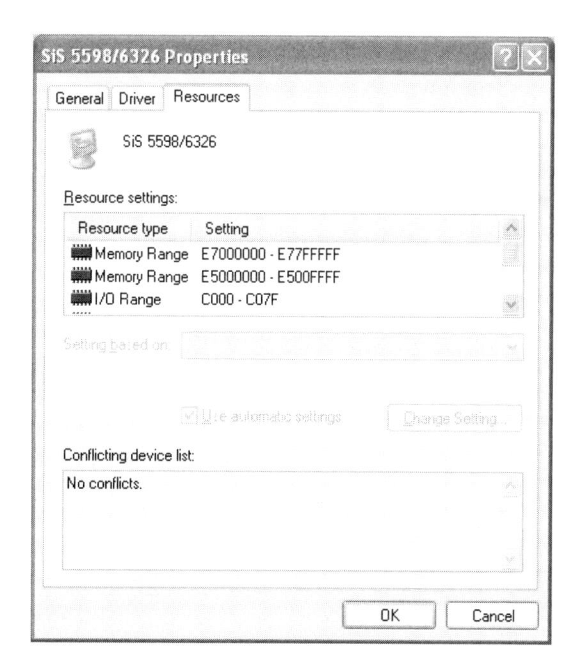

Configuring Hardware Profiles

While we are on the subject of general hardware installation, removal, and configuration, let's also consider hardware profiles. Hardware profiles are not new to Windows XP—they have been around since the days of Windows 9*x*, but they continue to be an important part of Windows XP hardware configuration—especially for laptop computers.

The purpose of hardware profiles is to enable a laptop computer to have different hardware configurations without having to install/uninstall hardware every time the computer is in use. Let's consider an example. Say that you use a laptop computer in an office setting. While connected to the local area network at the physical office, you use a mouse, keyboard, and desktop monitor with the laptop. You also have a local printer. However, when you are on the road, the external keyboard, mouse, monitor, and printer are, of course, not used. Using hardware profiles in this situation, you could configure a "docked" and "undocked" profile so that Windows XP knows what hardware to use when you are connected to the physical network and when you are traveling. The end result is that you save system resources when you are on the road by not loading additional hardware configuration data that is not needed, and your applications do not get confused about which device is available and which is not. You can easily configure hardware profiles for a computer, and Exercise 5-3 shows you how.

EXERCISE 5-3

CertCam 5-3

Creating a Hardware Profile

To create a hardware profile, just follow these steps:

1. Open Control Panel and open System Properties.
2. Click the Hardware tab and click the Hardware Profiles button. You see the Hardware Profiles window appear, as shown in the following illustration.

3. You see the current default profile. If you click the Properties button, you can see the basic properties of the default profile, shown in the following illustration. You have two basic options here: you can identify the profile as a profile for a portable computer and you can choose to always include the profile as an option when Windows starts. Both of these are not enabled by default. Click Cancel.

4. To create a new profile, click the Copy button. A Copy Profile dialog box, shown in the following illustration, appears. Enter a desired name for the new profile and click OK. The current configuration from the default profile is copied to the new profile. At this point, you now have two profiles that are the same.

5. You can now select the new profile and click Properties. In the provided dialog box, you can choose the portable computer option and the option to always include the profile when windows starts, as you can see in the following illustration:

6. On the Hardware Profiles window, you now see the two profiles. When you restart the computer, you'll see a boot menu that allows you to select the profile that you want. Click OK on the Hardware Profile window and again on the System Properties window and restart Windows XP.
7. During bootup, a hardware profile menu appears. Select the new hardware profile that you want to use and allow Windows XP to boot using that hardware profile. Log onto the computer.
8. Open System in Control Panel, click the Hardware tab and click the Device Manager option.
9. Now that you are in Device Manager, access the properties pages for the devices that you do not want to use under the new profile. On the General tab of those devices, choose the "Do not use this device in the current hardware profile (disable)" option. Continue this process until you have

disabled any devices that should not be part of the portable hardware profile configuration.

10. Close the properties pages for the device. Notice that the devices you have disabled now appear in Device Manager with a red X over them, indicating that the device is disabled, as shown in the following illustration.

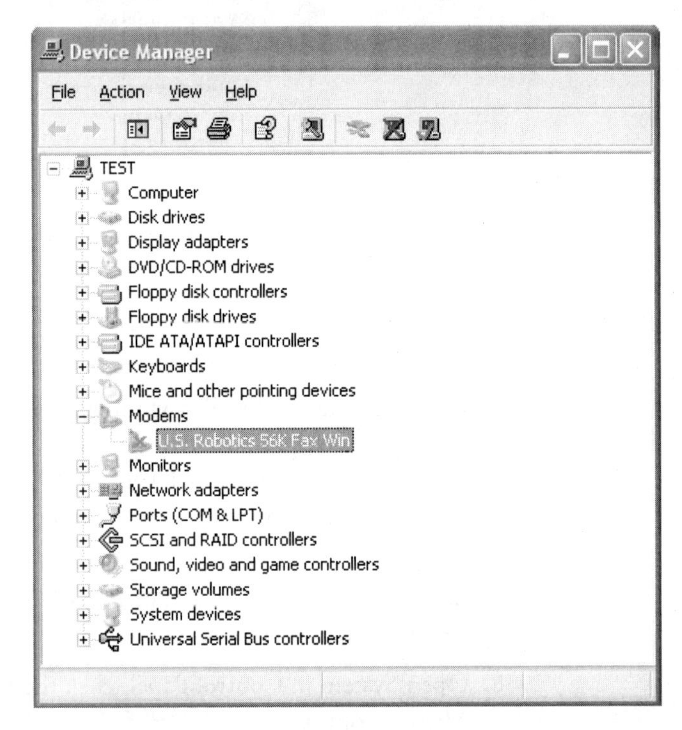

At any time, you can create additional hardware profiles by following these steps, or you can delete any hardware profiles by returning to the Hardware Profile window.

SCENARIO & SOLUTION	
Under Windows 2000, the Add/Remove Hardware wizard was typically used when installing new hardware. Is this not the case in Windows XP?	The Add Hardware wizard's role in Windows XP is to install and troubleshoot problematic hardware. Windows XP automatically installs compatible plug and play hardware without any user interaction. This feature allows Windows XP to further automate the hardware installation process.
What is the advantage of using the Hardware wizard over Device Manager when troubleshooting a device that will not work?	There is no advantage. Device Manager's General tab can give you the device's status and allow you to use the troubleshooter just as the Hardware wizard will.
Will Windows XP allow you to manually configure a device's resources, such as IRQ assignment?	Windows XP automatically handles resource assignment during plug and play installation. However, if two devices conflict with each other, the Resources tab of the device's properties will enable you to manually configure the settings. Otherwise, resource assignment is handled automatically.
How many hardware profiles can be used?	You can use as many hardware profiles as desired. In terms of laptop computer usage, users often have a docked and undocked profile and may even have a separate one for home use, so that a home printer can be used. Hardware Profiles are designed to be flexible and can be used to meet as many profile needs as you may have.

CERTIFICATION OBJECTIVE 5.02

Manage and Troubleshoot Device Drivers and Driver Signing

A *device driver* is simply software that allows Windows XP or other operating system to interact with a hardware device. The driver determines communication parameters and essentially acts as a bridge between the operating system code and the device driver. The driver, then, allows the operating system to "drive" the device so that the

FROM THE CLASSROOM

PCCards and IP Addresses

One really great feature of Windows XP (and 2000) that I really like is the ability to configure different PCCard slots with different IP configurations. As a notebook user, when I am at the office, I am required to use a static IP address, but at home, when I connect via cable modem, I am forced to obtain an IP via DHCP. One of the nice features of Windows 2000 and XP is that when my one PCCard NIC is in slot1, I can configure a static TCP/IP configuration, but when I move it to slot2, I can have a DHCP client configuration. Going to and from the office, I just have to switch PCCard slots and…voila! Network connectivity is working!

operating system can control the hardware device, which you then manage through the operating system interface.

Drivers are developed by hardware vendors, and from Microsoft's point of view, how well a driver operates with Windows XP is solely the responsibility of the hardware vendor. When Microsoft releases a new operating system, an updated device driver generally needs to be created so that the device can communicate with the new operating system. This is the primary reason that some devices fail to operate after an upgrade—the driver is incompatible with the new operating system.

Even though device drivers are the responsibility of hardware manufacturers, Windows XP still maintains a generic database of drivers so that hardware can function with Windows XP even if a manufacturer's driver is not available. Under most circumstances, the manufacturer's driver should be used if at all possible, since it is specifically developed for the hardware device's interaction with Windows XP. So, the short lesson here is to simply use hardware that is compatible with Windows XP and make sure you are using the most current driver designed by the manufacturer, if possible.

Because driver configuration and management can be difficult, Windows XP provides you with the Driver tab, found on each device's properties pages, which can be accessed from Device Manager. The Driver tab, as you can see in Figure 5-4, gives you a few different options that you can use to manage the device's driver.

FIGURE 5-4

The Driver tab for device properties

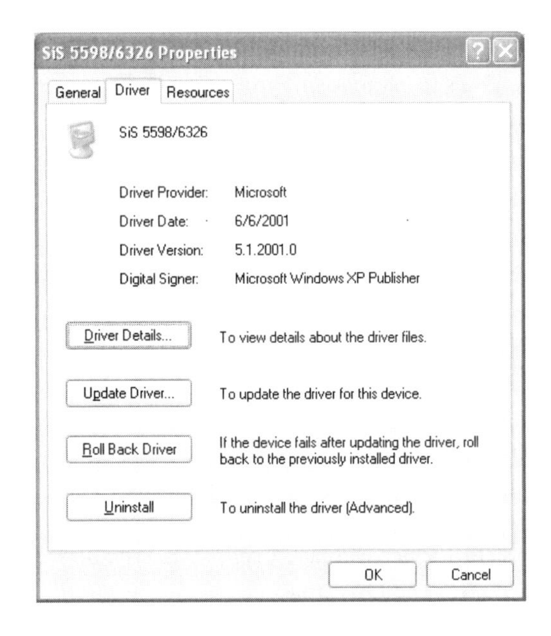

If you click the Driver Details button, you see information about the driver, such as the location, files used, provider, file version, copyright, and digital signer information, as shown in Figure 5-5. This data can be helpful when you simply

FIGURE 5-5

The Driver File Details window

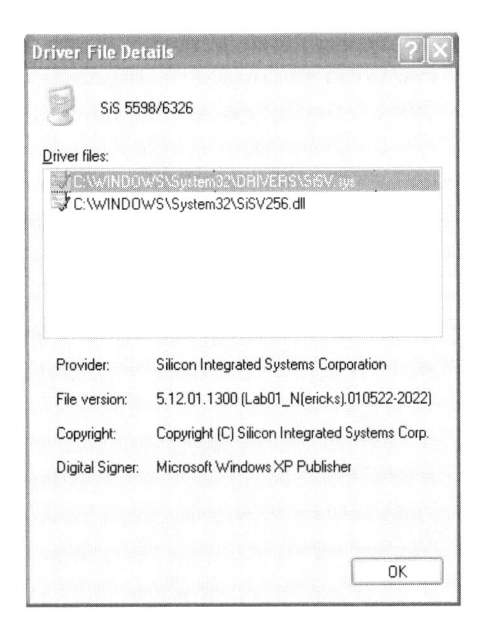

want to gain basic information about the driver. For example, if you want to know which files to remove—if you ever need to manually remove them—they are listed in the Driver files window.

Since drivers are updated periodically, you should strive to always use the most current one. To help with this process, Windows XP uses the Hardware Update wizard, which enables you to replace an older driver with a newer one. Exercise 5-4 walks you through the process of updating a driver.

EXERCISE 5-4

CertCam 5-4

Updating a Driver

To update a driver, just follow these steps:

1. In Device Manager, right-click the desired device and click Properties. Then, click the Driver tab.
2. On the Driver tab, click the Update Driver button.
3. The Hardware Update wizard appears, shown in the following illustration. Notice that you have two radio buttons on the Welcome screen. You can have Windows XP install the new driver automatically from a disk or CD, or you can install from a specific list of drivers or locations. If you choose the automatic option, Windows XP searches your CD and floppy drives for a new driver and installs the driver once it's found. If you want to update the driver manually, choose that option on the Welcome screen and click Next.

4. The Search and Installation options window appears, as shown in the following illustration. You can choose to have Windows XP search for the driver in specific locations, such as the floppy and CD-ROM, or you can specify the path to the driver. If you want to specifically choose the driver, choose the Don't Search radio button option. Click Next.

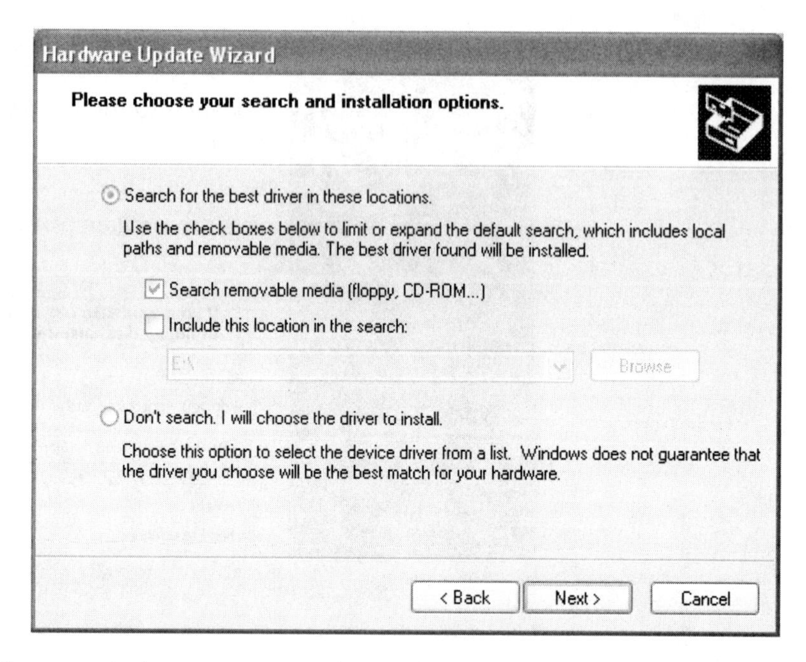

5. The next window gives you a selection list, as you can see in the following illustration. You can choose the kind of device that you are using and allow Windows to try to match a driver from its database to the device. If you have an installation disk, you can also use the disk here. However, if you do have an installation disk, keep in mind that you can simply use the automatic installation method on the Welcome screen of the wizard (which is faster and easier). Make the desired selection and click Next.

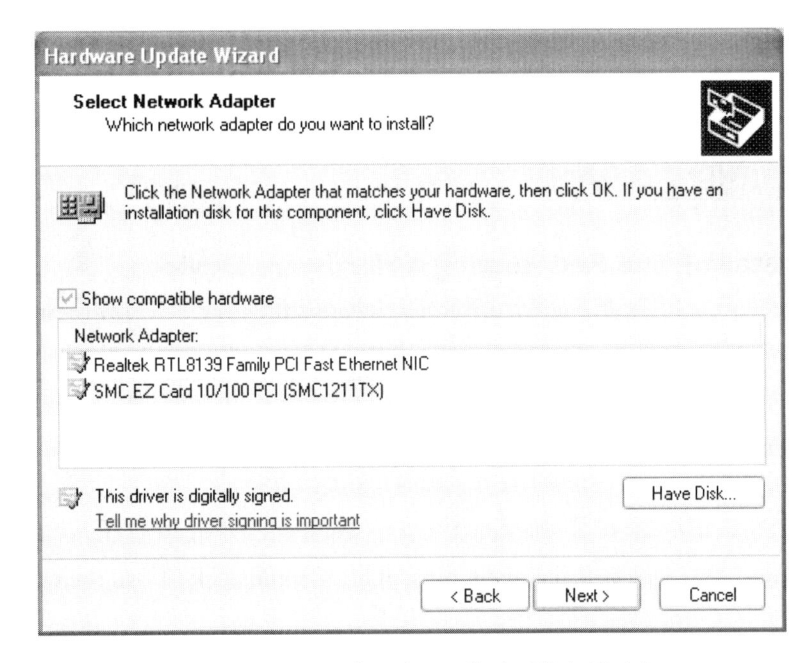

6. The files for the driver are copied and installed. Click Finish.

If you want to completely remove a driver, simply use the Uninstall button. You'll see a warning message that tells you that you are about to remove the device from your system, shown in Figure 5-6. When you uninstall the driver, the device is uninstalled as well. At this point, Windows XP plug and play will detect the uninstalled hardware device as new hardware and attempt to reinstall it. In some cases, this can

FIGURE 5-6

The warning before a device is removed

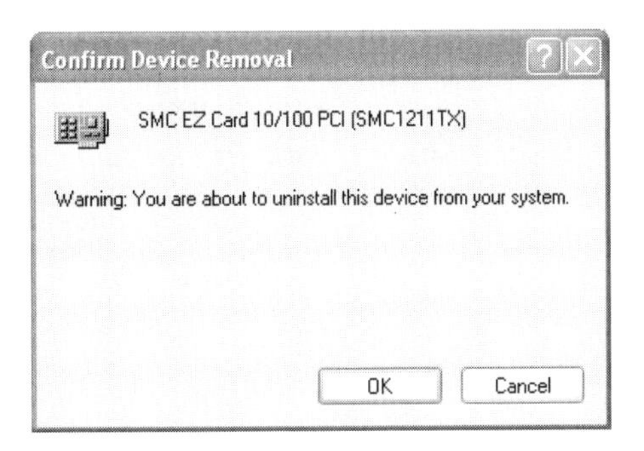

help you uninstall and reinstall a problematic device, especially if you are having driver problems. You can see an example of this process in Exercise 5-5.

EXERCISE 5-5

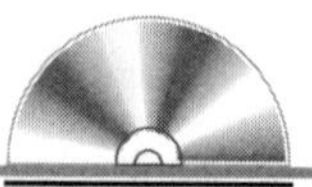

Uninstalling and Redetecting a Hardware Device

To uninstall a driver and redetect the device, follow these steps:

1. In Device Manager, expand the desired category and select the device that you want to uninstall. If you perform this exercise, choose a basic device, such as a standard network adapter, keyboard, mouse, or some other device that uses a simple generic driver.
2. Right-click the device and click Properties. Click the Driver tab.
3. Click the Uninstall button and click OK to the warning message that appears.
4. The device driver is uninstalled from your computer. Note that the device no longer appears in Device Manager.
5. To have Windows redetect and reinstall the device, on the menu bar click Action | Scan for Hardware Changes.
6. Windows scans the system and detects the device. A bubble message appears in the Notification Area telling you that a new device has been detected and is being installed. Once the installation is complete, the bubble message tells you so, as you can see in the following illustration—and that is all there is to it!

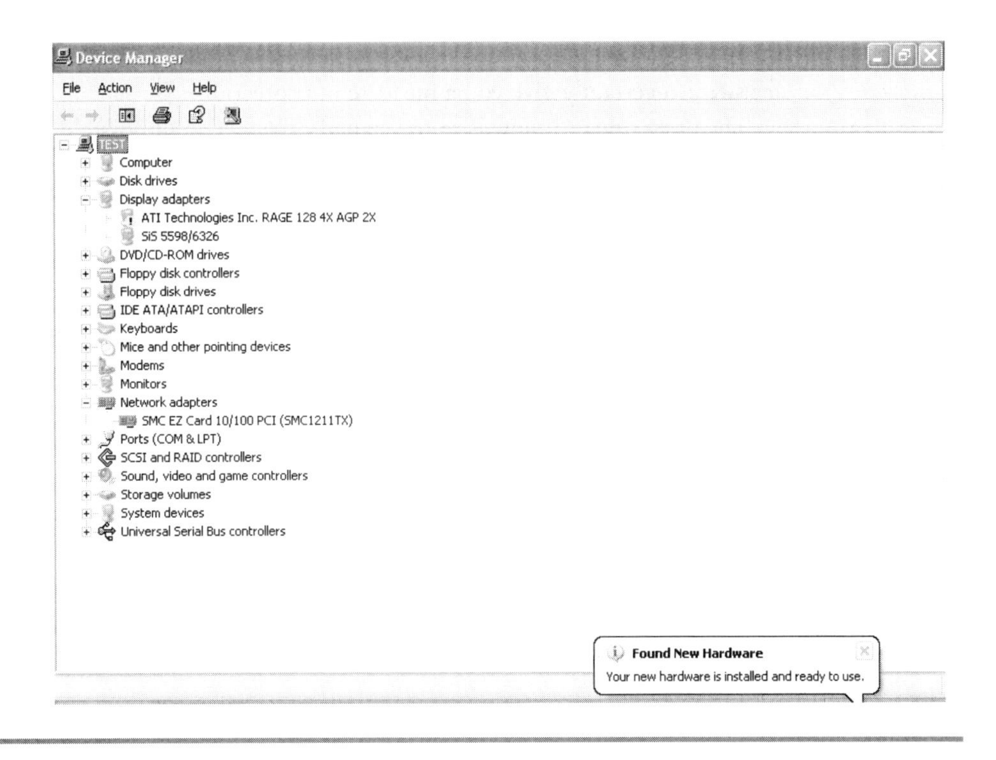

Aside from the driver management options found on the Driver tab, you can also manage driver signing in Windows XP. Driver signing, first introduced in Windows 2000 systems, enables you to make certain that you are installing and using only drivers that have been "signed," or certified, by Microsoft. This feature makes certain that the drivers have been tested and will work with specified hardware on Windows XP. The signing feature, however, certainly does not mean that unsigned drivers are damaging to your system or will not work—it just means that Microsoft has not approved or tested them, and you are on your own in terms of testing, compatibility, and troubleshooting.

Signed drivers have a digital signature stamp that cannot be altered without altering the entire driver package. The digital signature is basically a digital code that is able verify that the driver package is coming from a reliable source. This feature tells you that a signed driver is, in fact, a signed driver and that you can feel safe when using the driver on your system.

Another advantage of signed drivers, especially with Internet downloads, is that a signed driver tells you that the package is actually a verified driver—not a virus or other malicious code acting like a driver. For downloads of drivers, the signed driver feature can certainly give you a measure of protection.

The basic rule to follow is to use signed drivers if at all possible. With the signed driver, you can ensure that the driver has been tested and has received Microsoft's seal of approval. Of course, in some cases, it may not be possible to use a signed driver. This is fine, but it leaves you doing your own homework to determine if the driver will work and if the driver is safe to use.

You can manage how driver signing works in Windows XP so that Windows handles driver signatures in a way that works for you and your environment. If you open System Properties and click the Hardware tab, shown in Figure 5-7, you see a Driver Signing button.

If you click the Driver Signing button, you see a Driver Signing Options window, shown in Figure 5-8. You have the following options that you can invoke to determine how Windows XP handles driver signing.

- **Ignore** If the driver is not digitally signed, this option tells Windows to ignore the software's being unsigned and to install it anyway. You will receive no warning messages or prompts when using this setting.

FIGURE 5-7

Hardware tab of System Properties

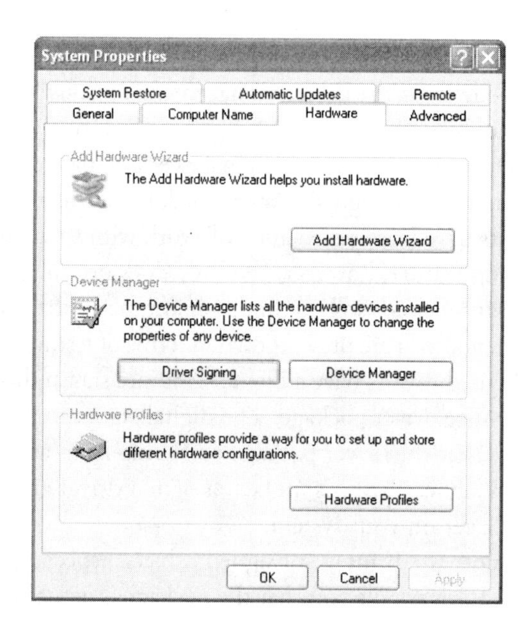

- **Warn** If the driver is not digitally signed, a warning dialog box appears alerting you to this and allowing you to choose to install the driver. This is the default setting.
- **Block** If the driver it not digitally signed, the operating system will not allow it to be installed.
- **Administrator Option** This check box option enables you to make the Ignore, Warn, or Block setting that you choose the default for all users on this particular Windows XP computer. You must be an administrator on the local computer to enable or disable this option.

Aside from the basic driver signing interface, you can also use the File Signature Verification utility to check existing files on your computer in order to make certain that they are digitally signed. This is a great way to check if any files have been altered on your computer. You can search for files, and you can also configure the tool to create a log file. The File Signature Verification utility is available on the Tools menu of System Information, or you can start it from the run line using the sigverif command. Exercise 5-6 shows you how to use the File Signature Verification utility.

FIGURE 5-8

The Driver Signing Options window

FROM THE CLASSROOM

Driver Signing on the Job

Driver signing is an excellent feature that helps you manage Windows XP desktop systems. Using the desired level of control, your options range from essentially ignoring driver signing to blocking drivers that are not digitally signed from being downloaded and installed on a computer. This flexibility enables you to use driver signing in your network environment in a way that is useful and appropriate. In many cases, administrators configure computers using the desired drivers, and then configure the driver signing option for Block so that users cannot download and install new drivers that are not signed.

The basic configuration, however, completely depends on your needs. In some environments, custom drivers are developed for specific hardware devices that are not signed by Microsoft. This is fine, and you can configure driver signing to ignore signatures so that the feature does not interfere with installations. The key point to remember is that driver signing is a safely mechanism built into Windows XP to help you manage and control what drivers are installed on a particular machine. As with all safety features, use the driver signing feature to protect your network computers while not interfering with any specific actions you need to complete.

EXERCISE 5-6

CertCam 5-6

Using the File Signature Verification Utility

To use File Signature Verification, just follow these steps:

1. Click Start | Run. Type **sigverif** and click OK.
2. The File Signature Verification utility appears, as shown in the following illustration. You can immediately start the utility by clicking the Start button, or you can click the Advanced button to configure options for the utility. Click Advanced.

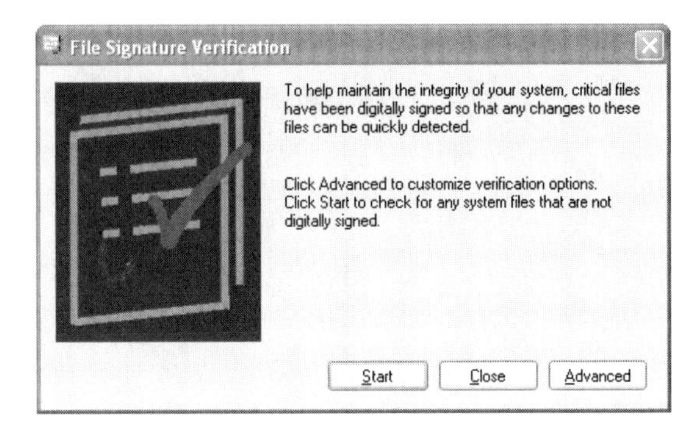

3. On the Advanced Search window, shown in the following illustration, you have two options. You can search the entire system for files that are not digitally signed, or you can look for specific types of files in specific locations that have signatures. This second option is helpful if you are suspicious about a particular file or group of files. You can quickly verify them without checking the entire system.

4. Click the Logging tab. You can choose to save the results of the File Signature Verification utility to a log file, which is named sigverif.txt by default. You can choose to append the scan to the existing log or overwrite the existing log (which is the default option). Make any desired changes and click OK.

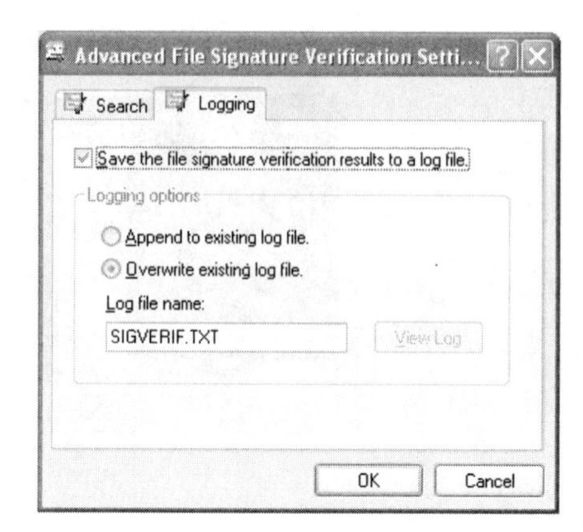

5. Click the Start button to begin the utility. When the utility begins, a file list is built, and then you'll see a status bar as files are verified. Once the utility completes, you see a completion window. If any files are not digitally signed, they will appear in the dialog box.

6. Once the scan is complete, you can also easily view the log file by clicking the Advanced button and then clicking the Logging tab. Click the View Log button, and the log file appears in a simple text format, as shown in the following illustration:

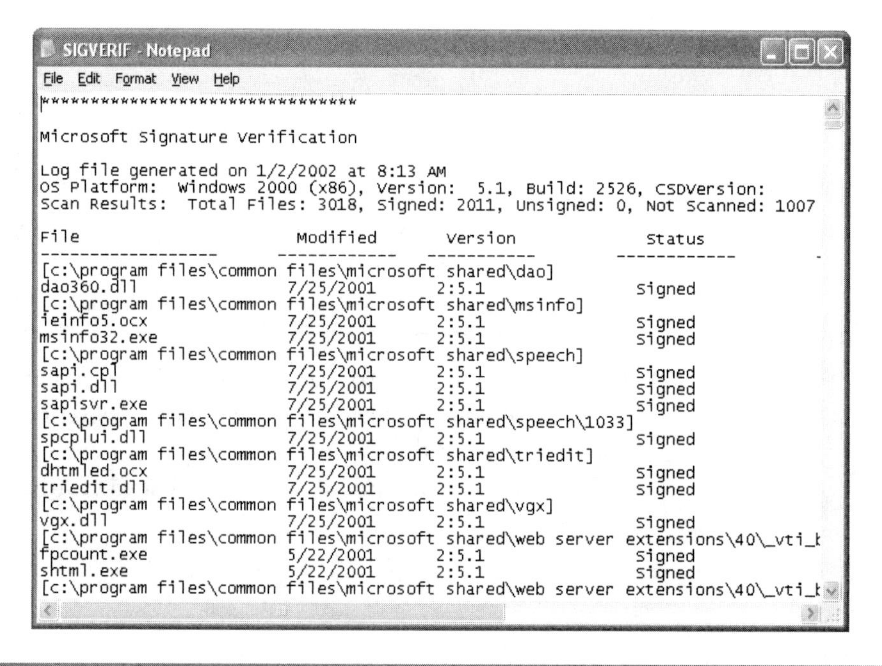

SCENARIO & SOLUTION	
Are Microsoft's drivers automatically signed?	Drivers installed on your system when you installed Windows XP that are taken from Windows XP's database are all digitally signed by Microsoft. You can run the File Signature Verification utility to check them. Driver files that you install from other vendors should be scanned for verification.
A new driver has been developed for a hardware device, but the old driver works fine. Do I need to install the new driver?	New drivers usually provide operating system compatibility upgrades or fix problems with older drivers. If you are not having problems, the choice is yours, but it is recommended to use the most current driver.
Should I use the manufacturer's driver when a Windows XP driver is working?	Under most circumstances, the manufacturer's driver, assuming it is compatible with Windows XP, is better than the generic driver included with Windows XP. A good example is video cards—Windows XP has an extensive video card driver database, but while one of the drivers may work with your video card, the manufacturer's driver is often better and will give you better results and enhanced options.
What is the best driver signing setting?	There is no "best" setting, but each setting can be used to meet specific needs. By default, the Warn setting is used. This lets Windows check driver files and then prompt you for an action. However, in some cases, you may want to ignore driver signatures or completely block any that are not signed. Your best bet is to start with the Warn setting as a default, then work from there in order to meet your specific needs.

CERTIFICATION OBJECTIVE 5.03

Configure Advanced Configuration Power Interface (ACPI)

Advanced Configuration and Power Interface (ACPI) is an industry standard designed to save power on computer operating systems. Developed by a number of companies, including Microsoft, Intel, and Compaq, ACPI enables a computer to automatically power down system components when they are not in use and then automatically power them up as they are needed.

In order to completely understand ACPI, we need to back up a moment and consider Advanced Power Management (APM). APM is an older power management scheme that was supported under Windows 95 and older computer Basic Input/Output System (BIOS). The idea behind APM is the same as ACPI, but it simply did not work as well. The computer could not make accurate inactivity assessments, and the hardware sometimes shut down at importune times, such as during a long file download. Also, APM could not detect when a device connected to the computer needed to be used. For example, let's say that you have a network printer attached to your computer using APM. Once APM shut the hardware down, the system could not detect that a network user needed the printer—it remained in sleep state until someone physically moved the mouse or touched the keyboard—and even then it sometimes would not wake up.

ACPI is a much better specification and gives the operating system more control over hardware power-down states and greater ability to power up hardware as needed. For example, let's say that you use ACPI on 100 computers running Windows XP. The computers power down during the night, but you want to run disk defragmenter once a month during the middle of the night. Under ACPI, this configuration is no problem because the system can power up the hard drive when it is needed, as in this case when the defrag needs to run. Once the utility has run, the system can power down again. This configuration is not possible under APM because manual mouse and keyboard strokes are required to wake the computer.

In an ACPI compliant system, power management is handled throughout the entire computer system, which includes computer hardware, software, and the operating system itself. ACPI works in Windows XP through operating system management and through the BIOS. In order for ACPI to work, the computer's BIOS must support ACPI. In today's computer market, this typically is not a problem, since basically all newer computers support ACPI. If the computer does not seem to support ACPI, you can check the computer's CMOS settings and make sure that "operating system control" is turned on so that Windows XP can control power management throughout the system. Check your computer documentation for details about accessing CMOS setup and how to configure the CMOS settings on your PC.

Users do not directly control whether or not a computer is ACPI compliant. During Windows XP installation, the operating system detects ACPI compliance and invokes the standard. However, you can manage how ACPI behaves by using Power Options in Control Panel. Exercise 5-7 explores Power Options.

exam Watch

If the BIOS does not support ACPI, you might be able to upgrade the BIOS so that it does. However, once you upgrade the BIOS, you will have to reinstall Windows XP.

EXERCISE 5-7

CertCam 5-7

Using Power Options

To use Power Options, just follow these steps:

1. Click Start | Settings | Control Panel | Power Options.
2. On the Power Schemes tab, you can configure which power scheme you want to use. If you click the drop-down menu, you see different power schemes that are configured by default, such as Portable/Laptop. You can create your own scheme by simply adjusting the Turn Off Monitor, Turn Off Hard Disks, and System Hibernates settings as desired, as shown in the following illustration.

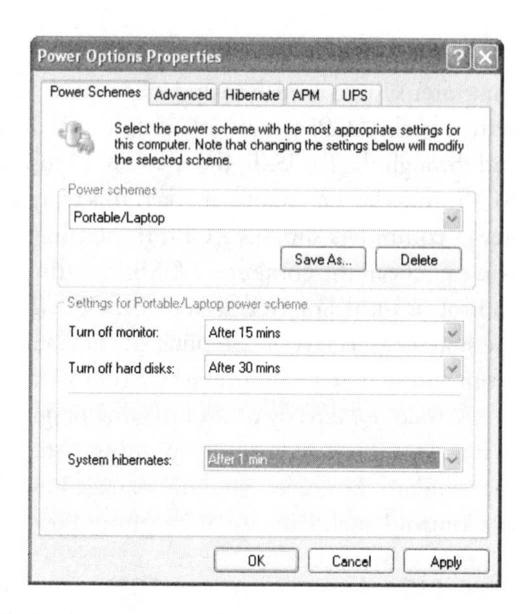

3. The Advanced tab, shown in the following illustration, gives you two check box options. You can choose to always show the power icon on the taskbar, and you can choose to prompt for a password when the computer resumes from standby. Click the check boxes if you want to use these options.

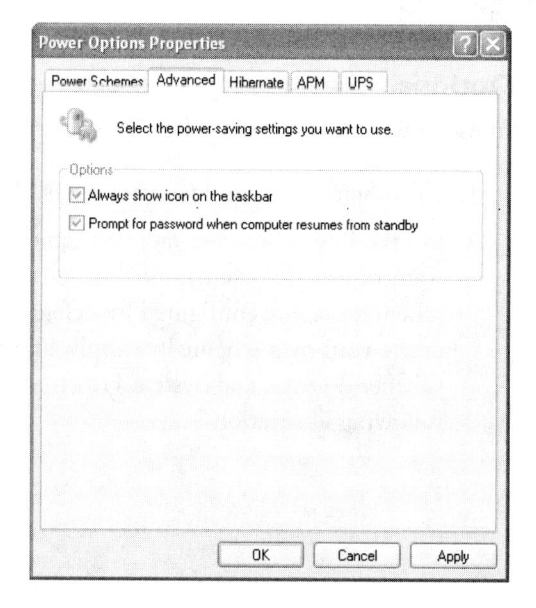

4. The next tab allows you to enable hibernation, as shown in the following illustration. Hibernation allows Windows XP to write information stored in memory to the hard disk and then power down the computer. When the computer is brought back online, the information on the disk is read back into memory so that the system appears just the way you left it. Hibernation requires 1MB of free hard disk space for each MB of RAM. For example, as you can see in the illustration, the computer has 256MB of RAM, and therefore requires 256MB of free disk space so that information in RAM can be written to the disk when hibernate mode is activated.

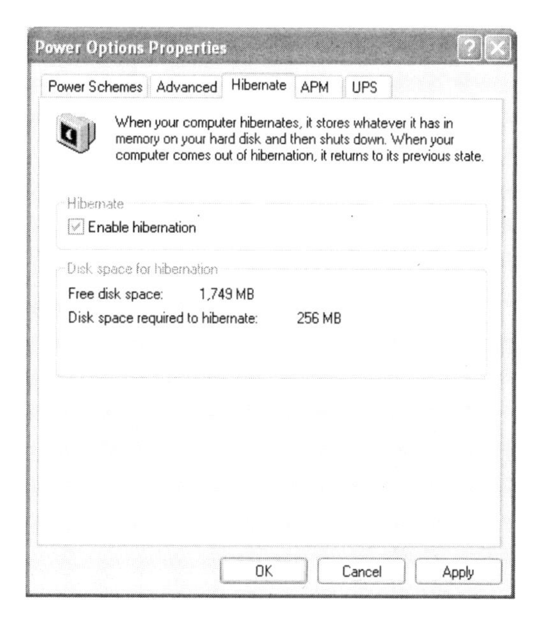

5. You also see tabs that enable you to use APM, if it is supported. For desktop systems, the option is not necessary with ACPI, but if you are using a laptop computer with a battery, you'll see options to manage power with the battery as well. Finally, if you have an Uninterruptible Power Supply (UPS) attached to your computer, you can configure it on the APM tab.

SCENARIO & SOLUTION	
Is ACPI compliant on all computer systems today?	ACPI has to be supported by the computer's BIOS and by the operating system. Most new computers from major manufacturers support ACPI. Using Windows XP and a computer that supports ACPI, you can take advantage of all of the power saving features offered.
Can ACPI and APM be used together?	Yes, especially on laptop computers where APM can be used to manage battery power. However, under most circumstances, do not enable ACPI on desktop systems, because APM requires a mouse or keyboard stroke in order to awake—which defeats the automated functions of ACPI.
Does ACPI experience the hardware lockups that sometimes happened with APM?	If you have used APM, you know that occasionally a computer would not wake up from standby, and you had to reboot the system. Although ACPI is not perfect, its power management scheme greatly reduces the likelihood of this happening.
Does hibernation work on all computers?	Typically, if the computer supports ACPI, hibernation will be supported as well. The Power Options feature in Control Panel tells you if the computer supports hibernation. Use Power Options to enable hibernation on the Hibernation tab; then use the Power Schemes tab to determine the amount of time that passes before the computer hibernates.

CERTIFICATION OBJECTIVE 5.04

Implement, Manage, and Troubleshoot Display Devices

Display devices have been a problem for years. Installed and configured correctly with the correct driver, they work great. Configured correctly with the wrong driver, you end up in Safe Mode. The trick with display devices, as with all hardware in Windows XP, is simply this:

- Use video cards that are compatible with Windows XP.
- Use the appropriate driver for the video card you are using.

If you follow these two simple rules, display device management is typically easy. However, in a not-so-perfect computing world, there are several different issues that this section addresses, most of which make great exam fodder.

Windows XP is the best operating system for display device management that Microsoft has produced. You can make changes to video cards without rebooting—you can reinstall drivers without rebooting (most of the time)—and Windows XP supports multiple monitors. Essentially, you are getting everything learned from Windows 98, Me, and 2000 in the XP operating system. The following sections explore the installation, configuration, and management of display devices.

Installing Video Cards

A video card is like any other internal card installed on a computer. Video cards are typically installed in an ISA or AGP slot on the computer. Upon reboot, Windows XP can automatically detect and install the video card. You can specify a driver for the card using Device Manager, and in many circumstances video cards will have their own setup routines that you run from a CD. These setup routines install the necessary drivers that provide features of the card, such as 3D graphics and related visual technologies.

As I mentioned, the trick to installation success is to use only video cards listed on the HCL at **www.microsoft.com/hcl**. The HCL changes often, so be sure to check the Web site for the latest iteration. Make sure you have the most current driver and that the driver is compatible with Windows XP. If the installation of the video card fails, you can reboot using the Last Known Good Configuration or Safe Mode/VGA Mode. See Chapter 13 to learn more about Safe Mode.

Configuring Display Properties

Display properties are configured using Display in Control Panel or, more easily, by right-clicking an empty area of the desktop and clicking Properties. As you can see in Figure 5-9, you have Themes, Desktop, Screen Saver, Appearance, and Settings

FIGURE 5-9

Display Properties

tabs available to you. You can configure the first four tabs in order to adjust the appearance of Windows XP (see Chapter 4 for more information on this). If you click the Settings tab, you see a few different options for configuring the display properties and video card performance in order to meet your needs. Exercise 5-8 shows you how to configure the display properties.

EXERCISE 5-8

Configuring Display Settings

To configure Display Settings, just follow these steps:

1. Right-click an empty area of the desktop and click Properties. Click the Settings tab. You see the basic settings options, as shown in the following illustration.

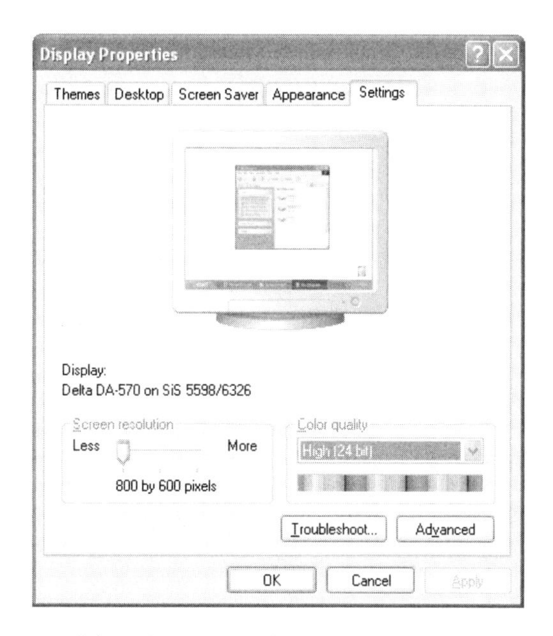

2. In the left portion of the tab, you see the option to adjust the screen resolution. In order to change the screen resolution, simply drag the slider bar to a different location. You can see an example of the new resolution in the test monitor portion of the tab. Click Apply. A Monitor Settings window appears, shown in the following illustration, where you can choose to keep the new settings (you have 15 seconds, or the setting will revert to the previous setting).

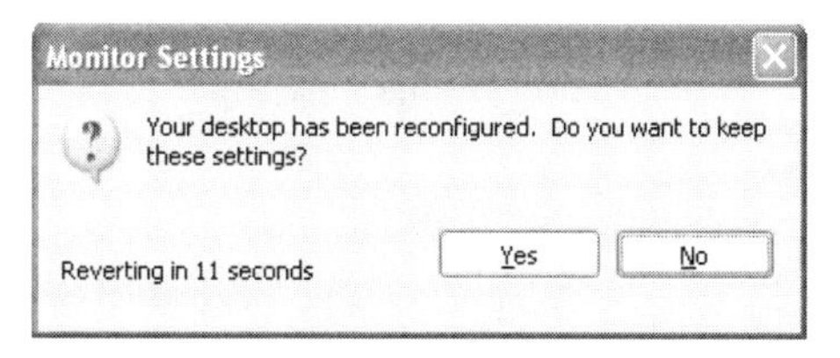

3. You can also adjust the color quality settings by using the drop-down menu. Generally, you want to use the highest color quality settings supported by the video card (such as 32 bit).

4. Click the Advanced button on the Settings tab. Several additional tabs appear. The standard tabs you see are General, Adapter, Monitor, Troubleshoot, and Color Management. As you can see in the following illustration, you may see additional tabs as well. These tabs are specific to the computer's video card and are determined by the video card software that you install.

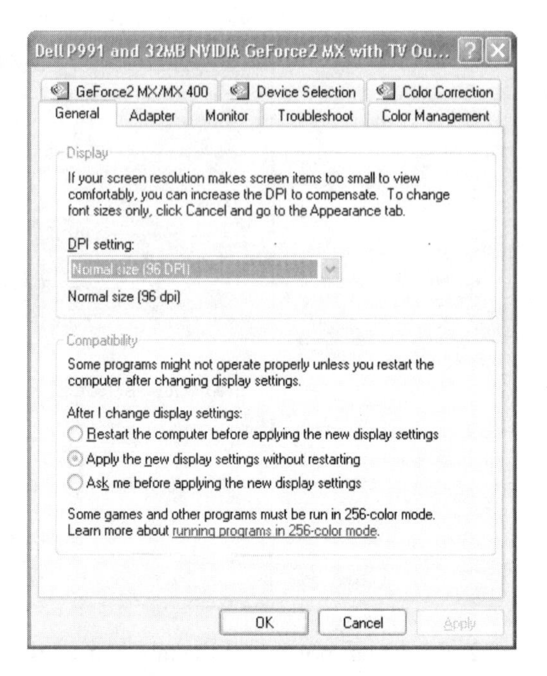

5. On the General tab, you have two sections, Display and Compatibility. Under Display, you can change the Dots Per Inch (DPI) setting to compensate for small screen items under your current resolution. The default is 96. This feature, however, does not adjust font/color sizes. Under Compatibility, you can have the computer restart after changes are made to display settings. This feature is available because some programs may not work correctly if there is no reboot after setting changes are made. The default setting is to Apply the New Display Settings without restarting, but you can choose a different radio button option depending on your needs.
6. On the Adapter tab, you can read basic information about your video adapter. You can also click Properties to access the Device Manager's properties pages for the video card. If you click the List All Modes button, you see all screen resolution modes that are supported by the video card, as shown in the following illustration:

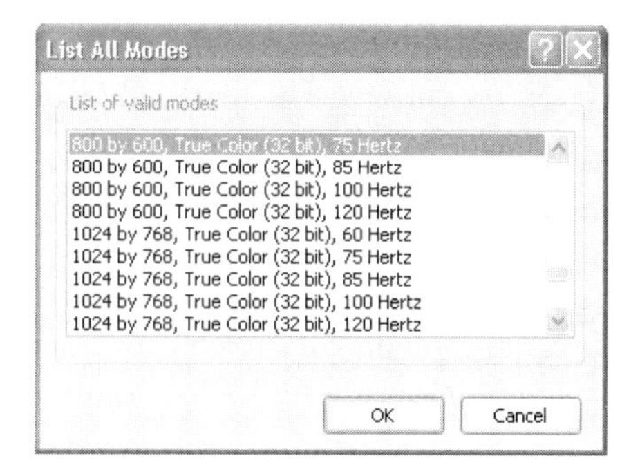

7. On the Monitor tab shown in the following illustration, you can access the Device Manager properties for the monitor by clicking the Properties button. You can also adjust the screen refresh rate. Higher refresh rates reduce "flicker" that may appear on the screen, and, naturally, you'll need a high quality video card for higher refresh rates. Default settings typically fall around 75 to 85 Hertz. Also note the setting that allows you to hide modes that are not supported by the monitor—this makes certain that incompatible settings cannot be accidentally selected on the Settings tab.

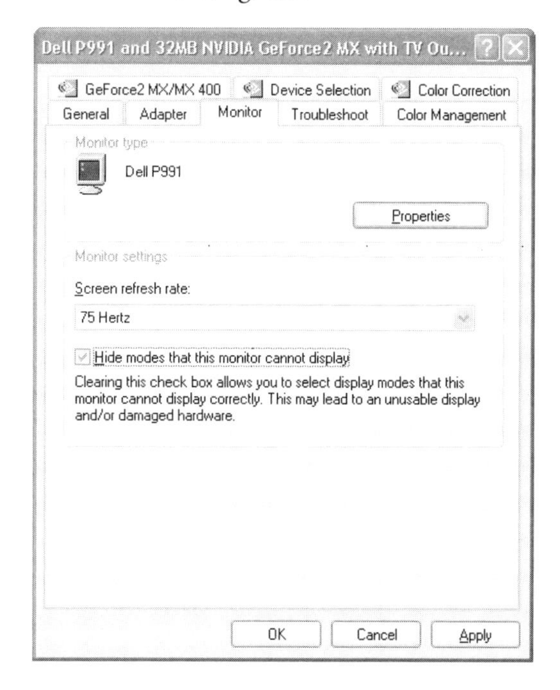

8. On the Troubleshoot tab, shown in the following illustration, you have two setting options. The first enables you to adjust the hardware acceleration of the video card. The typical setting is Full, but you can gradually decrease the setting in order to troubleshoot performance problems with the video card. Of course, lower acceleration settings also mean lower performance. When you move the slider bar down, you'll see a description of the impact the lower setting will have on video performance. You also have the option to use Write Combining as well. Write Combining provides graphics data to your screen faster, which improves performance. However, some video cards cannot keep up with this setting. If you are having distortion problems, try clearing this check box.

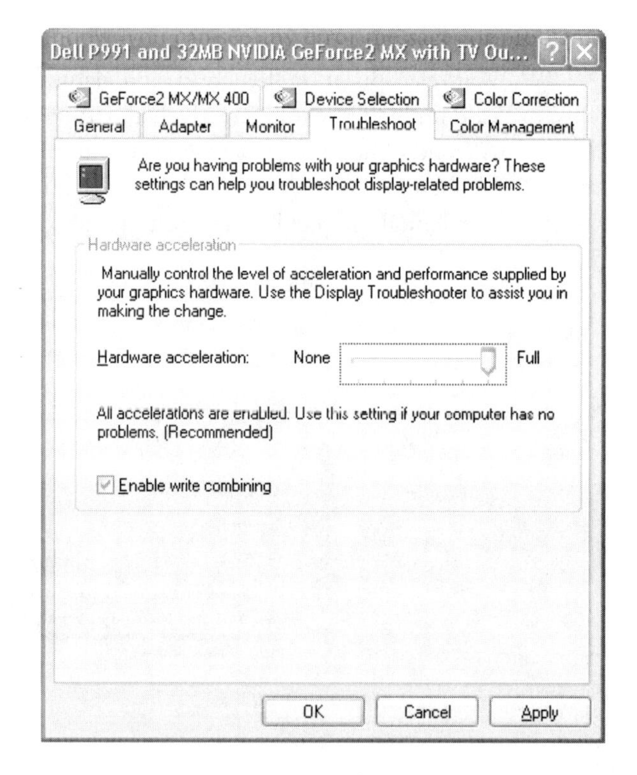

9. The Color Management tab, shown in the following illustration, allows you to choose a color profile that can manage the display of colors on your monitor.

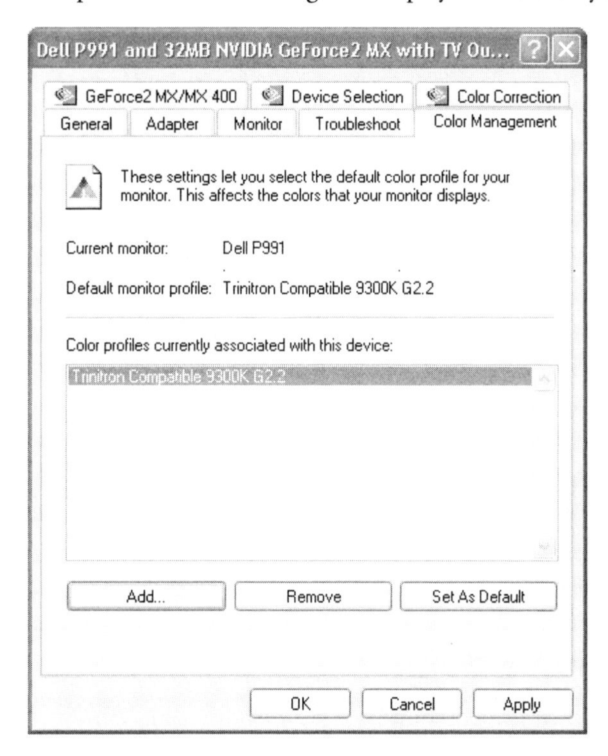

If you click the Add button, you see a list of profiles that are available by default, shown in the following illustration. As you can see, you can choose a color profile specific to your monitor's make and model, and this matching may improve color performance. As a general rule, unless you have color specific problems, do not use a color profile, as doing so may limit your monitor's color capabilities.

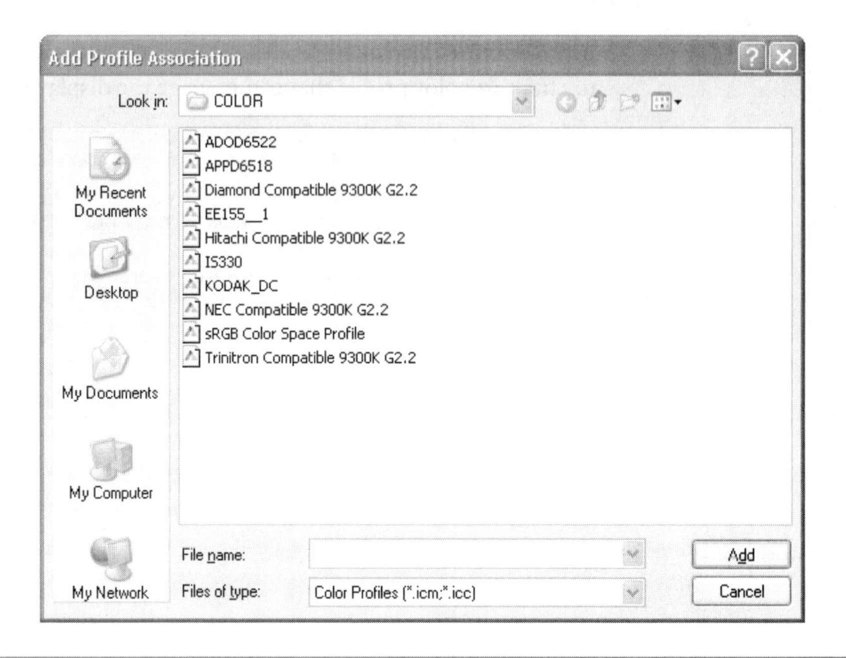

Using Multiple Monitors

Multiple monitors, first introduced in Windows 98, continues to be supported in Windows XP. With more than one monitor, you can run different applications on different screens and potentially increase work productivity. Multiple monitors are useful to many different people, especially those working with multiple documents and graphics files. With Windows XP and the right hardware, you can connect up to 10 individual monitors to a single PC.

When using multiple monitors, you can place different applications or files on different monitors and stretch items between monitors. For example, let's say you have a spreadsheet with many columns. You could use two monitors to stretch the file so that all columns are visible across the two monitors.

When using multiple monitors, one monitor serves as the primary monitor where older applications and the Windows logon screen will appear. You can use multiple video cards with different settings, or you can use a single video card that has multiple outputs where you can connect the monitors. Regardless of the configuration you choose, you use Display properties to adjust the appearance of each monitor.

exam Watch

Windows XP also supports a dual-view feature. Basically, this is the same as multiple monitors, but it is used on laptop computers where the LCD screen is always the primary monitor and the attached monitor serves as a second viewing area.

When setting up multiple monitors, there are a few basic rules you should keep in mind and have memorized for the exam:

- If the computer has a video adapter built into the motherboard, then the built-in adapter must be used as the VGA device.
- Monitors in the multiple monitor setup must use either PCI or AGP slots.
- The PCI and AGP cards cannot use any VGA resources.
- Only Windows XP compatible drivers can be used on the monitors.

To set up a multiple monitor configuration, follow the steps in Exercise 5-9.

EXERCISE 5-9

Setting up Multiple Monitors

To set up multiple monitors, just follow these steps:

1. Turn off the computer. Follow the manufacturer's instructions to install the new PCI or AGP video card.
2. Attach a monitor to the new card and boot the computer.
3. Windows XP plug and play will detect the new card and install it.
4. Right-click an empty area of the desktop and click Properties. Click the Settings tab. You'll see two monitor icons on the tab. Select the monitor that you want to use as the secondary monitor.

exam Watch

If the primary monitor is an onboard video adapter built into the motherboard, it must be the primary monitor.

5. Click the "Extend my Windows desktop onto this monitor" check box.
6. Adjust the resolution and color scheme settings as desired for the monitor. Click OK.
7. To add additional monitors to the configuration, repeat Steps 1–6.

SCENARIO & SOLUTION	
I need to use a particular screen resolution, but the resolution has made the icons too small. What can I do?	You can try to increase the DPI setting on the Advanced Properties, General tab for the video card. This may increase icon size. If you only need to make changes to the font size, then adjust the settings on the Appearance tab of Display Properties.
How can I make the video card display 256 colors for an older program if the option is not displayed in the Color Quality drop-down box?	Try using the Program Compatibility wizard to configure the 256 color option. The Program Compatibility wizard is found in Start | All Programs | Accessories.
On a particular monitor, I'm noticing distortion and corruption. What can I do?	Try removing the Write Combining setting on the Troubleshoot tab of the Advanced properties pages. If that does not work, try reducing hardware acceleration until the problem is solved.

CERTIFICATION OBJECTIVE 5.05

Monitor and Configure Multi-Processor Computers

Like Windows 2000, Windows XP supports multi-processor computers. The use of multiple processors on one computer increases the computer's ability to handle tasks and is particularly useful for Windows XP computers that function as network file and print servers. Simply put, the greater the processor speed and with two processors available to Windows XP, the faster it can work and meet the needs of local and network processes.

Essentially, Windows XP must be able to divide the workload between the processors into even pieces in order to utilize the processors. This process, which is called *multitasking*, enables the operating system to juggle processor requests between the two processors. Windows XP Professional is a true multitasking operating system that uses a type of multitasking called *preemptive multitasking*. Preemptive multitasking systems have the ability to manage and control applications and processor cycles. Because the Windows XP kernel remains in control of all resources, the operating system can halt applications or make them wait, or "preempt" them. With this kind of power and control, Windows XP can divide tasks between processors and determine which processor performs which task. This process, called *symmetric multiprocessing* and *processor affinity*, is the important concept to keep in mind when using multiple processor systems. After all, you want to maximize the use of both processors in order to get the best system performance. You can ensure that processor affinity is occurring by using Task Manager. You can right-click the desired task and choose the affinity setting, which enables the computer to use both processors for that particular task. For older applications that need their own memory spaces, you can also make sure that processor affinity does not occur.

on the job

You may also be familiar with *cooperative multitasking* ***from older versions of Windows—this simply refers to applications sharing the processor and waiting on each other for processor cycles. The difference with preemptive multitasking is that Windows XP can manage the entire process and direct which task is handled by which processor. For this reason, Windows XP Professional is a true multitasking operating system.***

Windows XP Professional can support two Intel-based processors. Windows XP does not support other processor types, such as Alpha or MIPS, so in order for multi-processor functionality to work, two Intel-based processors must be used. If you install Windows XP Professional on a computer with two Intel-based processors, the processors should be detected and installed during Windows XP setup. If you install an additional processor at a later time, follow the steps in Exercise 5-10 to get the new processor to work with Windows XP.

EXERCISE 5-10

Setting up Multiple Processors

To set up multiple processors, follow these steps:

1. Once the new processor is installed, access Device Manager.
2. Expand Computer and right-click the device listed under Computer (usually Standard PC) and click Properties.
3. Click the Driver tab. Click Update Driver.

4. In the Hardware Update wizard, choose the "Install from a list or specific location (Advanced)" radio button, as shown in the following illustration, and click Next.

5. In the Search and Installation Options window, choose the Don't Search radio button and click Next.
6. In the next window, select the manufacturer and model of the processor you have installed. If it does not appear, you may need to use an installation disk provided by the manufacturer. Click the Have Disk button to install the driver this way.
7. Click Next. The new driver is installed.
8. Click Finish. You will need to reboot your computer.

SCENARIO & SOLUTION

Can Windows XP support more than two processors?	No. Windows XP supports only two Intel-based processors.
How can I manage tasks between the two processors?	As with any task, you can access Task Manager to control and end tasks, regardless of which processor they are running on.

CERTIFICATION OBJECTIVE 5.06

Implement, Manage, and Troubleshoot Disk Devices

Disk management in Windows XP provides you a number of configuration options that are more flexible than ever before. Building on volume management first introduced in Windows 2000, Windows XP allows to use multiple hard disks and to create virtually unlimited numbers of volumes. Chapter 7 covers Windows XP hard disk configuration and management, so refer to that chapter to learn more about volume and disk management.

This section focuses on removable drive management, specifically CD/DVD-ROM drives and other removable media drives, such as tape drives. CD and DVD-ROM drives (or combo drives) are standard on computers today, and in many computer systems now have multiple CD/DVD drives and CD read/write drives. Like any hardware device, internal CD/DVD drives must be attached to the system and detected by plug and play. You can then install the manufacturer's driver—often you'll get additional software, such as third party media players and CD burner software. The good news is that CD/DVD-ROM drives and CD read/write drives work better than ever with Windows XP. With DVD drives, you can watch movies on your Windows XP's screen. Standard playback features, such as Dolby Digital, are supported and used for DVD playback. For CD-ROM drives, the CDFS file system is used. For DVD disks, the Universal Disk Format (UDF) file system is used. CDFS and UDF are industry standards natively supported in Windows XP.

As with all hardware, the trick when installing new internal or external CD-ROM devices is to use devices that are listed on the HCL and to make sure you have the most current driver. A further concern with installation involves audio playback. If you expand the CD/DVD category in Device Manager, you'll see your CD/DVD-ROM drives listed, as shown in Figure 5-10.

If you right-click the desired CD/DVD-ROM drive and click Properties, you'll see a Properties tab. As you can see in Figure 5-11, you can adjust the overall CD volume here, and you can also determine whether or not the drive is allowed to play CD music. If you are having problems with a CD-ROM drive not playing music, be sure and check the setting on this tab.

You can also check the Volumes tab, shown in Figure 5-12, and see the partition setup of the CD, its capacity and status, and other general information about the state of the disk.

FIGURE 5-10

The CD/DVD drives in Device Manager

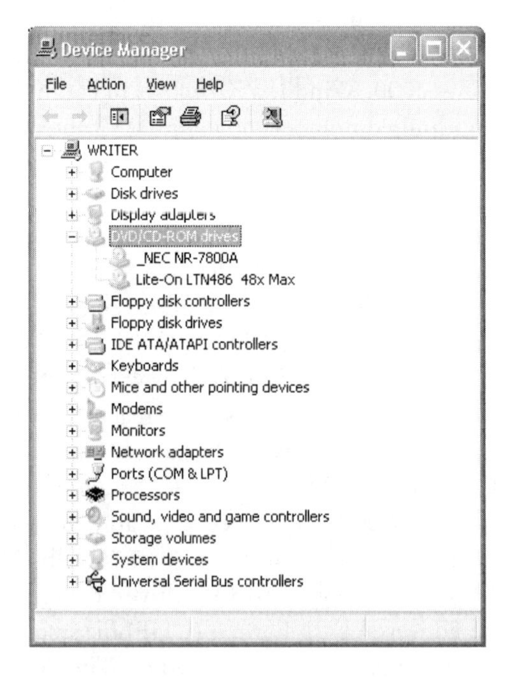

FIGURE 5-11

The CD-ROM Properties tab

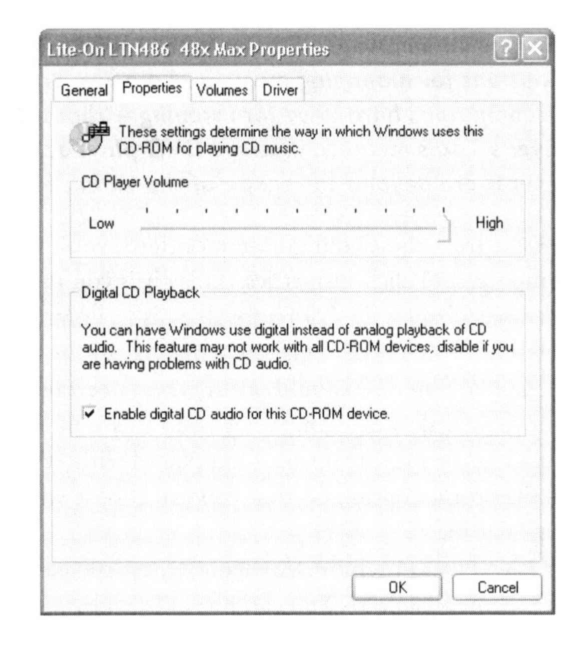

FIGURE 5-12

The Volumes tab

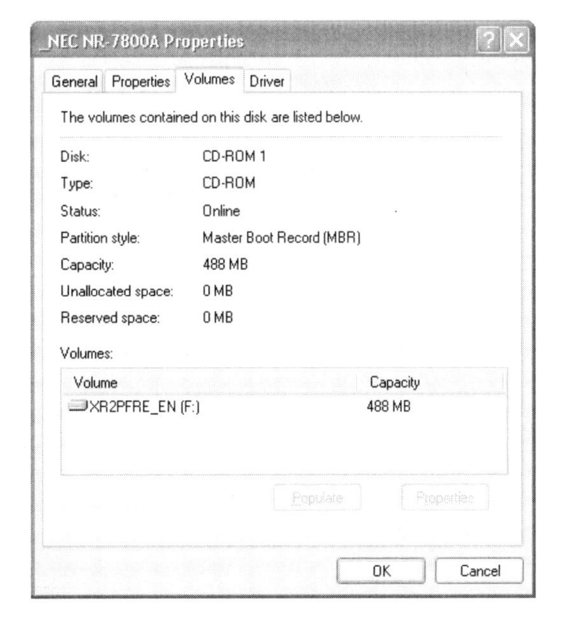

on the Job

Note that Windows Media Player, included in Windows XP, gives you a number of options for managing music and movies. You can copy entire audio CDs to the computer's hard drive for listening without the CD. You can also use Media Player's Tools menu to manage DVD playback and parental controls. These features are beyond the scope of the exam, but great features nonetheless.

Aside from these configuration options, you can also right-click the disk in My Computer and click Properties. This gives you the same tabs you see with other hard disks (see Chapter 7). For removable disks, however, you'll also see an AutoPlay tab, shown in Figure 5-13. This tab, which is new in Windows XP, enables you to select a default action that should occur when a certain type of file is opened from the removable disk. For example, as you can see in Figure 5-13, I am making certain that all music files are opened and played with Windows Media Player. You can also use the prompt option, so that you can choose which action you want to take for a particular file.

Other types of removable media drives, such as Zip, Jazz, or tape drives, function in the same basic way. You can install them by connecting them to an appropriate port and allowing plug and play to detect the drives. From that point, you can install an appropriate driver. Concerning tape drives for backup purposes, Windows XP

FIGURE 5-13

The AutoPlay tab

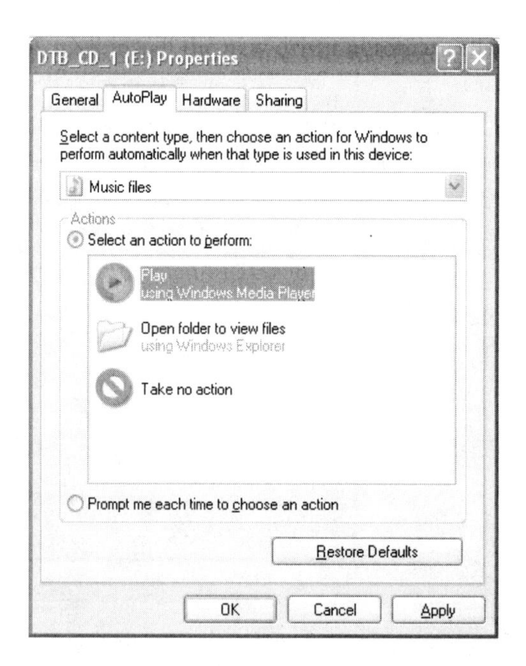

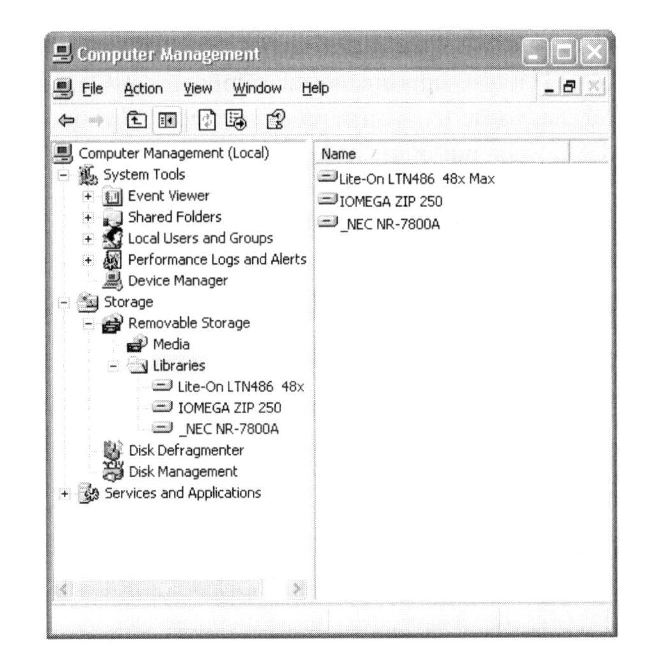

FIGURE 5-14 Removable Storage in Computer Management

supports a number of industry standard drives, and you can support them using Windows XP's Removable Storage console found in Computer Management and shown in Figure 5-14.

CERTIFICATION SUMMARY

Managing hardware on Windows XP is generally easy and problem free. The best advice is to always check the HCL for compatible hardware before making a hardware purchase decision. You also should ensure that you have the most updated driver for any hardware device. Windows XP plug and play can automatically install plug and play hardware with no intervention from the user, but in the case of non-plug and play or problematic hardware, the Add Hardware wizard can be used.

Every hardware device uses a driver so that it can interact with the Windows XP operating system. Using a device's properties from Device Manager, you can easily update drivers using the driver tab and even roll back drivers in the event of problems. Windows XP also supports driver signing and the File Verification utility, so you can ensure that all drivers on a computer are digitally signed by Microsoft.

Windows XP has the capability to use Advanced Configuration Power Interface (ACPI) if it is supported in the computer's BIOS. With ACPI, Windows XP can manage hardware, system processes, and applications so that they can be powered down when not in use and automatically powered up when needed.

Display devices are installed as any other hardware, and the correct driver certainly makes a difference. You can configure display devices using the Settings tab of Display Properties, and you can also use Advanced properties to make additional performance configurations. Multiple monitor support appears in Windows XP as well, with support for up to 10 monitors on the same computer. Windows XP also supports multi-processor computers where two Intel-based processors can be used with Windows XP.

Finally, Windows XP supports CD/DVD-ROM drives and makes use of the CDFS and UDF file systems. External Zip, Jazz, and tape drives are also supported, but always check the HCL first for compatibility.

TWO-MINUTE DRILL

Install and Remove Hardware on Windows XP

- ❑ Windows XP is a fully compliant plug and play system. Windows XP contains an extensive device driver database and can automatically install most plug and play hardware with no interaction from the user.
- ❑ In the event that a device cannot be automatically installed or is causing problems, the Add Hardware wizard can be used to manually install the device, assuming you have a driver.
- ❑ Device Manager can be used to manage devices on the computer. You can gain information about a device's status, driver, and resource usage. If there is a conflict between two devices, you can manually assign resources using Device Manager.
- ❑ Hardware profiles can be used with mobile computers. Different profiles can be used when the computer is in docked and undocked states to manage the hardware the computer uses and minimize battery consumption.

Manage and Troubleshoot Device Drivers and Driver Signing

- ❑ Device drivers enable an operating system to interact with a hardware device. You should use the latest driver that is compatible with Windows XP in order to get the best functionality. Although Windows XP has an extensive database of generic drivers, always try to use the manufacturer's driver built for Windows XP.
- ❑ You can easily update a device driver by accessing the Driver tab on the device's properties pages found in Device Manager. You can also roll back the driver from this location should problems occur, or you can uninstall the device.
- ❑ Windows XP supports driver signing so that you can verify that your device drivers are digitally signed by Microsoft. As a protective measure, you can have Windows XP warn or block the installation of unsigned drivers.
- ❑ You can use the File Signature Verification utility to verify that all drivers on your system are digitally signed. You can also inspect specific files in specific locations and even generate a log file.

Configure Advanced Configuration Power Interface (ACPI)

- ❑ ACPI is an industry standard that provides an operating system and computer system with a way to conserve energy by powering down components that are not in use. The operating system can then repower components as they are needed. ACPI is supported by Windows XP and must be supported by the computer's BIOS in order to work.
- ❑ You can configure Power Management options using the Power Options icon in Control Panel. You can use provided power schemes or create your own.
- ❑ Windows XP also supports hibernation, which must also be supported by the computer's BIOS in order to work. Hibernation allows a computer to write data that is in RAM to the hard drive and automatically power down. When the computer is repowered, the data is read from the hard drive back into RAM, thus returning the system to its previous state.

Implement, Manage, and Troubleshoot Display Devices

- ❑ Check any video cards for compatibility on the HCL and make sure you have a Windows XP compatible driver before installing them.
- ❑ You can configure video card settings on the Settings tab of Display Properties.
- ❑ You can configure advanced options by clicking the Advanced button on the Settings tab. The advanced options enable you to adjust appearance and performance settings, such as DPI settings and hardware acceleration.
- ❑ Windows XP supports the use of multiple monitors. Under this configuration, you can use up to 10 monitors connected to one or more video cards. Use the Settings tab of Display properties to configure the primary and secondary monitors.

Monitor and Configure Multi-Processor Computers

- ❑ Windows XP supports the use of multi-processor computers. Windows XP can support two Intel-based processors on a single computer.
- ❑ If the processors are present during installation, Windows XP will detect them both. If a second processor is installed later, use Device Manager to install the driver for the new processor.
- ❑ Use Task Manager to manage processes on the multi-processor computer.

Implement, Manage, and Troubleshoot Disk Devices

- ❑ CD/DVD-ROM drives are installed and managed as any other hardware device. When using CD-ROM drives, Windows XP uses the CDFS file system. For DVD drives, the UDF file system is used.
- ❑ External removable drives, such as Zip, Jazz, and tape drives, can be installed and used with Windows XP (assuming they are compatible). Removable media can also be managed using the Removable Storage Console.

SELF TEST

The following questions will help you measure your understanding of the material presented in this chapter. Read all of the choices carefully, as there may be more than one correct answer. Choose all correct answers for each question.

Install and Remove Hardware on Windows XP

1. Which statement is true concerning the use of device drivers?

   A. Always use the manufacturer's compatible driver when possible.

   B. Always use Windows XP's generic drivers over the manufacturer's drivers.

   C. Windows XP does not provide any drivers, so manufacturer drivers must always be used.

   D. Older drivers work well with Windows XP.

2. When installing plug and play hardware on Windows XP, which statement best describes the interaction of the user?

   A. The hardware is installed automatically with no intervention from the user.

   B. The user is prompted to run the Add Hardware Wizard.

   C. The user is prompted to load the correct driver.

   D. The user is prompted to choose the manufacturer from a list.

3. You are having problems with a new video card. You want to find out what might be causing the problem. What are two tools you can use to gain this information?

   A. Add Hardware wizard

   B. Device Manager

   C. Driver signing

   D. sigverif.exe

4. You want to use device manager in order to see resources by connection. Where can you change the default organization of device manager from Type to Connection?

   A. File menu

   B. Tools menu

   C. View menu

   D. List menu

5. You want to disable a particular device so that it does not function while you are troubleshooting the system. You do not want to uninstall the device. What can you do?

A. Remove the driver.

B. Use Device Manager, General Properties tab for the device and choose the Disable option from the drop-down menu.

C. Use Device Manager, Driver Properties tab for the device and choose the Disable option from the drop-down menu.

D. Use Device Manager, Resources Properties tab for the device and choose the Disable option from the drop-down menu.

6. For a particular device, you want to manually configure the IRQ and memory allocation settings. You access the Resources tab, as shown in the following illustration. The options to change the settings are grayed out. What is causing the problem?

A. You must enable the option to change resources on the General tab.

B. The driver is incorrect.

C. Windows XP does not allow manual changes unless there is a conflict.

D. The user is not an administrator.

7. Consider the Hardware Profiles window in the following illustration. You want to create a new hardware profile. What steps should you follow to create the new profile?

A. Click the Copy button on the Hardware Profiles window and click OK.

B. Use Device Manager to disable devices that are not needed under the new profile.

C. Click the Rename button on the Hardware Profiles window and name the profile "new."

D. Remove all devices that you do not want to use in the new profile.

E. Reboot the computer and use the Safe Mode option.

F. Reboot the computer and choose the new profile in the Hardware Profiles menu that appears.

Manage and Troubleshoot Device Drivers and Driver Signing

8. You have recently installed a new driver for a video card. After the driver was installed, the video card makes the screen difficult to read. You want to use the old driver again. How can you easily return to the old driver?

A. Run the Update Driver option on the Driver tab of the device's properties.

B. Uninstall the driver and allow Windows to redetect and assign a new driver.

C. Use the driver rollback feature.

D. You cannot return to the old driver.

9. Which statement is true concerning the removal of a driver from a device?

   A. Removing the driver effectively uninstalls the device from the system.

   B. The system can still work with the device after driver removal.

   C. The system will automatically assign a new driver once you remove an old one.

   D. You cannot remove a driver without physically removing the device from the computer.

10. Stan uses a computer running Windows XP for testing purposes. You want to make sure that Stan can install and test any driver without any warnings or interference from Windows XP. What can you do?

    A. Use Group Policy to give Stan the Driver Config permission.

    B. Use Driver Signing Options and choose the Ignore option.

    C. Use the Sigverif utility.

    D. Use Device Manager and choose the Allow All Drivers option.

11. You want to make certain that all unsigned drivers are not allowed on a particular Windows XP computer, and you want to make sure that the setting is applied to all users. What two configurations should you choose on the Driver Signing window? (Choose two.)

    A. Choose the Warn option.

    B. Choose the Block option.

    C. Choose the Reject option.

    D. Choose the Administrator option.

12. You want to use the File Signature Verification utility, shown in the following illustration, to scan only a particular directory for drivers that are not signed. What do you need to do?

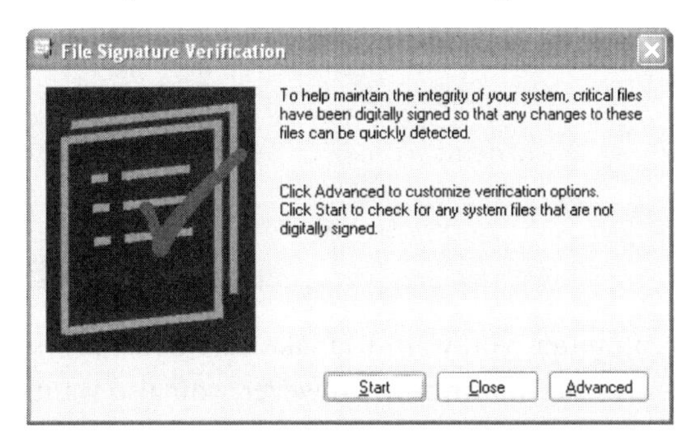

A. Simply click Start.

B. Click the Advanced button and configure the option on the Search tab.

C. Click the Advanced button and configure the option on the Logging tab.

D. Click the Advanced button and configure the option on the Directory tab.

Configure Advanced Configuration Power Interface (ACPI)

13. You want to use ACPI on a particular Windows XP computer, but the option does not seem to be available. What needs to be done?

A. Use Add/Remove Windows components to install it.

B. Enable ACPI through the Power Options icon in Control Panel.

C. Run the acpiconf.exe utility.

D. Upgrade the BIOS.

14. Consider the following Power Schemes tab:

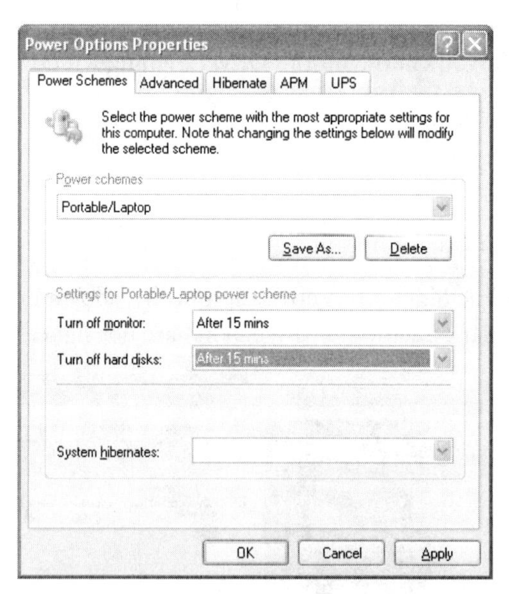

Using a laptop computer, you want to make sure that the system will shut itself down when it has not been used for 30 minutes. However, you also want to make sure that you do not lose any data that might in use when the automatic shutdown occurs. What do you need to do on this tab?

A. Under Power Schemes, choose the Auto Shutdown feature.

B. Change the hard drive "turn off" setting to 30 minutes.

C. Configure the Hibernate feature for 30 minutes.

D. You cannot configure this option without UPS support.

15. You want to use the hibernation feature on your computer, which contains 128MB of RAM. How much free hard disk space will be required in order to use hibernation?

A. 64MB.

B. 128MB.

C. 256MB.

D. No disk space is required.

Implement, Manage, and Troubleshoot Display Devices

16. After a change in the screen resolution, the icons on the desktop have become very small. What setting can you use to try to increase the size of the icons?

A. Write Combining.

B. Refresh Rate.

C. Use a Color Profile.

D. DPI.

17. You are having problems with a new video card. The screen appears distorted; then corrects itself. What setting should you clear first to try and resolve the problem?

A. Write Combining.

B. Refresh Rate.

C. Use a Color Profile.

D. DPI.

18. In a multiple monitor configuration, what is the maximum number of monitors that are supported under Windows XP?

A. 2

B. 4

C. 8

D. 10

Monitor and Configure Multi-Processor Computers

19. How many Intel-based processors can be used on a single computer under Windows XP?

A. 2

B. 4

C. 8

D. 10

20. You want to manage processes on a multi-processor computer. What tool can you use to manage processes?

A. Device Manager

B. Computer Management

C. Task Manager

D. Program Compatibility

Implement, Manage, and Troubleshoot Disk Devices

21. A CD-ROM on a computer running Windows XP will not play audio CDs. What can you do to fix the problem?

A. Install a driver that supports audio CDs.

B. Use Computer Management to configure the option.

C. Use Windows Media Player to initialize the CD.

D. Access the drive's properties in Device Manager and enable the audio CD option on the Properties tab.

22. When you insert a DVD into a DVD drive, you want to make sure that the DVD is automatically started and played with Windows Media Player. Where can you configure this option?

A. Access the drive's properties in My Computer and use the AutoPlay tab.

B. Access the drive's properties in Device Manager and use the AutoPlay tab.

C. Access the drive's properties in My Computer and use the Media tab.

D. Access the drive's properties in Device Manager and use the Media tab.

LAB QUESTION

On a computer running Windows XP, you are having problems with the video adapter. You are seeing distortion and experiencing generally sluggish behavior. You need to try to fix the problem without changing the video card or the current driver. What are some things you can try?

SELF TEST ANSWERS

Install and Remove Hardware on Windows XP

1. ☑ A is correct. If a manufacturer has a driver developed for Windows XP, use that driver. You are likely to get better results and more device features using the manufacturer's driver over Windows XP's generic driver.

   ☒ B, C, and D are incorrect. B is incorrect because the manufacturer's driver is typically better than the generic Windows XP driver. C is incorrect because Windows XP has an extensive driver database. D is incorrect because although older drivers may work, you are more likely to have compatibility problems.

2. ☑ A is correct. Under most circumstances, plug and play hardware is installed automatically on Windows XP with no interaction from the user. The hardware is detected, and a driver for the hardware is installed as well. In most cases, a reboot is not even necessary.

   ☒ B, C, and D are incorrect. Since Windows XP installs most hardware with no interaction from the user, all of these answer options are incorrect.

3. ☑ A and B are correct. The Add Hardware wizard and Device Manager can both give you status information about a device so you can see what might be causing the problem.

   ☒ C and D are incorrect. Although driver signing and the sigverif.exe tools are helpful concerning digital signatures, they cannot help you troubleshoot device problems.

4. ☑ C is correct. You can use the View menu to change the appearance and organization of device manager. Your options are to view devices by Type or Connection or to view Resources by Type or Connection.

   ☒ A, B, and D are incorrect. None of these menu options will enable you to change the view of device manager.

5. ☑ B is correct. You can easily disable a device by choosing the drop-down menu option on the General tab of the device's properties pages, found in Device Manager.

   ☒ A, C, and D are incorrect. A is incorrect because removing the driver will uninstall the device. C and D are incorrect because you cannot disable a device on the Driver and Resources tabs.

6. ☑ C is correct. Windows XP manages resource allocation when hardware is installed. The options on the Resources tab are grayed out unless there is a conflict with another device.

☒ A, B, and D are incorrect. Since resource allocation is handled automatically unless a conflict occurs, these answer options are incorrect.

7. ☑ A, B, and F are correct. In order to create a new hardware profile, copy the existing profile. Then reboot and choose the new profile on the Hardware Profiles menu. Then use device manager to disable devices that you do not want to use under the new profile.

   ☒ C, D, and E are incorrect. These actions are not part of the valid steps to create a hardware profile.

Manage and Troubleshoot Device Drivers and Driver Signing

8. ☑ C is correct. In the case when you want to return to an older driver after an upgrade, use the driver rollback feature.

   ☒ A, B, and D are incorrect. These actions will not return you to using the older driver.

9. ☑ A is correct. When you remove the device driver, the device is effectively uninstalled from the system. Windows XP can redetect and reinstall the device by rebooting or choosing the Scan For Hardware Changes option in Device Manager.

   ☒ B, C , and D are incorrect. These actions do not occur when you uninstall the driver.

10. ☑ B is correct. Change the Driver Signing option to Ignore so that Stan can install any driver without prompts or interference from Windows XP.

    ☒ A, C, and D are incorrect. A is incorrect because there is no Driver Config permission. C is incorrect because Sigverif will not manage driver signing. D is incorrect because there is no Device Manager option to Allow All Drivers.

11. ☑ B and D are correct. To configure the option to block all drivers for all users on a particular computer, choose the Block option on the Driver Signing window and also click the Administrator option.

    ☒ A and C are incorrect. The Warn option gives the user control, so A is incorrect. C is incorrect because the there is no Reject option.

12. ☑ B is correct. Click the Advanced button and choose the directory that you want to scan on the Search tab.

    ☒ A, C, and D are incorrect. These options will not allow you to scan only a single directory—and there is no Directory tab under Advanced options.

Configure Advanced Configuration Power Interface (ACPI)

13. ☑ D is correct. ACPI is configured automatically upon Windows XP installation if the BIOS supports it.

☒ A, B, and C are incorrect. Since ACPI is configured during installation with BIOS support, these answer options are not valid.

14. ☑ C is correct. The hibernation feature enables a computer to write data in RAM to the hard disk and automatically shut down. When the computer is booted, the data on the hard disk is read back into RAM in order to return the computer to its previous state.

☒ A, B, and D are incorrect. None of these options will meet the needs.

15. ☑ B is correct. Hibernation requires the same amount of free disk space as you have RAM. In this case, the amount of 128MB.

☒ A, C, and D are incorrect. Since you need the same amount of disk space as RAM, A and C are incorrect. D is incorrect, because you need free disk space for hibernation to work.

Implement, Manage, and Troubleshoot Display Devices

16. ☑ D is correct. You can increase the DPI setting on the Advanced properties, General tab to try to increase the icon size.

☒ A, B, and C are incorrect. None of these settings will increase icon size.

17. ☑ A is correct. Clear the Write Combining setting on the Troubleshoot tab of the Display Advanced properties to attempt to correct the problem.

☒ B, C, and D are incorrect. None of these settings will resolve the problem.

18. ☑ D is correct. Windows XP supports up to 10 monitors.

☒ A, B, and C are incorrect. Windows XP supports a maximum of 10 monitors.

Monitor and Configure Multi-Processor Computers

19. ☑ A is correct. Windows XP supports two Intel-based processors.

☒ B, C, and D are incorrect. Windows XP supports only two processors.

20. ☑ C is correct. Use Task Manager to manage processes.

☒ A, B, and D are incorrect. None of these applications will enable you to manage processes.

Implement, Manage, and Troubleshoot Disk Devices

21. ☑ D is correct. You can enable the use of digital audio CDs on a CD-ROM drive by clicking the check box on the Properties tab of the CD-ROM's properties sheets in Device Manager.

☒ A, C, and D are incorrect. These options are not valid and will not enable CD music.

22. ☑ A is correct. You can configure how Windows XP handles media by using the AutoPlay tab found on the CD/DVD drive properties pages in My Computer, as you can see in the following illustration. Choose the item you want from the drop-down menu and select an action.

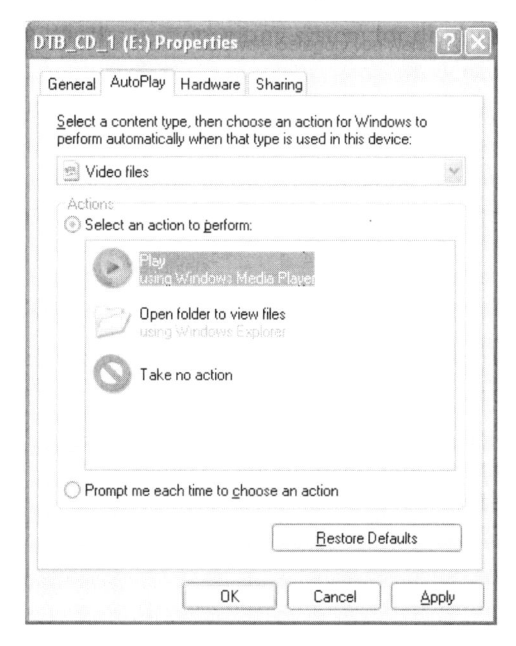

☒ B, C, and D are incorrect. These locations are not valid.

LAB ANSWER

You can try to correct the performance problem by following a few steps.

1. First, access the Troubleshoot tab, shown in the following illustration, and clear the Write Combining check box. Click Apply and Click OK to test the new configuration.

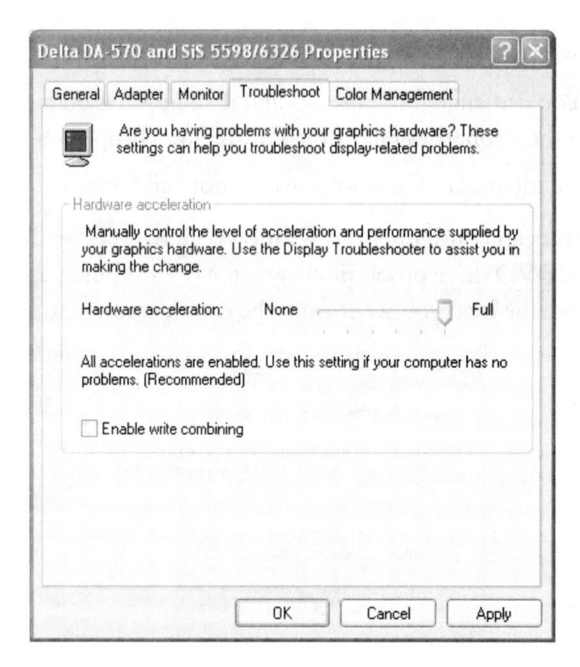

2. If this does not work, return to the Troubleshoot tab and incrementally reduce the hardware acceleration setting and test each one to see if you can find a setting that works better.
3. You can also access the Monitor tab and try reducing the Screen refresh rate.
4. Also, check the Settings tab of Display properties. You might try reducing the Color Quality to see if that resolves the problem.
5. If all of these actions fail, your best bet is to obtain an updated card or driver for the card. Under most circumstances, this is still your best choice.

6

Configure and Manage Windows XP Devices

CERTIFICATION OBJECTIVES

6.01	Configure Keyboards, Mice, and Smart Card Readers
6.02	Monitor, Configure, and Troubleshoot Multimedia Hardware, Such as Cameras and Handheld Devices
6.03	Install, Configure, and Manage Modems
6.04	Install, Configure, and Manage USB Devices
6.05	Install, Configure, and Manage Infrared Data Association (IrDA) Devices and Other Wireless Devices
✓	Two-Minute Drill
Q&A	Self Test

This chapter continues our discussion of Windows XP hardware in Chapter 5. In this chapter, you'll take a look at some specific devices and connection technologies that you'll need to know about for the real world and for the exam. Like previous versions of Windows, Windows XP supports typical hardware and peripherals, such as modems, printers, and other standard hardware. However, Windows XP also provides greater support for cameras, portable devices, and wireless devices. The good news about all of these devices is that configuration and usage is typically easy, but for some, you'll find a lot of different configuration options, which make great exam material, of course!

The information in this chapter tends to be more "hands on" in nature, so it is a good idea for you to get some practice with Windows XP installing and configuring different hardware and peripheral devices. Use the labs in this chapter as a guide for your hands-on study—this will greatly help you prepare for the exam.

CERTIFICATION OBJECTIVE 6.01

Configure Keyboards, Mice, and Smart Card Readers

Windows XP makes keyboard, mice, and smart card reader configuration easy. Under most circumstances, you simply plug in the device, boot the computer, and plug and play automatically detects and sets up the device for you—it's that simple. In today's marketplace, there are many keyboard and mouse styles and models from which to choose and a number of connection options, including serial, USB, and even wireless.

For installation of these devices, follow the manufacturer's instructions. You'll need to make sure the device is attached to the correct port and you have an appropriate driver for Windows XP. For standard keyboards and mice, Windows can assign one of its own drivers.

Once these devices are installed, you can access Control Panel icons for the keyboard and mouse in order to configure them. For smart card reader setup, just follow the manufacturer's instructions for port connections and drivers. Once the smart card reader is set up successfully, you'll see the option appear in Device Manager. The following two sections take a look at configuring the keyboard and the mouse.

Keyboard Configuration

Keyboard configuration, like mouse configuration, is rather easy and straightforward, but there are several important options, and you should be familiar with them for the exam. I suggest that you study this section, and then spend some hands-on time configuring a keyboard in a number of different ways so you see how the different options work.

Keyboard configuration is performed with the Keyboard icon in Control Panel, and by opening the icon you can see that two different tabs are available.

on the job

You can also access keyboard properties in Device Manager, where you can troubleshoot keyboard problems and manage the device driver for the keyboard.

On the Speed tab, shown in the Figure 6-1, you can adjust the keyboard repeat speed. As you can see in the figure, you have settings for Repeat Delay and Repeat Rate. The Repeat Delay slide bar determines how fast multiple characters are

FIGURE 6-1

Speed tab

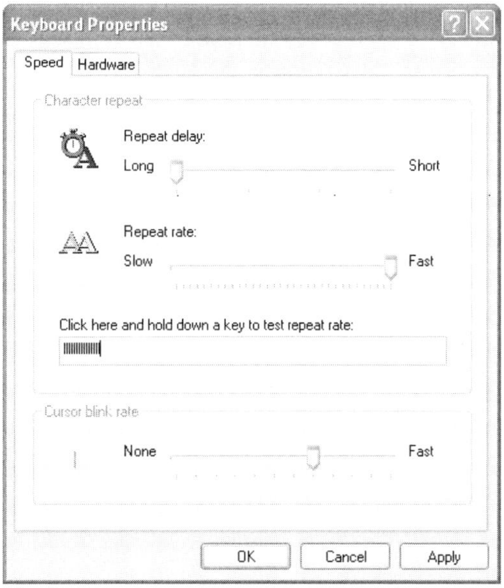

generated when you press a single key. A short delay means that characters occur quickly when you hold down a single key. The Repeat Rate determines how fast characters are repeated when you hold down a single key. While the Repeat Delay option determines how much time passes before the repeat begins, the Repeat Rate determines how fast characters are repeated. Finally, the Cursor Blink Rate at the bottom of the tab determines how fast the cursor blinks.

The Hardware tab, shown in Figure 6-2, simply tells you what hardware is installed, such as keyboard manufacturer, and what port the keyboard is plugged into. If you click Troubleshoot, the Windows Troubleshooter opens to help you solve problems, and the Properties button opens the device's General and Driver tabs from Device Manager.

Mouse Configuration

Mouse configuration, which is also available in Control Panel, contains several tabs that enable you to control how the mouse operates. As with the keyboard settings, the settings you'll see here are easy to understand, but you should be familiar with them so that you can sort through any convoluted exam questions you might come across.

FIGURE 6-2

Hardware tab

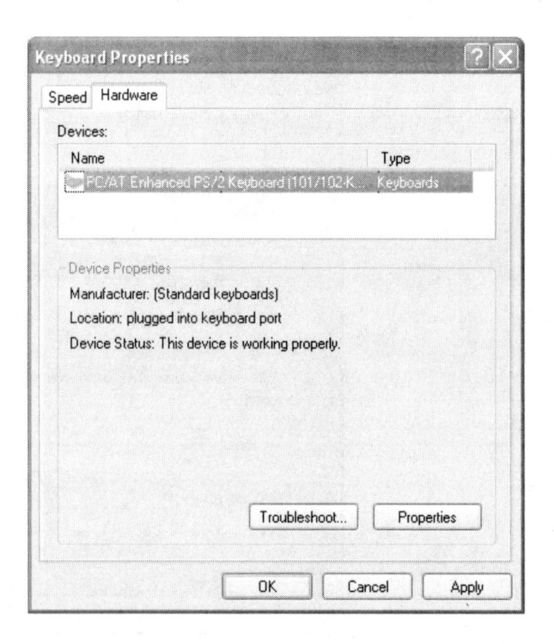

The Buttons tab, shown in Figure 6-3, contains three different options, which are as follows:

- **Button Configuration** By default, the right mouse button gives you menu options, while the left mouse button performs actions. You can switch this behavior by clicking the Switch Primary And Secondary Buttons check box.
- **Double-Click Speed** Use the slide bar to adjust how fast double-clicking occurs.
- **ClickLock** Click allows you to highlight or drag an item without holding down the mouse key. Using ClickLock, you can press the button once to lock and press it again to unlock it. If you turn on ClickLock, you can click the Setting button and adjust how long you need to hold down the mouse button for ClickLock to turn on.

On the Pointers tab, shown in Figure 6-4, you can determine what pointers and/or what pointer scheme that you want to use. As you can see in Figure 6-4, the Windows Default scheme is typically used, which gives you the NormalS, Hourglass Busy, and

FIGURE 6-3

Mouse Buttons tab

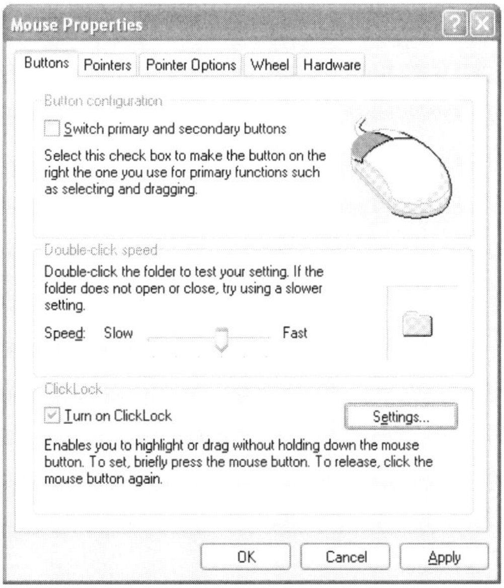

FIGURE 6-4

Mouse Pointers tab

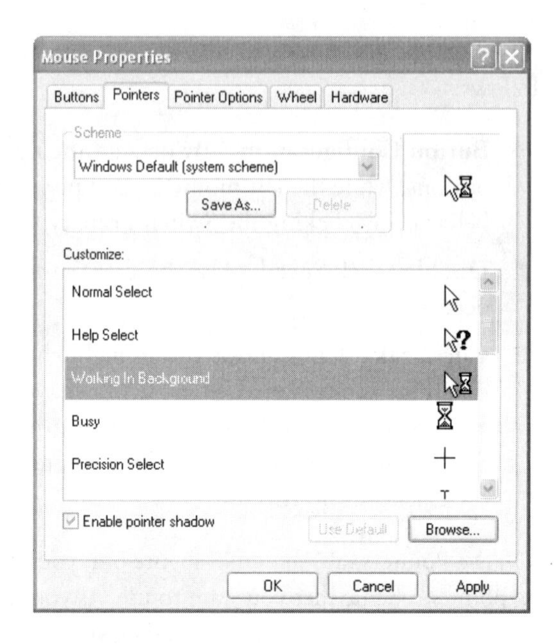

so forth. However, if you click the Scheme drop-down menu, you'll see there are many other schemes from which you can choose, including animated schemes.

You can also create you own scheme by selecting an item in the Customize window and clicking the Browse button. You'll see an extensive list of additional pointers that you can use, shown in Figure 6-5, and you can even download your own from the Internet if you like. Pointer files that function with Windows should be cursor files, such as *.ani or *.cur.

On the Pointer Options tab, shown in Figure 6-6, you have three different setting categories you can configure:

- **Motion** Use the slider bar to select pointer speed movement. You can also use the Enhance Pointer Precision check box, which gives you more control over the pointer when moving short distances.
- **Snap To** This check box automatically moves the pointer to the default button in any given dialog box.
- **Visibility** You can configure effects here, such as showing the pointer trail, hiding the pointer while you are typing, and showing the location of the pointer when you press the CTRL key.

FIGURE 6-5

Mouse Cursor files

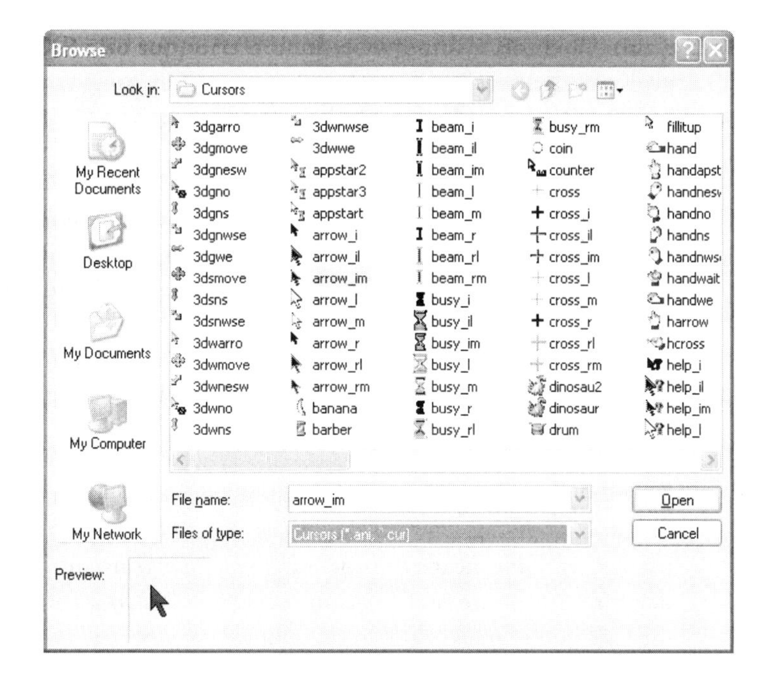

FIGURE 6-6

Mouse Pointer Options tab

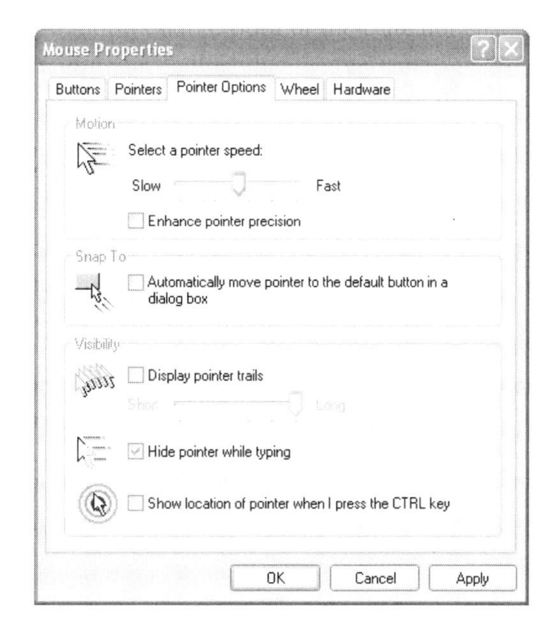

The Wheel tab, shown in Figure 6-7 and used for mice that have wheel controls, gives you the ability to control the scrolling when using the wheel. The default setting is typically three lines per wheel notch. You can increase the value; however, you can also choose to scroll one screen per notch.

on the job

It is important to keep in mind that Windows XP mouse options give you a number of features you can use; however, under most circumstances, the default settings are all most of your users will ever need.

Finally, the Hardware tab gives you the make and manufacturer of the mouse. You can access the Windows Troubleshooter from this tab and the Device Manager properties for the mouse. There is a particular tab on the Device Manager properties sheets called Advanced Settings that you should be familiar with. The Advanced Settings tab, shown in Figure 6-8, gives you some basic settings that determine how Windows XP interacts with the mouse. By default, the mouse is sampled 100 times per second. This means the operating system is constantly checking the mouse to determine its position. The default setting is 100, but you can increase the speed to increase mouse tracking. Typically, however, you don't need to change this setting unless mouse operations seem sluggish.

FIGURE 6-7

Mouse Wheel tab

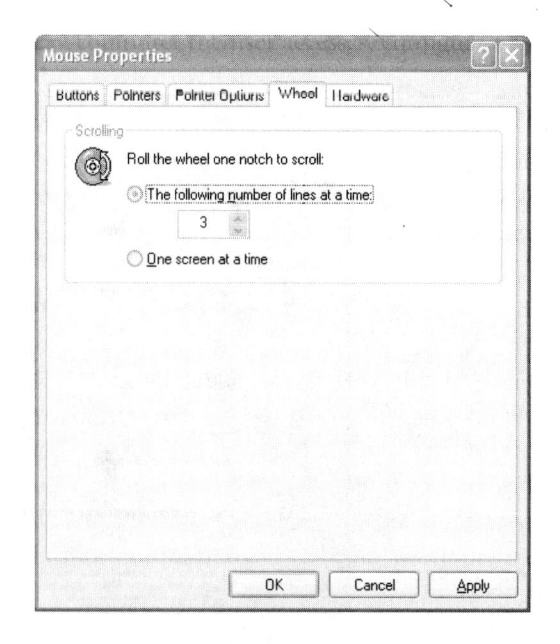

FIGURE 6-8

Advanced Options tab

Under Wheel Detection, the default setting assumes that a wheel is present on the mouse. You can change this setting so that the system does not try to detect the mouse wheel, which effectively disables it, and you have the operating system always check for the wheel. If the mouse has a wheel and it works correctly, you can leave the default setting configured.

Finally, the input buffer length, which is set to 100 by default, is the size of the input buffer that stores information about the position of your mouse. If the mouse seems to behave erratically, try increasing the input buffer length in order to fix the problem.

CERTIFICATION OBJECTIVE 6.02

Monitor, Configure, and Troubleshoot Multimedia Hardware, Such as Cameras and Handheld Devices

Multimedia hardware covers a number of different hardware devices, such as scanners, digital cameras, digital camcorders and even handheld devices, such as Palm and BlackBerry. These hardware devices generally fall under the category of multimedia,

SCENARIO & SOLUTION	
A user complains that mouse buttons are "sticking" when she tries to drag documents to folders. What is causing the problem?	ClickLock has been turned on. If the user does not want to use ClickLock, access the Buttons tab of Mouse Properties and clear the Turn On ClickLock check box.
How does Windows XP choose the default mouse options?	The default settings for mouse properties, and for most hardware in general, are set to the configuration that most people will find useful. Because of this, you typically do not need to make widespread configuration changes when Windows XP is rolled out—the default settings are often all your users will need.
A user complains that the mouse pointer always disappears when he is typing. The user wants the mouse pointer to stay visible in the foreground. How can you fix this problem?	Open Mouse properties and access the Pointer Options. Click the Hide Pointer While Typing check box found in the Visibility section.

and for the most part they are all managed and installed in the same way. You typically connect the device to a correct port and install software on Windows XP that allows XP to operate with the device. For example, if you want to use a digital camera, the camera typically plugs into a serial or USB port, and you install software that enables Windows XP to interact with the camera and download picture files from it.

If the multimedia device does not have a setup program, access the manufacturer's Web site and follow instructions for setup. For cameras and scanners, you can also use Windows XP Scanner and Camera Installation Wizard. Exercise 6-1 walks you through the process of using the wizard.

EXERCISE 6-1

CertCam 6-1

Installing a Camera or Scanner

To install a camera or scanner, just follow these steps:

1. Open the Scanners and Cameras folder in Control Panel.
2. In the left pane, click the Add An Imaging Device link.
3. The Scanner and Camera Installation Wizard appears. Click Next to continue.

4. In the Scanner and Camera Installation Wizard, shown in the following illustration, you can choose the manufacturer and model of the camera or scanner that you want to install. If you have an installation disk, you can click the Have Disk button. Make your selection and click Next.

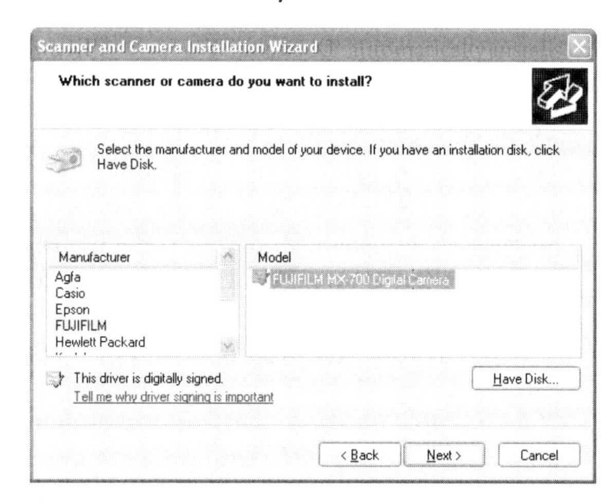

5. The Connection window appears, as shown in the following illustration. Connect the camera to the correct port on your computer and make a selection on the Available Ports window. Notice that you can choose to have Windows automatically detect the port as well. Click Next.

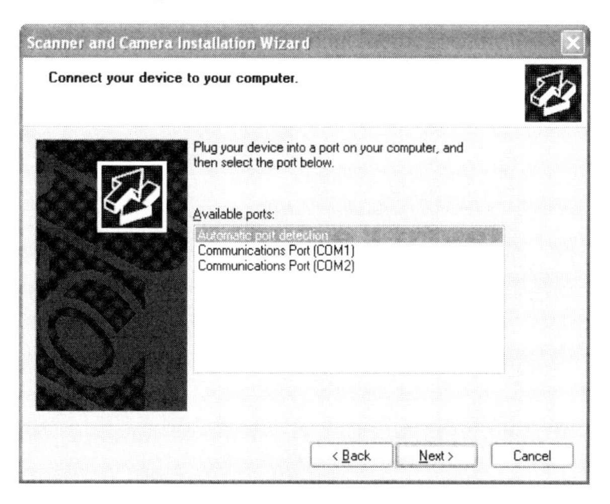

6. Click Next again and click Finish.

Once you have installed the scanner or camera, the icons for the devices appear in the Scanners and Cameras folder, shown in Figure 6-9. You can then access configuration properties by right-clicking the icon and clicking Properties. The properties for the device are device specific, and you will probably use manufacturer's software to manage the device over the options presented here. However, you can use the icons for specific actions, such as Get Pictures or Start Scan. Again, the trick with multimedia hardware is to follow the manufacturer's instructions for setup and use.

Concerning the exam, you should get some practice installing and removing multimedia devices if possible. On another exam note, keep in mind that hardware such as cameras and scanners consume system resources. If you have a docked laptop computer that makes use of multimedia hardware, you should consider using a different hardware profile that disables the multimedia devices when the computer is not docked. This will save system resources and possibly even battery power. See Chapter 5 to learn how to set up hardware profiles.

exam Watch

When multiple hardware devices and peripherals are used with laptop computers, creating different hardware profiles is often your best choice to control hardware and peripherals. Keep this in mind when you see exam questions concerning multimedia hardware and laptop computers.

FIGURE 6-9

Scanners and Cameras folder

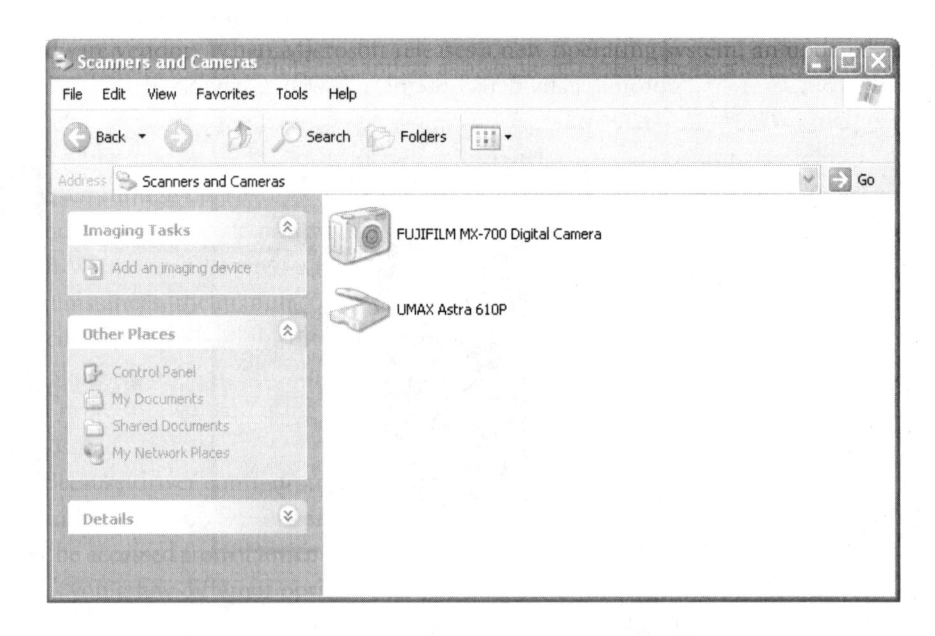

SCENARIO & SOLUTION	
Should the Scanner and Camera Wizard be used to install devices, or should the device's setup program be used?	The Camera and Scanner Wizard is provided to help you install multimedia hardware when a manufacturer's setup program is not available. If you have the setup program, your best choice is to use the manufacturer's setup routine, which typically installs additional applications that help you manage the device.
What is the best way to handle laptop computers that use digital cameras when traveling?	The best way, in general, to manage laptop computers is to create a hardware profile that disables any devices that are not in use while traveling. If camera connections and software are used, simply keep the desired device(s) enabled in the profile. See Chapter 5 to learn more.

CERTIFICATION OBJECTIVE 6.03

Install, Configure, and Manage Modems

Modems have been around since the early days of Windows, and in the past modem configuration was a big pain. You had to know something about IRQ settings, port data, and even scripting. Modems continue to be a big part of any computer system today and are used for access to the Internet, as well as corporate dial-up connections. The good news is that modem installation and configuration is rather easy these days, and like all hardware, if you are using modems and modem drivers that are compatible with Windows XP, you are not likely to have problems.

Plug-and-play modems are detected and installed automatically in Windows XP. However, if you are having problems installing a modem, Windows XP provides the Add Hardware Wizard / Install New Modem feature that can help you get the modem installed. The use of the Installation wizard works just like any other Installation wizard. The wizard scans for hardware changes. If the modem is found, the modem is installed. If not, you have the option of accessing the familiar selection list to select the manufacturer and model of the modem or using the Have Disk option. Once the modem is installed, it appears on the Modems tab of Phone and Modem Options in Control Panel, as shown in Figure 6-10.

As you can see, installation is generally easy. However, the Phone and Modems Options in Control Panel gives you a number of configuration options that determine how the modem operates. Naturally, these options make great exam fodder, so you'll need to know what setting controls what aspect of modem operation, and you'll need to know where and how to change those settings when necessary. The rest of this section explores modem configuration. Make sure you study this section carefully and get some hands-on practice before taking the exam.

exam Watch

The exam is most likely to ask you about minor configuration issues and problems. In order to solve those problems, you must know what to change and where the items are located on the Phone and Modems configuration tabs.

If you open Phone and Modems in Control Panel, you'll see the three-tab interface for Phone and Modem Options. The following sections explore these options individually.

Dialing Rules

The Dialing Rules tab enables you to configure dialing locations. For laptop users, the configuration on this tab can be very important for the modem to correctly dial

FIGURE 6-10

Modems tab

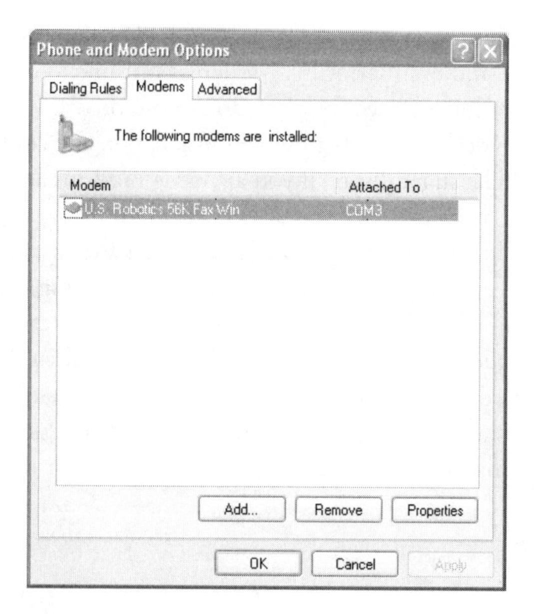

access numbers. Any existing dialing rules are found on the Dialing Rules tab, and you can click the Edit button to make changes to the existing rule, or you can create a new rule by clicking the New button. Exercise 6-2 walks you through the process of creating a new dialing rule.

EXERCISE 6-2

Creating a New Dialing Rule

To create a new dialing rule, just follow these steps:

1. Open Phone and Modem Options in Control Panel. On the Dialing Rules tab, click New.
2. The New Location window appears the three tabs. On the General tab, shown in the following illustration, enter a location name. Location names typically work well as calling locations (such as "Home, "Office," etc.). Enter the country/region and current area code. Then, enter any desired rules, such as outline line number, carrier code, etc. Also, use the check box at the bottom of the window to disable call waiting while you are using the line.

3. Click the Area Code Rules tab. You see an empty window with no current area code rules. To create an area code rule, click the New button.
4. In the New Area Code Rule window, shown in the following illustration, enter the area code you are calling, and then you can specify prefixes to include in the area code. Once you have added the prefixes that belong, you can then determine whether or not to dial 1 when making the call and whether or not the area code should be used. Once you are done, click OK.

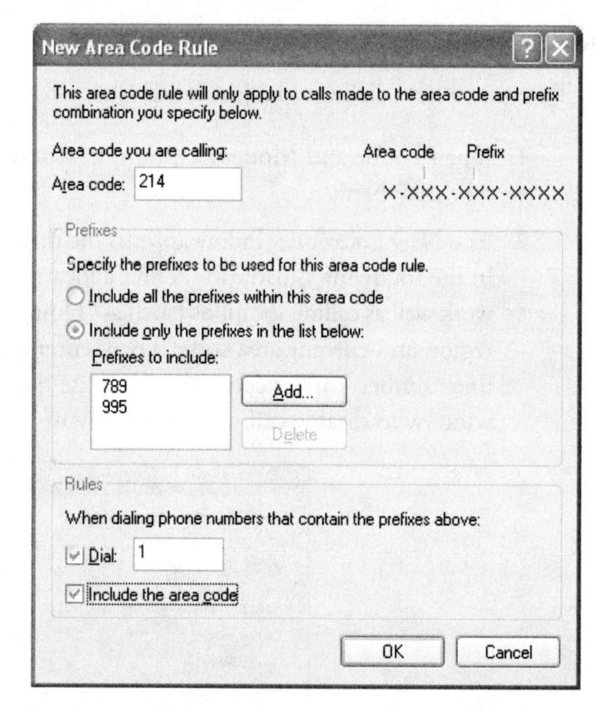

5. Now the new location appears in the Area Code Rules window, shown in the following illustration. At any time, you can edit the connection or delete it from this window.

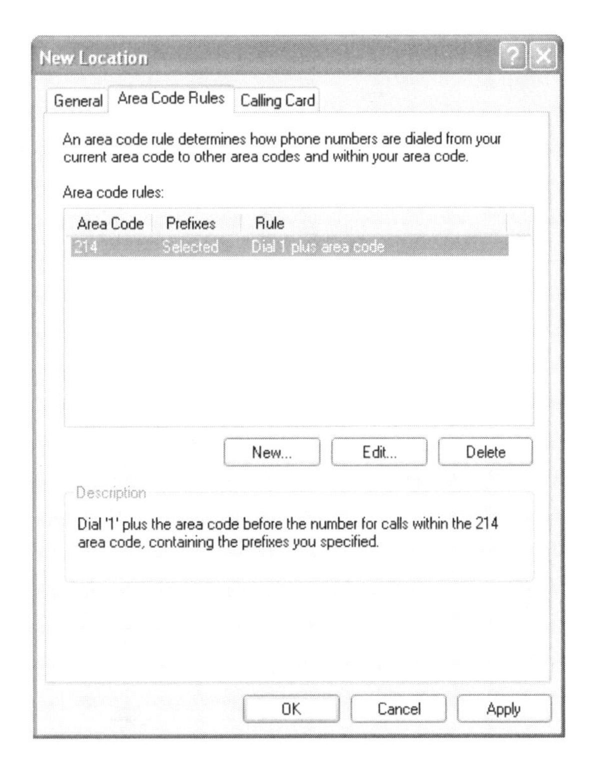

6. On the Calling Card tab, shown in the following illustration, you can configure a calling card type that should be used when calling from the location, if needed. Select an existing type and enter your account and PIN numbers to use the calling card. If the calling card is not listed, click the New button to enter the card and name and information so that it can be used. When you're done, click OK.

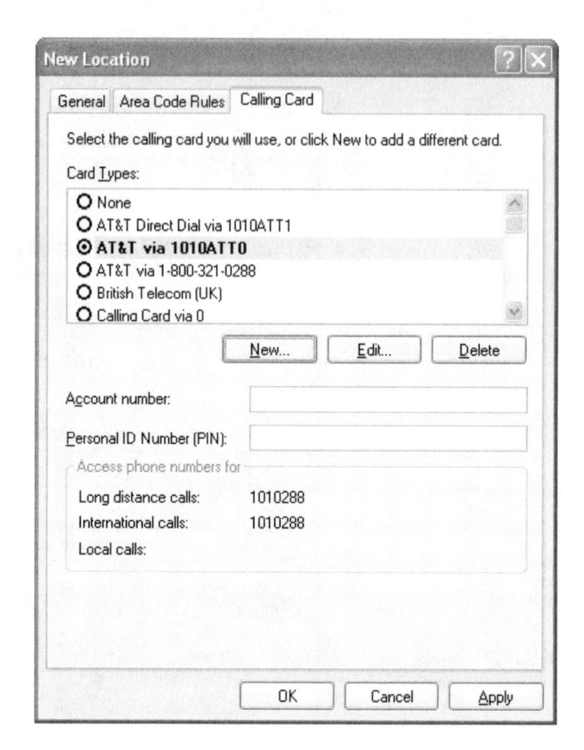

7. The New Location now appears in the Dialing Rules window. You can edit or delete the location at any time from this interface.

Modems

The Modems tab shows all modems that are installed on the computer. You can add and remove modems from the computer from this tab, and you can also click the Properties button to access the Properties sheets for the modem. There are several important configuration options you should note on the Modem properties tabs. The following sections outline the options available on the Modem properties tabs.

General

The General tab can be accessed through Phone and Modem Options in Control Panel or by right-clicking on the modem in Device Manager. You can see the Device

Status and Disable the device from this window. See Chapter 5 to learn more about Device Manager tabs.

Modem

The Modem tab, shown in Figure 6-11 gives you three important settings:

- **Speaker Volume** If you want to hear the connection noise, leave the volume turned up on the slider bar—if not, turn the volume down.
- **Maximum Port Speed** The maximum port speed setting determines how fast programs can transmit data to the modem, not the line speed from modem to modem. If you are having problems with a device connected to the modem or an application sending data over the modem, you can try lowering or raising the port speed value. The default setting is typically 115,200 Kbps
- **Dial Control** The Wait For Dial Tone Before Dialing check box is enabled by default and typically should remain enabled.

FIGURE 6-11

Modem tab

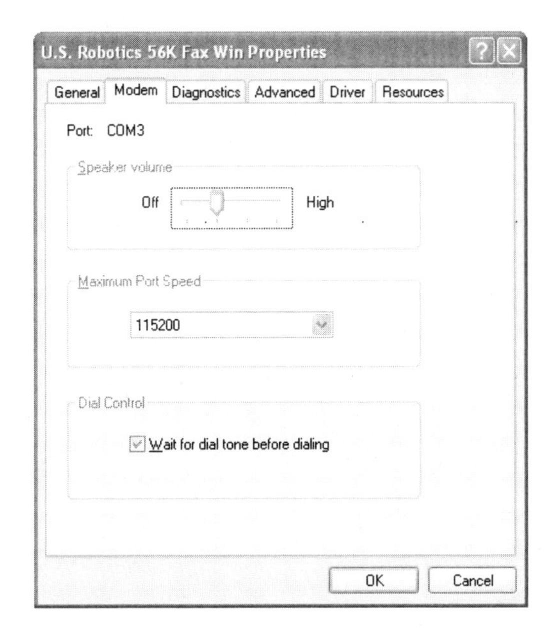

Diagnostics

The Diagnostics tab, shown in Figure 6-12, gives you a Query Modem option. The query performs several command tests in order to see if the modem is working correctly. Once the test is complete, you can see a list of commands that were issued and the response on this window. You can also click View Log in order to see test data from a log file.

Advanced

The Advanced tab provides you a place to enter additional initialization commands. Although unnecessary on most modems today, initialization commands can control the functions of the modem and can be used when the modem works too slowly or frequent hang-ups occur. The initialization commands vary from modem manufacturer to manufacturer.

You can also access Advanced Port Settings here by clicking the Port Settings button. The Advanced Settings window, as you can see in Figure 6-13, enables you to determine the FIFO buffer usage. The FIFO (first in, first out) buffer setting uses the universal asynchronous receiver/transmitter (UART) chipset, which is the primary component that buffers incoming information to the modem until it is transferred to the computer. The default settings for the Receive and Transmit buffers on this

FIGURE 6-12 Diagnostics tab

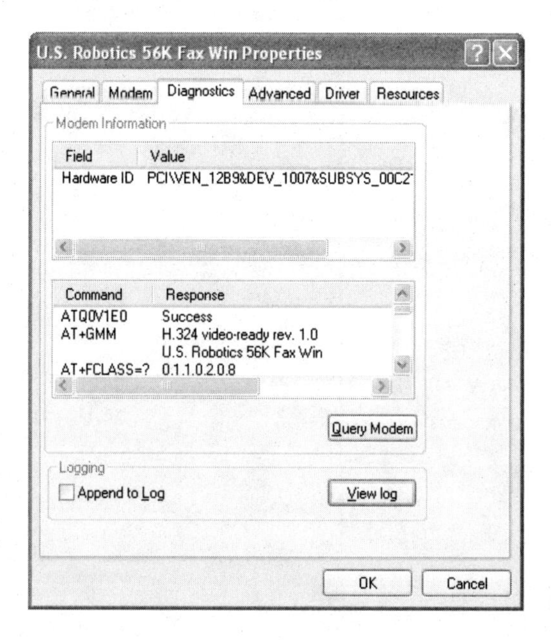

FIGURE 6-13

Advanced settings

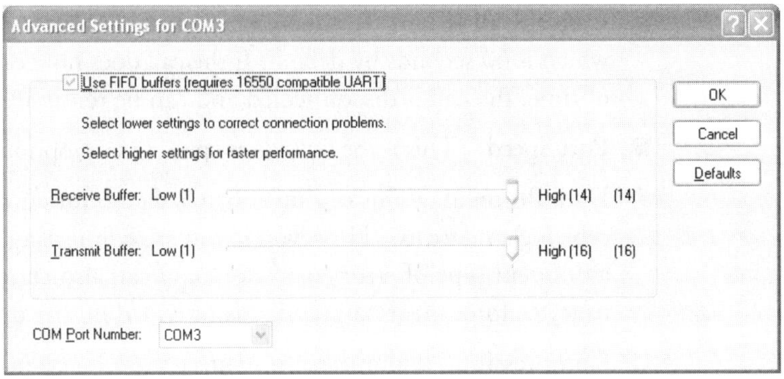

tab are High, but you can lower them to correct performance problems—however, the higher the setting, the higher the performance.

You can also choose to Change Default Preferences on the Advanced tab, and there are a few important configuration options here you should keep in mind for the exam. First of all, if you click the Change Default Preferences button, you see a General tab, shown in Figure 6-14. You have the following settings available:

- **Disconnect Call If Idle** This setting, when enabled, disconnects a call if it is idle for more than the number of defined minutes. If a user is getting disconnected during idle times, this is the setting to check.

FIGURE 6-14

General default settings

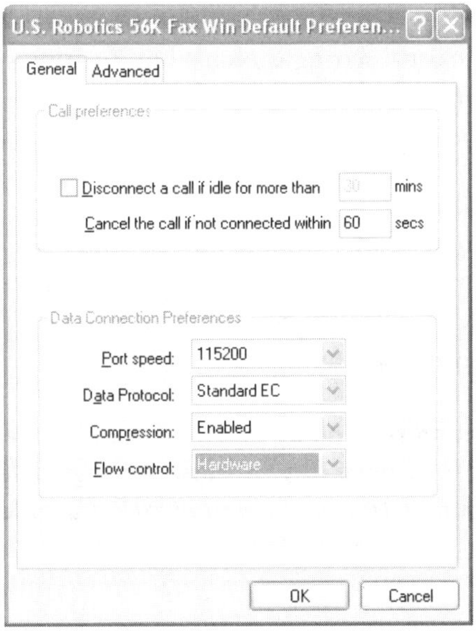

- **Cancel Call If Not Connected** You can configure a value for this setting, which is 60 seconds by default. If the call does not complete during this period of time, the call is disconnected and can be reinitiated.
- **Port Speed** This is the same port speed setting option seen on the Modem tab.
- **Data Protocol** This option controls data error correction. The common type is StandardEC. However, if you are connecting with a modem that uses a different type of error correction, you can also choose to disable the option or try to force error correction, as provided on the drop-down menu.
- **Compression** Compression reduces the KB size of data for transmission purposes. A standard configuration uses the Enabled option here, but you can disable it if specific connection issues call for it.
- **Flow Control** This setting specifies whether hardware or software flow control is used to manage the flow of data between the modem and the computer. RTS/CTS is hardware flow control, while XON/XOFF is software flow control.

If you click the Advanced tab, you see the option to manage hardware settings, shown in Figure 6-15. The options are as follows:

- **Data Bits** Determines the number of data bits that are used for each character that is sent and received. The default setting is 8, and the modem you are communicating with must have the same setting.
- **Parity** Determines the type of error checking that is used for the port. The usual setting is None, but if parity is used, the modem you are communicating with must have the same setting.
- **Stop Bits** This setting tells the system that a packet of information has been set. The standard setting here is 1.
- **Modulation** Modulation type must be compatible with the modem you are communicating with. Most modems use standard modulation, but if you are having problems communicating with a particular modem, you can try the nonstandard setting here.

on the job

Keep in mind that all of these settings are default settings. You normally do not need to change any of these settings unless you are trying to troubleshoot specific connection or communication problems.

FIGURE 6-15

Hardware settings

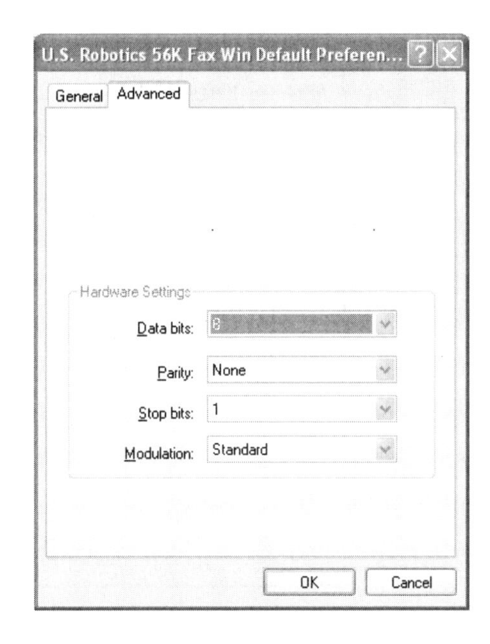

Driver and Resources

Finally, the Driver and Resources tab found on the modem's properties sheet is the same Driver and Resources tabs you see when accessing any device's properties from Device Manager. See Chapter 5 to learn more about the information found on these tabs.

Advanced

The Advanced tab, shown in Figure 6-16 lists the telephony providers that are installed on the computer. Telephony providers are applications that enable your modem to communicate with specific types of applications or even hardware. For example, you see the Microsoft H.323 Telephony Service Provider. H.323 is a protocol used by NetMeeting and related multimedia applications. When you select the provider and click the Properties button, you can configure the service provider so that your modem can connect with the appropriate server, as you can see in Figure 6-17. Of course, if you are not using any of these specific providers, there is nothing you need to configure here.

FIGURE 6-16

Advanced tab

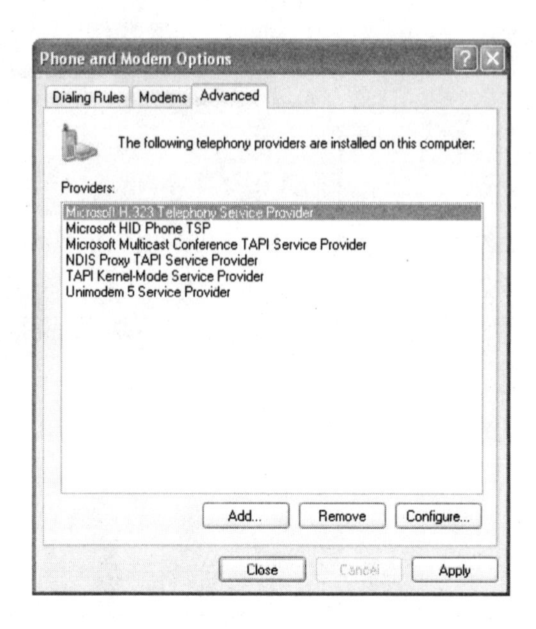

FIGURE 6-17

TAPI provider properties

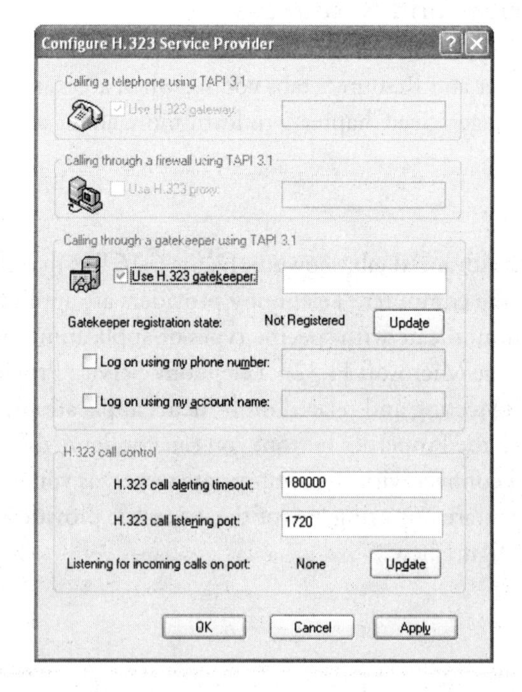

FROM THE CLASSROOM

Modem Configuration in the Real World

Depending on the corporate environment, many computers will be outfitted with modems and dial-up connections. In fact, because of the mobile networking environment in today's marketplace, many networks use only laptop computers. I previously worked for a company that only provided laptop computers to its employees—no desktop systems at all. The purpose was flexibility and mobility. For this reason, you may find yourself administering a network where most users are mobile and most access an RAS server for corporate connectivity when they are away from the office.

The good news is that Windows XP supports a wide range of modems and the options provided to network environments in terms of hardware needs are broad. As an IT specialist, you may be faced with modem configuration and troubleshooting on a regular basis. If the modem and the modem drivers are compatible with Windows XP, you are not likely to experience many help desk tickets from users, and even when those tickets arrive, the solutions are often simple check box options that need to be corrected. Depending on user permissions for your environment, you can also ensure that local computer users cannot make configuration changes to modem settings, which can only be performed by local computer administrators. In short, the modem is still an important part of the IT environment, but it need not be a focal point of your time and energies.

CERTIFICATION OBJECTIVE 6.04

Install, Configure, and Manage USB Devices

A few years ago, PCs had a real problem. Computer users were limited by the number of physical ports available for peripherals. In years past, this wasn't such a big deal, since the primary peripheral hardware was keyboards, mice, and printers. Today, computer users hook up multiple peripherals and hardware devices to their computers, such as scanners, external modems and hard drives, zip drives, digital cameras, game controllers, and the list goes on and on. However, the PC was limited by the number of physical connection ports, and the same slow serial bus had been used for years.

SCENARIO & SOLUTION	
A user reports that her modem always dials 1 before local numbers. How can this problem be fixed?	The user needs to configure a location that makes the desired numbers local numbers, or the user has configured a location and chosen to dial 1. Either way, a location needs to be created or the existing location needs to be correctly edited.
A user complains that her laptop computer seems to have unsteady behavior when trying to use the modem. What setting adjustment should be tried first?	Try adjusting the port speed, which will help reduce the time/amount of information flowing from the modem to the computer. You can change the setting on the Modem tab of the modem's properties sheets.
You want to make certain that the modem disconnects if calls are not completed within 30 seconds. How can you configure this?	If you access the modem properties, Advanced tab, you can click the Change Default Preferences button and change the Cancel The Call If Not Connected Within dialog box to 30 seconds.

Enter the USB, or Universal Serial Bus. USB is a faster serial bus technology that enables multiple USB devices to connect to a single port. In fact, you can connect up to 127 individual peripherals to a single interface on the computer using USB hubs. The idea is to make using a peripheral as easy as plugging a lamp into a wall socket. You don't have to worry about configuration and setup; you simply plug it in and use it. When you install USB hardware, you simply plug the hardware into the USB port. Windows XP automatically detects and installs it with no interaction from you and no rebooting. Overall, USB is a great technology that is here to stay, and one that you will use with more and more devices. Most all peripherals sold today are available in the USB format, and you can even expect PCs in the future to be primarily USB machines.

Overall, USB usage is easy and problem free, but there are a few facts and features you should know about USB in order to make the right choice in real-world connectivity and dealing with those picky exam questions. First of all, let's consider USB hub configuration. The USB port found on the front or back of a PC is referred to as the USB root hub. It is the hub that connects directly to the internal computer's motherboard. The USB root hub may have multiple USB ports available, and in many cases USB devices will even have their own ports so you can daisy-chain peripherals together off one port. These devices, called "compound devices," also form an additional hub. For example, a typical USB keyboard may plug directly into the USB root hub, but provide a USB port for the mouse to plug into the keyboard. This compound device acts as a hub.

From the USB root hub, you can connect several different devices, but you can also connect another external hub. USB hubs typically support up to seven additional connections, including another hub. For this reason, the USB has a tiered star topology. One hub feeds from the root hub, then the next hub feeds from the first hub and so forth. Using this tiered star topology approach, you can combine enough hubs to support up to 127 devices.

Of course, under most circumstances, no one is going to connect 127 devices to a single PC, but the point is that through additional USB hubs chained together, you can easily extend USB connections as you need them. One point concerning USB hubs that you need to keep in mind, however, is the distinction between bus-powered and self-powered. Bus-powered hubs draw their power from the USB bus, or essentially the power flowing into the computer system from the AC/DC outlet. For most U.S. peripherals, such as keyboards and mice, this is all you need. However, some USB devices may require more power. For example, let's say that you have a USB bus-powered hub. You purchase a USB external hard drive. However, the hard drive does not work when you plug it into the USB hub. The problem is that the external hard drive needs more power to operate than the USB bus-powered hub can provide. In this case, you need a USB self-powered hub, which connects to its own AC/DC connection. Of course, most peripherals that need their own power supply have their own AC/DC connection. But you can see the need for self-powered hubs, especially in situations where you are chaining several hubs together and attaching multiple peripherals. As a general rule, a bus-powered hub can support up to 100mA per port whereas a self-powered hub can support up to 500mA per port.

exam Watch

Keep the self-powered vs. bus-powered hub issue in mind for the exam. If you see questions that involve connecting several devices, especially scanners, disk drives, tape drives, and other peripherals such as these to a bus-powered hub, the answer is usually going to be that a self-powered hub is needed. Also, the importance of self-powered hubs cannot be understated in the case of a laptop computer using batteries. Since the bus-powered hub draws power from the system, the USB bus can drain laptop batteries when peripherals, especially those using a lot of power, are in use. You can use a self-powered hub to correct the problem if peripherals are needed when running on battery power.

As I mentioned, installing a USB device is as easy as plugging it in. Windows XP can automatically detect and install the USB without any help and without a reboot. When a device needs to be removed, simply unplug it. Windows XP can detect that the device is no longer available and remove it from the operating system.

You can gain a lot of helpful information about USB devices and USB configuration on a particular computer system by using Device Manager. If you open Device Manager, you can see a category for Universal Serial Bus Controllers, and if you expand that category, you see device options for the USB Root Hub and the USB Universal Host Controller, as you can see in Figure 6-18.

If you right-click the USB Universal Host Controller and click Properties, you see the standard Device Manager properties sheets, containing the General, Driver, and Resources tabs. However, you also see an Advanced tab, shown in Figure 6-19. The Advanced tab shows you how much bandwidth each USB controller is using. Since each device attached to the controller has to share the bandwidth, this is a good tab to check to see if a system is running low on USB bandwidth due to the number of devices attached to the USB port. If you choose, you can also check the Don't Tell Me About USB Errors check box, which will stop any bandwidth, power, and USB

FIGURE 6-18

USB in Device Manager

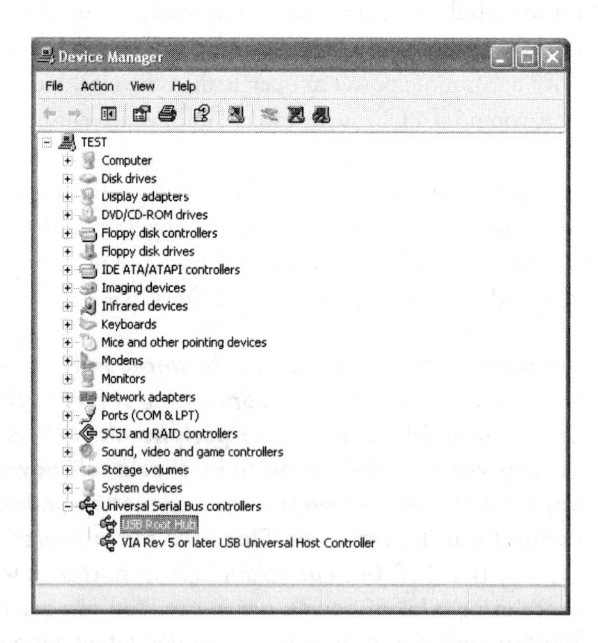

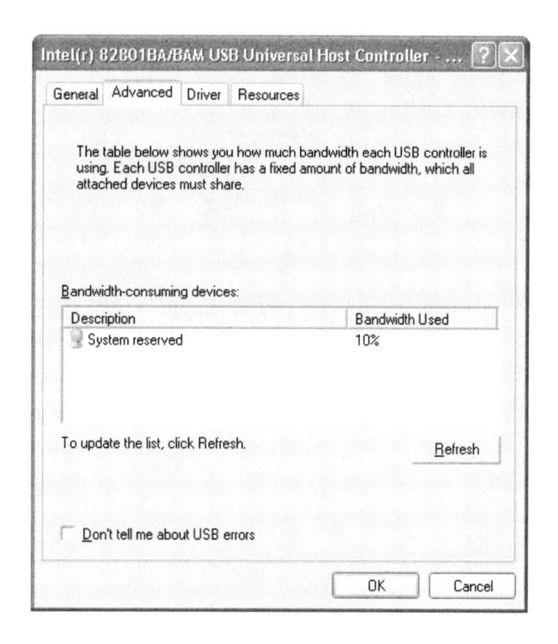

FIGURE 6-19 USB Host Controller Advanced tab

device errors from being reported. However, you should typically leave this box unchecked.

If you right-click the USB Root Hub option in Device Manager and click Properties, you also see the standard Device Manager tabs, with two additional tabs specific to the hub. The first is Power, which you can see in Figure 6-20. The Power tab tells you information about the hub type and power available per port. As you can see in Figure 6-20, I am using a self-powered hub that has 500mA available per port. You can also see a list of attached devices and the power required to run those devices. Again, this is a good place to gain overall information about the USB root hub and how power is being used on the hub.

The second tab is Power Management, shown in Figure 6-21. You have two check box options here. First, you can choose to allow the computer to turn off the device in order to save power, which is typically selected by default. Second, you can have the device bring the computer out of standby if standby is configured.

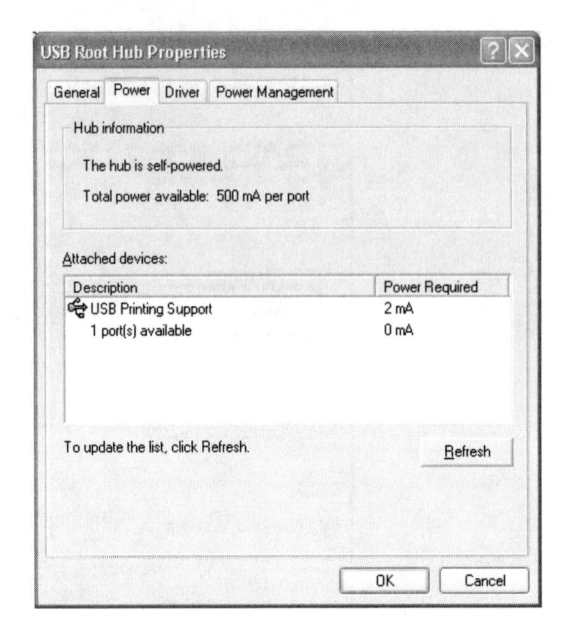

FIGURE 6-20

Power tab

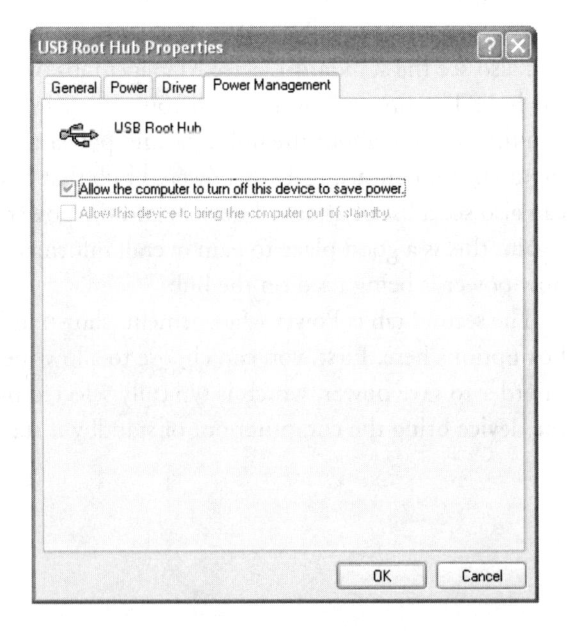

FIGURE 6-21

Power Management tab

FROM THE CLASSROOM

IEEE 1394

While we are on the subject of alternative bus and connection features, a newer connection technology, IEEE 1394, also commonly called Firewire, is also available and supported under Windows XP. IEEE 1394 is a high-performance serial bus designed for multimedia, such as audio and video transfer. The IEEE 1394 interface is capable of functioning without the computer's help. For example, you can connect a digital camera to an IEEE 1394 interface and send a digital picture directly to a printer. Data that travels along the IEEE 1394 interface remains in a digital format, which provides exact data transfer over the potential distortion problems with analog transmission.

IEEE 1394 supports data transfer rates of 100 Mbps, 200 Mbps, and 400 Mbps, The latter is designed for cable use and even provides traffic management features. At the time of this writing, IEEE1394b is under development, which supports data transfer speeds of up to 3.2 Gbps.

IEEE 1394 works like USB in that you can connect multiple devices to single interface—up to 63 to be precise. Devices are connected in a star or branching tree formation. Concerning IEEE 1394 cabling, the bus consists of two pairs of twisted-pair cabling, providing the high-speed transfer features. As with any Windows XP devices, make sure you have the correct cabling for the 1394 bus before attaching devices, and as always, check the manufacturer's specifications and instructions.

CERTIFICATION OBJECTIVE 6.05

Install, Configure, and Manage Infrared Data Association (IrDA) Devices and Other Wireless Devices

Windows XP supports infrared and other wireless devices. In the past, wireless connections were somewhat of a dream, something that would be helpful but not very practical. Today, wireless technology still has plenty of development room, but

SCENARIO & SOLUTION	
How many devices can be attached to a USB port?	Most USB root hubs allow you to connect two or three devices directly to the root hub. However, you can attach a secondary USB hub to the root hub, which supports seven connections. From that hub, you can also attach another hub and so forth. Under most circumstances, you'll see the best results using a self-powered hub that can handle the power pull from the USB devices.
How are USB devices installed?	USB devices are installed like any other device on Windows XP. Simply connect the device to the USB port. Windows XP will automatically detect the presence of the new device and install it on the system. You will not need to reboot. If you want to remove the device, simply unplug it.
Can you daisy chain USB devices together?	Usually. Some USB devices also contain USB ports so that other USB devices can connect to them. These devices, called compound devices, provide a way to combine device connections. You'll usually be physically limited to one or two devices in a USB chain, but the option is often available.

the use of infrared and other wireless technologies is becoming more and more common. Even among peripherals, you can locate all kinds of wireless keyboards, mice, and game controllers.

There are several different issues to consider concerning wireless connectivity and devices, and we'll take a look at those issues in this section. But first, a little background on wireless technology supported under Windows XP is necessary. Windows XP supports the use of infrared wireless technology for devices. You can install an infrared wireless link and use the wireless device to exchange information with Windows XP. Windows XP also supports wireless networking. Wireless networking is commonly used for communication with desktop computers and handheld devices (PDAs). If you have ever used a PDA, you know that you can synchronize with a desktop PC via a wire connection or an infrared wireless link. Wireless networking, however, is moving beyond these kinds of transfers to actual LAN networks, as well as WAN networks. Though not widely adopted at this time, wireless technology is the "coming attraction" for networking, and a number of network types are identified for wireless technology, such as the following:

- **Wireless wide area networks** Wide area networks use global wireless technologies to exchange information from geographical place to place. The transmission medium used is satellite communications, including common wireless technologies as Global System for Mobile Communications (GSM), Cellular Digital Packet Data (CDPD), and Code Division Multiple Access (CDMA).
- **Wireless metropolitan area networks** These kinds of networks establish wireless connections between offices in the same metropolitan areas. Using radio waves and infrared technologies, high-bandwidth transmissions can be made wirelessly over shorter distances. Many of the technologies for this kind of wireless transmission are still in development, and broadband wireless is a standard under development by IEEE 802.16.
- **Wireless LANs** Wireless LANS typically exist within a single building or complex and typically operate via wireless stations. The stations function as a network backbone to connect different wireless segments. Desktop systems are outfitted with radio wireless network adapter cards that communicate with the wireless station. Then, the wireless station transmits the data to the correct wireless network adapter card. You can think of the wireless station as a network hub that handles traffic on that segment and forwards wireless traffic to other segments. Though not widely used, the technology is promising and gives you the potential for future office environments without wires.
- **Wireless personal area network** The wireless personal area network simply refers to a computer system that is wireless communications capable. The operating system is able to communicate with wireless devices, such as keyboards and mice, and you could even use a wireless modem to connect with a cellular phone. The two driving technologies at this time are infrared devices and Bluetooth, which uses radio waves. Standardization for wireless personal area networks is established as 802.15.

The primary focus of wireless communication via devices is infrared with Windows XP, with Bluetooth becoming more and more popular. Infrared communication is commonly used in most computer systems and even in household appliances, such as VCR remote controls. Infrared technology is implemented according to the Infrared Data Association (IrDA) standards and infrared protocols. Windows XP can make full use of these standards and protocols. Most laptop computers now ship with infrared receivers; and for desktop systems that are not equipped with an infrared port, you can easily install an external infrared transceiver. For infrared data transfer, a few different features are used, which you should keep in mind:

- **Wireless Link File Transfer** Provides the ability to transfer files over a wireless link.
- **Infrared Printing (IrLPT)** Provides the ability to wirelessly send print files to a printer outfitted with an IrDA transceiver.
- **Infrared Image Transfer Protocol (IrTran-P)** Allows you to wirelessly transfer pictures from a digital camera to the PC.

exam watch

Some synchronization software automatically disables IrTran-P, which will keep you from using digital image transfer over the wireless link. If you suspect this is the case, you'll need to disable synchronization software before using the wireless link to transfer digital pictures. Check the synchronization software for more information about this issue.

- **Infrared Networking (IrNET and IrCOMM)** Provides the ability to communicate with other computers. IrNET allows point-to-point communication between two computers, while IrCOMM requires a central hub.

A common question about infrared usage concerns transfer speeds. There are several different possible transmission speeds with IrDA, depending on the IrDA implementation on the particular computer. You find these two basic types:

- **Serial IrDA** The most common, serial IrDA can provide data transfer speeds of up to 115.2 Kbps. Under this configuration, the existing serial hardware can be used without additional hardware costs, thus making it the most common—and often the most practical.
- **Fast IrDA** Fast IrDA can provide a maximum data transfer of 4 Mbps. Very fast IrDA can provide speeds of up to 16 Mbps half duplex.

If your computer has an IrDA port, it is detected and made available during Windows XP installation. You can check Control Panel for a Wireless Link icon, as shown in Figure 6-22. This tells you that IrDA is installed on your computer.

If a wireless link is not available on your computer, you can install one by purchasing an IrDA external device compatible with Windows XP. Check the HCL for a list of IrDA transceivers that will work with Windows XP. Once you purchase the device, simply attach it to the correct serial or USB port for installation to begin. You can also use the Add Hardware Wizard to install a wireless link, which is explored in Exercise 6-3.

FIGURE 6-22

Wireless Link icon

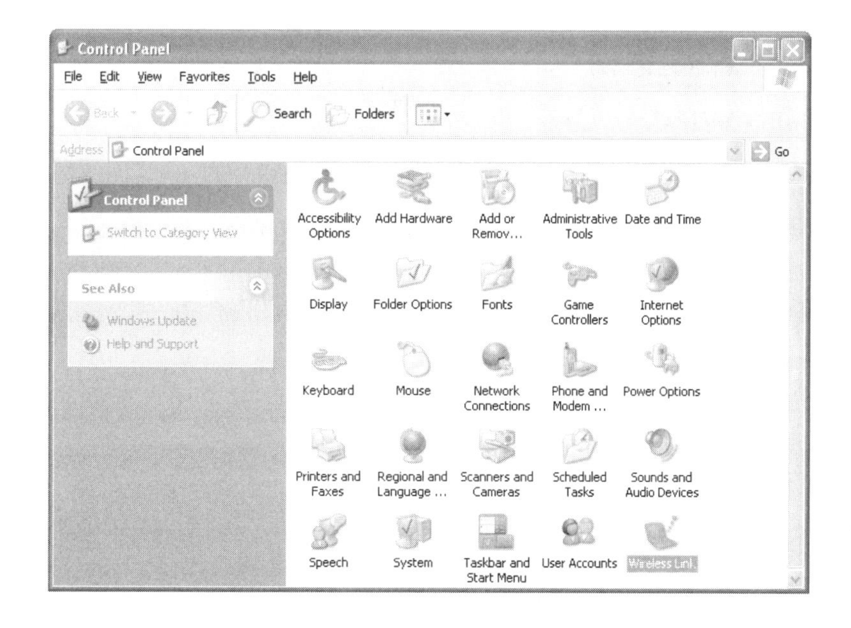

SCENARIO & SOLUTION

How do wide area networks function with wireless technologies?	Wide area networks function with the existing wireless infrastructure, which is based on satellite technology using different transfer methods. This is the same technology that governs cellular phone usage. As the technology matures, higher-bandwidth transfers will be easier, supporting large wide area networks.
Do most computers have an IrDA port?	Most laptop computers have an IrDa port built into them. Many desktop systems now ship with the IrDA port as well. However, if an IrDa port is not available, you can install an external infrared device so that your computer will support wireless communications.
Do I have to manually install the IrDA protocols in order for IrDA to work?	When you install an IrDA transceiver or if one is already available during Windows XP installation, then the protocols services needed for the wireless link are automatically installed. You not need to manually install or manage the services and/or protocols.

EXERCISE 6-3

Installing a Wireless Link

To install a wireless link, just follow these steps:

1. Connect the device according to the manufacturer's setup instructions. If the device is not automatically installed, follow the rest of the steps in this exercise.
2. In Control Panel, double-click Add Hardware Wizard.
3. Click Next on the Welcome screen.
4. Windows searches for any plug-and-play hardware. If the wireless device is not found, you'll be asked if you have connected the hardware. Click Yes and click Next.
5. In the Hardware selection window, shown in the following illustration, scroll to the bottom of the window and click Add a New Hardware Device.

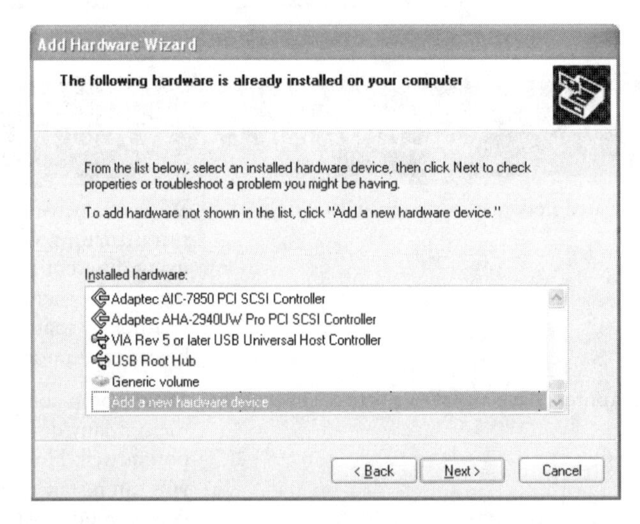

6. In the next window, choose to install hardware from a list and click Next.
7. In the Selection window that appears, choose Infrared Devices, as shown in the following illustration.

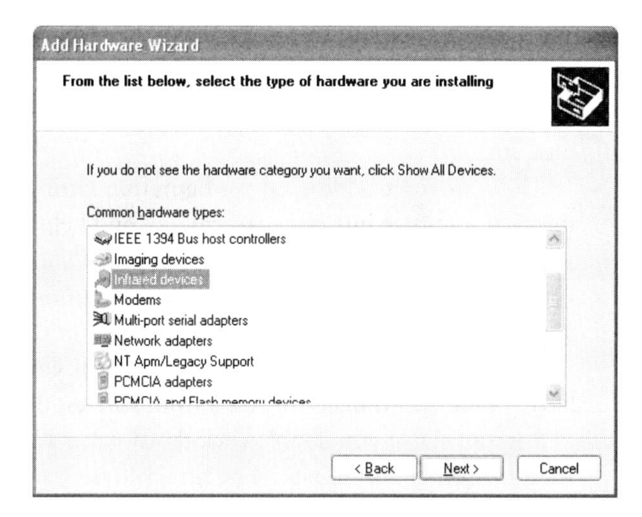

8. In the Infrared Device Selection window, shown in the following illustration, select the manufacturer and infrared device; or if you have an installation disk, you can attempt to use the disk by clicking the Have Disk button.

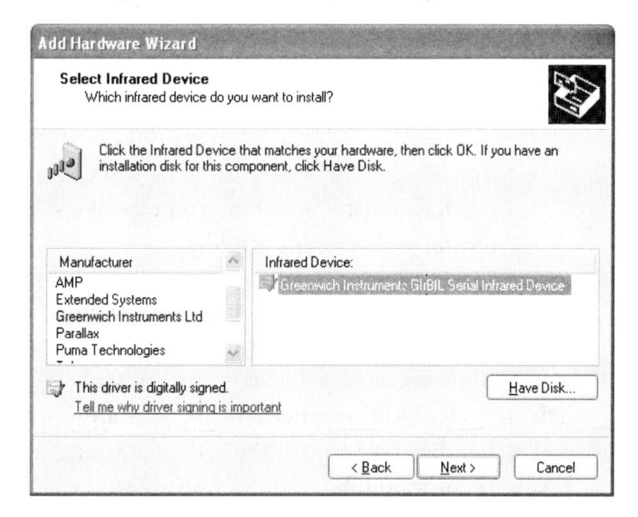

9. Click Next to begin the installation. You may be prompted to select the port the infrared device is attached to. Click Finish when the final window appears.

Once the infrared transceiver is installed, you can begin communicating with infrared devices. When an infrared device is in range of the port, an Infrared icon appears in your notification area where you can choose to use the device, transfer files, etc.

There are some additional configuration settings you should be aware of, since these can improve infrared performance and help solve problems. First of all, if you access the infrared device in Device Manager, you can access its properties sheets and you'll see an IrDA Settings tab, shown in Figure 6-23. The IrDA Settings tab enables you to control the maximum connection rate for the IrDA device. The typical setting is 115,200 Kbps, but like the modem settings, you can reduce this value if you are having problems transferring data from wireless devices.

Additionally, if you double-click the Wireless Link option in Control Panel, you'll see three configuration tabs. The first, Infrared, shown in the Figure 6-24, gives you a few different configuration options:

- Display An Icon On The Taskbar Indicating Infrared Activity.
- Play Sound When Infrared Device Is Near By.
- Allow Others To Send Files To Your Computer Using Infrared Communication.
- Notify Me When Receiving Files.
- You also have a default location you can configure where data received from wireless transfer is stored. You can choose a location by clicking the Browse button and selecting a folder.

On the Image Transfer tab, shown in Figure 6-25, you can choose to enable digital camera image transfer to the computer. This essentially turns on the IrTran-P service so that digital images can be received. As with the Infrared tab, you can choose a default folder location where the pictures are stored when they are received.

Finally, the Hardware tab tells the name and manufacturer of the infrared device. Like all Hardware tabs, you can also access the troubleshooter and Device Manager properties from this window.

FIGURE 6-23

IrDA Settings tab

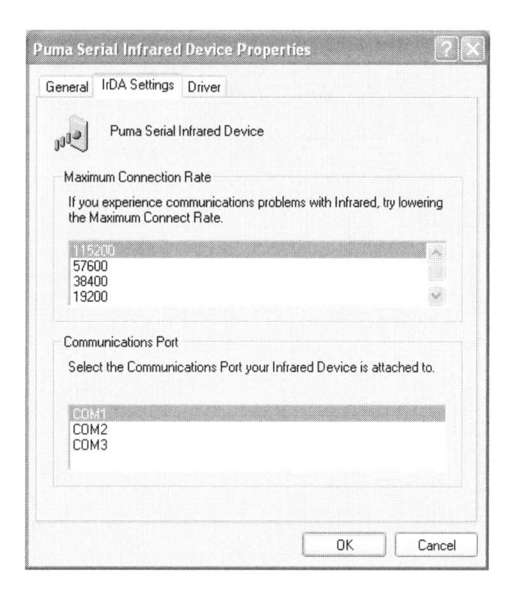

FIGURE 6-24

Infrared tab

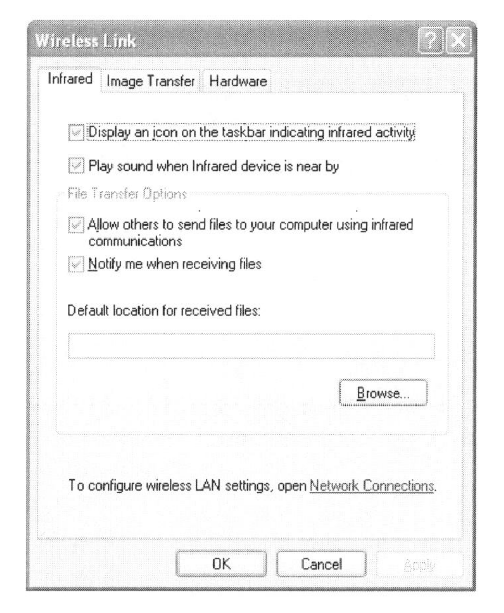

FIGURE 6-25

Image Transfer tab

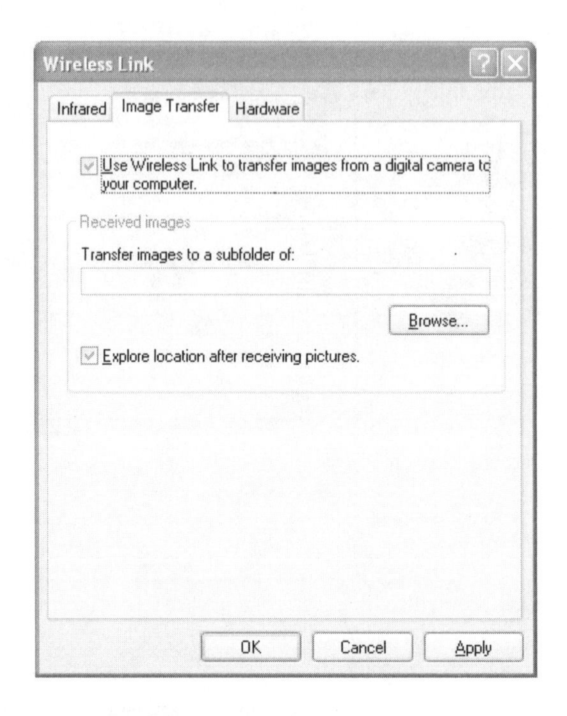

SCENARIO & SOLUTION

Do you need to use the Add Hardware Wizard under most circumstances when installing a wireless link?	No. Under most circumstances, Windows XP will be able to detect and install the plug-and-play device. You should follow the manufacturer's setup instructions. However, if you are having problems, the Add Hardware Wizard can help you get the device installed.
I want my computer to play a sound when an infrared device is near my computer. Where can I configure this option?	You can have your computer play a sound when an infrared device is in range by clicking the check box option on the Infrared tab, found on the Wireless Link properties in Control Panel.
How can I tell when a device is in range of my IrDA port?	An IrDA icon will appear in Windows XP's notification area when a wireless device is in range.

CERTIFICATION SUMMARY

In this chapter, you explored a number of device connection and configuration issues specific to Windows XP. For the exam, you must have a firm knowledge of device installation and management, so it is important that you get some hands-on practice with Windows XP.

Windows XP is compatible with most standard keyboards, mice, and smart card readers. You can check the HCL for specifics or just view the manufacturer's compatibility lists. As a general rule, you only need to attach keyboards, mice, and smart card readers to the correct port on the computer running Windows XP—installation occurs automatically. You can also access the keyboard and mice properties in Control Panel to further configure them if necessary.

Windows XP supports multimedia hardware, such as scanners and digital cameras. Again, you'll need to follow the manufacturer's installation instructions. Typically, installation is easy, but you can use the Add New Device feature in the Scanners and Cameras folder if you are having problems installing the device.

Modem installation and configuration remains important in Windows XP. You can install both internal and external compatible modems and then access Phone and Modem Options in Control Panel in order to configure the modem. You can configure dialing rules, as well as modem communication features, using Phone and Modem Options.

Windows XP continues to support USB devices. USB can support up to 127 devices using a series of hubs, beginning with the root hub. Hubs can be self-powered or bus-powered, and often need to be self-powered in order to provide the power flow to such USB devices as hard drives, scanners, cameras, and so on.

Finally, Windows XP supports wireless communications through IrDA. If the computer is not equipped with an IrDA port, you can install an external one so that communication can occur with wireless devices.

TWO-MINUTE DRILL

Configure Keyboards, Mice, and Smart Card Readers

- Windows XP can support many different kinds of keyboards and mice, including USB and wireless products.
- To install a keyboard, mouse, or smart card reader, attach the device to the correct port and allow plug and play to detect the device. If you have a setup program to run for the device from the manufacturer, you can run that program in order to install the manufacturer's drivers.
- You can configure a few keyboard options by accessing the Keyboard properties in Control Panel. You can control the repeat delay and repeat rate on the keyboard, and you can also access the troubleshooter and Device Manager properties for the device.
- You can also configure mouse properties by accessing the Mouse properties in Control Panel. You can control button behavior, install different pointers, control the wheel function, and also access the mouse troubleshooter and Device Manager properties.

Monitor, Configure, and Troubleshoot Multimedia Hardware, Such as Cameras and Handheld Devices

- Multimedia devices, such as cameras, scanners, and handheld devices are installed via plug and play. Follow the manufacturer's setup instructions. If you are having problems installing scanners and cameras, you can access the Scanners and Cameras folder in Control Panel and use the wizard to help you install the device.
- Once the scanner or camera is installed, you can access its properties sheets via the Scanner or Cameras folder in Control Panel. Since products are different from manufacturer to manufacturer, you'll need to follow the configuration instructions and operations issues for that particular device.
- Keep in mind for the exam that hardware profiles can be used to manage hardware on laptop computers when those computers are mobile.
- Although you can access pictures or start scanning features from the Scanners and Cameras folder, the manufacturer of the device often provides additional

applications that help you use and manage the device. Refer to the manufacturer's instructions for details.

Install, Configure, and Manage Modems

- ❑ Windows XP supports a wide variety of internal and external modems by many different manufacturers. Check the HCL for a complete list of supported modems.
- ❑ Modems are installed like any other hardware device. Plug-and-play modems can be automatically detected and installed, or you can use the Add Hardware Wizard if you are having problems. You use modems that connect to serial, USB, or even IrDA ports.
- ❑ Once the modem is installed, you can configure modem behavior using Phone and Modem Options in Control Panel. You'll see the option to configure Dialing Rules, Modem Setup, and Advanced Features.
- ❑ Under dialing rules, you can configure the way the modem dials numbers, depending on location. You can configure area code rules, calling cards, and additional calling features, such as whether or not to dial 1 in front of the number.
- ❑ On the Modems tab, you can install and remove modems from the computer and access modem properties. For modem properties, you can configure how the modem operates, such as speeds, flow control, parity, etc., and you can also update the driver.
- ❑ The Advanced tab enables you to configure and use telephony providers that are installed on the computer, as well as installing new ones. For some telephony providers listed on this tab, you can select them and click the Properties button to configure usage features.

Install, Configure, and Manage USB Devices

- ❑ USB enables you to connect multiple USB devices to a single USB port. Using a series of hubs, you can connect up to 127 devices to a single USB root hub.
- ❑ When USB devices are installed, they are automatically detected and installed by plug and play.

- ❑ You can connect up to seven devices to a single USB hub, one of those being an additional hub to which more devices can be connected. For this reason, the USB topology is often recognized as a branching star.
- ❑ USB hubs can either be self-powered or bus-powered hubs. Bus-powered hubs frequently do not have the power to handle many USB devices, such as cameras, disk drives, printers, and scanners. For this reason, the self-powered hub, which gets its power from an AC/DC outlet, is often a better choice.

Install, Configure, and Manage Infrared Data Association (IrDA) Devices and Other Wireless Devices

- ❑ Windows XP supports IEEE standards for wireless communication. This includes current standards for WWANS, WLANs, and even wireless personal area networks. IEEE standards govern wireless communications and determine how Windows XP handles different wireless communication protocols and methods.
- ❑ Windows XP supports the Infrared Data Association (IrDA) standard for infrared wireless communication. If a computer is outfitted with an IrDA port, Windows XP can automatically detect the presence of other wireless devices and display an icon in Control Panel.
- ❑ Windows XP supports IrDA features that enable file transfers using IrDA and digital picture transfers over IrDA.
- ❑ If an IrDA device was not originally installed on the computer, one can be added by using an external IrDA port. These external ports install like any other device, and plug and play can typically detect and set them up.

SELF TEST

The following questions will help you measure your understanding of the material presented in this chapter. Read all of the choices carefully, as there may be more than one correct answer. Choose all correct answers for each question.

Configure Keyboards, Mice, and Smart Card Readers

1. You want to install a new plug-and-play USB keyboard. You note that the keyboard is listed on the HCL as supported. What do you need to do to install the keyboard?

   A. Attach the keyboard to the USB port.

   B. Attach the keyboard to the USB port and run the Add Hardware Wizard.

   C. Attach the keyboard to the USB port, run the Add Hardware Wizard, and update the driver.

   D. Run the Add Hardware Wizard.

2. In your environment, you have a user who needs the Repeat Delay feature of the keyboard to function more slowly. Where can you configure this for the user?

   A. Keyboard properties, Speed tab

   B. Keyboard properties, Hardware tab

   C. Keyboard properties, Pointers tab

   D. Keyboard properties, Mouse tab

3. You have a user that needs to reverse the right and left keys of his mouse so that left-clicking opens item menus. Where can you make this change?

   A. Mouse properties, Buttons tab

   B. Mouse properties, Pointers tab

   C. Mouse properties, Pointer Options

   D. Mouse properties, Wheel

4. A certain user needs to be able to drag items on the desktop without holding down the left mouse key. What feature can you configure for the user on the Buttons tab of Mouse properties for the user?

   A. HoldLock

   B. ClickLock

C. Snap-To

D. DragLock

5. What kinds of files can be used for mouse pointers?

A. JPEG

B. CUR

C. ANI

D. BMP

6. A particular user is having problems managing the mouse pointer when trying to maneuver around a small portion of the screen. What setting can you use that may give the user more control over the mouse pointer?

A. ClickLock

B. Snap To

C. SlideLock

D. Enhanced pointer precision

7. A particular user scans many documents throughout the work day. The user likes to use the scroll wheel on her mouse, but the wheel moves very slowly. The user would like to be able to scroll through hundreds of pages easily, preferably, one page at the time with one wheel notch. How can you configure this?

A. Access Mouse properties, Pointer Options and change the pointer type to Wheel.

B. Access Mouse properties, Buttons tab and change the pointer type to Wheel.

C. Access Mouse properties, Wheel tab and change the option to One Screen At A Time.

D. Access Mouse properties, Hardware tab and change the option to One Screen At A Time.

Monitor, Configure, and Troubleshoot Multimedia Hardware, Such as Cameras and Handheld Devices

8. You need to install a PDA so that it can synchronize with your PC. What is the best way to install the PDA?

A. Run the Add Hardware Wizard.

B. Change the driver on the desired port.

C. Follow the manufacturer's instructions.

D. Configure a specific port.

9. You use a laptop computer at a docking station. The laptop also contains a PC card used for a digital video camera. When you traveling, you do not want to use the PC card. What is the easiest way to make the PC card available when you are docked and not available when you are traveling?

   A. Remove the driver when you are traveling.

   B. Use System Standby.

   C. Create a separate hardware profile.

   D. Create a separate user profile.

Install, Configure, and Manage Modems

10. You use a modem in your laptop computer and you have several locations configured, depending on how you need to use modem. For a particular location, the computer keeps dialing 1 in front of local numbers. You need to change this behavior. How can you change it?

    A. Access the Area Code Rule properties sheet and clear the Dial 1 option.

    B. Access the Area Code Rule properties sheet and clear the Treat All Numbers As Long Distance check box.

    C. Access the Area Code Rule properties sheet and include the area codes that are local.

    D. Access the Area Code Rule properties sheet and clear the Dial Properties check box.

11. In your environment, you need to access an outside line in order to make long-distance calls using your computer. Where can you configure this option?

    A. Access the Dialing Rules tab of Phone and Modem Options and click the check box option provided.

    B. Access the Edit Location from the Dialing Rules tab and enter the number for the outside line in the provided dialog box.

    C. Access the Edit Location from the Area Code Rules tab and enter the number for the outside line in the provided dialog box.

    D. Access the Edit Location from the Calling Card tab and enter the number for the outside line in the provided dialog box.

12. A particular user reports that several applications on his computer running Windows XP that send data to the modem seem to be having problems. What setting can you change to attempt to resolve this problem?

    A. Access Modem Properties, change the flow control setting on the General tab.

    B. Access Modem Properties, change the flow control setting on the Modem tab.

    C. Access Modem Properties, change the port speed setting on the General tab.

    D. Access Modem Properties, change the port speed setting on the Modem tab.

13. Consider the following settings on the Advanced Port Setting window. You want to make sure the modem is set for the best possible performance. What do you need to do here?

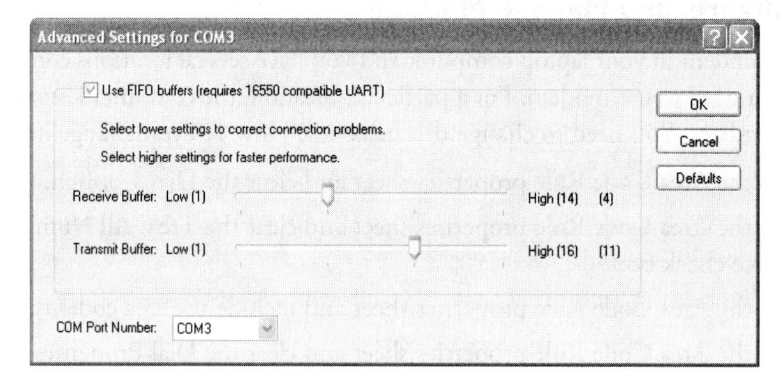

    A. Nothing—the options are set for best performance.

    B. Change both settings to High.

    C. Change both settings to Low.

    D. Change the Receive Buffer to High and the Transmit Buffer to Low.

14. You are transferring compressed files that were compressed with WinZip. You notice that transmission time is still slow. What can you try on the General Default Preferences tab, shown in the following illustration, to boost performance?

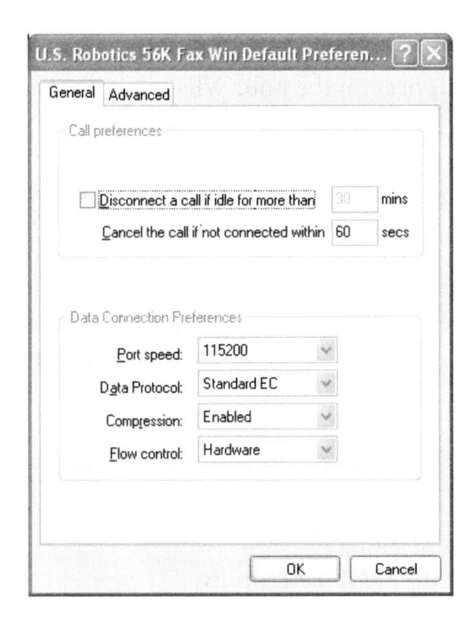

A. Change the Port Speed to 56,000 Kbps.
B. Change the Data Protocol to Forced EC.
C. Disable the Compression setting.
D. Change Flow Control to XON/XOFF.

15. A modem you are communicating with uses software flow control. You want your modem to be compatible. What flow control setting should you use?

A. None
B. Hardware
C. RTF
D. XON/XOFF

Install, Configure, and Manage USB Devices

16. What is the maximum number of USB devices you can have attached to a computer?

A. 7
B. 87
C. 127
D. 257

17. You are using a bus-powered hub for several USB devices. You want to see how much power is being consumed by the devices on the hub. Where can you gain this information?

A. Device Manager

B. Performance Monitor

C. Task Manager

D. System Information

18. You are using a bus-powered hub. You recently attached a digital camera to the hub, but you notice that the device does not work. All other devices seem to be working fine. What is the problem?

A. The camera is installed.

B. You need a self-powered hub.

C. The driver needs to be updated.

D. You need to run the USBCONF.EXE utility.

Install, Configure, and Manage Infrared Data Association (IrDA) Devices and Other Wireless Devices

19. What type of network uses GSM for wireless communication?

A. Wireless wide area network

B. Wireless metropolitan area network

C. Wireless local area network

D. Wireless personal area network

20. What wireless protocol is used for wireless printing?

A. Wireless FTP

B. IrLPT

C. IrTran-P

D. NetBEUI

21. Which wireless protocol is used for wireless digital image transfer?

A. Wireless FTP

B. IrLPT

C. IrTran-P

D. NetBEUI

22. You have a digital camera that you want to use to wireless transfer images over your computer's IrDA port. However, the option does not seem to work. All other IrDA communications are working. What do you need to so that the digital image transfer will work?

A. Update the IrDA port driver.

B. Enable the option on the Image Transfer tab of the Wireless Link's properties.

C. Enable IrTran-P on the Infrared tab of the Wireless Link's properties.

D. Install the multimedia protocols for the wireless link.

LAB QUESTION

You need to configure a certain computer in your Windows XP network so that the modem will function for some specialty needs. Considering the following requirements, how would you configure the modem?

- The configuration must have a dialing rule that accesses 9 for an outside line and makes the 817 area code local.
- The modem should use a maximum port speed of 57,600 Kbps.
- The modem should not use hardware compression.
- The modem should use software flow control.
- The modem should disconnect if it is idle for more than 15 minutes.
- The modem should use V.23 modulation.

SELF TEST ANSWERS

Configure Keyboards, Mice, and Smart Card Readers

1. ☑ A is correct. For most plug-and-play devices, all you need to do is attach the device to the USB port. Windows XP can automatically detect and install the keyboard.

   ☒ B, C, and D are incorrect. If you are having problems installing the device, you can use the Add Hardware Wizard. Under most cases, however, all you have to do is physically attach the device to the correct port, and Windows XP will handle everything else for you.

2. ☑ A is correct. You can change the repeat delay and repeat rate on the Speed tab of Keyboard properties.

   ☒ B, C, and D are incorrect. You can't configure anything on the Hardware tab, so B is incorrect. C and D are incorrect because there is no Mouse or Pointers tab on Keyboard properties.

3. ☑ A is correct. You can change the primary and secondary mouse buttons on the Buttons tab of Mouse properties.

   ☒ B, C, and D are incorrect. You cannot change the primary and secondary mouse buttons on any of these tabs.

4. ☑ B is correct. You can use the ClickLock feature to so that users can drag items on the desktop without having to hold down the left mouse key.

   ☒ A, C, and D are incorrect. None of these items are correct.

5. ☑ B and C are correct. Mouse pointer files can be animation or cursor files, which have the ANI or CUR extension, respectively.

   ☒ A and D are incorrect, because PEG and BMP files are picture files and cannot be used for mouse pointers.

6. ☑ D is correct. You can turn on Enhanced Pointer Precision, which is available under the Motion section of the Pointer Options tab on Mouse properties. This feature can give you more control when trying to navigate small areas with the mouse.

   ☒ A, B, and C are incorrect. None of these options will give you enhanced pointer control.

7. ☑ C is correct. You can change the wheel motion to One Screen At A Time on the Wheel tab of Mouse properties.

☒ A, B, and D are incorrect. You cannot change the wheel properties on any of these tabs.

Monitor, Configure, and Troubleshoot Multimedia Hardware, Such as Cameras and Handheld Devices

8. ☑ C is correct. The simplest answer is often the best. In the case of PDA connections, you typically attach the PDA to a serial, USB, or infrared port as instructed by the PDA documentation, and then you install software for synchronization to take place.

☒ A, B, and D are incorrect. These actions are not the best options for installing a PDA.

9. ☑ C is correct. You can create a separate hardware profile that disables the PC so that when you are traveling, the PC card is not available.

☒ A, B, and D are incorrect. None of these actions will disable the PC card.

Install, Configure, and Manage Modems

10. ☑ A is correct. You can simply access the area code rule and clear the Dial 1 check box. This will make the area code local.

☒ B, C, and D are incorrect. B and D are not real options on the Area Code Rule window. C is incorrect because you cannot include multiple area codes on this tab.

11. ☑ B is correct. You can access the Edit Location window from the Dialing Rules tab of Phone and Modem options. On the General tab, enter the number required to access an outside line for long distance, as shown in the following illustration.

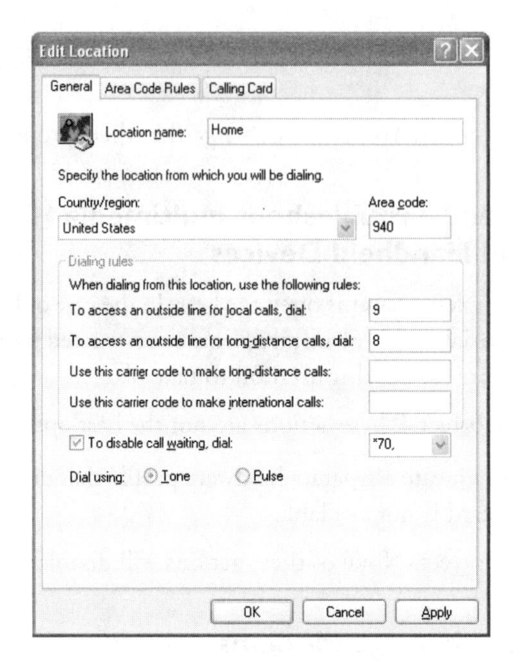

☒ A, C, and D are incorrect. You cannot configure the option on any of these tabs.

12. ☑ D is correct. You can reduce the port speed option on the Modem tab in order to try and resolve the problem.

    ☒ A, B, and C are incorrect. Flow control handles data transmission to other modems, not internal application transmissions, so A and C are incorrect. D is incorrect because you can only adjust port speed on the Modem tab.

13. ☑ B is correct. Both the Receive and Transmit Buffer settings should be set to High, unless there are connection problems, in which case you can try lower settings.

    ☒ A, C, and D are incorrect. These setting options will not give you the best performance.

14. ☑ C is correct. If you are transferring a lot of files that were compressed using software compression, such as WinZip, the hardware compression feature may actually slow down data transfer. Try turning off hardware compression to see if the problem is resolved.

    ☒ A, B, and D are incorrect. None of these options will meet the needs.

15. ☑ D is correct. XON/XOFF is software flow control. If the modem you are trying to communicate with is using software flow control, you can try this setting. Under most cases, however, hardware flow control is used.

    ☒ A, B, and C are incorrect. You cannot use software flow control with these settings.

Install, Configure, and Manage USB Devices

16. ☑ C is correct. Using a daisy chain of hubs, you can connect up to 127 devices to a USB interface.

☒ A, B, and D are incorrect. None of these numbers are correct.

17. ☑ A is correct. You can use Device Manager to access the properties of the root hub. Access the Power tab to find the information.

☒ B, C, and D are incorrect. You can't access the root hub's properties from any of these tools.

18. ☑ B is correct. If you attach a device to bus-powered hub that pulls too much power, the device will not work. In this case, you need to use a self-powered hub.

☒ A, C, and D are incorrect. You can tell from the question prompt that the device is installed, but it does not work; therefore, none of these solutions will solve the problem.

Install, Configure, and Manage Infrared Data Association (IrDA) Devices and Other Wireless Devices

19. ☑ A is correct. GSM, or Global System for Mobile Communications, is a wide area wireless technology used in many mobile phones and wireless networks.

☒ B, C, and D are incorrect. These types of networks do not use GSM.

20. ☑ B is correct. IrLPT enables wireless printing through IrDA.

☒ A, C, and D are incorrect. None of these answer options provide wireless printing.

21. ☑ C is correct. The IrTran-P protocol is used to wirelessly transfer digital photos from a camera to your computer.

☒ A, B, and D are incorrect. These protocols do not handle wireless digital photograph transfer.

22. ☑ A is correct. All protocols are available when the wireless link is installed. However, in order to enable digital image transfer over the wireless link, you need to enable the option on the Image Transfer tab of the Wireless Link's properties, as you can see in the following illustration.

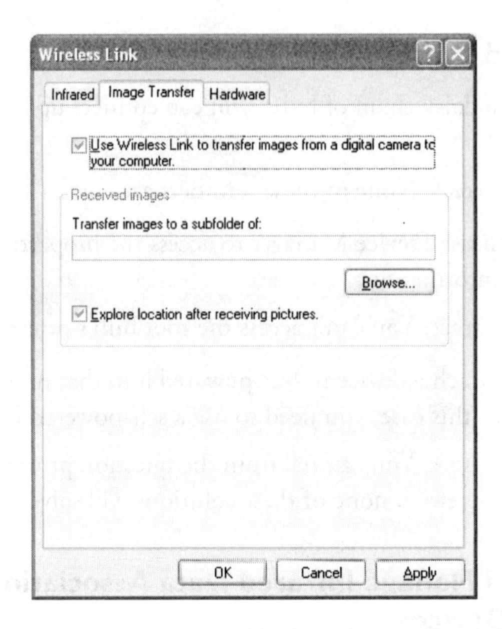

☒ B, C, and D are incorrect. You cannot enable digital image transfer in any of these ways.

LAB ANSWER

The lab question asked you to configure a modem to meet these specific requirements:

- The configuration must have a dialing rule that accesses 9 for an outside line and makes the 817 area code local that is dialed without 1.
- The modem should use a maximum port speed of 57,600 Kbps.
- The modem should not use hardware compression.
- The modem should use software flow control.
- The modem should disconnect if it is idle for more than 15 minutes.
- The modem should use V.23 modulation.

To configure the options, follow these steps:

1. Open Phone and Modem Options in Control Panel.
2. On the Dialing Rules tab, click New.
3. On the New Location window, give the new location a name. In the To Access An Outside Line For Local Calls, Dial dialog box, shown in the following illustration, enter **9**. Enter the current area code in the provided dialog box.

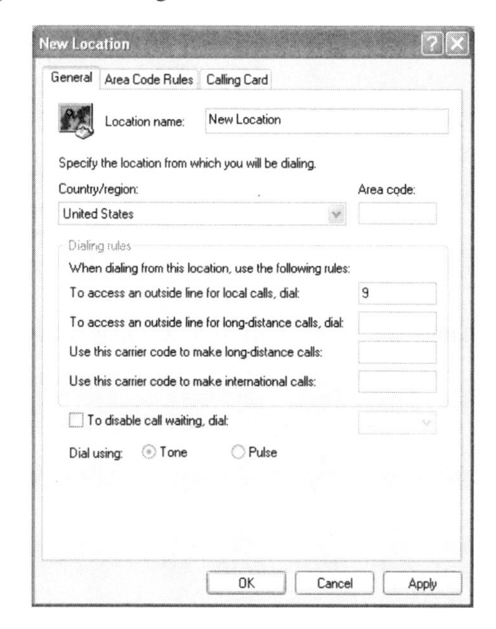

4. Click the Area Code Rules tab.
5. Click New. In the New Area Code window, enter **817** for the area code. At the bottom of the window, click the Include The Area Code check box, shown in the following illustration. Click OK and OK again.

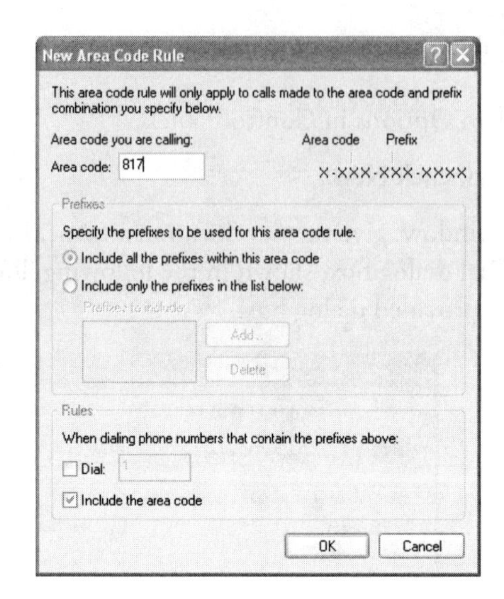

6. Click the Modems tab. Click Properties.
7. On the Modem tab, change the Port Speed to 57,600, as shown in the following illustration.

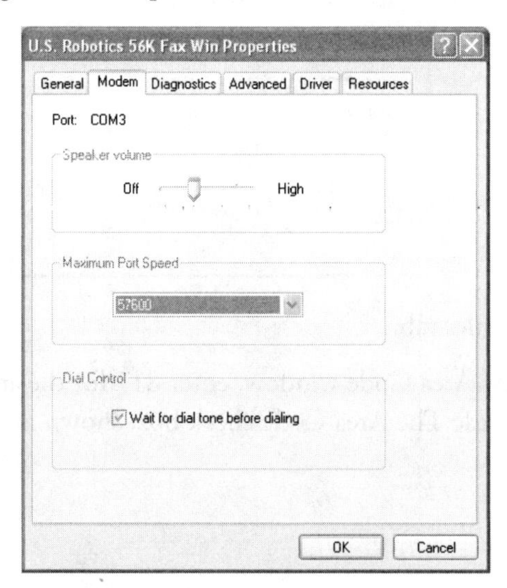

8. Click the Advanced tab and click Change Default Preferences.
9. On the General tab, change the following settings, as shown in the following illustration.

- Click the Disconnect A Call If Idle For More Than option and enter **15** in the dialog box.
- Change the compression setting to Disabled.
- Change the Flow Control setting to XON/XOFF.

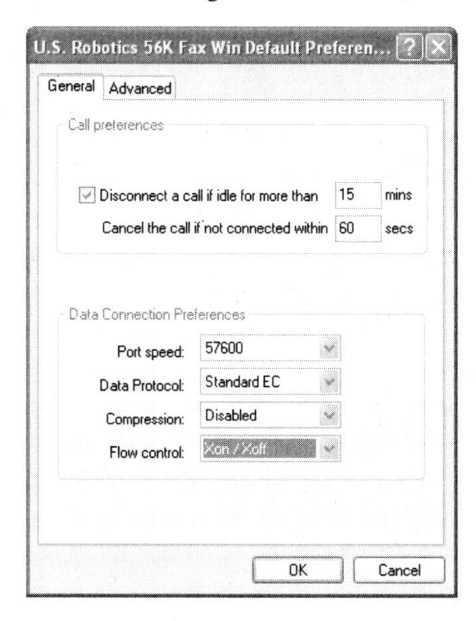

10. Click the Advanced tab. Change the Modulation type to V.23.

11. Click OK and OK again to save your changes.

a. Check the Disconnect a Call If Idle For More Than [illegible]

b. Change the Compression setting to Disabled.

c. Change the Flow Control setting to XON/XOFF.

[illegible]

[illegible]

7

Configuring Disk Drives and Volumes

CERTIFICATION OBJECTIVES

- 7.01 Configure NTFS, FAT, and FAT32 File Systems
- 7.02 Monitor and Configure Disks
- 7.03 Monitor and Configure Disk Volumes
- ✓ Two-Minute Drill
- Q&A Self Test

Windows XP Professional supports the same disk tools and volume technologies that were first introduced with Windows 2000. As operating system drives and storage have grown during the past several years, the need to effectively configure drives and use appropriate file systems is very important. Only a few years ago, common desktop computers featured a 50MB hard drive—today, drives in excess of 50GB are not at all uncommon. After all, the data stored in today's electronic world requires more space, and the management of that space and that data has become more critical.

As an IT professional, you will be expected to configure and manage hard drives under Windows XP Professional. Fortunately, with the tools and configuration options provided by Windows XP Professional, that job does not have to be a difficult task. In this chapter, you will explore file systems, drive management, and Windows XP volume configuration.

CERTIFICATION OBJECTIVE 7.01

Configure NTFS, FAT, and FAT32 File Systems

Windows XP Professional supports the NTFS, FAT, and FAT32 file systems. This means that Windows XP Professional can have drives configured with these operating systems and can read drives configured with these operating systems. During the installation of Windows XP Professional (which is explored in Chapter 1 of this book), you have the option to choose a desired file system, so for starters you should have a firm understanding of the features and limitations of each file system.

Understanding FAT and NTFS

Before looking at file systems, though, we should review the basics. First off, hard drives are typically installed in a computer in an unformatted state. This means that the operating system is unable to write and read data from the hard disk. Think of an unformatted hard disk as a filing cabinet with no file folders. Without file folders, there is no way to organize and store information on the hard disk. So, in order to use the hard disk, Windows XP Professional must write a signature to the hard disk and format it with a file system so that it can read and write to that disk.

When the hard disk is formatted, magnetic rings are created on the disk and the disk divided into circular areas called *sectors.* Sectors are then grouped together in *clusters,* which are logical areas of the disk that the operating system uses to write data to. How the operating system handles cluster size will affect the amount of disk storage space lost on cluster size configuration.

on the Job

When formatting the disk, the operating system writes a file system to the disk, which is a way to organize and manage data on that disk. The File Allocation Table (FAT) file system has been around for a number of years and currently offers 32-bit support. FAT (technically FAT16) is a basic file system that was designed to support small disks. Under Windows XP Professional, the FAT16 file system can grow up to 4GB in size and support file sizes up to 2GB. In other words, 4GB is maximum amount of cluster storage space and management functionality that FAT16 provides. This amount, of course, is too small in today's computing environments.

exam Watch

FAT16 is supported on Windows 3.1 and higher Microsoft operating systems. Under most circumstances, FAT16 would never be used on a Windows XP Professional operating system (or even relatively recent systems, such as Windows 98) unless you needed to dual-boot with an older operating system, such as Windows 3.1 and the original version of Windows 95. Considering the age of these operating systems, however, that scenario is unlikely.

FAT32 is significantly different from FAT16 in several ways. First available for Windows 95b, FAT32 supports larger hard drives and smaller file clusters. In other words, you can make use of a large hard drive while simultaneously conserving disk space by virtue of the small cluster size. There is less wasted room on the hard disk than when FAT16 is used. FAT32 supports 32GB drives. For these reasons, FAT32 is the operating system of choice for Windows 95b, Windows 98, and Windows Me operating systems.

The final operating system supported is NTFS, which is the preferred operating system for Windows XP Professional. NTFS has been around since the earlier days of Windows NT, but the new version, first supported in Windows 2000 (NTFS v5), provides additional features and functions. NTFS supports up to two terabytes of data, which is a theoretical level, since hard disks are not yet capable of supporting that much data. Essentially, there are no limitations with NTFS in terms of drive size, but that is only the beginning. NTFS also supports many features that are not available under the FAT (16 or 32) file system. The primary features of NTFS are as follows:

- **NTFS Security** NTFS supports both folder level and file level security. You can individually configure files and folders with their own security features, as well as individual security settings for users. Because of file attribute settings, you can finely control security.
- **Encryption** NTFS natively supports data encryption. You can encrypt a folder so that it cannot be read by someone else yet continue to use the data in that folder as normal (see Chapter 9).
- **Compression** NTFS natively supports data compression. This feature reduces the amount of disk space needed in order to store data, but allows you to continue using data as you normally would (see Chapter 9). However compression and encryption cannot be applied to the same file or folder.
- **Logging** NTFS maintains a disk log that holds information about the functioning of the NTFS file system. In the event of a hard disk crash, the log can be helpful in recovering and repairing data.

With these features, along with the unlimited amount of storage space available, it is easy to see why NTFS is the file system of choice for Windows XP Professional computers. The next obvious question: why ever use FAT? Although NTFS is the best file system and contains numerous features not found in FAT, there are some reasons that FAT may be needed.

The first and foremost reason concerns dual-boot systems. Windows 9*x* and Me do not support the NTFS file system. So, if you want to dual boot between Windows 9*x*/Me and Windows XP Professional, the Windows 9*x*/Me system will not be able to read any data on the Windows XP Professional partition. In dual-boot cases, it is usually best to find the common file system for the two operating systems, and in this case that is FAT32.

One other reason concerns small hard drives. NTFS has a complex structure with some overhead associated with it, so drives that are 2GB are smaller are best used with FAT. NTFS consumes too much disk space in overhead on such small drives and simply does not work that great. Under most circumstances, of course, you'll not be using drives smaller than 2GB, with the exception of floppy disks, but it is an important point to remember, and issues like this always make good exam fodder.

Formatting and Converting Drives

During the installation of Windows XP Professional, you can choose the operating system that you want to use. However, things change and from time to time, and you may need to change the file system that is used on a particular Windows XP Professional computer. There are two simple rules about formatting and converting drives that you should memorize:

- You can convert a FAT or FAT32 drive to NTFS while preserving your data. The exercise coming up in this section shows you how. Conversion is a one-way process, however. Once you convert to NTFS, you cannot revert back to FAT.
- You cannot convert an NTFS drive to FAT or FAT32 without reformatting the drive. This means that all of your data on the hard disk will be destroyed during the formatting process. You will have to restore all of the data from backup.

As you can see, the exam objective that says "convert from one file system to another" is somewhat of a misnomer. You can only convert to NTFS—you cannot convert from NTFS to anything. You have to reformat in order change an NTFS drive to FAT. To learn more about formatting drives, see the next section.

Exercise 7-1 shows you how to convert a FAT drive to an NTFS drive.

EXERCISE 7-1

CertCam 7-1

Converting a FAT Drive to an NTFS Drive

To convert a FAT drive to an NTFS drive, just follow these steps:

1. Click Start | Run. Type **command** and click OK.
2. At the command prompt, you will use the Convert command to convert the FAT drive to NTFS. Keep in mind that the conversion process is completely safe, and all of your data is will remain as it is. The command and syntax is **convert *driveletter:* /FS:NTFS**. For example, in the following illustration, I am converting drive D to NTFS.

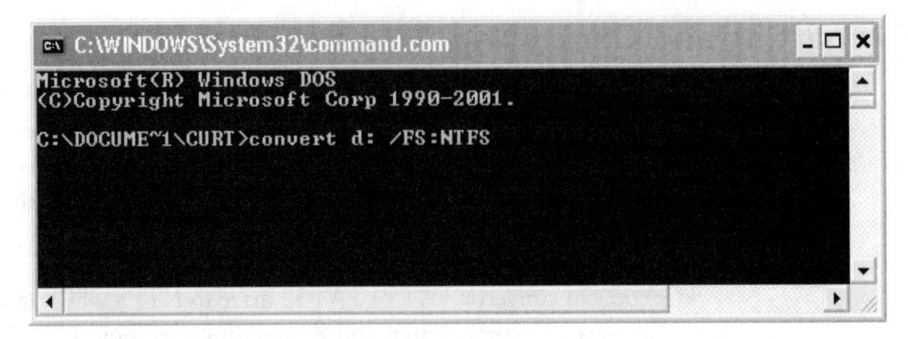

3. Conversion may take several minutes, depending on the size of the drive. When the process is complete, simply exit the command interface. If you converted the boot partition, you will be prompted to reboot the computer.

Although the conversion process is safe and effective, volumes that are converted lack some of the performance benefits of drives that were initially formatted with NTFS. Also, the Master File Table is different on converted volumes, which also somewhat affects performance. Still, conversion is the easiest way to change a FAT drive to NTFS without reformatting and having to restore data currently held on the FAT volume.

SCENARIO & SOLUTION	
I have a 40GB hard drive, and I am interested in using two different partitions. Which file system should I use?	NTFS. FAT will not make the best use of drives of this size, so there is no reason to use the FAT file system.
In a computer that dual boots between Windows 98 and Windows XP Professional, can I use both FAT and NTFS and have a common partition formatted with FAT where data is stored?	This is a possible alternative, but do keep in mind that any data stored on the NTFS partition will be inaccessible by the Windows 98 computer. Depending on your needs, however, this common drive option may be very effective.

CERTIFICATION OBJECTIVE 7.02

Monitor and Configure Disks

Windows 2000 introduced several new disk technologies to Windows and made the configuration and management of hard disks much easier than it has been in the past. You can configure, reconfigure, and adjust hard disk settings without rebooting, and you can make a number of changes that were once only available if you chose to reformat the disk.

The same capabilities are available in Windows XP Professional. You can access the disk management console through Computer Management, which is available in Start | Control Panel | Administrative Tools | Computer Management. Select Disk Management in the left console pane, as shown in Figure 7-1, and you can see the disks and their configuration in the right console pane.

The following sections explore some of the major disk management features you should be aware of for the exam.

FIGURE 7-1

Selecting Disk Management

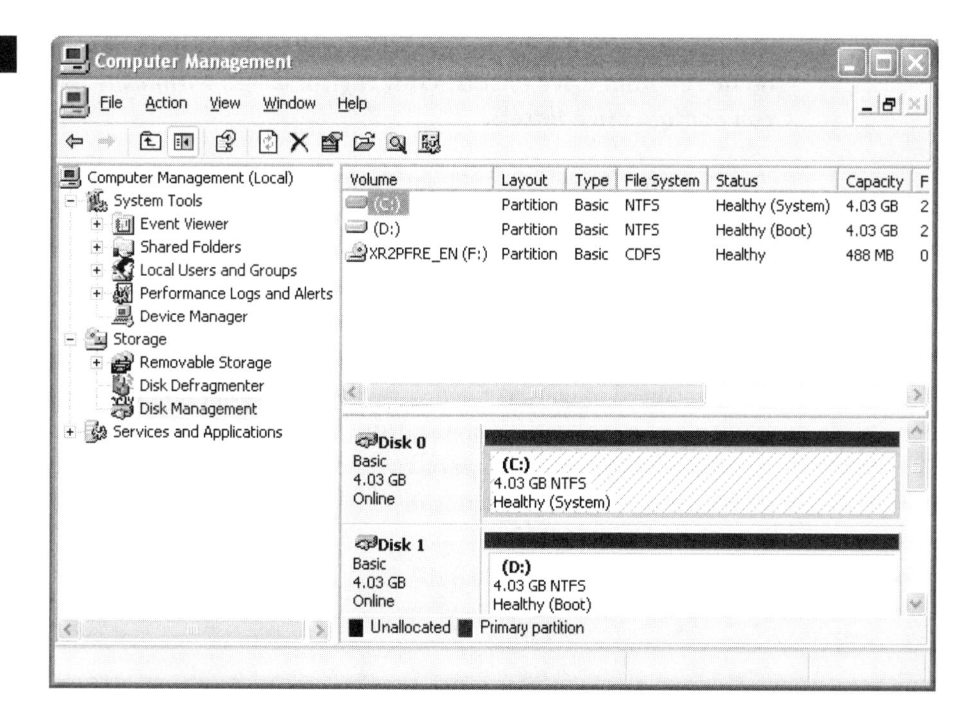

Basic and Dynamic Disks

Windows XP Professional, like Windows 2000, continues to support basic and dynamic disks, and it is important to define the two types. *Basic disks* are the same kinds of disks that we have always worked with in the past and are the standard hard disks that support standard configuration. A basic disk can have a primary partition and extended partitions that make up logical disk drives. For example, you can configure a basic disk so that it has a C drive (primary) and a D drive (extended). You can use the D drive for storage or other purposes (or to set up a dual-boot configuration). On a basic disk, you can have up to four primary partitions or alternative configurations, such as three primary partitions and one extended partition. One of the primary partitions is considered active and is used to start the computer. In other words, this active partition contains your boot files and the master boot record. Basic disks behave as disks have in the past and do not provide the advanced management features supported under Windows XP Professional. Disks are always basic when first installed, but you can convert them to dynamic in order to take advantage of all Windows XP Professional has to offer.

exam Watch

Keep in mind that on basic disks extended partitions are "logical" partitions—they are a logical organization of an existing partition. For this reason, they do not contain drive letters. Only logical drives within the extended partition can contain drive letters.

A *dynamic disk*, which is supported only on Windows 2000 and XP systems at this time, is a drive configured by the Disk Management console so that it can support volume management. In other words, the Disk Management utilities configure the drive so that it can make use of Windows XP Professional's disk management features, such as unlimited volumes and spanned volumes. In essence, if you want to take advantage of volume management and avoid the partition restrictions placed on basic disks, you need to convert the disk to a dynamic disk. If not, there are no performance features associated with dynamic disks, so there are no reasons to convert. However, if you want to take advantage of volume management, then you can easily convert your existing drives to dynamic disks by following the steps in Exercise 7-2.

EXERCISE 7-2

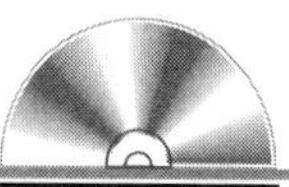

Converting a Basic Disk to a Dynamic Disk

To convert a basic disk to a dynamic disk, just follow these steps:

1. In Disk Management, right-click the Disk number is the graphical portion of the Disk Management display and click Convert to Dynamic Disk. You can also click Action | All Tasks | Convert to Dynamic Disk.
2. In the Convert to Dynamic Disk window, shown in the following illustration, select the disk that you want to convert and click OK.

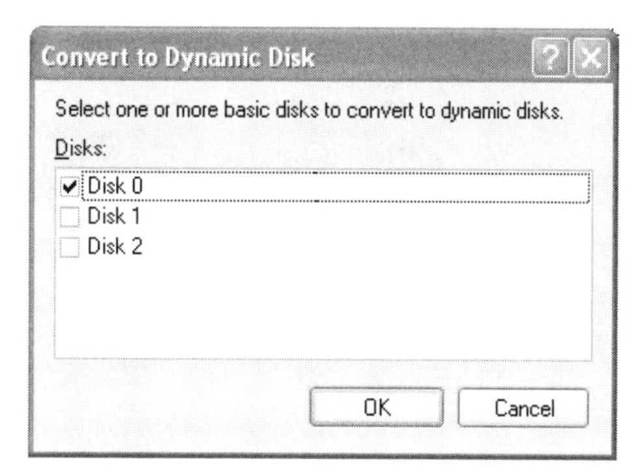

3. In the Disks to Convert window, review the settings, as shown in the following illustration. Click Convert to continue.

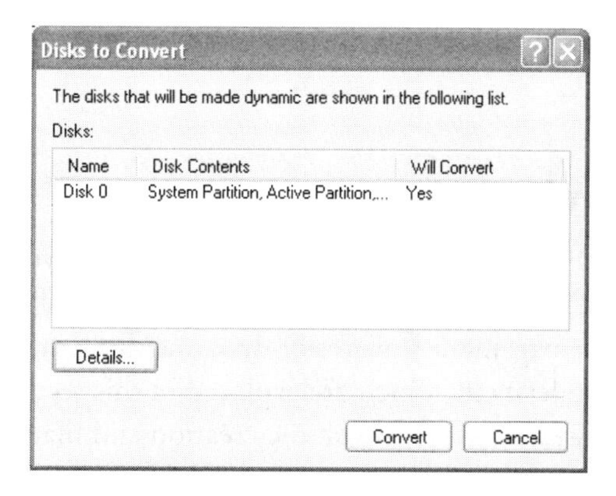

4. You will see a message telling you that other operating systems will not be able to start from the disk once the conversion has taken place (this means all other operating systems such as NT, 9*x*, and Me). Click OK to continue.
5. You may see a message telling you that any mounted disks will need to be dismounted. Click OK to continue.
6. The conversion process occurs, and you are prompted to reboot the computer. Once you reboot, you can see that the disk's status has changed from basic to dynamic, as shown in the following illustration:

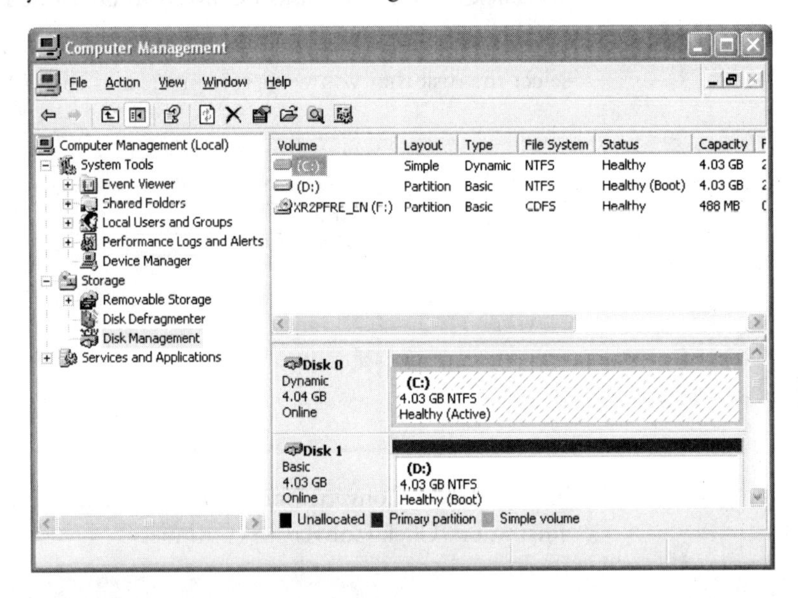

Using Dynamic Disks

Once a basic disk has been converted to a dynamic disk, you can begin taking advantage of the features of dynamic disks. First of all, there are a number of monitoring and management features of dynamic disks that you should be able to interpret and understand, which are explored in this section. Your primary work with dynamic disks, however, is volume creation and management, which you can explore in the next section.

Dynamic Disk States

Dynamic disks are capable of displaying several different states. This information tells you the current status of the disk and helps you understand problems that may exist. The following bullet lists explains the states that a dynamic disk may display:

- **Online** The disk is online and functioning with no errors.
- **Online (Errors)** The disk is online, but there have been some errors. These errors are usually minor and can be fixed by running the Error Checking tool found on the Tools menu of the disk's properties.
- **Offline** The disk is not accessible. This problem can be due to corruption or an I/O problem. Try right-clicking the disk and clicking Reactivate Disk in order to bring the disk back online.
- **Missing** The disk is not accessible or disconnected, or corruption has caused the disk to not be readable. Try right-clicking the disk and clicking Reactive Disk in order to bring the disk back online.
- **Initializing** This message occurs when the disk is temporarily unavailable because of a conversion to dynamic state.
- **Not Initialized** This message means that the disk does not have a valid signature and occurs when you install a new disk. When the Disk Management utility appears, the disk appears as Not Initialized. To write a valid signature so that you can format and begin using the disk, simply right-click the disk and click Initialize.
- **Foreign** This status appears when a physical, dynamic disk is moved from a Windows 2000/XP Professional computer to another Windows 2000/XP Professional computer. When this message appears, right-click the disk and click Import Foreign Disk.
- **Unreadable** This status appears when I/O errors keep the disk from being readable. Access Action | Rescan Disks to fix the problem.
- **No Media** This status appears on removable drives when no media is inserted into the drive.

exam watch

You should have the different disk states and the actions you should take memorized for the exam.

Configuring Drive Letters and Paths

Windows XP makes drive letter and path configuration easy. You can assign a drive any alphabet letter, and you can also assign a drive to an empty NTFS folder. First of all, if you want to make a change to a dynamic disk volume, simply right-click the volume in the Disk Management console and click Change Drive Letter and Paths. A simple Change Drive Letter and Paths window appears, as you can see in Figure 7-2.

You can do the following actions:

- **Add** If you click the Add button, a second window appears where you can mount the drive to an empty NTFS folder (which is discussed later in this section). Since a drive can only have one drive letter, you cannot assign multiple drive letters for the same drive.
- **Change** If you click the Change button, the Change Drive Letter Or Path window appears, as you can see in Figure 7-3. You can choose a different drive letter from the drop-down menu.
- **Remove** You can also remove the drive letter. Dynamic Disks do not require that a drive be identified by a drive letter or path. However, some programs may not function if you remove the drive letter, and you will not be able to access the drive

Besides assigning a different drive letter, you can also mount a volume to a local, empty NTFS folder. The purpose of this is to give you freedom and flexibility beyond the 26-letter alphabet limitation. When you mount a volume to an empty NTFS folder, a drive path is used instead of a drive number. For example, let's say that you have a local volume that is only used for storage. You could create a folder called

FIGURE 7-2

Change Drive Letter And Paths for the C drive

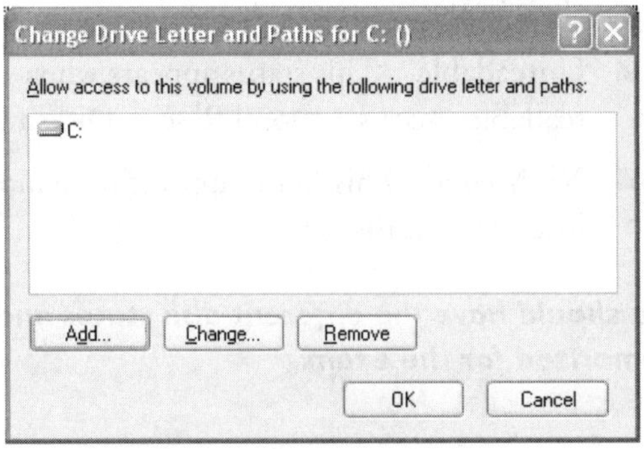

FIGURE 7-3

The Change Drive Letter Or Path window

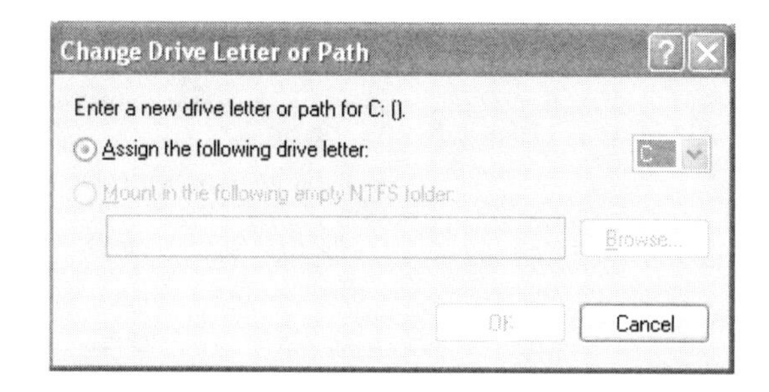

Storage and mount the drive to the empty storage volume. You can then access the drive by simply accessing C:\Storage, just as you would a folder. The end result is that you can have an unlimited number of drives and use them like folders rather than having standard drive letters that you must keep track of. You can use both a drive letter and a mounted volume on the same drive, it you like.

exam Watch

Keep in mind that the drive must be mounted to an empty folder. Once the mount takes place, you can move data to that folder in order to store it on the volume. Also, remember that the folder must be on an NTFS volume—not FAT.

To configure a mounted volume, follow the steps in Exercise 7-3.

EXERCISE 7-3

CertCam 7-3

Mounting a Drive to an Empty NTFS Folder

To mount a drive to an empty NTFS folder, just follow these steps:

1. In the Disk Management window, right-click the volume that you want to mount to an empty NTFS folder and click Change Drive Letter And Paths.
2. In the Change Drive Letter And Paths window, click the Add button.
3. In the Add Drive Letter Or Path window, shown in the following illustration, select the Mount radio button and then enter the path to the folder that you want to mount, or click the Browse button to select the folder.

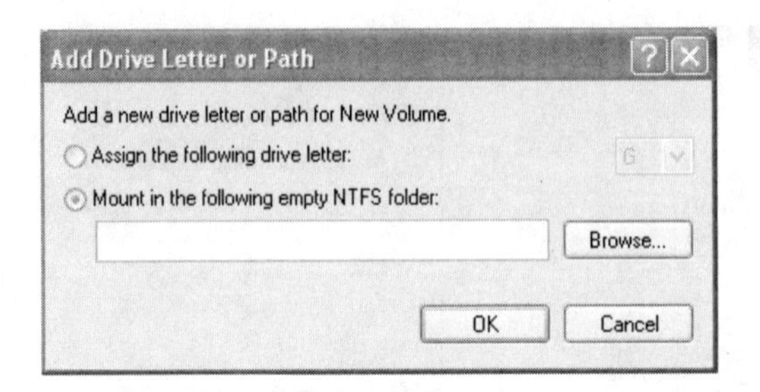

4. If you Browse for the folder, a browse window appears, shown in the following illustration. You can locate the folder or create a new one by clicking the New Folder button. Make your selection and click OK.

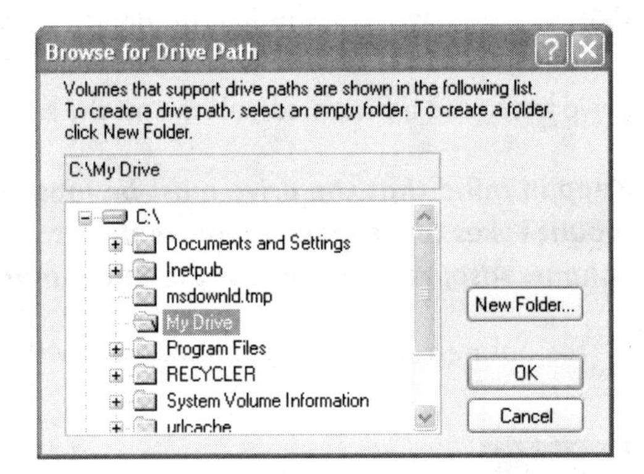

5. Click OK again on the Add Drive Letter Or Path window.

SCENARIO & SOLUTION	
If a disk is displayed as "Online (Errors)," what is the problem?	"Online (Errors)" means that the disk is functioning, but minor errors have been detected. These are typically file system errors and nothing critical. You can run the Error Checking tool to correct them.
What is the benefit of mounting a drive to an empty NTFS folder if the drive already has a drive letter?	The benefit with this type of configuration is that you can access the drive with a common name instead of drive letter. This can be helpful on computers where there are many volumes in use for different purposes. Instead of remembering what drive letter is for what drive, you can simply remember a folder name, which can be descriptive of the volume's purpose.

CERTIFICATION OBJECTIVE 7.03

Monitor and Configure Disk Volumes

Volumes are the lifeblood of dynamic disks. Using dynamic disks, you open a world of management possibilities and lose the restrictions you often face with basic disks. When a disk is first converted to a dynamic disk, it will appear in the disk console as unallocated space. This means that the disk has no volumes and has not been formatted. In other words, the disk is not usable by the operating system in its current state. Figure 7-4 shows you the appearance of an unallocated disk.

Creating Simple Volumes

In order to use the disk, you must first create a simple volume on the disk. Exercise 7-4 guides you through this process.

FIGURE 7-4

Dynamic disk with unallocated space

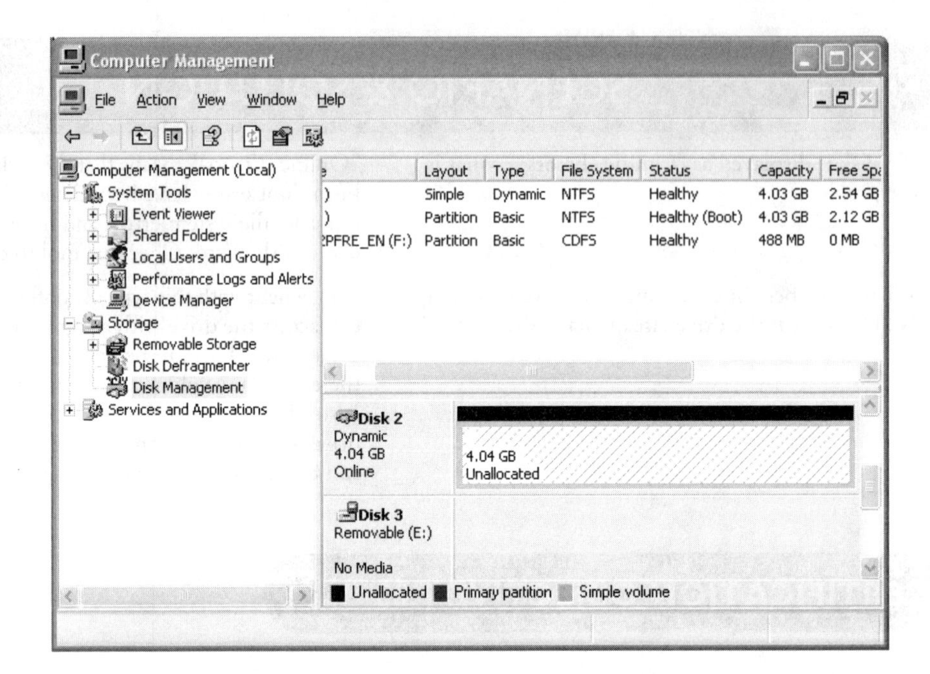

EXERCISE 7-4

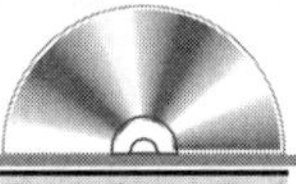

Creating a Simple Volume

To create simple volume, just follow these steps:

1. In the Disk Management console, right-click the Dynamic disk's unallocated space and click New Volume.
2. The New Volume wizard appears. Click Next to continue.
3. In the Select Volume Type window, shown in the following illustration, click the Simple radio button and click Next.

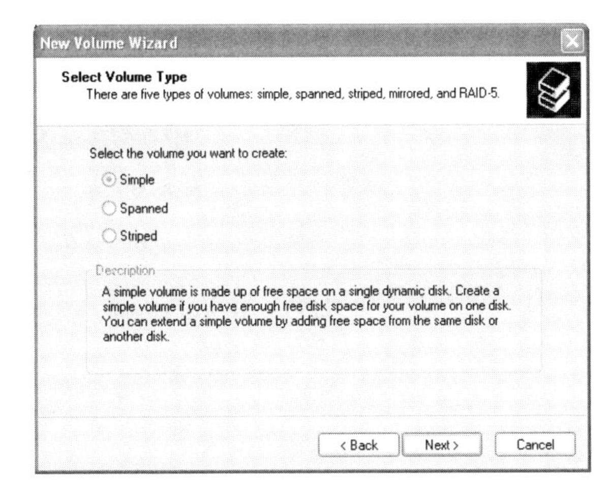

4. In the Select Disks window, shown in the following illustration, select the disk that you want to configure (which is already selected for you under this wizard) and then enter the size of the volume (in megabytes) that you want to create. The maximum amount of space available is listed here for you as well. Click Next.

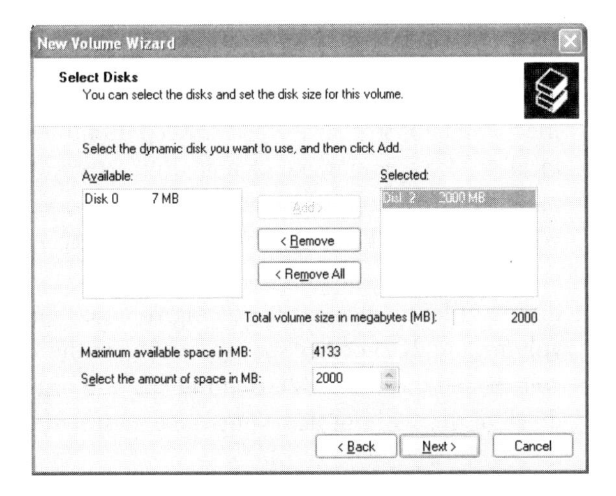

5. In the Assign Drive Letter or Path window, choose a drive, assign an empty NTFS folder, or do not assign either. Click Next.

6. In the Format Volume window, shown in the following illustration, you can choose to format the volume or not, and you can choose to use the quick

format feature and enable file and folder compression for the volume. Make your selections and click Next.

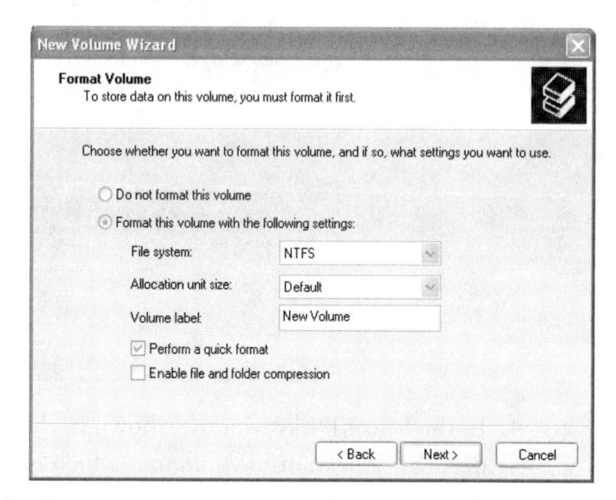

7. Click Finish. The new volume is created and appears in the Disk Management window.

Once the dynamic volume has been created and formatted, you can begin using the volume for storage purposes. Keep in mind that you can right-click the volume in Disk Management and change drive letters and paths, extend the volume (adds more free space to it), format the volume (erases all existing data), or delete the volume (erases all existing data), as well as access the volume's properties.

If you want to extend the volume, you select another area of free space on the same disk in order to enlarge the existing volume. For example, let's say you have a 10GB volume and 2GB of free space available on the same disk. You can extend the 10GB volume and include the 2GB of free space in order to create a 12GB volume. You can do all of this without damaging the data stored on the original 10GB volume.

Creating Spanned Volumes

Besides the simple volume, Windows XP Professional also supports spanned volumes. A spanned volume combines areas of unallocated space on multiple disks into one logical volume. You can combine between 2 and 32 areas of unallocated space from different drives. For example, let's say that a computer has three hard drives. On each drive there is about 500MB of unallocated free space. A 500MB volume is rather small and not very practical for everyday use. However, using the spanned volume option, you can combine all three 500MB areas of unallocated space to create a 1.5GB volume. You can then use the volume, just as though the storage was located on a single disk. Essentially, this configuration gives you more flexibility and fewer volumes (and drive letters to keep up) and makes good use of leftover space.

Once the spanned volume has been created, you see it as any other volume in My Computer or Disk Management. It is important to note, however, that spanned volumes are storage solutions only—they do not provide any fault tolerance. If one disk in the spanned volume is lost, all data on the spanned volume is lost. However, you can back up a spanned volume just as you would any other volume.

exam Watch

Remember for the exam that a spanned volume is a storage solution—not a fault tolerant solution.

Exercise 7-5 shows you how to create a spanned volume.

EXERCISE 7-5

CertCam 7-5

Creating a Spanned Volume

To create spanned volume, just follow these steps:

1. In the Disk Management console, right-click one of the areas of unallocated disk space on one of the disks and click New Volume.
2. The New Volume wizard appears. Click Next to continue.
3. In the Select Volume Type window, shown in the following illustration, click the Spanned option, and then click Next.

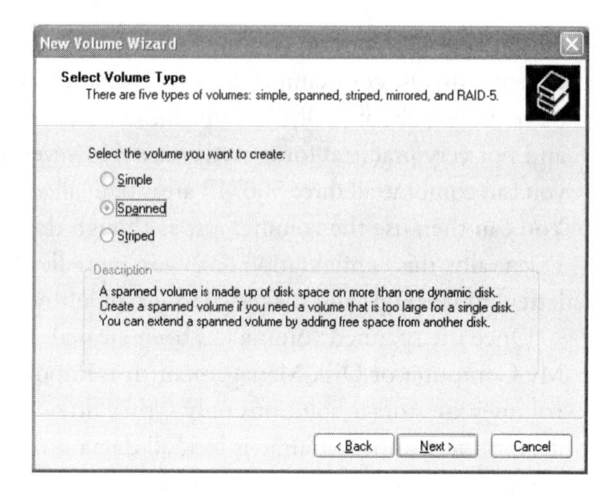

4. In the Select Disks window, the current disk appears in the selected dialog box. Choose the free space on the desired disks that appear on the Available window and click the Add button. Repeat the process until all unallocated areas that you want to use appear in the Selected box. Click Next.
5. In the Assign Drive Letter or Path window, choose a drive letter or mount the drive to an empty NTFS folder. You can also choose not to assign a drive letter or path at this time. Click Next.
6. In the Format Volume window, choose whether or not to format the volume at the time and whether or not to perform a quick format and enable file and folder compression. Click Next.
7. Click Finish. The volume is created and now appears in the Disk Management console.

---

exam Watch

As with a simple volume, you can extend a spanned volume by adding more unallocated space to it. Simply right-click the volume in Disk Management and click Extend Volume. Follow the wizard steps that appear to add more unallocated space. Also, keep in mind that you cannot reclaim a portion of disk space once it has been added to a spanned volume without deleting the entire spanned volume—once you are in the club, you are there to stay!

Creating Striped Volumes

Striped volumes are similar to spanned volumes in that they combine areas of free disk space (between 2 and 32 areas of unallocated space on different drives) in order to create one logical volume. However, the big difference is that striped volumes write data across the disks instead of filling one portion of free space first, then the next portion, and so on. The big difference is that you are likely to see faster read and write performance than you will with a simple spanned volume. As with a spanned volume, you can create a striped volume by right-clicking one of the areas of unallocated space and clicking Create Volume. In the Create New Volume wizard, choose to create a striped volume and follow the same steps that appeared in Exercise 7-5.

Another important point concerning striped volumes is that the areas of unallocated free space must be the same size. For example, let's say that you want to use 500MB, 800MB, and 900MB areas of unallocated disk space to create a striped set. Since the areas have to be the same size, Disk Management will configure 500MB from each disk, which means that you will still have some unallocated space left over. This configuration enables data to be written evenly across the disks.

exam watch

A striped volume provides no fault tolerance, but it does provide better performance than a spanned volume.

About Fault Tolerance

Windows XP Professional does not support any kind of disk fault tolerance, unlike Windows 2000/.NET server. The exam may try to trick you on this point, so it is important for you to understand the two types of fault tolerance supported under Windows 2000/.NET server. When you see these options on the exam, you'll know that Windows 2000/.NET server provides support for these features, but they are not available on Windows XP (or Windows 2000 Professional for that matter).

The first type of fault tolerance supported by Windows 2000/.NET server is disk mirroring. Disk mirroring (also called RAID 1), which is supported on dynamic disks in Windows 2000 Server, requires two physical disks. When a disk mirror is configured, one disk volume maintains an exact copy of the first disk. In the event that one of the disks fails, you always have a redundant copy. The good feature of disk mirroring is that you have a redundant disk copy that can be easily used in the event that a single disk failure occurs. The bad news about disk mirroring is the megabyte cost. Since you are maintaining an exact copy of a volume, everything you save requires much storage space as it normally would. Still, for critical servers that must be up and running quickly, disk mirroring is a great choice.

The second type of fault tolerance supported under Windows 2000/.NET server is RAID-5 volumes. RAID stands for Redundant Array of Inexpensive Disks, and it is a standard that uses three or more dynamic disks in order to store data. Using a parity bit, which is a mathematical accuracy check, data is written across the disks in stripe fashion. Should a single disk fail, then the data can be regenerated from the remaining disks. You can use up to 32 physical drives for a RAID-5 volume, but RAID-5 volumes cannot hold the system or boot partition.

exam Watch

Remember, disk mirroring and RAID-5 volumes are not supported under Windows XP Professional.

Managing Remote Disks

Using Disk Administrator, you can also manage remote disks on Windows XP Professional computers. This feature enables you to manage disks on other Windows XP Professional computers in a Windows domain. In order to access disk management on other Windows XP Professional computers, you must be a member of at least the domain administrators group or the server operators group. In a workgroup environment, you can also remotely manage disks by having the same administrative account name on the computers that you wish to manage. Exercise 7-6 shows how to manage a disk remotely.

EXERCISE 7-6

CertCam 7-6

Managing Disks on a Remote Computer

To manage a disk on a remote computer, just follow these steps:

1. Log on to the Windows XP Professional with the proper permissions.
2. Click Start | Run and type **MMC**. Click OK.
3. In the MMC that appears, click Console | Add/Remove Snap-In.
4. In the Snap-ins window, click Add and select Disk Management from the selection list. Click Add.

5. In the Select Computer window that appears, shown in the following illustration, choose a different computer and then enter the computer's name (or browse and select it). Click Finish.

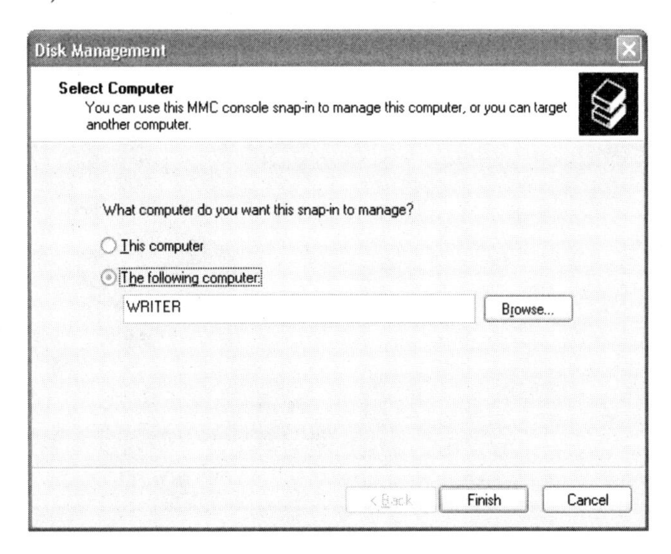

6. Click Close on the Snap-in list window and click OK to begin using the Disk Management snap-in.

Using Disk Properties

Each disk contains properties pages that you can use to configure different aspects of the disk. Most of the items found on the disk properties pages are rather easy to understand, but they are important for both your real world work and for the exam. You can access a disk's properties pages by right-clicking the disk in Disk Management and clicking properties, or you can right-click the disk and click properties in My Computer. The following sections explore the features that are available to you.

General Tab

The General tab, shown in Figure 7-5, gives you a quick way to view information about the disk, such as disk type, file system, used space, and free space. You can also launch the Disk Cleanup wizard here, which inspects the drive for items that can possibly

FIGURE 7-5

The General tab

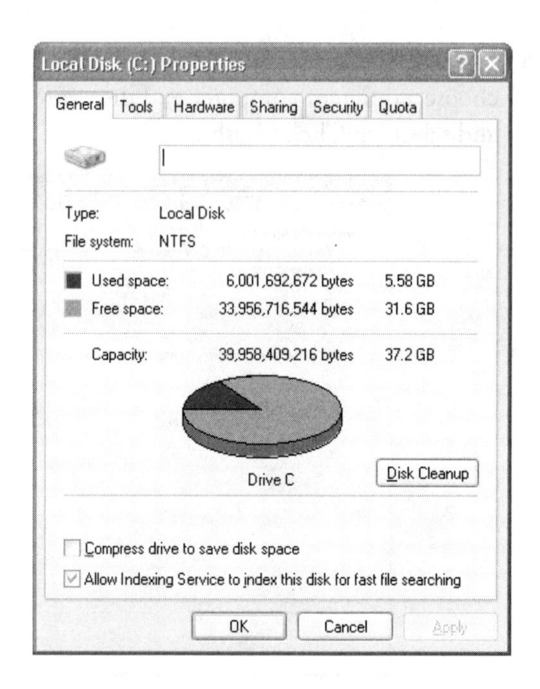

be deleted in order to free up space on the disk. Notice at the bottom of the window that you can compress the entire disk in order to conserve space, and you can index the drive so that searches work better and faster. See Chapter 9 to learn more about disk compression.

Tools Tab

The Tools tab gives you three different tools that you can use to administer and manage the physical disk, as shown in Figure 7-6. The first tool is the Error Checking tool, formerly called ScanDisk. Error Checking inspects the disk for file system problems and disk surface problems. As you can see in Figure 7-7, when you choose to use the Error Checking tool, you have the option to fix file system errors and scan for and fix bad disk sectors. This tool can be very helpful if you are experiencing disk problems, but it does need exclusive access to the disk, which may require a reboot before it can run.

The next tool is the disk defragmenter. Disk defragmenter is able to correct fragmentation in the file system, which occurs over time as files are saved, changed, and moved. Since disk defragmentation is a performance issue, this tool is examined in more detail in Chapter 13.

FIGURE 7-6 The Tools tab

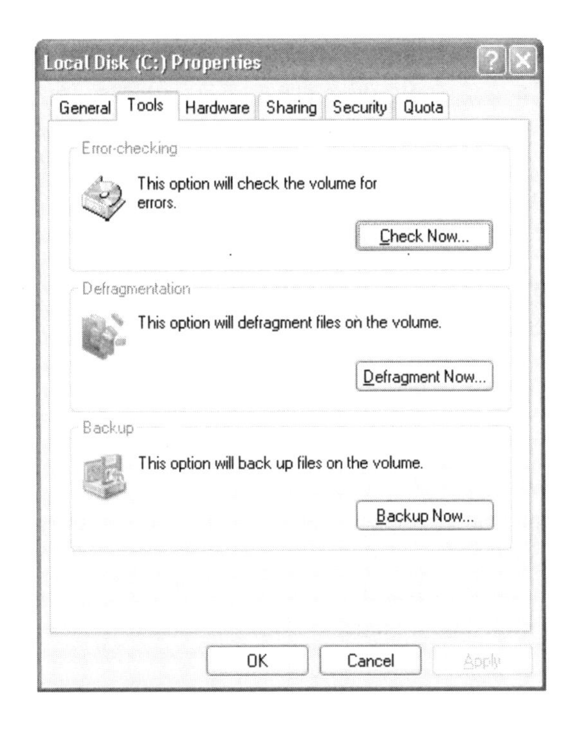

exam watch

Always remember: if disk reads and writes seem to have become slower and slower over time, the problem is almost always fragmentation.

The final tool is the Backup utility, which can also be accessed from the Computer Management console. There are a number of Backup features you need to know about for the exam, and you'll learn all about them in Chapter 13.

FIGURE 7-7 The Error Checking tool

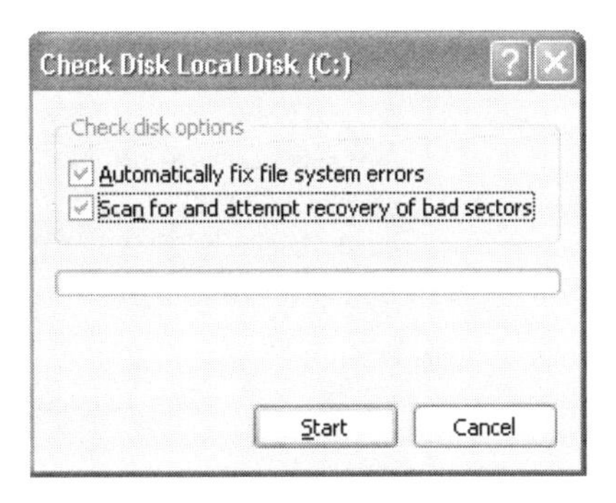

Hardware Tab

The Hardware tab, shown in Figure 7-8, gives you a listing of all disk drives on the computer. You can select a disk and click Properties to access the Device Manager properties pages for the disk, or you can click the Troubleshooter if you want Windows XP to try to help you solve problems with the disk.

Sharing Tab

The Sharing tab, shown in Figure 7-9, enables you to share the entire disk and configure permission and cache settings in effect when the disk is shared. You can learn all about resource sharing in Chapter 10.

Security Tab

If simple file sharing is not in use, you'll see a Security tab, which is simply the standard Security tab you see on all shared resources. Using the security tab, you can configure access to the disk and permissions for local and domain users. See Chapter 12 to learn more about security.

FIGURE 7-8

The Hardware tab

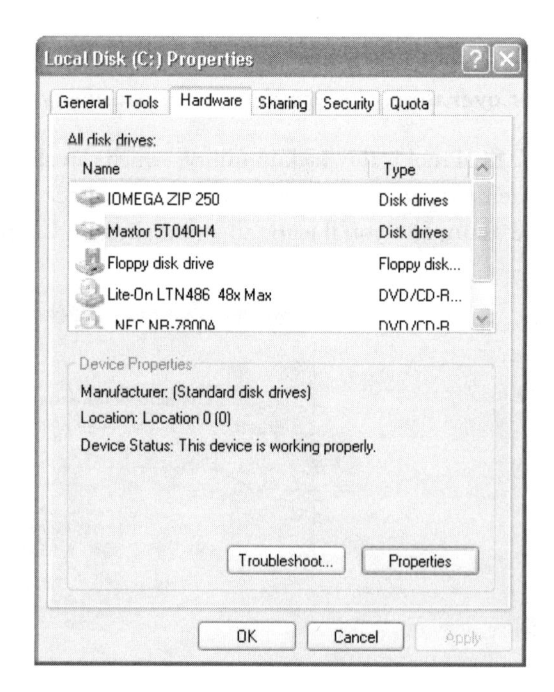

FIGURE 7-9

The Sharing tab

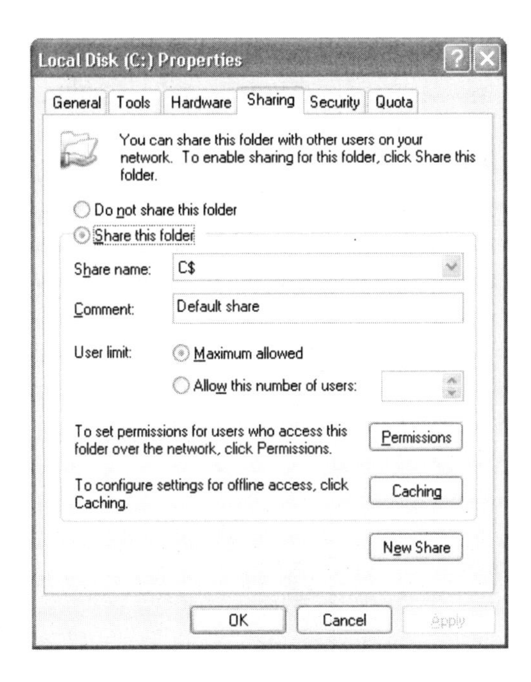

Disk Quota Tab

Disk Quota is a feature first introduced in Windows 2000 that enables you to control user storage capabilities. Let's consider an example. Say you are using Windows XP as a file server and user storage center. You want to have users store files and folders on the shared hard disk, but you do not want users storing more than 500MB of data. This restriction keeps users from wasting a lot of disk space storing items they no longer need. Using Disk Quota, you can easily configure this restriction.

You can enable disk quota management on the Disk Quota tab by clicking the Enable Quota Management check box, shown in Figure 7-10. Once you enable Quota Management, you have a few configuration options that are available to you:

- **Deny disk space** Quota management can be used to deny disk space to users who exceed the quota limit, or it can be used to warn users without actually denying them disk space. If you want to strictly enforce quota management, you can choose the Deny option by clicking this check box.

- **Set disk space and warning levels** You can set the amount of disk space a user can have in the quota and a warning level. The warning level is generally an amount slightly lower than the quota so that users receive warning messages when the quota limit is near.
- **Log events** You can use the final two check boxes to log events to the event log when users exceed their storage limits or reach the warning level. These options are not available by default, but you can enable them if you like.

Once you have configured the basic setup for disk quotas, you can then configure quota entries to establish the quota settings that apply to users. These settings, called *quota entries*, are explored in Exercise 7-7.

FIGURE 7-10

The Quota tab

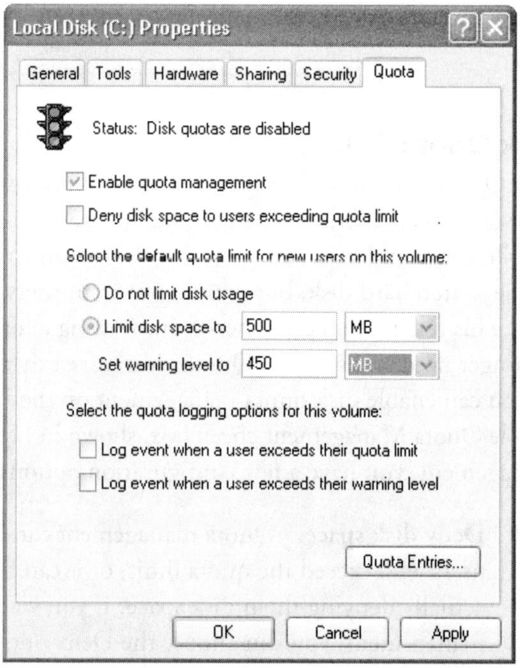

EXERCISE 7-7

Configuring a Quota Entry

To configure a quota entry, just follow these steps:

1. On the Quota tab, click the Quota Entries button. Doing this opens the Quota Entries window, as shown in the following illustration:

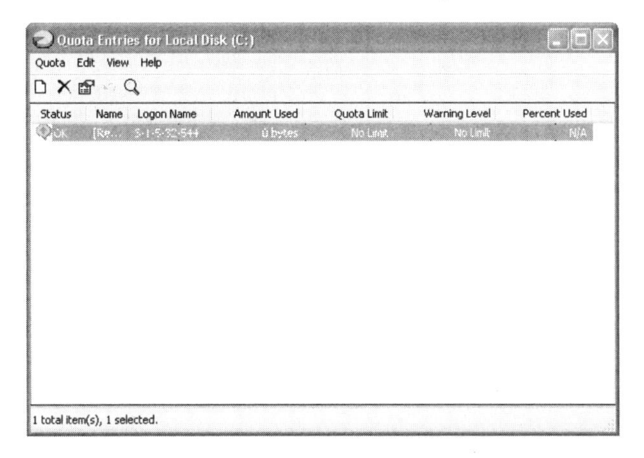

2. To create a quota entry, click the Quota tab and click New Quota Entry. A search window opens, shown in the following illustration, where you can search for and select the user that you want to add.

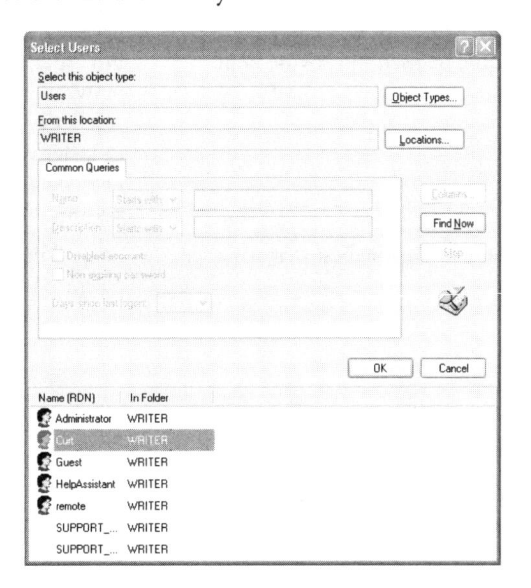

3. Select the user and click OK.
4. The Add New Quota Entry window appears, as shown in the following illustration. You can choose to not limit disk space, or you can set the quota and warning level for that particular user. This feature allows you have flexibility in dealing with users who need more storage space.

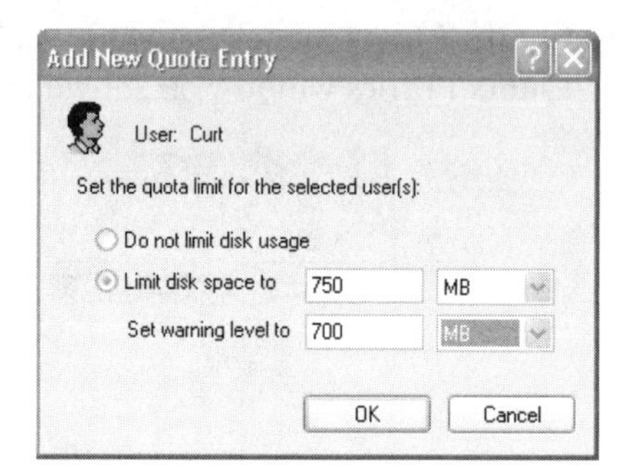

5. The new entry now appears in the Quota entries window. You can edit, change, or delete the entry at any time using this console.

SCENARIO & SOLUTION

Can a spanned volume be used to provide fault tolerance?	No. Spanned volumes are storage solutions that use between 2 and 32 drives. You can logically combine smaller pieces of unallocated space across the drives in order to create an effective storage solution. However, no fault tolerance is provided by spanned volumes.
Which volume type provides the best performance: spanned or striped?	Striped volumes provide the best read and write performance.

CERTIFICATION SUMMARY

Windows XP Professional provides an easy to use Disk Management console, available through Computer Management. Supporting both basic and dynamic disks, Windows XP Professional can provide any number of disk configurations, including simple volumes, spanned volumes, and striped volumes. The console also provides a number of disk status indicators that can help you troubleshoot disk problems, as well as helpful tools and features found on the disk's properties pages.

For the exam, keep in mind the differences between the different volume types and status indicator messages. Also, remember that spanned volumes and striped volumes are storage solutions—not fault tolerant solutions.

Finally, you can also remotely administer another Windows XP Professional computers via the Disk Management console by simply connecting to the other computer. You must have domain administrator or server operator permission in order to remotely manage a Windows XP Professional computer on a Windows 2000 network.

TWO-MINUTE DRILL

Configure NTFS, FAT, and FAT32 File Systems

- ❑ Windows XP Professional supports NTFS, FAT32, and FAT16.
- ❑ Windows XP Professional is designed to function best with NTFS. NTFS provides a number of features, such as file level permissions, encryption, compression, and disk quotas, that are not supported under FAT16 or FAT32.
- ❑ Use FAT32 when you need to dual-boot Windows XP Professional with a downlevel operating system that does not support NTFS.
- ❑ You can convert FAT drives to NTFS without losing any data by using the Convert command line tool.

Monitor and Configure Disks

- ❑ Windows XP Professional supports both basic and dynamic disks. Basic disks use partitions, while dynamic disks use volumes. Volumes are not limited and can be configured without rebooting. Additionally, volumes provide a number of configuration options not supported under basic disks.
- ❑ Dynamic disks provide a number of status messages that can help you determine the current state of the disk.
- ❑ Dynamic and basic disks can be configured with drive letters and/or can be mounted to an empty NTFS folder so that they can be accessed in the same way as a local folder.

Monitor and Configure Disk Volumes

- ❑ Disk volumes are available only on dynamic disks.
- ❑ You can create simple volumes using the Disk Management console. Volumes can be formatted, reformatted, and deleted, and you change drive letters and paths without rebooting.
- ❑ Spanned volumes are used when you have unallocated space on multiple disks (up to 32). You can create a spanned volume that creates one logical volume across the disks. Spanned volumes provide no fault tolerance.

- ❑ Striped volumes can be created on 2 to 32 disks. Striped volumes require each unallocated space to be the same size, but data is written in a striped fashion across the disks, which improves performance. Striped volumes provide no fault tolerance.
- ❑ You can remotely manage the disk(s) of another Windows XP Professional computer within a Windows 2000 domain with domain administrator or server operator permissions.

SELF TEST

The following questions will help you measure your understanding of the material presented in this chapter. Read all of the choices carefully, as there may be more than one correct answer. Choose all correct answers for each question.

Configure NTFS, FAT, and FAT32 File Systems

1. For testing purposes, you would like to dual-boot Windows XP Professional with the original version of Windows 95. What file system do you need to use so that Windows 95 can access data on the Windows XP Professional partition?

A. FAT16

B. FAT32

C. NTFS

D. CDFS

2. Aside from the ability to support larger hard drives, what is another advantage of FAT32 over FAT16?

A. Partition size

B. Cluster size

C. NTFS support

D. Encryption

3. Which is not a feature of NTFS?

A. NTFS security

B. Encryption

C. Fault tolerance

D. Logging

4. You want to convert a FAT32 drive to NTFS. The drive is currently labeled D. What command can you use to convert this drive?

A. Convert D

B. Convert D: NTFS\FS

C. Convert D: FS/NTFS -A

D. Convert D: /FS:NTFS

5. You need to convert an NTFS drive to a FAT32 drive. The drive letter is D. How can this be done?

   A. Convert D: /FAT32: NTFS.

   B. Convert D: FAT32.

   C. Convert D: FS:/FAT32/NTFS -D.

   D. Reformat the drive.

Monitor and Configure Disks

6. What is the maximum number of primary partitions allowed on a basic disk?

   A. 1

   B. 2

   C. 3

   D. 4

7. What is the maximum number of volumes you can configure on a dynamic disk?

   A. 5

   B. 11

   C. 21

   D. Unlimited

8. On a particular dynamic disk, you notice that the status says "Online (Errors)." What should you do?

   A. Reformat the disk.

   B. Reactivate the disk.

   C. Import the disk.

   D. Run the Error Checking tool on the General properties page.

9. On a particular dynamic disk, you notice that the disk status is Offline. What is the first thing you should do to try to bring the disk back online?

   A. Reformat the disk.

   B. Reactivate the disk.

   C. Import the disk.

   D. Run the Error Checking tool on the General properties page.

10. You want your company employees to be able to access a particular volume by running \\xp\docs. Your computer is named XP. What else do you need to do in order to configure this option (Choose two answers—each answer represents part of the solution.)

A. Format the drive as a folder.

B. Assign a drive letter of Z.

C. Mount the drive to the Docs folder.

D. Create a folder called Docs on an NTFS drive. Share the folder and assign permissions as desired.

E. Run the MntDrpt—R command.

F. Create a folder called Docs on a FAT32 drive. Share the folder.

Monitor and Configure Disk Volumes

11. You want to change a simple volume's drive letter. Which statement best describes what will happen when you change the drive letter?

A. The volume and all data will be lost.

B. The volume's drive letter will be changed, but you will need to reboot.

C. You can only change the drive letter to C.

C. You can change the drive letter without any danger to data and without a reboot.

12. You would like to create a spanned volume. What is the minimum number of disks that you can use?

A. 1

B. 2

C. 3

D. 8

13. You want to create a striped volume across three disks. One disk has 600MB of free disk space, the second has 400MB, and the last disk has 950MB. You create the striped volume, but you notice that only 1.2GB of disk space is used in the striped volume. What is wrong?

A. One disk is offline.

B. All portions of unallocated space must be the same size.

C. The disks are not using compression.

D. There are I/O errors on the disk.

14. You want to create a RAID-5 volume on a computer that has five dynamic drives. How many drives will actually be available for data storage when you create the volume?

A. 5

B. 4

C. 3

D. None, RAID-5 is not supported on Windows XP.

15. You have a shared volume on your Windows XP Professional computer. Five network users access the volume to store data. You want to limit the amount of data the user can store. What feature do you need to use on this volume?

A. Compression

B. Encryption

C. Quotas

D. Permissions

16. What two fault tolerance solutions are supported on Windows 2000/.NET Server?

A. Disk Mirroring

B. Compression

C. RAID-1

D. RAID-5

17. You want to use disk quotas on a particular Windows XP Professional computer. You would like users warned when they are close to reaching their quota limit, but you do not want users denied access if they go over the limit. Currently, users are denied access. What do you need to do in order to fix this problem?

A. On the Disk Quota tab, change the warning level to 10GB.

B. Clear the Deny option on the Disk Quota tab.

C. Create separate quota entries.

D. Set the quota limit to 10GB.

18. A particular user travels with a Windows XP Professional laptop. Many different files are used on the computer, and updates and changes are made frequently. The user complains that the laptop seems to be running slower, particularly when recalling files. What do you need to do?

A. Disable quotas.

B. Run the Error Checking tool.

C. Defragment the disk.

D. Create a simple volume.

19. A particular user reports that file system errors occur on his Windows XP Professional computer. What tool can you run to attempt to resolve the problem?

A. Run the Error Checking tool.

B. Defragment the disk.

C. DSKFIX.exe

D. Convert the disk to dynamic.

20. A user would like to create a spanned volume over an NTFS disk and a FAT32 disk. The user reports that she cannot create the spanned volume. What is the problem?

A. The disks are basic.

B. FAT32 disks cannot be used for spanned volumes.

C. The user is not a Power User.

D. The user needs to defragment the disk.

LAB QUESTION

A user on your network has several small pieces of unformatted free space on three hard disks that she has used to create a single spanned volume. Later, the user wants to move one of those portions of free space out of the volume to use for other purposes. What does the user need to do?

SELF TEST ANSWERS

Configure NTFS, FAT, and FAT32 File Systems

1. ☑ A is correct. The original version of Windows 95 only supported FAT16.

☒ B, C and D are incorrect. B and C are incorrect because the original version of Windows 95 did not support FAT32 or NTFS. D is incorrect because CDFS is not a file system used for operating system partitions.

2. ☑ B is correct. The cluster size of FAT32 is smaller than FAT16, which conserves disk space.

☒ A, C, and D are incorrect. Partition size has nothing to do with FAT16 to FAT32 differences, so A is incorrect. C and D are incorrect because both NTFS and encryption are not supported under FAT32.

3. ☑ C is correct. NTFS is not fault tolerant in and of itself.

☒ A, B, and D are incorrect. These are all features of NTFS.

4. ☑ D is correct. To convert a drive, use the **convert *driveletter*: /FS:NTFS** command.

☒ A, B, and C are incorrect. None of these options provides the proper syntax.

5. ☑ D is correct. You cannot convert an NTFS drive to a FAT32 drive. The only option is to reformat the drive.

☒ A, B, and C are incorrect. You cannot convert an NTFS drive to a FAT32 drive.

Monitor and Configure Disks

6. ☑ D is correct. A basic disk allows up to four primary partitions or three primary partitions and one extended partition.

☒ A, B and C are incorrect. Four primary partitions are allowed.

7. ☑ D is correct. There is no limit on dynamic volumes. Even if you use all available drive letters, you can still mount volumes to an empty NTFS folder—or not label them at all.

☒ A, B and C are incorrect. There is no limit on the number of volumes you can configure on a single drive.

8. ☑ D is correct. The Online (Errors) message indicates that some I/O errors have been detected. This is usually nothing serious, and running the Error Checking tool will usually solve the problem.

☒ A, B, and C are incorrect. Reformatting the disk will cause data loss, and reactivation is not necessary under this message. You do not need to import the disk, since it is not foreign.

9. ☑ B is correct. When a disk is offline, the first action you should take is to try to reactivate the disk.

   ☒ A, C, and D are incorrect. These actions will not bring an offline disk back online.

10. ☑ C and D are correct. You can mount a drive to an empty NTFS folder by creating the folder and mounting the drive to the folder using Disk Management. In the case of a network share, share the folder and assign desired permissions.

    ☒ A, B, E, and F are incorrect. These actions are not part of the solution.

Monitor and Configure Disk Volumes

11. ☑ D is correct. You can change drive letters of a dynamic volume at any time without any danger to data and without rebooting the computer.

    ☒ A, B and C are incorrect. These actions are not accurate.

12. ☑ B is correct. In order to create a spanned volume, you must have unallocated space on at least two dynamic disks.

    ☒ A, C, and D are incorrect. At least 2 disks are required.

13. ☑ B is correct. Striped volumes require the same amount of disk space on each disk. In this case, the smallest amount of available space is 400MB, so Disk Management will use 400MB on each disk, for a total of 1.2GB.

    ☒ A, C, and D are incorrect. There are no problems with the configuration, so these answers are incorrect.

14. ☑ D is correct. RAID-5 is a fault tolerant solution on Windows 2000 Server, but is not supported under Windows XP.

    ☒ A, B, and C are incorrect. RAID-5 is not supported.

15. ☑ C is correct. You can invoke disk quotas in order to control how much storage space is used.

    ☒ A, B, and D are incorrect. None of these features will control disk storage space.

16. ☑ A and D are correct. The Windows 2000 Server platform supports both disk mirroring and RAID-5 volumes for fault tolerant purposes.

☒ B and C are incorrect. Compression is not a fault tolerant strategy, and RAID-1 is not supported.

17. ☑ B is correct. If you do not want users blocked from storing data on the disk when the quota is met, simply clear the Deny option on the Quota tab.

☒ A, C, and D are incorrect. These options will not solve the "deny" problem and keep the current configuration.

18. ☑ C is correct. If users report that a particular disk has slowed down over time, especially when reading and writing, the disk needs to be defragmented.

☒ A, B, and D are incorrect. These options will not resolve problems with slow disk reads and writes.

19. ☑ A is correct. If file system errors and other problems with the disk are occurring, run the Error Checking tool to fix bad sectors and file system problems.

☒ B, C, and D are incorrect. Disk defragmenting and dynamic conversion will not resolve file system or disk problems. DSKFIX.exe is not a real tool.

20. ☑ A and B are correct. You cannot create spanned volumes on FAT32 disks. The FAT32 disk can be converted to NTFS; then the spanned volume can be created. Also, if the disks are not both dynamic disks, then spanned volumes cannot be created.

☒ C and D are incorrect. The user must be an administrator on the local computer to create a spanned volume, so C is incorrect. A fragmented disk would not prevent you from creating a spanned volume, so D is also incorrect.

LAB ANSWER

Once you place areas of unformatted space into a spanned volume, they become a part of the spanned volume. Data is written to those areas of unformatted free space, so you cannot remove a portion of the spanned volume at will. The only way to reclaim the free space is to back up the data stored on the volume and then delete the entire spanned volume.

8

Configure and Manage Windows XP Printing and Faxing

CERTIFICATION OBJECTIVES

8.01	Install Local Printers
8.02	Connect to Network and Internet Print Devices
8.03	Manage Printers and Print Jobs
8.04	Control Access to Printers with Permissions
8.05	Configure and Troubleshoot Fax Support
✓	Two-Minute Drill
Q&A	Self Test

Printing is one of those subjects and tasks that has caused a lot of people a lot of problems over the years. The concept is simple—connect a printer to a computer and use the printer, and even share that printer on the network for others to access. However, printing can be a complicated and difficult support issue for IT professionals because there are so many options and possible configuration issues. As an IT professional, however, you'll spend your fair share of time installing, configuring, and troubleshooting printers and printer access, and you can expect to see a few exam questions on this topic as well.

In addition to printing, Windows XP includes a new fax console that enables you to easily send, receive, and manage faxes. Since this is a new Windows XP feature, it is included on the exam. In this chapter, we will take a look at both printing and fax support. Keep in mind that you should get some hands-on practice with both of these features for your real-world knowledge and for the exam.

CERTIFICATION OBJECTIVE 8.01

Install Local Printers

Before we get into the topic of installing a printer on a Windows XP computer, we should briefly consider a few conceptual issues that will strengthen your understanding and simplify your work with Windows XP printing. First, if you have been around Microsoft technology for any period of time, you are probably familiar with the basic definitions of "printer" and "print device." If not, consider this your first lesson. Microsoft refers to a "printer" as the software on a computer running Windows XP that drives and manages a "print device." Microsoft refers to a print device as the physical printer hardware. In common terms, we typically refer to a "printer" as the hardware device that generates the printed pages, but in Microsoft terms, this is the "print device," and the "printer" is the software installed on Windows XP.

So how does Windows XP handle printing? When you are using an application—let's say WordPad—and you want to print something, the application sends the document you want to print as a print job to the printer driver. Commonly, a series of calls are made to the graphical device interface (GDI), which handles the printing. The printer driver takes the GDI data for the printer driver and converts it into instruction-specific data for the printer. This information tells the printer what to do in order to re-create the document and output it on paper. This information then goes to the print processor, which routes the data to the correct local or network printer. The job then goes to a spooler, which can either be local or on the network. The job of the spooler is to hold the print job until the print device is ready to process it. You can think of the spooler as a queue in which the data is held until the print device is ready. When the print device is ready, the print job goes to the print monitor, which then sends it to the print device where it is actually printed. As you can see, the process of printing an item is rather complex, but all of these actions are hidden from the user's view. To the user, it appears as though a job is sent and printed. You, as the IT professional, however, know that the process is more complex—and managing those processes can be even more complex.

First things first; a print device must be installed, along with the correct printer software in order to use a printer on Windows XP. Print devices are like all other hardware devices—you should check the HCL and only use print devices that are compatible with Windows XP. Typically, a print device is installed by connecting the device to the correct port, such as the LPT port or USB port (IrDA options are also available), and then installing the printer manufacturer's software that accompanies the print device. This sets up the printer on Windows XP so that applications can use it and network users can access it, if you choose to share it for network use. If you have problems installing the printer this way, you can also use the Add Printer wizard, found in the Printers And Faxes folder in Control Panel. Exercise 8-1 shows you how to use the Add Printer wizard.

EXERCISE 8-1

CertCam 8-1

Using the Add A Printer Wizard

To install printer, just follow these steps:

1. Attach the print device to the correct port and turn it on.
2. Open the Printers And Faxes folder in Control Panel. Click on the Add Printer Wizard link to launch the Add Printer wizard.
3. The Welcome screen appears. Note that if you are using a USB, infrared, or IEEE 1394 print device, Windows XP can install it automatically without the help of this wizard. Click Next.

4. In the Local Or Network Printer window, shown in the following illustration, choose whether the printer is a local or network print device. For the exercise, we will assume that the print device is Local. When you choose the Local option, you can also click the check box for plug-and-play detection so that Windows can automatically detect and install the print device. Click Next.

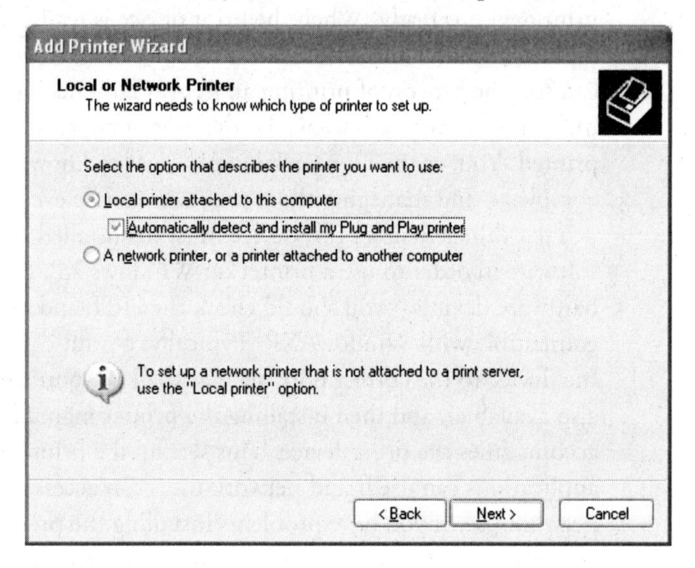

5. Windows searches for a new plug-and-play print device. If Windows XP detects the device, it is installed automatically. If not, you see a message telling you that you can install the print device manually. Click Next.
6. In the Select a Port window, you can use an existing port or create a new port type. Typically, you are going to use the LPT1 port, as shown in the following illustration. Click Next.

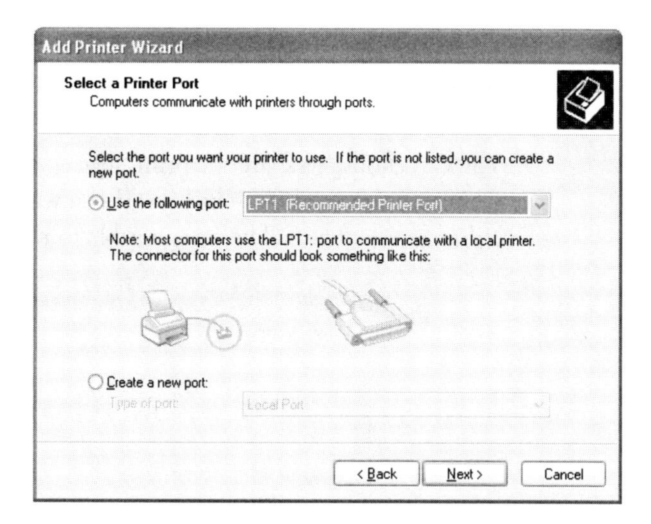

7. In the Install Printer Software window, choose the manufacturer and print device model to install, as shown in the following illustration. You can also click the Have Disk button to install the software from a disk provided by the manufacturer if you have one. Make your selections and click Next.

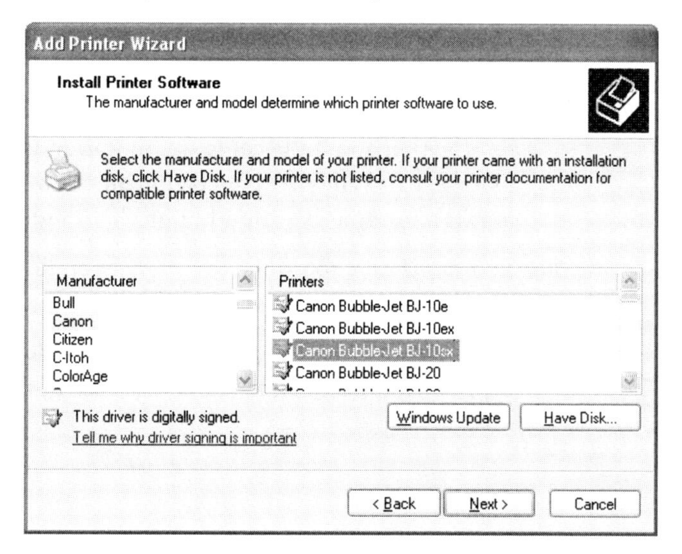

8. Enter a desired name for the printer (or you can accept the default). If you want to use the printer as your default printer, click the Yes button—or No if you do not want to use it as the default. Click Next.
9. You can choose to share the print device, shown in the following illustration. Choose the desired radio button. If you want to share the print device, give it a share name that will be recognizable to network clients.

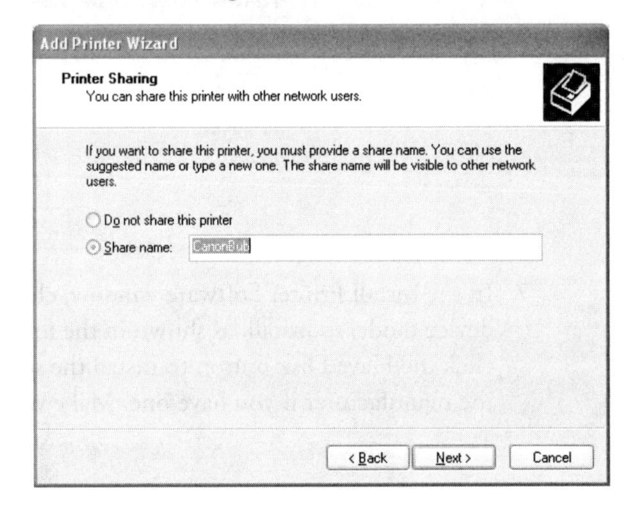

10. If you chose to share the print device, a window appears where you can enter information about the computer's location (such as "Marketing Group – Floor 2") and any necessary comments. This information can be read by network users. Make any additions here and click Next.
11. You can choose to print a test page if you like. Choose Yes or No and click Next.
12. Click Finish. The new print device is installed and now appears in the Printers And Faxes folder, as you can see in the following illustration.

on the job

Printer drivers are updated regularly by the manufacturer, and if you are trying to use a printer driver that is pre–Windows XP, you can probably find an updated driver on the manufacturer's Web site. Although you may be able to use an older driver, you are much more likely to experience problems. Always check the manufacturer's Web site and download the latest printer drivers that are available.

CERTIFICATION OBJECTIVE 8.02

Connect to Network and Internet Print Devices

Aside from installing a local printer on a computer running Windows XP, you can also configure a printer for print devices connected directly to a network with their own IP address or to an Internet print device. Keep in mind that a printer is simply the software that allows you to connect to a print device, whether that print device is local, network, or even on the Internet. Additionally, you can even configure several

SCENARIO & SOLUTION	
When should the Add Printer wizard be used?	Under most circumstances, Windows XP can detect and install the printer automatically. You can also use the manufacturer's installation disk to help you get the printer installed. If you are having problems installing the printer, the Add Printer wizard can be used to assist you.
Once a print device has been installed, how can I update the driver at a later time?	You can update printer drivers just like any other device. Access the printer's properties in the Printers And Faxes folder and click the Advanced tab. You'll see an option to install a New Driver here. You can learn more about configuring printer properties later in this chapter.

printers that use different configurations for the same print device. Confusing, yes, but necessary to keep in mind for the Microsoft exams.

Aside from connecting to a local print device, users on a Microsoft network can also connect to another printer on the network. This feature allows multiple users to access a single printer, or even multiple printers when necessary. You can easily connect to a network printer by using the Add Printer wizard in the Printers And Faxes folder. Exercise 8-2 walks you through the process.

EXERCISE 8-2

Installing a Network Printer

To install a network printer, just follow these steps:

1. Open the Printers And Faxes folder in Control Panel. Click the Add Printer Wizard link.
2. Click Next on the Welcome screen.
3. In the Local Or Network Printer window, select the Network Printer radio button, and click Next.

4. In the Specify a Printer window, shown in the following illustration, you have a few different options. First, you can choose to "Browse for a printer."

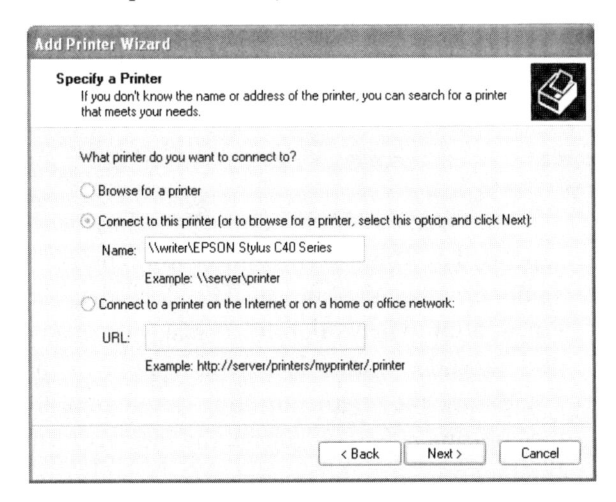

If you click this option and click Next, you see a selection window, shown in the next illustration. You can select a shared network printer that you see in the window and click Next to install it. If you know the UNC path of the printer that you want to connect to, select the radio button option and enter the path. As you can see in the first illustration, I am connecting to a computer named Writer and using the Epson printer attached to it. If you want to connect to an Internet print device, see Exercise 8-3. Make your selection and click Next.

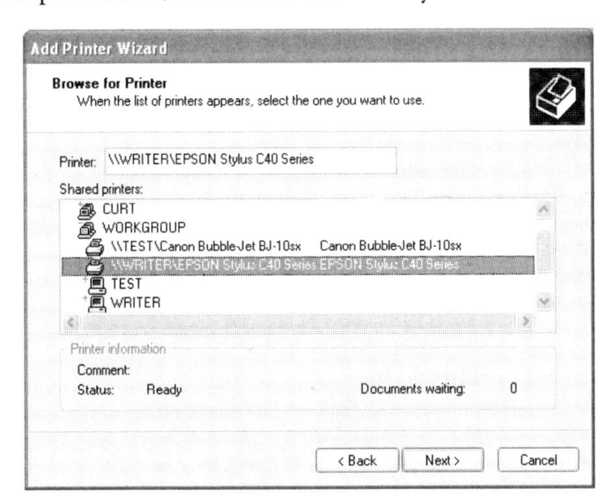

5. The printer is now installed on your computer. This simply means that the print driver for the network print device has now been installed on your computer, allowing you to use that network print device. The Test Page window appears. If you want to print a test page, choose Yes and click Next.
6. Click Finish.

First introduced in Windows 2000, Internet Printing Protocol (IPP) is also supported in Windows XP. This allows computers running Windows XP to print to a print device on the Internet. The idea is that networks can use the Internet as a free way to print to network printers in a wide area network. For example, let's say you want to send a series of documents to a user in Spokane, but you are located in Dallas. You can use the Internet printing feature to print to an Internet-enabled printer in the Spokane office. Of course, the Internet printer has to be configured to allow Internet printing, and you'll learn about that in the next section. If you want to connect to an Internet printer, you simply use the Add Printer wizard again, and follow the steps outlined in Exercise 8-3.

EXERCISE 8-3

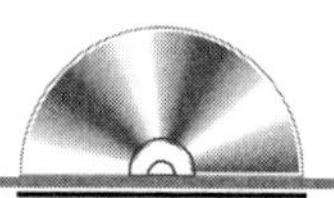

CertCam 8-3

Installing an Internet Printer

To install an Internet printer, just follow these steps:

1. Open the Printers And Faxes folder in Control Panel. Click the Add Printer Wizard link.
2. Click Next on the Welcome screen.
3. In the Local Or Network Printer window, select the Network Printer radio button and click Next.
4. In the Specify a Printer window, choose the option to connect to a printer on the Internet, and enter the URL of the printer, shown in the following illustration.

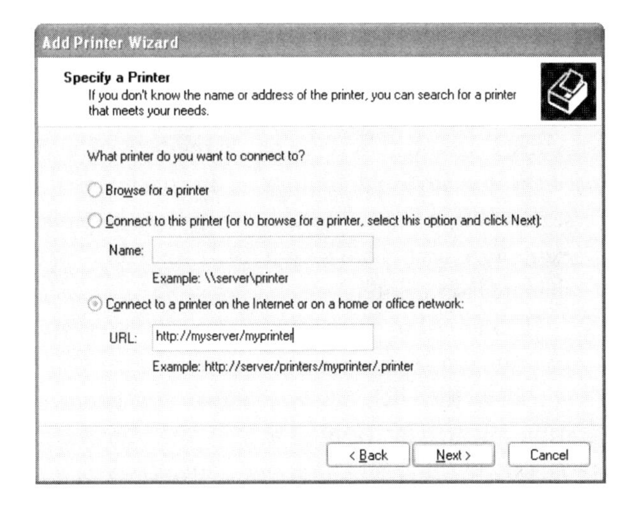

5. Click Next and click Finish.

Once the printers are set up, you can then print to them as you would a local printer. If you have more than one printer configured, you'll see a selection screen when you print that allows you to choose what printer you want to print to, as you can see in Figure 8-1.

FIGURE 8-1

Print screen

In Windows domain environments, users can also search the Active Directory to locate printers. Printers configured and shared on computers running Windows 2000 and Windows XP that are members of a domain are automatically published in the Active Directory. Users can search the Active Directory on computers that are members of the domain and look for certain characteristics, called attributes. The printers search option is not available when the computer is not a member of a domain. For example, a user could search for "print color" and find all printers in the network that are laser printers.

If you need to print to an Internet printer, you can follow this same format, but you can also connect to an Internet printer using a browser (IE 4.0 or later only). If you know the URL, simply enter it in the address line. If you do not, enter the server's name followed by **/printers** to see a list of Internet printers on that server. For example, let's say that I know the server is **http://myserver**. If I don't know the printer name, I can type **http://myserver/printers** to see a list of print devices available on that server. If you know the name of the printer, you can simply type the server name and printer name, such as **http://myserver/internetprint**, to directly access the Internet printer. Once you locate the printer you want, you can click the Connect button. Windows XP will copy the necessary drivers, and the new printer will appear in your Printers And Faxes folder. This is a simple way to use a Web browser to access the Internet printer, rather than using the Add Printer wizard to set it up.

exam Watch

Keep the* http://servername/printers *URL in mind for the exam. This is the best way to locate the desired printer on a print server when using Internet/intranet printing.

Concerning the troubleshooting of network and Internet printer connections, keep the following points in mind:

- If you cannot connect to a network printer, you need to verify that the printer and server are online and that the UNC path information has not changed.
- If the network server and UNC path information is correct, check your computer's network connectivity and connectivity to the print server using the ping command.
- If you have connectivity and the server/print device is connected and ready, you can try rebooting to restart services or delete the printer and re-create it using the Add Printer wizard.

- For Internet printing, make sure you are using IE 4.0 or later. If you do not know the actual URL of the printer, you can access **http://servername/printers** to see what printers are available. If you know the exact URL, you can access it directly from the browser using **http://servername/printername** or you can set up the Internet printer using the Add Printer wizard. Either way, once the printer is recognized, you can use it as if the printer is local.
- If you cannot connect to the Internet printer, you'll need to verify Internet connectivity and if the print server and printer are online.

CERTIFICATION OBJECTIVE 8.03

Manage Printers and Print Jobs

Once you have installed a local printer on a computer running Windows XP, you can then configure and manage the operation of the print device. This includes the functionality of the print device and print jobs sent to the print device, and you can share that printer so that others on your network—or even the Internet can access it. In this section, you'll learn about a number of important configuration features and issues concerning print device and print job management.

SCENARIO & SOLUTION	
The print server's name on my network has changed. Now I cannot connect. What do I need to do?	Just delete the existing printer and use the Add Printer wizard to re-create the printer with the correct UNC path.
Can I access an Internet printer using Netscape?	No. You can only access Internet printers using IE 4.0 or later.

Configuring a Printer

Once the printer is installed on the local computer running Windows XP, you can configure how the printer operates by accessing the printer's properties, found by right-clicking the printer icon in the Printers And Faxes folder and clicking Properties. You'll see primary tabs of General, Sharing, Ports, Advanced, Security, and Device Settings. Depending on the printer, you may see additional tabs that are installed by the manufacturer's setup program. The following sections explore the primary tabs and show you what is available to configure. For the exam, it is important that you have a firm understanding of the configuration options and where you can configure certain options within the properties sheets. Study these sections carefully and be sure to get some hands-on practice.

General Tab

The General tab, shown in Figure 8-2, gives you the printer name and any location/comment information that has been configured. Under Features, you can see if color printing is supported, staple features, speed, and any paper types that might be available.

FIGURE 8-2

General tab

EPSON Stylus C40 Series Properties
Color Management | Version Information
General | Sharing | Ports | Advanced
EPSON Stylus C40 Series
Location: Writer
Comment: For use by all workstations
Model: EPSON Stylus C40 Series
Features
Color: Yes
Double-sided: No
Staple: No
Speed: Unknown
Maximum resolution: Unknown
Paper available:
Printing Preferences... | Print Test Page
OK | Cancel | Apply

If you click the Printing Preferences button, you can configure paper orientation (portrait or landscape), page order, paper quality, and other basic settings. Depending on the printer, you may see additional information here that is made available by the manufacturer's software, as you can see in Figure 8-3. The options provided on these tabs are self-explanatory, but keep in mind that most of the printing features are configured here.

You can also send a test page to the printer for testing purposes by clicking the Print a Test Page button on the General tab.

Sharing

The Sharing tab enables you to share the printer. See "Configuring Network Printers" later in this chapter for more information about sharing setup and configuration.

Ports

Windows 2000 introduced additional printing features in a number of different areas, including port configuration. If you click the Ports tab of the printer properties, shown in Figure 8-4, you see several different port options and the ability to add, delete, or configure a port. Port configuration can be a little on the confusing side,

FIGURE 8-3

Printing Preferences screen

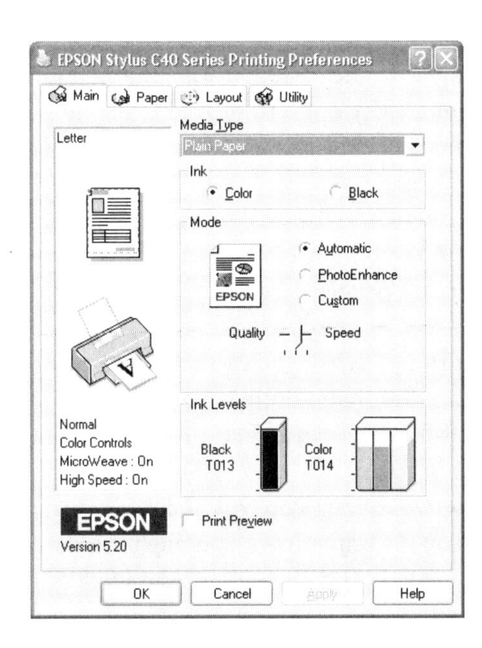

FIGURE 8-4

Ports

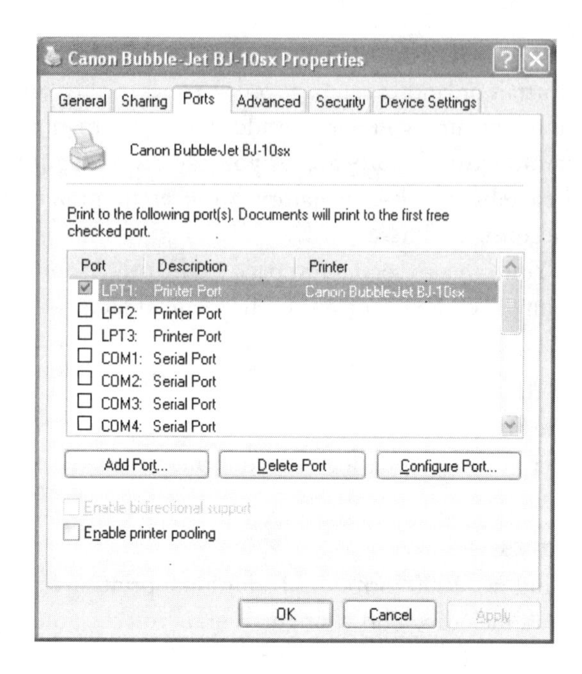

which makes it great exam question fodder, so in this section you can explore all you need to know about printer ports and what the configuration options are.

A printer port, like other kinds of ports, is a point of connection for a computer to a printer. In the past, that was almost always an LPT port, but with today's new port connectivity options, such as USB and IrDA, a number of different ports can be used. You can also configure serial ports for printing, as well as TCP/IP ports on your network.

When you install a local printer, the port option here is configured according to what port the printer is attached to. However, you can configure multiple ports as necessary for printer device connections, such as in the case of printer pooling or for troubleshooting purposes.

First things first—you can select the existing port that is in use and click the Configure Port radio button. You see a simple Configure Port dialog box, shown in Figure 8-5. The Transmission Retry value is listed here. The timeout value is the amount of time that passes before you are notified that the printer is not responding to the print request. The typical default setting here is 90 seconds. If you are using plotters on the printer port, you might need to increase this value to allow the plotter more time to buffer, or configure and hold, print data. Again, this is one of those tricky setting options that you need to remember for the exam.

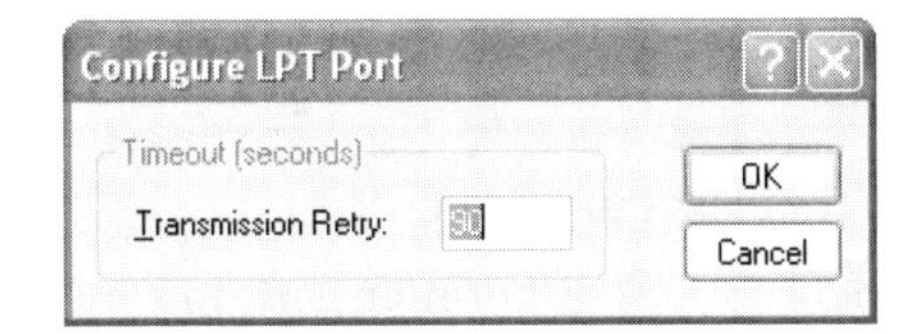

FIGURE 8-5 Configure Port screen

Also notice at the bottom of the dialog box in Figure 8-4 that you have two check box options that you can enable. They are as follows:

- **Enable Bidirectional Support** If the printer supports bidirectional communication between the printer and the computer, you can enable that option here so that Windows XP can receive data from the printer about problems.
- **Enable Printer Pooling** You can configure a printer pool, which is two or more identical print devices that function through one logical printer. For example, the pool acts like one printer to the user, but may actually be made up of three print devices. This feature is often used when a number of users are supported over a shared printer. To enable the feature, click the check box and select the other ports each with additional, identical print devices connected on them. It's a good idea when configuring printer pooling to physically locate all print devices in the same location to avoid users running all over the place trying to find their print job.

You can also add new ports. If you click the Add Port button, a window appears where you can configure a new local port or a TCP/IP port. The new local port option enables you to configure a new port type. For example, if you recently installed an IrDA device, you could configure the new port here so that IrDA enabled printers could use the port.

You can also choose to install a standard TCP/IP port. A TCP/IP port is a logical port made up an IP address of a network printer. For example, let's say your environment uses a network printer that has a network adapter card. The TCP/IP port feature enables your computer to print to the IP port found on the printer's network adapter, assuming you have permission to do so. The end result is that through TCP/IP, your computer can send print jobs directly to the network printer. Exercise 8-4 shows you how to configure a TCP/IP port.

EXERCISE 8-4

Configuring a TCP/IP Printer Port

To configure a TCP/IP printer port, just follow these steps:

1. Open the Printers And Faxes folder in Control Panel. Right-click the desired printer and click Properties.
2. Click the Ports tab and then click the Add Port button.
3. In the provided Printer Ports dialog box, shown in the following illustration, select Standard TCP/IP port and click the New Port button.

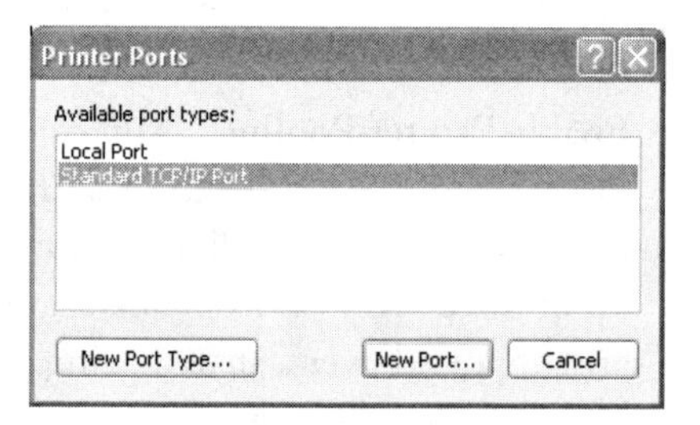

4. The TCP/IP Printer Port wizard appears. Note that the network device must be turned on and the network must be connected and configured. Click Next.
5. In the Add Port window, shown in the following illustration, enter the printer name or IP address of the printer. You can also enter the port name, if necessary. Click Next.

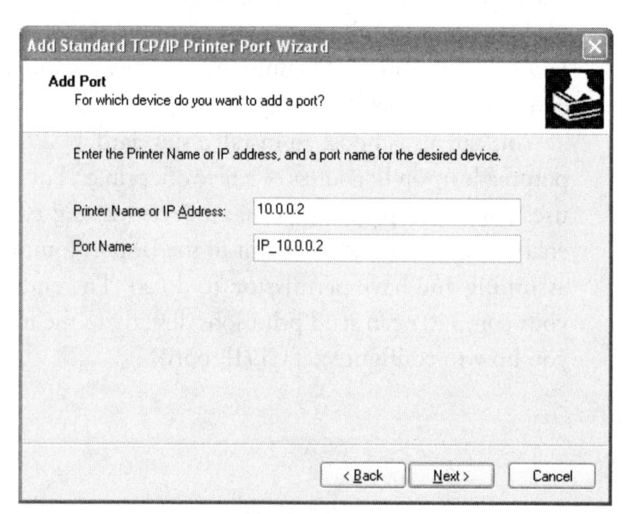

6. If the port is found, Windows XP will install the port. Click Finish.

---

exam watch

Do not forget about the bidirectional support and printer pooling options available on this tab and the purposes for these settings.

Advanced Tab

The Advanced tab gives you a number of different settings that impact printing availability and functionality. You should be very familiar with the options found on this tab, shown in Figure 8-6.

You have several different options here, and the following list describes them:

- **Availability** By default, a local printer is always available. However, you configure the printer so that it is only available for certain hours. This feature is helpful when you want to control user access to the printer so that it is restricted to certain hours of the day or certain days of the week.
- **Priority** This setting establishes a priority setting for the printer. In the case where there are multiple printers that print to the same print device, you can

FIGURE 8-6

Advanced tab

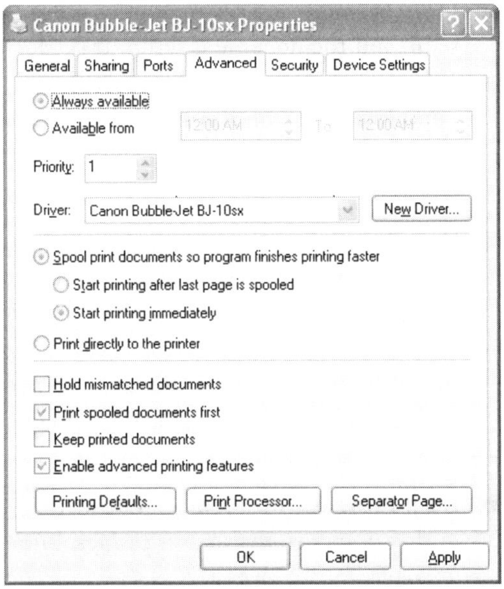

control which printer has priority by entering a value here—1 is the lowest priority, while 99 is the highest priority.

- **Driver** If you need to update the driver, click the New Driver button. This opens the Add Printer Driver wizard, which will walk you through the steps of installing a new printer driver.
- **Spool Settings** By default, documents are spooled and they start printing immediately. This means that documents are held on the hard disk spooler until the printer is available to print. Essentially, this frees up the application and the user can return to work. You can choose to hold the document until the last page is spooled, but this may slow printing down a bit.
- **Print Directly** This radio button option prints directly to the printer without using the spooler. The application will remain busy the entire time the print job is being run, and the user will not be able to continue working with the application. You should only use this option in cases where you are having problems with the print spooler. Also, this setting can cause a lot of problems for shared printers. For example, if two users print at the same time, their documents could be printed at the same time, resulting in a mess of print jobs that are not usable. Again, this setting should not be used except in troubleshooting situations.
- **Hold Mismatched Documents** Mismatched documents refer to the printer setup and the document setup. If the formats do not match, the document is considered mismatched. Use this option to hold the document so that it will not be printed. This feature does not stop other documents from printing, and it is not selected by default. Typically, this setting is helpful for troubleshooting purposes.
- **Print Spooled Documents First** Let's say that five users have sent print jobs to the spooler. Which print job does the spooler take first? In this case, the spooler will take the first job that finishes spooling. In the case that none of the print jobs have finished spooling, the printer chooses the larger documents over smaller ones. This option is chosen by default and should remain selected for printer efficiency. If you clear the setting, document printing order is based solely on priority.
- **Keep Printed Documents** This setting holds documents that print correctly in the spooler so that a user can resubmit it for printing again. For example,

if a user has to print the same document several times, this setting can be helpful, since the job is already in the spool. Of course, under most circumstances, this setting is not used, and this option is not selected by default.

- **Enable Advanced Printing Features** Advanced printing features enables metafile spooling, which allows different kinds of print options such as page ordering, booklet printing, and other types, depending on your printer. This option is selected by default and should remain enabled unless you are having computer/printer compatibility problems, in which case turning off this setting may help.
- **Printing Defaults** This option enables you to control paper orientation and related settings. These are the same settings you see under Printing Defaults on the General tab.
- **Print Processor** If you click Print Processor, you see a window that shows the print processor used and the default data type, shown in Figure 8-7. The default data type is typically RAW, but you may choose a different data type if your printer documentation tells you to do so.
- **Separator Page** Use this option if you want a separator page to print between print jobs.

Security

The Security tab enables you to determine what users or groups have access to the printer and what they can do with the printer. See the "Control Access to Printers with Permissions" section later in this chapter for details.

FIGURE 8-7

Print Processor screen

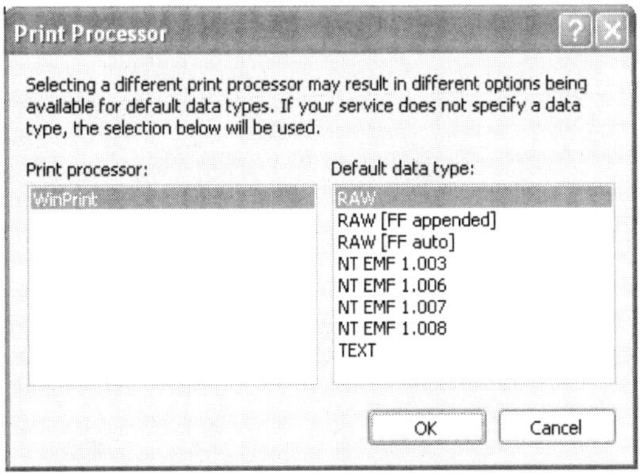

Device Settings

The Device Settings window, shown in Figure 8-8, contains basic settings for the device, such as paper feed and envelope usage. This tab may not be available on all printer models.

Managing Print Queues

The process of printer configuration and setup is typically a one-time event, assuming everything works like you want it to. However, you may have to manage the print queue from time to time in order to manage and control documents. The "queue" refers to the holding area—documents that are either currently printing or are waiting to be printed. Assuming you have permissions to access the print queue on a computer running Windows XP, you can do so by double-clicking the Printer icon in the Printers And Faxes folder, or you can click the Printer icon that appears in the System Tray when items are being printed.

exam watch

You must have permission to open, view, and modify the print queue. If you do not, an access denied message appears if you try to open the printer in the Printers And Faxes folder, and you will not see a Printer icon in the Notification Area.

FIGURE 8-8 Device Settings window

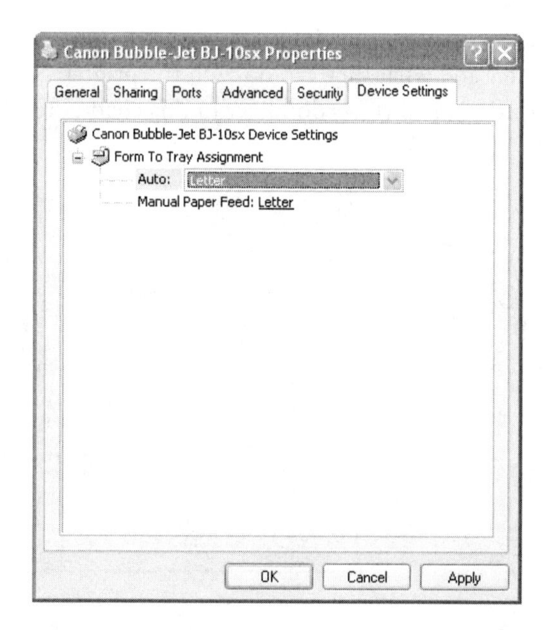

The print queue, as you can see in Figure 8-9, gives you a listing of documents that are printing or are waiting to be printed. You can manage the print queue in a few different ways. First, you can click the Printer menu and choose Pause Printing or Cancel All Documents. The pause feature is good if you need to perform maintenance on the printer without deleting everything that is waiting in the queue. You can use the Document menu to manage individual documents. For example, you can select a document and click the Document menu, where you can Pause, Resume, Restart, or Cancel the document's print. In this case, a Cannel print order deletes the file from the printer spool, and the file is not printed. These features can be helpful if a document seems to be stuck in the queue—you can cancel it, and the other documents should resume printing. You can also easily perform these same actions by simply right-clicking on the Document icon in the print queue.

You can also make a few adjustments to a document's printing by right-clicking the document and clicking Properties. As you can see in Figure 8-10, you have a standard properties sheet with several tabs. The noteworthy items are found on the General tab. As you can see in Figure 8-10, you can change the priority of the document in the queue. Under most circumstances, documents are set to a priority of 1. What if there are 15 documents in the print queue, but one particular document needs to be printed first? No problem, just access the document's properties and change the priority setting to Highest (99)—this will ensure that the document prints first, assuming no other documents have a similar or higher priority setting.

Also notice that you can configure a schedule for a particular print job. Let's say that someone in the Research group has sent a 300-page research paper to the printer during peak printing hours. You can access the document's properties and change the time restriction so that the job is held in the queue until after hours. As you can see, you have a lot of power when you have rights to manage the print queue, and it is a task that should only be assigned to a few people.

FIGURE 8-9

Print Queue screen

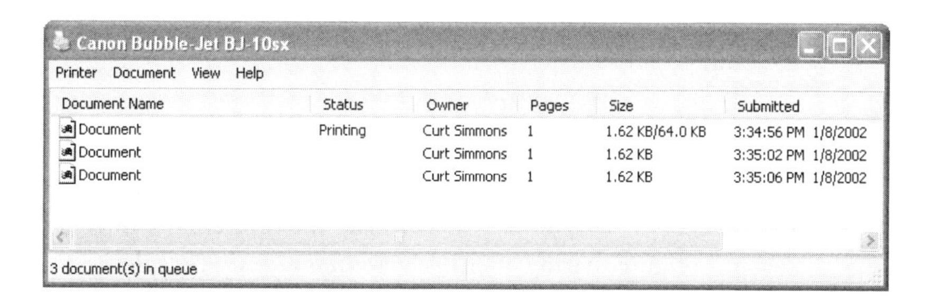

FIGURE 8-10

Document properties

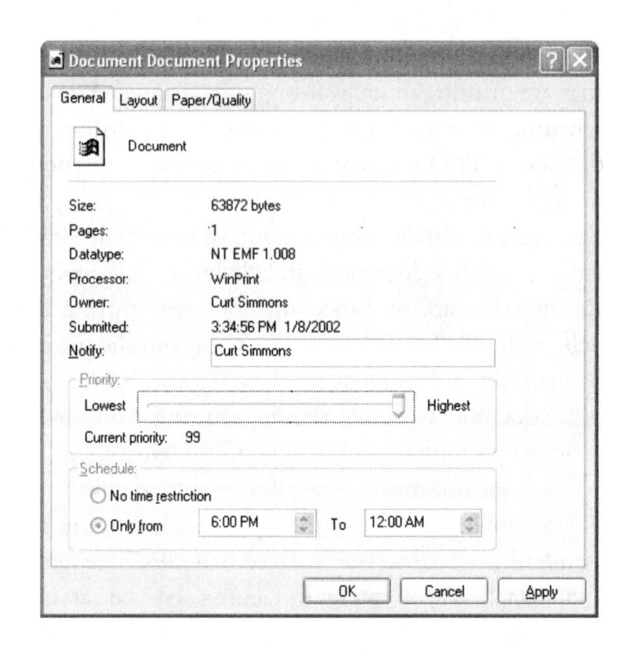

In larger networks, managing print queues can be very important. After all, you have the power to pause, restart, delete, and even reorder jobs in the print queue. Many larger networks have administrators whose sole job is to manage printing and solve problems with network printers and printing bottlenecks.

Configuring Network Printers

Local printer management is a relatively easy task, but as an IT professional, your job will be to troubleshoot and manage shared printers on a Microsoft network. That task, in and of itself, does not have to be monumental, as long as your print devices are able to handle the printing load that will be placed on them and as long as you have configured permissions appropriately (see the next section to learn more about permissions).

Configuring Local Area Network Printers

You can configure a local area network printer when you install the printer using the Add Printer Wizard, or you can share the printer later once installation is complete. To configure sharing after installation is already complete, access the printer's properties and click the Sharing tab, shown in Figure 8-11. Click the Share This Printer radio button and enter a desired share name in the dialog box.

If you have network clients other than Windows XP or 2000, you can also use this tab to install additional drivers. When a down-level computer connects to a printer local to the computer running Windows XP, the down-level computer downloads the drivers it requires to print. If you click the Additional Drivers button, you see a list of options. Simply click the check box next to the drivers you want to install and click OK. You may be prompted to insert your Windows XP CD-ROM or asked to provide the driver you want to make available. You can usually obtain down-level drivers from the manufacturer's Web site.

Once the printer is shared, network users can begin accessing the printer, typically using the default permissions. See the next section to learn more about permissions.

Aside from a local area network printer, you can also configure a printer for Internet/intranet access. This feature enables users to print to a URL and open a printer from Internet Explorer. In order to configure a printer so that it can be accessed via URL, IIS must be installed on your Windows XP computer (see Chapter 11 to learn more about IIS). When IIS is installed, the printer is automatically made available via Web services when you share the printer. You can think of the Internet printing

FIGURE 8-11

Sharing tab

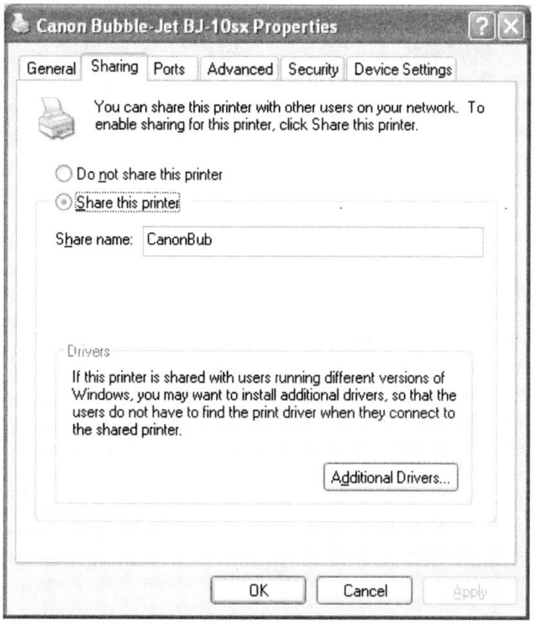

options as just another way for users to access the shared printer, which can be helpful in the case of intranet printing. All permissions and related configurations apply to an Internet printer as they do for a standard printer.

exam Watch

If a user is accessing your Internet printer through Internet Explorer, the user can see his or her documents in the print queue and delete them if necessary. However, unless the user has the Manage Documents permission, he or she can make no changes to other documents in the print queue.

CERTIFICATION OBJECTIVE 8.04

Control Access to Printers with Permissions

The preferred method for managing any network resource in a Windows 2000/.Net environment is through NTFS permissions, and the same rule holds true for shared printers. Depending on your network needs, you may have several print devices that you want to make available to all users at all times. Alternatively, you may have

SCENARIO & SOLUTION	
On a particular shared printer, I want to make sure that a separator page is printed with each print job. Where can I configure this?	Access the printer's properties and click the Advanced tab. At the bottom of the window, you will see a button for Separator Page. Click the button and configure the page as desired.
I want to set up a printer pool that uses three identical print devices attached to a computer running Windows XP. Where can I configure this option?	Access the printer's properties and click the Ports tab. Click the Enable Printer Pooling check box and select the ports that the printer should print to.
I need to connect to an Internet printer, but I only know the name of the server. What can I do?	Type **http://servername/printers**. This will give you the printers directory in IIS, where you can see all shared printers available on that server.
I am having some compatibility problems with Windows XP and an older print device. What is one action I can take that might resolve some of the compatibility problems?	You can access the Advanced tab of the printer's properties sheets. Remove the check box from Enable Advanced Printing Features. This might help resolve some of the problems.

certain print devices that should be available to some users only some of the time and others at other times—or not at all. The possible permission scenarios with any shared resource are limitless, and printer sharing is certainly no exception.

First things first—in order to modify the permissions of a shared printer, you must be the administrator or owner of that printer on the local machine. If you needed to configure the permissions through the Active Directory, you will need to be at least a member of the Server Operators or Print Operators group.

In order to modify the permissions of a printer, you need to access the Security tab of the printer's property pages, as you can see in Figure 8-12. There are three primary print permissions that you can either allow or deny:

- **Print** This permission allows a user to print to a printer and manage their own documents.
- **Manage Printers** This permission allows a user to open the printer's properties pages and configure options.
- **Manage Documents** This permission allows a user to open the print queue and manage all documents, not just their own.

FIGURE 8-12

Security tab

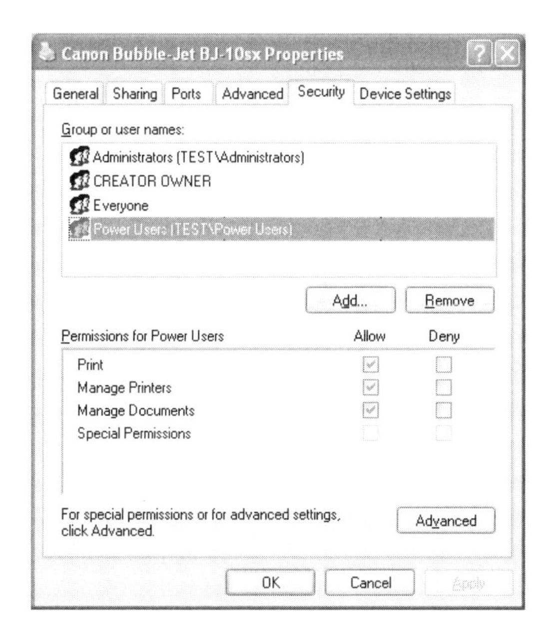

In Windows XP, local administrators are given all three permissions. The Creator/Owner is given the Manage Documents permission, Everyone is given the Print permission, and Power Users are given all three permissions. Obviously, most users in your environment will have Print permission for the printer, while only a select few will be given the Manage Printers and Manage Documents permissions.

Like all permission features, you can also click the Advanced button and view a listing of permission entries for particular groups, as you can see in Figure 8-13. You can select a desired group, click the Edit button, and reconfigure the default permissions for that group if necessary. You can also set up auditing, view the owner, and view the Effective permissions for a group by using the Effective permissions tab. The tabs you see here are standard, and they work for printer permissions as they do for any other shared object. It is important to note here that if no permission is expressly applied to the group, the group can inherit its permission from the Active Directory. If there is no inheritable permission, the group is simply denied any access.

As you can see, printing permissions are rather straightforward. However, in most cases, your permission problems will not be so cut and dried. For example, let's say that two different groups—Marketing and Accounting—use a certain shared printer.

FIGURE 8-13 Advanced Permissions screen

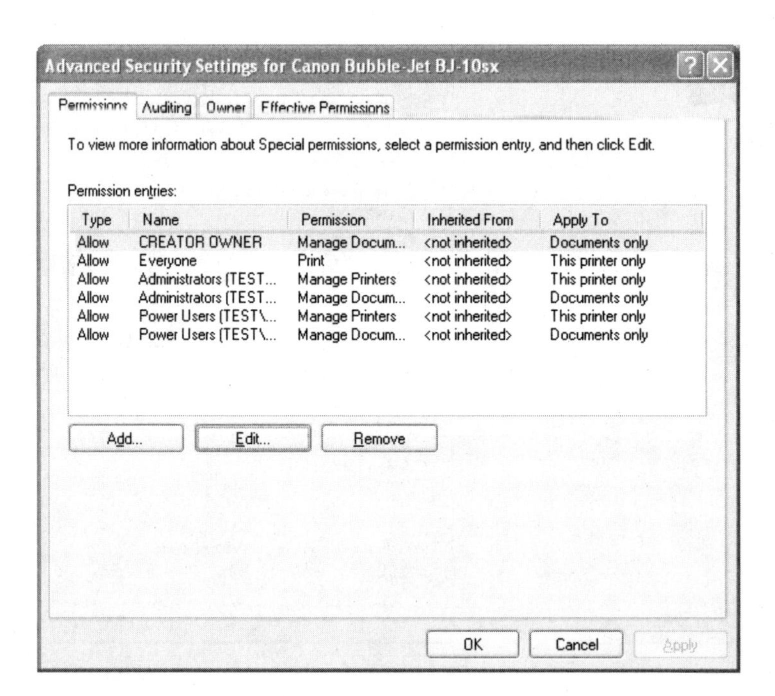

You want to make certain that the Marketing group can only access the printer from 3:00 P.M. until 10:00 P.M., but Accounting has full access. Also, when the printer is available to both groups, how can you ensure that the Accounting group's jobs are given preferential treatment? These are the kinds of scenarios that you are likely to encounter on the exam and in the real world. In cases such as this, you use a combination of multiple printers, different priorities, and different availability options in order to make the configuration work. Keep in mind that you cannot single out a group for certain time access through the available security permissions—that has to be done using multiple printers for the same print device. Fortunately, the configuration for situations like this is easy, once you determine your plan of attack. Exercise 8-5 walks you through a scenario like this one—and you should keep this one in mind when you take the exam!

EXERCISE 8-5

Configuring Printer Permissions

The Scenario:

In your network, a certain printer is accessed by the Management group and by the Research group. Although the Research group technically uses the printer more often, they frequently print documents in excess of 100 pages that are not considered critical print needs. The Management group needs the printer all of the time, and their documents should be printed first. You would like to configure the printer so that the Research group's print jobs do not print until after 2:00 P.M. each day, keeping the morning hours open when the printer is most busy. Also, if a user in the Management group needs the printer in the late afternoon, that user's print job should be favored over any jobs from the Research group. How can you configure this?

The Solution:

In this scenario, you need two different printers, one for each group. To configure the printer for the Management group, just follow these steps:

1. Create the first printer. You can label the printer "Management." Then access the Security tab.
2. On the Security tab, as shown in the following illustration, give the Management group Allow Print permission. Make sure no other group is granted Allow Print permission.

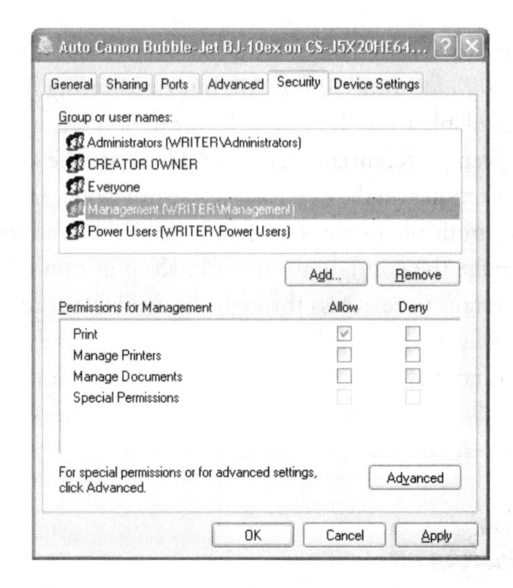

3. Click the Advanced tab. Ensure that the printer is always available and that that the Priority level is set to 50, as shown in the following illustration. Click OK.

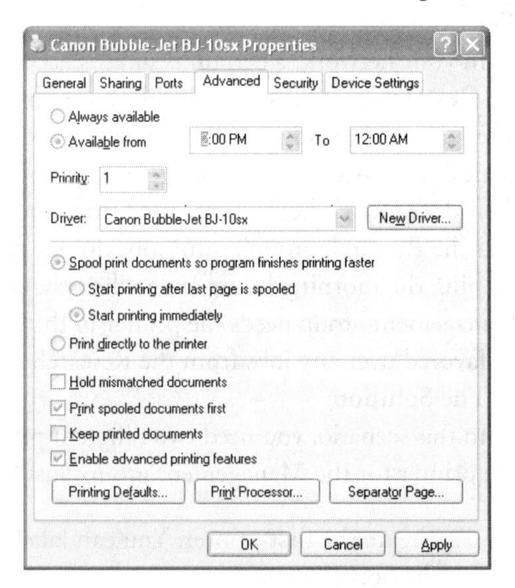

To configure a printer for the Research group, follow these steps:

1. Create the second printer. You can label the printer "Research." Then access the Security tab.

2. On the Security tab, assign the Research group Allow Print permission. Make sure that Allow Print permission is not given to any other groups.
3. Click the Advanced tab. Change the schedule so that the printer is available only from 2:00 P.M. to 12:00 A.M. Under Priority, leave the value configured as 1.

CERTIFICATION OBJECTIVE 8.05

Configure and Troubleshoot Fax Support

Windows XP Professional includes a new fax console that can make the use of Windows XP as a fax server much easier than it has been in the past. With the new fax console, you can manage incoming and outgoing faxes in much the same way you handle e-mail in an e-mail client. This feature makes fax sending/receiving and archiving much easier and streamlined.

SCENARIO & SOLUTION	
If a user has Print permission, can the user also manage his or her own documents in the queue?	Yes, a user with Print permissions can delete his or her own documents in the print queue, but cannot access or see other user documents.
I want a certain user to be able to manage documents in the print queue, but not change any printer configuration. What permission is needed?	The user should be given the Manage Documents permission. The user will be able to make changes in the print queue, but the user will not be able to alter the printer configuration.
I need to assign different groups different printer availability restrictions. How can I do this?	You need to create a different printer for each group. Assign the permission to use the printer to that particular group and configure the availability options as needed.

FROM THE CLASSROOM

Managing Printers

Printer management is similar to the management of any other resource in a Windows 2000/.NET network. Once you establish the shared resource, you then determine who can access the shared resource and under what conditions. As a general rule, you should make certain that printer permission assignment is as simple as possible. This rule holds true with any kind of shared resource.

The more complex the permissions and the more cross-group memberships you have in your environment, the more likely you are to have problems. If a user is a member of one group that has Print permissions but a member of another group that also has the Manage Documents permission, the user's effective permission is both Manage Documents and Print permission. For this reason, Windows networking groups should be clearly and carefully defined, and then permissions to resources (including printers) based on those groups. Careful and logical permission assignment makes your life as an administrator much easier and simpler.

Installing and Setting Up the Fax Console

The new fax console is not installed by default when you install Windows XP, so you'll need to install it using Add/Remove Windows Components. Exercise 8-6 shows you how.

EXERCISE 8-6

CertCam 8-6

Configuring Printer Permissions

To install the fax console, follow these steps:

1. Open Control Panel and double-click Add/Remove Programs.
2. In the Add/Remove Programs window, click the Add/Remove Windows Components button.

3. Windows XP Setup appears. On the Windows Components page, shown in the following illustration, select Fax Services and click Next.

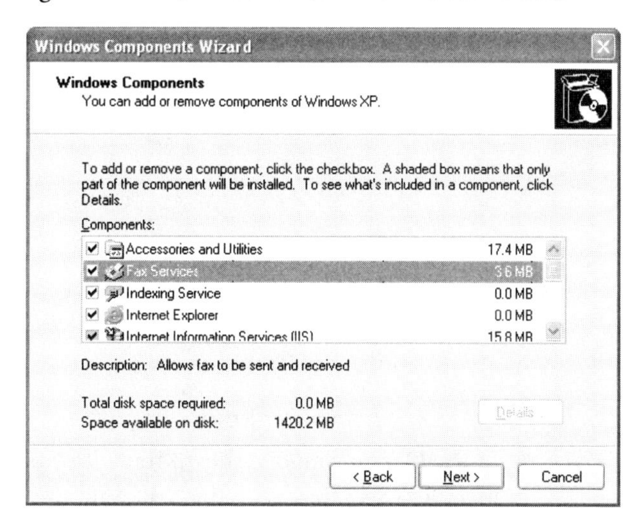

4. The Fax services are installed (you may be prompted for your Windows XP installation CD-ROM). Click Finish.

Once the installation of the fax console is complete, you see an icon appear in your Printers And Faxes folder. If you double-click the icon, a wizard appears that helps you set up the fax console. Exercise 8-7 walks you through the process.

EXERCISE 8-7

Configuring the Fax Console

To configure the fax console, follow these steps:

1. Double-click the Fax Console in the Printers And Faxes folder.
2. The Fax Configuration wizard appears. Click Next.
3. In the Sender Information window, shown in the following illustration, enter any information that is desired. Keep in mind that any information entered here will appear on the fax cover page when you send a fax.

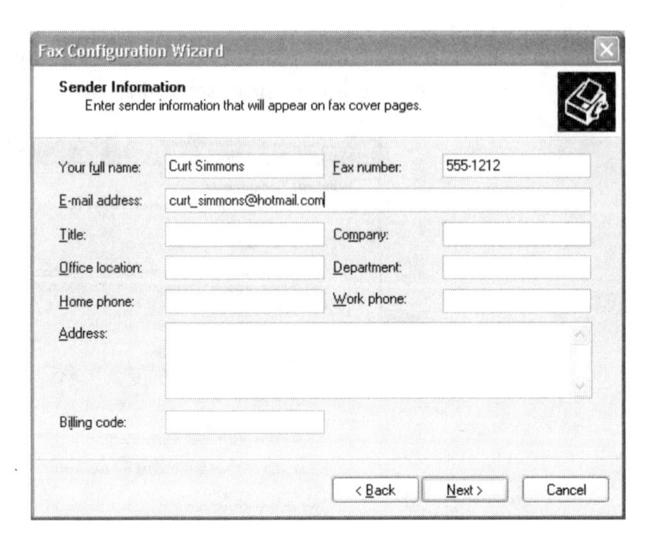

4. In the Device window, shown the following illustration, use the drop-down menu to select the device that you want to use for faxing, such as a fax modem. Notice that by default, the device is only set to send faxes—if you want the device receive faxes, select the check box option and determine if you want manual or automatic answering. Click Next.

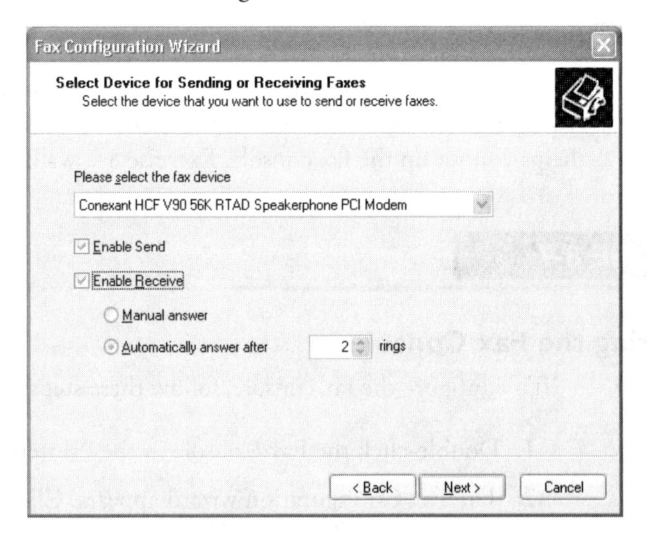

5. In the Transmitting Subscriber Identification (TSID) window, enter a business name and/or your fax number, as shown in the following

illustration. This information will be transmitted to recipients when you send a fax. Click Next.

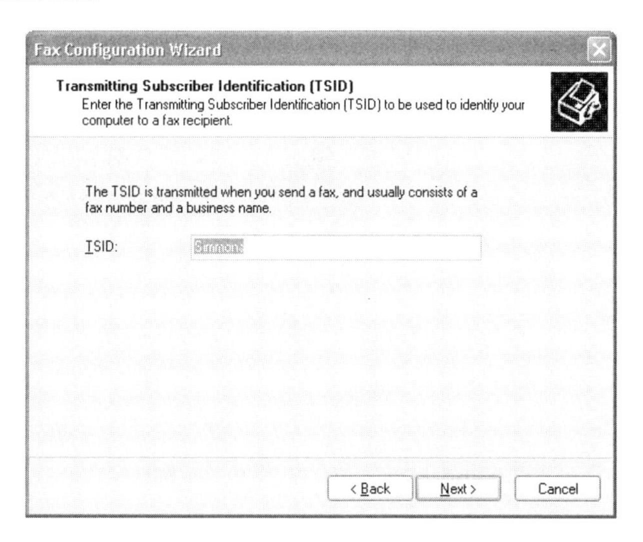

The Telephone Consumer Protection Act of 1991 makes it unlawful for any person to use a computer or electronic device to send any message via a telephone fax machine unless such messages clearly contain, in a margin at the top or bottom of each transmitted page, or on the first page of transmission, the date and time it is sent and an identification of the business or other entity or other individual sending the message and the telephone number of the sending machines or such business, other entity, or individual.

6. In the Called Subscriber Identification (CSID) window, enter a name or number to identify your computer. This information is transmitted back to the sender when you receive a fax in order to identify you. Click Next.
7. In the Routing Options window, you can choose to print the fax when it arrives and you can also choose to save the fax to a specified folder, as you can see in the following illustration. Note that received faxes are automatically archived in the inbox of the fax console, but this option enables you to save an additional copy to a different folder. Make your selections and click Next.

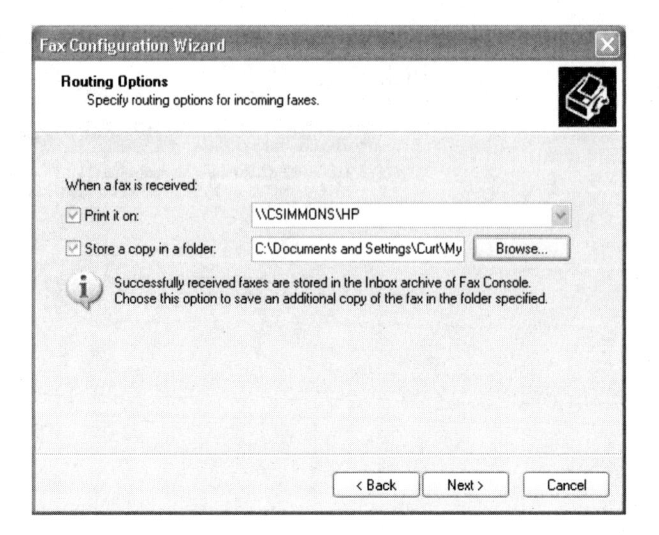

8. Click Finish to complete the wizard.

Using the Fax Console

Once installation is complete, you see the Fax Console screen, which contains Incoming, Inbox, Outbox, and Sent Items, shown in Figure 8-14. As you can see, the console looks like a typical e-mail client, such as Outlook or Outlook Express.

At this point, you can begin using the fax console. Overall, the fax console is very intuitive and easy to use, and you should spend some hands-on time working with the fax console before you take the exam. As you practice using the fax console, keep the following points in mind:

- To send a fax, use the File menu. A wizard will help you set up the fax you want to send and apply a cover sheet. You can also choose to send the fax at a later time and assign a higher priority so that the fax will be sent before other faxes in the queue.
- If you want to import older faxes into the console, Use the Import/Export feature on the File menu.

FIGURE 8-14 Fax Console screen

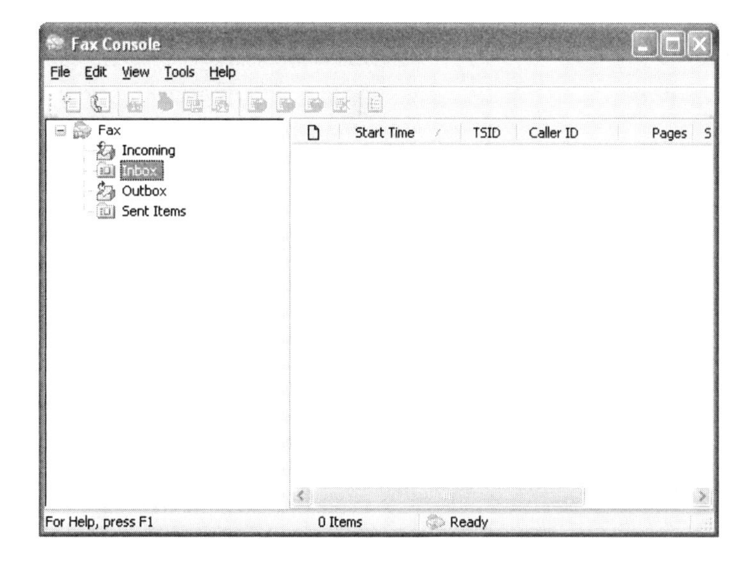

- Like an e-mail client, you can right-click faxes in your Inbox, Outbox, and Sent Items folders and perform actions, such as printing, Mail To, Save As, Delete, and so forth.
- On the Tools menu, you'll find a number of helpful features. You can configure sender information, which provides more information about you to the recipients. You can also configure personal cover pages. You can click the Fax Printer Status option to determine if the fax is online or if there are problems.
- Also found on the Tools menu is the Fax Monitor, shown in Figure 8-15. The Fax Monitor tells you the current status of the fax and enables you to answer calls and find out about transmission problems.

Configuring the Fax Console

Once you have initially set up the fax console, you can perform additional configuration options as necessary by using the Tools menu. If you click Tools | Configure Fax, the same Fax Configuration wizard appears that you saw in Exercise 8-7. However, if you click Tools | Fax Printer Configuration, you see a standard properties page with a number of important configuration tabs. The following sections point out what is available to you and what you need to know for the exam.

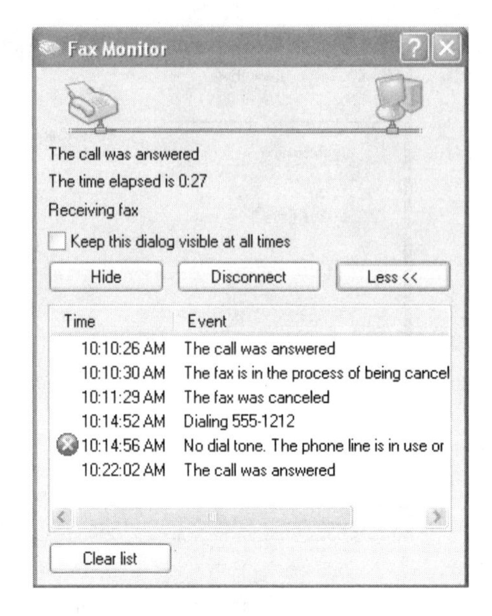

FIGURE 8-15 Fax Monitor screen

General

The General tab contains basic information about the fax. You can click the Printing Preferences button here and configure portrait or landscape printing when faxes are printed.

Sharing

You may see a Sharing tab, which simply tells you that sharing of the fax console is not supported.

Security and Fax Security

You'll see Security and Fax Security tabs that govern how people can use the fax printer. The Security tab lists basic printing permissions, discussed previously in this chapter, and the Fax Security window, shown in Figure 8-16 lists the fax permissions. As you can see, they are essentially the same as print permissions in that users and groups can be assigned Fax, Manage Fax Configuration, or Manage Fax Documents permission, depending on how you plan to assign permissions. You manage permissions for the fax console in the same way you would for a print device, so refer to the "Control Access to Printers with Permissions" section for more information about using permissions.

FIGURE 8-16

Fax Security screen

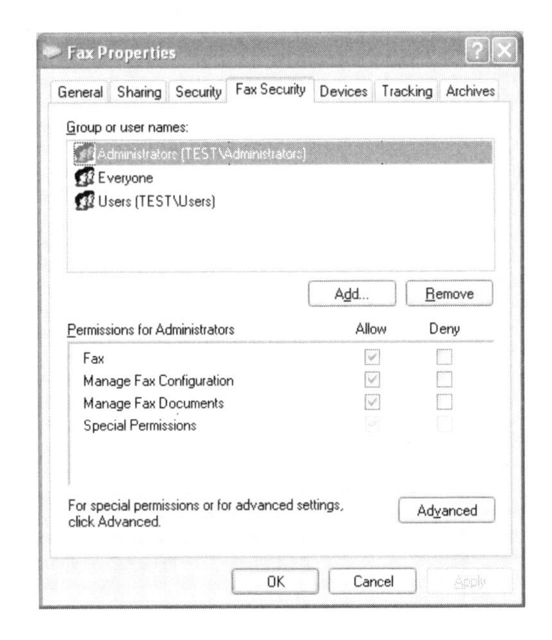

Devices

On the Devices tab, you see the fax device that is used for the console. If you click the Properties button, you have a few important additional tabs that appear.

First, the Send tab, which you can see in Figure 8-17, enables the device for fax sending. You can configure the Number Of Retries, Retry Interval, and Discount Rate Start and Discount Rate Stop if discount rates are used for faxing.

On the Receive tab, shown in Figure 8-18, you see the same basic configuration you made when you used the Fax Console Setup wizard. You make changes here as desired.

exam Watch

You may see an exam question concerning a fax console that will send but not receive faxes. Keep in mind that the fax console does not receive faxes by default—you must enable the receive feature by using the Fax Configuration wizard or by enabling the receive feature on this tab.

Finally, the Cleanup window enables you to determine how long failed faxes are kept before they are deleted.

FIGURE 8-17

Send tab

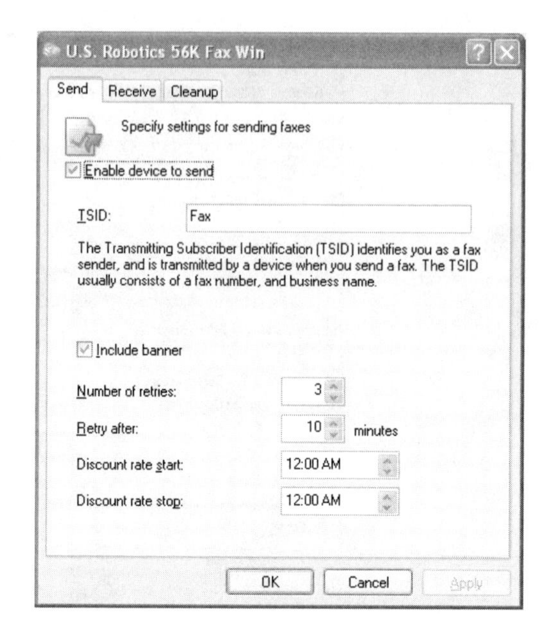

FIGURE 8-18

Receive tab

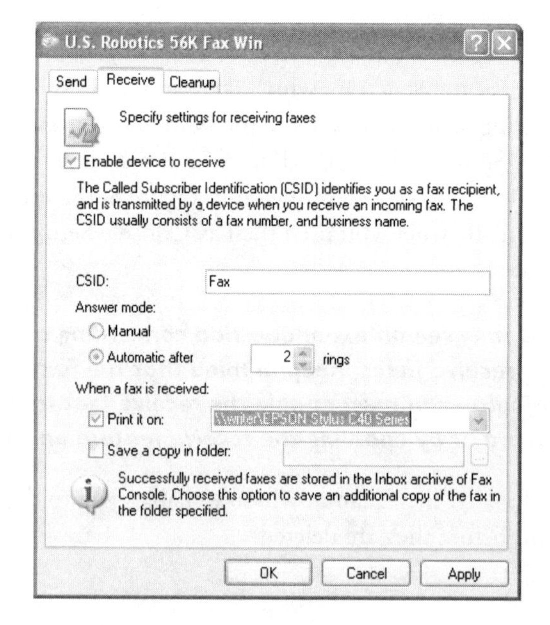

Tracking

On the Tracking tab, shown in Figure 8-19, you can configure a few different options that keep you informed about fax activity. First, you can have the Notification Area show progress of sent faxes and status information about incoming faxes. You can also have Fax Monitor automatically open when a fax is sent or received, and you can also configure sound events that alert you to fax activity. These settings are self-explanatory.

Archives

The Archives tab tells you the default archive locations for sent and received faxes, which are held in the Sent Items and Inbox folders by default.

FIGURE 8-19

Tracking tab

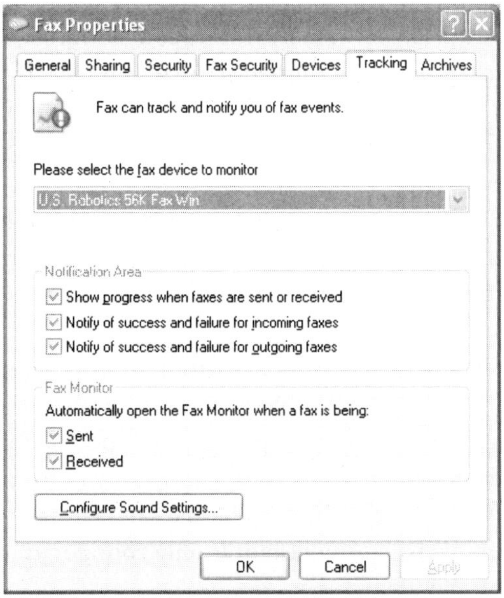

CERTIFICATION SUMMARY

In this chapter, Windows XP printing and faxing was explored. Keep in mind that Microsoft defines a "printer" as the software used to manage and configure a "print device." Thus, you can have multiple printers for a single print device in order to meet your configuration needs.

Windows XP has rich support for many different brands and models of printers, using different kinds of technologies and connection ports. You can easily install compatible local printers using plug and play or the manufacturer's installation program, or you can use the Add Printer wizard in the Printers And Faxes folder in Control Panel.

You can connect to network and Internet printers using Windows XP. You can connect to printers on your network using the UNC path. Use the Add Printer wizard to help you set up the printer. You can also connect to printers on the Internet using Internet Explorer 4.0 or later. Windows Internet printers are available through the **http://servername/printers** convention. You can use this option to see what printers are shared on that particular server. If you connect to an Internet printer with IE, you can manage documents in your print queue using the Web browser. If you have proper permissions, you can manage other documents in the queue in the same manner.

Documents that are waiting to printed can be managed by accessing the print queue. From the print queue, with proper permissions, you can individually pause and delete documents in the queue, or you can delete all documents in the queue or pause all printing.

You can manage user and group print permissions, including Print, Manage Printers, and Manage Documents. Multiple printers can be used for the same print device in order to meet specific group permission configuration needs.

Finally, the new fax console enables you to easily manage sent and received faxes on Windows XP. The fax console can be installed using Add/Remove Windows components, but by default is only configured to send faxes; however, it can be enabled to also receive faxes.

TWO-MINUTE DRILL

Install Local Printers

- ❑ The term "printer" refers to the software configured on Windows XP that manages a "print device." You can configure multiple printers for a single print device in order to meet user and configuration needs.
- ❑ The Windows XP printing system includes the Graphical Device Interface (GDI), print driver and processor, and the print spooler.
- ❑ Local print devices can be connected and installed on a number of local ports, including the LPT, USB, and even IrDA ports. Follow the manufacturer's setup and configuration instructions.
- ❑ If you have problems installing local plug-and-play printers, use the Add Printer wizard in the Printers And Faxes folder in Control Panel.

Connect to Network and Internet Print Devices

- ❑ You can connect to multiple network printers as needed using Windows XP.
- ❑ You can connect to network printers on your local area network via the UNC path. You can use the Add Printer wizard to easily locate and connect to network printers. Keep in mind that you must have appropriate permission to connect to and use a network printer.
- ❑ You can print to a printer located on the Internet using Internet Explorer 4. You can connect to the print device using the URL **http://servername/printername**. If you do not know the printer name, you can find the shared printers on a particular server by typing **http://servername/printers**.

Manage Printers and Print Jobs

- ❑ You can configure printers individually by accessing the printer's properties sheets in the Printers And Faxes folder. You can have different configurations for each printer configured here, even if the printers work with the same print device.

- You can configure basic printing preferences and settings via options on the General tab. This includes paper orientation and printing quality.
- On the Sharing tab, you can configure a printer so that it is shared on the network, and you can also include additional drivers for down-level operating systems, which can be downloaded to those clients when they connect to the networked printer.
- You can configure the ports that the printer can use on the Ports tab. You can also configure a TCP/IP port here so that a printer prints directly to a TCP/IP address for printers with their own network adapter card.
- You have a number of configuration options on the Advanced tab. These options determine basic printer functionality, such as availability, priority, spool settings, and driver.
- You can use the print queue to manage documents that are waiting to be printed. With proper permissions, you can pause and delete individual documents in the queue, or you can pause or delete all documents in the queue.
- In order to share a printer on the Internet, you must have IIS installed on the computer and a proper Internet connection and presence in order for users to connect. This configuration can also be used for intranet connectivity.

Control Access to Printers with Permissions

- You can manage access to shared printers with permissions. In order to configure permissions, you must be the administrator on the local computer, or you must have Server Operator or Print Operator permissions to configure permissions via the Active Directory.
- The Print permission enables a user or group to print documents on the printer. The user can manage his or her own documents in the print queue.
- The Manage Printers permission enables a user or group to manage the properties pages of printer and make configuration changes on that printer.
- The Manage Documents permission enables a user or group to manage the print queue and all user documents in that queue.

Configure and Troubleshoot Fax Support

- ❑ Windows XP provides a new fax console that makes the management of faxes much easier. With the new fax console, you can manage incoming and outgoing faxes in much the same way you manage e-mail with an e-mail client.
- ❑ The fax console is not installed by default in Windows XP, but you can install it using Add/Remove Windows Components.
- ❑ Once the console is installed, a Configuration wizard will help you set up the service. By default, the fax service is only configured to send faxes, not receive them. You must enable the receive feature with the wizard or by accessing the fax console's properties pages.
- ❑ Permissions for the fax console are similar to printer permissions. The available fax permissions are Fax, Manage Fax Configuration, and Manage Fax Documents.

SELF TEST

The following questions will help you measure your understanding of the material presented in this chapter. Read all of the choices carefully, as there may be more than one correct answer. Choose all correct answers for each question.

Install Local Printers

1. In Microsoft terms, what is the device called that you connect a computer to in order to generate printed documents?

A. Printer

B. Print device

C. Print job

D. Printer output

2. Three users send items to the printer at the same time. Once those items are processed, which printer component holds those items until they can be sent to the print device?

A. GDI

B. Print processor

C. Print spooler

D. Printer driver

3. You have just connected a USB printer to a local USB port on a computer running Windows XP. What is the next action that might be necessary?

A. Run the Add A Printer Wizard.

B. Restart the computer.

C. Update the driver, if necessary.

D. Configure an IRQ for the printer.

Connect to Network and Internet Print Devices

4. What Windows 2000/.NET domain directory service enables a user to locate a certain printer on the network without knowing the printer's actual name?

A. PrintDiscover

B. Active Directory

C. Printer Find

D. PrintAttrib

5. You have a printer configured on a computer running Windows XP that connects directly to a network printer configured with a network adapter. The printer has been working correctly over the past two weeks, but today you cannot connect. Which test could you perform to determine if you have network connectivity with the printer?

A. Traceroute

B. Ipconfig

C. Ping

D. Prntrun

6. A user needs to connect to an Internet printer. The user is running an older laptop computer that uses Internet Explorer 3.0. What is the minimum upgrade the user needs to perform in order to connect to the Internet printer?

A. IE 4.0

B. IE 5.0

C. IE 6.0

D. Netscape

7. A user accesses a printer called "print33" on a server called "pntser4" located at a branch office. The printer is configured for Internet printing. Using a browser, what is the correct URL for accessing the printer?

A. **http://print33**

B. **http://pntser4/printers**

C. **http://prntser4/print33**

D. **http://prntser4/print33/printers**

8. You need to access a certain printer on print32, an Internet print server. However, you do not know the name of the printer you want to use. In Internet Explorer 4.0, what URL can you enter to see a list of shared printers on the server?

A. **http://print32**

B. **http://servers/print32**

C. **http://print32/pntshare**

D. **http://print32/printers**

Manage Printers and Print Jobs

9. You manage a number of different printers on several computers running Windows XP. You want to quickly check your printers to determine which ones provide staple support. You want to gain this information through the printers' properties sheets. Which tab can you check to find this information?

A. General

B. Ports

C. Sharing

D. Advanced

10. On a particular computer running Windows XP, you install three identical printers that you want to manage as one logical printer in a printer pool. You configure the printer but pooling is not provided under the default configuration. Which printer properties tab do you need to access in order to turn on printer pooling?

A. General

B. Ports

C. Sharing

D. Advanced

11. For a particular printer, you want to make certain that users can only use the printer between 11:00 A.M. and 2:00 P.M. Monday–Friday. Which configuration tab for the printer will enable you to configure this option?

A. General.

B. Ports.

C. Advanced.

D. This must be configured at the actual print device.

12. You have two different printers configured for the same print device. One printer is configured for the Marketing group and one printer is configured for the Advertising group. You want to make certain that the Advertising group's print jobs always print before the Marketing group's print jobs. What can you configure on the printer assigned to the Advertising group so that their print jobs will always print first?

A. Choose the Print Directly radio button option.

B. Change the priority to 50.

C. Choose the Hold Mismatched Documents option.

D. Choose the Print Spooled Documents First option.

13. You want to make certain that documents are printed on a priority basis, not on which documents are spooled and in what order. In order to make certain that spooling does not affect document print order, which option on the printer's Advanced properties tab needs to be cleared?

A. Enable Advanced Printing Features.

B. Keep Printed Documents.

C. Print Spooled Documents First.

D. Set the priority to 1.

14. Curt has a LaserJet printer attached to his computer. Curt notices that it sometimes takes a few minutes for the printer to start printing when a job is sent, especially if the job is lengthy. Curt wants the job to start printing as soon as possible. What setting can you configure on the Advanced tab that will help speed up the printing process?

A. Change the priority value to 99.

B. Clear the Hold Mismatched Documents check box.

C. Choose the Print Directly To The Printer option instead of using the spool.

D. Under Spool Settings, make sure the Start Printing Immediately option is selected.

15. On a computer running Windows XP that you manage, a group of users print to the shared printer. You receive a call from a user that a document she wanted to print never arrived at the printer. Now, it seems that other users are reporting the same problem. The print device is in working order and has paper. What do you need to do first?

A. Reinstall the printer.

B. Restart the computer.

C. Open the print queue and try pausing and restarting the print queue.

D. Open the print queue and delete all of the documents.

16. You are configuring a network print device. You want to make certain that users who run the Windows Me system can connect and use the print device connected to your Windows XP system. You have the drivers for Windows Me. What can you do so that those drivers will be available to Me clients?

A. Distribute them manually.

B. Configure the option on the Sharing tab of the printer's properties.

C. Add the driver using the Advanced tab.

D. Use Device Manager to configure the additional driver.

17. You want to configure Internet printing for a certain Windows XP computer so that the shared printer will be made available on the local intranet. What do you need to install on Windows XP to configure an Internet printer?

A. Nothing

B. IIS

C. ICF

D. ICS

Control Access to Printers with Permissions

18. You want a certain user to be able to print documents to a printer but also manage documents in the queue. You do not want the user to be able to configure the printer's properties. What two permissions should be assigned?

A. Print

B. Manage Printers

C. Manage Documents

D. Deny

19. You need to configure permissions for two groups. The first group, Accounting, needs a printing priority of 1 and the second group, Marketing, needs a printing priority of 50 so that their print jobs are always printed over accounting. You have a printer configured for the print device. What do you need to do?

A. Simply set the priorities and assign permissions.

B. Give the Marketing group the Manage Documents permission so they move their documents up in the print queue.

C. Create a second printer and assign a group to each printer—then configure priorities appropriately.

D. Configure multiple priorities based on the group permission.

Configure and Troubleshoot Fax Support

20. You set up and configure a fax console on a computer running Windows XP. You want to include older faxes that are stored in a folder on your computer. How can you include the old faxes in the fax console?

A. Use the Import option on the File Menu.

B. Use the Merge option on the File Menu.

C. Choose the Import option on the Tools menu.

D. Choose the Merge option on the Tools menu.

21. After fax installation and configuration, you notice that the fax will not receive faxes—it only sends them. You need to enable your fax to receive faxes, as well as send faxes. Where can you enable this?

A. Use the Receive option on the File menu.

B. Access the fax properties and enable the feature on the General tab.

C. Access the fax properties and enable the feature on the Properties button of the Devices tab.

D. Access the fax properties and enable the feature on the Security tab.

LAB QUESTION

On a computer running Windows XP, the fax console was installed with the default settings. Now that you have started using the fax console, you need to make a number of configuration changes. These changes are as follows:

- The fax console should receive calls automatically after two rings.
- When sending faxes, the number of retries should be 10 when a busy signal is encountered.
- You want a sound to play when a fax is received.
- You want the Notification Area to tell you if there is incoming or outgoing faxes.

How can you configure these options?

SELF TEST ANSWERS

Install Local Printers

1. ☑ B is correct. The physical device that generates printed output is called the print device. This may seem trivial, but it is easy to misunderstand configuration issues and options if you think of the print device as a "printer." Keep in mind that multiple printer configurations can be generated for the same print device, which can meet a variety of needs when network access is provided to users.

   ☒ A, C, and D are incorrect. These terms do not correctly identify the print device.

2. ☑ C is correct. The print spooler holds documents in the order they should be printed until the print device is available.

   ☒ A, B, and D are incorrect. None of these items hold documents until they can be printed.

3. ☑ C is correct. Plug and play can automatically detect and install plug-and-play printers. The next action you might need to perform is a driver upgrade, using the manufacturer's driver.

   ☒ A, B, and D are incorrect. These actions are not necessary when installing a plug-and-play printer.

Connect to Network and Internet Printers

4. ☑ B is correct. In Windows 2000 domains, the Active Directory maintains a listing of all computers and resources on the network. Users can search the Active Directory and locate desired printers by attribute, such as color printers or printers belonging to certain departments or groups.

   ☒ A, C, and D are incorrect. None of these items are correct.

5. ☑ C is correct. In this case, you should use the ping command to test network connectivity between the printer and the computer's network adapter card. This will tell you if the problem is a simple connectivity issue.

   ☒ A, B, and D are incorrect. Although ipconfig and traceroute are helpful network tools, they will not help you troubleshoot this situation. Prntrun is a not a valid command.

6. ☑ A is correct. In order to connect to an Internet printer, you must be running IE 4.0 or later.

   ☒ B, C, and D are incorrect. None of these browser versions are the minimum required.

7. ☑ C is correct. If you know the server and printer name, you can access the printer directly with the **http://servername/printername** convention.

   ☒ A, B, and D are incorrect. These options will not give you direct access to the printer.

8. ☑ D is correct. You can view the printers that are available on an Internet print server by using the **http://servername/printers** convention.

   ☒ A, B, and C are incorrect. These options will not give you access to the printers directory.

Manage Printers and Print Jobs

9. ☑ A is correct. You can gain general information about the printer on the General tab. This tab will tell you if the printer supports staple features.

   ☒ B, C, and D are incorrect. These tabs will not give you the requested information.

10. ☑ B is correct. Printer pooling can be enabled by clicking the check box on the Ports tab. Printer pooling requires two or more identical print devices. The printer then distributes print jobs to them, even though they appear as one printer to users.

    ☒ A, C, and D are incorrect. Printer pooling cannot be enabled on these tabs.

11. ☑ C is correct. You can use the Advanced tab to configure scheduling of when the printer can be used.

    ☒ A, B, and D are incorrect. You cannot configure this option on the General or the Ports tabs, so A and B are incorrect. In most cases, time features are not configured directly on the print device, unless the device is a standalone network printer, so D is also incorrect.

12. ☑ B is correct. Priority levels determine which print jobs print first, based on 1 (lowest) to 99 (highest). When multiple printers exist for the same print device, you can change the priority of one printer so that users who can access that printer have priority over other users.

    ☒ A, C, and D are incorrect. These settings will not change priority levels.

13. ☑ C is correct. Clear the Print Spooled Documents First check-box option to ensure that only priority settings impact document printing order.

    ☒ A, B, and D are incorrect. These settings will not ensure priority configuration.

14. ☑ D is correct. Make sure the Start Printing Immediately setting is selected under spool settings, instead of the Hold Document Until Last Page Is Spooled option. This causes the user to have to wait on the spool process instead of getting printer output immediately.

☒ A, B, and C are incorrect. These options will not resolve the problem.

15. ☑ C is correct. You first option should be to open the print queue, pause it, and restart it to see if you can get the documents flowing to the printer again.

☒ A, B, and D are incorrect. You do not need to reinstall or restart, so A and B are incorrect. Although you may need to delete all of the documents in the print queue, you should try to stop and restart it first so that users to not have resubmit print jobs. Therefore, D is also incorrect.

16. ☑ B is correct. If you share a printer that will be available to down-level clients, you can easily provide the additional drivers by using the Sharing tab of the printer's properties pages.

☒ A, C, and D are incorrect. These actions will not make the printer driver available and configured correctly for down-level client use.

17. ☑ B is correct. IIS is required before you can configure an Internet printer.

☒ A, C, and D are incorrect. These options are not correct.

Control Access to Printers with Permissions

18. ☑ A and C are correct. You should assign the Print and Manage Documents permissions. This allows the user to print to the fax and manage documents in the queue, but not the actual printer properties.

☒ B and D are incorrect. The Manage Printers permission gives the user access to the printer's properties, so C is incorrect. D is incorrect because the Deny permission simply denies access, which does not meet the needs in this situation.

19. ☑ C is correct. The only possible configuration in this case is to configure two different printers. Assign each group permission Print from a printer and configure the priorities as desired for each printer.

☒ A, B, and D are incorrect. None of these options will provide the desired configuration.

Configure and Troubleshoot Fax Support

20. ☑ A is correct. You can import and export data to and from the fax console using the Import/Export options on the File menu.

☒ B, C, and D are incorrect. You cannot import from these locations.

21. ☑ C is correct. If you do not enable the Receive option during the wizard setup, you can enable it at any time by accessing the Fax Properties, clicking the Devices tab, clicking the Properties button, clicking the Receive tab, and placing a check mark next to Enable Device To Receive.

☒ A, B, and D are incorrect. You cannot enable receive support from these locations.

LAB ANSWER

The lab question asked you to configure the fax to meet these specific requirements:

- The fax console should receive calls automatically after two rings.
- When sending faxes, the number of retries should be 10 when a busy signal is encountered.
- You want a sound to play when a fax is received.
- You want the Notification Area to tell you if there is incoming or outgoing faxes.

To configure these options, follow these steps:

1. Open the fax console and click Tools | Fax Printer Configuration.
2. Click the Devices tab and click the Properties button.
3. On the Send tab, shown in the following illustration, change the number of retries to 10.

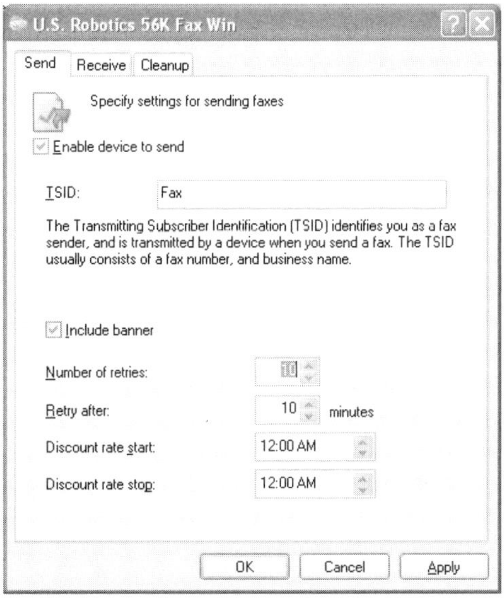

4. On the Receive tab, click the Enable Device To Receive check box and choose the automatic/two rings setting, as shown in the following illustration. Click OK.

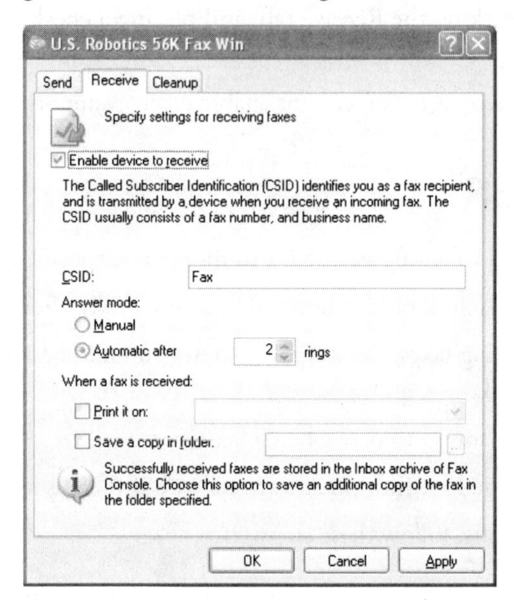

5. Click the Tracking tab. Ensure that the Notification Area settings are selected.

6. Click the Configure Sound Settings button at the bottom of the Tracking tab. Ensure that the Play A Sound When A New Fax Is Received check box is selected. Click OK and OK again.

9

Resource Administration

CERTIFICATION OBJECTIVES

9.01	Configure, Manage, and Troubleshoot File Compression
9.02	Create and Remove Shared Folders
9.03	Control Access to Files and Folders Using Permissions
9.04	Manage and Troubleshoot Web Server Resources
9.05	Manage and Troubleshoot Access to and Synchronization of Offline Files
✓	Two-Minute Drill
Q&A	Self Test

Windows XP Professional is designed for networking, and the primary feature of any network is the ability to share information. After all, computers networked together that cannot share information or peripherals (such as printers) are not much use to anyone. With file and folder management and sharing comes the issues of security and administration. It is helpful to think of file and folder management in terms of home security. You would not open your front door and let just anyone walk into your home. In the same manner, even those people whom you invite in the door cannot do whatever they want while they are guests. The same idea holds true for file and folder management and sharing—administration is the key to successful management and implementation. In this chapter, we'll take a look at resource administration and explore the objectives and resource management issues you are most likely to see on Exam 70-270.

CERTIFICATION OBJECTIVE 9.01

Configure, Manage, and Troubleshoot File Compression

I remember my first "real" computer, which had a hard drive capacity of about 30 megabytes. Today, I have folders that contain more than 30 megabytes of data, and I'm sure you do as well. Sure, computers today often have 40GB hard drives and higher, but the need to conserve storage space is as important today as ever. Fortunately, Windows XP Professional makes file compression easier than ever. It is fast and can be done automatically and, to the local user running applications and files on the computer, there is seemingly no difference between compressed and non-compressed files or, even, volumes.

Windows XP Professional supports two different types of file/folder compression, NTFS compression and Compressed (zipped) folders. Since there are differences between these methods, we will explore them individually in the following two sections.

NTFS Compression

NTFS compression is available to compress individual files or folders, as well as entire drives. Of course, to use NTFS compression, you must have an NTFS drive.

The good thing about NTFS compression is that it is fast and easy—and it gives you a lot of compression options. Consider the following points:

- NTFS compression enables you to compress a single file, a folder, or an entire NTFS drive. You can compress a folder without compressing its contents as well.
- All compressed items remain in a compressed state unless you move the contents to a FAT volume. FAT does not support NTFS compression, so compression is lost when the file/folder is moved.
- If you want to work with a compressed file, Windows XP automatically decompresses it for you while the file is in use. When you close the file, Windows XP automatically compresses the file again. This, of course, consumes more system resources, and, depending on the state of your system, you may see a performance hit.
- If you move or copy a file into a compressed folder, it is compressed automatically. If you move a file from a different NTFS drive to a compressed folder, it is also compressed. However, if you move a file from the same NTFS drive into a compressed folder, it retains its original state, either compressed or uncompressed.
- You cannot encrypt an NTFS compressed file.

You need to memorize these bullet points for the exam. You may see tricky compression questions that test your in-depth knowledge of NTFS file compression.

As you can see, these are fairly straightforward rules, but it is important that you keep them in mind as you are working with NTFS compression. Beyond these rules, compression is rather easy. The following exercises walk you through the compression of drives, folders, and files.

EXERCISE 9-1

Compressing an NTFS Volume

To compress an NTFS volume, just follow these steps:

1. Click Start | My Computer.

2. In My Computer, right-click the desired NTFS drive and click Properties.
3. On the General tab, shown in the following illustration, click the "Compress drive to save disk space" check box in order to compress the entire drive. Then, click OK.

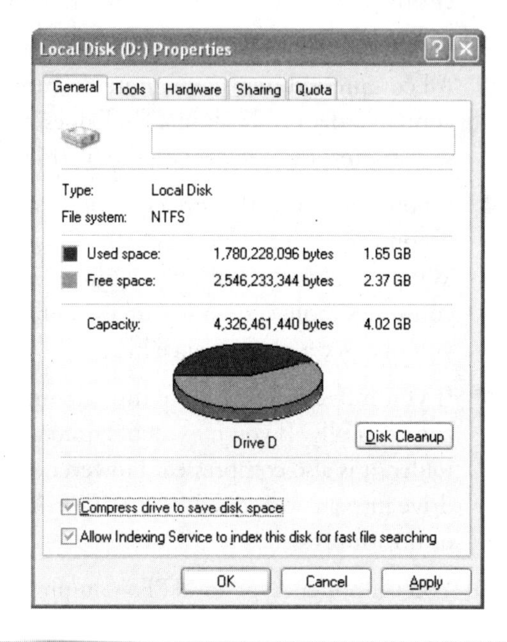

Exercise 9-2 shows you how to compress the contents of a file or folder.

EXERCISE 9-2

Compressing an NTFS File or Folder

To compress an NTFS file or folder, just follow these steps:

1. Browse to the desired file or folder that you want to compress. Remember that the file or folder has to reside on an NTFS drive in order for compression to be available.

2. Right-click the desired file or folder and click Properties.
3. On the General tab, click the Advanced button.
4. In the Advanced Attributes window, shown in the following illustration, click the "Compress contents to save disk space" check box and click OK.

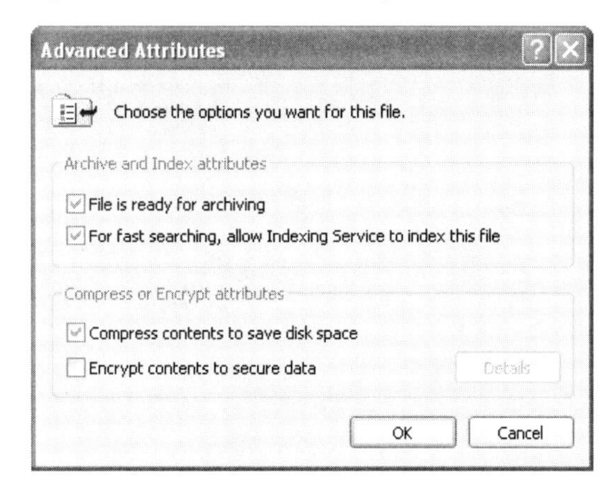

Another helpful feature of NTFS compression is that in Windows XP you can make compressed drives, files, and folders appear in a different color so you can recognize them as compressed. Exercise 9-3 shows you how to configure this option.

EXERCISE 9-3

Configuring Color for Compressed Items

To configure color for compressed folders, just follow these steps:

1. Open Control Panel and double-click Folder Options.
2. Click the View tab.
3. Scroll and locate the "Show encrypted or compressed NTFS files in color" check box, shown in the following illustration. Select the check box and click OK.

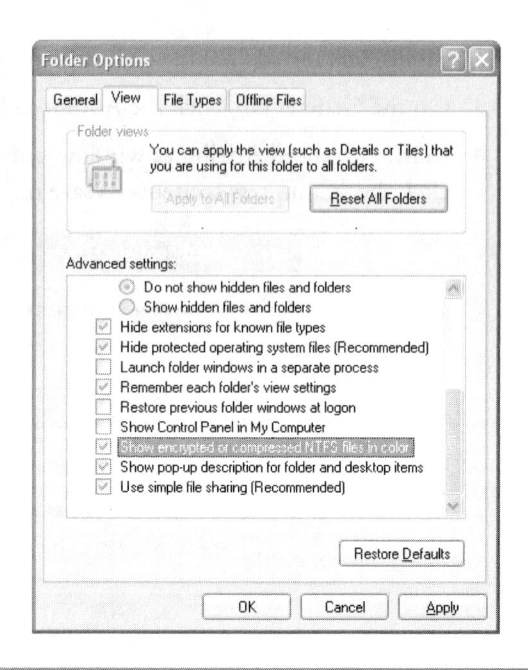

on the Job ***Typically, NTFS compression reduces drive, file, and folder size by about 50 percent. Applications are reduced by about 40 percent. As you can see, the judicious use of NTFS compression can provide significant savings in drive storage space.***

Aside from the Windows XP interface options, you can also use a command line utility, compact.exe, to manage compressed files and volumes in Windows XP. Using compact.exe, you can compress, decompress, and view the compression attributes of a folder, file, or drive. The syntax for compact.exe is

```
compact.exe [/c] [/u] [/s[:dir]] [/a] [/i] [/f] [/q] [filename [...]]
```

Table 9-1 defines each of the command switches.

Compressed (Zipped) Folders

First introduced in Windows Me and included in Windows XP Professional, Compressed (zipped) folders is a built-in compression feature that allows you

TABLE 9-1 compact.exe Switches

Switch	Explanation
C	Compresses the specified file
U	Uncompresses (decompresses) the specified file
S	Performs the specified operation on the files in the given folder or subfolder
A	Displays file with hidden or system attributes
I	Continues performing the specified operation even after errors have occurred
F	Forces the compress operation on all specified files, including currently compressed files
Q	Reports only the most essential information
Filename	Specifies a pattern, file, or folder

to compress folders on the fly. This folder compression, which is built on WinZip technology, gives you a quick and easy way to copy files to a compressed folder, which can then be e-mailed or stored. At first glance, it may not seem like there is a need for zipped folders when NTFS compression is available, but there are several advantages:

- Compressed (zipped) folders can reside on either NTFS or FAT volumes, unlike NTFS compression, which only works on NTFS volumes.
- Files that reside in a compressed folder can be directly opened without unzipping them, and some applications can also run in a zipped state.
- Zipped folders can be moved to any drive/folder on your or another computer or to the Internet or be sent via e-mail and remain in their compressed state. Additionally, you'll see no performance hits when using zipped folders.
- Files cannot be individually compressed using the zip feature. You must place them in a compressed folder in order to compress the files.
- Compressed zipped folders can be password protected.

exam Watch

You need to keep the differences between compressed folders and NTFS compression clear for tricky exam questions.

SCENARIO & SOLUTION	
I have compressed my boot and system partitions on a Windows XP Professional computer, but I have noticed a performance hit. Is this normal?	Yes. All things come with a cost, and compression is no exception to the rule. When the boot and system partitions have been compressed, the system must uncompress, read the files, and recompress them. This takes time and causes extra work for the operating system. Take a look at your compression plan and consider only compressing data drives and folders as an alternative.
I moved a compressed file to an encrypted folder and the compression was lost.	Compression and encryption are not compatible with each other, so any files moved to an encrypted folder will lose the compressed state. The file becomes encrypted, as opposed to compressed, because encryption overrides compression.
If I copy a compressed file to a folder, will it retain its compressed state?	That depends. If the folder is uncompressed, then the copied file inherits the target location's properties, which is uncompressed in this instance. If the folder is compressed, then the copied file is compressed under the folder's properties
On a particular folder, the compression option is not available. Why?	The folder is stored on an FAT volume. Files, folders, and FAT volumes cannot use NTFS compression.

Using the Compressed (zipped) folder feature is very easy. If you have a folder that you want to compress, simply right-click the folder and click Send To | Compressed (zipped)Folder. This will create the zipped folder with all of the original folder's contents compressed, but the original folder remains. In other words, you'll see your original folder and a copied, compressed folder of the same contents. If you want to create an empty compressed folder to which you can copy items, simply click File | New | Compressed Folder from within the desired folder or Windows Explorer. If you want to create the new compressed folder on your desktop, simply right-click an empty area of the desktop and click New | Compressed folder.

CERTIFICATION OBJECTIVE 9.02

Create and Remove Shared Folders

Shared folders are the primary way of making data available to users on a network. Shared data can include files, documents, applications, and essentially anything else you might store in a folder. By sharing folders, users can access data on different network computers. For the exam, as well as your real world experience, you should know how to create and remove shared folders from a local Windows XP Professional computer. Fortunately, the process is easy.

If Windows XP Professional is connected to a network, whether a Windows 2000 domain or a workgroup setting, the ability to share folders is automatically available. If the computer is not configured for networking, then the sharing feature does not appear until the computer is configured for network access (network card, IP address configuration, client for Microsoft networks, and File and Printer Sharing for Microsoft networks). See Chapter 10 to learn more about networking with Windows XP Professional.

To share a folder, simply right-click the desired folder, click Properties, and then click the Sharing tab. As you can see in Figure 9-1, the Sharing tab gives you two

FIGURE 9-1

The Sharing tab

My Music Properties
General
Sharing
Local sharing and security
To share this folder with other users of this computer only, drag it to the Shared Documents folder.
To make this folder and its subfolders private so that only you have access, select the following check box.
Make this folder private
Network sharing and security
To share this folder with both network users and other users of this computer, select the first check box below and type a share name.
Share this folder on the network
Share name: My Music
Allow network users to change my files
Learn more about sharing and security.
OK
Cancel
Apply

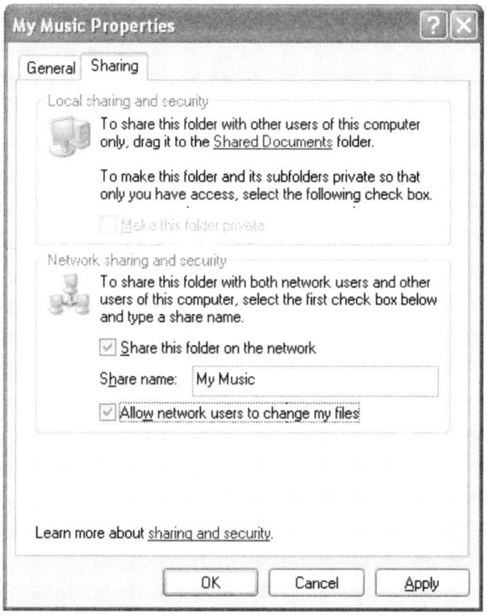

options. First, you can share the folder locally. This means that if you want only users of your local computer to be able to access the folder, you simply need to drag the folder to the Shared Documents folder that is available in Windows XP. When a user logs on the computer, the Shared Documents folder is available to the user, and anything stored in the folder is also available. To share the folder on the network, select the "Share this folder on the network" check box and then enter a desired share name. To stop a folder from being shared, simply clear this check box.

You can also use the Computer Management console's Shared folder feature to manage shared connections. For example, you can see how many users are connected to a particular shared folder and view open files. You can forcefully disconnect sessions from this console as well. Exercise 9-4 shows you how to use the Computer Management console.

EXERCISE 9-4

Using Shared Folders

To manage shared folders, just follow these steps:

1. Log on as an administrator.
2. Open Control Panel | Administrative Tools | Computer Management.
3. In the Computer Management console, shown in the following illustration, expand shared folders. You can then view the shares, sessions, and open files. To close sessions and open files, right-click Sessions or Open Files in the left console pane and choose either Disconnect All Sessions or Disconnect All Open Files.

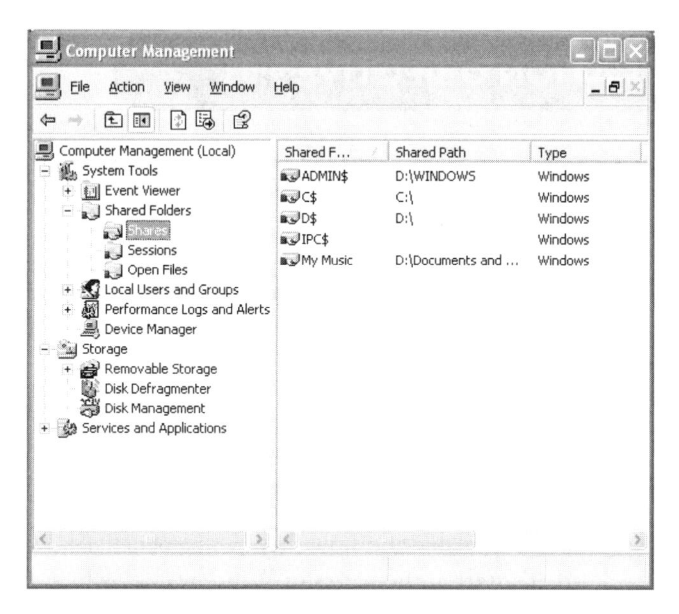

4. Close the console when you're done.

SCENARIO & SOLUTION

I want to prevent any user on the local Windows XP Professional computer from sharing folders. How can I do this?	You can use Group Policy on the local Windows XP Professional, as well as on a Windows 2000 OU, domain, or site configuration from Windows 2000 Server and prevent users from sharing folders. You'll find a Shared Folders option under the User Configuration node in Administrative Templates in the Group Policy console.
I moved a compressed file to an encrypted folder, and the compression was lost.	Compression and encryption are not compatible with each other, so any files moved to an encrypted folder will lose the compressed state.
Why does Windows XP Professional give the local folder sharing option?	In an attempt to make folder sharing easier for end users, any shared folder can be placed in Shared Folders so that all local users can access the folder. This feature provides an easy way for local computer users (such as those in a small workgroup or family system) to use the same data.

CERTIFICATION OBJECTIVE 9.03

Control Access to Files and Folders Using Permissions

Once you share files and folders on a network, you'll want to manage those files and folders in a way that is both practical and useful. Typically, you will want to control what users are allowed to do with the folders you have shared and their contents. Using NTFS permissions, you can finely control what users can and cannot do with a locally shared folder. If you have spent any time on a Microsoft network, you know the issue of permissions can certainly get complicated and difficult, and you can expect the exam to reflect this. In the next section, you'll explore the file and folder permissions that are available and how they can be beneficial.

Let's start at the basics of Windows XP, which handles permissions somewhat differently from previous versions of Windows. Keep in mind that while Windows XP Professional is designed to be a network operating system, many home and small office users are expected to take advantage of Windows XP Professional as well. Therefore, Windows XP Professional attempts to make networking features as easy as possible for the end user. Consider the Sharing tab in Figure 9-2.

Notice that you have the option to share the folder on the network and the option to allow network users to change the files in the folder. When you share a folder using this tab, the permission of Read is assigned to the folder. You can override this setting by allowing Write permission by clicking the "Allow network users to change my files" check box option. Good enough, but is that all there is? Not hardly.

These easy permission options are provided for users on a home network or small office workgroup. If your computer is connected to a domain, you will also see a Security tab on the shared folder/drive's properties sheets. Even if your computer is not a domain member, you can still enable the Security tab. Just follow the steps in Exercise 9-5.

FIGURE 9-2

The Sharing tab

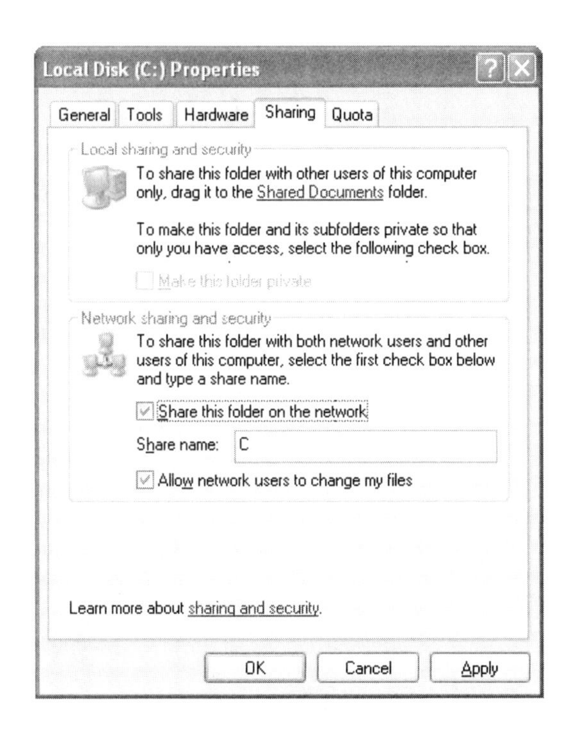
Local Disk (C:) Properties
General
Tools
Hardware
Sharing
Quota
Local sharing and security
To share this folder with other users of this computer only, drag it to the Shared Documents folder.
To make this folder and its subfolders private so that only you have access, select the following check box.
Make this folder private
Network sharing and security
To share this folder with both network users and other users of this computer, select the first check box below and type a share name.
Share this folder on the network
Share name:
C
Allow network users to change my files
Learn more about sharing and security.
OK
Cancel
Apply

EXERCISE 9-5

CertCam 9-5

Enabling Advanced Security Options for Computers Not Connected to a Domain

To enable advanced security settings for computers not connected to a domain, just follow these steps:

1. Log on as an administrator.
2. Open Control Panel and double-click Folder Options.
3. Click the View tab and clear the "Use simple file sharing (recommended)" check box option, shown in the following illustration. Click OK.

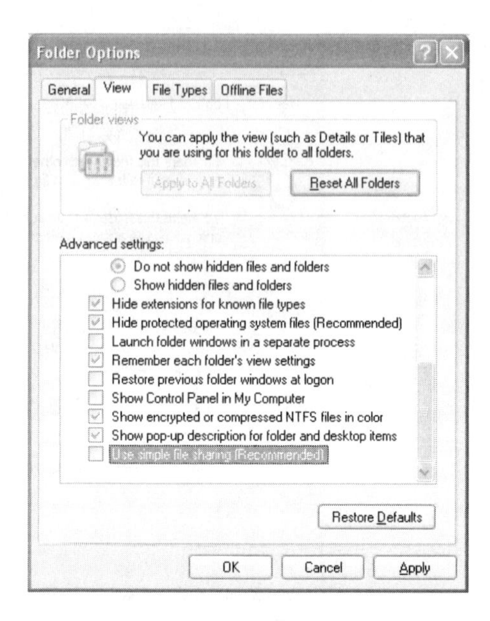

Once you enable the advanced file sharing option, you'll see that the Sharing tab changes its appearance, as shown in Figure 9-3.

FIGURE 9-3

The advanced Sharing tab

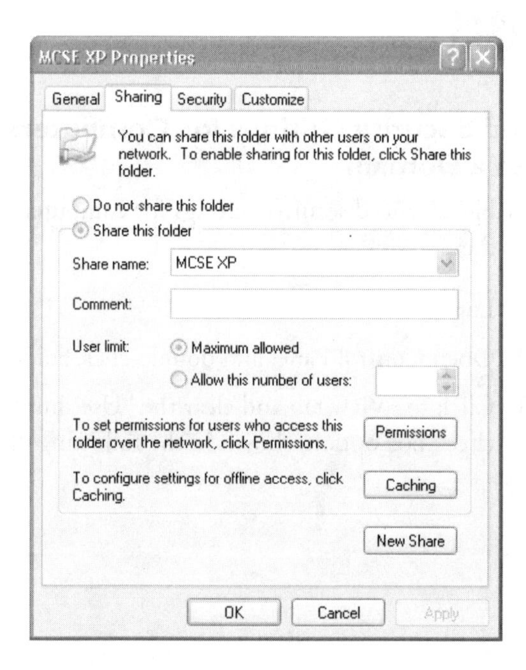

As with the previous Sharing tab, you can still select to share the folder and assign a desired name, and you can even limit the number of users who can connect to the share at the same time. You can also set folder permissions, which brings us to our discussion of file and folder permissions in Windows XP.

There is no difference in file and folder permission in Windows XP and in Windows 2000, so if you have worked with Windows 2000 Server or Professional, you'll see no differences here. The following sections take a look at file and folder permissions and advanced NTFS permissions. In the following sections, you'll learn about shared folder and file permissions, as well as individual NTFS permission that you can apply to users.

File and Folder Permissions

File and folder permissions are set on the Security tab found on the Properties sheet of the file or folder. Simply right-click the desired file or folder, click Properties, and then click the Security tab, shown in Figure 9-4. As you can see, you can select a desired group or an individual user and configure the desired file level permissions for that file.

FIGURE 9-4

The Security tab for an individual file

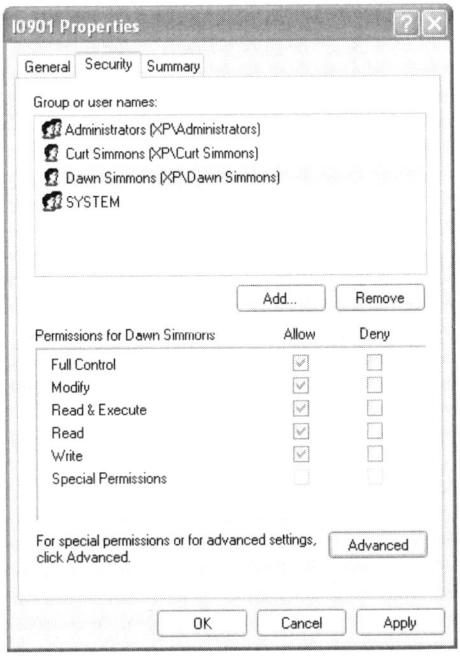

The standard permissions are Full Control, Modify, Read & Execute, Read, Write, and Special Permissions. In truth, each of these permissions is actually made up of a combination of certain special permissions. Before looking at what special permissions make up these standard permissions, let's first consider the special permissions and their definitions, which are described in Table 9-2. You'll need to know these for the exam, so I suggest that you commit them to memory.

exam watch

When configuring permissions, keep in mind that if a permission is grayed out, the permission has been inherited from a parent folder.

TABLE 9-2 Special Permissions

Special Permission	Explanation
Traverse Folder, Execute File	Allows or denies browsing through folders to reach other subfolders and the execution of files.
List Folder, Read Data	List Folder allows or denies viewing file/subfolder names. Read Data allows or denies reading data in a file.
Read Attributes	Allows or denies the reading of attributes of a file or folder.
Read Extended Attributes	Allows or denies the reading of extended attributes of a file or folder.
Create Files, Write Data	Create Files allows or denies the right to create a file in a particular folder. Write Data allows or denies the creation of new data to a file or the overwriting of existing information.
Create Folders, Append Data	Create Folders allows or denies the ability to create subfolders in a folder. Append Data allows or denies the appending of data to an existing file (does not allow the changing of existing data in the file).
Write Attributes	Allows or denies the editing of attributes in a file or folder.
Write Extended Attributes	Allows or denies the writing of extended attributes for a file or folder.
Delete Subfolders and Files	Allows or denies the power to delete subfolders and files within a folder.
Delete	Allows or denies the power to delete a file or folder.
Read	Allows or denies reading of a file or folder.
Change permissions	Allows or denies the ability to change permission for a file or folder.
Take Ownership	Allows or denies the power to take ownership of a file of folder.
Synchronize	Allows or denies the power to synchronize data.

Now that you have taken a look at the special permissions, let's return to the standard permissions I mentioned previously. Standard permissions are combinations of special permissions that give users or groups certain rights. The following bullet list tells you which special permissions are included in which standard permissions.

- **Full Control** Full Control permission contains all special permissions.
- **Modify** Modify permission contains the following special permissions:
  - Traverse Folder/Execute File
  - List Folder/Read Data
  - Read Attributes
  - Read Extended Attributes
  - Create Files/Write Data
  - Create Folders/Append Data
  - Write Attributes, Write Extended Attributes
  - Delete
  - Read
  - Synchronize
- Read and Execute
  - Traverse Folder/Execute File
  - List Folder/Read Data
  - Read Attributes
  - Read Extended Attributes
  - Read
  - Synchronize
- List Folder Contents
  - Traverse Folder/Execute File
  - List Folder/Read Data
  - Read Attributes
  - Read Extended Attributes

    - Read
    - Synchronize
- Read
    - List Folder/Read Data
    - Read Attributes
    - Read Extended Attributes
    - Read
    - Synchronize
- Write
    - Create Files/Write Data
    - Create Folders/Append Data
    - Write Attributes
    - Write Extended Attributes
    - Read

So now that we have taken a look at the file and folder standard permissions and what special permissions make up the standard permissions, it is important for you to know how the permissions work together. There are two important rules that you must memorize for the exam and for your real world work with NTFS permissions:

- File and Folder permissions are cumulative. This means that if a user has Read permission and that same user is a member of a group that has Full Control permission, then the user's effective permission is Full Control. In situations where multiple permissions apply to the same user, then the least restrictive permission takes effect.
- Deny permission overrides all other permissions. This is an exception to the first rule. For example, let's say that a user has Full Control permission but is a member of group that is denied access. In this case, the user's effective permission is Deny. The user has no access to the file at all.

exam Watch ***You are very likely to see questions concerning these rules on the exam. Just remember to sort through the questions carefully and apply the two rules to arrive at the correct answer.***

Advanced NTFS Permissions

Under most circumstances, the standard permissions of Full Control, Modify, Read & Execute, List Folder Contents, Read and Write are all you need to effectively manage user access to shared folders and files. However, in some cases, you may need to customize the security settings for a particular user or group. For example, suppose you want to give a particular group Full Control to a shared folder without the special permission of Take Ownership. How can you do it? The answer is through advanced permissions.

You can easily set advanced permissions for any desired file or folder and apply those advanced permissions to a desired user group. Exercise 9-6 shows you how to configure advanced settings, but first I want to explain the issue of *inheritance.* By default, objects in Windows XP Professional, as well as Windows 2000, inherit the properties of the parent object. For example, let's say that a particular folder called Docs resides in a shared folder called Company. By default, the properties and permissions of Company are enforced on the Docs folder as well. This inheritance behavior keeps administrators from having to configure folder after folder. Instead, you configure the top-level folder, and all subfolders inherit those settings. As you can guess, this is a great time-saving feature. However, there may be times when you need to override this feature, and you can do so with the advanced security settings. See Exercise 9-6 for a walkthrough.

EXERCISE 9-6

Configuring Advanced Permissions

To configure advanced permissions, follow these steps:

1. Log on as an administrator.
2. Right-click the desired file or folder and click Properties. Click the Security tab.
3. Choose the desired user or group from the provided list and click the Advanced button.
4. The Advanced Security Settings window appears, as shown in the following illustration. Note that the "Inherit from parent the permission entries that apply to child objects…" check box is selected by default. If you want to override inheritance for this object, remove the check box option here. Select

the user/group in the window whose permissions you want to change and click the Edit button.

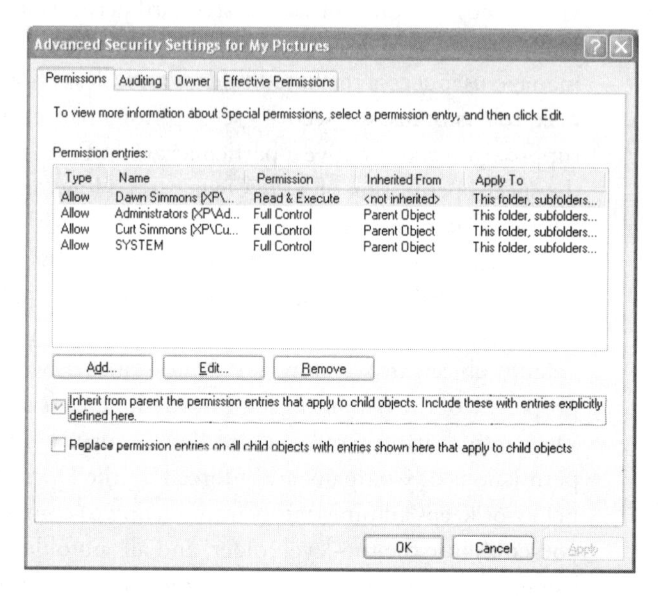

5. In the Permission Entry window, shown in the following illustration, click the Apply Onto drop-down menu and select one of the following, as applicable:
   - Apply onto this folder, subfolders, and files
   - Apply onto this folder only
   - Apply onto this folder and subfolders
   - Apply onto this folder and files
   - Apply onto subfolders and files only
   - Apply onto subfolders only
   - Apply onto files only
6. Once you have made your selection, click the desired check boxes in order to configure the permissions of the user or group. Also note that at the bottom of the page, as shown in the following illustration, you can choose to apply these permissions to objects and/or containers within the existing container. Once you are done, click OK and OK again to leave the Advanced settings window.

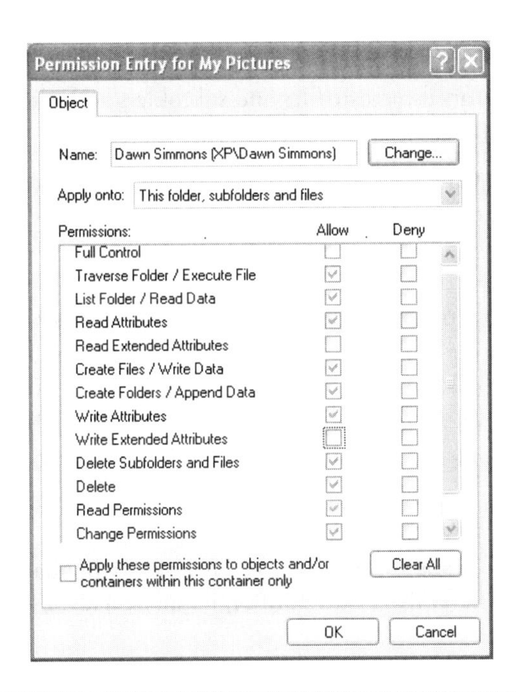

Share Level vs. NTFS Permissions and Access Optimization

As you learned in the previous section, a user's effective NTFS permission is the least restrictive permission available. For example, if a user has Read, Write, and Full Control permissions from different group settings, then the user has Full Control permission because it is the least restrictive.

Now let's muddy the waters a bit. Windows XP Professional, like Windows 2000, also supports share level permissions. Share level permissions are the only permissions available for shared folders that reside on non-NTFS volumes, such as FAT or FAT32. They are a weaker form of permissions without all of the advanced options found in NTFS permissions. There are three types of share level permissions:

- **Read** The user can view a list of what resides in the shared folder and subfolders, providing the ability to view data and run applications in the shared folder.

- **Change** The user can do everything provided by Read permissions, but the user can also create files and subfolders and edit existing files. The user can also delete files and subfolders in the share.
- **Full Control** The user can do everything provided by Read and Change, but the user can also take ownership of the folder and change any existing NTFS permissions.

Share level permissions can be configured by clicking the Permissions button on the Sharing tab for the folder; doing this opens a basic window where you can configure the permission based for a user or group, as you can see in Figure 9-5.

Like NTFS permissions, a user's least restrictive share level permission provides the effective permission. For example, if a user has Read permission from one group membership and Full Control from another group membership, then the user has Full Control over that folder.

This all sounds simple enough. However, what happens when Share and NTFS permissions are mixed, which often happens. For example, let's say a user belongs

FIGURE 9-5

Share level permissions

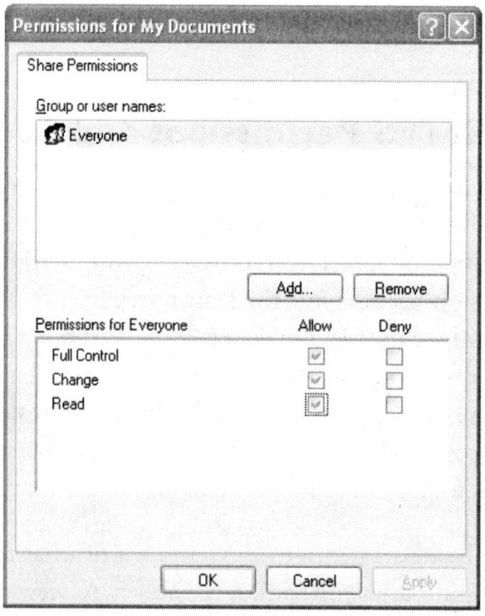

to a group that has Read share level permission of a folder but Full Control NTFS permission. Which permission does the user get? When there is a combination of share and NTFS permissions, the most restrictive permission is the effective permission—which is Read in this case. As you'll notice, this is the opposite of the approach of NTFS permissions and share level permissions. How can you keep it all straight? Here's a quick list you can memorize.

exam Watch

You should memorize the following bullet list for the exam—it will help you stay on track when you experience complicated and tricky permissions questions.

- NTFS permissions are cumulative. When a user has several different permissions for the same shared folder, the least restrictive permission applies. The exception is Deny, which overrides all other permissions.
- Share level permissions are cumulative. When a user has several different permissions for the same share, the least restrictive permission applies. The exception is Deny, which overrides all other permissions.
- When share level permissions and NTFS permissions are combined, the user receives the most restrictive permission. For example, if a user has Modify NTFS permission for a shared folder but Read shared folder level permission, the effective permission is Read. Again, Deny overrides everything.

As a general rule, both share level and NTFS permissions are configured at the group level. This makes the application of permissions easy for administrators, less confusing, and more streamlined. For example, may environments contain a standard Users group in which network users belong. Permissions and restrictions to network resources are then configured for the group as a whole—not on an individual level. Users who should have more rights are often placed in different group structures, such as Power Users, while administrators belong to administrative groups. Great variations occur from network to network, of course.

As a part of your administrative tasks, you must also consider the concept of "access optimization." How can you use shared folders and permissions in order to make access faster for network users. There are many different strategies, but here are a few you might see on the exam:

- Remember to keep groups and permissions as simple as possible. Having users belong to multiple groups with different permissions tends to cause conflicting permissions and difficulty troubleshooting access problems. The simpler the group membership configuration, the easier your job is to configure and manage permissions and access.

- Consider placing users' home folders on a network shared folder, with subfolders for each user, instead of sharing each user's individual home folder. This speeds access and makes network access to the home folder easier.
- For users who access different computers using roaming user profiles, it is not usual to redirect the My Documents folder to a network share so that access is faster.
- The most restrictive permission should always be the file system (NFTS) permission, as opposed to share permissions. You have a greater level of control with NTFS permissions, and they apply both locally and when accessing shared folders from the network.

exam Watch

As a general rule, it is important to review permissions and keep them as simple as possible. Complex permissions require more administrative time and tend to cause access problems. You can optimize user access by keeping users strictly organized into groups and making certain that permissions on shares are simple and straightforward.

CERTIFICATION OBJECTIVE 9.04

Manage and Troubleshoot Web Server Resources

Windows XP Professional is capable of performing on a network as a Web server through Internet Information Services (IIS), which is available in Windows XP Professional. You can learn more about setting up IIS and IIS functionality in Chapter 11, but we'll take a brief look at resource management via the Web server in this section.

Essentially, Web sites are made up of files and folders, just like any other directory structure on the local computer. Depending on how complicated the Web site is, resources offered to users may span many different computers or be stored locally. You'll find that managing those Web folders is not much different from managing any other shared folder on Windows XP Professional.

SCENARIO & SOLUTION

As a general rule, what is the best way to apply permissions for shared folders?	Permissions should be applied at the group level in a domain environment. In a workgroup setting, they can be applied individually. In a domain environment, you can always override group settings with more liberal permissions for an individual user as needed, but as a general rule, users should be managed via groups.
I need to configure advanced permissions for a user, but I am concerned about effective permissions. Is there an easy way to get this information?	Yes. On the Advanced Security settings dialog box, click the Effective Permissions tab and choose the user's name to see the effective permissions.
A user has NTFS Read, Write, and Modify permissions for a file as a result of different group memberships. What is the user's effective permission?	NTFS permissions are cumulative, with the exception of Deny. The least restrictive permission applies, so in this case, the user has Modify permission (which includes Read and Write).
A user has the NTFS permission of Read and the share level permission of Full Control on a particular share. What is the user's effective permission?	The combination of NTFS and share level permission results in the most restrictive permission, which is Read in this case.

FROM THE CLASSROOM

Inheritance in the Real World

Inheritance is an important issue in Windows 2000 networks that affects not only permissions and subfolders, but larger networking divisions as well, such as domains and OUs. In Group Policy, inheritance is very important because child OUs and OUs residing under a domain policy inherit the domain policy unless the policy is explicitly overwritten by an OU policy. In terms of permissions, the same concept applies. A subfolder may inherit the parent's permissions, but you can individually override the inheritance feature if necessary. From an administrative point of view, however, inheritance is designed to be an effective and time saving feature of Windows 2000. If you have to override inherited permissions on a regular basis, you probably have a faulty folder structure. As a general rule, folders should be organized and grouped in such a way that permissions inheritance is normal and appropriate. If you have to override permission on a regular basis, your folder structure probably needs some work.

In order to share resources on a Web site via IIS, you typically create a virtual directory that points to a real directory located on the local computer or even another shared directory located on the network. In order to set up Web shares, IIS provides a virtual directory wizard that helps you configure the directory and its security. Exercise 9-7 walks you through this process.

EXERCISE 9-7

Configuring Advanced Permissions

To configure advanced permissions, follow these steps:

1. Log on as an administrator.
2. Access the IIS console by clicking Start | Control Panel | Administrative Tools | Internet Information Services.
3. In the IIS console, expand Web sites and select the desired Web site where you want to add the virtual directory, as shown in the following illustration.

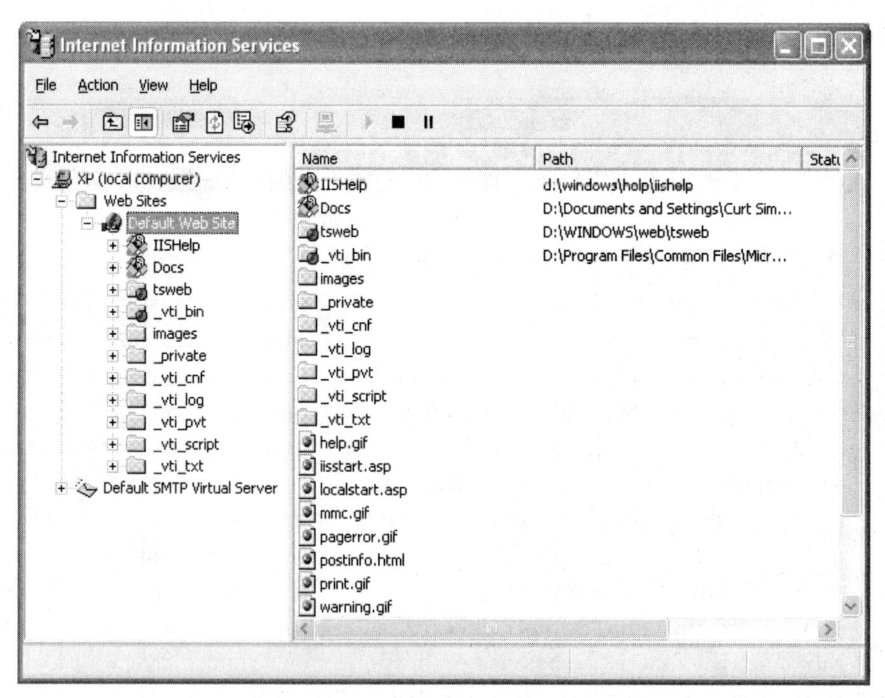

4. Right-click the Web site in the left console pane and then click New | Virtual Directory.
5. The Virtual Directory Creation wizard appears. Click Next.
6. In the Virtual Directory Alias window, enter a name for the directory. This is the directory name that users will access via the Web browser, so something friendly is preferred. Make your entry and click Next.
7. In the Web Site Content Directory, enter the path to the directory that contains the content. You can use the Browse button to locate the folder on your local computer or the network. Make your entry and click Next.
8. In the Access Permissions window, shown in the following illustration, choose the desired level of permissions. By default, Read and Run Scripts are selected. You can also choose Execute, Write, and Browse, depending on your security needs. Make your selections and click Next.

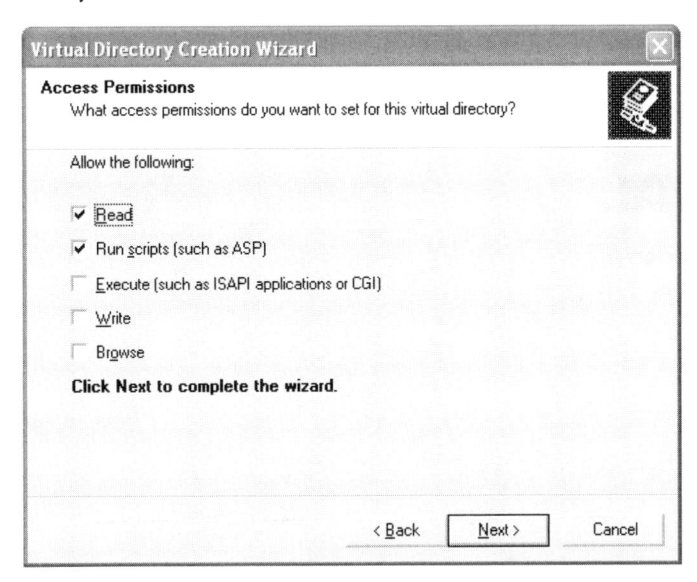

9. Click Finish to complete the wizard. The new directory appears in the IIS console.

Once the directory is created, you can right-click the directory name and click Properties, where you can further configure security and access needs as desired. On the Virtual Directory tab, shown in Figure 9-6, you can easily make changes to the settings you configured when you created the directory with the wizard.

You can also further configure security settings using the Directory Security tab. If you click the Edit button under "Anonymous access and authentication control," you see the Authentication Methods window, shown in Figure 9-7. From this location, you can either allow or not allow anonymous access and configure the desired authentication control. By default, anonymous access is configured so that users do not have to provide a username and password, as with typical Web folder access. However, you can choose to use NTFS ACLs so that users have to be authenticated before accessing Web sites. If you choose this option, Integrated Windows authentication is used by default.

As you can see, you can manage access to Web resources in much the same way you would any other network access folder. The primary difference here is that typical Web access is read only and anonymous. For the exam, however, you need to know where to change these configurations.

FIGURE 9-6

Virtual Directory tab

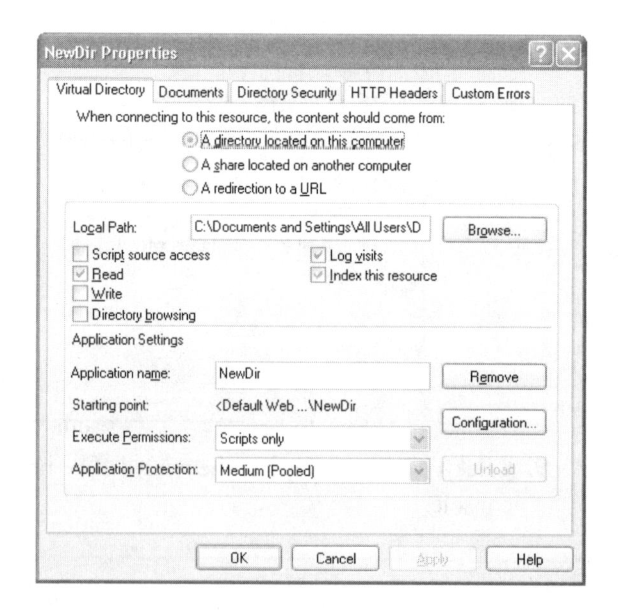

FIGURE 9-7

The Authentication Methods window

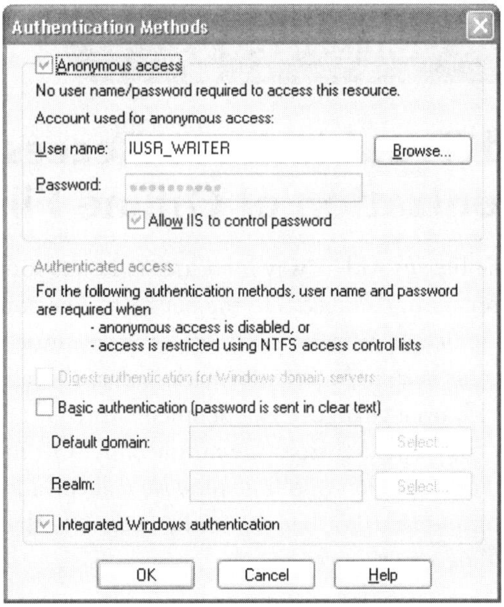

SCENARIO & SOLUTION

How is Windows XP Professional typically used with IIS?	In most cases, IIS is used to host intranet sites on Windows XP Professional. Windows 2000 Server is more suited to handling Internet sites, but Windows XP Professional can be an effective system for managing Internet sites
Why is anonymous access allowed by default?	Anonymous access is the typical way users access a Web folder—much the same way as accessing Web sites on the Internet. However, if you want to impose Windows authentication methods, you can do so on the Directory Security tab of the virtual directory's properties pages.

CERTIFICATION OBJECTIVE 9.05

Manage and Troubleshoot Access to and Synchronization of Offline Files

Offline files provide a way for a user to access some resources on the network when the user is not connected to the network. The concept of offline files is certainly nothing new in Windows XP, but they continue to serve important purposes. How can a user keep network information stored locally? Offline files. How can a user make editorial changes to a document stored on a network server and then have the server copy updated from the offline copy? Offline files.

In our discussion of offline files, we will consider two different offline file methods, caching and actual offline file configuration, both of which can be very effective tools for offline access.

Caching

When a folder is shared on the network, you have the option of configuring a caching level for the information in that folder. This feature enables network documents to be stored locally on the user's computer in a "cache," which is a temporary storage location. The benefit is network performance. Because cached files are stored locally, not as much information must traverse the network. While caching is not a great tool for user information that changes frequently, for network data and files it can keep network traffic problems at bay and provide access to network resources when the user is not connected to the network.

You can configure caching on a shared folder by right-clicking the folder and clicking Properties. Return to the Sharing tab and click the Caching button. You'll see the Caching Settings window, shown in Figure 9-8. To enable caching, simply click the check box and choose one of the three options from the Setting drop-down menu. The options are:

- **Automatic Caching Of Documents** This option is recommended for folders containing user documents. With this setting, the documents are automatically downloaded and made available when working offline.

FIGURE 9-8

Caching settings

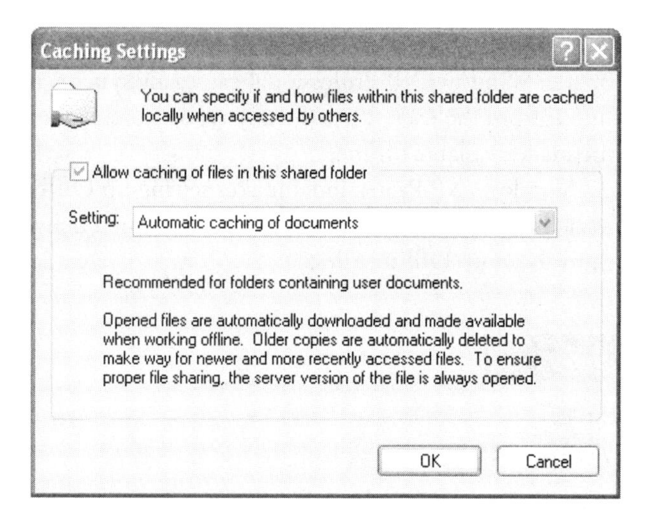

- **Automatic Caching Of Programs And Documents** This option is recommended for folders with read-only data or applications that are run over the network. Opened files are automatically downloaded and made available offline.
- **Manual Caching Of Documents** With this option, users must specify any files that they want to make available when working offline. The only difference here is that documents are not automatically downloaded.

Offline Files

While the network caching function is very useful for network documents and files that seldom change, the Offline Files feature is more suited for collaborative work or files that are updated regularly. Let's consider an example. A certain document is stored on a Windows 2000 File server. During the day, four users access the file and make editorial changes to it. One user needs to work on the file in the evening using her laptop computer, which will not be connected to the network. She simply downloads the file, makes any desired changes, and synchronizes with the server when she returns to work. The server recognizes the new changes and incorporates them. When other users access the file, they see the new changes. In the meantime, if other users have also modified the file, the file is synchronized in the same way and the original user would see the additional changes that have been made by other users. Overall, using the Offline Files feature is easy, and it provides a great tool for collaborative work.

Users do not have to keep track of which file is new and what changes have been made. Windows XP Professional can easily synchronize with the server without any input from the user. Virtually any type of file, from documents to Web pages, can be made available offline.

Windows XP Professional makes setting up Offline Files easy, providing a wizard tool that helps the user connect with the desired network file. Exercise 9-8 shows you how to set up Offline Files.

EXERCISE 9-8

CertCam 9-8

Configuring Offline Files

To configure offline files, follow these steps:

1. Log on as an administrator.
2. Open Control Panel and open Folder Options. Click the Offline Files tab. If you see a message telling that Fast User Switching is enabled, you'll need to change the option in User Accounts so that Fast User Switching is disabled. Offline Files is not compatible with Fast User Switching.
3. On the Offline Files tab, click the Enable Offline Files check box, as shown in the next illustration. You can then set these Offline File options:

   - Synchronize all offline files when logging on
   - Synchronize all offline files before logging off
   - Display a reminder every *x* minutes
   - Create an Offline Files shortcut on the desktop
   - Encrypt offline files to secure data

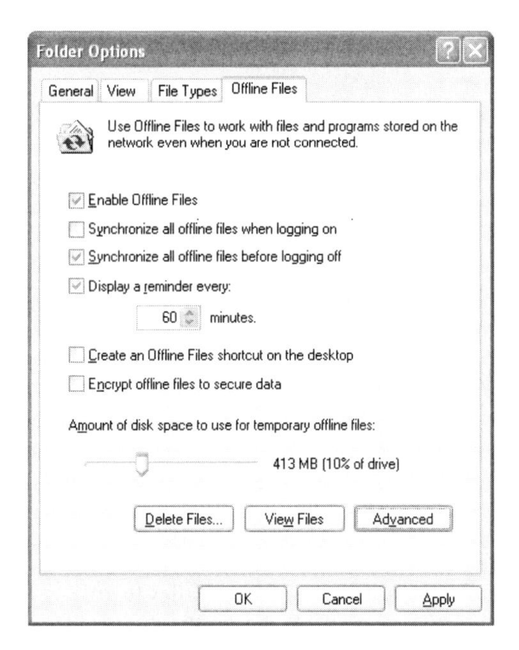

4. By default, offline files use 10 percent of your hard drive's disk space for storage. You can raise or lower this amount as desired by moving the slider bar.
5. Using the Delete Files button, you can delete previously stored offline files. Using the View Files button, you can view any currently stored offline files.
6. If you click the Advanced button, you see an Advanced Settings window, shown in the following illustration. This option enables you to be notified when a network connection has been lost so that you can begin working offline. You also have the radio button option to never go offline. You can also generate an exception list. For example, let's say that I always want my computer to go offline if a network connection is lost, unless I am working with a particular computer. I can add that computer to my list so that I do not begin working offline in that particular case. Make any desired configuration changes and click OK.

7. Now that the Offline Files feature is enabled, you can choose what file/folder you want to make available offline. Using My Network Places or any desired window, simply browse to the network resource, right-click it, and click Make Available Offline.
8. The Offline Files wizard appears. Click Next on the Welcome screen.
9. The Synchronization window appears. If you want to automatically synchronize when you log off and log on, leave the check box selected and click Next. If not, clear the check box and click Next.
10. The final window, shown in the following illustration, allows you to enable reminders and create a shortcut to the desktop. You can enable these if you like. Click Finish.

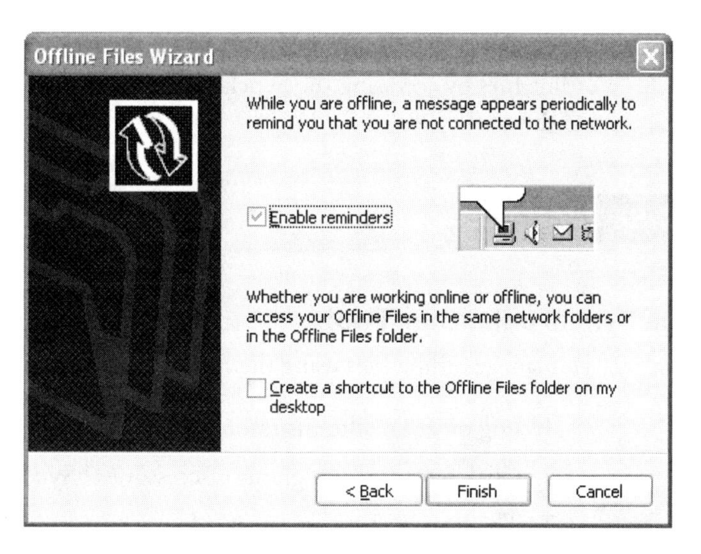

11. The files are copied to your computer, as you can see in the following illustration:

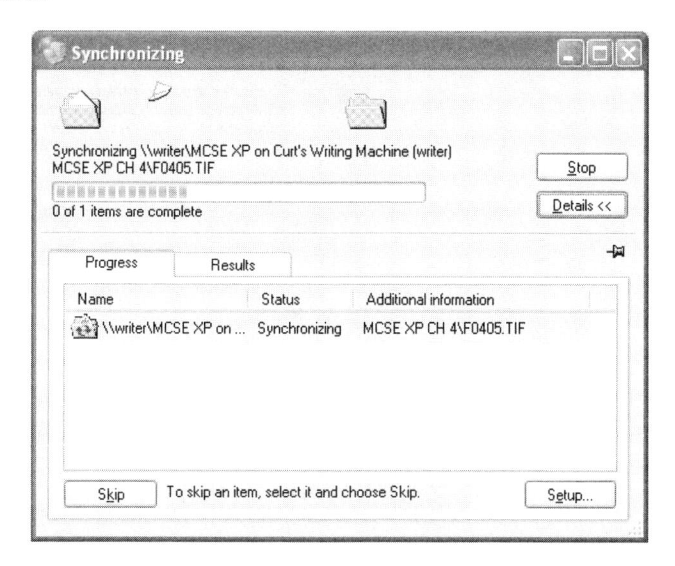

Once you set up offline files, you simply use the file as desired. Depending on your settings, the file is automatically synchronized with the original file that resides on the file server. You can manually enforce synchronization at any time by simply right-clicking the file or folder and clicking Synchronize. You can also further manage offline files by accessing the Synchronization tool. Exercise 9-9 shows you how to use this tool.

EXERCISE 9-9

Using the Synchronization Tool

To manage offline files using the Synchronization tool, follow these steps:

1. Log on as an administrator.
2. Click Start | All Programs | Accessories | Synchronization.
3. The Items to Synchronize window appears, as shown in the following illustration. As you can see, any current offline files/folders appear here. You can select any items that you want to manually synchronize and click the synchronize button.

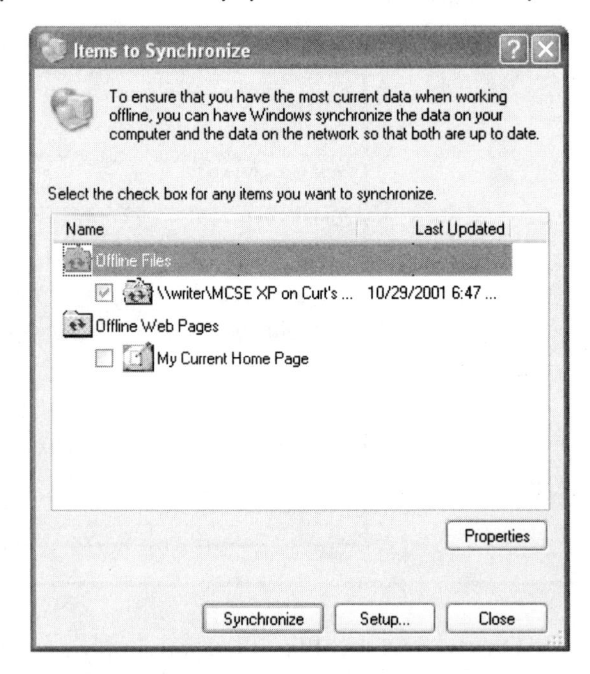

4. You can also click the Setup button to Synchronization the settings, which you can change at any time. As you can see in the following illustration, you have a Logon/Logoff tab, an On Idle tab, and a Scheduled tab. These tabs are self-explanatory, and you can use them to determine the way and the times that synchronization occurs. Make any desired changes and click OK.

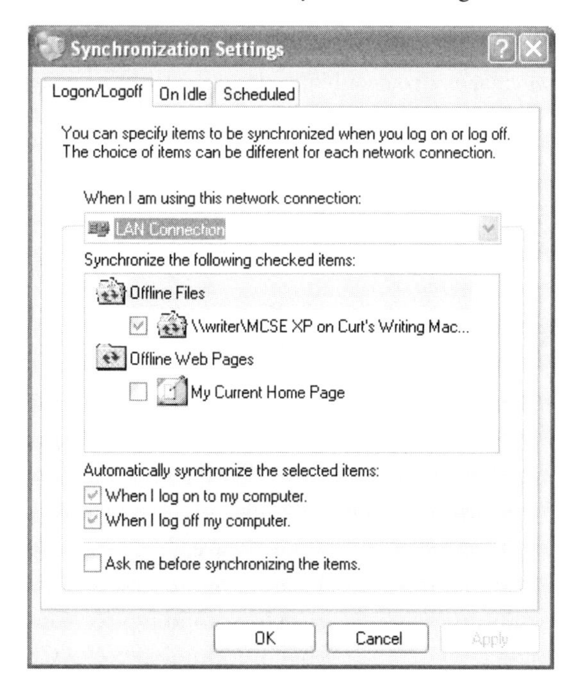

As you can see, Offline Files is easy to configure and use. Just keep in mind the following for the exam:

- Offline Files is not compatible with fast-user switching. In order to use Offline Files, you must disable fast-user switching in Users (in Control Panel).
- The Synchronization tool only allows you to synchronize items and configure how they are synchronized; you cannot add new items from this location—that must be done with Windows Explorer or My Network Places.
- You can cache data, such as Web pages, from the Internet. Just add the desired site to your Favorites folder in Internet Explorer, right-click the Web page in Favorites, and choose make the page available offline.

SCENARIO & SOLUTION	
What is the benefit of caching when Offline Files are available?	The caching feature can be configured for automatic downloading and caching. This helps reduce network traffic, but it is not suited for files and folders that change regularly.
Why is fast-user switching not compatible?	Fast-user switching allows another user to log on and still see your application and open files. It is a way for several people to quickly use the same computer. Since offline files are tied to your username and require complete logons/logoffs to close, they do not work with fast-user switching.

CERTIFICATION SUMMARY

Resource administration is an ongoing task for IT professionals. With Windows XP Professional, you can easily share all kinds of data and information on the network and then control access to that data.

Windows XP Professional supports two different compression methods that enable you to conserve disk storage space. The first is NTFS compression. You can compress individual files, folders, and even hard drives using NTFS compression, but it only works on NTFS drives. The second type of compression is Compressed (zipped) folders, which uses WinZip technology. The Compressed (zipped) folders feature works on any drive, and the compressed folders can be e-mailed or stored on different computers.

With Windows XP Professional, you can easily share folders and files. Once sharing is enabled, you can place security settings on those folders so that you can control what users and groups do with the folders and the contents. Windows XP Professional supports both share level security and NTFS permissions. NTFS and share level permissions are cumulative for the user—the least restrictive permission applies. The exception to the rule is the Deny permission, which overrides all other permissions. If NTFS and share level permissions are combined, then the most restrictive permission applies.

Web server resources work a lot like shared folders. When administering IIS on Windows XP Professional, you can create virtual directories and assign the desired permissions to those directories. Typically, the anonymous permission is applied, but you can even use Integrated Windows authentication.

Finally, Windows XP Professional supports offline file content through caching and the Offline Files feature. Caching stores network information locally, which speeds network usage and reduces traffic. Caching is most appropriate for resources that do not change often. Offline Files enables you to work with a file locally and then synchronize that file with the original network copy. The Offline Files feature is very helpful for users who need to work collaboratively on a single document.

TWO-MINUTE DRILL

Configure, Manage, and Troubleshoot File Compression

- Windows XP Professional provides NTFS compression, which reduces file and application size by about 50 percent.
- NTFS compression is specific to NTFS drives. Compressed data moved from an NTFS drive loses it compression attribute.
- If you move or copy a file to a compressed folder, the file is compressed automatically.
- If you move a file from a different NTFS drive to a compressed folder it is also compressed.
- If you move a file from the same NTFS drive to a compressed folder, it retains its original state.
- NTFS compression and encryption are not compatible.
- Compression may cause a performance hit, especially compression of the boot and system partitions.
- Windows XP Professional also supports Compressed (zipped) folders. Compressed folders can be stored on any drive and on the Internet and can even be sent via e-mail without losing the compressed state.

Create and Remove Shared Folders

- If a Windows XP Professional computer is configured for networking, you can easily share files and folders.
- Windows XP Professional provides a local share feature so that users of the same computer can access the Shared Documents folder and see shared files.
- The Computer Management console provides an additional location to manage shared folders.

Control Access to Files and Folders Using Permissions

- ❑ If a Windows XP Professional computer is not connected to a Windows 2000 domain, then simple file sharing is in use and there is no security tab on shared folders. You can override this setting on Folder Options | View Menu.
- ❑ Standard NTFS permissions for files and folders are Full Control, Read & Execute, Read, and Write.
- ❑ Standard permissions are made up of special permissions, which are Traverse Folder/Execute File, List Folder/Read Data, Read Attributes, Read Extended Attributes, Create Files/Write Data, Create Folders/Append Data, Write Attributes, Write Extended Attributes, Delete Subfolders And Files, Delete, Read, Change, Take Ownership, and Synchronize.
- ❑ You can configure advanced NTFS permissions so that you individually select special permissions that you want to apply. You can also override inheritance.
- ❑ NTFS permissions are cumulative, with the exception of Deny. This same rule also applies to share level permissions.
- ❑ When share and NTFS permissions are combined, the most restrictive permission applies.

Manage and Troubleshoot Web Server Resources

- ❑ IIS is provided with Windows XP Professional so that you can use Windows XP Professional as a Web server, but IIS is not installed by default.
- ❑ You can create virtual directories and assign a number of different permission levels to those directories, from anonymous access to Integrated Windows authentication.

Manage and Troubleshoot Access to and Synchronization of Offline Files

- ❑ Windows XP Professional supports cached network files, which help reduce network traffic. Caching is especially useful for documents and folders that seldom change.
- ❑ Offline files can be used for collaboration. You can work with offline files, and Windows XP can synchronize those files automatically with the network copy.

- The Offline Files feature is not compatible with fast-user switching.
- You can enable the use of offline files on the Offline Files tab of Folder Options, and you can use the Synchronization tool to manage synchronization of offline files.

SELF TEST

The following questions will help you measure your understanding of the material presented in this chapter. Read all of the choices carefully, as there may be more than one correct answer. Choose all correct answers for each question.

Configure, Manage, and Troubleshoot File Compression

1. In your network environment, you receive a request from a user for help. It seems that the user's NTFS compressed folders are losing their compressed state when they are moved to a FAT32 volume. What is the problem?

   A. You cannot move an NTFS compressed folder to a FAT32 folder—you can only copy it.

   B. The user must recompress the folder after the move.

   C. NTFS compression does not work on FAT32 drives.

   D. The user has fast-user switching enabled.

2. You compressed all drives on your Windows XP Professional computer. However, you notice a decrease in performance. What statement best explains the issue?

   A. Compression consumes more memory.

   B. Compressed files must be decompressed, read, and then recompressed. This takes more time reading uncompressed files.

   C. The compression algorithm interferes with processor threads.

   D. The computer's hardware does not meet Windows XP Professional standards.

3. A user copies a file from one NTFS drive to a compressed folder on a different NTFS drive. What is the file's state?

   A. Compressed.

   B. Uncompressed.

   C. You cannot copy a file to an NTFS compressed folder.

   D. The file is replaced with an uncompressed copy.

4. A user moves a file from the same NTFS drive into a compressed folder. The file was previously uncompressed. What is the state of the file after the move?

   A. Compressed.

   B. Uncompressed.

C. You cannot move a file to a compressed NTFS folder.

D. The moved file is replaced with a copy.

5. You want to use compact.exe to compress folders on your system. Which switch enables you to see hidden or system files?

A. /c

B. /u

C. /s

D. /a

6. A user on your network reports a problem with compression. The user wants to store several compressed files in an encrypted folder so they will be protected. When the files have been moved, the user accesses the advanced properties of the file and sees the window shown in the following illustration. Why is the compression being removed?

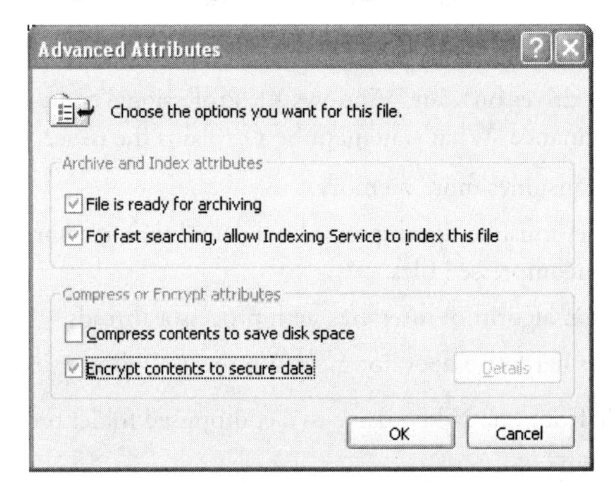

A. The user needs to copy the compressed files to retain compression.

B. The user needs to recompress the files once they are placed in the encrypted folder.

C. NTFS compression and encryption are not compatible.

D. The user needs to encrypt the entire folder.

7. You create a Compressed (zipped) folder. You want to move that folder to a Zip disk. What will happen to the compression?

A. The compression will be lost.

B. The compression will remain in place.

C. You can't move a compressed folder to a Zip drive.

D. The folder will become encrypted.

Create and Remove Shared Folders

8. A friend using Windows XP Professional at home complains that no Sharing tab exists on any folders or drives. What is the problem?

A. Networking is not configured.

B. The drives and folders are compressed.

C. The drives and folders are encrypted.

D. There is a system error.

9. You want to make a folder available to all users of your Windows XP Professional computer. How can you configure this?

A. Use Local folders.

B. Use Shared folders.

C. Use User folders.

D. Drag the folder to the Shared Documents folder.

Control Access to Files and Folders Using Permissions

10. You want to give a particular user the ability to make editorial changes to a document in a shared folder. However, you do not want the user to be able to delete the file. What permission should you use?

A. Full Control.

B. Read and Write.

C. Modify.

D. You can't assign this permission.

11. On a Windows XP Professional computer connected to a workgroup, you notice that the Security tab is not available on any shared folders. What do you need to do the enable the Security tab?

A. Turn off simple file sharing.

B. Run the Network Sharing wizard.

C. The option is not available unless you are connected to a domain.

D. Turn on Advanced Security under Users in Control Panel.

12. You want to assign a certain user all rights to a particular file, except the Take Ownership right. How can you configure this?

A. Assign Full Control.

B. Assign Modify.

C. Assign Read and Write.

D. Configure the rights individually under Advanced permissions.

13. A user has NTFS permissions of Read, Write, and Modify for a particular folder as a result of several group memberships. What is the user's effective permission?

A. Read

B. Write

C. Modify

D. Full Control

14. A particular user has share level permissions of Read, Change, and Deny Full Control as a result of several group memberships. What is the user's effective permission?

A. Read

B. Change

C. No access

D. Modify

15. A user has share level permission of Full Control for a particular folder and Modify and Read NTFS permission for the same folder. What is the user's effective permission?

A. Full Control

B. Modify

C. Read

D. No access

Manage and Troubleshoot Web Server Resources

16. By default, what access method is applied to virtual directories in IIS? (Choose two.)

A. Full Control

B. Anonymous

C. Windows Integrated

D. SSL

17. Consider the following illustration. What do you need to do so that users can run scripts in this virtual directory?

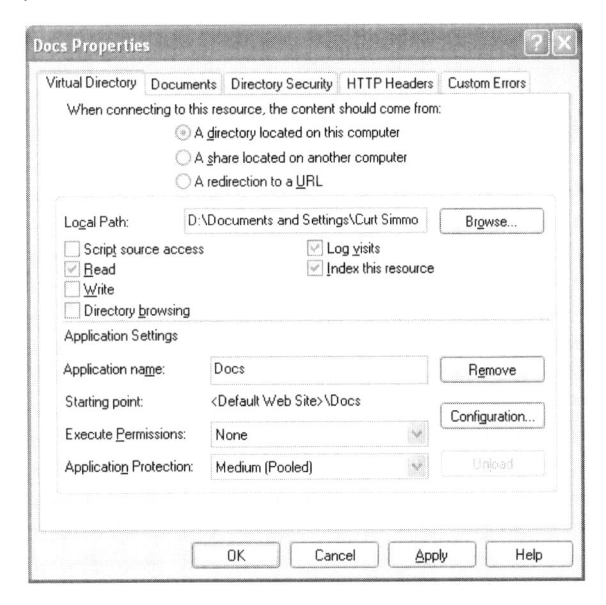

A. Choose the " A redirection to a URL" radio button

B. Choose the "Directory browsing" check box

C. Change the Execute Permissions

D. Change the Application protection

Manage and Troubleshoot Access to and Synchronization of Offline Files

18. For a particular network folder, you want to make sure that files in the folder are automatically cached on the user's hard drive when they are accessed. Where can you configure this?

A. On the folder's sharing tab.

B. In Internet Explorer on the user's computer.

C. Move the folder to an offline folder.

D. Change the permissions on the folder to Full Control.

19. What Windows XP feature is not compatible with Offline Files?

A. Encryption

B. Compression

C. Fast-user switching

D. Caching

LAB QUESTION

Consider the following two illustrations:

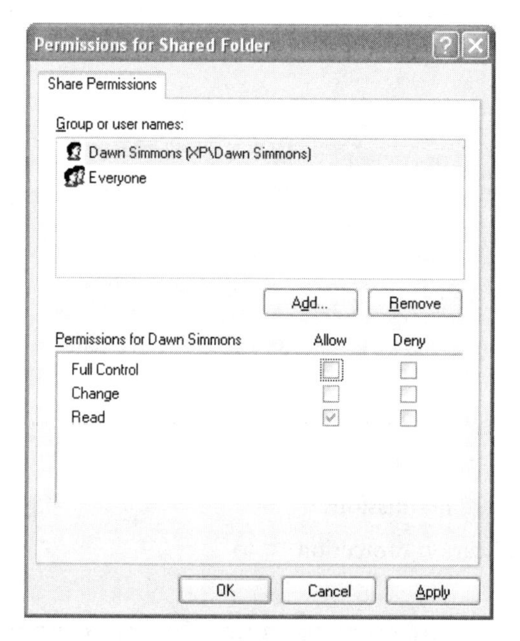

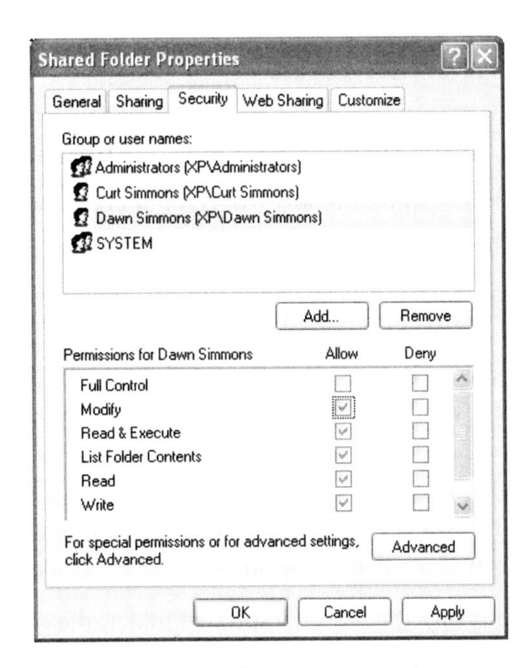

A particular user has share level Read permission for a particular shared folder. The user also has Modify NTFS permission for the same folder resulting from membership in an additional group. Answer the two following questions:

A. What is the user's effective permission?

B. If an administrator changes the user's share level permission to Deny, what will this do to the effective permission?

SELF TEST ANSWERS

Configure, Manage, and Troubleshoot File Compression

1. ☑ C is correct. NTFS compression only works on NTFS drives. NTFS compression is always lost when a folder is moved or copied to a FAT drive.

   ☒ A, B, and D are incorrect. Moving or copying is not an issue here because NTFS compression does not work on FAT drives. Fast-user switching does not affect compression.

2. ☑ B is correct. Compressed files must be decompressed, read, and recompressed. When all drives are compressed, you'll see a performance hit because more time is needed to read the files.

   ☒ A, C, and D are incorrect. Compression may require more memory, but this is not the primary issue, so A is incorrect. C is incorrect because compression does not interfere with processor threads. D is also incorrect because the performance problem is not a hardware issue.

3. ☑ A is correct. If you copy a file to a compressed folder, the file inherits the attributes of the folder and becomes compressed.

   ☒ B, C, and D are incorrect. The file is not uncompressed because it inherits the target folder's attributes, so B is incorrect. C and D are "answer distracters."

4. ☑ B is correct. When you move a file into a compressed folder on the same NTFS drive, it retains its original state, which is uncompressed in this case.

   ☒ A, C, and D are incorrect. The file is not compressed because of the "same drive move" rule, so A is incorrect. C and D are "answer distracters."

5. ☑ D is correct. The /a switch displays files with hidden or system attributes.

   ☒ A, B, and C are incorrect. The /c switch compresses a file, the /u switch uncompresses a file, and the /s switch performs the specified operation on the files in a given folder.

6. ☑ C is correct. NTFS compression and encryption are not compatible. When a file is moved to an encrypted folder, the compression on the file is removed.

   ☒ A, B, and D are incorrect. Compression and encryptions are simply not compatible, so these answers are all incorrect.

7. ☑ B is correct. Compressed (zipped) folders remain compressed, even when they are moved to non-NTFS volumes.

☒ A, C, and D are incorrect. The compression remains in place, so A is incorrect. C and D are "answer distracters."

Create and Remove Shared Folders

8. ☑ A is correct. The Sharing tab does not appear unless the computer has a configured network adapter.

☒ B, C, and D are incorrect. Compression and encryption do not affect sharing, and there is no system error in this case.

9. ☑ D is correct. Simply drag the folder to the Shared Documents folder so that it will be available to other users of the local system.

☒ A, B, and C are incorrect. None of these folder options provides local shared use.

Control Access to Files and Folders Using Permissions

10. ☑ B is correct. In this case, assign the permission of Read and Write so that the user can read the file and make changes to it.

☒ A, C, and D are incorrect. Both Full Control and Modify give the user the ability to delete the file. D is an "answer distracter."

11. ☑ A is correct. You need to turn off simple file sharing, found on the View tab of the Folder Options

☒ B, C, and D are incorrect. The only solution is to turn off simple file sharing, so all of these answers are incorrect.

12. ☑ D is correct. Advanced permissions enable you to specifically assign or deny special rights. In this case, you can use advanced permissions to assign all rights except the Take Ownership permission.

☒ A, B, and C are incorrcct. None of these permissions will meet the requirements.

13. ☑ C is correct. NTFS permissions are cumulative. In this case, you apply the least restrictive permission, which is Modify.

☒ A, B, and D are incorrect. The least restrictive permission is applied; therefore, A and B are incorrect. D is incorrect because Full Control is not assigned.

14. ☑ C is correct. In both NTFS and share level permissions, the least restrictive permission is applied, except in the case of Deny, which overrides all other permissions. The user has no access in this case.

☒ A, B, and D are incorrect. Read and Change are incorrect, because the user has no access. Modify is incorrect because it is not a share level permission.

15. ☑ B is correct. When share and NTFS permissions are applied, the most restrictive permission is the user's effective permission. In this case, the user has only Modify access because of the combination of NTFS permission and share level permission, with Modify being the most restrictive.

☒ A, C, and D are incorrect. These permissions are not the most restrictive in terms of the share level and NTFS permission combination.

Manage and Troubleshoot Web Server Resources

16. ☑ B and C correct. By default, the anonymous permission is used with Web directories so that users can access them without a username and password. Windows integrated permission is also configured by default.

☒ A, and D are incorrect. These are not the default permissions.

17. ☑ C is correct. Change the Execute Permissions drop-down menu to Scripts only.

☒ A, B, and D are incorrect. These selection items will not allow scripts to be run.

Manage and Troubleshoot Access to and Synchronization of Offline Files

18. ☑ A is correct. You can enable the automatic caching feature on the folder's Sharing tab by clicking the Caching button.

☒ B, C, and D are incorrect. These options will not enable automatic caching for the folder.

19. ☑ C is correct. Fast-user switching is not compatible with Offline Files.

☒ A, B, and D are incorrect. All of these features are compatible.

LAB ANSWER

For this lab question, you only need to remember the simple permissions rules explored in this chapter. The answers are

- The combination of share level and NTFS permissions results in the most restrictive permission being the effective permission. In this case, the user's effective permission is Read.
- The Deny option overrides all other permissions. Since it is the most restrictive here, the user will have no access.

10

Networking

CERTIFICATION OBJECTIVES

Windows XP Professional contains all of the features and functions that enable it to participate on a network, ranging from the complex environment of a Windows 2000 domain to a simple workgroup or home network. The beauty of Windows XP Professional is that it can meet the most stringent networking requirements, and is still simple enough for the home user who wants to connect two PCs together. Hopefully, the end result is less support time, less troubleshooting time, and less user configuration errors for IT people like you and me.

In today's networking environments, TCP/IP is the protocol of choice, and Windows XP Professional is optimized to take full advantage of TCP/IP. Beyond simple wired networking, Windows XP can easily function via dial-up connections, VPN, RAS, and even ICS. In this chapter, we'll explore all of these areas and point out the content you are likely to see on the exam. Let me offer one disclaimer: this chapter is not a networking primer. Since you are taking a certification exam, I assume you have some networking experience under your belt. If not, you should consider studying a networking book to get your feet on solid ground. You can, however, gain a networking overview from Chapter 1.

CERTIFICATION OBJECTIVE 10.01

Configure and Troubleshoot TCP/IP

TCP/IP has had a bad reputation to overcome. In the past, it was labeled as difficult, problematic, and not very friendly to IT professionals, who often found maintaining a TCP/IP network to be a real headache. Today's IP environments are different. Since TCP/IP is the protocol of choice for Internet communications, it has become the protocol of choice in most major networks today. In fact, most major operating systems produced today, including Microsoft and Novell, are designed for TCP/IP networking; after all, TCP/IP is a suite made up of over one hundred communication protocols, so it is very robust. Like wise, TCP/IP is very scalable. An IP network can meet the needs of a handful of clients or of thousands.

Why has TCP/IP become the protocol of choice? There are a number of important reasons:

- **Scalability** As I mentioned in the previous paragraph, IP address schemes essentially have no limit. You can create subnets to manage IP clients and any number of IP address ranges. TCP/IP addressing can easily scale to the millions in terms of network clients.

- **Robustness** TCP/IP is a suite of protocols. This means there are many other protocols besides Transmission Control Protocol and Internet Protocol that make up the suite. Some common examples are File Transfer Protocol (FTP), Simple Mail Transfer Protocol (SMTP), Post Office Protocol (POP), User Datagram Protocol (UDP), and many others. In fact, there over 100 protocols in the TCP/IP protocol suite.
- **Internet Standard** TCP/IP is the standard protocol for Internet communications. The HTTP protocol is a part of the TCP/IP suite, and the vast functionality you experience on the Internet is due to the protocols available in TCP/IP. Since TCP/IP is the standard for Internet communication, the use of TCP/IP makes sense for private networking environments, since the use of TCP/IP allows for intranet use and a cohesive approach with Internet communications.

The good news for IT administrators is that TCP/IP is easier than ever to manage. Sure, planning an IP network infrastructure can be challenging and confusing, but once that infrastructure is in place, managing an IP network is rather easy. Fortunately, network infrastructure planning is beyond the scope of Exam 70-270, and your IP management is limited to managing the local Windows XP Professional client. DHCP configuration and related IP management issues are typically saved for the Server exam, although I can't promise that none will pop up on Exam 70-270.

With all of that said and without this turning into an IP configuration book, let's take a look at Windows XP Professional's use of TCP/IP, how it is configured, and the tactics you can use to solve problems.

Configuring Windows XP Professional for Automatic IP Addressing or DHCP

Once again, I'll assume you are up to date on your TCP/IP skills—if not, you'll find a wide variety of introductory level books at any bookstore. As you are working with Windows XP Professional, it's important to remember that all of the old TCP/IP rules apply. Each client on your network needs a unique IP address, an appropriate subnet mask, and possibly a default gateway if the client's requests must travel to a different subnet. The good news is that Windows XP Professional can configure this addressing automatically if you are one of the following:

- On a home or small office network with no domain controllers
- In a Windows 2000 network that has DHCP up and running

Let's consider the first option. Windows XP Professional is designed to use TCP/IP in a small workgroup or office setting. Because the users in this type of setting are typically not IT professionals who can configure TCP/IP, Windows XP Professional can configure it automatically through the Automatic IP Addressing (APIPA). When APIPA is used, Windows XP Professional first checks the network for the presence of a Dynamic Host Configuration Protocol (DHCP) server that can lease an IP address to it. If a DHCP server is not available, then Windows XP Professional uses APIPA. When APIPA is used, an IP address from the address range of 169.254.0.0 to 169.254.255.255 is used, along with a subnet mask of 255.255.0.0.

on the Job

You can disable APIPA in the registry by changing the IP Autoconfiguration value from 1 to 0.

Windows XP Professional automatically assigns itself an IP address from this range so that it can participate on the network. Before assigning itself a random IP address from this range, the client broadcasts a network message to see if another APIPA client is already using that same IP address. Of course, if a different range of IP addresses or subnet masks are used on the network, the client still may not have IP connectivity with other clients. The point here is that Windows XP Professional can use APIPA in environments where no DHCP server is used and where static IP address configurations are not used. The end result is that a user can have a home network running TCP/IP without even knowing what TCP/IP is or that it even exists—and that's the real beauty of APIPA.

exam Watch

APIPA assigns only the IP address and subnet mask—not a default gateway. APIPA assumes that communication is limited to the local subnet. Again, this feature is great in home or small office networks or in the case a DHCP server failure, but it is not designed as a large networking solution.

In the same way that Windows XP Professional can automatically assign itself an IP address, Windows XP Professional is configured to search for a DHCP server so that it can lease an IP address. DHCP is a Windows 2000 Server service. Administrators can configure DHCP with a pool of IP addresses that can be leased to network clients. The client receives a unique IP lease and keeps that lease for a specified period of time, after which the lease must be renewed. If the lease cannot be renewed, then the client can receive a new IP address. The end results are a system that is relatively easy to configure, unique IP addresses that all clients receive, and for administrators the freedom from having to worry about unique IPs.

By default, Windows XP Professional configures itself for APIPA if a network adapter card is present in the computer. For the exam, however, you should also know the correct setting that APIPA and DHCP use. Fortunately, the configuration is a single radio button, and you learn how to set it in Exercise 10-1.

EXERCISE 10-1

CertCam 10-1

Using APIPA or DHCP

To configure TCP/IP to use APIPA or DHCP, follow these steps:

1. Click Start | Control Panel | Network Connections.
2. Right-click the Local Area Connection and click Properties.
3. On the General properties tab, shown in the following illustration, select Internet Protocol (TCP/IP) in the list and click the Properties button.

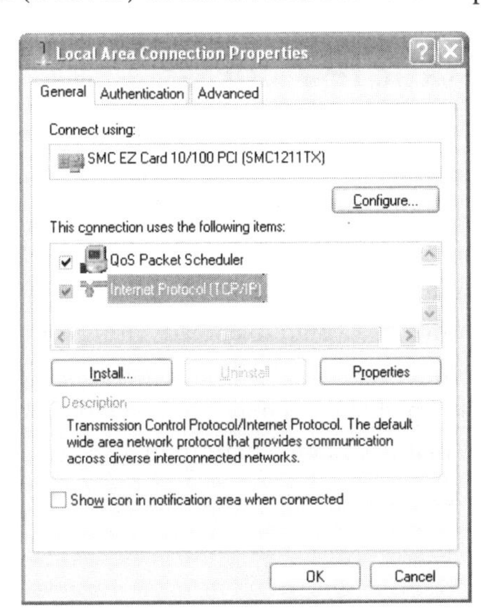

On the Internet Protocol (TCP/IP) Properties General tab, ensure that the "Obtain an IP address automatically" and the "Obtain DNS server address automatically" radio buttons are selected, as shown in the following illustration:

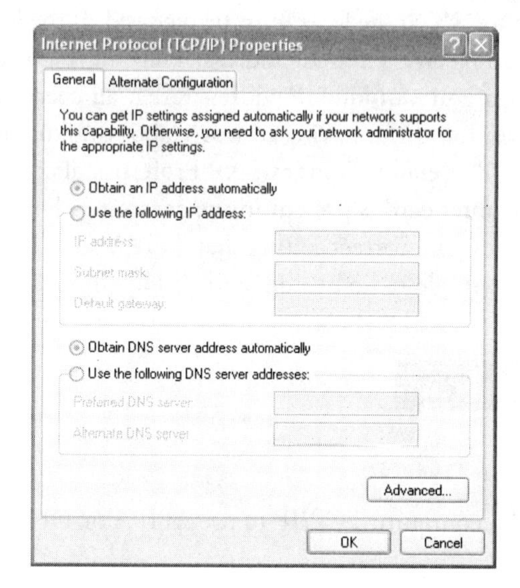

Once these are selected, Windows XP Professional looks for a DHCP server. If no DHCP server is found, then an APIPA address is configured.

Configuring a Static IP Address

APIPA and DHCP are designed to provide automatic IP addressing so that configuration never needs to be static. By *static*, I mean that you manually enter an IP address, subnet mask, and a default gateway if necessary. In the past, this manual form of IP addressing was required, and a simple keystroke error could cause a number of connectivity errors. As you can imagine, for this reason TCP/IP was known as a "high overhead" protocol. With automatic addressing mechanisms, however, you will typically not perform manual assignment. However, there are cases in which clients may want a workgroup to have a certain IP address range and subnet masks. When a handful of computers are used (or even up to 100), you can reasonably perform a manual assignment if necessary, and the exam expects you to know how to configure a Windows XP Professional computer with a manual IP address.

Not to sound like a broken record, but let me again say that you are unlikely to see IP addressing and subnet mask configurations on this exam. You might see a network configuration and the IP addresses of certain clients in order to troubleshoot a problem, but the important point to remember is that each client must have a unique IP address and the same subnet mask when they are on the same subnet. Keep in mind that in order for a client computer to find its way off the local subnet, a default gateway must be configured. Also, you might consider manually entering the IP addresses of DNS servers on your network, since this information is typically provided by the DHCP server. Exercise 10-2 shows you how to manually configure a Windows XP Professional computer's IP settings.

EXERCISE 10-2

CertCam 10-2

Manually Configuring TCP/IP

To manually configure TCP/IP settings, follow these steps:

1. Click Start | Control Panel | Network Connections.
2. Right-click the Local Area Connection and click Properties.
3. The Local Area Connection Properties window, select Internet Protocol (TCP/IP) in the list and click Properties.
4. On the Internet Protocol (TCP/IP) properties window, shown in the following illustration, click the "Use the following IP address" radio button and manually enter the desired values for the IP address, subnet mask, and default gateway. If desired, you can also enter a preferred and alternate DNS server IP address in the provided boxes.

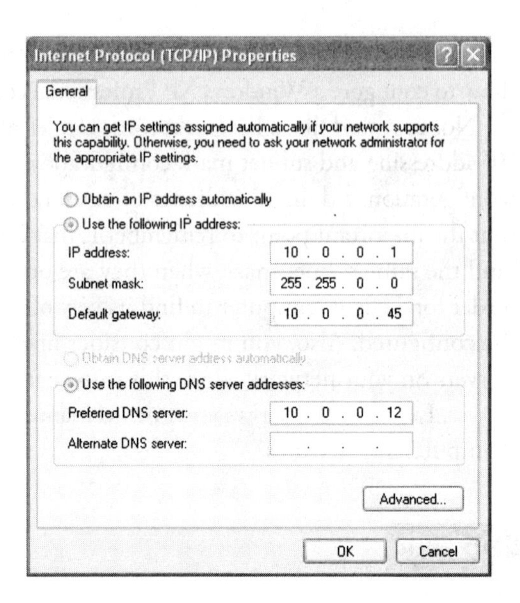

5. If you click the Advanced button, you can configure some additional TCP/IP settings. On the IP Settings tab, you can add, edit, and remove IP addresses and default gateways for the computer, shown in the following illustration. This feature enables you to use multiple IP addresses and default gateways on the same computer and may be especially helpful in the case of a laptop computer that you move from one network to the next.

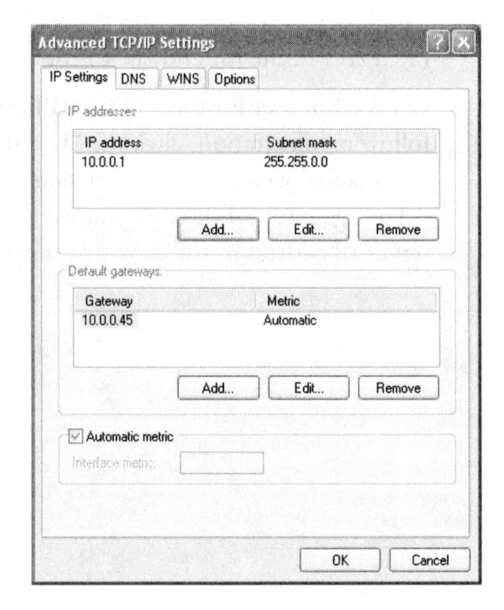

6. On the DNS tab, you can enter the additional addresses of other DNS servers that can be used. You can also determine how DNS handles names that are unqualified. The default settings are typically all you need here.
7. On the WINS tab, you can add the names of WINS servers, if they are still in use on your network, and you can enable LMHOSTS lookups.
8. On the Options tab, you have a TCP/IP filtering feature. If you select TCP/IP Filtering on this tab and click Properties, you see a simple TCP/IP Filtering window. TCP/IP filtering functions like a miniature firewall through which you can allow or deny traffic on desired TCP and UDP ports or on a protocol basis. These settings are not needed in a network environment where a firewall is in use, but they can be helpful in a workgroup setting if you want to place some IP restrictions on the computer's network adapters. Keep in mind that any filters you configure here apply to all network adapters in the computer, not just the adapter being configured. Click OK and OK again once you have configured these options.

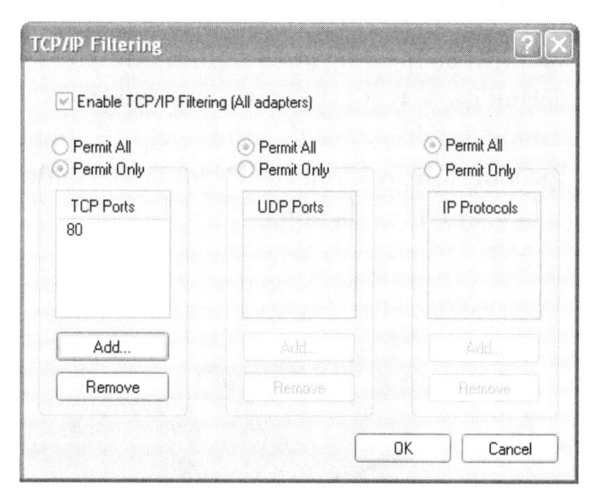

Helpful TCP/IP Troubleshooting Tools

Troubleshooting TCP/IP connectivity and problems can be a moderately difficult task. The good news, however, is that there are several command line tools that can help you. The following sections explore these troubleshooting tools, and you should spend some hands-on time with them as you prepare for Exam 70-240.

Ping

Ping is a network connectivity tool that allows you to test network connectivity against another computer or even your computer's local network adapter card. Ping sends an ICMP echo request to the desired IP address or name and provides you with a response as to whether the ping was successful or the host was unreachable. At the Windows XP Professional command prompt, simply type **ping *ipaddress***, such as ping 10.0.0.1, or you can ping via a name such as **ping computer**7. You can also perform a loopback test against your computer's network adapter card by typing **ping 127.0.0.1**. To see all of ping's options, type **ping -?** at the command prompt. Figure 10-1 shows you an example of a successful ping test.

Ipconfig

Ipconfig reports the IP configuration of your computer. At the command prompt, simply type **Ipconfig** and press ENTER. You'll see the IP address, subnet mask, and default gateway for the local area connection. If you type **Ipconfig /all**, you can see a more detailed list of the computer's IP configuration, shown in the Figure 10-2. Ipconfig also gives you some additional command line parameters, which you can review by typing **Ipconfig /?**.

FIGURE 10-1

A successful ping test

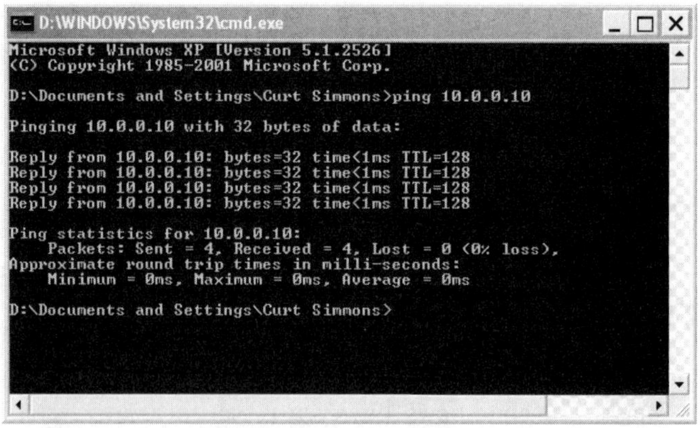

```
D:\WINDOWS\System32\cmd.exe
Microsoft Windows XP [Version 5.1.2526]
(C) Copyright 1985-2001 Microsoft Corp.

D:\Documents and Settings\Curt Simmons>ping 10.0.0.10

Pinging 10.0.0.10 with 32 bytes of data:

Reply from 10.0.0.10: bytes=32 time<1ms TTL=128
Reply from 10.0.0.10: bytes=32 time<1ms TTL=128
Reply from 10.0.0.10: bytes=32 time<1ms TTL=128
Reply from 10.0.0.10: bytes=32 time<1ms TTL=128

Ping statistics for 10.0.0.10:
    Packets: Sent = 4, Received = 4, Lost = 0 (0% loss),
Approximate round trip times in milli-seconds:
    Minimum = 0ms, Maximum = 0ms, Average = 0ms

D:\Documents and Settings\Curt Simmons>
```

FIGURE 10-2 The results of Ipconfig /all

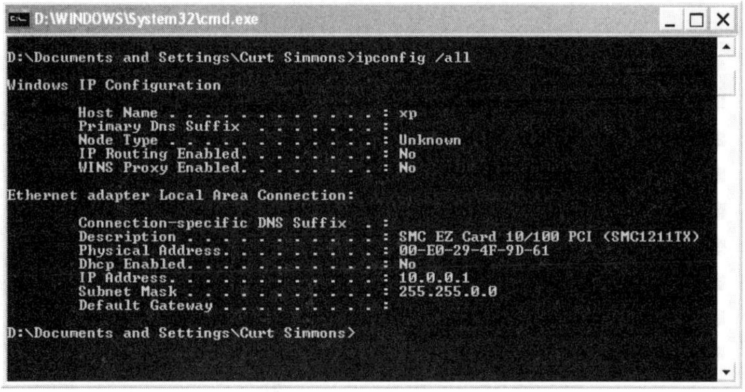

```
D:\WINDOWS\System32\cmd.exe

D:\Documents and Settings\Curt Simmons>ipconfig /all

Windows IP Configuration

        Host Name . . . . . . . . . . . . : xp
        Primary Dns Suffix  . . . . . . . :
        Node Type . . . . . . . . . . . . : Unknown
        IP Routing Enabled. . . . . . . . : No
        WINS Proxy Enabled. . . . . . . . : No

Ethernet adapter Local Area Connection:

        Connection-specific DNS Suffix  . :
        Description . . . . . . . . . . . : SMC EZ Card 10/100 PCI (SMC1211TX)
        Physical Address. . . . . . . . . : 00-E0-29-4F-9D-61
        Dhcp Enabled. . . . . . . . . . . : No
        IP Address. . . . . . . . . . . . : 10.0.0.1
        Subnet Mask . . . . . . . . . . . : 255.255.0.0
        Default Gateway . . . . . . . . . :

D:\Documents and Settings\Curt Simmons>
```

Netstat and Nbtstat

Netstat is a connectivity tool that displays all connections and protocol statistics for TCP/IP. You can use a number of switches with Netstat, which you can view by typing **netstat ?**. For example, you can view the protocol local address, foreign address, and the current state of the connection.

Similarly, Nbtstat is helpful in cases where you need to troubleshoot NetBIOS naming and connectivity problems. This tool checks the status of NetBIOS over TCP/IP connections and can give you information about the NetBIOS caches, the current sessions, and statistics. There are a number of switches, which you can view by simply typing **nbtstat** at the command line. The –RR switch (ReleaseRefresh) was first introduced in Windows NT 4.0 in order to send name release packets to WINS and then perform a refresh.

Tracert

Tracert is a simple utility that traces the route from one host to another. You can trace routes over the local network, or even to a Web site, such as **www.osborne.com**, shown in Figure 10-3. You can also view a listing of tracert switches by simply typing **tracert** at the command line.

Pathping

First appearing in Windows 2000, pathping combines the functionality of ping and tracert. You can ping an address or DNS name and see the actual route of the ping,

FIGURE 10-3

Tracert

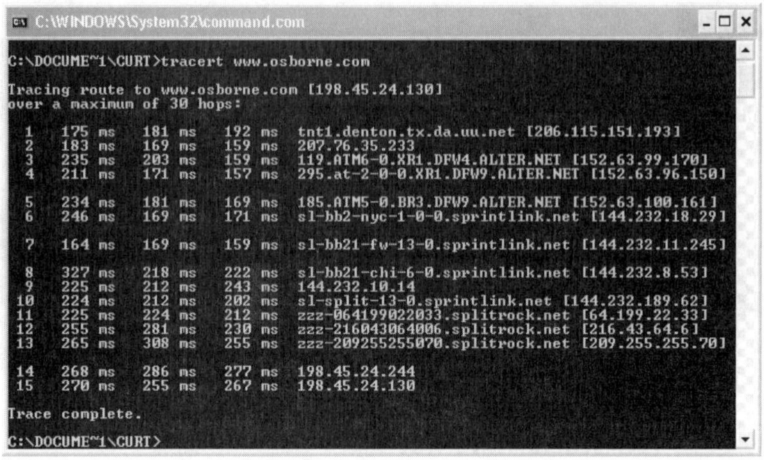

```
C:\WINDOWS\System32\command.com

C:\DOCUME~1\CURT>tracert www.osborne.com

Tracing route to www.osborne.com [198.45.24.130]
over a maximum of 30 hops:

  1   175 ms   181 ms   192 ms  tnt1.denton.tx.da.uu.net [206.115.151.193]
  2   183 ms   169 ms   159 ms  207.76.35.233
  3   235 ms   203 ms   159 ms  119.ATM6-0.XR1.DFW4.ALTER.NET [152.63.99.170]
  4   211 ms   171 ms   157 ms  295.at-2-0-0.XR1.DFW9.ALTER.NET [152.63.96.150]

  5   234 ms   181 ms   169 ms  185.ATM5-0.BR3.DFW9.ALTER.NET [152.63.100.161]
  6   246 ms   169 ms   171 ms  sl-bb2-nyc-1-0-0.sprintlink.net [144.232.18.29]

  7   164 ms   169 ms   159 ms  sl-bb21-fw-13-0.sprintlink.net [144.232.11.245]

  8   327 ms   218 ms   222 ms  sl-bb21-chi-6-0.sprintlink.net [144.232.8.53]
  9   225 ms   212 ms   243 ms  144.232.10.14
 10   224 ms   212 ms   202 ms  sl-split-13-0.sprintlink.net [144.232.189.62]
 11   225 ms   224 ms   212 ms  zzz-064199022033.splitrock.net [64.199.22.33]
 12   255 ms   281 ms   230 ms  zzz-216043064006.splitrock.net [216.43.64.6]
 13   265 ms   308 ms   255 ms  zzz-209255255070.splitrock.net [209.255.255.70]

 14   268 ms   286 ms   277 ms  198.45.24.244
 15   270 ms   255 ms   267 ms  198.45.24.130

Trace complete.

C:\DOCUME~1\CURT>
```

including percentage information on the packets lost. This troubleshooting tool can be useful in a large network environment with connectivity problems. The pathping utility can help you isolate where the connectivity problem is so that it can be repaired.

Route

The Route command can be used to view local routing tables and change them if there are errors present. This troubleshooting tool can be used to verify correct routing information and correct IP routing data in the host's routing table. You can view all the switches available for Route by typing **route** at the command prompt.

Nslookup

Nslookup is used to look up IP address-to-DNS mappings in a DNS database. Of course, this tool works only in domain environments where DNS is in use. You can gain the DNS server's name and IP address by simply typing **nslookup** at the command prompt. To see a listing of available switches, type **nslookup** so that the DNS server is found; then simply type ? to see the options available to you.

SCENARIO & SOLUTION	
There are two subnets on my network. What must be done to enable communication between the two?	There has to be physical connectivity between the two IP subnets, and then you'll need to configure the client's with a default gateway. This can be done manually in small environments but is typically handled by DHCP in larger environments.
In a workgroup setting, how does APIPA function? After all, since the computers are auto-assigning themselves an IP address, couldn't two have the same IP?	No. When APIPA is used, the computer that is about to auto-assign itself an IP address broadcasts the auto-generated IP address on the network to determine if that IP address is already in use.
Can you ping a host name?	Yes, you can ping a host name, such as **www.osborne.com**, a computer name, or an IP address.

exam Watch

The use of TCP/IP troubleshooting tools will likely appear in scenario type questions, or even as possible troubleshooting solutions. It is important that you know what each tool does and have a good feel for how to use it. There is no substitute for hands-on practice!

CERTIFICATION OBJECTIVE 10.02

Connect to Computers Using Dial-Up Networking

Dial-up networking, which enables two computers to communicate with each other via telephone lines, has been around for years now. It all began with terribly slow modems, and because of telephone line restrictions, dial-up connectivity is unfortunately not very fast today either. However, millions of users maintain dial-up accounts to access the Internet, and corporations use dial-up accounts for remote user access. If dial-up access is generally slow, then why is it still in widespread use? Economics and convenience have a lot to do with it. After all, for dial-up connectivity to work, your computer needs a modem. No problem—most come equipped with one anyway as a standard feature. You already have the network infrastructure in place—the telephone system—so you can understand why dial-up networking continues to be an important force. It is very inexpensive and convenient.

Like previous versions of Windows, Windows XP Professional fully supports dial-up networking, and you can even configure Windows XP Professional to accept incoming calls as well. Windows XP also supports Remote Access Service for dial-up and authentication to a Windows 2000 Server. In the following sections, we'll take a look at these configuration issues.

Connecting to Other Computers via Dial-Up Networking

As with many things in XP, you'll find a helpful wizard that can assist you in setting up dial-up connections. Before getting started, you'll need to know the name of the computer/ISP you are connecting to, the phone number(s) that can be used, and the user name and password that are used to gain access. Exercise 10-3 shows you how to set up a dial-up connection. In order to configure a dial-up connection, you'll need to have an installed modem on your computer. See Chapter 6 for more information about installing modems.

EXERCISE 10-3

CertCam 10-3

Setting up a Dial-Up Connection

To set up a dialup connection, follow these steps:

1. Click Start | Control Panel | Network Connections.
2. If you have the Windows XP view turned on, you'll see a Create a new connection option in the Network Tasks pane. If it's not turned on, you'll see a Create a New Connection icon. Click or double-click the option. This opens the New Connection Wizard. If this is the first time the user has tried to create a new connection, a dialog box may appear asking the user for dialing preferences. Click Next on the Welcome screen.
3. In the Network Connection Type window, shown in the following illustration, you can choose the type of connection that you want. For a dial-up connection,

you'll typically choose the first option to connect to the Internet or to connect to the network at your place of work. In truth, both options are rather similar because the connections need the same type of information from you. For this exercise, we will choose the "Connect to the network at my workplace" radio button. Click Next.

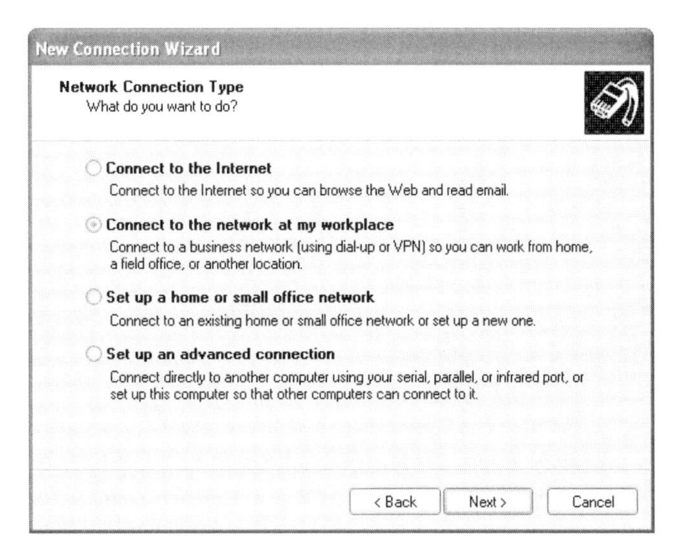

4. In the Network Connection window, you are asked if you want to use a dial-up connection or a Virtual Private Network Connection. Choose dial-up connection and click Next.
5. In the Connection name window, enter a friendly, recognizable name for the connection and click Next.
6. In the "Phone number to dial" window, enter the phone number. Include the area code and the 1 for a long distance call, if necessary, and click Next.
7. Click Finish.
8. The Connect window appears, shown in the following illustration. Enter the user name and password needed for the connection. You can also choose to save the password for yourself only for all users of the computer. This feature enables a single connection for anyone using the computer, or keeps the connection private for one user. When you are done, just click Dial.

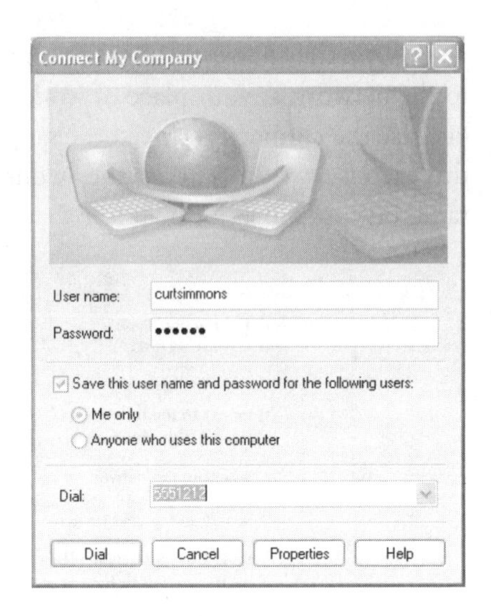

Once the connection has been created, you can right-click the connection icon in the Network Connections folder and click Properties. Here, you have some additional configuration options that you need to be aware of for both the real world and the exam.

First, on the General tab, shown in Figure 10-4, you can set up alternative phone numbers and configure dialing rules. In case of connectivity failure to one phone number, the "Alternates" feature enables the connectoid to rotate through phone numbers until it can connect to one of them. This feature is helpful for both remote access connectivity, as well as Internet connectivity.

The dialing rules, which are largely self-explanatory, enable you to configure certain ways for your computer to behave with regard to certain numbers or area codes. Dialing rules enable the computer to access an outside line, to distinguish local area codes ones from ones for long distance calls, and even to use calling cards for long distance or international calls. To configure dialing rules, just enable the check box option on the General tab, then click the Dialing Rules button. You'll see several different windows for you to configure, but the setting options are self-explanatory.

FIGURE 10-4

Connection Properties, General Tab

exam watch

Even though dialing rules are rather easy to configure, you should spend some time creating them for your own background knowledge. You never know what question might pop up on the exam. Also, see Chapter 7 to learn more about modem and dialing rule configuration.

The Options tab gives you some additional options that might be helpful when connecting. For example, you can do the following:

- Display progress while connecting
- Prompt for name and password, certificate, and so on
- Include Windows logon domain
- Prompt for phone number

You can also configure how Windows XP handles redial attempts. By default, there are three redial attempts with one minute between each attempt. Also, the connection can be configured to hang up a call if it is idle for a certain period of time, and the line can be redialed automatically if it is dropped.

If users complain that their calls are disconnected, always check the Options tab and the setting for "Idle time before hanging up." Users may place a value here that causes the line to be disconnected when they stop working for a moment or two.

The Security tab, shown in Figure 10-5, gives you several different security options for the dial-up connection. By default, the typical settings are used, which allow unsecured passwords. You can use the drop-down menu to require a secure password or a smart card. If you choose to use security settings, the "Automatically use my Windows logon name and password (and domain, if any)" radio button is available. You also see the check box available for requiring data encryption. Depending on how RAS is configured on Windows 2000 Server, you may want to configure these options on the client computer. Of course, the use of secure and encrypted data transfer is a policy issue and not something you can invoke individually on Windows XP Professional computers without the same server configuration.

FIGURE 10-5

Connection Properties, Security tab

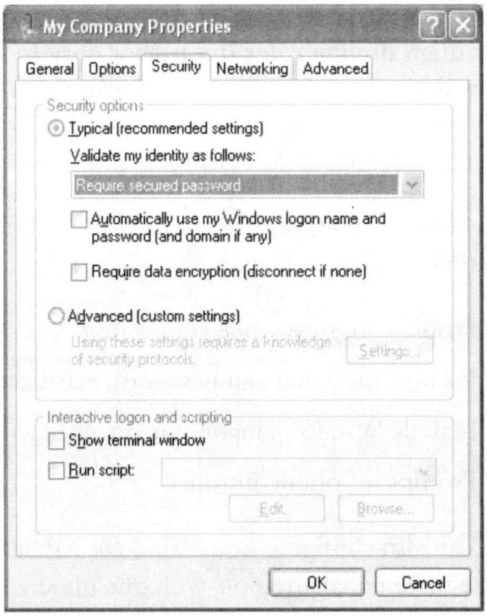

The security settings available here can be used for Remote Access connections to Windows 2000 networks. In the case of an ISP dial-up connection, the unsecured password setting is almost always used. On the Typical Settings drop-down menu, you need to memorize the settings, which are Allow Unsecured Password, Require Secure Password, or Use Smart Card.

Aside from the secure password features available under typical settings, you can click the Advanced button and then Settings to configure different security protocols for use with dial-up networking, as shown in Figure 10-6.

The Advanced Security Settings window gives you a number of options, and you need to know these for the exam.

exam watch

You are very likely to see the items in the Advanced Security Settings window on the exam. I strongly encourage you to memorize everything on this tab, including the data encryption levels you see in the Data Encryption drop-down menu.

FIGURE 10-6 Advanced Security Settings window

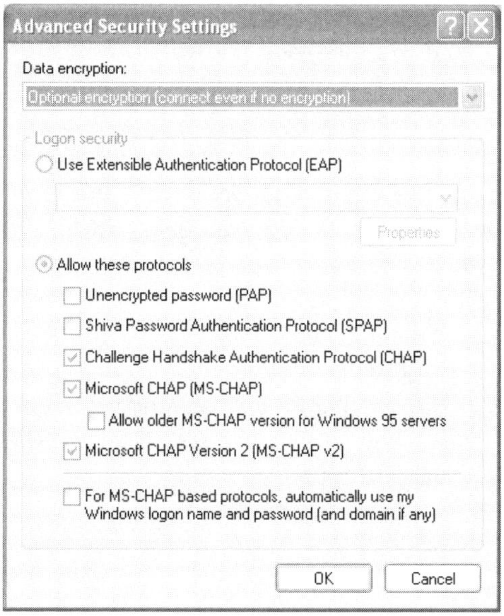

The following list explains the options and security protocols available to you:

- **Data encryption** You can choose to use data encryption if it is available by the server. The levels available are No Encryption Allowed, Optional Encryption (connect even if no encryption is available), Require Encryption (disconnects if server declines), and Maximum Strength Encryption (disconnect if server declines).
- **Use Extensible Authentication Protocol (EAP)** EAP is used with other security devices, such as smart cards and other certificates, as well as MD5 Challenge.
- **Security protocols** You can also choose to use different security protocols, depending on the level of security desired in your environment. The available protocols are these:
  - **Unencrypted password/Password authentication protocol (PAP)** PAP uses plain text passwords, an approach that basically provides no authentication protection.
  - **Shiva Password Authentication Protocol (SPAP)** If your server is using SPAP, you can enable the protocol here. Note however, that required encryption does not work with SPAP.

exam Watch ***These are the kinds of sticky details the exam likes to throw at you: SPAP cannot be used with required encryption, although the configuration tab here may not tell you that fact.***

  - **Challenge Handshake Authentication Protocol (CHAP)** CHAP negotiates a secure form of encryption with the server using Message Digest 5, an industry standard in encryption, so that that private data, such as a user's password, cannot be decrypted. The challenge-response uses MD5 hashing to prove to the server that you know your password without actually sending the password over the network.
  - **Microsoft CHAP (MS-CHAP)** Microsoft built on the CHAP standard with MS-CHAP. MS-CHAP is more suitable for Windows workstations on Windows networks. You can also enable older MS-CHAP versions for compatibility with Windows 95 if necessary.
  - **Microsoft CHAP Version 2 (MS-CHAP v2)** This version provides stronger data encryption and mutual authentication. MS-CHAP v2 is

offered first in VPN connections, and current Windows clients can use MS-CHAP v2 when it is offered.

The Networking tab enables you to configure typical networking services, such as File and Printer Sharing for Microsoft networks. Also, the Advanced tab enables you to use the new Internet Connection Firewall (ICF) and/or ICS (we'll get to ICS later in this chapter and ICF in Chapter 11).

Configuring Incoming Connections

Just as you can configure Windows XP Professional to dial up to corporate networks or the Internet, you can also configure Windows XP Professional to receive calls. This feature enables Windows XP Professional to accept up to three connections at a time, provided they are different types of connections. For example, you can accept a VPN connection, a dial-up connection, and an ICS connection at the same time. To create the incoming connection, you once again use the New Connection wizard. Exercise 10-4 walks you through this process.

EXERCISE 10-4

CertCam 10-4

Configuring Incoming Connections

To set up an incoming connection, just follow these steps:

1. Click Start | Control Panel | Network Connections.
2. If you have the Windows XP view turned on, you'll see a Create a New Connection option in the Network Tasks pane. If it's not turned on, you'll see a Create a New Connection icon. Double-click/single-click the Create a New Connection, then click Next on the New Connection wizard's Welcome screen.
3. In the Network Connection Type window, click the "Set up an advanced connection" radio button and click Next.
4. In the Advanced Connection Options window, click the "Accept incoming connections" radio button and click Next.
5. In the Devices for Incoming Connections window, select your modem and click Next.
6. In the Incoming Virtual Private Network Connection window, you can choose whether or not to allow VPN connections over this connection.

For the purpose of this exercise, click the "Do not allow virtual private connections" radio button and click Next.

7. In the User Permissions window, shown in the following illustration, select the Users that are allowed to access the computer via a dial-up connection.

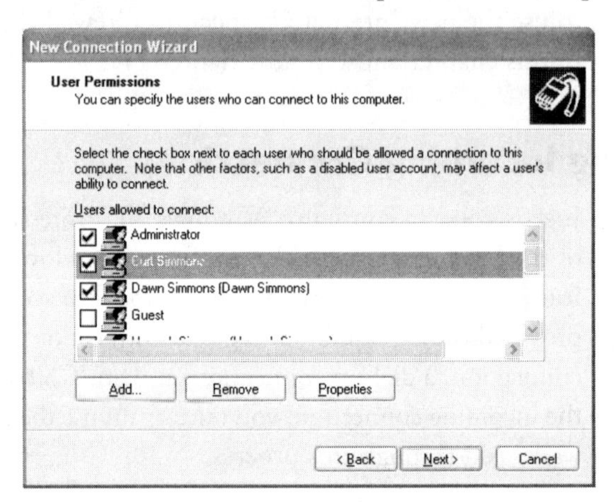

8. In the Networking Software window, shown in the following illustration, choose which Network Software items you want to enable over this connection by clicking or clearing the check box next to the item. You can install additional services by clicking the Install button. For example, if you wanted to use the IPX/SPX compatible transport on this connection, you would click Install and click Protocol to install it. Make your selections and click Next.

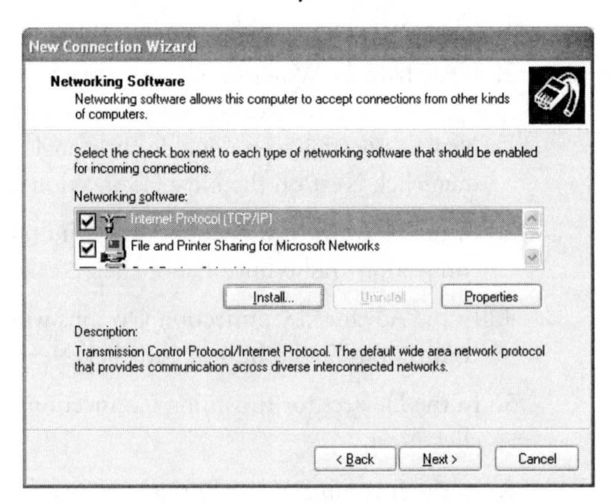

Internet Protocol cannot be uninstalled.

9. Click Finish.

Once you have configured the connection, you can adjust the incoming connection's settings by accessing the connection's properties sheets. In Network Connections, right-click on the Incoming Connections icon and click Properties. The property sheets contain a General, a Users, and a Networking tab. The options you see are the same options presented in the wizard, so I'll not repeat that information here. However, there are two check boxes on the Users tab I would like to point out.

The Users tab, shown in Figure 10-7, enables you to make changes to the users who are allowed or not allowed to access the computer via the incoming connection. You also see two check box options. The first requires all users to secure their passwords and data. If this option is selected, a user who is connecting must have the "Require data encryption (disconnect if none)" setting enabled on the Advanced security window of the user's dial-up connection. The second option states "Always allow directly connected devices such as palmtop computers to connect without providing a password." If you'll be using mobile devices to connect to Windows XP, you'll probably need to enable this option.

FIGURE 10-7

The Users tab

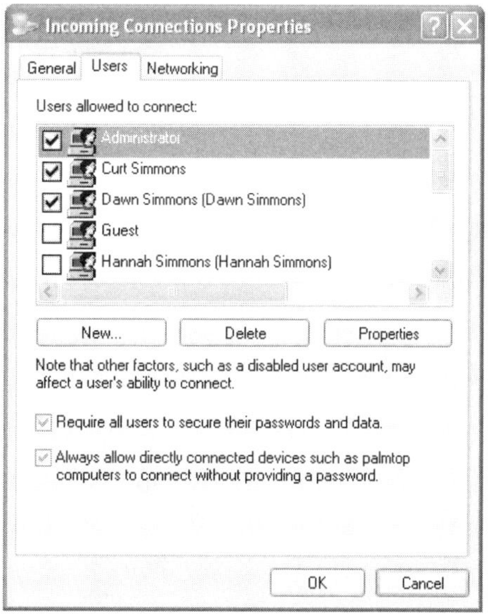

SCENARIO & SOLUTION	
I want to enable the IPX/SPX compatible protocol for my incoming connection. Will this also affect my outgoing connection?	No. You can configure a protocol or service to be used on the incoming connection, but the outgoing connection will not be affected—the two work independently of each other.
Does Windows XP Professional support the callback feature?	Yes. Callback can be used for security purposes. The user makes a connection with the computer and then disconnects. The computer then calls the user back to continue the session. If you want to enable the callback feature for a user, access the Users tab on the Incoming Connection's properties, select the user, and click Properties. On the Callback tab, you can choose to let the user select the callback number, or you can enter a static callback number.
I want to make sure that users log on with a secured password when using dial-up networking. How can I configure this?	On the Security tab of the dial-up networking connection's properties, choose the Typical settings and choose Require Secured password from the drop-down menu. You can also choose to automatically use a Windows logon name and password, and you can also require data encryption.
For a particular user, I want to make sure that a dial-up connection logs on with the most encryption available and that a smart card is used. What settings are needed?	On the Security tab of the dial-up networking connection's properties, click the Advanced Settings radio button and click Settings. Under Data Encryption, choose Maximum Strength Encryption. Under Logon Security, choose EAP and choose Smart Card or Other Certificate.

CERTIFICATION OBJECTIVE 10.03

Connect Using VPN or ICS

Virtual Private Networking (VPN) and Internet Connection Sharing (ICS) are two very different technologies that I have placed together for organizational purposes. In truth, these types of connections are simply another way to use Windows XP

Professional for different kinds of network connectivity. You are likely to see a question or two on the exam concerning both of these connection types, and the following sections explore them and give you opportunities to practice using them.

Connect Using VPN

Virtual Private Network connections have been around for some time now, and with good reason. VPN connections enable you to use an existing public network, such as the Internet, freely and in a way that is private. When a VPN connection is used, the actual network data that you are transferring is encapsulated in a Point-to-Point Tunneling Protocol packet (PPTP) or a Layer 2 Tunneling Protocol (L2TP) packet. The packet has a typical header destination for a typical PPP packet traveling the Internet. The PPTP or L2TP packet can traverse the Internet as a PPP packet. When the packet reaches the destination network, the PPTP or L2TP encapsulation is stripped away, and the true data is revealed. The end result? You can connect to segments of your network using the Internet without paying WAN link charges. This feature works great for a company who has a satellite office where a few people need to send data over the VPN connection each day. Of course, the VPN connection is not designed for high levels of traffic, but in many connectivity cases it is an easy and cost-efficient solution.

I mentioned that PPTP and L2TP are used in VPN connections. Let's consider these two protocols in a bit more detail. First, PPTP allows tunneled traffic through an IP network, such as the Internet. The second type, L2TP, provides more functionality. For example, PPTP can be used only on IP networks, whereas L2TP can be used on any type of PPP packet network, such as ATM or X.25. Also, L2TP supports header compression and tunnel authentication, as well as the use of IP Security (IPSec). PPTP does support encryption, whereas L2TP supports encryption only when IPSec is used. The end result is that L2TP gives you more options and functionality than PPTP, but both are highly effective VPN protocols.

You can configure Windows XP Professional to make VPN connections or to allow incoming VPN connections. Exercise 10-5 walks you through the process of configuring Windows XP Professional to make VPN calls.

EXERCISE 10-5

Configuring VPN Connectivity

To set up a VPN connection, follow these steps:

1. Click Start | Control Panel | Network Connections.
2. Start the New Connection wizard and click Next on the Welcome screen.
3. In the Network Connection Type window, click "Connect to the network at my workplace" and click Next.
4. In the Network Connection window, choose the "Virtual Private Network connection" radio button and click Next.
5. In the Connection Name window, enter a friendly name for the connection and click Next.
6. In the Public Network window, choose which existing dial-up connection you want to dial so that the VPN tunnel can be established. For example, if you had a dial-up connection configured to access a RAS server, you could select that connection so that VPN connectivity can be used. Make your selection and click Next.
7. Enter the host name or IP address of the VPN Server to which you are connecting.
8. Click Finish. The VPN connection is created and now appears in the Network Connections folder.

The VPN connection's properties pages are the basically the same as a typical dial-up connection. You have the same security-setting options, calling options, and so on. The General tab lists the host name or IP address of the destination and the dial-up connection that should be used to generate the VPN connection. If you want to accept incoming VPN connections, you can use the New Connection wizard to create an incoming connection and allow VPN connections during the wizard steps.

It is important to keep in mind that VPN connectivity can be managed with authentication protocols, just as a typical dial-up connection. This feature enables you to use VPN solutions without compromising network security standards.

Connect Using ICS

Internet Connection Sharing, a technology first introduced with Windows 98, has come a long way in the past couple of years. ICS, which is designed for the home network or the small office workgroup, enables one computer to have an Internet connection while the other computers share that connection. Essentially, the physically connected computer acts as a host to the other workgroup computers. As a general rule, ICS is easy to set up and use, but there are some requirements that must be kept in mind and memorized for the exam:

- ICS is not designed for a Windows domain. ICS is designed for the home or small office network that does not use Windows 2000 Servers, DHCP Servers, or DNS Servers. As a part of ICS configuration, the ICS host computer will function as a DHCP Allocator and assign IP addresses to the client computers that will use ICS. The IP address range is 192.168.0.2–192.168.0.254; a subnet of 255.255.255.0 is used to assign IP addresses to client computers. The ICS host will assign itself the static IP address of 192.168.0.1. The point is that you cannot have a statically configured IP network or one managed by a DHCP Server, because ICS will reassign all of the IP addresses, resulting in lost network connectivity. The Network Setup Wizard can configure the IP settings for the host and clients, which is why the Network Setup Wizard is the preferred method of network installation and configuration for end users. The clients must be aware of the ICS host's IP address in order to access the host.
- ICS can be used on a dial-up, LAN, VPN, Point-to-Point over Ethernet (PPPoE), or broadband Internet connection. The host computer has a connection to the Internet, as well as a network adapter card for local network connectivity. Client computers only need have a network adapter card in order to connect to the ICS host.

- You must use Internet Explorer 5 or later. Configure Internet Explorer to access the Internet via a LAN connection and use the Proxy Server check box option.
- Outlook and Outlook Express are supported for mail access. The mail client must be configured to access mail through the LAN.
- Windows XP's version of ICS also uses a Discovery and Control feature. The Discovery and Control feature gives client computers more power over the connection in the sense that clients can launch an Internet connection, disconnect it, and monitor the status of the connection. When ICS is installed and configured, client computers have an icon in their notification area for viewing statistics about the connection and making a disconnection. Additionally, all the client needs to do in order to establish the Internet connection is launch the browser.

In order to establish an ICS host, you first configure the Internet connection that you want to share, whether that is a broadband connection, dial-up, or other type. Access the connection's properties sheets in the Network Connections folder and click the Advanced tab, shown in Figure 10-8. On the Advanced tab, click the Allow check box in the ICS section. You can also allow clients to automatically establish a dial-up connection when an access attempt is made, and you can allow other users

FIGURE 10-8

Advanced connection properties

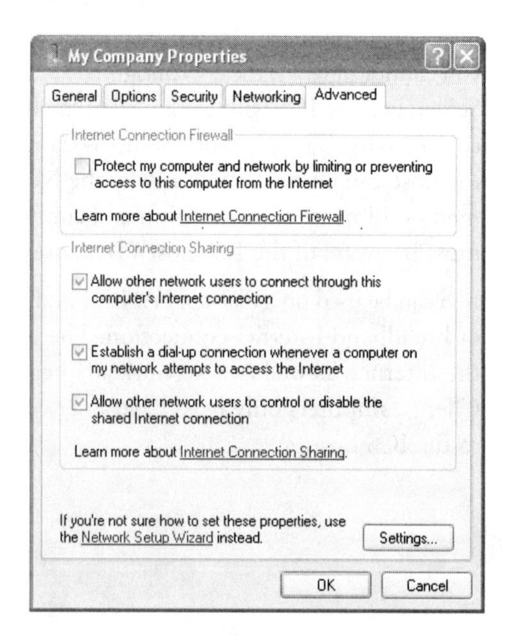

to control or disable the connection. For always-on broadband connections, these two check boxes are not necessary. To stop the host computer from sharing the Internet connection, just clear the check box on this tab.

To configure Internet Explorer to access the ICS host, open Internet Options in Control Panel. Click the Connections tab and click the LAN Settings button. In the Local Area Network (LAN) Setting, click the "Automatically detect settings" check box and the "Use a proxy server" check box, shown in Figure 10-9.

CERTIFICATION OBJECTIVE 10.04

Troubleshoot Network Connections

In addition to the network troubleshooting tools I mentioned earlier in the chapter, there are troubleshooting tips for the different kinds of connections we have explored, which will be briefly described here.

For connectivity in a Microsoft network, the client computer must have a properly installed network adapter card and an appropriate IP address and subnet mask. The best way to troubleshoot network connections is to use the ping and IPconfig tools to determine the connectivity problem. First, check for connectivity against your network adapter card by using ping 127.0.0.1, and then test for connectivity against

FIGURE 10-9

Local Area Network (LAN) settings

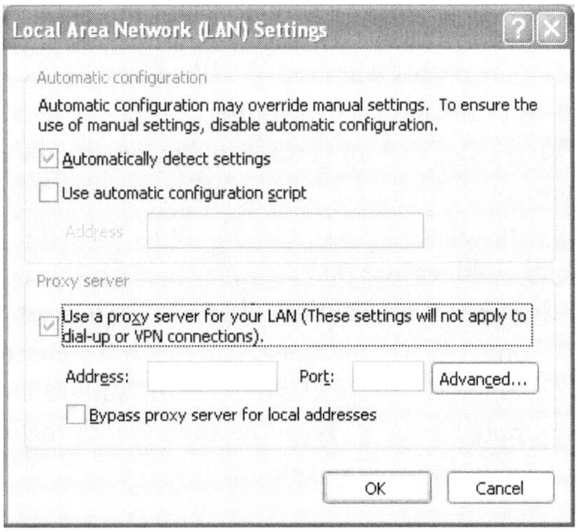

FROM THE CLASSROOM

ICS Configuration

ICS is a helpful tool that enables one computer to have a configured Internet connection and the necessary connection hardware—such as a modem, DSL hardware, Internet satellite hardware, and so on—and have other linked computers use that connection. The good news is that having the other clients can use the single connection saves money and allows multiple users to access the Internet at the same time.

However, it is important to keep in mind that Internet connectivity speed depends on available bandwidth. Let's say that the ICS host is configured with a 56 Kbps modem. If you have three users actively using the Internet at the same time, the modem has three times the amount of data to download than it would with one user. The end result—the Internet can become very slow for your workgroup users.

In a home situation, this may not be a problem, but when ICS is used in a small office setting, broadband connectivity usually becomes necessary so that information can be retrieved from the Internet in a timely manner. The trick is to experiment with the connection and client usage so you can make a wise decision about the type of Internet connectivity that is right for you.

other network hosts using an IP address, then WINS/DNS names. Make sure your IP Properties sheets are configured with the appropriate IP addresses of WINS and DNS servers that are in use in your network. If your network has more than one subnet, the clients will need the IP address of the default gateway in order to communicate on different subnets.

When using dial-up networking, make sure the modem is configured properly and is functional. If you are having problems, you may need to slow down the modem's connection speed by accessing the modem's properties sheets. Once the connection is configured, ensure that a correct user name and password is used and that the security settings are configured to match those of the computer you are dialing into. If the computer will not stay connected but seems to automatically disconnect, check the Dialing Rules properties to see if the auto-disconnect feature is enabled. The same issues apply for the VPN connection. Check the security settings to ensure that they match with the VPN server.

Finally, if there are connectivity problems when ICS is in use, first verify that the host computer has Internet connectivity. If the host computer does but clients or a single client does not, the problem is almost always an IP configuration problem. Remember that IE and any mail applications must be configured to access the Internet via the LAN connection. Use your TCP/IP troubleshooting tools to resolve the IP connectivity problem.

CERTIFICATION SUMMARY

Windows XP Professional is designed for networking in Microsoft Windows domains, as well as in peer-to-peer networks. TCP/IP is installed automatically on Windows XP Professional computers and is the protocol of choice for today's Microsoft networks. Windows XP Professional supports APIPA and is able to assign itself an IP address in a workgroup setting. Windows XP Professional can also receive the IP address assignment from DHCP, or you can configure the settings manually.

Dial-up networking provides dial-up support that conforms to major security standards. You can configure dial-up connections that support password security and data encryption. Additionally, dial-up connections also support logon security and protocols such as EAP, PAP, SPAP, CHAP, and MS-CHAP.

Windows XP Professional also supports VPN connections, where the Windows XP Professional can connect to a VPN server using PPTP or L2TP. Windows XP can be configured to receive VPN connections as well. You can set the same levels of security on VPN connections as you can for dial-up connections.

Finally, ICS can be used to provide Internet connection sharing for workgroup clients. ICS changes the computer IP address to the 192.168.0.2–192.168.0.254 range, with a subnet of 255.255.255.0. ICS clients must be configured to access the Internet via LAN settings in Internet Explorer. Outlook Express and Outlook, as well as other mail applications, must also use LAN settings to connect. The Network Setup Wizard can help end users automatically configure these settings.

✓ TWO-MINUTE DRILL

Configure and Troubleshoot TCP/IP

- ❑ Windows XP Professional is designed for TCP/IP networking. TCP/IP settings can be configured automatically via APIPA or via a DHCP server. You can also configure them manually.
- ❑ Connectivity in TCP/IP networks depends on a properly configured IP address, subnet mask, and an optional default gateway (if there is more than one subnet).
- ❑ You can troubleshoot IP connectivity and functionality via a number of command line tools. Common command line tools are ping, ipconfig, netstat, nbtstat, tracert, pathping, route, and nslookup.

Connect to Computers Using Dial-Up Networking

- ❑ Dial-up networking uses the computer's modem to establish connections with other computers over the phone, including RAS and ISP connections.
- ❑ Dial-up networking supports a number of features, including dialing rules and encryption and authentication mechanisms. Common logon security features that can be used include EAP, PAP, SPAP, CHAP, and MS-CHAP (v2).
- ❑ Through EAP, certificate authentication and smartcard authentication can be used with dial-up connections.
- ❑ You can configure inbound connections so that a user can connect to the Windows XP computer. You must select which users are allowed to dial in to the computer, and you can even enable the callback feature if desired.

Connect Using VPN or ICS

- ❑ Windows XP Professional supports PPTP and L2TP for secure VPN connections. Windows XP Professional can receive VPN connections as well.
- ❑ ICS is designed for workgroups in which a single computer can host an Internet connection. Clients receive a specialized IP address, and Internet Explorer must be configured for LAN access in order to use ICS.

- ❑ The ICS host acts as a DHCP Allocator in order to provide IP addresses to network clients. Network clients can use the Discovery and Control feature, which enables them to view information about network statistics, as well as establish and disconnect sessions. The host, however, can prevent sessions from being established or disconnected.

Troubleshoot Network Connections

- ❑ Troubleshooting network connections should begin at the hardware level to ensure that such items as modems and network adapter cards are functioning properly.
- ❑ Use the TCP/IP troubleshooting to tools to isolate network-specific connectivity problems and bottlenecks.

SELF TEST

The following questions will help you measure your understanding of the material presented in this chapter. Read all of the choices carefully, as there may be more than one correct answer. Choose all correct answers for each question.

Configure and Troubleshoot TCP/IP

1. APIPA assigns IP addresses in the 169.254.0.0–169.254.255.255 range. What default gateway address is assigned when APIPA is used?

   A. 169.254.1.1

   B. 131.107.2.200

   C. 10.0.0.1

   D. Thc dcfault gateway is not assigned.

2. You want to manually configure the IP addresses and subnet masks for a certain workgroup. For the workgroup, however, you want to make certain that only certain IP protocols can be used. How can you configure this?

   A. LAN connection settings, General tab.

   B. You must set up third-party firewall software.

   C. By running the **noipprot / b** command.

   D. By accessing the advanced IP properties, Options tab, and using IP filtering.

3. A user reports a problem with her Windows XP Professional computer. The computer is unable to contact any network resource. You attempt to contact resources and cannot do so. What command should you run first?

   A. Ping 127.0.0.1

   B. Ipconfig /x

   C. Ping 131.107.2.200

   D. Tracert

4. A particular WINS server seems to have the wrong "NetBIOS name to IP" mapping in its database. You need to issue a command so that the computer can release name mappings and perform a refresh. What do you need to do?

   A. Netstat -t

   B. Nslookup

C. Nbtstat -RR

D. Ipconfig /all

5. You work in a WAN environment. You verify that the clients and the server both have network connectivity. Clients report some problem accessing a remote server. You want to view the IP path to that server and see if you can locate the source of the communication failure. What tool will help you do this?

A. Nbtstat

B. Tracert

C. Ipconfig

D. Pathping

6. You need to view some DNS mappings on a DNS Server. What command line tool will allow you to do this?

A. Nbtstat

B. Route

C. Nslookup

D. Pathping

Connect to Computers Using Dial-Up Networking

7. For a configured dial-up connection, you need to ensure that a certain area code is considered local by your computer. Where can you configure this?

A. Dialing Rules

B. Connection properties, Security tab

C. Modem Properties

D. Internet Options in Control Panel

8. A manager at your company uses a laptop computer to dial up to a RAS server when traveling. You want to make certain that a secure password is used and that data is encrypted. Further, you want the connection to be dropped if encryption is not available. What do you need to do to configure this?

A. On the connection's security tab, use the Typical setting and choose "Require secure password" from the drop-down menu. Click the Advanced Settings button and choose the Encryption option.

B. On the connection's security tab, use the Typical setting, choose "Require secure password" from the drop-down menu, and click the "Require data encryption" check box.

C. On the connection's security tab, click the Advanced button and click Settings. Choose EAP as the logon security and choose MD-5 Challenge.

D. You can't configure a secure password with encryption.

9. Consider the Advanced Security Settings, shown in the following illustration. You want to use settings that allow a specific user to log on to an RAS server using a smart card with encrypted data. What do you need to do?

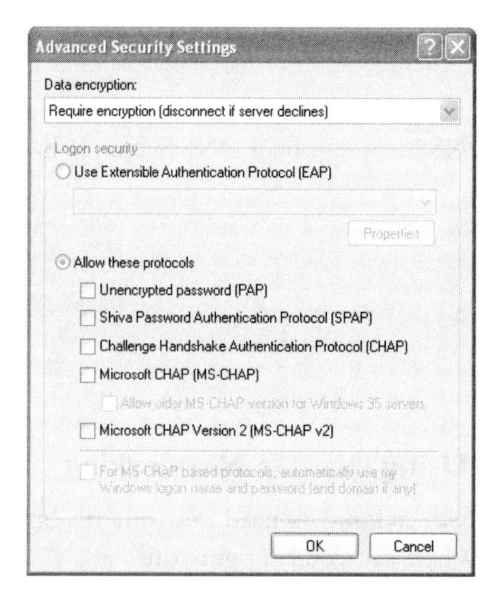

A. Use EAP and choose the Smart Card option from the drop-down menu.

B. Use PAP and choose the Require Encryption setting from the Data encryption drop-down menu.

C. Use SPAP.

D. Use MS-CHAP v2.

10. A particular user logs onto an RAS server when traveling in different locations. You want to require the user's computer to use encryption when it is available from the server. However, you do not want the user locked out of the network if encryption is not available. What encryption setting should you use on the connection's Security tab?

A. Required

B. Optional

C. Nominal

D. Choice

Connect Using VPN or ICS

11. What two VPN protocols are supported in Windows XP Professional? (Choose two)

A. PPP

B. PPTP

C. L2TP

B. APIPA

12. You have your Windows XP Professional computer configured to accept incoming VPN connections. You want to make sure that users who access your computer log on with secure passwords and data. What do you need to do? (Choose two answers. Each answer contains part of the solution).

A. Access the incoming connection's properties.

B. On the Users tab, click "Require all users to secure their passwords and data."

C. On the Advanced tab, click "Require strong security."

D. On the General tab, click "Require encrypted password authentication."

13. In an emergency situation, you want stop VPN connections on your incoming connection on your Windows XP Professional computer. How can you stop the VPN connections without deleting the entire connection?

A. Shut down the computer.

B. Clear the VPN check box option on the connection's General tab.

C. Remove the VPN protocols from the connection's Networking tab.

D. You cannot do this without deleting the connection.

14. A particular user has Share level permissions of Read, Change, and Deny Read resulting from group memberships. What is the user's effective permission?

A. Read

B. Change

C. No access

D. Modify

15. A small workgroup contains ten Windows XP Professional computers. A user decides to implement ICS. However, once ICS is enabled, the host computer loses contact with the rest of the network. All computers have a static IP address. What is the problem?

    A. The firewall has been enabled.

    B. ICS changed the IP address of the host.

    C. The computer is not connected to the Internet.

    D. ICS has disabled the computer's network adapter card.

16. In a small office environment, ICS is in use. One user, John, keeps disconnecting the ICS connection when other users are accessing the Internet. As the administrator of the ICS computer, you want to make sure that John (and no other user) can disconnect a session. What can you do?

    A. Give all users Read permission.

    B. Change the users' browsers to connect automatically.

    C. Clear the check box option on the Advanced tab of the dial-up connection's properties.

    D. Disable the "logon locally" option.

Troubleshoot Network Connections

17. In a workgroup environment, ICS is used. Clients access the Internet via Internet Explorer 6. Eudora mail is used for e-mail. Since the ICS connection was configured, users cannot access their e-mail via ICS. What is wrong?

    A. Eudora is not configured for LAN connectivity.

    B. Eudora is not supported.

    C. The firewall is blocking the SMTP protocol.

    D. Mail is not available when using ICS.

LAB QUESTION

A small company contains 30 Windows XP Professional and 15 Macintosh computers. The company hires you as a consultant. The company wants to implement Internet connectivity with ICS. One Windows XP Professional computer will have a DSL connection. All other computers need to access the Internet via the Windows XP Professional host. A variety of browsers are used, and the network is made of statically assigned IP addresses. What issues would you point out to the company?

SELF TEST ANSWERS

Configure and Troubleshoot TCP/IP

1. ☑ D is correct. APIPA is designed for small workgroups using a single IP subnet. No default gateway is auto-assigned with APIPA.

☒ A, B and C are incorrect. No default gateway is assigned.

2. ☑ D is correct. You can control the TCP and UDP ports that can be used and the IP protocols through TCP/IP filtering. The filtering options are available on the Advanced TCP/IP Settings dialog box, Options tab, Properties button.

☒ A, B, and C are incorrect. TCP/IP filtering is not available on any General tab, so A is incorrect. B is incorrect because you do not need a third-party firewall to configure filtering options. Finally, there is no **noipprot** command.

3. ☑ A is correct. If there is no connectivity, first check the computer's network adapter card by running the loopback test, which is ping 127.0.0.1.

☒ B, C, and D are incorrect. There is no ipconfig /x command, so B is incorrect. Pinging a network IP address is not the first action, so C is also incorrect. Finally, tracert will not help solve this problem, so D is incorrect.

4. ☑ C is correct. Nbtstat, which is NetBIOS over TCP/IP, is the tool you would use here, and the –RR (ReleaseRefresh) switch will do the job.

☒ A, B, and D are incorrect. These tools will not troubleshoot NetBIOS over TCP/IP.

5. ☑ D is correct. Pathping combines the output of tracert and ping so you can determine where network packets are being lost.

☒ A, B, and C are incorrect. These tools will not help you solve this particular problem.

6. ☑ C is correct. Use Nslookup to view DNS mappings.

☒ A, B, and D are incorrect. These tools will not enable you to view DNS mappings.

Connect to Computers Using Dial-Up Networking

7. ☑ A is correct. You can configure Area Code rules by accessing dialing rules from the General tab of the connection's properties sheets.

☒ B, C, and D are incorrect. You can't configure area code rules from any of these locations.

8. ☑ B is correct. You can use typical settings and require a secure password and an encryption level.

   ☒ A, C, and D are incorrect. None of these options is the best answer when you simply need a secure password and encryption.

9. ☑ A is correct. If you want to use a Smart Card with encryption, your only option on this window is the EAP protocol. Choose Smart Card or other Certificate from the drop-down menu, which also enables encryption.

   ☒ B, C, and D are incorrect. None of these protocol options will meet the smart card/encryption need.

10. ☑ B is correct. In order to use encryption but still be able to log on in the event that it is unavailable, choose Optional Encryption.

    ☒ A, C, and D are incorrect. Required encryption will disconnect the user if encryption is not available; therefore, A is incorrect. C and D are not encryption options.

Connect Using VPN and ICS

11. ☑ B and C are correct. PPTP and L2TP are the supported VPN protocols.

    ☒ A and D are incorrect. PPP is not used over VPN connections, and APIPA is not a transport protocol.

12. ☑ A and B are correct. In order to configure this option, access the incoming connection's properties, click the Users tab, and click "Require all users to secure their passwords and data."

    ☒ C and D are incorrect. The listed options do not exist on the General and Networking tabs.

13. ☑ B is correct. If you want to stop VPN connectivity from an inbound connection, simply clear the VPN check box on the General tab.

    ☒ A, C, and D are incorrect. While shutting down the computer and removing VPN protocols will work, they are not the most effective solution.

14. ☑ C is correct. Share permissions are cumulative, with the exception of a deny permission, which overrides all others. In this case, the user has Deny Read and effectively has no access.

    ☒ A, B, and D are incorrect. The least restrictive permission is applied; therefore, A and B are incorrect. D is incorrect because Full Control is not assigned.

15. ☑ B is correct. When setting up ICS, all computers should be configured to obtain an IP address automatically. ICS assigns a static IP address to the host computer, and then acts as a DHCP Allocator to assign IP addresses to the other computers.

☒ A, C, and D are incorrect. These answer options do not explain why the host has lost connectivity.

16. ☑ C is correct. Because of Discovery and Control, users may able to disconnect sessions. You can stop this behavior by clearing the check box option on the connection's Advanced tab.

☒ A, B, and D are incorrect. None of these actions will solve the problem.

Troubleshoot Network Connections

17. ☑ B is correct. Only Outlook and Outlook Express are supported with ICS. Eudora cannot be used.

☒ A, C, and D are incorrect. These options do not explain the problem.

LAB ANSWER

For this lab question, there are a few important issues you should point out:

☑ Only Windows computers can use an ICS connection. ICS is not supported for Macintosh.

☑ Only IE 5 and later can be used.

☑ All clients must be configured to obtain an IP address automatically, so the static assignments must be removed.

Troubleshooting Network Connections

11

Internet and Remote Networking

CERTIFICATION OBJECTIVES

11.01	Connect to Resources Using Internet Explorer
11.02	Configure, Manage, and Troubleshoot Internet Explorer Security Settings
11.03	Configure and Manage Remote Assistance and Remote Desktop
11.04	Configure the Internet Connection Firewall
11.05	Configure, Manage, and Implement Internet Information Services
✓	Two-Minute Drill
Q&A	Self Test

In the previous chapter, we focused on network connectivity issues in LAN and workgroup settings. While Windows XP Professional provides all of the tools and features you might need on a LAN or workgroup, it is also designed for Internet usage and provides new Remote Assistance and Remote Desktop features. Also, Windows XP Professional includes a personal firewall, called the Internet Connection Firewall (ICF).

These services give you a rich landscape of networking features and options, many of which will be very helpful in your personal use of Windows XP Professional, as well as in network support of the operating system. This rich landscape of features also provides the exam with a number of complicated and difficult questions related to the objectives we'll cover in this chapter. Be sure to pay special attention to the details we discuss and to the exam watches as we take a look at the usage, connectivity, and security features found in these services.

CERTIFICATION OBJECTIVE 11.01

Connect to Resources Using Internet Explorer

Internet Explorer (IE) is a Web browser, meaning that you can connect to Web pages and local shares using the Internet Explorer interface. Internet Explorer provides an easy way for end users to access what they need on the Internet and on intranets. This exam objective, connect to resources using Internet Explorer, simply is intended to ensure that you are familiar with Internet Explorer and how to use it to connect with local and remote resources. This is one of those vague exam objectives that you are likely to see combined with another exam objective. For example, "A user need to access your computer over the Internet using Internet Explorer, however, ICF is in use on your computer…" However, if you have not used Internet Explorer very much, you should certainly spend some time surfing the Web with it and using it to connect to shares on the local network. To use IE on the Internet, you'll need an Internet connection, which is explored in the next section.

Configuring an Internet Connection

Today's Internet connections come in either dial-up access or broadband access. Dial-up access uses the computer's modem and the public phone lines to connect to an ISP, while broadband solutions use different broadband hardware and provide "always on, always connected" solutions—common examples are DSL, cable, and Internet satellite. How the connection is configured is determined by the type of connection you want to establish. For a modem connection, simply install the modem and run the New Connection wizard in the Network Connections folder. Choose the Connect to the Internet option and follow the instructions that appear. For broadband connections, you will usually receive an installation CD and specific instructions on how to establish the connection.

If you are on a network that uses a proxy server/firewall or that uses ICS, you'll use the LAN settings in Internet Explorer to configure connectivity. You can configure how you want IE to manage and use the connections on your computer, and Exercise 11-1 shows you how.

EXERCISE 11-1

CertCam 11-1

Configuring Connections in IE

To configure a connection in IE, just follow these steps:

1. Click Start | Control Panel | Internet Options.
2. Click the Connections tab.
3. On the Connections tab, shown in the following illustration, you have three different options when configuring connections. First, you see a Setup button at the top of the tab. If you click the Setup button, you are taken back to the New Connection wizard, which will then help you configure a connection.

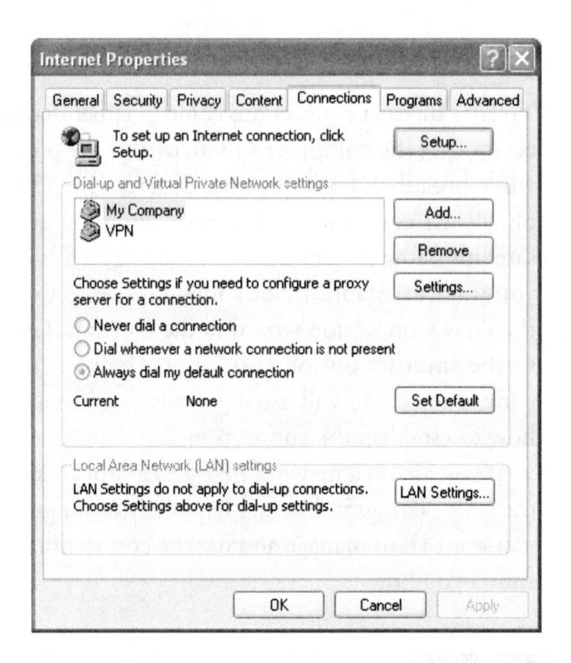

4. In the second section of the tab, you can manage dial-up and Virtual Private Network (VPN) connections. A list of your currently configured connections appears in the dialog box. You can Add and Remove connections using the provided buttons, and you can check the settings of a connection by selecting it and clicking the Settings button. If you click the Settings button, a Settings window appears where you can configure a proxy server to be used with the connection, as shown in the following illustration. You can have IE try to detect proxy server settings, or you can provide the proxy server's IP address. Users will need to follow network administrator instructions to configure these options, and the use of a proxy server will often fall under LAN settings as well. Also notice on the Connections tab that you have these radio button options: never dial a connection, dial whenever a network connection is not present, and always dial the default connection.

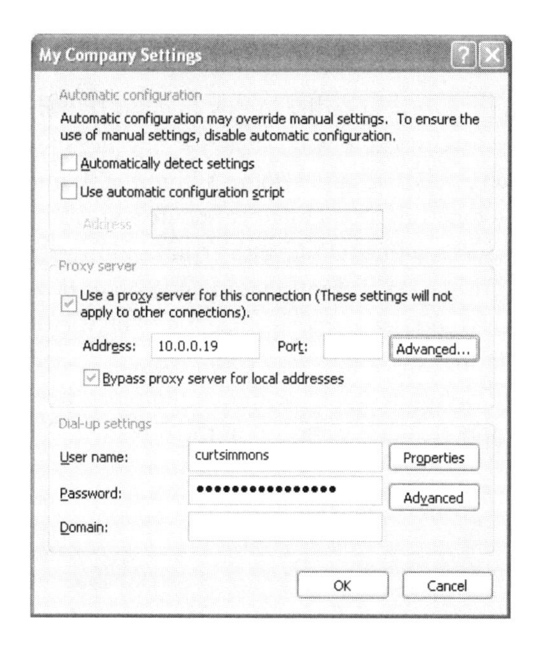

5. Finally, you see a LAN settings button at the bottom of the tab. If you access the Internet through a LAN or via ICS, you'll need to use this option instead of dial-up networking. Click the LAN Settings button to view the Local Area Network Settings window, shown in the following illustration. You can choose to automatically detect settings or configure the IP address of the proxy server/ firewall IE needs to access for Internet connectivity.

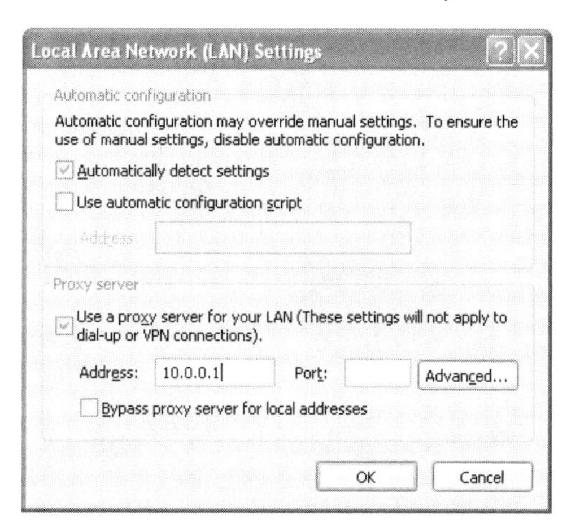

Accessing Resources Using Internet Explorer

As I mentioned earlier in this chapter, IE has become a versatile tool in Windows networks because you can access Internet sites, network shares (even printers), and even local drives and resources from the IE interface. As Figures 11-1 and 11-2 show, you can easily access Internet resources with a URL, while you can access local network resources with a UNC path. You can browse your local file structure as well.

Also, keep in mind that integration of the Internet with local network resources/ local computer sources is a major goal of Microsoft networking. In Windows XP, you'll find that any folder works much like Internet Explorer. You can be working in the My Computer folder and then jump to a network resource or Internet Resource by simply typing the address in the provided dialog box.

FIGURE 11-1

Internet Explorer accessing an Internet site

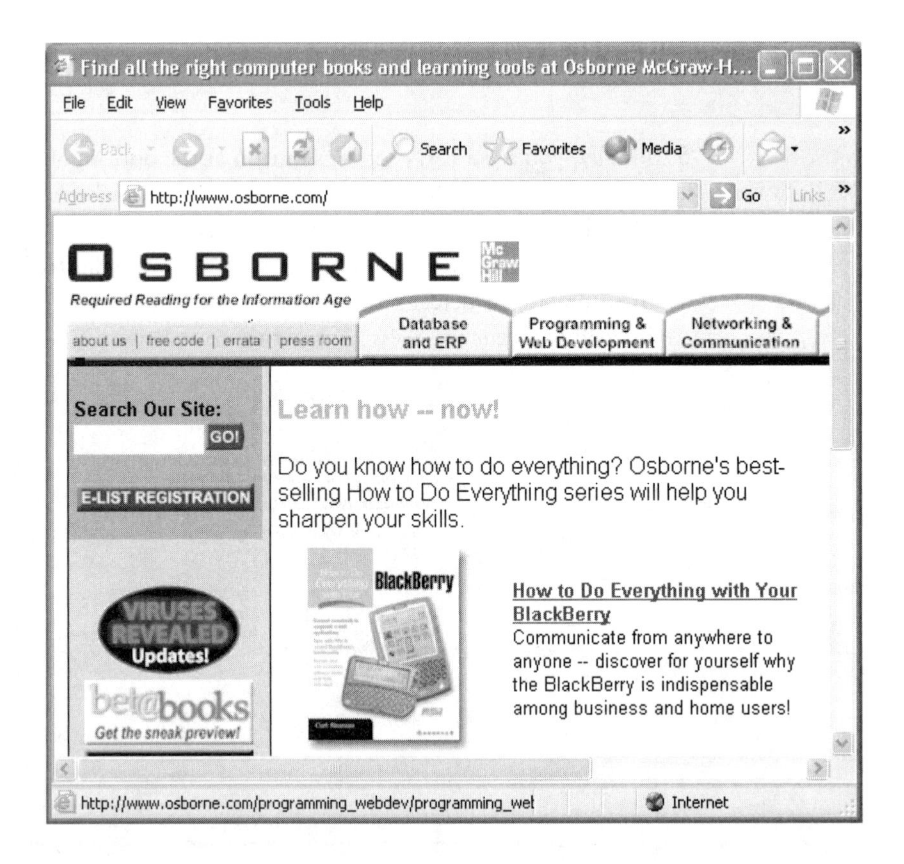

FIGURE 11-2

Internet Explorer accessing a network share

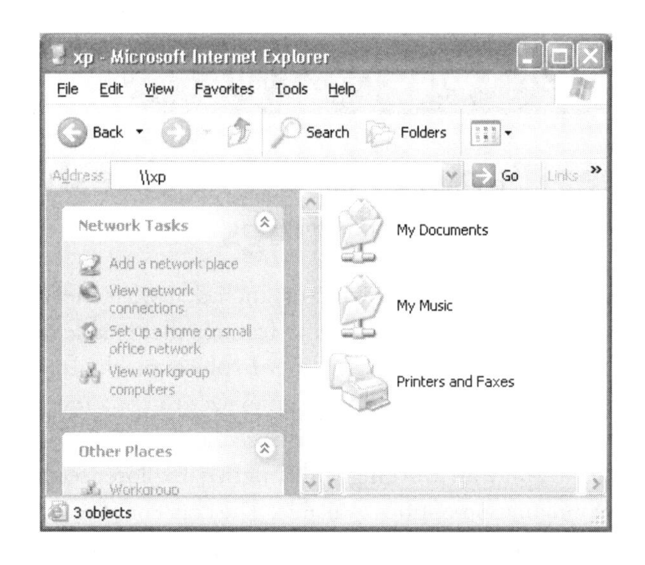

SCENARIO & SOLUTION

I have primary LAN connection to the Internet. Can I also configure a dial-up connection	Yes. Configure the LAN connection first and then configure the dial-up connection on your computer. The dial-up connection will appear in the Connections tab of Internet Explorer. If you want to make certain that IE always uses the LAN connection first, click the "dial whenever a network connection is not present" check box.
Why does Windows XP allow Internet site access from practically any folder?	Windows XP's interface works like a Web browser in that you can access an Internet site directly from a folder's Address bar, just as you can access a network resource. The idea behind this design is to integrate network resources with Internet resources. Users can easily access both local network and Internet resources using the same folder tools, thus achieving more network integration with the Internet.
Why do IE's tool bars change when switching from an Internet site to a network share?	IE's toolbars are specific for Internet use. This is a downside of using a regular folder for Internet access: you do not have all of IE's features available. When you use IE to access a network share, the toolbar options specific to Internet usage disappear. Simply access another Web site to have them reappear.

CERTIFICATION OBJECTIVE 11.02

Configure, Manage, and Troubleshoot Internet Explorer Security Settings

Internet Explorer 6, which is included with the Windows XP operating system, includes a number of security features that enable network clients and home clients to be able to safely use Internet Explorer on the Internet. There are several different options available, and you can expect to see a few exam questions on the security settings. You should study this section carefully, and make sure you spend some hands-on time working with Internet Explorer security and are comfortable with the configuration options available. The concept of security with Internet Explorer covers two primary areas: general security settings and privacy settings. The following sections examine these issues.

General Security Settings

You can configure the general security settings for Internet Explorer by accessing the Security tab of Internet Options in Control Panel, which is also available from within IE by clicking Tools | Internet Options. The Security tab, shown in Figure 11-3, has configuration options for Internet, intranet, trusted sites, and restricted sites. You can select a desired zone and then use the slider bar to select a security setting, or you can configure a custom setting.

For the exam, you need to know the different security levels that are available. The following bullet list explains them, and you should commit them to memory.

- **Low** Appropriate for sites that you completely trust. The Low setting allows all Active X content to run, allows content to be downloaded without security prompts, and provides only minimal safeguards and warning prompts.
- **Medium Low** Appropriate for sites on your local intranet. Unsigned ActiveX controls are not downloaded, but most content can be run without prompts, and only minimal security prompts appear.

FIGURE 11-3 The Security tab of Internet Options

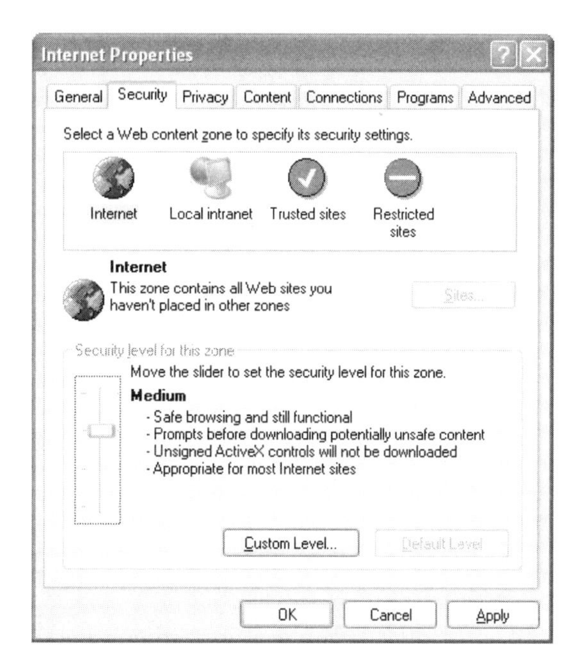

- **Medium** Appropriate for most Internet sites. Unsigned ActiveX controls are not downloaded, and the user is prompted before downloading potentially unsafe content. This setting gives you the best mix for safe browsing.
- **High** Appropriate for sites that might have harmful content. All less secure features are disabled. This is the safest way to browse, but it provides the least amount of functionality.
- **Custom** If you click the Custom Level button, the Security Settings window appears, shown in Figure 11-4, where you can enable, disable, or prompt ActiveX controls, content, and a variety of other settings.

exam watch

The exam is likely to give you a scenario question that asks you to choose which security level is best for a particular user who needs certain security settings. The exam may also mix in privacy settings here, so it is important that you memorize the options on these tabs. Not very practical for the real world perhaps, but that's the exam for you!

You can use Trusted Sites and Restricted Sites to override the security settings configured on this tab for those sites. If you select the Trusted Sites Zone icon,

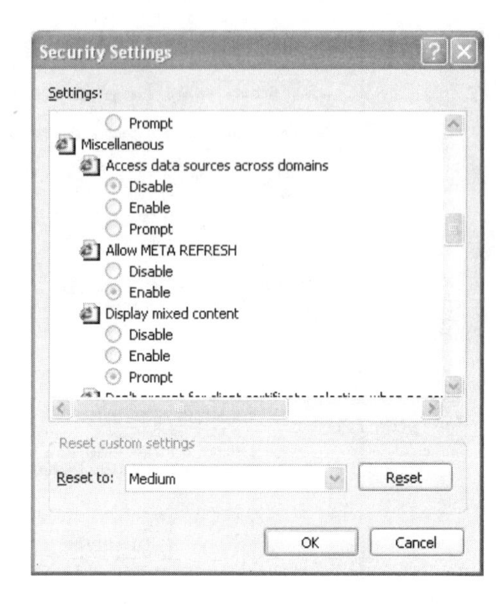

FIGURE 11-4 The Custom level Security Settings window

you'll see that the default security setting is Low (if you click on the Default Level button). If you click the Sites button, the Trusted Sites window appears, shown in Figure 11-5. Enter the name Web address of the trusted site and click Add to begin generating a list. Also note that you can require server verification (https) for sites in the zone for security purposes.

Under Restricted Sites, the default security setting is High. If you click the Sites button, you see the same kind of dialog box as in Figure 11-5, where you can generate a list of sites that are restricted. Note that these sites are not forbidden; they are simply configured with the High security setting.

Privacy

Privacy settings in Internet Explorer enable you to control how cookies are used on the Internet. *Cookies* are small text files that contain personal information about the user or computer. Cookies are a great feature of the Internet, because they allow Web sites to recognize you and invoke personalized settings. Many online stores use cookies so that they can provide personalized preferences and shopping recommendations when you access their sites. The problem with cookies is that they put private information out on the Web that may be stolen or even traded with other users. Cookies are a big reason e-mail spam is so prevalent. One click on a banner ad, and the Web site can get your e-mail address without your knowledge…if cookies aren't managed and controlled.

FIGURE 11-5

The Trusted sites window

The Privacy tab provides this control in the same manner as the general security settings. You can use the slider bar to select a security level, import security settings from another IE configuration, and configure advanced settings. First things first: the slider bar, shown in Figure 11-6, provides an easy way for most users to configure cookie handling settings.

FIGURE 11-6

The Privacy tab

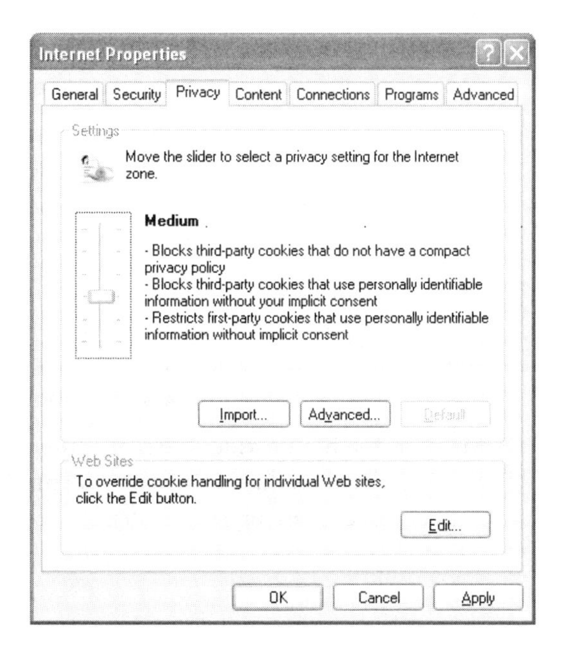

Before we explore the cookie settings that are available, you should understand a few terms:

- **Persistent cookie** A persistent cookie is stored as a file on your computer. The cookie can be read by the Web site that created it whenever you visit the site.
- **Temporary cookie** A temporary cookie is stored on your computer during a browsing session and is removed once the browsing session ends.
- **First-party cookie** A first-party cookie originates or is sent from the Web site you are viewing. In other words, it is generated out of contact between your browser and the Web site.
- **Third-party cookie** A third-party cookie originates or is sent from a Web site that you are not viewing. Typically, the cookie is generated because you clicked on some content on the first-party site, such as an advertisement.
- **Unsatisfactory cookie** An unsatisfactory cookie might allow access to information that personally identifies you that could be used without your consent.

The following bullet list explains the slider settings that are available to you. You should have these memorized for the exam:

- **Accept All Cookies** This setting saves all cookies on the computer, and any existing cookies can be read by the Web sites that created them. This setting basically provides no privacy setting control.
- **Low** Restricts third-party cookies that do have a compact privacy policy. A compact privacy policy ensures that cookies are not exchanged with third-party Web sites. Also, third-party cookies that use personal information that can identify you without your implicit consent are not allowed.
- **Medium** Blocks third-party cookies that do not have a compact privacy policy and blocks third-party cookies that use personal information that can identify you without your implicit consent. This setting also restricts first-party cookies that use personal identification information without your implicit consent.
- **Medium High** Provides the same protection as the Medium setting, but first-party cookies that use personal identification information without your implicit consent are blocked instead of restricted.

- **High** Blocks all cookies that do not have a compact privacy policy and blocks all cookies that use personal identification information.

exam watch

The High setting will prevent users from using cookies at online stores.

- **Block All Cookies** Cookies from all Web sites are blocked. If existing cookies reside on the computer, they can be read only by the Web site that created them.

There are also a couple of advanced setting options that you need to be aware of. First, if you click the Advanced button, you see an Advanced Privacy Settings dialog box, shown in Figure 11-7. You can choose to override automatic cookie handling so that all first or third party cookies are automatically accepted, blocked, or trigger a prompt. When security is an issue, the prompt setting can be very helpful, since no cookies can be transmitted without your explicit approval. However, all of the prompt dialog boxes can get aggravating and hinder Internet browsing.

You can also override settings for individual Web sites. For example, let's say that you have a Medium privacy setting, but you want all cookies blocked from a certain Web site. Simply click the Edit button at the bottom of the Privacy window to access the Per Site Privacy Actions window, shown in Figure 11-8. Enter the Web site address and click either Block or Allow. You can manage your exception list from this window as well.

FIGURE 11-7

The Advanced Privacy Settings window

FIGURE 11-8

Controlling cookies from specific sites

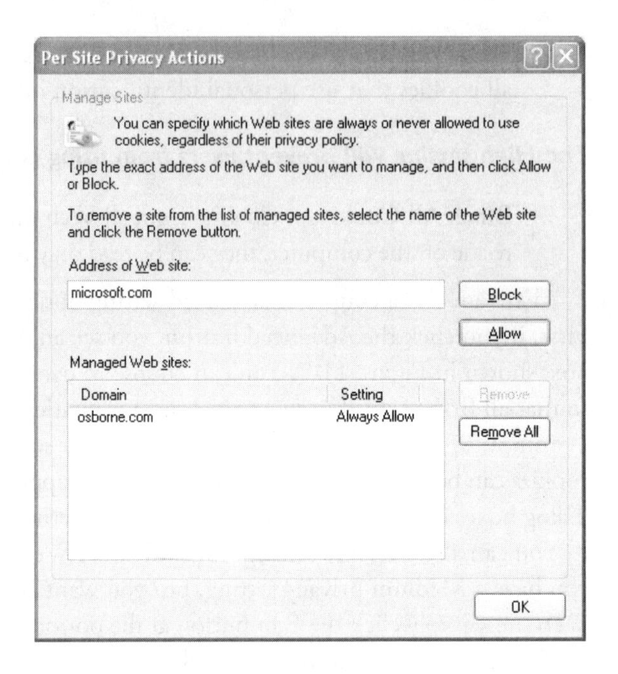

EXERCISE 11-2

Configuring IE Security

A user in your company accesses a number of Web sites for research purposes. You want to make certain that the user's IE settings meet the following needs:

- You want to maximize browsing, but you want prompts before any unsafe content is downloaded. Also, you do not want to allow unsigned ActiveX controls.
- You want to make sure that all third party cookies are automatically blocked and that no first-party cookies with personal information are allowed.
- For all other first-party cookies, you want the user to be prompted.
- You want to make sure that cookies for **www.ourcompetitor.com** cannot be generated.

In order to meet the needs in this situation, configure IE's security and privacy settings as follows:

1. Click Start | Control Panel | Internet Options.
2. Click the Security tab. Since you want both the best browsing available and prompts for potentially unsafe content and no unsigned ActiveX controls, move the slider bar to the Medium setting.
3. Click the Privacy tab. You want all third party cookies blocked and all cookies blocked with personal information. To meet these needs, choose the Medium High setting.
4. Click the Advanced button. To enable prompting for first-party cookies, click the Override automatic cookie handling check box, then click the Prompt radio button under First-party cookies. Under Third-party cookies, ensure that the Block radio button is selected. Click OK
5. On the Privacy tab, click Edit under Web Sites. Enter **www.ourcompetitor.com** in the dialog box, click Block, and click OK.
6. Click OK on Internet Properties.

SCENARIO & SOLUTION

What is the best way to use the High Security Setting?	The High Security Setting provides the best security but the least amount of browsing functionality. The High setting is best used with zones where there may be threatening content.
I am the local administrator for my Windows XP Professional computer. How can I configure security settings for other users of my computer?	This can be done through Group Policy, which can be configured either at the local computer level, or at the OU, domain, or site level by an enterprise administrator.

CERTIFICATION OBJECTIVE 11.03

Configure and Manage Remote Assistance and Remote Desktop

Windows XP Professional introduces two new remote management features called Remote Assistance and Remote Desktop. The first, Remote Assistance, allows you to access another person's Windows XP computer remotely, such as over the Internet or a WAN, so that you can troubleshoot and solve problems. The second, Remote Desktop, enables you to open a terminal session with a Windows XP Professional system so that you can use the computer remotely. Both of these features are helpful in a wide variety of situations, and since they are new, you can expect to see an exam question or two on them. The following two sections explore Remote Desktop and Remote Assistance.

Configuring Remote Assistance

Let's say you have a cousin in New York, but you live in San Diego. How can you help your cousin solve his computer problems? Sure, you can use the phone, but if you could actually see his desktop, you could fix the problem yourself. Let's say you are technician in a Help center for a large international company. A user in Toronto calls you for help, but you are in Houston. What if you could access her computer and fix the problem yourself without those painstaking verbal steps over the telephone? The solution to both of these scenarios is the goal of Remote Assistance. With Remote Assistance, a user can access another user's computer over a WAN, such as the Internet, and actually configure the other user's computer.

Remote Assistance works only with Windows XP computers. In other words, you can't use Remote Assistance from your XP computer and assist someone using a Windows Me computer. Also, each XP computer must use Windows Messenger or an MAPI-compliant e-mail account like Outlook or Outlook Express. The two computers must be configured for Remote Assistance, and both must have connectivity at the same time in order for Remote Assistance to work.

To enable Remote Assistance, access System Properties in Control Panel and click the Remote tab, shown in Figure 11-9. Click the Remote Assistance check box to enable the feature on your Windows XP computer.

FIGURE 11-9

The Remote tab

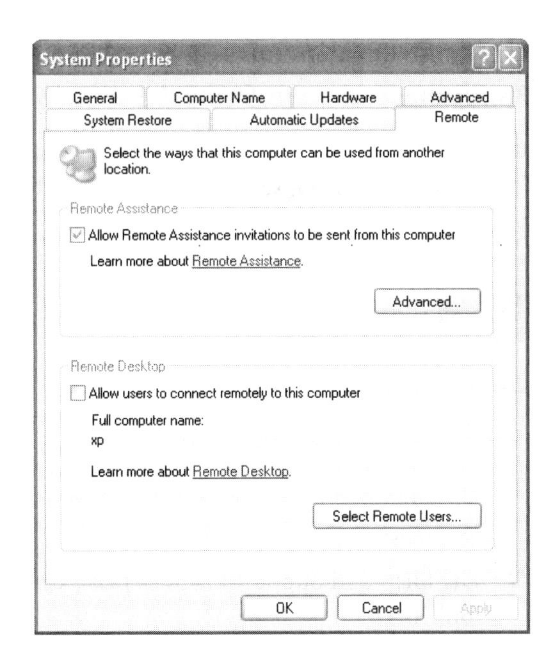

Next, click the Advanced button. You will see a Remote Assistance Settings dialog box, shown in Figure 11-10. Ensure that the "Allow this computer to be controlled remotely" check box is selected if you want your computer to be controlled remotely. Next, you see a maximum amount of time that invitations can remain open. Remote Assistance works with invitations. You send an invitation to another user, who can then access your computer via the invitation. This setting places a time limit on the invitation, which is 30 days by default.

FIGURE 11-10

The Remote Assistance Settings dialog box

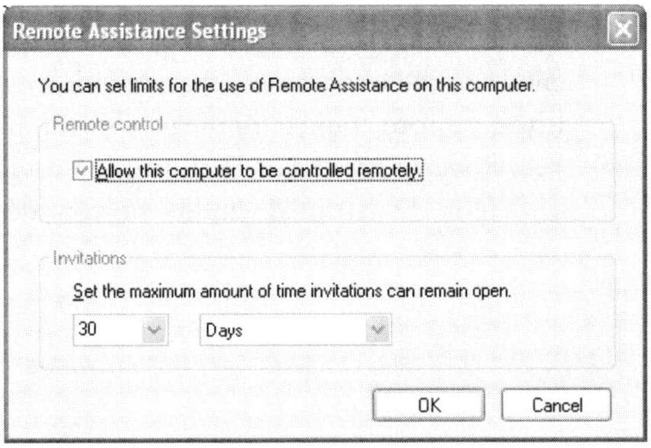

exam Watch

If you want to connect to a computer from behind a firewall, a network administrator must allow communication over TCP port 3398.

Once the computer is ready for remote assistance, the next step is to simply send an invitation to a desired user or accept an invitation from a user. Exercise 11-3 walks you through this process.

EXERCISE 11-3

Using Remote Assistance

To use Remote Assistance, follow these steps:

1. To send a Remote Assistance invitation, click Start | All Programs | Remote Assistance.
2. The Help and Support Center opens. Click the "Invite someone to help you" link.
3. You can send an invitation using Windows Messenger, Outlook, or Outlook Express. Click the Sign-in button to sign in to Windows Messenger or enter the e-mail address of the user you want to invite under Outlook Express.
4. Follow the instructions that appear. You can enter additional message text as desired, set the message expiration date, and establish a password that the user will enter in order to access your computer. You must give the password to the user—it is not sent via Windows Messenger or Outlook Express.
5. If you want to answer an invitation that you receive, click the link in Windows Messenger or open the invitation attachment that you see in the invitation e-mail. The invitation, an example of which appears in the following illustration, gives you the user's name, the expiration date, and the password dialog box. If you want to connect to the user's computer, enter the password and click Yes. Once you are connected, you can navigate through the user's computer as seen on the terminal window on your desktop.

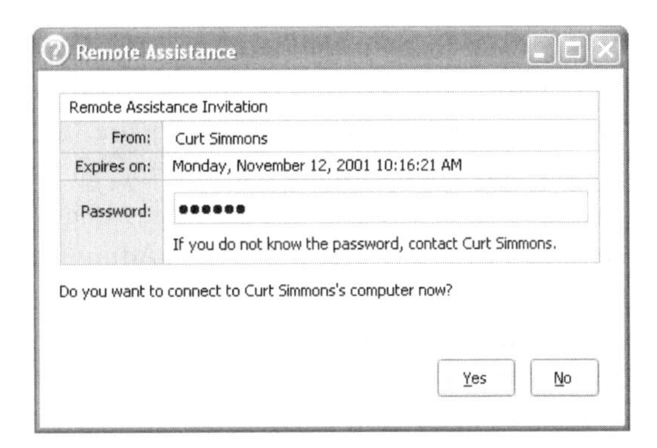

exam watch ***Although you can access the user's computer and make configuration changes via the remote connection, the user always retains control of the connection and can forcefully terminate it at any time by pressing Stop in Windows Messenger or the ESCAPE key on the keyboard.***

Configuring Remote Desktop

Remote Desktop, which is built on Windows terminal services, enables you to connect to and use another computer from a remote location. As you might imagine, this capability has a number of benefits. For example, let's say that you have a desktop system at your office, but you travel to branch offices a lot with a laptop. You can use Remote Desktop to connect to your desktop computer as needed. Let's say you have a desktop system at home and one at work. You could use Remote Desktop to access your home computer. You could even work on collaborative applications with another user on the same desktop. All of this assumes you have administrative or Remote Desktop group permissions on the computers. Remote Desktop allows multiple sessions on the same PC, so you could even have a number of users connected to one computer, collaborating on a project. As you can see, the potential uses of Remote Desktop are many.

In order to use Remote Desktop, you need two Windows XP computers. However, you can also connect a Windows XP computer to a Windows 9*x*, 2000, NT, or Me computer by installing the Remote Desktop client on those downlevel systems, which is available on the Windows XP Professional installation CD-ROM. You can connect computers that are on the same network, and you can use the Internet or VPN connection as well.

To set up Remote Desktop, you access System Properties | Remote tab and click the "Allow users to connect remotely to this computer" check box under Remote Desktop connections, as shown in Figure 11-11.

Click the Select Remote Users button. In the Remote Desktop Users window, click the Add button and select the user(s) to whom you want to give access to your computer remotely. Any members of the local Administrators group can automatically connect without assigning permission here. Simply add the users you want to give access to, and, if no account currently exists for the user, create one using User Accounts in Control Panel or in Computer Management.

An important item to note concerns passwords. In Windows XP, you can allow users to log on locally without a password. However, Remote Desktop requires the user to have a password, so make sure you configure a password for each user so that access via Remote Desktop will be available.

FIGURE 11-11 The Remote tab

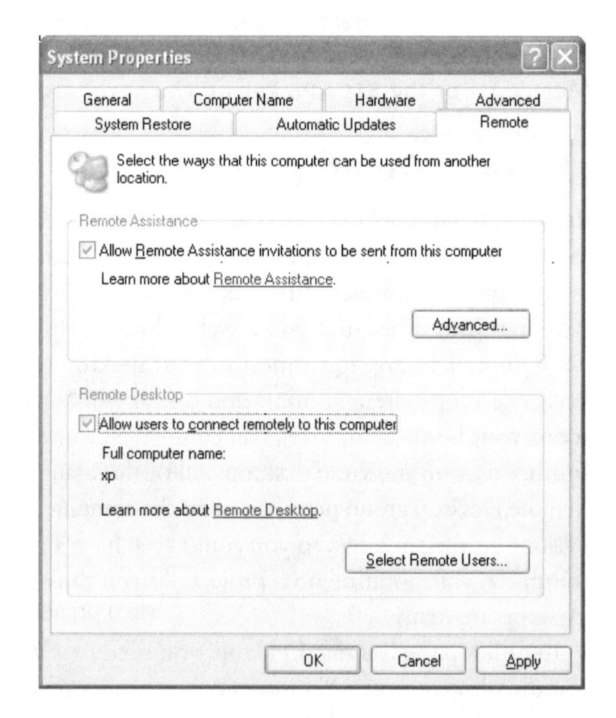

exam watch

By default, the Internet Connection Firewall does not allow Remote Desktop connections. If ICF is in use, you must enable Remote Desktop on the firewall in order for the remote connection to work. See the ICF section later in this chapter for configuration details.

As I mentioned, you can also enable Remote Desktop on downlevel clients, specifically Windows 9*x*, Me, 2000, and NT. To do so, you set up the Remote Desktop software on those clients. Exercise 11-4 walks you through the steps.

EXERCISE 11-4

Configuring Downlevel Clients for Remote Desktop

To configure downlevel clients to use Remote Desktop, follow these steps:

1. Insert the Windows XP Professional CD-ROM into the drive and click Perform Other Tasks on the Welcome screen.
2. Click the Set up Remote Desktop Connection option, as seen in the following illustration:

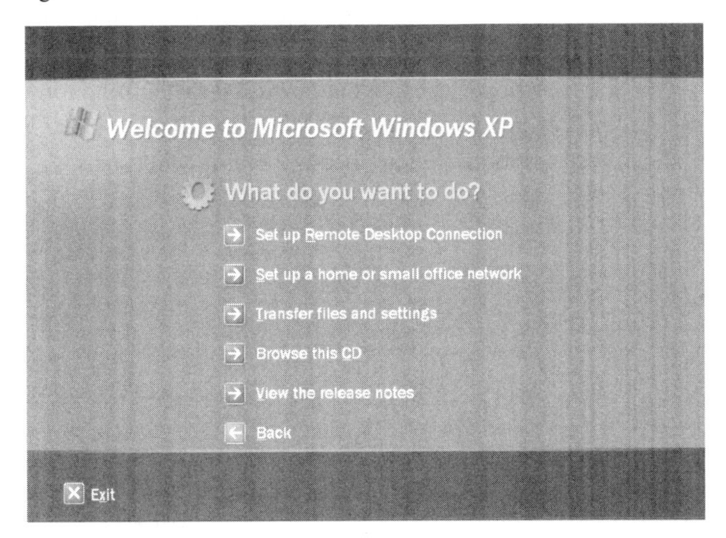

3. Review the EULA and click Next.
4. Enter your user name and any desired organization information and click Next.
5. Click Install to begin the installation.
6. Once the installation is complete, click Finish.

Once the computer has been set up to allow remote desktop connections, user accounts have been configured, and ICF has been set to allow Remote Desktop connections (if ICF is in use), you can connect to the computer from a Windows XP computer. Exercise 11-5 shows you how to establish the connection.

EXERCISE 11-5

Creating a Remote Desktop Connection

To create a Remote Desktop connection, follow these steps:

1. Click Start | All Programs | Accessories | Communications |Remote Desktop Connection.
2. In the Remote Desktop Connection window that appears, shown in the following illustration, enter the computer name, user name, password, and domain (if necessary) in the General tab. You can save the connection settings or open existing ones by using the buttons at the bottom of the screen. At this time, you can simply click Connect if you like, or you can configure additional options as described in the following steps.

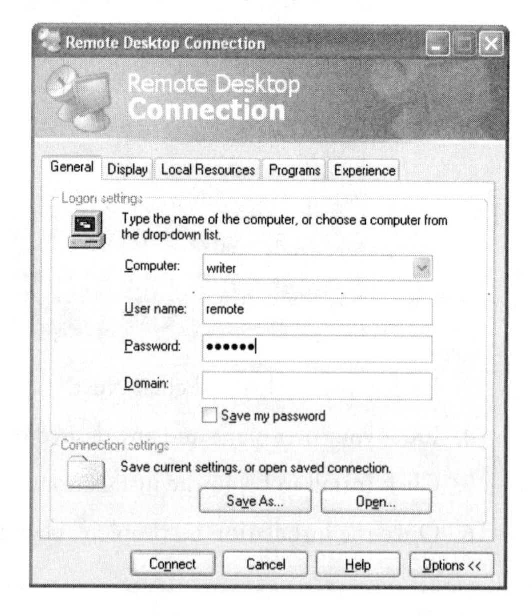

3. If you click the Display tab, shown in the following illustration, you can choose the style and color usage of your remote desktop. Remember that higher resolution settings may cause the connection to run more slowly.

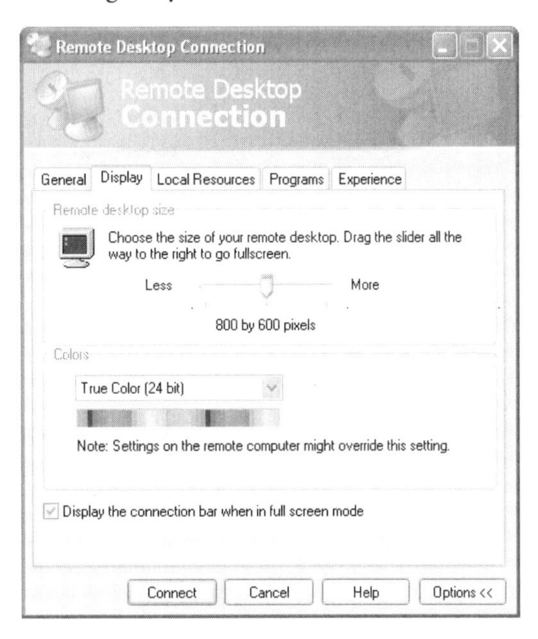

4. On the Local Resources tab, you can choose to use the remote computer's sound, keyboard combinations, and local devices (such as any printers attached to the remote computer), as well as disk drives and serial ports.

5. On the Programs tab, you can choose to start a program when the connection is made. This feature is helpful if you connect via Remote Desktop primarily to run a certain application.

6. On the Experience tab, shown in the following illustration, you can choose the connection speed from the drop-down menu to see what features are used. You can select them individually via the check boxes. Keep in mind that these features are bandwidth intensive, so if you are on a slow connection, you might consider removing some of these.

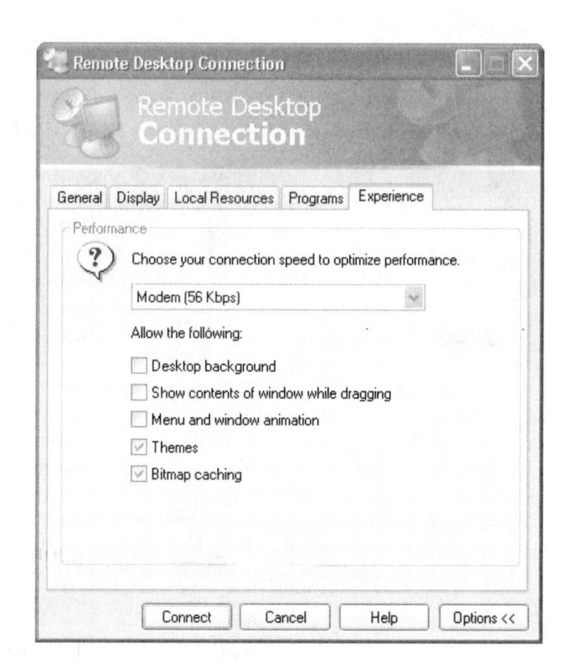

7. Once you are done, simply click Connect.

---

exam Watch

Again, keep in mind that if you want to connect to a computer that uses ICF, ICF must be configured to allow the Remote Desktop connection. See the next section to learn more about ICF.

Once you have finished with a remote desktop session, you can click the Save As tab on the General tab to save you work. The work is saved as an .rdp file, and you can simply open this file next time you want to connect.

on the Job

One issue with Remote Desktop that you should keep in mind is the screen saver. The screen saver that is configured on the remote computer will not run on the desktop connection on your computer—you'll simply see a blank screen saver.

Configuring the Remote Desktop Web Connection

Remote Desktop Web Connection is a Web application made up of an ActiveX control and sample ASP pages. It is designed to be deployed on a Web server. Once it's deployed, users on the network can create a remote desktop connection to another computer within Internet Explorer. With this feature, users of other operating systems can generate remote desktop connections without the Remote Desktop software being installed. Also, operating systems not supported by the Remote Desktop software can use the Web connection feature, providing cross-platform capabilities.

In order to set up and use the Remote Desktop Web Connection, you must be working on a network with a Web server available, such as IIS. To install the Remote Desktop Web Connection, follow these steps:

1. Open Add/Remove Programs in Control Panel.
2. Click Add/Remove Windows Components.
3. In the Windows Components window, select IIS and click Details.
4. In the Details window, select World Wide Web Service and click Details.
5. In the World Wide Web Service window, select the Remote Desktop Web Connection, shown in the following illustration:

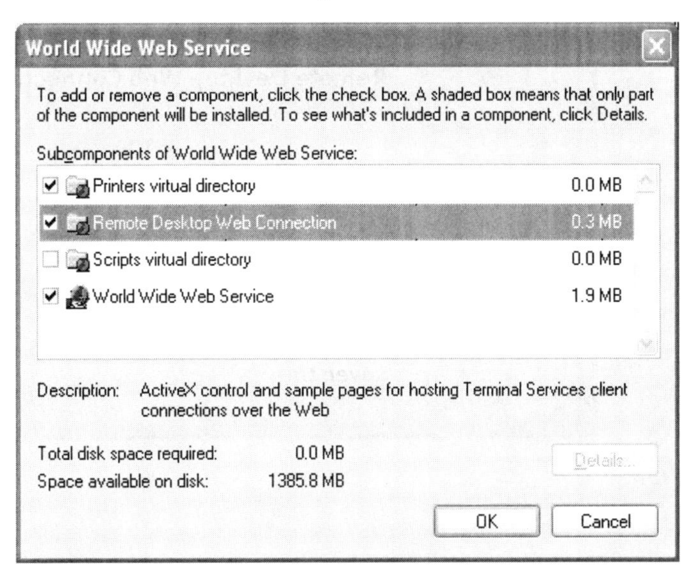

6. Click OK out of the Details boxes and click Next. The component is installed on your computer.
7. Click Finish.

Once the Remote Desktop Web connection is set up on the Web server, clients can connect to the Web server and the Remote Desktop Web Connection directory on the Web server using the http://*servername*/*directoryname* convention. When this connection is used, an HTML page appears, as shown in Figure 11-12. In the Server dialog box, enter the name of the computer you want to connect to and click Connect. The Remote Desktop session will then begin within Internet Explorer.

FIGURE 11-12

A Remote Desktop Web page

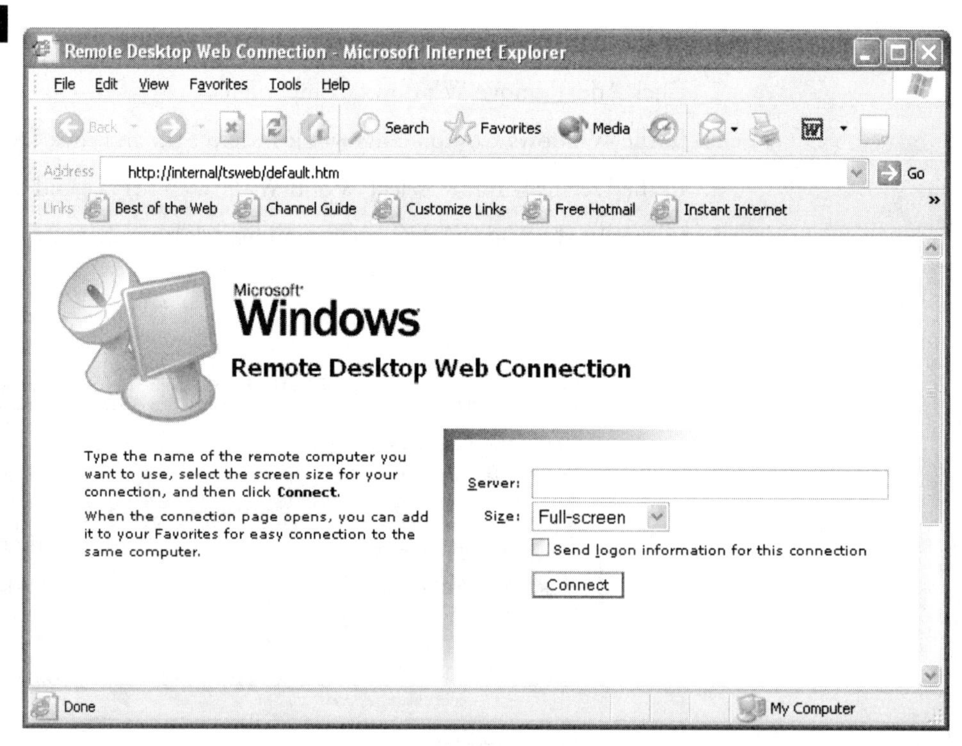

SCENARIO & SOLUTION	
Using Remote Assistance, what can I do with the other user's computer?	Remote Assistance is designed for individuals to provide assistance to another person's computer. With the user's permission, you can use your mouse and keyboard to make changes to the user's computer, thus making it possible to solve problems.
I want to use Remote Desktop to access my home computer via a DSL connection. Can I do this?	Yes. Your home computer must be configured to allow Remote Desktop communication through the Internet Connection Firewall. If you are using another personal firewall, you'll need to see if you can enable the necessary ports to allow communication. See the next section to learn more about ICF.

CERTIFICATION OBJECTIVE 11.04

Configure the Internet Connection Firewall

The concept of a personal firewall is not new; after all, companies such as Symantec and McAfee have been offering personal security products and firewalls for some time. Microsoft makes its first stab at a personal firewall in Windows XP with a product called Internet Connection Firewall (ICF). Before we take a look at ICF, let's quickly review our terminology. A *firewall* is a piece of hardware or software that is designed to control the traffic flowing in and out of a computer or a network. The purpose of a firewall is to protect the network or individual computer from hackers and other malicious attacks or content. Network firewalls, sold as both hardware and software solutions, have been around for years, and Microsoft even sells its own firewall and caching server: Internet Security and Acceleration Server. The concept of a personal firewall has become more important, however, as more and more users access the Internet via "always on" broadband connections and as small office and home networks become more prevalent. After all, personal PCs connected to the Internet need hacker protection as well.

Microsoft attempts to meet this challenge with ICF. ICF functions by filtering TCP/IP traffic that is not expressly requested from you or someone on your ICS network. Essentially, ICF works like all firewalls in that it inspects TCP/IP traffic at the packet level, then determines what IP packets are allowed on your network. ICF monitors all traffic that leaves the computer and creates a table of the Web requests made. When a return reaches the ICF, ICF inspects the table to determine if the information was requested. If it was, the traffic is allowed to pass. If it wasn't, the packets are dropped and they do not enter the computer. So, any traffic that reaches the firewall that is not explicitly requested by the user is dropped. The exception to the rule involves some services, such as Remote Desktop, which we will get to later in this section. The ICF is considered a *stateful* firewall in that it can inspect individual packets in terms of how they are used. In other words, packets are examined in transit and the ICF is aware of the packets' "state" during transit.

ICF works with Web browsers and with Internet mail. However, some mail clients will not function correctly with ICF. Mail clients that poll the mail server in order to see if mail should be downloaded have no problems, since they are making a request to the server and accepting a response. However, mail clients that can receive RPC messages from a mail server, such as is the case with Outlook with Microsoft Exchange, do not function with ICF, because the mail application is not polling server. Instead, the server's communication is direct, which is not allowed by ICF. The only workaround for these clients is to poll the server for mail instead of receiving it automatically. Of course, ICF is not designed for a larger LAN environment. It works great for the home user or even small office user. ICF is enabled on the dial-up connection or broadband connection to the Internet, but not internally on client network adapter cards. In other words, the ICF handles traffic coming from the Internet to the network, but not internal network traffic. If a user enables ICF on an internal network adapter, network communication will be impaired, since ICF will not allow traffic to enter the network adapter card that is not expressly requested by the user. In short, ICF only works on the Internet connection—not internal network connections.

Overall, ICF is easy to configure and use. There are a few important points you should keep in mind about ICF usage that will be helpful for both the real world and the exam:

- Firewall any connection to the Internet. This includes primary connections and any backup connections as well. In an ICS network, only the Internet connection(s) should be firewalled, not the internal network adapters.
- You can use ICF without using ICS. The two components are compatible but not dependent on each other.

To configure ICF, you simply turn on the feature and then configure features as desired for your needs. For most users, a simple check box enabling ICF is all they need, but you can enable a number of additional options. To turn on ICF, open the properties sheets for your Internet connection and click the Advanced tab, shown in Figure 11-13. Click the check box to enable the Internet Connection Firewall.

Once you enable ICF, you can click the Settings button at the bottom of the tab to access the Advanced firewall settings, which gives you Services, Security Logging, and ICMP tabs. The following sections take a look at your configuration options.

Services

The Services tab enables you to allow several different services that might be running on your network. For example, you could allow the Remote Desktop service so that you can manage your home computer from the office. With ICF enabled, your computer would be protected from other types of access, but the Remote Desktop service would be allowed. Essentially, the Services tab is an override feature that

FIGURE 11-13

Enabling ICF

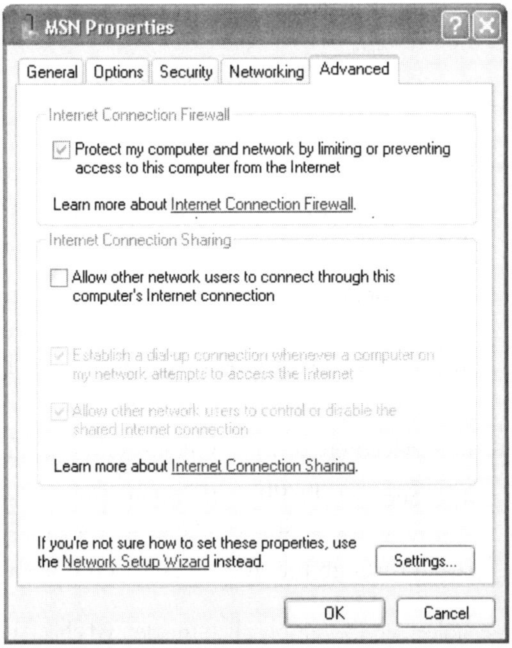

enables the firewall to allow different kinds of traffic that would normally not be allowed. By default, you can enable the following preconfigured services:

- **FTP Server** FTP, or File Transfer Protocol, enables users to upload or download information from a Web site. When enabled, FTP servers within your network can be contacted by Internet clients through ICF.
- **Incoming Connection VPN (L2TP or PPTP)** If you want to allow VPN traffic to enter the firewall, enable the service here.
- **Internet Mail Access Protocol Version 3(IMAP3)** If you are providing an IMAP3 mail server and clients need to access their mail through ICF, you can enable this option.
- **Internet Mail Access Protocol Version 4 (IMAP4)** If you are providing an IMAP4 mail server and clients need to access their mail through ICF, you can enable this option.
- **Internet Mail Server (SMTP)** If you are providing an SMTP mail server and clients need to access their mail through ICF, you can enable this option.
- **IP Security (IKE)** This service allows IP security tools to function though the firewall.
- **Post Office Protocol Version 3 (POP3)** If you are providing a POP3 mail server and clients need to access their mail through ICF, you can enable this option.
- **Remote Desktop** If you want an Internet user to be able to run a Remote Desktop session on your computer, enable this service.
- **Secure Sockets Layer (HTTPS)** If you are hosting a Web site on a computer on your network that uses secure HTTP, you need to enable this service in order for HTTPS traffic to get through ICF.
- **Telnet Server** If you are running a telnet server on your network, enable the service here so that ICF allows the traffic.
- **Web Server (HTTP)** If you are providing a Web site via a Web server on your network, enable the Web Server service so that HTTP requests can be passed through the firewall and to the Web server on your network.

To enable a service, simply click the desired check boxes, as you can see in Figure 11-14. This brings up the Service Settings dialog box where you specify the name or IP address

FIGURE 11-14

The Services tab

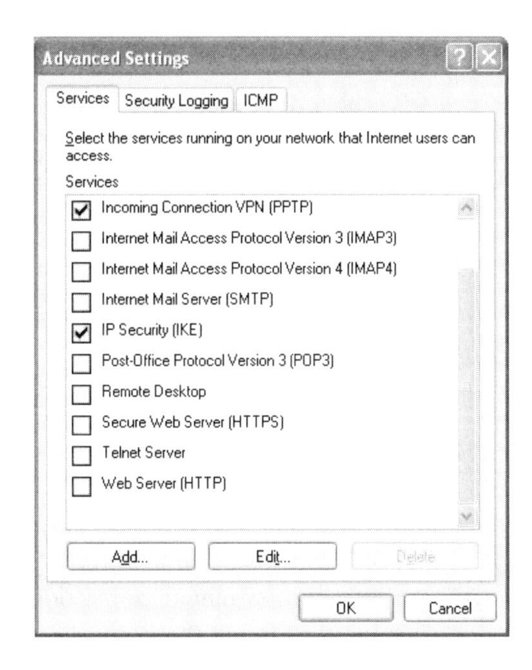

of the internal computer running the service that you wish to provide access to and the specific port numbers. Also, you can configure a custom service as well, as explored in Exercise 11-6.

EXERCISE 11-6

Configuring a Custom Service or Editing an Existing Service

To configure a custom service or edit an existing service, follow these steps:

1. On the Advanced Settings Services tab, click the Add button.
2. In the Service setting dialog box, shown in the following illustration, enter a description of the service, the name or IP address of the computer hosting the service, and the internal/external TCP ports used for the service.

3. If you want to edit an existing service, select the service in the list and click the Edit button. For example, in the previous illustration, you see the Remote Desktop service. The service name and TCP port (3389) are configured automatically, but I have entered the IP address of the computer on the network that will allow remote connections. When port 3389 traffic arrives at the firewall, the firewall checks for the service and then forwards the traffic to the IP address I have configured here.

As you'll notice, the existing services have either a TCP or UDP port configuration that cannot be changed. In the case of custom services, you'll need to make sure the port information is correct. For the purpose of the exam, it doesn't hurt to have the port numbers memorized for the standard services, and here they are:

- FTP = TCP 21
- L2TP = UDP 1701
- PPTP = TCP 1723
- IMAP3 = TCP 220
- IMAP4 = TCP 143
- SMTP = TCP 25
- IKE = UDP 500
- POP3 = TCP 110

- Remote Desktop = TCP 3389
- HTTPS = TCP 443
- Telnet = TCP 23
- HTTP = TCP 80

Security Logging

The Security Logging tab, shown in Figure 11-15, provides a way for you to log all packets that are dropped and/or all successful connections. Simply click the desired check box to begin logging. By default, the logfile is named pfirewall.log and is stored in the Windows directory. The log file can be viewed with any text editor, such as Notepad. The default log file size is 4096KB, which can be changed as desired. Once the log file begins to run out of room, the log is renamed pfirewall.log1 and a new log is created. In other words, logging does not stop, but rather new log files are created.

FROM THE CLASSROOM

TCP Ports and ICF

It is easy to get bogged down in the specifics of the TCP/IP protocol As you are working with ICF, or any firewall for that matter, it is important to remember that TCP/IP is actually a suite of protocols (in fact, there are over 100). These protocols all make up the TCP/IP suite, which gives us the vast networking functionality we see on the Internet and now on private networks.

In order to keep the protocols and services straight, different logical IP ports are used. Different services are assigned to different logical ports, and in this manner you can manage IP traffic at the port level.

With ICF, a port has to be enabled before traffic can arrive on that port without being solicited. As such, care should be taken not to enable ports that are not really needed. In other words, don't enable Remote Desktop if it is actually not in use. The more ports that are open to outside users, the easier it becomes for a hacker to break through one of the ports and invade the local network or computer.

FIGURE 11-15

The Security Logging tab

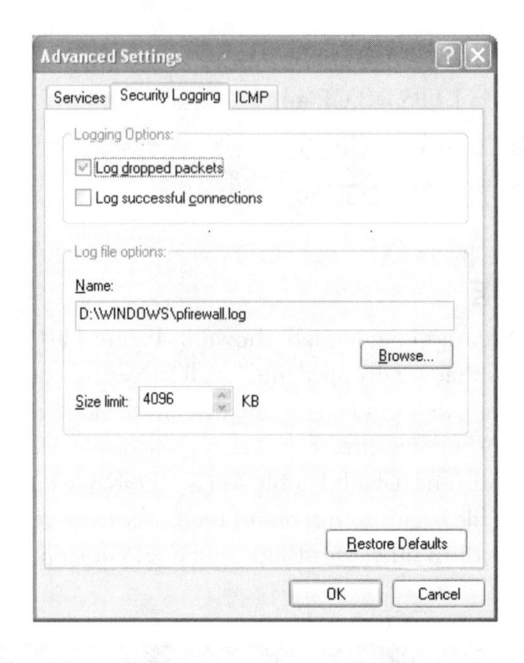

exam Watch

It is important to remember that excessive logging can slow your computer down, especially if the computer is the ICS computer. While logging dropped packets is a good idea because you can see what the computer is refusing, logging everything may cause you some performance problems.

The log file is recorded in the W3C Extended Log File format, an example of which appears in Figure 11-16. Data is stored in a field format, with the following fields in use:

- **Date** Provides the year, month, and day that the record occurred and is displayed as YYYY-MM-DD. For example an entry on November 15, 2001 would read 2001-11-15.
- **Time** Provides the hour, minute, and seconds when the record occurred and is displayed as HH:MM:SS in a 24 hour format. For example, an entry recorded at 2:15, 34 seconds in the afternoon would read 14:15:34.
- **Action** Displays the action that occurred, which can be one of the following:
  - **Open** Connection is opened.
  - **Close** Connection is closed.
  - **Drop** Packets are dropped at the firewall.

FIGURE 11-16

A Pfirewall.log

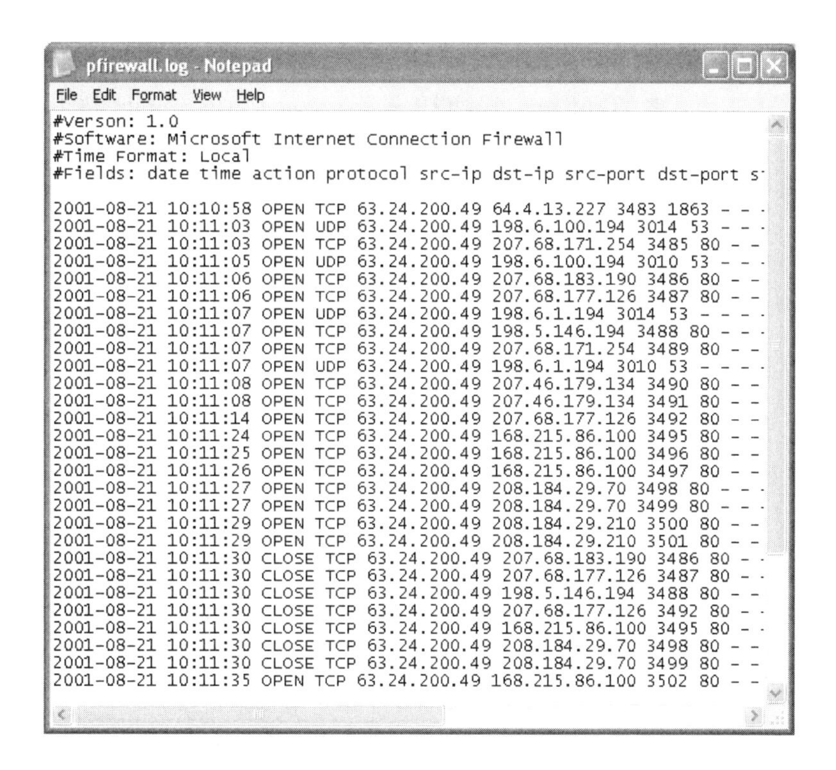


```
#Verson: 1.0
#Software: Microsoft Internet Connection Firewall
#Time Format: Local
#Fields: date time action protocol src-ip dst-ip src-port dst-port s

2001-08-21 10:10:58 OPEN TCP 63.24.200.49 64.4.13.227 3483 1863 - - -
2001-08-21 10:11:03 OPEN UDP 63.24.200.49 198.6.100.194 3014 53 - - -
2001-08-21 10:11:03 OPEN TCP 63.24.200.49 207.68.171.254 3485 80 - -
2001-08-21 10:11:05 OPEN UDP 63.24.200.49 198.6.100.194 3010 53 - - -
2001-08-21 10:11:06 OPEN TCP 63.24.200.49 207.68.183.190 3486 80 - -
2001-08-21 10:11:06 OPEN TCP 63.24.200.49 207.68.177.126 3487 80 - -
2001-08-21 10:11:07 OPEN UDP 63.24.200.49 198.6.1.194 3014 53 - - - -
2001-08-21 10:11:07 OPEN TCP 63.24.200.49 198.5.146.194 3488 80 - - -
2001-08-21 10:11:07 OPEN TCP 63.24.200.49 207.68.171.254 3489 80 - -
2001-08-21 10:11:07 OPEN UDP 63.24.200.49 198.6.1.194 3010 53 - - - -
2001-08-21 10:11:08 OPEN TCP 63.24.200.49 207.46.179.134 3490 80 - -
2001-08-21 10:11:08 OPEN TCP 63.24.200.49 207.46.179.134 3491 80 - -
2001-08-21 10:11:14 OPEN TCP 63.24.200.49 207.68.177.126 3492 80 - -
2001-08-21 10:11:24 OPEN TCP 63.24.200.49 168.215.86.100 3495 80 - -
2001-08-21 10:11:25 OPEN TCP 63.24.200.49 168.215.86.100 3496 80 - -
2001-08-21 10:11:26 OPEN TCP 63.24.200.49 168.215.86.100 3497 80 - -
2001-08-21 10:11:27 OPEN TCP 63.24.200.49 208.184.29.70 3498 80 - - -
2001-08-21 10:11:27 OPEN TCP 63.24.200.49 208.184.29.70 3499 80 - - -
2001-08-21 10:11:29 OPEN TCP 63.24.200.49 208.184.29.210 3500 80 - -
2001-08-21 10:11:29 OPEN TCP 63.24.200.49 208.184.29.210 3501 80 - -
2001-08-21 10:11:30 CLOSE TCP 63.24.200.49 207.68.183.190 3486 80 - -
2001-08-21 10:11:30 CLOSE TCP 63.24.200.49 207.68.177.126 3487 80 - -
2001-08-21 10:11:30 CLOSE TCP 63.24.200.49 198.5.146.194 3488 80 - -
2001-08-21 10:11:30 CLOSE TCP 63.24.200.49 207.68.177.126 3492 80 - -
2001-08-21 10:11:30 CLOSE TCP 63.24.200.49 168.215.86.100 3495 80 - -
2001-08-21 10:11:30 CLOSE TCP 63.24.200.49 208.184.29.70 3498 80 - -
2001-08-21 10:11:30 CLOSE TCP 63.24.200.49 208.184.29.70 3499 80 - -
2001-08-21 10:11:35 OPEN TCP 63.24.200.49 168.215.86.100 3502 80 - -
```

- **Info-Events Lost** Reports that several events occurred that were not recorded in the log.
- **Protocol** Reports what protocol was used for the connection. The entry can show TCP, UDP, or ICMP.
- **Src-ip** Reports the source IP address of the connection. The source IP address is the IP address of the computer attempting the connection (your computer or a computer on your network).
- **Dst-ip** Reports the destination IP address of the connection. The destination IP address is the IP address of the computer that the local computer (your computer or a computer on the network) is making.
- **Src-port** Reports the source TCP or UDP port of the sending computer. If ICMP is used, there is no port information and a dash (–) will be displayed in this field.
- **Dst-port** Reports the source TCP or UDP port of the destination computer. If ICMP is used, there is no port information and a dash (–) will be displayed in this field.

- **Size** Reports the size of the packet in bytes.
- **Tcpflags** Each IP packet header may contain TCP control flags. These control flags give the computer some instruction about how to handle the packet. See RFC 793 to learn more about Tcpflags. Typical control flags are
  - **Ack** Acknowledgement.
  - **Fin** Data is finished.
  - **Psh** Push Function.
  - **Rst** Reset the connection.
  - **Syn** Synchronize sequence numbers.
  - **Urg** Urgent Pointer field significant.
  - **Tcpsyn** Provides the TCP sequence number.
  - **Tcpack** Shows the TCP acknowledgement number in the packet.
  - **Tcpwin** Presents the TCP window size (bytes) in the packet.
  - **Icmptype** Shows a number that represents the Type field in an ICMP message.
  - **Icmpcode** Specifies a number that represents the Code field of an ICMP message.
  - **Info** Provides an information entry for the type of action that occurred.

ICMP

Internet Control Message Protocol (ICMP) is a TCP/IP management protocol that computers use to exchange messages with each other. ICMP can be used to exchange network condition information and failure information concerning transmission. Overall, ICMP can be important and helpful; it is also a common hacker method, so by default ICF does not allow ICMP messages. You can use the ICMP tab to enable different kinds of ICMP messages, such as echo requests, timestamp request, and so on. Of course, the need for ICMP and the potential security hole should be carefully evaluated. If you do want to use ICMP messages with ICF, simply enable the kinds of messages you want to receive on the ICMP tab, shown in Figure 11-17.

FIGURE 11-17

The ICMP tab

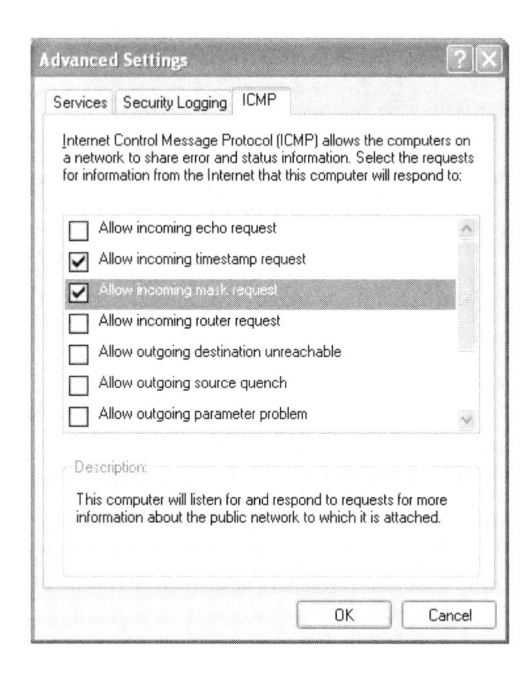

SCENARIO & SOLUTION

ICF does not seem to work on my broadband connection.	As a general rule, ICF will function on any connection to the Internet, but you should check any broadband hardware for known incompatibility issues with ICF. Your ISP should be able to provide you with this information.
What is the most secure way to use a service, such as Remote Desktop, that is only accessed from time to time?	For security purposes, you do not want any more TCP ports open than necessary, and configuring a service opens ports. The best way to use the service feature is to open ports only on days when the Remote Desktop will be used. Otherwise, clear the service check box so that the port remains closed when the service is not needed.

CERTIFICATION OBJECTIVE 11.05

Configure, Manage, and Implement Internet Information Services

Internet Information Services (IIS) is included with Windows XP Professional so that you can use Windows XP Professional as a network intranet server or enable Web applications or services on the Windows XP Professional computer. IIS on Windows XP Professional is mostly used to run Web-based applications over a network and for development and testing purposes. IIS in Windows XP does not contain all of the features and user support of IIS running Windows 2000 Server. As such, you are not likely to see exam questions directly relating to IIS. You may see a question that refers to IIS but the substance of which relates to some other topic. I'll give you the basics of IIS to get you started, but you should spend some time working with the software on Windows XP to get a feel for what is available. Of course, the implementation of a Web site using IIS deserves an entire book on its own and is outside of the scope of this one.

IIS may have been installed by default when you install Windows XP Professional. If it hasn't, you can install it, along with additional components, by access Add/Remove Windows Components from Add/Remove Programs in Control Panel. Once it's installed, you can test the functionality of IIS and explore the IIS documentation by typing **http://*computername*** in a Web browser. You'll see a page, such as the one shown in Figure 11-18, that tells you that IIS is now running, but no default Web page has been configured. At this point, you can create Web pages and save them in your default Web site, found in \inetpub\wwwroot. IIS is fully functional with FrontPage so that Web sites can be easily created.

You can manage your Web site by accessing the Internet Information Services console, an MMC snap-in that is found in Administrative Tools in Control Panel, as shown in Figure 11-19. From the console, you can manage the Web site, access the Web site's properties, configure security, and create and share virtual directories. You can also enable logging, manage ISAPI filters, and perform a number of other Web site management tasks.

FIGURE 11-18

An initial status report on IIS

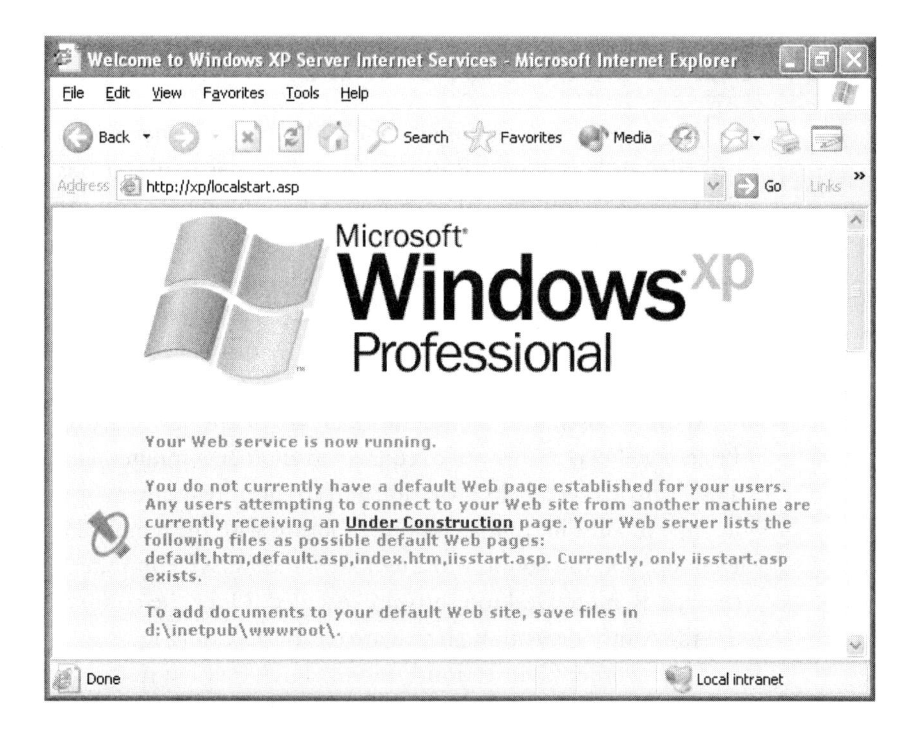

FIGURE 11-19

The IIS console

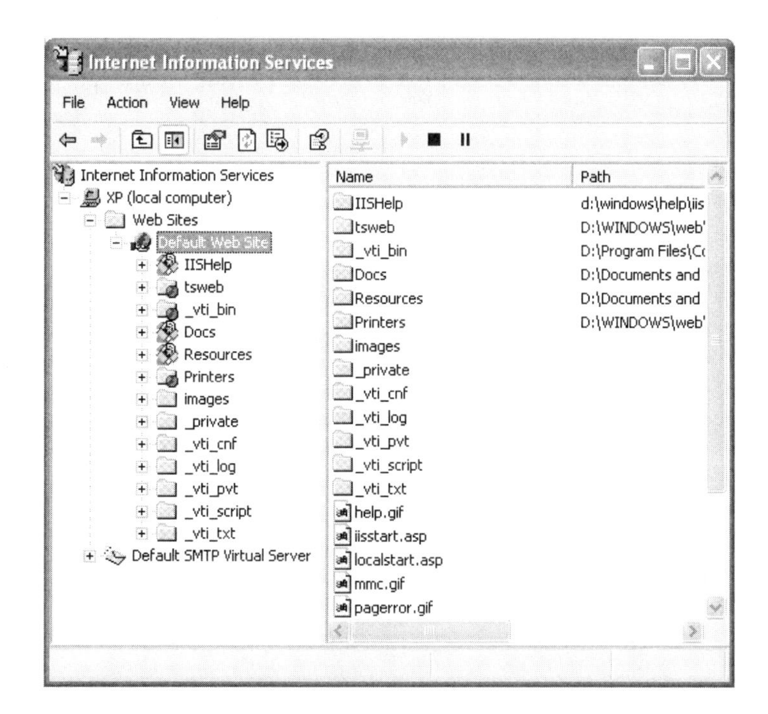

CERTIFICATION SUMMARY

In this chapter, you explored some additional Internet and networking features provided in Windows XP Professional. Internet Explorer 6 is provided with the Windows XP Professional operating system. Using IE, you can connect to and use Internet resources, as well as resources on your local network. Because of Windows XP Professional's Internet integration, HTML content can be read and used seamlessly between your computer and the Internet. IE also provides zone level security, as well as custom security settings. IE also provides privacy control so that you can control cookies used on the Internet.

Remote Assistance and Remote Desktop are new features of Windows XP Professional that enable you to connect to another computer. Using Remote Assistance, a user can answer a help invitation and connect to another computer over the Internet in order to assist in troubleshooting problems with the remote computer. Using Remote Desktop, you can connect to a remote Windows XP computer or to a downlevel client that has Remote Desktop software installed. Once the connection is made, you can use the computer as though you are locally accessing it.

The Internet Connection Firewall (ICF) is also a new feature of Windows XP. Designed for home and small office users, ICF can protect the Internet connection from unsolicited TCP/IP traffic. ICF can work with ICS as well.

Finally, Internet Information Services is included with Windows XP Professional so that Windows XP Professional can provide intranet pages and host Web applications.

TWO-MINUTE DRILL

Connect to Resources Using Internet Explorer

- ❑ Windows XP Professional is integrated with Internet Explorer 6, which can meet the user's Internet, intranet, and local network connectivity needs.
- ❑ IE works seamlessly with the Internet and the local network, allowing access to local folders via the UNC path. Users can also access Internet and local resources from any folder by simply typing the address in the To box.
- ❑ Internet connections can be configured via the Network Connections folder. IE can function with any type of Internet connection, including LAN/proxy server connections.

Configure, Manage, and Troubleshoot Internet Explorer Security Settings

- ❑ Internet Explorer provides zoned security for the Internet, the intranet, trusted sites, and restricted sites.
- ❑ The available settings for the zones are Low, Medium Low, Medium, High, and Custom.
- ❑ You can override zone security settings with the Trusted Sites and Restricted Sites options.
- ❑ IE 6 contains a privacy setting that enables you to set a security level for cookie usage.
- ❑ Using privacy settings, you can manage IE's use of persistent cookies, temporary cookies, first-party cookies, third-party cookies, and unsatisfactory cookies.
- ❑ The available cookie settings are Block All Cookies, High, Medium High, Medium, Low, and Accept All Cookies.

Configure and Manage Remote Assistance and Remote Desktop

- ❑ Remote Assistance provides a way for a Windows XP computer to connect to another XP computer over the Internet, allowing a user to assist in troubleshooting a remote user's computer. With the user's permission, you can manage and configure the system remotely.

- Remote Assistance uses invitations. A user who would like assistance sends an invitation to the helper via Windows Messenger or Outlook Express.
- The assisting user connects to the computer via Windows Messenger or via an e-mail link in Outlook Express. The user must know the password to complete the connection. The password is generated by the user who needs help and must be transmitted to the user manually (the password is not provided via Windows Messenger or the e-mail invitation).
- Remote Desktop enables you to connect to another computer remotely over the Internet, an intranet, or a local LAN. In order to connect, you must have an administrator account on the local computer or you must be a member of the Remote Desktop group.
- If you are connecting to a computer that uses ICF, ICF must be configured to allow Remote Desktop communication.
- Remote Desktop is natively available in Windows XP, and you can install the Remote Desktop software from the Windows XP installation CD on Windows 9*x*, Me, NT, and 2000 computers.
- Remote Desktop also provides a Web connection via IIS so that remote connectivity can be handled via an intranet. This feature resolves compatibility issues and is an excellent choice for cross-platform environments.

Configure the Internet Connection Firewall

- ICF is designed for home users or small workgroups using ICS. ICF and ICS are independent, but they can work together.
- ICF only allows traffic to enter your computer that has been expressly requested. A table is kept that records HTTP requests made. Any traffic arriving that does not match an HTTP request is rejected.
- ICF can support a number of services, such as FTP, SMTP, and Remote Desktop. These services basically override the default ICF setting that rejects all traffic not requested by the user.
- You can configure log files to function with ICF that can record dropped packets and/or all successful connections.
- You can allow ICMP traffic if desired.

Configure, Manage, and Implement Internet Information Services

- IIS is available on Windows XP Professional and can be installed via Add/Remove Windows Components.
- IIS can be used to serve intranet pages or provide a workspace for HTML applications.
- IIS supports a number of security features and is easily integrated with FrontPage.

SELF TEST

The following questions will help you measure your understanding of the material presented in this chapter. Read all of the choices carefully, as there may be more than one correct answer. Choose all correct answers for each question.

Connect to Resources Using Internet Explorer

1. Which of the following items can you use Internet Explorer to connect to?

   A. Web pages

   B. Printers

   C. Intranet pages

   D. Shared folders

2. You need to configure a certain user's IE browser so that the browser connects to the Internet through a proxy server. Where can you configure this?

   A. On the dial-up connection's properties.

   B. On Internet Options, Security tab. Click the Proxy button.

   C. On Internet Options, Connections tab. Click the LAN Settings button.

   D. On Internet Options, Programs tab. Click the LAN button.

Configure, Manage, and Troubleshoot Internet Explorer Security Settings

3. For a particular user, you want to make certain that IE's security settings do not allow any unsigned ActiveX controls and you want prompts before downloading potentially unsafe data. However, you want the most browsing functionality as well. What setting is best?

   A. High

   B. Medium

   C. Medium Low

   D. Low

4. For a particular user, you want to make certain that IE's security settings do not allow unsigned ActiveX controls and that prompts before downloading potentially unsafe content are provided.

However, for **www.yoursite.com**, you want to make certain that no restrictions are placed, including download prompts. How can you configure this?

A. On the Security tab, choose the High setting.

B. On the Security tab, choose the Medium setting. Add **www.yoursite.com** to the list of trusted sites.

C. On the Security tab, choose the Medium setting. Add **www.yoursite.com** to the list of restricted sites.

D. On the Security tab, choose the Medium Low setting. Add **www.yoursite.com** to the list of trusted sites.

5. You want to make certain that all third-party cookies are blocked for a particular user. However, you only want to restrict first-party cookies. What do you need to do in Internet Options to configure this?

A. On the Privacy tab, choose the Medium High setting.

B. On the Privacy tab, choose the Medium setting.

C. On the Security tab, choose the Medium setting.

D. On the Security tab, choose the Medium Low setting.

6. You want to make certain that all first-party cookies are accepted with no restrictions, but all third party cookies are blocked. What is the easiest way to configure this in Internet Options?

A. Choose the High setting on the Privacy tab.

B. Choose the Low setting on the Privacy tab.

C. Choose the Medium setting on the Privacy tab.

D. Choose the Advanced button and enable the desired radio buttons on the Advanced Privacy Settings window.

7. You need to configure IE security settings so that there are no restrictions in the local intranet, but the Internet has high security settings. Also, you want to completely restrict **www.yourcompany.com**. Finally, you want to make certain that **www.yourcompany.com** is completely blocked from using cookies. What do you need to do to configure these settings? (Choose three answers. Each answer represents part of the solution.)

A. Choose the High setting on the Privacy tab.

B. On the Privacy tab, click Edit and add **www.yourcompany.com** to the list. Choose the Block option.

C. On the Security tab, select local intranet and choose High. Then select Internet and choose Medium.

D. On the Security tab, select the local intranet and choose Low. Then select Internet and choose High.

E. Choose Restricted Sites on the Security tab and add **www.yourcompany.com** to the list.

F. Choose Restricted Sites on the Privacy tab and add **www.yourcompany.com** to the list.

Configure and Manage Remote Assistance and Remote Desktop

8. You need to instruct a user on a remote network to enable Remote Assistance on a Windows XP Professional computer. Where can you enable Remote Assistance?

A. Internet Options, Advanced tab

B. System Properties, Remote tab

C. Connection Properties, Remote tab

D. Network Properties, Advanced tab

9. You want to send a remote assistance invitation using Outlook. However, you want to the invitation to expire in three days. What do you need to do?

A. Nothing. Invitations automatically expire after three days.

B. On the Remote tab of System Properties, click the Advanced button under Remote Assistance and change the expiration time to 3 days.

C. On the Remote tab of Internet Options, click the Advanced button under Remote Assistance and change the expiration time to 3 days.

D. Edit the e-mail invitation from 30 days to 3 days.

10. You want to use Remote Desktop to connect to a Windows Me computer using your Windows XP Professional computer. Which statement is true concerning this connection?

A. Windows Me natively supports Remote Desktop.

B. You must download a security patch from **Microsoft.com**.

C. You must install IIS on the Windows Me computer.

D. You must install the Remote Desktop client software on the Windows Me computer.

11. Your LAN uses a firewall. You need to use Remote Desktop to connect to a computer on the Internet via the firewall. By default, the network firewall does not allow this kind of traffic.

What TCP port will the firewall administrator need to open so that Remote Desktop traffic can pass?

A. 80

B. 21

C. 3398

D. 54

12. You are using Remote Desktop to connect to a computer on the Internet using a 56K modem. You notice that performance is very slow. You access the connection's properties. What can you change that will help increase performance?

A. Run the **remote – fb** command.

B. Change the display to true color.

C. Change the options on the Environment tab to Modem.

D. You cannot increase performance over this kind of connection.

13. You want to use Remote Desktop to connect your office computer to your home computer. Both computers run Windows XP Professional. The home computer uses a modem that is configured to receive calls. ICF and ICS are both used on your home network. You call the computer, but the Remote Desktop does not work. What do you need to do?

A. ICS does not work with Remote Desktop. Remove ICS.

B. ICF does not work with Remote Desktop. Remove ICF.

C. Configure the Services tab of ICS to allow Remote Desktop

D. Configure the Services tab of ICF to allow Remote Desktop

Configure Internet Connection Firewall

14. A user on your LAN enables ICF on his network adapter card used on the internal network. What is likely to happen?

A. No changes will take place.

B. The user will not be able to access network resources.

C. Users on the network will not be able to access the user's computer.

D. The user will see extensive connection failures on outgoing connections.

15. You want to use ICF with an incoming PPTP connection. What can you do?

    A. ICF does not allow VPN connections.
    B. ICF allows PPTP connections by default. Do nothing.
    C. Enable the PPTP service connection option on the Services tab of the Advanced ICF settings.
    D. Select all options on the ICMP tab of Advanced ICF settings.

16. You notice that ICF is generating an excessive number of log files on your Windows XP ICS host computer. There are 10 other computers that use the ICS connection. You examine the Security Logging tab, shown in the following illustration. What action can you take so that the security log will not grow so large, yet still provide you with useful data?

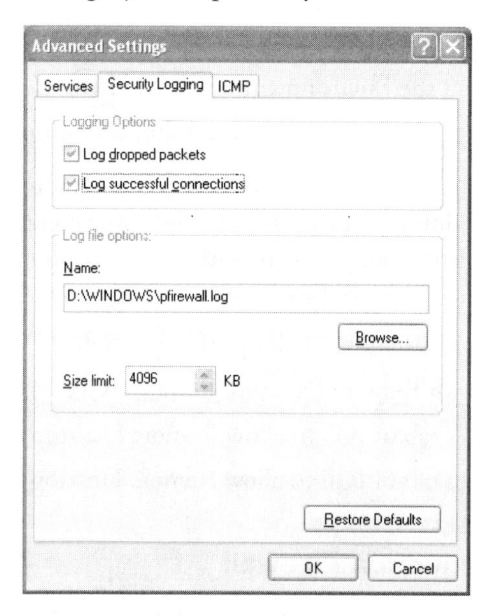

    A. Clear the "Log dropped packets" setting.
    B. Clear the "Log successful connections" settings.
    C. Change the default firewall log name to pfirewall.log1.
    D. Change the log file size to 10096KB.

Configure, Manage, and Implement Internet Information Services

17. You have just installed IIS on a local Windows XP computer. What can you do to see if IIS is functioning and ready for use?

A. Run the **iistest –p** command.

B. Type **http://** ***localhostname*** in a browser.

C. Run the **iisdebug** command.

D. Upload a Web page.

LAB QUESTION

You want to set up ICF on an ICS network with the following configuration:

- Allow an incoming PPTP connection on a computer named "VPN."
- Allow Remote Desktop on a computer named "XP."
- Log dropped packets in a log file named ICSnet.log.
- Allow echo requests.

How can you configure these options?

SELF TEST ANSWERS

Connect to Resources Using Internet Explorer

1. ☑ A, B, C, and D are correct. You can use Internet Explorer to connect to resources on the Internet, an intranet, and on the local network.

   ☒ All answers are correct.

2. ☑ C is correct. You can configure IE to connect to the Internet via a proxy server. Access the Connections tab in Internet Options, and then click the LAN Settings button. Here you can enter the IP address of the proxy server or have IE discover the settings.

   ☒ A, B, and D are incorrect. You cannot configure LAN Settings from any of these locations.

Configure, Manage, and Troubleshoot Internet Explorer Security Settings

3. ☑ B is correct. The Medium setting is appropriate for most users and provides the best browsing flexibility while not allowing ActiveX controls and providing download prompts.

   ☒ A, C, and D are incorrect. These settings do not meet the question's requirements.

4. ☑ B is correct. Since you want no unsigned ActiveX controls and prompts for potentially unsafe content, you need the Medium setting. Then, add **www.yoursite.com** to the list of trusted sites in order to override the restrictions.

   ☒ A, C, and D are incorrect. There is no reason to use the High setting, so A is incorrect. C is incorrect because the restricted sites would further restrict **www.yoursite.com**. D is incorrect because the Medium Low setting does not provide prompts for potentially unsafe downloads.

5. ☑ B is correct. Use the Medium setting on the Privacy tab. This setting blocks third-party cookies, but only restricts first-party cookies.

   ☒ A, C, and D are incorrect. A is incorrect because the Medium High setting blocks first-party cookies. C and D are incorrect because you cannot configure cookies security levels on the Security tab.

6. ☑ D is correct. If you want to allow all first-party cookies with no restrictions, but block all third-party cookies, open the Advanced Privacy Settings and choose to override automatic cookie handling. Then, choose the Accept radio button under First-party cookies and the Block radio button under Third-party cookies.

   ☒ A, B, and C are incorrect. The automatic settings will not provide the settings required.

7. ☑ B, D, and E are correct. To configure these requirements, choose the Low setting for intranet on the Security tab and High setting for the Internet on the Security tab. Also on the Security tab, add **www.yourcompany.com** to the list of restricted sites. On the Privacy tab, click the Edit button and add **www.yourcompany.com** to the list of blocked sites so that no cookies may be used with that site.

   ☒ A, C and F are incorrect. The High setting on Privacy will restrict all cookies, not just those for the desired site, so A is incorrect. C is incorrect because High on the intranet setting will greatly restrict the zone, while the Medium setting for Internet is too low. F is also incorrect because you cannot configure a restricted site on the Privacy tab, only set cookie restrictions.

Configure and Manage Remote Assistance and Remote Desktop

8. ☑ B is correct. You can enable Remote Assistance by clicking the check box on the Remote tab of System Properties.

   ☒ A, C and D are incorrect. You cannot enable Remote Assistance in these locations.

9. ☑ B is correct. On the Remote tab of System Properties, click the Advanced button under Remote Assistance. By default, invitations are extended for 30 days, but you can change this value using the drop-down menus.

   ☒ A, C, and D are incorrect. You can change the invitation time only on the Remote Assistance Settings dialog box, which is available on the Remote tab of System Properties by clicking the Advanced button under Remote Assistance.

10. ☑ D is correct. Windows Me can be used with Remote Assistance, along with Windows 9*x*, NT, and 2000 by installing the Remote Desktop client software, available on the Windows XP Professional installation CD-ROM.

    ☒ A, B, and C are incorrect. These answers are incorrect because the Remote Desktop software must be installed from the Windows XP Professional CD-ROM.

11. ☑ C is correct. Remote Desktop uses TCP port 3398.

    ☒ A, B, and D are incorrect. These are not the correct port numbers.

12. ☑ C is correct. The Environment tab gives you a number of options that help you improve performance. In this case, use the drop-down menu and select 56K so that Windows XP's intensive graphics will not be used.

    ☒ A, B, and D are incorrect. None of these actions will help increase performance.

13. ☑ D is correct. ICF does not allow Remote Desktop communication by default. However, you can enable it on the Services tab of ICF Settings

☒ A, B, and C are incorrect. ICF must have Remote Desktop enabled.

Configure the Internet Connection Firewall

14. ☑ C is correct. ICS keeps a communication table, and no communication that is not explicitly requested is allowed. Therefore, users on the network will not be able to access resources on the user's computer.

☒ A, B, and D are incorrect. The user is not likely to experience connectivity problems, so B and D are incorrect. A is incorrect because problems will occur.

15. ☑ C is correct. PPTP, which allows a VPN connection, can be used by enabling the PPTP service on the Services tab of ICF settings.

☒ A, B, and D are incorrect. None of these items correctly explains how PPTP can be used.

16. ☑ B is correct. If you log successful connections, you'll use up a lot of log space, especially when ICS is in use and a number of computers are accessing the Internet. You can clear this option and still log dropped packets.

☒ A, C, and D are incorrect. None of these actions will reduce log file size.

Configure, Manage, and Implement Internet Information Services

17. ☑ B is correct. Once IIS installed, just type **http://*localhostname*** in a browser to see if IIS is functioning.

☒ A, C, and D are incorrect. None these commands or actions is valid.

LAB ANSWER

To configure these options, follow these steps:

1. Enable ICF on the Advanced tab of the Internet connection's properties. Then, click the Settings button.
2. On the Services tab, click the Incoming Connection VPN (PPTP) check box and then click the Edit button.
3. In the Service Settings window, shown in the following illustration, enter **VPN** for the computer's name and click OK.

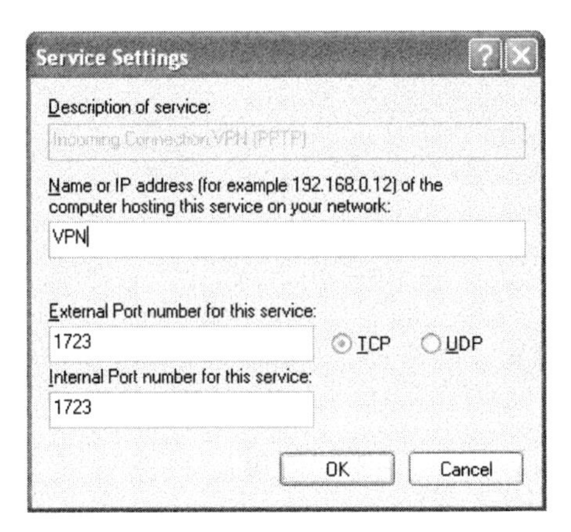

4. On the Services tab, click the Remote Desktop check box and click the Edit button.
5. In the Service Setting window, enter **XP** for the computer's name and click OK.
6. Click the Security Logging tab. Enable the "Log dropped packets" check box and change the security log name to ICSnet.log, as shown in the following illustration.

7. Click the ICMP tab. Click the "Allow incoming echo requests" check box. Click OK to save the configuration.

12

Configuring, Managing, and Troubleshooting Security

CERTIFICATION OBJECTIVES

12.01	Configure, Manage, and Troubleshoot Encrypting File System (EFS)
12.02	Configure, Manage, and Troubleshoot Local User and Group Accounts
12.03	Configure, Manage, and Troubleshoot Local Security Policy
12.04	Configure, Manage, and Troubleshoot a Security Configuration
✓	Two-Minute Drill
Q&A	Self Test

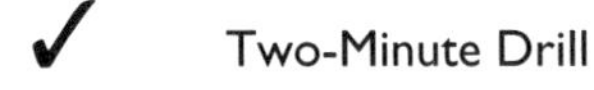

Windows XP Professional provides the security features necessary in today's complex networking environments. Even in workgroup environments, Windows XP Professional provides tools that enable users to keep data safe and allow you to control how users and groups function on the system. As an IT professional, you'll need to know how to configure the various security features and options and how to solve security issues and problems. It is also important to note here that the exam explores security configuration and management at the local computer level. In a domain environment, you will most likely configure security settings at the server level through Group Policy and related tools. However, for obtaining your MCSE credentials, this exam expects you to know how to manage Windows XP Professional at the local level, including how to employ user and group security settings, security templates through local Group Policy, and the Encrypting File System (EFS). In this chapter, you'll explore all of these issues.

CERTIFICATION OBJECTIVE 12.01

Configure, Manage, and Troubleshoot Encrypting File System (EFS)

Encrypting File System (EFS) is a feature of the NTFS file system. Encryption enables Windows XP Professional to store data so that it cannot be opened by users who do not possess an encryption key. Essentially, the data is locked away in a mathematical algorithm that uses a public key and a private key. In order to decrypt the data, the user has to have the private key. This kind of encryption scheme, known as asymmetrical encryption, uses one key to encrypt a file and to decrypt the file. When EFS encrypts a file, a random key is generated that can only be decrypted by the private key attached to the user's account. Of course, the user does not have to be aware of any keys or the underlying encryption technology. The user simply selects to encrypt data, but can open the data and use it seamlessly without any kind of manual decryption. If another user attempts to access the encrypted data, that user's key will not decrypt the data and it will not be readable.

There are a couple of important issues to consider when working with EFS. First off, EFS is a feature of NTFS and only works on NTFS drives. However, encryption and compression are not compatible—you can either encrypt a drive or compress it, but you cannot do both. Also, encryption tends to slow access down—using encrypted files is slower than using regular files because Windows XP Professional must encrypt and decrypt files as they are needed, when opened/closed. Finally, a new feature in Windows XP enables you to encrypt a file so that several different users can still access the encrypted file.

In order to use encryption, simply right-click the file or folder that you want to encrypt, click Properties, and then click the Advanced button on the General tab. The Advanced Attributes window, shown in Figure 12-1, gives you a simple encryption check box that you can use in order to turn on EFS.

exam Watch

You can encrypt a folder in the same way, the folder itself is not actually encrypted—only the files within the folder. Also, you can manage encrypted files and folders using cipher.exe.

As you will see, encrypting data is rather easy. At any point, you can permanently decrypt a file or folder by returning to the Advanced Attributes window and clearing the check box. However, what if you need to access your encrypted data over the network via several different workstations? You can do so in a couple of different ways. First, if you set up a roaming user profile; then the encryption key will be available no matter where you log on. Alternatively, you can copy your key and carry it with you on a floppy disk. Then, you can use the key to open your encrypted data. This export process is rather easy, and the following exercise walks you through the steps.

FIGURE 12-1 The Advanced Attributes window

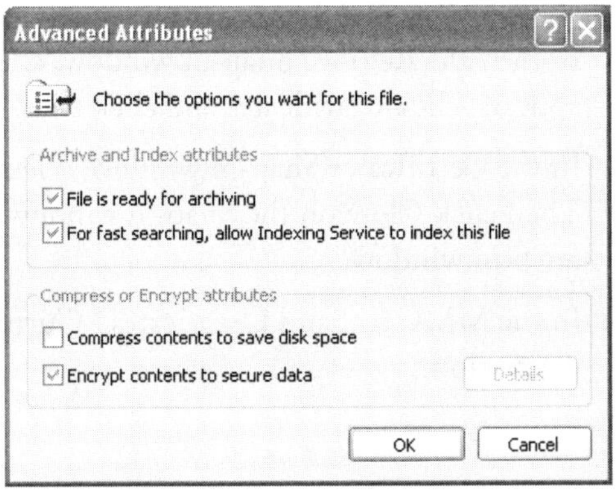

FROM THE CLASSROOM

Encryption

As network security concerns have become more and more important, tools such as Windows XP encryption have become more and more important. Although no security measure is foolproof, encryption is a great way to protect private data from the eyes of others. In network environments, it is not uncommon for a number of people to use the same computer, and encryption enables a user to keep data private on a computer that might be less than private.

In its wider application, encryption protects data from internal network hackers and threats such as corporate espionage. Although Windows XP's encryption scheme is certainly not the most complex in the security world, it does provide a measure of strong security that is impenetrable by most computer users.

EXERCISE 12-1

Exporting a Private Key

To export a private key, just follow these steps:

1. Click Start | Run. Type **MMC** and click OK.
2. In the MMC, click File | Add/Remove Snap-in.
3. In the Add/Remove Snap-in window, click Add. In the snap-in list that appears, click Certificates and click Add.
4. In the Certificates Snap-in window, select My User Account and click Finish. Then click Close on the Snap-in window and OK on the Add/Remove Snap-in window.
5. In the MMC, expand Certificates - Current User, as shown in the following illustration:

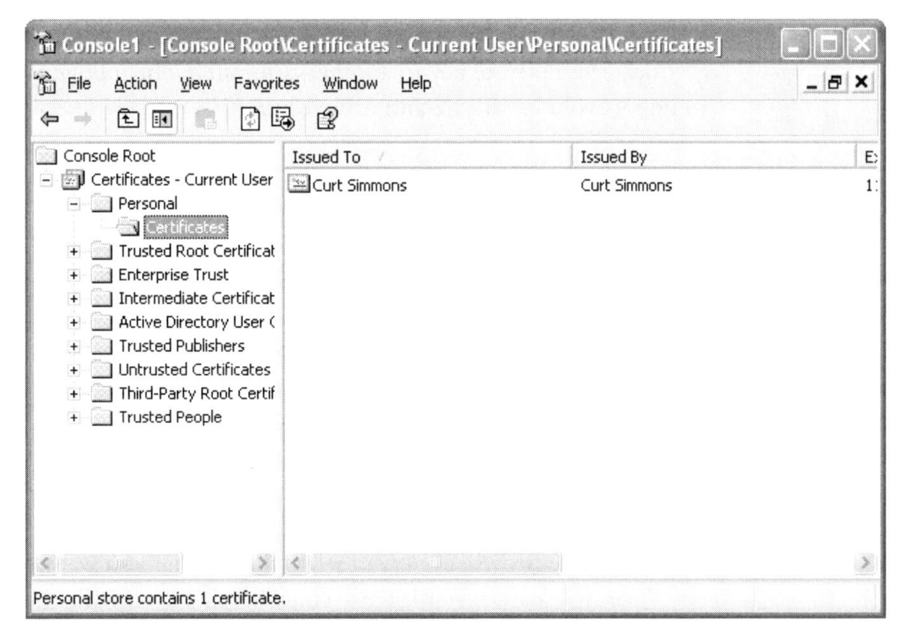

6. Expand the Personal folder and then select the Certificates folder.
7. Click Action | All Tasks | Export, which will start the Export Certificate Wizard.
8.

   e key with your digital certificate. If you are moving to another Windows XP, 2000, or NT 4.0 (with SP4) system, choose the Enable Strong Encryption option.
9. Choose a password, which you will need to import the certificate in the new location.
10. The wizard saves your certificate and private key to a file (*.pfx, which is a Personal Information Exchange file). You can now copy this file to a floppy disk and move it to a new computer.

Once you have copied your certificate and private key, you can import the certificate and private key to another computer. The following steps show you how to import your certificate and private key.

EXERCISE 12-2

Importing Your Private Key

To import your private key, just follow these steps:

1. Use the steps in Exercise 9-1 to open the Certificates MMC.
2. Open Certificates—Current User. Expand the Personal folder and select the Certificates folder.
3. Click Action | All Tasks | Import. This will begin the Import Wizard.
4. Use the Browse option to select the file that you want to import and complete the wizard steps. You will need to provide the password you assigned to the file when you were exporting.

Windows XP Professional also provides Recovery Agents in the event that the user who originally encrypted a file or folder leaves the company, and the file or folder cannot be unencrypted. Consider this example: A certain user who knows just enough to be dangerous accidentally deletes his private key. The computer is full of company-sensitive encrypted data that no one can read without the user's private key. What can you do? The answer is to use the Recovery Agent.

Because in an imperfect world things happen that can leave encrypted data stranded, a Recovery Agent can be assigned so that the data can be recovered in the event that the user's private key is lost or corrupted or if the user suddenly decides to never return to work. In order to prevent data from being hopelessly lost in encryption, a Recovery Agent can decrypt the data. It is important to note that the agent can only decrypt data, not re-encrypt it.

In order to configure a Recovery Agent, you must be logged onto Windows XP Professional as an Administrator, and you need to know the location of the certificate of the person who will become the Recovery agent. If you are part of a domain, a network administrator will need to assist in this process, since certificates are most often stored in the Active Directory in Windows domain networks. To configure the Recovery Agent, follow these steps:

EXERCISE 12-3

Configuring a Recovery Agent

To configure a recovery agent, just follow these steps:

1. Click Start | Run. Type **MMC** and click OK.
2. In the console window, click File | Add/Remove Snap-in.
3. In the snap-in window, click Add. In the Add Standalone snap-in window, click Group Policy and click Add.
4. In the Group Policy Object window, leave the Local Computer option selected, as shown in the following illustration, and click Finish.

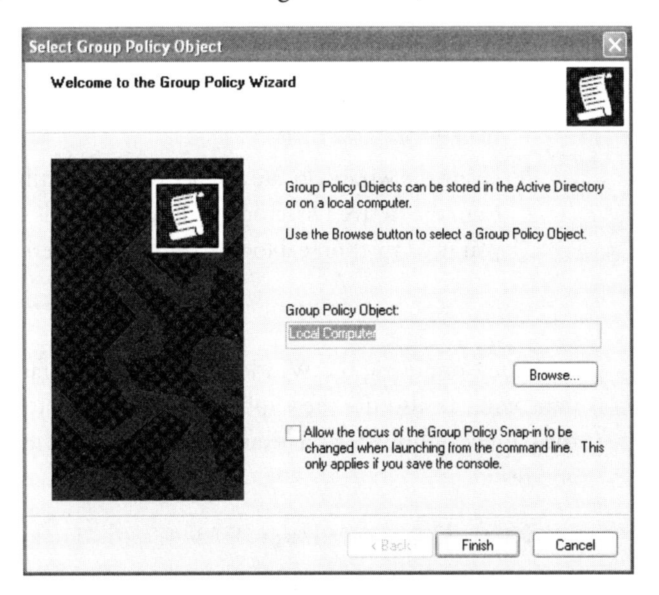

5. Click Close on the Add Standalone snap-in window and OK on the Snap-in window. You now see the Local Computer Policy in the MMC. Expand Local Computer Policy | Computer Configuration | Windows Settings | Security

Settings | Public Key Policies | Encrypting File System, as shown in the following illustration:

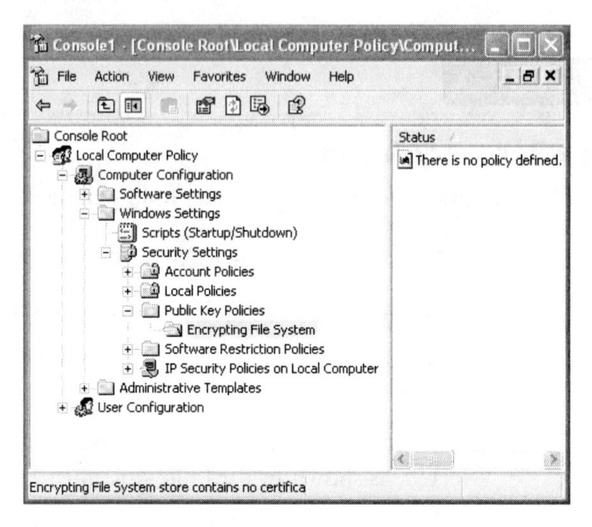

6. Right-click the Encrypting File System folder and click Add Data Recovery Agent. This starts the Add Recovery Agent wizard. Click Next on the Welcome screen.
7. Using the wizard, locate the desired user certificate. You can select the certificate from the Active Directory. If the certificate is not located in the Active Directory, you need to choose a local *.cer file. The certificate must be saved as a *.cer file.

Aside from using the Windows XP GUI interface for encrypting and decrypting data, you can also use the Cipher command line tool. You should be familiar with the Cipher options for the exam, and I have provided them here for quick reference and review.

```
Cipher [/e] [/d] [/s[:dir]] [/a] [/i] [/f] [/q] [/h] [pathname [...]]
```

Table 12-1 defines each of the command switches.

TABLE 12-1 Cipher Command Switches

Switch	Explanation
/e	Encrypts the specified file
/d	Decrypts the specified file
/s: dir	Performs the selected operation an all folders and subfolders in the specified directory
/a	Performs the selected operation on all files with the specified name
/i	Continues the selected operation even if errors occur
/f	Forces the encryption operation on all specified files, including currently encrypted files
/q	Reports only the most essential information
/h	Performs the selected operation on hidden files

SCENARIO & SOLUTION

How are encryption and decryption handled when a user accesses an encrypted file?	When a user encrypts a file, the file appears as it normally would to the user. The user does not have to manually decrypt the file when he or she accesses it—Windows XP handles this process automatically. The only difference the user may notice is a slight decrease in performance.
Can a compressed file be encrypted?	No. Compression and encryption are not compatible.
For a particular file, I noticed that the Advanced button is not available on the General tab. Why?	The file is stored on a FAT drive. FAT drives do not support advanced NTFS features, such as encryption.
How many recovery agents can I designate?	You can designate as many recovery agents as you like. However, keep in mind that recovery agents can decrypt files at will and basically provide a security hole. So, take care when assigning the recovery agent role to users or administrators—the fewer the better.

CERTIFICATION OBJECTIVE 12.02

Configure, Manage, and Troubleshoot Local User and Group Accounts

In Windows domain environments, user and group accounts are handled at the server level via the Active Directory. However, Windows XP Professional also enables you to configure and manage accounts at the local level. For example, on the local computer, you can configure user and group accounts with certain rights, permissions, and features in a way that is helpful in your environment. In workgroup settings, this configuration can be very helpful in user management. From a domain perspective, local user and group configuration can also provide additional layers of security and policy management. Of course, you can easily create and manage user and group accounts using the Computer Management console, and in a limited manner, you can configure user and group accounts with the User icon in Control Panel. This utility is designed for the end-user, and most of your work with Windows XP Professional local user and group accounts will be handled from the Computer Management console.

User Accounts

Windows XP Professional allows you to create as many local user accounts as you need, with the administrator and guest accounts provided by default. The rest, then, depends on you and the needs of your environment. From a simple home computer where different family members access the computer to a workgroup setting where several different accounts may be necessary, Windows XP Professional gives you a number of user and group configuration options via Computer Management and Group Policy, as you will see in the next section.

User names must be unique and can contain up to 20 characters, including numbers. However, user accounts cannot contain " ? \ [ ] : ; | = + * . In Windows XP Professional, you can assign a user a password if you like, and Windows XP Professional does allow users to log on without passwords. Of course, while this kind of configuration is good for home or very small office use, it is not secure.

If you open the Computer Management console, which is found in Administrative Tools in Control Panel, you see a Local Users and Groups node in the left console pane. If you expand Local Users and Groups, you'll see the Users and Groups Container.

FIGURE 12-2

Local User and Groups

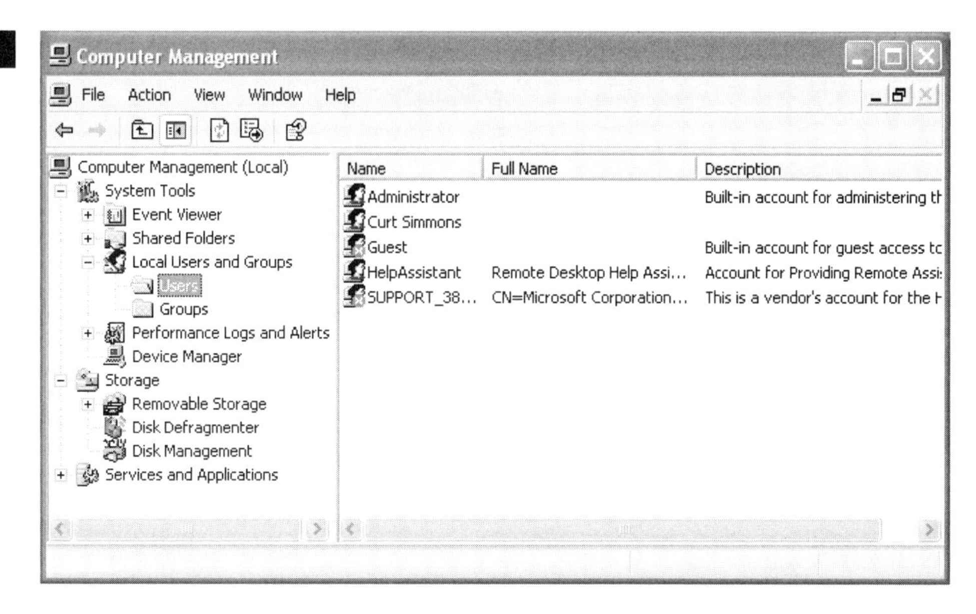

you open the Users container, you can see the current local users that are configured, as shown in Figure 12-2.

Excercise 12-4 shows how to easily create a new user.

EXERCISE 12-4

CertCam 12-4

Creating a New User

To create a new user, just follow these steps:

1. In the Computer Management console, expand Local Users and Groups. Right-click the Users container and click New User.
2. In the New User window, enter a user name, full description, and password and confirm the password. Then, you can choose from the following options:
   - User Must Change Password At Next Logon
   - User Cannot Change Password
   - Password Never Expires
   - Account Is Disabled

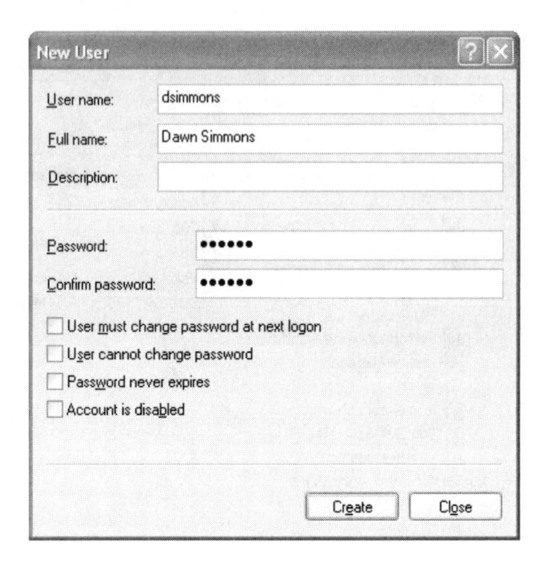

3. Once your selections are made, click the Create button and the new account will appear in the Local Users container.

Once you have created a new user account, you can manage it from within the Users container by simply right-clicking on the User account. From this menu, you can reset the user's password, rename the account, delete it, or access its properties. Concerning the resetting of user passwords: in case a user forgets his or her password, you can reset the password using the Set Password option. However, resetting the password will keep the user from accessing some personal data that is tied to the original password. Once the user logs off, this data will become inaccessible. Specifically, the user will lose access to encrypted files, stored passwords, and personal security certificates. As you can see, resetting the password is a "last straw" action and one that should be avoided. Instruct your users to create password reset disks that enable them to recover forgotten passwords, and if the user simply wants to change the password, he or she can use User Accounts in Control Panel to change it (assuming the user knows the current password and is able to log on in the first place).

On the properties sheets of the User Account, shown in Figure 12-3, you can manage the password restrictions and you can disable the account on the General tab. Using the Member Of tab, you can add the user to desired local groups. Finally, on the

FIGURE 12-3

User Account properties

Profile tab, you can configure a local or roaming user profile. See Chapter 4 for more information about profiles.

Group Accounts

Group Accounts are used on the local computer to assign certain rights and permissions to certain users. Group configuration is an easy way to manage group rights and permissions. Windows 2000 groups are extremely important in domain environments, where thousands of users may need different types of rights and access. The group is the preferred method of managing these users. They are also useful, and much simpler to manage, at the local level.

Windows XP Professional has several built-in groups that you can use.

- **Administrators** Administrators have complete and unrestricted access the computer.
- **Backup Operators** Backup Operators can override security restrictions in order to back up and restore data.

- **Users** Users are restricted to their own individual folders in terms of system configuration. Therefore, Users are restricted from making system-wide changes.
- **Guests** Any Guests have the same permissions as the Users group by default.
- **Network Configuration** Members of this group have some administrative features that enable them to manage and configure networking.
- **Power Users** Power Users have most administrative rights, with certain restrictions. They can run most applications, including legacy applications.
- **Remote Desktop Users** Group members have the right to log on remotely.

Just as with user accounts, you can easily create a new group by right-clicking on the Group container and clicking New Group. Enter the group name, and a description if desired, and then Add members to the group. You can manage the membership of the group by accessing the group's properties.

SCENARIO & SOLUTION

Scenario	Solution
Do I need to configure local user and group accounts in a domain environment?	Not usually. In a domain environment, user and group membership and configuration is handled at the server level. There may be some administrative reasons for using a local user or group, but under most circumstances, local management is not necessary.
Why would you choose to disable an account?	You can disable an account so that no one can log on using the account. This feature is useful if the user of that account is out of the office for an extended period of time, or if the account is not needed, but you do not want to delete it.

CERTIFICATION OBJECTIVE 12.03

Configure, Manage, and Troubleshoot Local Security Policy

You can individually configure users and groups for the local Windows XP Professional computer system. However, you can also configure a local security policy that determines what users and security features are invoked on that system. The policy that you create will then apply evenly to all users. This configuration ensures that the same security settings and features are applied to all and helps prevent security loopholes. There are a few different items that you will want to consider, and the next section begins by configuring user and group accounts using Group Policy.

User and Group Policy

Group Policy enables you to control user and group accounts. Group Policy is configured via a Windows 2000 domain controller in the Active Directory and is applied at the site, domain, or OU level. You can also configure local Group Policy that applies to your computer.

exam Watch

Local Group policy is the weakest form of Group Policy. In domain environments, OU, domain, and site GPOs will overwrite local Group Policy.

To access the local Group Policy console, click Start | Run. Type **gpedit.msc** and click OK. The Group Policy console opens, as shown in Figure 12-4.

As you can see in Figure 12-4, there are two subfolders—Computer Configuration and User Configuration. Most of our work involving configuring security settings will occur in the Computer Configuration subfolder. If you expand Windows Settings | Security Settings under Computer Configuration, you see that you can configure a number of different policies that affect users and groups, as shown in Figure 12-5. The following sections explore these policies.

FIGURE 12-4

Group Policy console

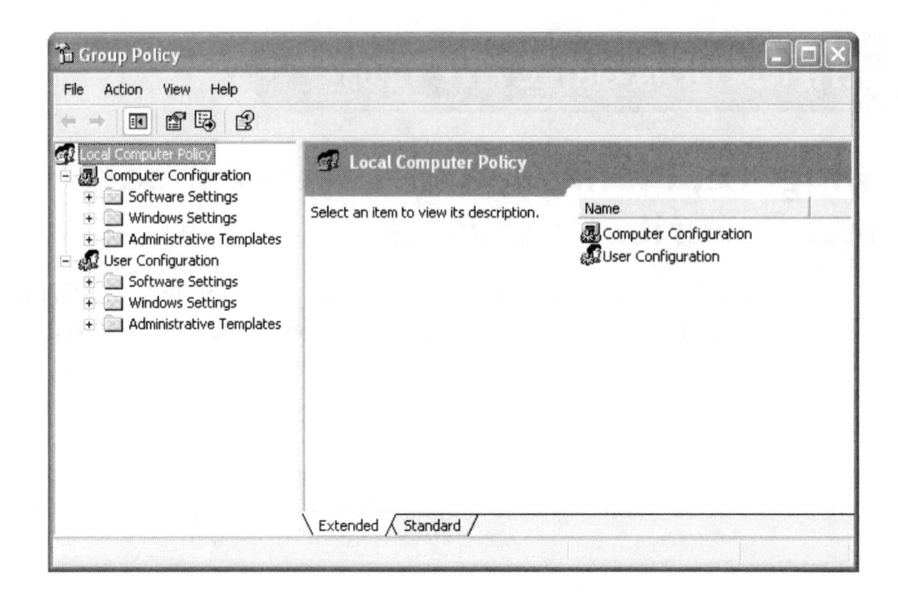

Account Policies

If you expand Account Policies, you have two subfolders—Password Policy and Account Lockout Policy. If you expand Password Policy, you see a listing of policies you can

FIGURE 12-5

Security Settings

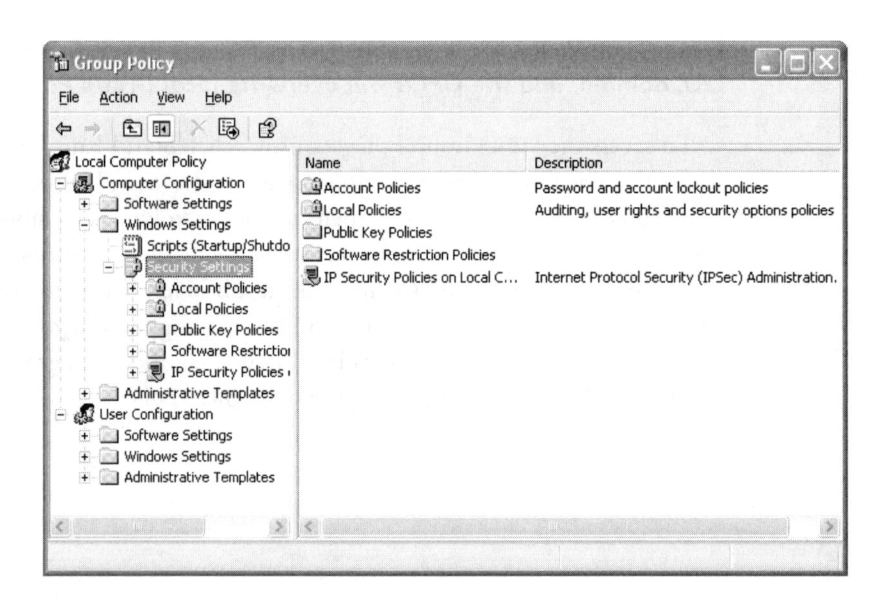

choose to invoke as well as any default settings that may be in effect. The options and the defaults are as follows:

- Enforce Password History (none)
- Maximum Password Age (42 days)
- Minimum Password Age (0 days)
- Minimum Password Length (0 characters)
- Password Must Meet Complexity Requirements (disabled)
- Store Password Using Reversible Encryption (disabled)

If you double-click one of the security templates, you see a simple window where you can enter a desired property. For example, in Figure 12-6, you see the template for minimum password length properties. By default, this setting is zero, but you can change it here and click OK in order to invoke a new minimum length requirement.

All template settings provide you with a simple window, like the one you see in Figure 12-6. The second category under account policies is Account Lockout. If you expand the Account Lockout container, you have three template options, which are (with the default settings):

- Account Lockout Duration (not applicable)
- Account Lockout Threshold (0 invalid logon attempts)
- Reset Account Lockout Counter After (not applicable)

FIGURE 12-6

Minimum Password Length Properties

on the Job

The account lockout feature is a good security measure because it can lock an account for a period of time if logon failure occurs. For example, if a user attempts to log on and enters the incorrect password for three times, the account can lock, preventing login at all. This is a good security feature that prevents someone from trying to guess a user's password. To use the lock out option after a certain number of invalid logon attempts, use the Account Lockout Threshold template and then configure the lockout duration and the lockout reset.

Audit Policy

Windows XP Professional gives you the ability to audit security events on your Windows XP system. This feature enables you to see what users are doing and/or accessing. When you turn on auditing for the desired events, the audit data is recorded to the Security Log, which is available in Event Viewer.

If you expand Local Policies under Security Settings, you see the Audit Policy container, shown in Figure 12-7.

You have the following audit policy options, all of which are turned off by default:

FIGURE 12-7

The Audit Policy container

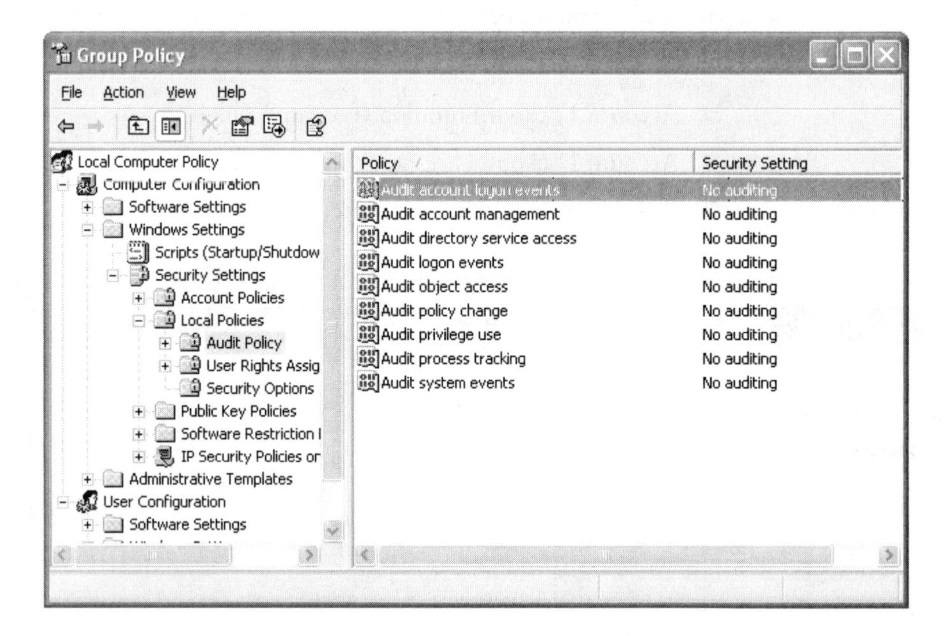

- Audit Account Logon Events
- Audit Account Management
- Audit Directory Service Access
- Audit Logon Events
- Audit Object Access
- Audit Policy Change
- Audit Privilege Use
- Audit Process Tracking
- Audit System Events

Each template window gives you either a Success or Failure check box. For example, in Figure 12-8, you can choose to audit the success or failure of logon events. If you choose the Success option, then each logon event that is successful will be written to the Security Log. Conversely, if you choose Failure, only logon event failures will be written.

You should think carefully about what events you want to audit, or you will end up with a Security log that is full all of the time. As you consider auditing, try to only invoke audit policy settings that will give you useful data that you intend on monitoring regularly.

FIGURE 12-8

Audit Account Logon Events Properties

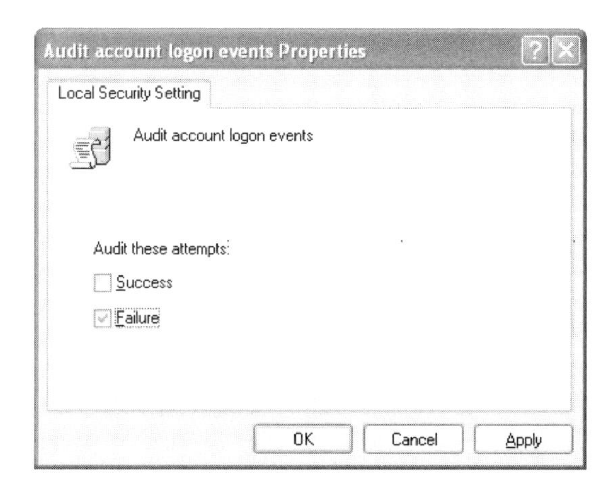

Aside from auditing user logon events and account management issues, you can also audit access to objects, specifically folders. This feature enables you to audit the success or failure of users attempting to access a particular folder and can be a great security tool if you suspect that a user is attempting to break security. Exercise 12-5 shows you how to audit access to an object.

EXERCISE 12-5

CertCam 12-5

Auditing Access to Objects

To audit access to an object, such as a folder, just follow these steps:

1. In Group Policy, expand Windows Settings, Security Settings, Local Policies, Account Policy.
2. In the right pane, double-click Audit object access.
3. In the Audit object access window, choose either Success or Failure (or both) and click OK. Close the Group Policy console.
4. On the desired folder or object, right-click and click Properties. Click the Security tab and click Advanced.
5. On the Advanced Security window, click the Auditing tab, as shown in the following illustration.

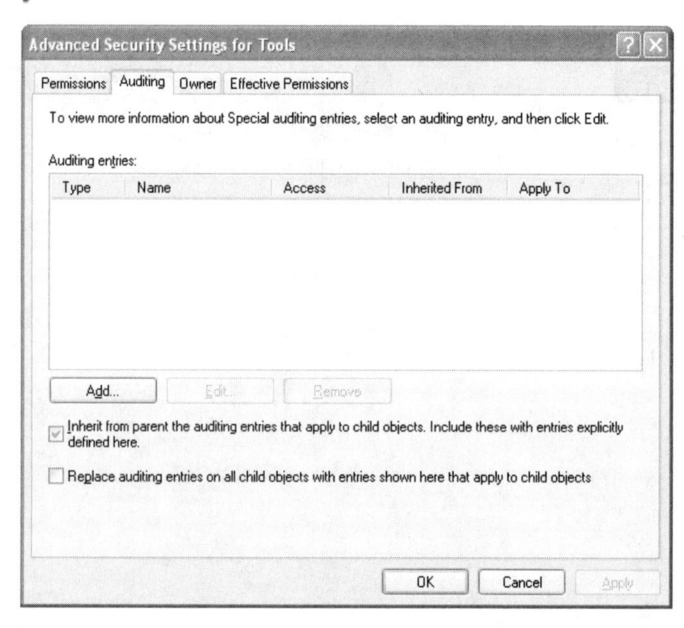

6. Click the Add button. In the Select User, Computer, or Group window, you can select who you want to audit. For example, you might choose Everyone or Users. This will audit all user accounts in the Everyone or the Users group. You could also choose to audit administrators only. Make a selection and click Next.
7. The Auditing Entry for the Tools window appears. In this window, shown in the following illustration, you can choose the specific success/failure events that you want to audit. Simply make your selections and click OK, then OK again on the Advanced Security window.

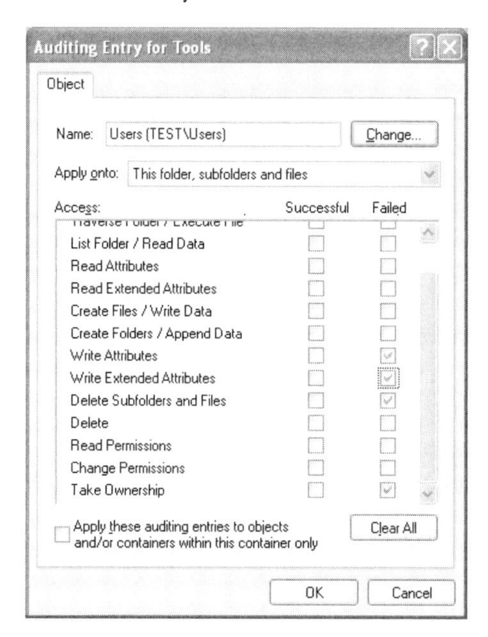

User Rights Assignment

User Rights Assignment is a simple portion of the Group Policy, Local Policies settings. Essentially, user rights assignment enables you to assign certain rights to users via groups. Basically, you double-click a desired template and add or remove groups from the template in order to restrict or permit users. For example, as you can see in Figure 12-9,

FIGURE 12-9

User Rights Policy

the "Access this computer from the network" provides default privileges to major groups. However, you can add new groups or remove any default groups.

There are a number of user rights assignment templates—too many to review here. However, here are some of the more common ones, and you should spend some time using Group Policy and getting familiar with the rights features available.

- Take ownership of files or other objects
- Log on locally
- Log on as a service
- Deny logon locally
- Act as a part of the operating system
- Access this computer from the network

SCENARIO & SOLUTION	
I want to make sure that user passwords expire after 30 days. Where can I configure this option in Group Policy?	Access Computer Configuration | Windows Settings | Security Settings | Account Policies | Password Policy. Open the Maximum Password Age option and change the value to 30.
I want to record an event when a user fails to access something in the Active Directory in my domain. Where can I configure this?	Access Audit Policy under Local Policies. Open the Audit Directory Service Access and click Failure.
I want to allow a certain group to back up files and directories without giving them any additional administrative privileges. How can I do this?	In Group Policy | Local Policy, access User Rights Assignment. Double-click the Back up Files and Directories option and add the group to the list.

CERTIFICATION OBJECTIVE 12.04

Configure, Manage, and Troubleshoot a Security Configuration

Aside from configuring security settings via Group Policy, you can also enforce a standardized security configuration using security templates. Security templates, which are available in the Security Templates MMC snap-in, give you a single place where a number of important security settings can be configured.

You can open the Security Templates MMC by opening an empty MMC and then adding the Security Templates snap-in. As you can see in Figure 12-10, several default security templates appear in the left console pane, and the content of the selected security template appears in the right console pane.

The default templates are configured with standard Windows XP settings; however, you can modify them to meet your needs. You can also create new templates and export existing templates so that they can be used on other Windows 2000/XP Professional computers. The default templates all serve specific purposes, and it is possible that you may run into exam questions that throw these template names around. The list on the following page describes each of them and will help keep you on track for the exam.

FIGURE 12-10

Security Templates snap-in

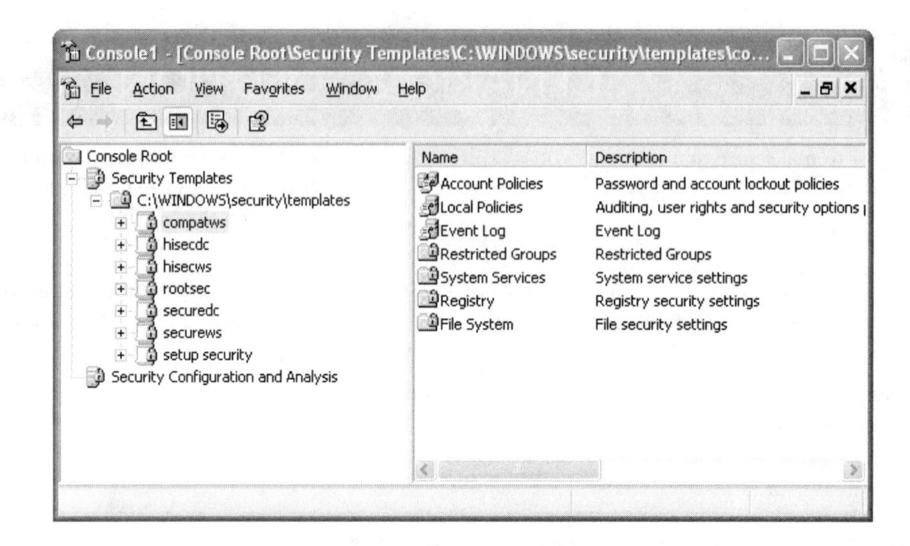

on the job

The easiest way of working with Security Templates is via the Security Templates snap-in, which you can also directly open by typing *Secedit.exe* ***at the command prompt. By default, security templates are stored in systemroot\Security\Templates.***

- **Setup Security** This template applies default computer settings during installation, which include file permissions for the root of the system drive.
- **Compatws (Compatibility)** This template provides default permissions for workstations and is primarily applied to Administrators, Power Users, and Users. This template makes certain that Administrators have the most power, while Users have the least amount of power. The Compatibility template is designed for Windows 2000/XP workstations only and should not be used on domain controllers.
- **Securedc And Securews (Secure Domain Controller And Secure Workstation)** This template should be applied to domain controllers and workstations and defines the security settings that are least likely to affect application compatibility. This template also limits the use of LAN Manager and NTLM authentication protocols.
- **Hisec (Highly Secure)** This template is a superset of Securedc And Securews and imposes further restrictions on encryption levels and signing. The settings for this template primarily affect domain controllers.

- **Rootsec (System Root Security)** This template specifies the new root permissions that were provided during setup. This template can be used to reapply root permissions, but it does not overwrite explicitly assigned permissions for the root.

exam watch

Keep the security templates in mind for the exam and know what they do! Know how to apply which security template under which situation.

Under each default template, you can modify the default settings as desired. Each template contains the same category of settings, which are as follows:

- Account Policies—includes password policy, account lockout policy, and Kerberos policy
- Local Policies—includes audit policy, user rights assignment, and security options
- Event Log
- Restricted Groups
- System Services
- Registry
- File System

For each template, you can modify the default settings found under each category. However, for safety purposes, you should consider saving the template under a different name and then editing it. This will enable you to experiment with the template without affecting the original, default template. Exercise 12-6 walks you through this process.

EXERCISE 12-6

CertCam 12-6

Copying and Editing a Security Template

To copy and edit a security template, just follow these steps:

1. In the Security Templates MMC, right-click the desired security template and click Save As.
2. In the Save As dialog box, enter a name for the copy of the template. Note that the template is saved as an .inf file. Click Save

3. The new template now appears in the Security Templates console. Expand the template.
4. You can now double-click the categories as desired and begin editing the template according to which settings you want to invoke.

CERTIFICATION SUMMARY

Security is a constant concern for networking professionals. As an MCSE, you'll be expected to make the most of Windows XP Professional's local security features.

Windows XP provides file and folder encryption. Using a private and public encryption scheme, Windows XP enables users to encrypt data and then use that data seamlessly without having to constantly encrypt and decrypt files. In the event that a private key is lost or unavailable, Windows XP Professional also provides recovery agents so that the data is not permanently lost.

User and group accounts can be configured and controlled using Local Users and Groups in the Computer Management console. For end users, the Users tool in Control Panel is also available. Using Local Users and Groups, you can configure user and group accounts, group memberships, account password and lockout features, and user profiles. Using local Group Policy, you can configure security policy settings for users and groups that apply to all users logged onto the computer. These settings are effective, but they can be overwritten by site, domain, and OU policies in domain environments.

Finally, Windows XP Professional provides the Security Templates MMC snap-in, where you can configure predefined security templates, create your own, and export security templates so that they can be imported to other Windows 2000/XP computers.

TWO-MINUTE DRILL

Configure, Manage, and Troubleshoot Encrypting File System (EFS)

- ❑ EFS enables users to store data so that others cannot access the data. EFS enables the user to encrypt and decrypt data seamlessly.
- ❑ You can encrypt a file or folder by clicking the option on the Advanced dialog box, found on the General tab of the file or folder's properties sheets.
- ❑ Windows XP uses a private key/public key encryption scheme, known as *public key cryptography.*
- ❑ A Recovery Agent can be used to rescue encrypted data when a user's private key has been lost.
- ❑ You can also configure encryption using the Cipher command.

Configure, Manage, and Troubleshoot Local User and Group Accounts

- ❑ You can configure local users and groups in Computer Management or via the end-user utility found in Control Panel.
- ❑ When creating users, you can determine how passwords should be handled. You can assign the user a static password, or you can configure the account so that the user has to create a new password during the first logon.
- ❑ Windows XP groups determine user permissions and access. There are a number of standard built-in groups: Administrators, Backup Operators, Users, Guests, Network Configuration, Power Users, Remote Desktop Users.

Configure, Manage, and Troubleshoot Local Security Policy

- ❑ You can use local Group Policy to configure security settings that apply to all users. Local Group Policy is the weakest form of Group Policy. In a Microsoft network, any Group Policies from the site, domain, or OU level will overwrite the local Group Policy in the event of conflicting settings.

- Using Group Policy, you can configure standardized settings for Account Policies, such as minimum password age, password history, password complexity, and other settings.
- Group Policy can be used to turn on auditing as well. Then, you can choose to audit desired folders by accessing the Advanced | Auditing tab from the folder's Security tab. You can audit system events, user logon events, and even user access (such as to the Active Directory or to a local folder).
- Using Group Policy, you can configure user rights assignment, which is a part of Group Policy Local Policy settings. This feature enables you to assign permissions and rights via groups.

Configure, Manage, and Troubleshoot a Security Configuration

- You can apply a standardized security template to a computer running Windows XP Professional and even export that template to other computers using the Security Templates MMC console.
- Windows XP provides you with several default security templates, which are Setup Security, Compatws, Securedc And Securews, Hisec, and Rootsec.
- Under each template, you can review common configuration items, such as account policies, event logs, restricted groups, system services, the registry, and file systems.

SELF TEST

The following questions will help you measure your understanding of the material presented in this chapter. Read all of the choices carefully, as there may be more than one correct answer. Choose all correct answers for each question.

Configure, Manage, and Troubleshoot Encrypting File System (EFS)

1. Which statement is true concerning EFS?

   A. The user must manually decrypt encrypted files when he or she wants to use them.

   B. The user must have administrative rights to decrypt a file.

   C. The user can seamlessly open encrypted files that he or she has encrypted.

   D. Files are encrypted with the user's password.

2. You want to encrypt a certain file. You access the General tab of the file's properties sheets, but you notice that there is no Advanced button. What is wrong?

   A. Encryption has not been installed using Add/Remove Programs.

   B. The file is on a FAT drive.

   C. The file is compressed.

   D. Group Policy is restricting encryption.

3. In order to configure a recovery agent on a local Windows XP computer, what group membership do you need?

   A. Administrator

   B. Backup Operator

   C. User

   D. Remote Desktop

4. What command can you use the decrypt a file at the command line?

   A. cipher /e

   B. cipher /d

C. cipher /a

D. cipher /f

Configure, Manage, and Troubleshoot Local User and Group Accounts

5. You are currently creating several new local accounts on a Windows XP Professional computer. You need to make certain that a user account you have created for jsmith cannot be accessed until a later date. What can you do?

   A. Delete the account.

   B. Remove the password.

   C. Disable the account.

   D. Use the Cipher utility.

6. A certain user has forgotten his password. This user does not have a password reset disk. You need to reset the password. Which of the following statements are true concerning this action?

   A. The password can be easily reset with no data loss.

   B. The user will lose access to application data.

   C. The user will lose personal data, such as certificates.

   D. The user will lose all data.

7. You want to make certain that a local user has the right to add and delete user accounts on the local Windows XP computer. The user should also be able to change security settings. To what group membership should the user be added?

   A. Administrators

   B. Backup Operators

   C. Power Users

   D. Users

Configure, Manage, and Troubleshoot Local Security Policy

8. Consider the following illustration:

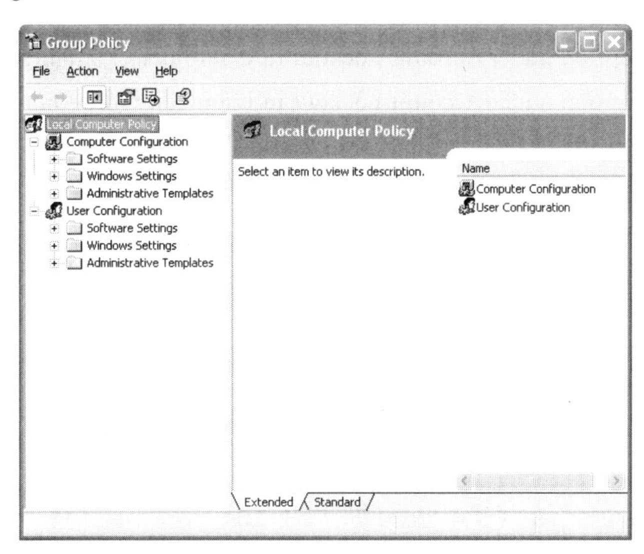

You want to change the local Group Policy so that all user passwords expire every 15 days. Where can you access this policy option?

A. User Configuration | Windows Settings | Account Policies | Accounts.

B. Computer Configuration | Windows Settings | Local Policies | Accounts.

C. Computer Configuration | Windows Settings | Security Settings | Account Policies | Password Policy.

D. You can't configure this in Group Policy.

9. A computer running Windows XP Professional resides in an OU in a Windows domain. An administrator configures a local policy that applies to users that access the computer. However, the administrator notices that portions of the local policy are not being applied correctly. What is the most likely explanation of this problem?

A. The policy is configured incorrectly.

B. The policy does not apply to Windows XP Professional.

C. The policy conflicts with another policy setting.

D. An OU, domain, or site policy is overwriting it.

10. You want to make certain that an account is locked after three unsuccessful logon attempts. How can you configure this?

    A. Set the option on the General tab of the user's properties sheets.
    B. Set the option under Account Lockout in Computer Configuration in Group Policy.
    C. Set the option under Account Lockout in User Configuration in Group Policy.
    D. Configure the setting on the Profile tab on the user's properties sheets.

11. Consider the following illustration:

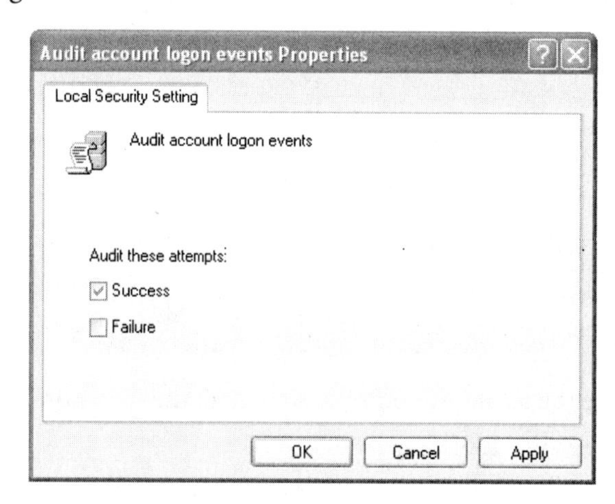

    Which statements concerning this policy are *not* true?

    A. All users who successfully log onto the computer will be logged.
    B. All users who do not successfully log onto the computer will be logged.
    C. Failed attempts will not be logged.
    D. The events will be written to the Security Log.

12. On a computer running Windows XP Professional, you want to audit several events concerning access to a particular folder. What do you need to do first in Group Policy to enable this?

    A. Audit privilege use.
    B. Audit process tracking.
    C. Audit policy change.
    D. Audit object access.

13. Which statement best describes the use of user rights assignment policy?
    - A. Use this policy to apply changes to all users.
    - B. Use this policy to manage user rights via Groups.
    - C. Use this policy to globally manage users.
    - D. Use this policy to manage administrative access.

Configure, Manage, and Troubleshoot a Security Configuration

14. What default security template makes certain that Administrators, Power Users, and Users have the rights and permissions that they should have on a default system?
    - A. Compatws
    - B. Setup Security
    - C. Securews
    - D. Hisec

15. You want to experiment with some changes to Compatws. What two steps should you perform (choose two—each answer is a part of the solution).
    - A. Make editorial changes as desired to the test template settings.
    - B. Choose "testing mode" from the File menu of the Security Templates snap-in.
    - C. Save Compatws as a test template so the original is not overwritten.
    - D. Run Compatws –a at the command line.

LAB QUESTION

As a consultant, you have been asked to configure a lockout policy for a local Windows XP computer. The desired results are that a lockout will occur after four unsuccessful logon attempts. The lockout should last for 30 minutes and automatically reset after 30 minutes as well. How can you configure this?

SELF TEST ANSWERS

Configure, Manage, and Troubleshoot Encrypting File System (EFS)

1. ☑ C is correct. Once a user encrypts a file, the user can open and read (decrypt) the file just as any other file. The user does not have to manually decrypt the file to use it.

☒ A, B, and D are incorrect. The user does not have to manually decrypt the file to read the file, so A is incorrect. B is incorrect because administrative rights are not required. C is also incorrect: encryption uses a uniquely generated encryption key created that is unique to each file or folder that is encrypted—not the user's password.

2. ☑ B is correct. Encrypted files can reside only on NTFS drives, as they are a feature of NTFS.

☒ A, C, and D are incorrect. A is incorrect because encryption is automatically available on NTFS drives. C is incorrect because you would still see an Advanced button even if compression were in use. D is incorrect as well: although Group Policy could restrict encryption, you would still see an Advanced button on the General tab.

3. ☑ A is correct. You must be an administrator on the local computer to configure a recovery agent.

☒ B, C, and D are incorrect. The group memberships do not have enough permission to configure a recovery agent.

4. ☑ B is correct. Use the cipher /d command to decrypt a file.

☒ A, C, and D are incorrect. The /e switch encrypts a file, so A is incorrect. The /a switch performs the selected operation on all files with the specified name, so C is incorrect. D is incorrect because the /i command is used to continue the operation, even if errors occur.

Configure, Manage, and Troubleshoot Local User and Group Accounts

5. ☑ C is correct. When you create the account, use the Account is disabled check box, as shown in the following illustration:

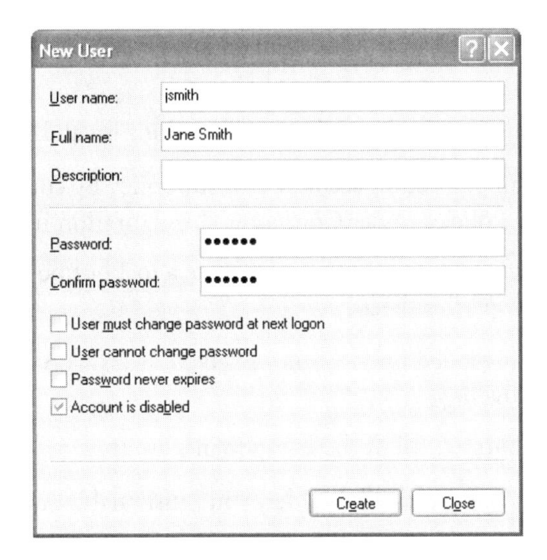

☒ A, B, and D are incorrect. Although you can delete the account, doing so removes it, which does not accomplish your intended goal. Using Cipher and removing the password will not disable the account.

6. ☑ B and C are correct. In the event that a password reset has to occur by a computer administrator, certain secure information—such as certificates, e-mail encrypted with the user's public key, Internet passwords saved on or remembered by the computer, and files that the user has encrypted—may be lost.

☒ A, and D are incorrect. The user will not lose all data; however the user may lose some personal security data, such as certificates.

7. ☑ A is correct. Only the administrators group can add and delete user accounts and change security settings.

☒ B, C, and D are incorrect. None of these group memberships will provide the required permissions.

Configure, Manage, and Troubleshoot Local Security Policy

8. ☑ C is correct. You can configure account policies by expanding Computer Configuration | Windows Settings | Security Settings | Account Policies | Password Policy.

☒ A, B, and D are incorrect. You cannot configure Password Policy using a different path.

9. ☑ D is correct. In this situation, an OU, domain, or site policy is probably overwriting the local Group Policy.

   ☒ A, B, and C are incorrect. None of these explanations is valid.

10. ☑ B is correct. You can enforce an account lockout policy by configuring the lockout policy, found under Account Policies under Computer Configuration in local Group Policy.

    ☒ A, C, and D are incorrect. You cannot configure a lockout policy under User Configuration or on the account's properties sheets.

11. ☑ B is correct. Since the failed option is not selected, users who do not successfully log on to the computer will *not* be logged.

    ☒ A, C, and D are incorrect. All of these statements are true.

12. ☑ D is correct. If you want to audit a folder, you must enable Audit object access.

    ☒ A, B, and C are incorrect. None of these items will turn on object auditing.

13. ☑ B is correct. User rights assignment enables you to manage rights and permissions to system processes through groups.

    ☒ A, C, and D are incorrect. These statements do not accurately describe user rights assignment.

Configure, Manage, and Troubleshoot a Security Configuration

14. ☑ A is correct. Compatws checks for compatibility among Administrators, Power Users, and Users rights assignment.

    ☒ B, C, and D are incorrect. These templates do not provide default permissions among these groups.

15. ☑ A and C are correct. If you want to edit an existing template, you should first use Save As to make a different copy and then begin editing the template.

    ☒ B and D are incorrect. These are not valid options that you can perform.

LAB ANSWER

For this lab question, you need to use local Group Policy to configure the desired result. Follow these steps:

1. Open Local Group Policy and expand Computer Configuration | Windows Settings | Security Settings | Account Policies | Account Lockout, as shown in the following illustration:

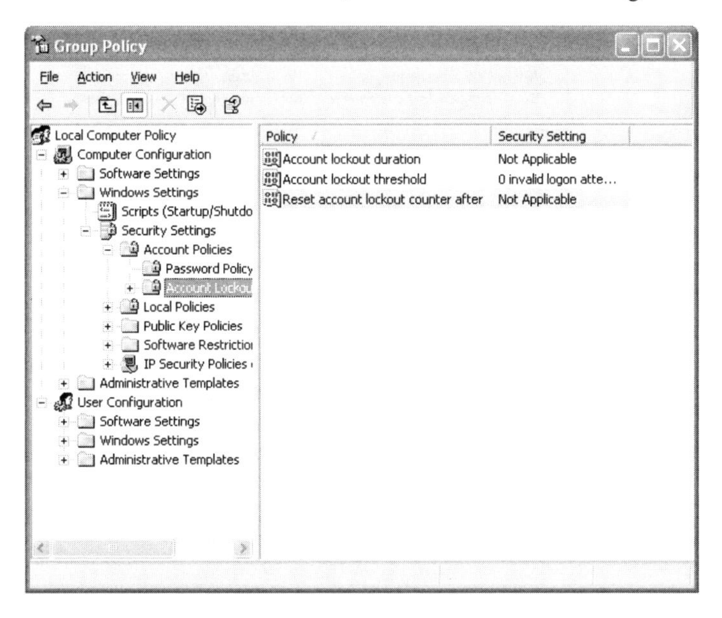

2. Open the Account Lockout Threshold policy. Change the value from 0 to 4, as shown in the following illustration.

3. A Suggested Value Changes dialog box appears, shown the following illustration. The suggested values for lockout duration and account reset are 30 minutes, so you can accept this default, since the customer wants to use the 30-minute values. Click OK.

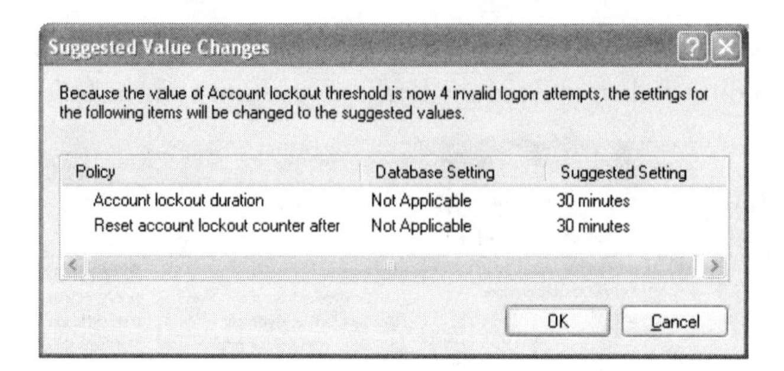
Suggested Value Changes
Because the value of Account lockout threshold is now 4 invalid logon attempts, the settings for the following items will be changed to the suggested values.
Policy
Database Setting
Suggested Setting
Account lockout duration
Not Applicable
30 minutes
Reset account lockout counter after
Not Applicable
30 minutes
OK
Cancel

13

Monitoring and Optimizing System Performance and Reliability

CERTIFICATION OBJECTIVES

13.01 Monitor, Optimize, and Troubleshoot Performance of the Windows XP Professional Desktop

13.02 Manage, Monitor, and Optimize System Performance for Mobile Users

13.03 Restore and Back Up the Operating System, System State Data, and User Data

✓ Two-MInute Drill

Q&A Self Test

Performance monitoring, management, and optimization can be an ongoing task for IT professionals. After all, complicated operating systems such as Windows XP Professional require intensive system resources to complete necessary operations. Also, users need protection from the possibility of data loss in the event of hardware failure, such as a disk crash. Fortunately, Windows XP Professional gives you the tools to manage performance issues successfully and to back up and protect both user data and operating system data in the event of a failure. The information provided in this chapter will allow you to make the most of managing operating system performance and data backup.

As with all exam objectives, hands-on practice is very important for the performance and backup issues. As you study the tools and features in this chapter, make sure you practice the labs and physically practice the objectives on a Windows XP Professional computer. With the issues of performance and data backup, hands-on practice is necessary for getting the full impact of the tools and resources provided by Windows XP.

CERTIFICATION OBJECTIVE 13.01

Monitor, Optimize, and Troubleshoot Performance of the Windows XP Professional Desktop

Windows XP Professional gives you the tools and resources you need to monitor, optimize, and troubleshoot desktop performance. The concept of "desktop" performance refers broadly to processes and components that affect how well a user is able to interact with the operating system. For example, memory performance is a critical factor because it affects how well Windows XP can operate and handle applications. Processor performance is critical because it determines how well Windows XP can respond to the load placed on it by the operating system, applications, and network resources. In this section, we will take a look at several different desktop performance issues, focusing on how to monitor and optimize a system's performance.

Using Performance Monitor

The Performance tool, otherwise known as *Performance Monitor*, is the same Performance tool that is found in the Windows 2000 operating system. Using Performance Monitor, you can gain real-time data about the performance of different system components and identify potential bottlenecks. Performance Monitor can provide you with information in a chart, report, or histogram format. You can also log data to a log file and configure administrative alerts, which can alert you when performance falls below a preconfigured baseline.

exam Watch

Administrative alerts can be sent in the form of an entry to the application event log or a network message. They can also start a performance data log or run a program.

Before getting into the use of the Performance tool, let's spend a moment considering the idea of performance monitoring. The purpose of performance monitoring is to gain information about the performance of various system components and hardware, such as memory and processor utilization. Typically, performance monitoring is best used with a *baseline of performance*. You determine a baseline by monitoring performance over a period of time during peak and non-peak times. Your results should include high and low peaks of performance so that you can effectively determine what is "normal" and satisfactory operation for a particular component. With the baseline, you can later use Performance Monitor to see if the component is functioning within normal parameters. If it is not, then you know that a problem exists with the component or that the load placed on the component has increased. Either way, you can effectively identify what component is not keeping up with the demand placed on it and creating a condition that is commonly called a *bottleneck*.

Let's consider an example. A computer running Windows XP Professional has 128MB of RAM. During initial testing, the 128MB was enough to meet the demands placed on it by the operating system and applications. With a baseline established, you are aware of what the memory can handle on a daily basis. However, several custom applications have recently been added to the system, which are used extensively throughout the workday. Now, the user complains that the system is running slowly. You use Performance Monitor to check the performance of memory and see that it is consistently running high. This simply means that the 128MB of RAM is now not enough to keep up with operating system and application demands. The memory has become a bottleneck because it cannot handle the demands placed on it by the operating system and applications in a timely manner. Your action: install more RAM to reduce the load on the system.

This example may not seem that complicated, but you'll certainly run into performance problems that are not so easily identifiable. The trick is to have baselines of performance established. With those baselines, you can begin using Performance Monitor to find bottlenecks that need to be corrected.

Though extensive use of Performance Monitor is beyond the scope of the exam, and therefore this book, you'll need to know the basics of how to use it and to have a general understanding of Performance objects and counters. In Performance Monitor, "objects" represent certain performance categories, such as memory, the physical disk, the processor, and related categories of system components and hardware that can be monitored by the Performance tool. Under each object, there are specific counters that you can monitor. *Counters* represent what you are actually monitoring under a particular object, such as "bytes per second." Some objects have only a few counters, while others may have 10 or more. The idea is to provide you with specific counters so that you can monitor specific actions of the object. For example, you can monitor the "memory" object, or you could monitor the "available bytes" counter and the "pages/sec" counter to gain information about memory availability and current usage, or you could use a combination of a number of other memory counters.

In this section, we'll take a look at a few lab exercises that show you how to use Performance Monitor. From this point on, you should spend some time working with it and getting to understand all of its capabilities.

Before getting into the exercises, let's first take a quick look at the basic Performance Monitor interface. If you click Start | Control Panel | Administrative Tools | Performance, the Performance tool opens, as you can see in Figure 13-1.

As you can see, the Performance Monitor is a basic MMC interface. The left console pane contains the System Monitor node and the Performance Logs and Alerts node. However, you primarily interact with Performance Monitor by using the right console pane. There are three basic divisions of this pane, starting at the top, which are as follows:

- **Toolbar** The toolbar contains icons you will use regularly to generate the types of charts and information that you want. The toolbar contains the following button options, which are seen from left to right in the illustration here. They are New Counter Set, Clear Display, View Current Activity, View

Log File Data, View Chart, View Histogram, View Report, Add Counter, Delete, Highlight, Copy Properties, Paste Counter List, Properties, Freeze Display, Update Data, and Help.

- **Information Area** The information area contains the chart, histogram, or report that you want to view. Just click the desired button on the toolbar to view counter information in the desired format.
- **Counter List** The bottom portion of the window contains a counter list, shown here. All of the counters displayed in the list are currently being reported in the information area. You can easily remove or add counters to the list using the toolbar. Each counter in the counter list is given a different color for charting and histogram purposes.

	1.000	Pages/sec	---	---	Memory	\\TEST
	1.000	% Processor Time	_Total	---	Proces...	\\TEST
	100....	Avg. Disk Queue...	_Total	---	Physic...	\\TEST

The primary functionality of Performance Monitor rests in objects and counters. You choose the counters that you want to monitor and then view those counters in

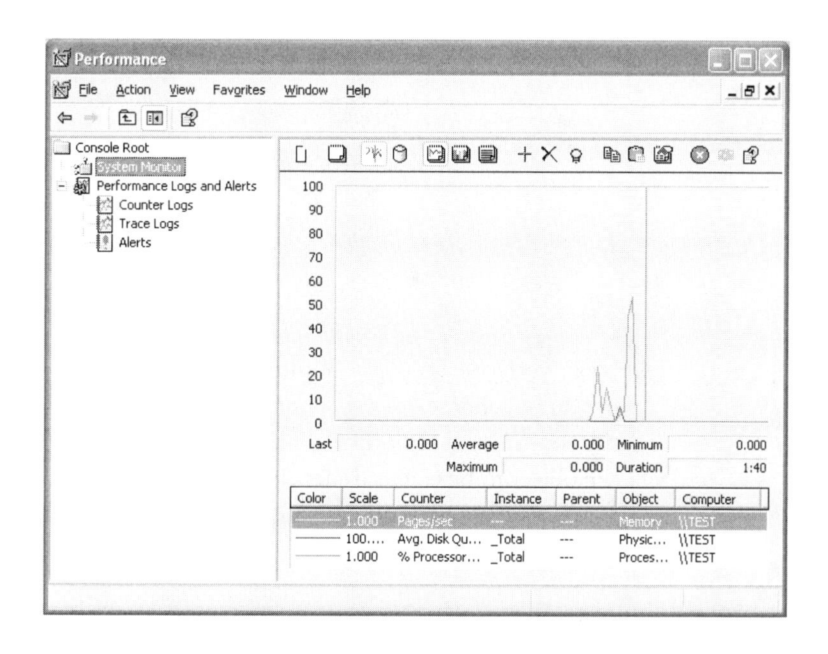

FIGURE 13-1 The Performance Monitor

either a chart, histogram, or report format. The following exercise shows you how to add counters to the Performance Monitor interface.

EXERCISE 13-1

Creating a New Chart

To create a new Performance Monitor chart, just follow these steps:

1. Click Start | Control Panel | Administrative Tools.
2. In the Performance MMC, click the New Counter Set button on the toolbar. Then, click the Add button on the toolbar.
3. In the Add Counters window, shown in the following illustration, use the drop-down menu to choose a performance object. For this exercise, you can see that I have chosen the PhysicalDisk counter.

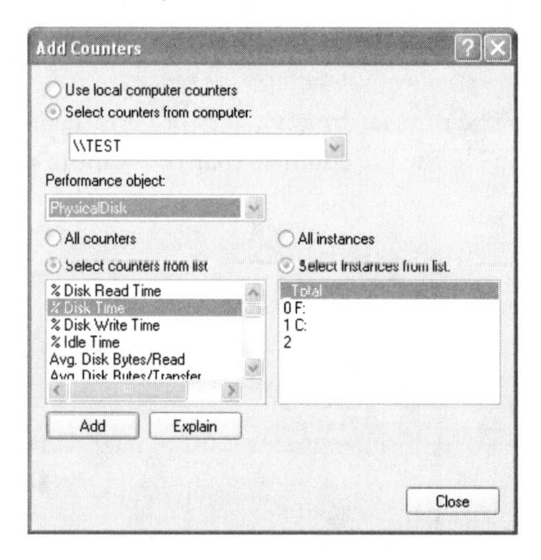

4. Next, you can choose to monitor all counters under the object you selected, or you can choose desired counters. To select individual counters, simply select the counter and click the Add button. Notice that there may be instances of the object to be counted, depending on your selection. The "Select instances from list" dialog box allows you to choose from among instances of the object,

if multiple ones are available. For example, as you can see in the previous illustration, I have three physical disks on the computer. I can monitor all disks or a selected one if I choose.

5. Repeat the counter Add process until you have added all desired counters, then simply click Close.

You can see that the counters you are adding are being monitored. You can change the chart/histogram/report view by simply clicking a different option button on the toolbar. As you can see in the following illustration, I am currently using the Report feature.

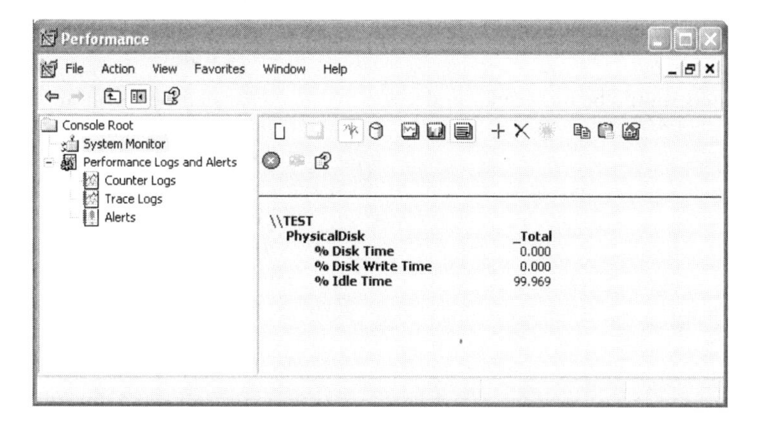

As you monitor various counters, you can gain information about the performance of the system processes and components that you selected. Generally, consistently high readings mean that the component or hardware is not able to meet the burden placed on it by the operating system's processes. Although high spikes are normal, consistently high readings on counters usually mean that a problem exists. This is, of course, where your baseline data is important. Using the baseline, you can tell if a component has higher readings than normal and what those reading might mean for system performance.

While the chart view helps you see readings in a graphical format, be sure to experiment with the report view—you can often gain more specific data from the report view.

SCENARIO & SOLUTION	
Is a baseline necessary in order to use Performance Monitor?	The baseline gives you information about the "normal" operation of an object. The baseline lets you know the normal range of performance that an object has experienced in the past. When there seems to be a performance problem, the baseline data will help you identify what object might be causing the performance problem. Of course, you can use Performance Monitor to examine counters without establishing a baseline of performance, but you will certainly have more trouble interpreting the data without a baseline to work from.
What counters should be monitored under an object?	That all depends on the data you want to gather. Keep in mind that counters monitor specific aspects of a particular object. You can monitor all counters under an object, or specific counters in order to gain specific performance information. The purpose is to not only to find the object that is causing performance problems, but also to determine what function of the object is not able to keep up with the demand placed on it.

So, if baseline performance is important to establish, how can you gain that data without sitting in front a screen all day; or if a particular object seems to be causing problems, how can you monitor that object during an entire day's operations without physically watching the screen? Performance Monitor gives you the ability to log data over a period time, which is a great way to gain performance data over a period of time without physically sitting at the machine. The performance data for the desired object(s) and counter(s) can be sampled over a period of time and then recorded in a log file. You can then use the log file to examine the data at a time that is convenient for you. Fortunately, using the log file is rather easy, and the following exercise walks you through the process.

EXERCISE 13-2

Creating Performance Logs

To generate a performance log, just follow these steps:

1. In Performance Monitor, expand Performance Logs and Alerts in the left pane. Right-click Counter Logs and click New Log Settings.
2. In the New Log Settings dialog box that appears, give the log file a name and click OK.
3. The Settings window for the log appears. On the General tab, shown in the following illustration, you can change the default log filename and storage location if you like. Next, use the Add Objects and Add Counters buttons to add the desired objects/counters that you want to log. As you can see in the illustration, I am logging several memory counters. Under the sample data heading, choose how often you want the log file to sample data. For example, in the illustration, I am sampling memory data every 15 seconds.

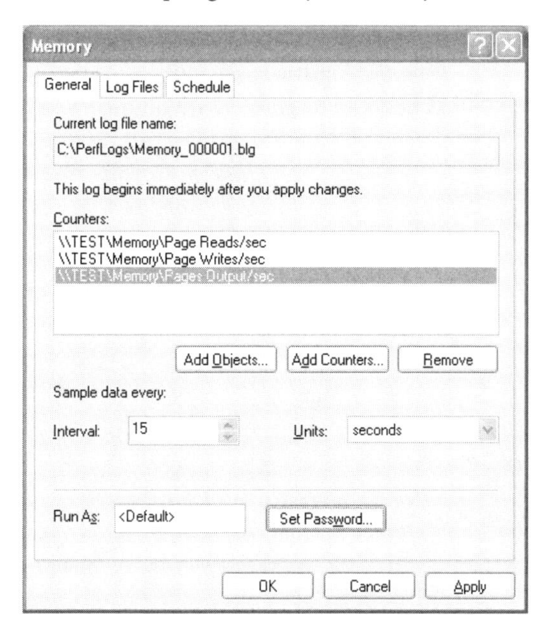

4. On the Log Files tab, shown in the following illustration, you can choose the type of log file that you want to produce, which would be a binary file by default. You can use the drop-down menu, however, to configure a text file, binary

circular file, or even an SQL database file. You can use the rest of the tab to adjust the file naming scheme.

5. The Schedule tab, shown in the following illustration, allows you to configure how the log file is started or stopped. The settings here are self-explanatory. When you are done with all of the settings for the log file, just click OK.

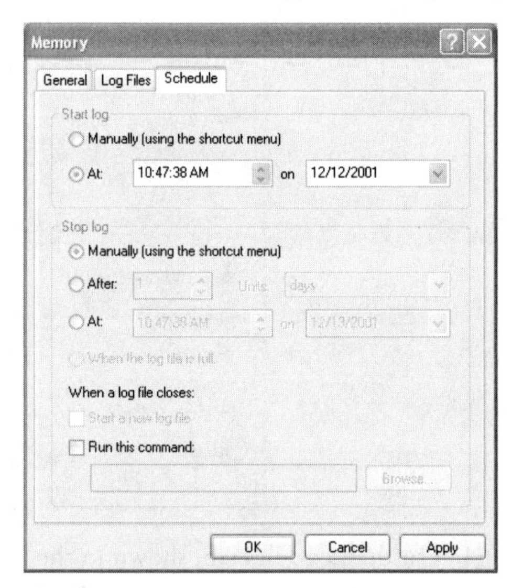

Let's say that you are using a computer running Windows XP Professional for certain network tasks. In order to make sure that the computer is functioning at its peak, you want to be notified when a certain performance object falls below the baseline of performance. Performance Monitor can provide you with this information though an alert. An alert is simply an action that the Performance Monitor carries out when "triggered." The trigger occurs when an object or counter falls below a certain baseline of performance. You configure the alert to carry out a particular action, such as send a network message or record an event to the Event Log, when the alert is triggered. This is a great way to keep track of objects that fall below baseline standards, and in critical scenarios, it is a great way to find out about the baseline failures as they occur. Like log files, alerts are rather easy to configure, and the following exercise shows you how.

EXERCISE 13-3

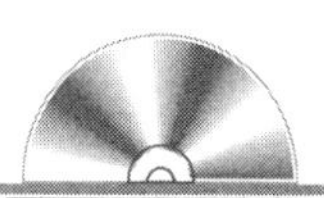

CertCam 13-3

Creating a Performance Alert

To generate a performance alert, just follow these steps:

1. In Performance Monitor, expand Performance Logs and Alerts in the left pane. Right-click Alerts and click New Alert Settings.
2. Give the new alert setting a name in the dialog box that appears and click OK.
3. On the General tab that appears, shown in the following illustration, you add counters to the alert, just as you do for a log file. Once the counters are added to the list, choose a baseline limit and a data sample rate.

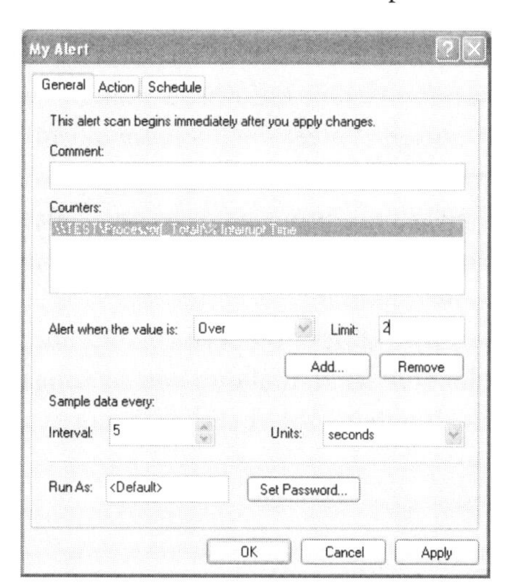

4. On the Action tab, shown in the following illustration, choose an action that occurs when the event is triggered. If you want to use the option to send a network message, the Messenger Service must be running.

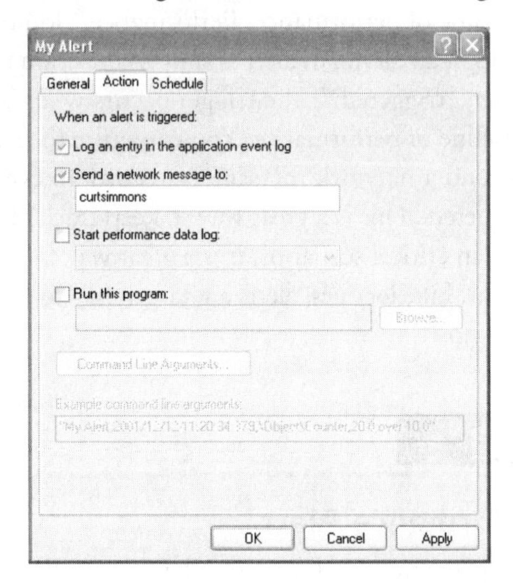

5. On the Schedule tab, you can configure a schedule as desired. This is the same Schedule tab you see when configuring a log file.

Optimize and Troubleshoot Memory and Processor Performance

When we think about a computer system's performance, the amount of physical memory and the speed of the processor are typically our first concerns. After all, a computer system must have enough physical RAM to run the operating system itself, as well as meet the requirements of any applications. The same is true for the processor—it must be able to keep up with the demands that the operating system and applications/processes place on it. Although memory and processor performance are not the only performance issues that you may face with Windows XP, they are certainly important.

As a part of desktop performance and configuration, Windows XP gives you a simple interface that allows you to adjust the graphical nature of Windows XP in order to conserve RAM and processor cycles. If a system seems sluggish, this may be

FIGURE 13-2

The Visual Effects tab

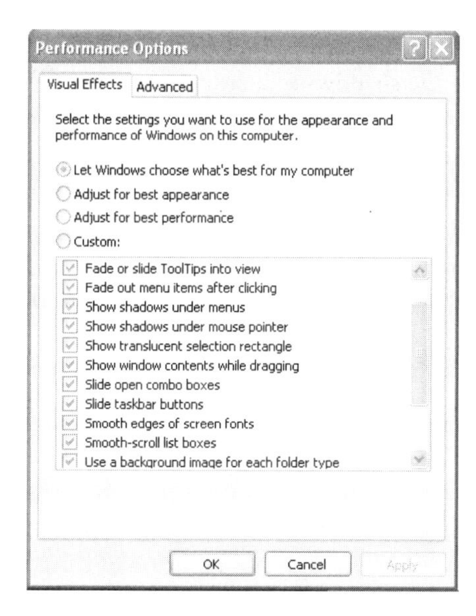

your first line of defense. If you right-click My Computer and click Properties, or just open System in Control Panel, you can click the Advanced tab and then click the Settings button under Performance. This opens the Performance Options window, as shown in Figure 13-2. As you can see on the Visual Effects tab, Windows XP attempts to choose its own settings by default. However, you can choose alternative settings that adjust Windows XP's visual effects for best appearance or best performance. You can also click the Custom button and clear the desired visual effects check boxes in

SCENARIO & SOLUTION

If you use a Custom configuration on the Visual Effect tab, which settings have the most system performance impact?	Any settings that have animated features, such as shading, tend to have an impact on performance. You can also clear the "Use visual styles on windows and buttons" option to help reduce some of the visual hits.
What does Windows XP do when the "Adjust for performance" option is used?	When this option is used, the system will look more like Windows 98/Me. You'll lose the basic XP interface appearance.

order to reduce RAM and processor usage on certain items. For example, you might remove the shadows and fading features of Windows XP.

If you click the Advanced tab, you can also manage a few additional memory and processor settings, shown in Figure 13-3. First, Windows XP is set to provide more processor cycles to applications than to Windows XP background processes. As a general rule, you should keep this setting to ensure that performance is optimized for applications, but you can change it so that the processor is used more efficiently for background services by simply clicking the radio button.

Next, you see that memory usage is also set to programs. This allows programs to get the most power from memory instead of system cache processes. However, depending on your RAM needs, you can optimize memory for system cache if so desired.

You also see the Page File (Virtual Memory) Change button. If you click the Change button, you see the Virtual Memory window, shown in Figure 13-4. Virtual memory allows Windows XP to use a portion of the computer's hard disk as a memory storage area. As data is loaded into memory and memory becomes low, pages of data are written to the hard disk and recalled as they are needed. This feature allows Windows XP to keep more frequently accessed information readily accessible in physical memory, even when physical memory begins to run low. This virtual memory tactic is certainly

FIGURE 13-3

The Advanced tab

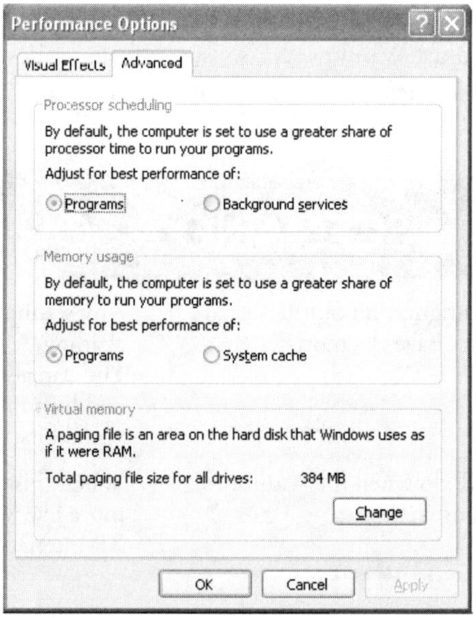

FIGURE 13-4

The Virtual Memory window

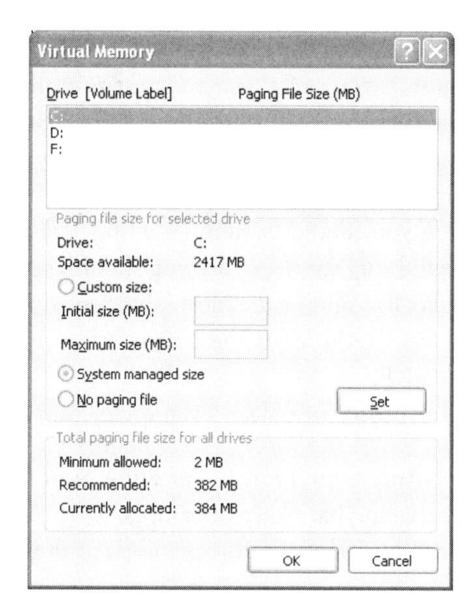

nothing new in Windows (it has been around since even the days of Windows 95), and the process still works the same in Windows XP.

As you can see, Windows XP is set to manage its own virtual memory settings, and it does a good job of this. However, you can manually input a minimum and maximum size for the page file, if you like. The commonly recommended amount is 1.5 times the amount of physical RAM installed on the computer. So, if you have 128MB of RAM, the recommended initial paging file size is 192MB.

It is important to note here, however, that Windows XP does a good job of managing its own memory settings, and as a general rule, you should allow Windows XP to handle those settings on its own. Incorrectly setting the virtual memory or choosing the "No paging file" setting option is likely to have adverse affects on system performance. Also, providing more paging file room is not a replacement for physical RAM. If the computer is running too slowly because there is not enough physical RAM installed on the system, then the paging file will not provide a cheap solution. In short, the paging file is used to help Windows XP physical memory—not replace it.

Aside from these basic settings features, you can use Performance Monitor to check out the performance of memory and the processor—and even the paging file. By monitoring these objects, you can get a clear view of system and application usage and of how memory and the processor are holding up under the demands placed on them. The counters you can check are great troubleshooting tools.

To use Performance Monitor, simply create a new chart and choose to monitor the desired object, such as processor, memory, or paging file. For the exam, it is not necessary for you to know about every counter that is available under each object. However, you should be familiar with some primary counters that can help you, and as with all things for the exam, you should get some hands-on practice. The following three bullet lists outline the most important counters for each of these objects. I suggest you memorize these for the exam and spend some time working with them on Windows XP.

For the processor object, keep these counters in mind:

- **% Interrupt Time** The amount of time the processor spends receiving and servicing hardware interrupts. This counter can help you see if the processor can handle the hardware needs of the system.
- **% Processor Time** The percentages of time the processor spends to execute a non-idle thread. This counter tells you how much time the processor requires to meet system and application threads.
- **Interrupts/sec** The average rate at which the processor receives and services interrupts.
- **% Idle Time** The amount of time that the processor is idle during a sampling period. If there seems to be no idle time, this may indicate that the processor cannot keep up with system, application, and hardware demands.

For the memory object, keep these counters in mind:

- **Page Reads/Sec** The amount of pages read in a monitored second.
- **Page Writes/Sec** The amount of pages written in a monitored second.
- **Pages/Sec** The rate at which pages are written to or read from a disk.

For the paging file object, keep these counters in mind (which are the *only* two):

- **% Usage** The amount of page file instances in use.
- **% Usage Peak** The peak usage of the paging file as a percentage. A high percentage is an indicator that more RAM may be needed on the system because the paging file is being used excessively.

SCENARIO & SOLUTION	
Is virtual memory necessary if I have a lot of RAM on the system?	Yes. All Windows computers use virtual memory, and the fact that a system seems to have enough physical RAM does not mean that a page file is not necessary. Never disable virtual memory unless you do so for troubleshooting purposes.
Can I use a custom setting and give the page file a greater size?	Yes, you can, but under most circumstances Windows XP will still manage the size for the best system performance. You can manually increase the size, however, and check for any performance gains. Just keep in mind that the page file is not a replacement for RAM upgrades.

Optimize and Troubleshoot Application and Disk Performance

For application and disk performance, you have a few different options that can help you optimize performance and troubleshoot problems. The following two sections examine these.

Application Performance

For application performance, first visit the Performance Options, Advanced tab window to make sure that the system is configured for programs in terms of processor scheduling and memory usage (which are the default settings). From that point, you can further manage application performance and troubleshoot application problems using Task Manager.

Task Manager is available in the Administrative Tools folder in Control Panel, or you can just press CTRL-ALT-DEL to access it. When Task Manager first opens, you'll see an Applications tab, as shown in Figure 13-5.

As you can see, a list of applications that are currently running appears in the window. If you look at the bottom of the tab, you can see the amount of CPU usage the applications are currently consuming. You can stop an application by selecting it and clicking the End Task button, and you can start new applications with the New Task button.

FIGURE 13-5

The Applications tab

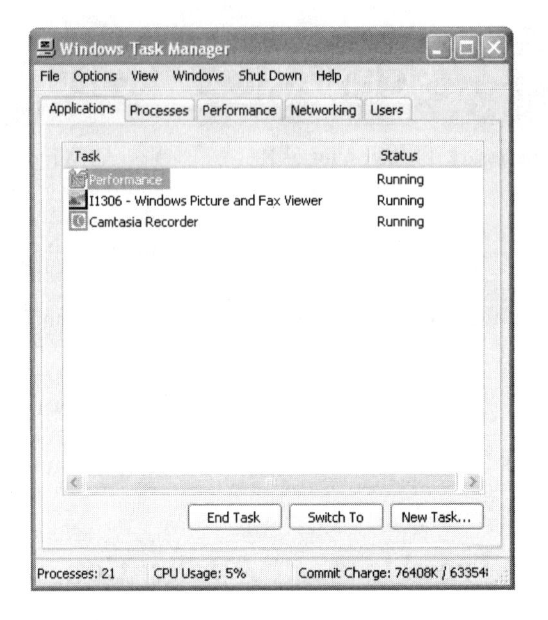

Of course, the best way to stop an application from running is to close the application from within the application. The option provided by Task Manager enables you to stop an application that is not functioning correctly or has locked up and is not responding.

If you click the Processes tab, you can see a list of processes that are currently running on the system, shown in Figure 13-6. As a general rule, this is a good troubleshooting tab because you can scan the list of processes running and identify any processes that are consuming an inordinately high amount of memory and CPU cycles.

Finally, you can also check out the Performance tab here for quick information. Although not as detailed as Performance Monitor and not limited to applications, this tab gives you a quick look at PCU usage and page file usage, as well as the total amount of memory in use and related values, as you can see in Figure 13-7.

Aside from using Task Manager to handle application performance and stop applications that are not responding, you can also use Windows XP's new Application Compatibility tool to ensure that older applications can function with Windows XP. This feature enables you to run applications on Windows XP that were designed for older operating systems, such as Windows 98 or even Windows 95. It is important

FIGURE 13-6

The Processes tab

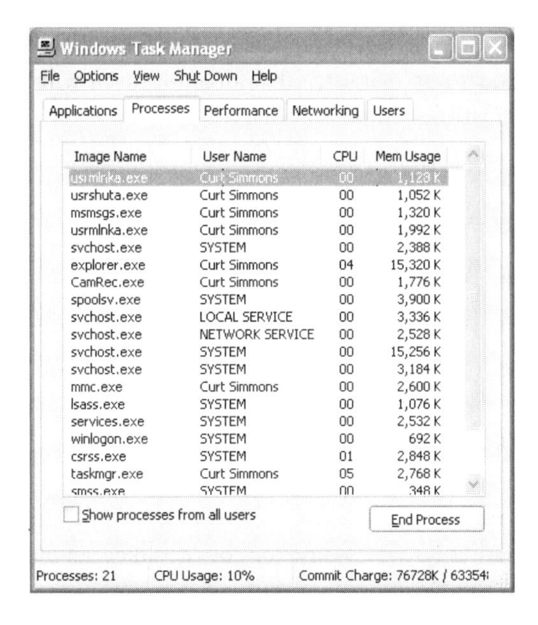

FIGURE 13-7

The Performance tab

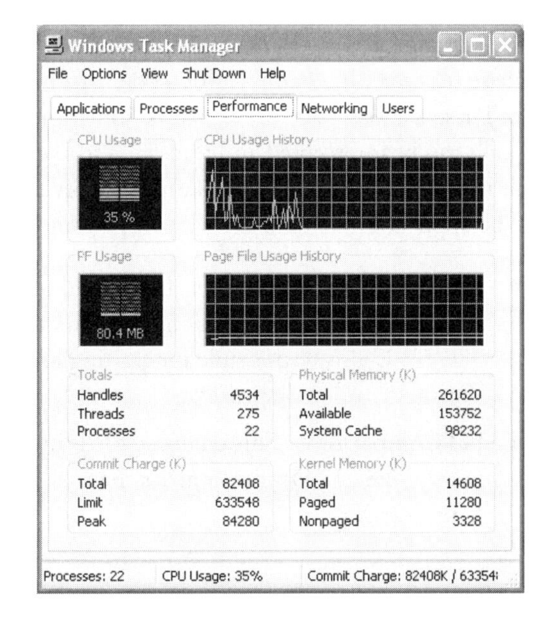

to note here that the Application Compatibility tool is a fix for some applications, but does not guarantee that an application will function with Windows XP. The Compatibility modes available are these:

- Windows 95
- Windows 98/Me
- Windows NT 4.0
- Windows 2000
- 256 Colors (reduces video card color to 256 for applications cannot handle higher color schemes)
- 640 By 480 (restricts screen resolution to 640 × 480)

From a technical point of view, the Application Compatibility tool enables the operating system to function, or "act like," an older version of Windows. Applications expect the Windows operating system to react in certain ways to application code that is being run. Incompatibility occurs when an operating system is upgraded so that code functions differently. The application still expects the same behavior, and when those API calls are not handled in the same way, the result is often a system lock (which we are all familiar with). The Application Compatibility tool uses four application database files to "filter" application code before it reaches the operating system core code. These databases act as translators, sometimes called "shims," so that application API calls can be intercepted and translated to and from the operating system. The end result is that Windows XP acts like a down-level operating system to the application, and the application is none the wiser. The four database files used are

- **MigDB.inf** This database file is used for Windows 9x and Me applications. This file examines applications and can determine what incompatibilities exist. The file is also responsible for alerting users to application incompatibilities during the upgrade process.
- **NTCompat.inf** This database file is used for Windows NT and Windows 2000. Like MigDB.inf, it alerts the user to potential incompatibilities with Windows XP.

- **SysMain.sdb** This database file contains matching incompatibility fixes that can be used with the Application Compatibility tool.
- **AppHelp.sdb** Help files that give the user clues about compatibility and how to solve problems.

The compatibility modes and shims provided with Windows XP typically meet the needs of around 100 popular applications. However, this does not mean that other applications will not work with a compatibility mode. Software developers can also create custom shim files that can be used by Windows XP so that other applications can be made compatible. If you are curious about compatibility customization, there is a QFixApp tool and a CompatAdmin tool that can be used to customize compatibility. You can download these tools via the Application Compatibility toolkit, available at *http://msdn.microsoft.com.*

From the user's point of view (or the administrator setting up compatibility for the user), Windows XP provides a Program Compatibility Wizard that helps you set up Windows XP for compatibility mode with a particular application. Exercise 13-4 walks you through the process.

EXERCISE 13-4

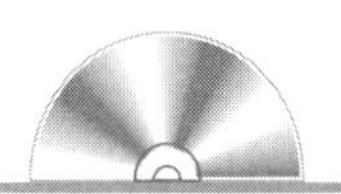

Configuring Program Compatibility

To configure program compatibility, just follow these steps:

1. Click Start | All Programs | Accessories | Program Compatibility Wizard.
2. The Welcome screen appears, shown in the following illustration. Notice that the wizard is a subset of the Help and Support system and also that older antivirus, backup, and system programs should not be used with the Application Compatibility tool. Click Next.

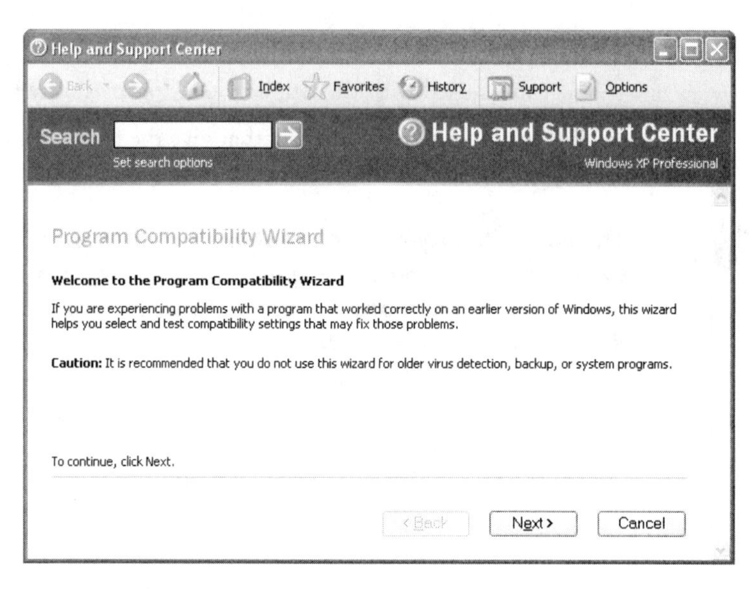

3. In the next window, you can select a radio button that allows you to choose from a list of programs or the program currently in your CD-ROM drive, or you can locate the program manually. Make a selection and click Next.
4. In the next window, shown in the following illustration, choose the operating system environment that you want Windows XP to emulate. Click Next.

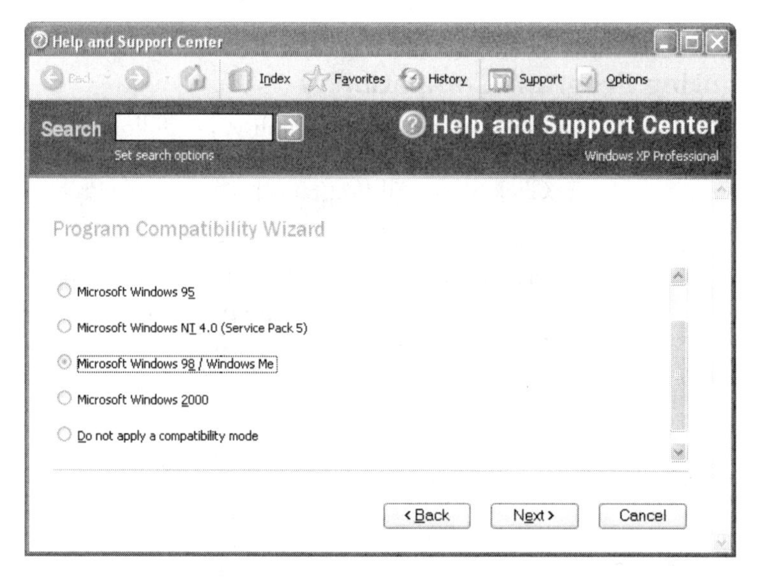

5. In the next window, you can choose to use 256 colors only, to use 640 × 480 resolution, or to disable visual themes. If any of these settings are necessary, select the desired ones and click Next.
6. In the next window, the settings will be tested with the application. Click Next.
7. Once the test is complete, answer whether or not the program appeared correctly; then click Next.
8. Data is collected. Click Finish.

Physical Disk Performance

For physical disk performance, you can monitor disk performance using Performance Monitor. You'll find a PhysicalDisk object and a number of potential counters. The following bullet list points out some of the major ones:

- **%Disk Read Time** The percentage of elapsed time that the disk was busy servicing read requests.
- **% Disk Write Time** The percentage of elapsed time that the disk was busy serving write requests.
- **% Disk Time** Shows both read and write time.
- **% Idle Time** The amount of time that the disk was idle during a sampling. A very low idle time may tell you that the disk cannot keep up with the demands being placed on it by the operating system.

In addition to using Performance Monitor to monitor hard disks, you should get in the habit of running a few tools that will correct problems and fragmentation—namely the Error Checking tool and Disk Defragmenter. The Error Checking tool, which is available on the Tools tab of the hard disk's properties sheets, gives you simple check box options to check for file system errors and recover bad sectors, as you can see in Figure 13-8.

FIGURE 13-8

The Error Checking tool

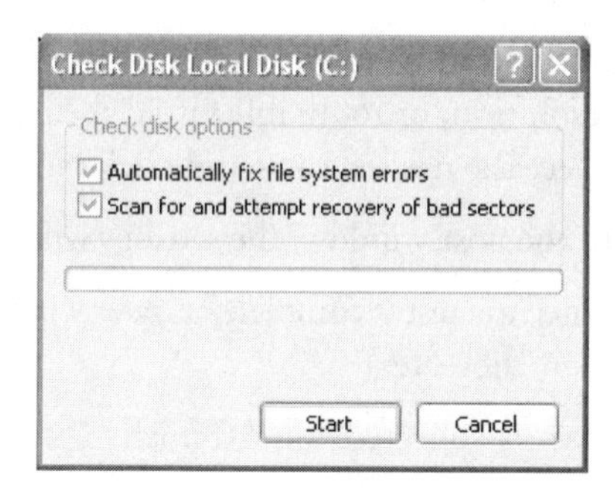

exam Watch

The Error Checking tool needs complete access to the disk in order for it to work. Applications must be closed, and in some cases Error Checking will ask you to reboot before it starts, in order to gain complete access to the disk.

The second tool is Disk Defragmenter, which is also available on the Tools tab of the disk's properties sheets. Fragmentation occurs over time in any file system. Windows XP attempts to store files in a contiguous format. However, as files are changed and resaved, the file system has to move data to different blocks of free space. The end result is that a typical file might have "pieces" scattered over the disk. When you open the file, the disk must work harder to retrieve all of the pieces and assemble them. When this happens, the disk is referred to as a "fragmented" disk. The Disk Defragmenter tool is used to defragment the drive and rearrange data so that is stored in a contiguous manner. Bear in mind that the defrag tool is not perfect, and the drive will not be completely defragmented after the utility is run. However, for very fragmented drives, you are likely to notice a performance improvement after Disk Defragmenter is run.

Exercise 13-5 walks you through the process of using Disk Defragmenter.

EXERCISE 13-5

CertCam 13-5

Using Disk Defragmenter

To defragment a drive, just follow these steps:

1. Open My Computer. Right-click the disk that you want to defragment and click Properties. On the Tools tab, click the Defragment Now button.

2. The Disk Defragmenter window appears, shown the in the following illustration. Click the Analyze button.

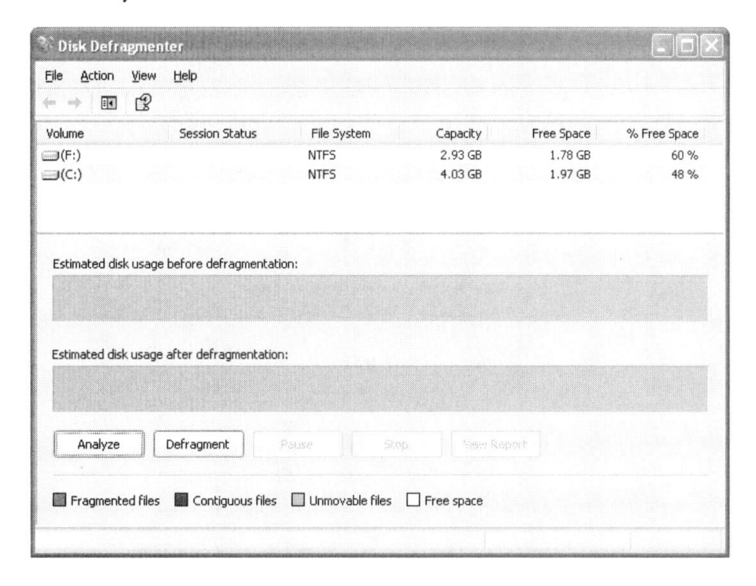

3. An analysis of the drive is performed, and a message appears telling you whether or not you should defragment the drive, as you can see in the following illustration:

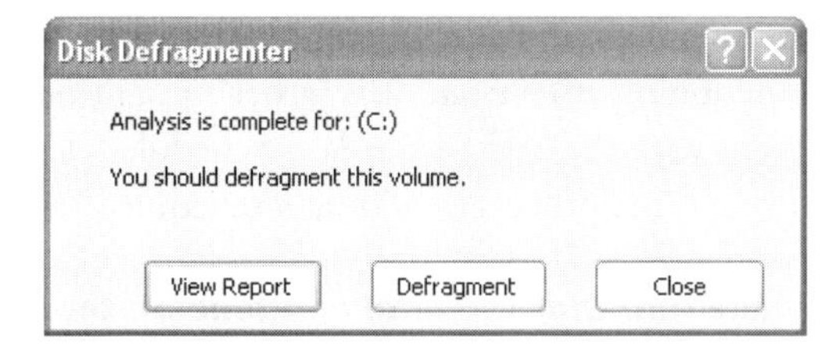

4. If the drive needs to be defragmented, click the Defragment button. The defragmentation process begins, as shown in the following illustration. It may take some time, depending on how badly the drive is fragmented, so defragmentation is best performed during off-peak hours Once the process is complete, you can view a report if you like.

Configure, Manage, and Troubleshoot Scheduled Tasks

The Scheduled Tasks feature gives you a way to schedule certain tools and utilities to run at certain times so you can automate the process of keeping Windows XP functioning at its peak. It is rather straightforward and easy to configure Scheduled Tasks with the help of the Add Scheduled Task Wizard. Exercise 13-6 walks you through the process of adding a scheduled task.

Make sure that the date and time on the computer's clock are accurate so that scheduled tasks will actually run when you want them to.

EXERCISE 13-6

Adding a Scheduled Task

To add a scheduled task, just follow these steps:

1. Click Start | All Programs | Accessories | System Tools | Scheduled Tasks.
2. In the Scheduled Tasks folder, double-click the Add Scheduled Task Wizard.

3. Click Next on the Welcome screen.
4. In the Scheduled Task window, select the task that you want to schedule, as shown in the following illustration. You can also browse for other programs if necessary. Click Next.

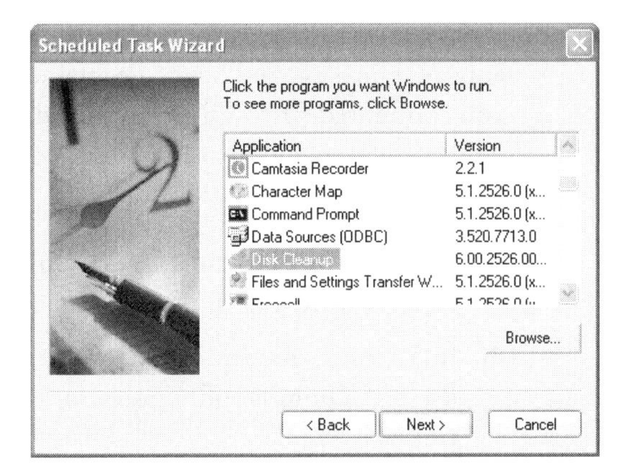

5. In the next window, give the task a name and choose when you want to run the program (such as daily, weekly, monthly, when you log on). Click Next.
6. Depending on your selection, an additional window may appear where you configure the time and day of the week, as shown in the following illustration. Make any necessary selections and click Next.

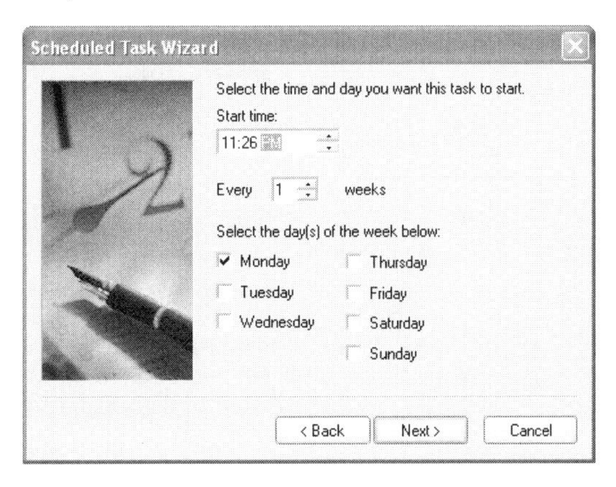

7. Your user name is listed in the next screen. Enter your password, if required for your account. Note that scheduled tasks are configured for a certain user—

multiple users on the same computer can have different scheduled tasks configured. Click Next.

8. Review your settings and click Finish. If you want to see advanced properties for the scheduled task, click the check box before clicking Finish.
9. If you chose to view Advanced properties, the properties pages for the task appear. The Task and Schedule tabs allow you to make changes to the values you configured when using the wizard. However, the Settings tab, shown in Figure 13-9, enables these additional configuration options:
   - "Delete the task if it is not scheduled to run again."
   - "Stop the task if it runs for *X* number of hours and *X* minutes." This is a safety feature that stops a task that is taking too long to complete.
   - Idle Time: you can choose to start the task only if the computer has been idle for *X* number of minutes, and you can stop the task if the computer ceases to be idle.
   - Power Management: you can choose not to start the task if the computer is running on batteries and to stop the task if the computer enters battery mode.

FIGURE 13-9

The Settings tab

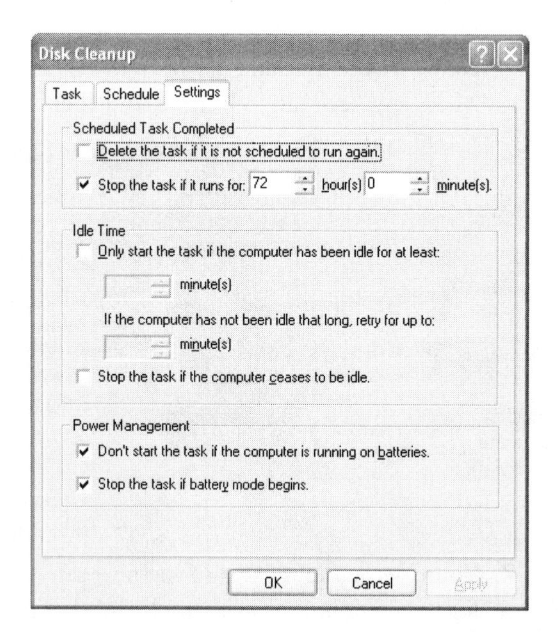

Once you create a scheduled task, it appears in the Scheduled Tasks folder. You can right-click the task and run it manually, delete it, or change the properties of the scheduled task.

exam Watch

Scheduled tasks run at the time they are configured to run, even if the user who created the scheduled task is not logged onto the computer. In such cases, the scheduled task runs, but is invisible to the currently logged on user.

If you are having problems with Scheduled Tasks, or if you want to suspend all Scheduled Tasks, you can easily do so in the Scheduled Tasks folder. Notice the Advanced menu. This menu contains the options to stop using scheduled tasks, pause scheduled tasks, and receive notification of missed tasks; you can also change the service account and view a log file.

SCENARIO & SOLUTION	
Does using Performance Monitor create a performance hit on a system?	Performance Monitor is a program, like any other kind of programs. The more programs you have running, the greater the drain on system resources. So, yes, running Performance Monitor itself contributes to system resource consumption, but the benefits are usually worth the performance hit.
On a system that barely meets the recommended hardware requirements, what can I do to increase performance?	Windows XP's new interface tends to be a resource hog. On a system that is barely limping along, I would access the Performance Options window and choose to adjust for best performance. This will cause you lose most of sleek interface appearance features, but you will not be wasting system processes on looks.
I want to use the Program Compatibility Wizard on a custom application. Will this work?	Maybe. The Program Compatibility Wizard uses common fixes for applications written for different environments. Depending on the custom application, the compatibility mode may enable the application to work without difficulty. However, there is no way to immediately tell without testing the application.
I have several scheduled tasks configured, but they seem to conflict with each other. What is the problem?	Some scheduled tasks, such as error checking and disk defragmentation, require complete access to the drive. Other utilities may interrupt the task, preventing it from running. As a general rule, schedule different tasks to run at different times.

CERTIFICATION OBJECTIVE 13.02

Manage, Monitor, and Optimize System Performance for Mobile Users

As corporate computer users have become more mobile, the importance of mobile optimization for laptop computers is increasing. In many networking environments, laptop computers are the desktop and mobile systems of choice, so it is important that laptop computers perform well both when connected to the network and when "on the road."

As an exam objective, system performance for mobile users primarily is concerned with hardware and power management. In terms of hardware, you may consider creating different hardware profiles for the laptop computer—one of which can be used when the computer is docked and one when the computer is not docked. This feature tells the laptop computer what hardware is available under docked or undocked conditions. See Chapter 5 to learn more about hardware profiles.

Beyond the hardware profile option, you should also keep a number of settings in mind for laptop computers. First, on the Performance Options window, Visual Effects tab, consider choosing the "Adjust for best performance" setting option. Doing this will remove a lot of Windows XP's graphical features, but will help conserve power. On the Advanced tab, be sure that Programs is selected for Processor and Memory usage.

Aside from these basic settings, you should take a look at power settings in order to make the best use of battery power when the laptop computer is running off batteries. In Control Panel, open Power Options. You'll see the Power Options properties sheets, shown in Figure 13-10.

On the Power Schemes tab, you can choose a power scheme that is appropriate for the laptop computer, such as the Portable/Laptop option. By default, this option turns off the monitor after 15 minutes and the hard disks after 30 minutes, but you can also adjust these settings to create your own specific scheme. If you have enabled hibernation, you'll also see a hibernation scheme option here as well, which is to hibernate after three hours of inactivity by default.

The hibernation feature that Windows XP supports enables the computer to write current memory data to the hard disk and then effectively shut down. When you reboot the computer, the data stored on the disk is loaded back into memory so that

FIGURE 13-10

The Power Options Properties sheets

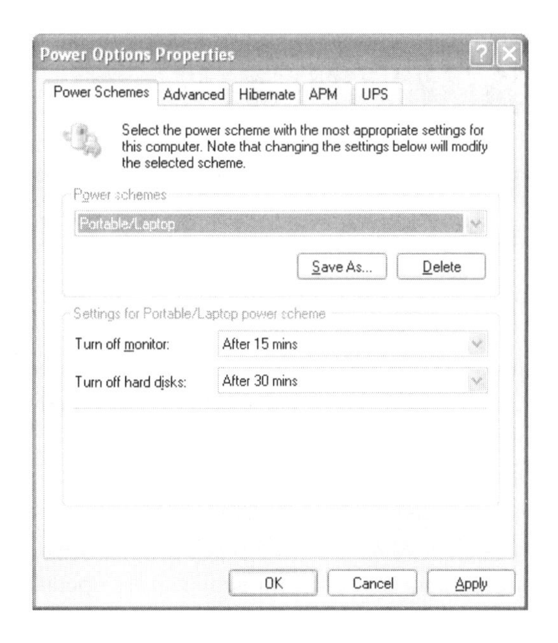

your computer appears just as you left it. This is a great energy saving feature. You can enable hibernation by clicking the check box option on the Hibernate tab.

A number of additional features also affect performance in situations where users move from computer to computer, such as profiles and Group Policy settings. You can learn more about these features in Chapters 4 and 9.

SCENARIO & SOLUTION

Can I use performance monitor on a laptop?	Yes. Performance Monitor works on a laptop computer just as it does on a desktop system.
What are the most important aspects of performance with a laptop?	Just as with a desktop system, your laptop must have enough physical RAM and processor speed in order to meet the demands placed on it. Beyond these requirements, you should make sure your laptop is configured to make the most of battery power when not connected to a power source.

CERTIFICATION OBJECTIVE 13.03

Restore and Back Up the Operating System, System State Data, and User Data

Windows XP Professional supports the same backup and restore features that were first introduced in Windows 2000 Professional. As you can read about in almost any technical book, the importance of an effective backup plan cannot be overstated. By effectively backing up data and following an effective backup plan, you can recover a failed operating system without any data loss.

For the exam, it is important to understand the different kinds of backup and restore features that are available and how to back up and restore data on a computer running Windows XP Professional. The following sections explore the issues and skills you need concerning backup and restore operations.

Types of Backup

Windows XP Professional supports several different types of backups, all of which can be performed on NTFS and FAT drives. You should be familiar with these types of backup for both the exam and the real world.

- **Normal** A normal backup backs up all selected files and marks them as having been backed up. All files you select are backed up, regardless of their previous backed up state. This type of backup is also known as a "full backup" and is the type of backup you initially use to back up data.
- **Incremental** An incremental backup backs up all selected files that have changed since the last backup. Commonly, a normal backup is performed, followed by several incremental backups, which only back up the changes. This backup strategy reduces overall backup time and storage space.
- **Differential** A differential backup is the same as an incremental backup, but the files backed up are not marked as having been backed up. The result is that a differential backup may re-back up files that have not changed because they are not being marked. The difference between an incremental backup and a differential backup is in recovery time. A differential backup

takes longer than an incremental backup, but in the event of a failure, you only need run the normal backup job for recovery with the differential backup. If you were using an incremental backup job, you have to recover the normal backup and every incremental backup that was created since the last normal backup.

on the Job

Incremental and differential backups can be confusing, but they are really about* time. *Incremental backups are faster, but it takes more time to fully restore data in the event of a failure, because you may have to run several different incremental backup jobs. Differential backups are slower to create, but faster when recovery is needed, because you only have to run the single differential backup, along with the normal backup. So, it is simply a time tradeoff. You can make backups faster, but recovery slower, or you can make recovery faster and backups slower—it's just a matter of choice.

- **Copy** A copy backup backs up selected files without marking them as having been backed up. This option is useful when you want to back up certain files in between normal and incremental backups without altering the incremental backup jobs.
- **Daily** This backup backs up all selected files that have changed during the day without marking them as having been backed up.

Creating a Backup Job

When you are ready to back up data, you can do so easily with Windows XP Professional's Backup Wizard. Exercise 13-7 walks you through the process of creating a backup job.

EXERCISE 13-7

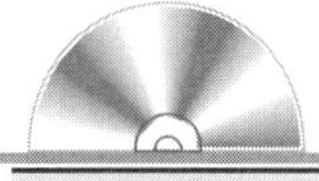

CertCam 13-7

Creating a Backup Job

To create a backup job, just follow these steps:

1. Click Start | All Programs | Accessories | System Tools | Backup.
2. The Backup and Restore Wizard appears. Click Next on the Welcome screen.

3. In the Backup Or Restore window, choose the "Back up files and settings" radio button and click Next.
4. In the What To Backup window, shown in the following illustration, you can choose a category to back up, or you can choose the custom option. Make a selection and click Next.

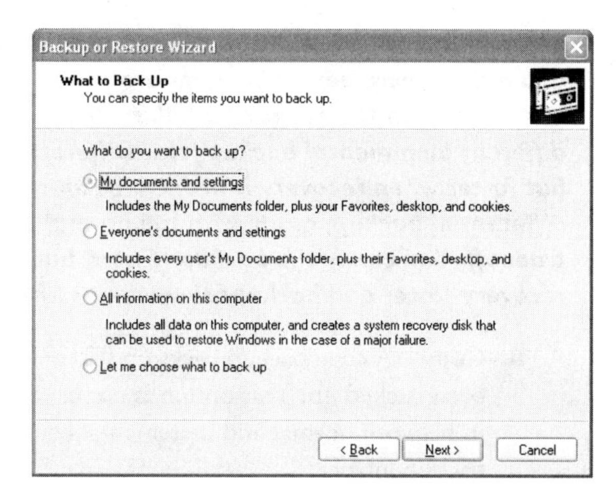

5. If you choose what to back up, the Items To Backup window appears, shown in the following illustration. In this Explorer-based window, browse in the left pane and select the files that you want to back up in the right pane. Click Next.

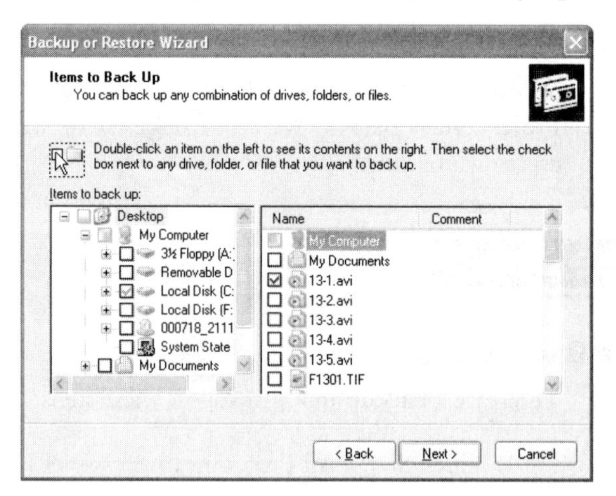

6. In the Backup Type, Destination, and Name window, choose a backup location and give the backup job a name. Click Next.
7. In the Completion window, click the Advanced button instead of clicking Finish.
8. In the Type Of Backup window, use the drop-down menu and choose Normal, Incremental, Differential, Copy, or Daily backup.
9. In the How To Backup window, you can choose to "Verify data after backup," "Use hardware compression" (if available), and "Disable volume shadow copy" (which allows a backup to occur, even if the file is currently being written to). Click Next.
10. In the Backup Options window, shown in the following illustration, you can choose to append this backup job to an existing backup job or replace an older backup job. Also note that you can allow only the owner and administrator to have access to the backup (if you are overwriting an older job). Make your selection and click Next.

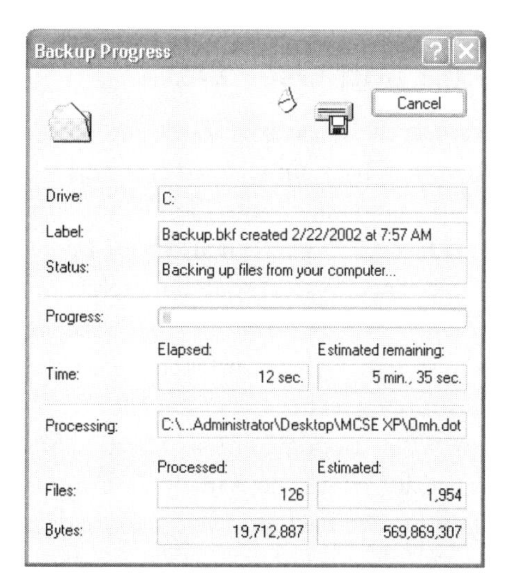

11. In the When To Backup window, you can choose to run the backup job now or at a scheduled time. Make any desired selections and click Next.
12. Click Finish. The backup job completes, as shown in the following illustration. Click Close when the job is complete.

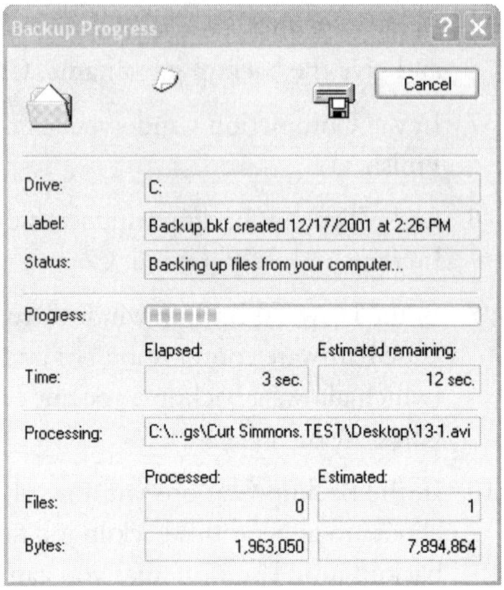

System State Data and User Data

As you see in the Backup Wizard, you have options to back up everything on your computer or to back up selected files and folders. In the event that you simply want to back up user data, choose the Documents and settings option in the wizard (or Custom). However, you can also back up everything on the computer, including system state data. System state data refers to a collection of operating system data, which includes the registry, COM+ Class registrations, system boot files, and related operating system data. In order to back up specific user data or System State Data, you can simply select the "Let me choose what to back up" option in the wizard and then choose the user data or select System State data. However, you may find it easier to make the desired selections manually instead of using the Backup Wizard. Exercise 13-8 shows you how to back up System State data without using the Backup Wizard.

exam Watch

Just as a point of reference, Windows 2000 Server domain controllers also hold the Active Directory database in System State data—but this, of course, does not apply to Windows XP Professional.

EXERCISE 13-8

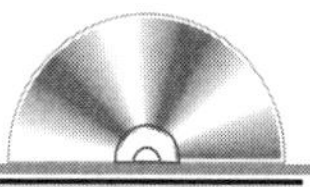

Manually Creating a Backup Job

To manually create a backup job, just follow these steps:

1. Click Start | All Programs | Accessories | System Tools | Backup.
2. In the Backup Utility, click the Backup tab, shown in the following illustration. In the left pane, select the System State check box. Notice the backup destination and backup media/file name at the bottom of the window. You can change these values if desired. Click the Start Backup button.

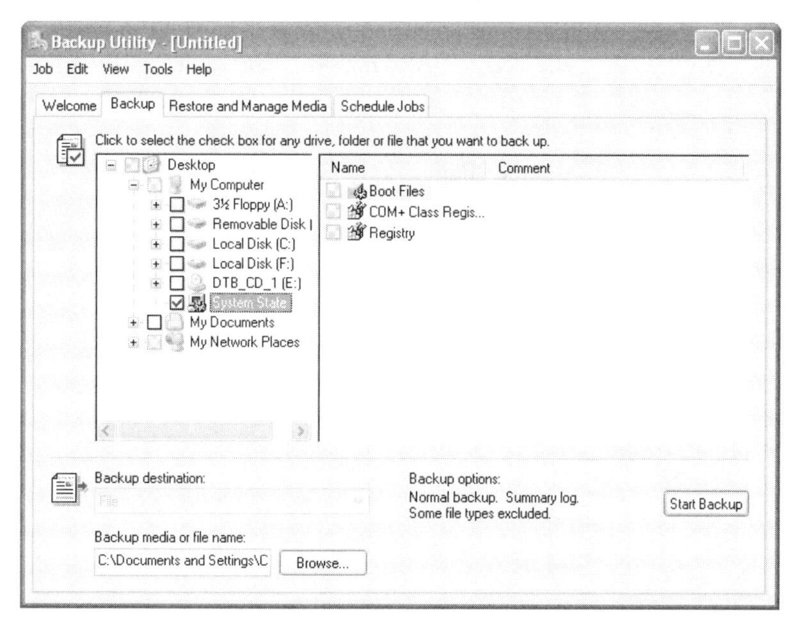

3. In the Backup Job Information window, you'll see a place to enter a backup description and options to append to or replace former backup jobs, as shown in the following illustration. Make any desired changes.

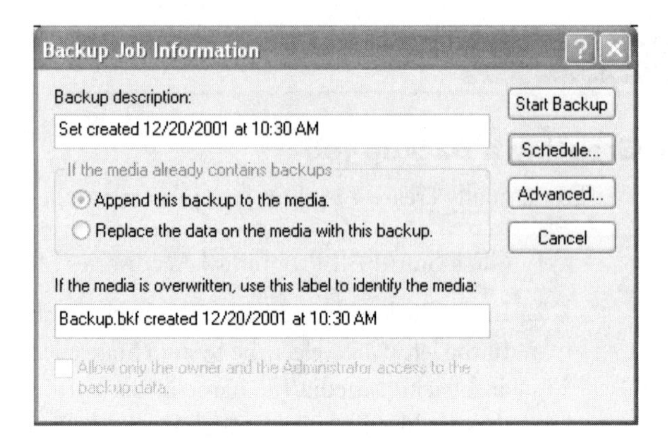

4. If you click the Schedule button, you can create a schedule when the backup should start. Also note that you can click the Advanced button and choose the Advanced backup options you saw when using the wizard, such as Verify data after backup and Backup Type, shown in thc following illustration. Make any desired changes and click OK.

5. Click the Start Backup button to begin the backup job.

Although the Backup Wizard can be really helpful, you'll probably want to manually select the items you want to back up and simply start the backup manually from the Backup tab once you are familiar with the process. You can manually select the backup settings and files and more quickly start the backup process this way.

Restoring Data

In the event of failure involving user data, system state data, or the complete operating system, you can use the backup jobs that you have created to restore the data to the computer. In the event of a disk failure or operating system failure, you can reinstall Windows XP and then use your backup jobs to restore the data or the complete operating system that has been saved in your backup jobs. As with backing up data, you can also restore data with the help of a wizard.

When you restore data, you choose the backup file that you want to restore using the Restore Wizard (or you can simply use the Restore and Manage Media tab on the Backup utility), shown in Figure 13-11. You can choose to restore the data to its original location or you can choose a different location.

FIGURE 13-11

The What To Restore window

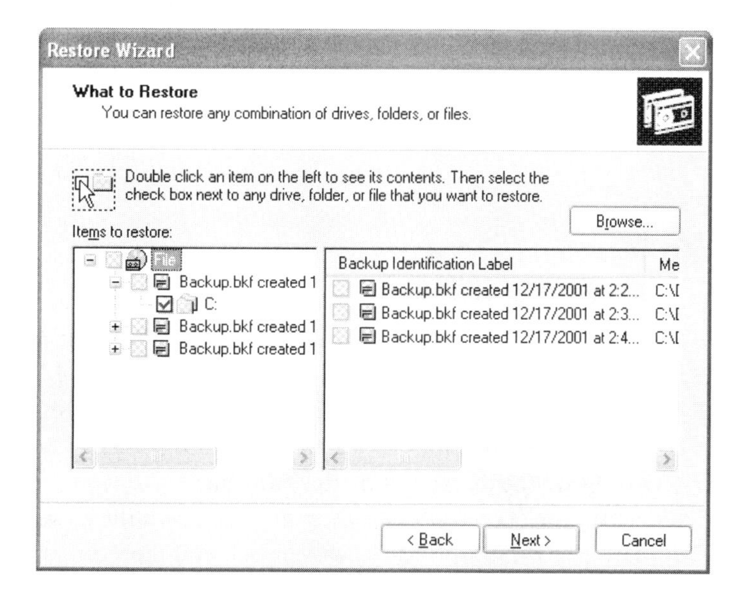

FROM THE CLASSROOM

Backup and Recovery

Backup files are always a tradeoff in terms of time and storage space. After all, backup jobs require time to run and storage space so that they can be effectively retained for use—if the need should ever arrive. From an administrator's point of view, backup can be an aggravating process that takes up time—yet a necessary one that can save your neck in the event of a system failure. This is particularly true when managing servers.

I usually refer to backups the same way I do to antivirus software: they both something you can easily forget about until a disaster occurs—then you wish you had kept the data or antivirus application current! The truth is that backups are a very important part of computer systems administration. The backup plan ensures that data can be recovered in the event of a system failure, which happens more often than you might think.

The backing up and storage of user data is rather easy and should be regularly scheduled. In network environments, backup files can be saved to a network server, which can also back up all of the client backup jobs. Regardless of the process you choose to take, the overall goal is to have important data readily available in the event of loss or failure. As with many administrative issues, there are several different ways to meet your goal, and the backup media and types of backups you choose to use depend on the needs of your company and the importance of the data.

Using Safe Mode

Safe Mode enables you to boot Windows XP with a minimal number of drivers and basic VGA interface. In short, it is useful when you are having problems getting Windows XP to start normally. Once booted into Safe Mode, you can then begin troubleshooting the system and resolving problems. In many cases, an incorrect video driver will keep Windows XP from booting normally, and Safe Mode can be used to remove the driver and fix the problem.

You can access Safe Mode by holding down the F8 key on the keyboard during startup. The Startup Menu will appear, and then you choose from a few different startup options, which are as follows:

- **Safe Mode** The normal Safe Mode option, in which a minimal number of drivers are loaded
- **Safe Mode With Networking** Boots into Safe Mode, but loads networking services and protocols so that you can access information on the network
- **Safe Mode With Command Prompt** Provides Safe Mode with Command Prompt access so that you can run command line utilities
- **Enable Boot Logging** Creates a log file of the boot process that can be used for troubleshooting
- **Enable VGA Mode** Uses a basic VGA driver and is good when an incompatible video card has caused the system to fail
- **Last Known Good Configuration** Loads the most recent settings that worked
- **Debugging Mode** Attempts to debug the boot process

Although the exam is not likely to ask you specific questions about Safe Mode, you may encounter scenarios in which Safe Mode is used or should be used. You should spend some time getting used to Safe Mode and the different startup options available to you.

If you choose to boot into Safe Mode, the Windows XP Help and Support center appears in order to help you solve problems. You'll also see the option to use System Restore (which is available outside of Safe Mode by clicking Start | All Programs | Accessories | System Tools | System Restore). System Restore, which was first introduced in Windows Me, creates restore points on the computer. The restore points are essentially a snapshot of the computer's configuration. In the event that something happens, you can use System Restore to restore the computer to an earlier time when the computer was working. System Restore restores system files and may remove recently installed applications; however, it does not remove user data files, documents, e-mail, IE history or favorites, or other user-generated data.

on the job

Although Windows XP creates its own restore points periodically, you can also manually create them. This is a good idea if you are about to try a new configuration. You can create a restore point when the system is working well, and then use that restore point in the event that your new configuration changes are not good. This feature allows Windows XP to solve the problems for you, instead of you having to manually solve them yourself.

System Restore is an easy tool to use. Exercise 13-9 walks you through a System Restore process.

EXERCISE 13-9

Using System Restore

To use System Restore, just follow these steps:

1. Click Start | All Programs | Accessories | System Tools | System Restore.
2. In the Welcome to System Restore window, shown in the following illustration, you can choose to restore your computer to an earlier time or manually create a restore point. Choose the "Restore my computer" radio button and click Next.

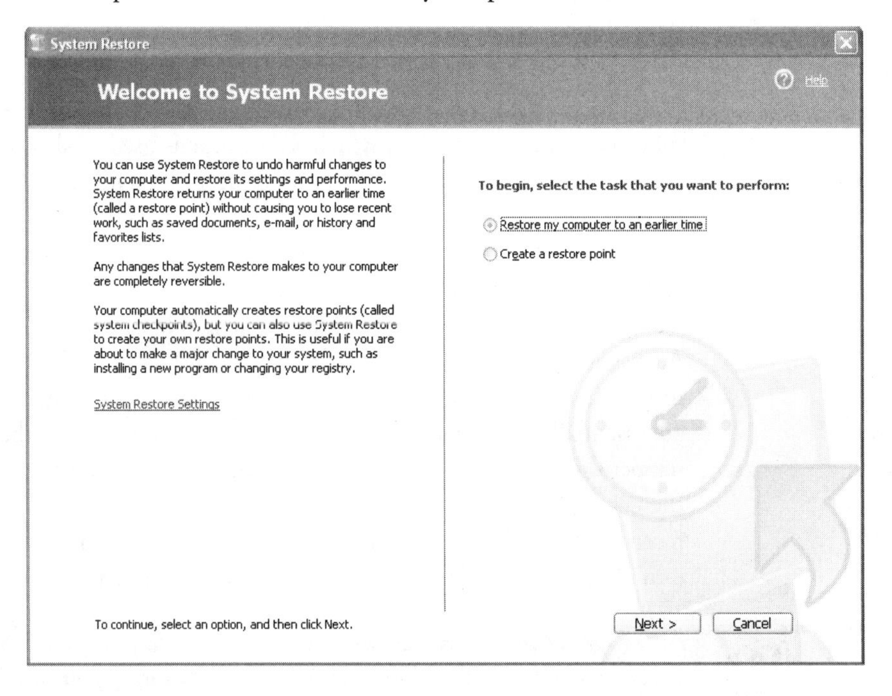

3. In the calendar interface that appears, as shown in the following illustration, select a date on the calendar and a restore point from that date that you want to use. Typically, you should use the most recent restore point, unless you have specific reasons to move further back to an earlier restore point.

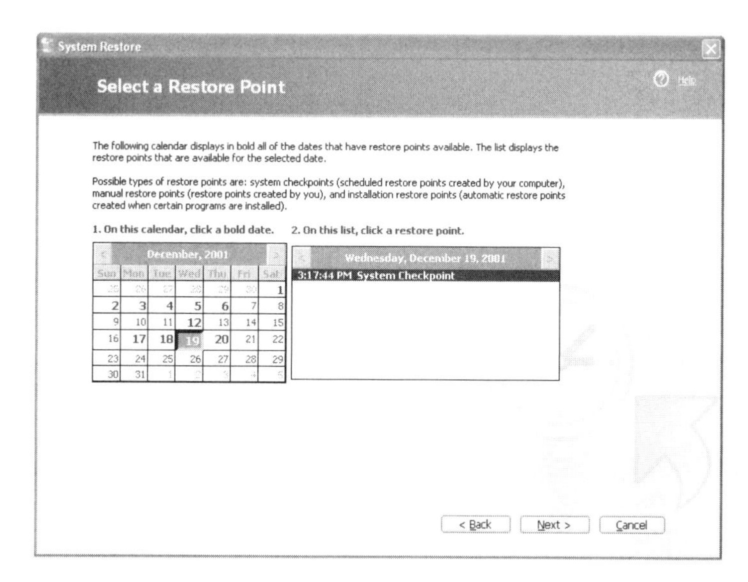

4. The next window tells you to close any currently open programs. Do so, and then click Next.
5. System Restore will configure your system and the computer will reboot.

---

on the Job

System Restore is a great tool and is probably the easiest way to correct user problems or incorrect user configurations. It is fast and easy and saves IT troubleshooting/help desk ticket time.

SCENARIO & SOLUTION	
Will System Restore correct faulty application problems?	If you install an application that is causing the system problems, System Restore will most likely uninstall the application—this should allow the system to boot normally.
Do users need to be worried about backup when using System Restore?	Like any computer process, System Restore is not foolproof. Problems can occur, and there is always the potential for data loss. For this reason, there is no exception for an effective backup plan that protects system and user data.

Recovery Console

The Recovery Console, first introduced in Windows 2000 Professional, is a command line tool that you can use to repair Windows XP Professional when it will not start. With the Recovery Console, you can access volumes on your hard disks, start and stop services, access files and folders, repair the master boot record, repair Windows XP Professional, and even format drives. As such, the Recovery Console is a powerful tool and one that should be used with care—but one that that can certainly get you out of a jam when you are experiencing problems starting Windows XP Professional.

The Recovery Console requires an administrator's password in order to use it. This prevents users who are not authorized from poking around with the tool. As such, the Recovery console is not installed with Windows XP Professional by default, but it is available on the Windows XP Professional installation CD-ROM. To install the Recovery console, just type ***D*:\i386\winnt32.exe /cmdcons** at the run line or command prompt, where *D* is the letter of your CD-ROM drive. The Recovery Console requires about 7MB of disk space, and once the installation is complete, you will need to reboot your computer. When you reboot, you can select the Recovery Console option on the operating system selection menu. If you choose the option, you'll be prompted to choose a Windows XP installation (usually 1) and enter your administrator password. At this point, you are ready to begin using the Recovery Console.

From an exam point of view, you may see direct questions about Recovery Console commands. More than likely, you'll see issues where a problem exists and an attempted recovery is made using the Recovery Console. Therefore, you'll need to have a good understanding of the commands that are available to you. Table 13-1 outlines these for you.

exam Watch

As with all exam objectives, there is no replacement for hands on experience with the Recovery Console. Spend some time using it before taking the exam!

TABLE 13-1 Recovery Console Commands

Command	Explanation
attrib	Sets file attributes
batch	Runs commands in a text file
CD/chdir	Changes directories
chkdsk	Checks and repairs volumes
cls	Clears screen
copy	Copies files from one location to the next
del/delete	Deletes a file or folder
dir	Displays a directory
disable	Stops a service or driver
diskpart	Adds or deletes partitions
enable	Enables a service or driver
exit	Exits from the Recovery Console
expand	Expands a CAB or compressed file/folder
fixboot	Enables you to fix or rewrite the boot sector of a hard disk
fixmbr	Allows you to fix the master boot record of a startup disk
format	Allows you to format a disk volume
help	Displays Recovery Console Help files
listsvc	Displays a list of services and drivers
logon	Allows you to log on to different installations of Windows XP/2000/NT
map	Displays a list of information about drivers on the hard disk
md/mkdir	Creates a directory
more/type	Displays a text file on the screen
rd/rdmdir	Deletes a directory
ren/rename	Renames a file or directory
set	Displays and sets Recovery Console values
systemroot	Changes to the Systemroot directory

SCENARIO & SOLUTION	
What kind of backup plan do most environments use?	Backup plans vary from environment to environment, but in most cases, a normal backup is run at least once a week, and then incremental and/or differential backups are used on other days. The idea is to have duplicate information with the least amount of administrative effort and least consumption of storage space.
Specifically, when should the Recovery console be used?	The Recovery console is a powerful tool; however, it is always best to try less intrusive methods first. Try Safe Mode and System Restore before delving into the Recovery Console.

CERTIFICATION SUMMARY

Windows XP gives you the tools you need to effectively monitor and optimize the operating system. Performance Monitor is an effective tool that can give you baseline data, which you can then use in the event that performance problems occur. Baseline data helps you determine what system objects/components are causing performance bottlenecks, so that you can then solve those problems. Performance Monitor allows you to view information in a chart, histogram, or report format, and you can even log data and configure alerts.

Windows XP also gives you a Performance Options window, found in System Properties, that allows you to adjust the performance of the Windows XP desktop. The visual impact of Windows XP can be a problem on systems with lower memory and processor speeds, and this tab enables you to make changes so that the visual effects and the drain on system resources are reduced.

Also, you can configure the system to optimize applications or system processes, and you can manually configure virtually memory (although manual configuration is not recommended). These settings also apply to mobile computers as well.

Next, Windows XP provides you with a backup utility so that user and system state data can be protected in the event of a catastrophic failure. Along with Safe Mode and the Recovery Console, the Windows XP backup utility makes system data recovery and boot failure recovery easier than in previous versions of Windows.

TWO-MINUTE DRILL

Monitor, Optimize, and Troubleshoot Performance of the Windows XP Professional Desktop

- ❑ Windows XP includes the Performance utility, which enables you to view real-time data about the performance of various system components and hardware.
- ❑ The Performance utility enables you to view data in chart, graph, or histogram formats.
- ❑ Performance uses objects to represent system components, such as memory and processor, and counters to monitor objects in order to gain an understanding of their performance.
- ❑ Performance baselines can help establish "normal" performance operation so that problematic components can be identified.
- ❑ Log files can be configured to sample data at desired intervals in order to gain a look at performance over a period of time.
- ❑ Performance alerts can be configured so that you can be alerted to performance events that occur in real time.
- ❑ For Windows XP's visual effects, on the Visual Effects tab of the Advanced tab of System Properties you can configure the system to optimize for visual effects or performance or you can choose a custom plan.
- ❑ On the Advanced tab of Performance Options, you can configure the system for program optimization or background services/system cache optimization for the processor and memory.
- ❑ You can configure Windows XP's virtual memory settings manually, or you can allow the operating system to manage the settings, which is the preferred method.
- ❑ You can manage application and system process performance using Task Manager.

- Applications that may not be compatible with Windows XP can use the Program Application Compatibility Wizard in to function with Windows XP.
- In order to make certain that hard disks are performing at their peak, periodically run the Error Checking tool to fix file system errors and use the Disk Defragmenter tool to defragment drives.
- Scheduled Tasks can be configured with the New Task Wizard, found in the Scheduled Tasks folder. Scheduled tasks may conflict with each other, so care should taken with schedules.

Manage, Monitor, and Optimize System Performance for Mobile Users

- For mobile computers and users, use Performance Monitor and the Performance Options settings in order to meet RAM and CPU usage needs.
- Use hardware profiles and configure power settings to make the best use of battery power.

Restore and Back Up the Operating System, System State Data, and User Data

- Windows XP supports normal, incremental, differential, copy, and daily backups.
- The backup utility can help you configure backup jobs that can be scheduled for later times.
- You can use the backup utility to back up everything on a computer or just selected user data. You can also back up System State data, which contains the registry, COM + Component Registration, and boot files.
- In order to restore data, use the Backup Wizard and run the Restore option. You can restore data to its original location or choose a different storage location.

- ❑ Safe Mode provides a way to boot Windows XP when it will not boot otherwise. Safe Mode boot options include Safe Mode, Safe Mode With Networking, Safe Mode With Command Prompt, Boot Logging, VGA Mode, Last Known Good Configuration, and Debugging Mode.
- ❑ You can use System Restore in order to return a Windows XP system to an earlier time when the system was functioning normally.
- ❑ Windows XP Professional provides the Recovery Console, a command line tool that can be used to fix Windows XP when it will not start normally.

SELF TEST

The following questions will help you measure your understanding of the material presented in this chapter. Read all of the choices carefully, as there may be more than one correct answer. Choose all correct answers for each question.

Monitor, Optimize, and Troubleshoot Performance of the Windows XPDesktop

1. What three viewing formats are supported by Performance Monitor?

   A. Chart

   B. Report

   C. Spreadsheet

   D. Histogram

2. What should you first establish in order to find object bottlenecks?

   A. A counter

   B. A baseline

   C. An object

   D. A growth plan

3. Which of the following statements are true concerning objects and counters?

   A. Counters are used to monitor objects.

   B. Objects are used to monitor counters.

   C. Multiple objects are used to determine a counter baseline.

   D. Each object has one counter.

4. Consider the following illustration:

Which of the following statements are *most* true concerning this window?

A. The PhysicalDisk object is monitored with all counters.

B. The PhysicalDisk object is monitored with all counters and all instances.

C. The PhysicalDisk object is monitored with the % Disk Time counter.

D. The PhysicalDisk object is monitored with the % Disk Time counter and Instances 0 and 1.

5. Which of the following options are not valid Performance Monitor alert actions?

A. Log an entry in the Application Event Log.

B. Run a program.

C. Shut down the computer.

D. Send a network message.

6. Consider the following illustration:

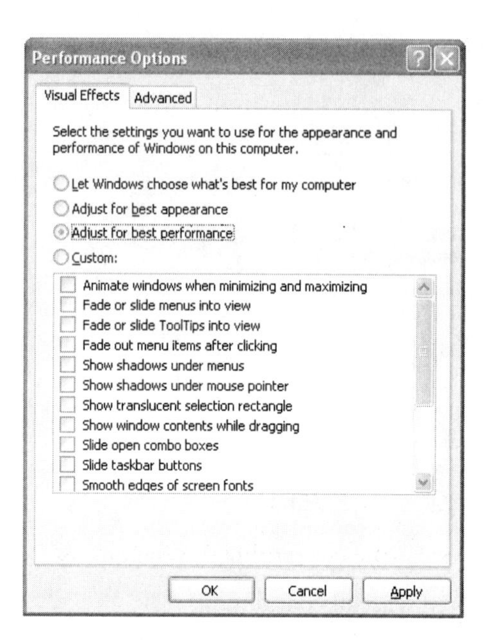

Which statements are true?

A. Performance settings take precedence over appearance settings.

B. Appearance settings take precedence over performance settings.

C. All XP visual effects are used.

D. Minimal to no XP visual effects are used.

7. Consider the following illustration:

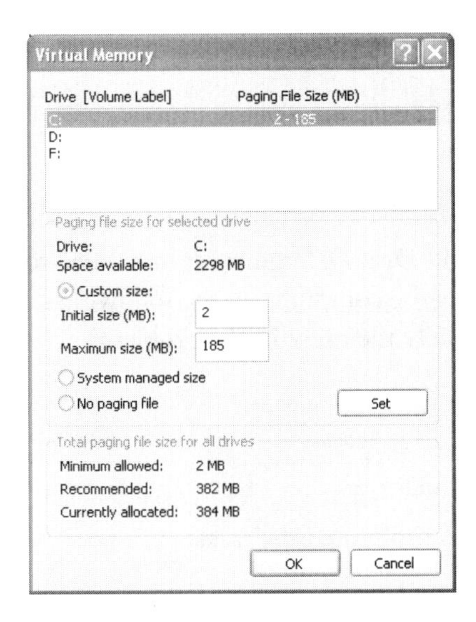

The user reports that the system is running very slowly. What needs to be changed on this tab?

A. The initial size needs to be changed to 4.

B. The maximum size needs to be changed to 78.

C. The System Managed Size needs to be selected.

D. The No Paging File needs to be selected.

8. What is the best tool or action to use when an application stops responding?

A. Application Compatibility.

B. Task Manager.

C. Restart the computer.

D. Group Policy.

9. Which database files are used for application compatibility?

A. MigDB.inf

B. NTCompat.inf

C. AppHelp.sdb

D. SysMain.sdb

10. A user complains that her computer has started slowing down. Simple tasks such as opening files seem to take longer than normal. What is the first thing you should do?

A. Run Error Checking.
B. Run Disk Defragmenter.
C. Create a performance baseline.
D. Format the drive with NTFS.

11. A user has Error Checking and Disk Defragmenter scheduled to run at 2:00 A.M. once a month. When the user checks the computer on the following day, he discovers that neither task has run. What is most likely the cause of the problem?

A. The computer was shut down.
B. The tasks need exclusive drive access.
C. The user was not logged on.
D. Group Policy security has prohibited the tasks.

Manage, Monitor, and Optimize System Performance for Mobile Users

12. A user travels with a laptop computer that was recently upgraded to Windows XP. The user is complaining that the system runs slowly. You verify that the minimum hardware requirements have been met, but the computer does not have extensive system resources. What is an easy configuration option that can help free up RAM and processor cycles?

A. Run Disk Defragmenter.
B. Create a baseline.
C. Change the paging file settings.
D. Choose the performance option on the Visual Effects tab of Performance Options.

13. What Windows XP feature can automatically turn a computer off after a specified period of inactivity and return it to its previous state upon reboot?

A. Sleep.
B. Hibernation.
C. Standby.
D. There is no such option in Windows XP.

Restore and Back Up the Operating System, System State Data, and User Data

14. Which answer option is not a part of System State data?

A. Registry
B. User Profile
C. Boot Files
D. COM + Registration

15. Which backup type(s) mark selected files as having been backed up?

A. Normal
B. Differential
C. Full
D. Incremental

16. Which backup type(s) do not mark selected files as having been backed up?

A. Normal
B. Differential
C. Copy
D. Daily

17. On a computer running Windows XP, a disk failure occurs on Thursday. You ran a full backup on Monday and incremental backups on Tuesday and Wednesday. You replace the disk and run restore using the full backup and Wednesday's incremental backup. However, the data is incomplete when the restore completes. What is wrong?

A. You needed a differential backup.
B. The old full backup overwrote the incremental backup.
C. You need to run each incremental backup in the restore process.
D. You needed a daily backup.

18. Which Safe Mode option will load the most recent settings that worked?

A. Safe Mode With Networking
B. VGA Mode
C. Last Known Good
D. Debugging Mode

19. You install a new video driver on a computer that prevents Windows XP from booting normally. Which Safe Mode option should you use so that you can change the driver?

A. Safe Mode With Networking

B. VGA Mode

C. Last Known Good

D. Debugging Mode

20. You are about to install a custom application on Windows XP Professional. You are unsure of the results of your actions. What two actions should you take before installing the new application?

A. Run a backup.

B. Create a recovery GPO.

C. Shut down optional services.

D. Create a restore point.

21. You want to install the Recovery Console on a Windows XP Professional computer. You have the Windows XP Professional CD-ROM inserted in the computer's CD-ROM drive, which is drive D. Which command will install the Recovery Console?

A. D:\i386\cmdcons

B. D:\i386\winnt32.exe /cmdcons

C. D:\winnt32.exe / cmdcons

D. D:\winnt32.exe\i386\cmdcons

22. Using the Recovery Console, you want to delete a partition on the hard drive. Which command will enable you to perform this action?

A. dir

B. chkdsk

C. diskpart

D. fixboot

23. Using the Recovery Console, you want to see a listing of drivers. What command can you use?

A. dir

B. batch

C. attrib

D. listsvc

LAB QUESTION

A company has engaged you as a consultant to configure a backup plan for a computer running Windows XP Professional that holds critical company data. A tape drive has been configured and installed on the computer. The company has the following requirements:

- One full backup must be performed each week.
- Data should be recoverable each day. In other words, changes made yesterday should be recoverable tomorrow in the event of a failure.
- Backup jobs should be verified after completion.
- Shadow copy backup should be used.
- Restore should be as fast as possible in the event of a failure.

How would you configure these options?

SELF TEST ANSWERS

Monitor, Optimize, and Troubleshoot Performance of the Windows XP Desktop

1. ☑ A, B, and D are correct. You can view data in a chart, histogram, or report format.
   ☒ C is incorrect. There is no "spreadsheet" format.

2. ☑ B is correct. First, establish a baseline in order to determine what objects are not performing within the baseline range. Doing this will help you identify bottlenecks.
   ☒ A, C, and D are incorrect. Objects and counters are used to monitor system components, but they do not establish a baseline for you. A "growth plan" is not relevant here.

3. ☑ A is correct. A performance object typically contains multiple counters that you use to monitor the performance of the object.
   ☒ B, C, and D are incorrect. You do not monitor counters with objects and objects can have more than one counter.

4. ☑ D is correct. In this example, the PhysicalDisk object is being monitored with the % Disk Time counter. Instances 0 and 1 are both being monitored.
   ☒ A, B, and C are incorrect. These answer options are not the *most* true concerning the object and counter configuration.

5. ☑ C is correct. A Performance Monitor alert can log an entry to the Application Event log or start a Performance data log, send a network message, or run a program. There is a not a direct option to shut down the computer.
   ☒ A, B, and D are incorrect. These are all valid alert actions.

6. ☑ A and D are correct. When the Visual Effects tab is set to adjust for best performance, performance is favored over visual effects. Under this setting, most if not all of XP's visual effects are not used.
   ☒ B and C are incorrect. Visual Effects are not favored under this configuration.

7. ☑ C is correct. The paging file configuration is too small in the illustration. The best choice is to allow Windows to handle the paging file size.
   ☒ A, B, and D are incorrect. The sizes are still too small in A and B, and D is incorrect because there is no reason not to use a paging file here.

8. ☑ B is correct. Use Task Manager to end an application that has stopped responding.
   ☒ A, C, and D are incorrect. Although you can end an application by restarting the computer, this is not the best choice. You cannot end an application with the Application Compatibility Wizard or Group Policy.

9. ☑ A, B, C, and D are correct. All of these files are used by application compatibility in Windows XP.
☒ No answers are incorrect.

10. ☑ B is correct. If a computer has become slower, and opening files occurs more slowly, your first line of defense is Disk Defragmenter, since fragmentation tends to slow computer systems down.
☒ A, C, and D are incorrect. Error Checking will not resolve this kind of performance problem, so A is incorrect. C is incorrect because it is too late to create a baseline once there are already performance problems. D is also incorrect, since formatting the drive with NTFS will destroy all of the data.

11. ☑ B is correct. Disk Defragmenter and Error Checking each require exclusive access to the drive. Since they were configured to run at the same time, they both would stop functioning.
☒ A, C, and D are incorrect. There is no indication that the computer was shut down, so A is incorrect. C is incorrect because the user does not have to be logged on for the tasks to run. D is incorrect because Group Policy restrictions are unlikely here. *Remember to take questions at face value and do not assume that additional configurations, such as Group Policy, have been made.*

Manage, Monitor, and Optimize System Performance for Mobile Users

12. ☑ D is correct. For laptop computers barely meeting the hardware requirements, configure the Visual Effects tab so that performance is selected over appearance.
☒ A, B, and C are incorrect. None of these options will improve system performance in this case.

13. ☑ B is correct. Hibernation is a feature that will write the information in memory to the hard disk and shut down automatically. When the computer is rebooted, the information is read back into memory.
☒ A, C, and D are incorrect. None of these options are correct.

Restore and Back Up the Operating System, System State Data, and User Data

14. ☑ B is correct. User Profiles are not a part of System State data.
☒ A, C, and D are incorrect. These options are all part of System State data.

15. ☑ A and D are correct. Both incremental and normal backups mark selected files as having been backed up.
☒ B and C are correct. These backup types do not back up selected files marked as backed up.

16. ☑ B, C, and D are correct. Differential, copy, and daily backups all back up selected files without having marking them as backed up.
☒ A is incorrect. A full backup backs up all files on the computer and marks them as having been backed up.

17. ☑ C is correct. If incremental backups are used, you have to run each incremental backup in the restore process to get all of the data.
☒ A, B, and D are incorrect. These issues do not accurately describe the problem.

18. ☑ C is correct. The Last Known Good configuration uses the last settings that worked.
☒ A, B, and D are incorrect. These options do not use the last settings that worked.

19. ☑ B is correct. VGA mode uses a basic VGA driver so that you can load Windows XP and change the faulty video driver
☒ A, C, and D are incorrect. These options are not best to use when a video driver problem has occurred.

20. ☑ A and D are correct. You should perform a backup and create a restore point—these actions will give you protection for data and the operating system should a failure occur.
☒ B and C are incorrect. These actions will not protect the system or user data.

21. ☑ B is correct. The correct command is D:\i386\winnt32.exe /cmdcons
☒ A, C, and D are incorrect. These commands are not accurate.

22. ☑ C is correct. The diskpart tool enables you to add or delete partitions.
☒ A, B, and D are incorrect. These tools do not allow you to add and delete partitions.

23. ☑ D is correct. The Listsvc command enables you to see a list of services and drivers.
☒ A, B, and C are incorrect. These tools do not show lists of services and drivers.

LAB ANSWER

To complete the requirements of the company, configure the backup in the following manner:

- Use a normal backup on Monday and a differential backup every other day of the week. The differential backup takes longer to run than an incremental backup, but in the event of a failure, you will only have one normal backup and one differential backup to run—not multiple incremental backups.
- When configuring the backup job, choose the "Verify data after backup" option. Ensure that volume shadow copy is not disabled.

A

About the CD

The CD-ROM included with this book comes complete with MasterExam, MasterSim, CertCam movie clips, the electronic version of the book, and Session #1 of LearnKey's online training. The software is easy to install on any Windows 98/NT/2000 computer and must be installed to access the MasterExam and MasterSim features. You may, however, browse the electronic book and CertCams directly from the CD without installation. To register for LearnKey's online training and a second bonus MasterExam, simply click the Online Training link on the Main Page and follow the directions to the free online registration.

System Requirements

Software requires Windows 98 or higher, Internet Explorer 5.0 or above, and 20MB of hard disk space for full installation. The electronic book requires Adobe Acrobat Reader. To access the Online Training from LearnKey, you must have RealPlayer Basic 8 or Real1 Plugin, which will be automatically installed when you launch the online training.

LearnKey Online Training

The LearnKey Online Training link will allow you to access online training from **Osborne.Onlineexpert.com**. The first session of this course is provided at no charge. Additional sessions for this course and other courses may be purchased directly from **www.LearnKey.com** or by calling (800) 865-0165.

The first time that you run the Training, you will required to register with the online product. Follow the instructions for a first-time user. Please make sure to use a valid e-mail address.

Prior to running the Online Training, you will need to add the Real plugin and the RealCBT plugin to your system. This will automatically be facilitated to your system when you run the training the first time.

Installing and Running MasterExam and MasterSim

If your computer CD-ROM drive is configured to auto-run, the CD-ROM will automatically start up upon inserting the disk. From the opening screen you may install MasterExam or MasterSim by pressing the *MasterExam* or *MasterSim* buttons.

This will begin the installation process and create a program group named LearnKey. To run MasterExam or MasterSim use Start | Programs | Learnkey. If the auto-run feature did not launch your CD, browse to the CD and click on the RunInstall icon.

MasterExam

MasterExam provides you with a simulation of the actual exam. The number of questions, the type of questions, and the time allowed are intended to be an accurate representation of the exam environment. You have the option to take an open book exam, including hints, references, and answers, a closed book exam, or the timed MasterExam simulation.

When you launch the MasterExam simulation, a digital clock will appear in the top center of your screen. The clock will continue to count down to zero unless you choose to end the exam before the time expires.

MasterSim

The MasterSim is a set of interactive labs that will provide you with a wide variety of tasks to allow the user to experience the software environment, even if the software is not installed. Once you have installed the MasterSim, you may access it quickly through this CD launch page or you may also access it through Start | Programs | Learnkey.

Electronic Book

The entire contents of the Study Guide are provided in PDF. Adobe's Acrobat Reader has been included on the CD.

CertCam

CertCam AVI clips provide detailed examples of key certification objectives. These clips walk you step-by-step through various system configurations. You can access the clips directly from the CertCam table of contents by clicking the CertCam button on the Main Page.

The CertCam AVI clips are recorded and produced using TechSmith's Camtasia Producer. Since AVI clips can be very large, ExamSim uses TechSmith's special AVI Codec to compress the clips. The file named tsccvid.dll is copied to your Windows\ System folder during the first auto run. If the AVI clip runs with audio but no video, you may need to re-install the file from the CD-ROM. Browse to the Programs\CertCams folder and run TSCC.

Help

A help file is provided through the Help button on the main page in the lower-left corner. Individual help features are also available through MasterExam, MasterSim, and LearnKey's Online Training.

Removing Installation(s)

MasterExam and MasterSim are installed to your hard drive. For *best* results for removal of programs, use the Start | Programs | Learnkey | Uninstall options to remove MasterExam or MasterSim.

If you desire to remove the Real Player, use the Add/Remove Programs icon from your Control Panel. You may also remove the LearnKey training program from this location.

Technical Support

For questions regarding the technical content of the electronic book, MasterExam, or CertCams, please visit **www.osborne.com** or e-mail **customer.service@mcgraw-hill.com**. For customers outside the 50 United States, e-mail: **international_cs@mcgraw-hill.com.**

LearnKey Technical Support

For technical problems with the software (installation, operation, removing installations), and for questions regarding LearnKey Online Training and MasterSim content, please visit **www.learnkey.com** or e-mail **techsupport@learnkey.com**.

B

About the Web Site

At Access.Globalknowledge, the premier online information source for IT professionals (**http://access.globalknowledge.com**), you'll enter a Global Knowledge information portal designed to inform, educate, and update visitors on issues regarding IT and IT education.

Get *What* You Want *When* You Want It

At the Access.Globalknowledge site, you can do the following:

- Choose personalized technology articles related to your interests. Access a news article, a review, or a tutorial, customized to what you want to see, regularly throughout the week.
- Continue your education, in between Global courses, by taking advantage of discussion groups with other users or instructors. Get the tips, tricks, and advice that you need today!
- Get instant course information at your fingertips. Course calendars show you the courses you want, and when and where you want them.
- Obtain the resources you need with online tools, trivia, skills assessment, and more!

All this and more is available now on the Web at **http://access.globalknowledge.com**. Visit today!

Glossary

Accessibility Options Windows XP supports a number of Accessibility options that provide a way for people with disabilities to more easily use Windows XP. Accessibility options are configured through the Accessibility Options icon in Control Panel or via the Accessibility wizard. Options include StickyKeys, ToggleKeys, and FilterKeys.

ACPI *See* Advanced Configuration and Power Interface.

Active Directory The Active Directory is the Windows 2000 network directory service. It's a tree-like, hierarchical structure that is used by administrators to store information about sites, domains, and organizational units, as well as about users, services, and resources. The Active Directory serves as a central repository for information about the network and provides a single location for resources on the network. The Active Directory is highly scalable and can hold millions of objects. It is a highly efficient system and resolves many of the complex domain problems that were found in Windows NT networks.

Activation Activation is the process that uses the unique product code and unique computer hardware information to create an "installation ID" that is submitted to Microsoft as a way to "activate" your software and prevent software piracy. Once activated, that copy of the operating system can only be installed on that one computer. Once Windows XP is installed, users can activate the product during the initial boot of Windows XP, or at a later time during the 30-day grace period. Activation can be performed automatically over the Internet or manually by calling Microsoft customer service.

Advanced Configuration and Power Interface (ACPI) ACPI is an industry standard for power management and is supported in Windows XP. ACPI works with plug and play to manage system hardware devices and services so that power can be reduced to those devices and services when they are not needed. The operating system retains control of ACPI and provides the power saving features we enjoy, such as hibernation and system standby. ACPI must be supported in the BIOS of the computer where it is to be used, and it is automatically set up if supported in the BIOS during the installation of Windows XP.

Advanced Power Management (APM) APM is an older power management scheme that allows applications to control the amount of power used with hardware. APM was particularly helpful on laptop computers where battery power conservation was very important.

Alert Performance Monitor in Windows XP enables you to configure performance alerts that trigger when certain components fall below a performance baseline established by the administrator. The alert can trigger a number of events, including sending a network message and writing the event to the application event log.

Answer File A file that answers the Windows XP Professional's setup routine prompts. The answer file enables you to perform an unattended installation (*see* Unattended Installation). Answer files can be created with Setup Manager, which has a helpful and easy to use wizard interface. The use of answer files in unattended installations is a common method for large rollouts of Windows XP in network environments.

APIPA *See* Automatic Private IP Addressing.

APM *See* Advanced Power Management.

Assigned Software Using Group Policy, you can assign software to users and computers so that it is installed automatically on the users' computers in a desired site, domain, or OU. When the assigned option is used, software installation is applied during bootup or user logon, depending on the configuration. Users have no control over software that is assigned.

Auditing In Windows XP, you can audit security events, as well as specific files and folders. This feature is particularly useful in a network environment where it enables you to see what resources users are accessing and how those resources are being utilized. You can use auditing to detect unsuccessful or successful access and view a security log where the data is generated.

Authorization In order for an RIS Server or DHCP Server to function on a Windows 2000 network, the server must be authorized in the Active Directory, a process that can be performed only by a member of the Enterprise Admins group. Authorization for both types of servers is performed via the DHCP console on a Windows 2000 Server. The purpose of authorization is to prevent a "rogue" DHCP or RIS server from participating on the network. This is a security feature of Windows 2000 that can help prevent both DCHP and RIS problems.

Automatic Private IP Addressing (APIPA) Windows XP Professional has the capability to auto-configure an IP address via the APIPA feature when a DHCP server is not available. Designed for home and small office networks, APIPA enables a workgroup to use TCP/IP without the configuration issues or overhead found in a large IP network. When APIPA is used, a client computer first looks for a DHCP server. If no server is found, the client then assigns itself an IP address in the reserved 169.254 range. This allows all clients to have a valid IP address on the same subnet, with no interaction or configuration from the user.

Backup Windows XP provides a backup utility. Using the backup utility, you can create a backup job that backs up the data you specify. In the event of a catastrophic failure, the backup job can be used to restore data on Windows XP. The Backup utility provides a wizard to help you create and use backup jobs, or you can configure them directly using the Backup console.

Basic Disks A basic disk in Windows XP Professional is a standard disk type that supports partitions and extended partitions. Basic disks do not have the management features of dynamic disks.

Basic Input/Output System (BIOS) A computer's BIOS is a set of instructions that are burned on the ROM of a PC. The BIOS handles hardware setup and management, as well as the Power On Self Test (POST).

BIOS *See* Basic Input/Output System.

Bottleneck In terms of performance, a bottleneck is any hardware device or service that cannot handle the load placed on it. The result is that the system slows down while different processes or network requests have to wait to have their turn. You can locate bottlenecks on a computer using the Performance program to monitor specific hardware devices and system processes.

CA *See* Certificate Authority (CA).

Certificate Authority (CA) A CA is a server that is capable of issuing storing and managing digital certificates. A certificate authority server's digital certificate can be purchased from a recognized CA root, such as Verisign, and used for authentication or encryption.

Challenge Handshake Authentication Protocol (CHAP) CHAP negotiates a secure form of encryption with a server using Message Digest 5 encryption. The challenge-response feature of the protocol allows a client to prove to the server that the password is known without actually transmitting the password over the network. Later revisions of CHAP include MS-CHAP and MS-CHAP v2.

Change Permission The Change Permission is a standard Windows XP permission that allows a user to change permissions on files and folders. However, the user holding the change permission does not have full control to the file or folder.

Cipher Cipher is a command line utility that you can use to encrypt, decrypt, and manage the encryption of files and folders; the utility can also be accessed through the Windows Explorer interface. Cipher, which has a number of switches used to perform encryption/decryption functions, can be helpful in circumstances in which you are managing a number of encrypted files and folders.

Client Installation Wizard The Client Installation Wizard can be used during RIS installations. When a connection to the RIS Server is made, the Client Installation Wizard is downloaded to the client computer. The user can then use the Client Installation wizard to make installation option selections, assuming they are allowed under the Group Policy.

Compressed (Zipped) Folders Windows XP Professional provides folder compression based on zip technology. You can compress folders on any drive and even save them on the network or the Internet or send them via e-mail. These compressed folders retain their compression regardless of their location.

Computer Account A computer account is a security principal object created in the Active Directory that identifies a specific computer on a network by a friendly name. The security principal object is identified by a unique SID. The computer name is the user friendly name that can be changed but is always tied to the SID. Computer accounts are used with Group Policy so that specific configurations can be applied to computers within a site, domain, or organizational unit.

Cookie A cookie is a text file that is used with Internet Explorer in order to exchange information with Web sites. You can manage cookie behavior on the Privacy tab of Internet Options. Cookies can be either persistent, meaning they remain as a file on the computer, or they can be temporary, meaning that they are used only during the browser session. The Privacy tab of Internet options enables you to control cookies.

Cooperative Multitasking This is when two or more applications share processor threads so that both applications can, seemingly, function at the same time.

Copy Backup When using the Backup utility, you have the option to create a copy backup. A copy backup makes copies of the files that you select. Unlike other backup options, it does not read, make, or clear markers, thus not interfering with other incremental or differential backup jobs. This type of backup is a great way to back up specific data without causing problems with other backup jobs and current backup schedules.

Counter Logs In Performance Monitor, you can configure counter logs that sample data at predetermined intervals. That data is then recorded to a log file so that you can view it at a later time. Counter logs are a helpful feature if you want to see the performance of some process in Windows XP over a period of time without having to physically view Performance Monitor as data is sampled.

Daily Backup The Daily Backup, which can be instituted using Windows 2000's Backup utility, backs up selected files and folders without using any markers. The files are simply backed up each day, whether they have changed are not. This type of backup does not affect other backup jobs.

Debugging Mode Windows XP provides several boot menu options that you can use in the event that you are having problems starting Windows XP normally. Debugging mode requires that your computer be connected to another computer with a serial cable. Debugging information is read from the problem computer and is recorded on the connected computer. You can then use the debugging information to troubleshoot the system.

Default Gateway A default gateway is an IP address that leads to a router that can then carry messages off a particular subnet. If a default gateway is used on a network, the default gateway entry can be added to the TCP/IP address properties of client computers. DHCP can handle default gateway assignments automatically so that client computers always know the correct default gateway address.

Defragmentation Defragmentation is the process of reorganizing files on a hard disk so that they are stored in a contiguous manner. Windows XP includes a Disk Defragmenter utility that can defragment hard disks.

Deny Permission This standard Windows XP permission denies access to a file or folder. Deny permissions override all other permissions. For example, if a user is a member of the Marketing group and has Full Control permission of a folder, but is also a member of the Production group that is denied access, then the user has no permissions to the folder.

DHCP *See* Dynamic Host Configuration Protocol.

Differential Backup A differential backup checks for the "difference" in files that have changed each day. Using a differential backup with a normal backup, you would need to use the normal backup tape and the last differential tape to create the restore. Differential backups speed up the restore time, but they take longer to create than an incremental backup.

Disk Defragmenter Disk Defragmenter is a Windows XP utility that can defragment hard disks so that files are stored in a contiguous format. *See also* Defragmentation.

DNS *See* Domain Name System.

Domain In a Windows 2000/.Net environment, a domain is logical grouping of computers and users for management purposes. Domains function as security and replication boundaries as well. Networks are often divided into domains so that users, computers, and resources in that domain can be controlled and secured. Different domains in the same environment can have different security and administrative needs, and the domain structure allows diversity and flexibility of administrative control and management in the same network.

Domain Name System (DNS) DNS is a network service that maps host names to IP addresses, such as **www.osborne.com** to a TCP/IP address. DNS is used on the Internet for all host naming and is now the standard for Windows 2000/.NET networks as well. DNS is highly scalable and provides a logical structure for network naming and name resolution.

Driver A driver is a piece of software that allows a hardware device to communicate with an operating systems such as Windows XP. Manufacturers produce drivers for their hardware products that make them compatible with Windows XP. However, Windows XP also contains an extensive database of drivers so that devices can be automatically installed and configured via plug and play.

Driver Signing Windows XP supports driver signing, which allows Windows XP to check the digital signature of a device to ensure that it is compatible with Windows XP. Driver signing is extremely helpful when downloading drivers from the Internet, because Windows XP can inspect them for a digital signature before you install them on your system.

Dynamic Disks Dynamic Disks are Windows 2000/XP hard disks that support a number of additional disk management features. Dynamic disks in Windows XP Professional support volume management, which does not limit you with four primary partitions per disks. Volumes can be managed and reformatted using the Disk Management console without rebooting the computer.

Dynamic Host Configuration Protocol (DHCP) DHCP is an industry standard that is used to dynamically assign IP addresses to network clients. DHCP, is a network service that runs on a Windows 2000 Server and dynamically leases client computers IP addresses. DHCP administrators determine the period of time and the scope of IP addresses that can be used for leasing. In order to enable Windows XP to use a DHCP server, simply click the "Obtain IP address automatically" radio button in TCP/IP properties.

EAP *See* Extensible Authentication Protocol.

Encryption Encryption is the process of scrambling data so that it cannot be read or decrypted with out the encryption key. The NT file system included in Windows XP supports the Encrypting File System, allowing data stored locally to be encrypted.

Encrypting File System (EFS) Encrypting File System enables you to encrypt files and folders seamlessly so that data remains private. Other users of the computer cannot open and read files that have been encrypted by another user, unless the encrypted item is configured for multi-user access. EFS is not compatible with compression under Windows XP.

Extended Partition In basic disks, extended partitions are a logical way to extend the four-partition limit of basic disk configuration. The extended partitions appear as separate drives to the user, although they are physically part of the same partition.

Extensible Authentication Protocol (EAP) EAP is an authentication protocol that is used with security devices, such as smart cards and digital certificates. EAP is a certificate-based authentication method.

FAT *See* File Allocation Table.

Fault Tolerance Fault tolerance is the ability of a computer system to tolerate disks faults or failures. In a fault tolerant system, multiple disks are used. If a single disk fails, the data can still be accessed from another disk or can be regenerated from the other disks. Windows 2000/.NET Server supports RAID 1 and 5, but no fault tolerant methods are supported under Windows XP.

File Allocation Table (FAT) FAT is an older file system that divides a disk into sectors for data management purposes. FAT16 and FAT32 are both supported in Windows XP, but FAT does not contain all of the file management features found in the NTFS file system, specifically encryption and file level permissions. However, FAT can be used with Windows XP in the case of dual-boot operating systems. FAT16 is the early version of FAT implemented for MS-DOS. FAT16 cannot support partitions larger than 4GB. FAT32 became the default file system for Windows 95OSR2 and was used on Windows 98 and Windows Me as well. It can support up to 2TB partitions, but for practical and performance purposes, its limit is about 32GB per partition.

FQDN *See* Fully Qualified Domain Name.

Fully Qualified Domain Name (FQDN) A FQDN is the complete DNS name of a domain or site. In other words, the domains making up the name can be completely resolved through DNS. For example, "east.trition.com" is a FQDN.

Graphical User Interface (GUI) GUI is an acronym for "graphical user interface," which is descriptive of the Windows XP/user interface. The desktop, Start Menu, folders, and so on are all considered part of the GUI.

Group Policy Group Policy is a Windows 2000/.Net implementation that enables administrators to finely control computers and users in a Windows network. However, Group Policy can also be implemented at the local computer level so that a local computer administrator can control and manage other users who access the local computer. Group Policy is always implemented at the Site, Domain, OU, and computer levels, with lower levels inheriting settings from higher levels. Because of this structure, the local Group Policy level is the weakest form of Group Policy.

GUI *See* Graphical User Interface.

Handheld Device Windows XP supports a number of handheld devices, otherwise called Personal Digital Assistants or Pocket computers. Examples of such handheld devices are Palm and BlackBerry and devices using Windows CE.

Hardware Compatibility List (HCL) The Hardware Compatibility List is a listing generated by Microsoft and regularly updated. The list contains hardware that is compatible with Windows XP as well as other versions of Windows. However, just because a device does not appear on the HCL does not mean that it is not compatible with Windows XP—it just may not have been tested as such. You should always check out the HCL before installing any new hardware to see if it's compatible. You can access the most up-to-date HCL at **www. Microsoft.com/hcl**.

Hardware Profile A Hardware Profile is a collection of hardware settings (enabled/disabled) that is used on a computer system. A default profile exists for each computer, but you can create additional hardware profiles that define how the computer is used. Hardware profiles are typically used on laptop computers. The laptop computer may have a docked and undocked hardware profile that defines what hardware is used when the computer is at a docking station and when the computer is mobile.

HCL *See* Hardware Compatibility List.

HTML *See* HyperText Markup Language.

HTTP *See* HyperText Transfer Protocol.

HyperText Markup Language (HTML) HTML is the default language used to create documents on the Internet. A Web page is made up of HTML data. Web browsers, such as Internet Explorer, interpret the HTML and display it graphically to the user.

HyperText Transfer Protocol (HTTP) HTTP is the Internet standard for transferring HTML documents from one place to another. Each time a document is downloaded from the Internet to a Web browser, HTTP is used.

ICF *See* Internet Connection Firewall.

ICS *See* Internet Connection Sharing.

IEEE 1394 IEEE 1394, otherwise called "Firewire," is a standard for a high-speed bus that can support up to 63 devices. Commonly used for high-speed multimedia transfers, IEEE 1394 is supported in Windows XP.

IIS *See* Internet Information Services (IIS).

Image In installation scenarios, an image is a copy of a disk that has an operating system and possibly applications installed. This image can then be transferred to another disk on another computer so that an exact replica is made. You can use Windows XP's Sysprep utility to prepare a computer for disk imaging, but the actual imaging process must be accomplished by third party software.

Incremental Backup An incremental backup backs up selected files, but first clears the markers on those files before backing them up. An incremental backup does not back up files that have not changed since the last backup. In order to restore data using incremental backup, you must use the last Normal backup and each incremental back that has been run since the last Normal backup. Incremental backups reduce daily backup time, but they take more time in the event that a restoration is required.

Internet Connection Firewall (ICF) Windows XP provides an Internet Connection Firewall that protects Internet connections from hackers and malicious attacks. ICF is designed for the home computer or the small office computer and can work in conjunction with ICS. ICF uses a table mechanism that keeps track of Internet documents that have been requested by IE. If any communication arrives that has not been requested, the information is dropped before entering the computer.

Internet Connection Sharing (ICS) ICS is a Windows XP Professional service that allows a computer to share an Internet connection with users on the local network. Designed for home and small office networks with no domain controllers or DHCP servers, the ICS host acts as a DHCP allocator for the network clients, and all clients can access the Internet through the ICS host.

Internet Information Services (IIS) Internet Information Services is the Web, FTP, SMTP, and NNTP implementation included with Windows XP that allows for Web site hosting and management. In Windows XP, IIS can act as a development platform and is a good way to publish files and folders on an intranet.

Internet Protocol Security (IPSec) IPSec is a security feature available in Windows XP that encrypts data before it travels between two points. Because that data is encrypted, IPSec guarantees that it is safe as it travels along any public or private IP network.

Interrupt Request (IRQ) An IRQ is signal sent to the computer's processor in order get the computer processor to perform some function. Different devices use different IRQ numbers so that conflicts do not occur, and in Windows XP, IRQ assignments to hardware are managed automatically by Windows XP plug and play.

IPSec *See* Internet Protocol Security (IPSec).

Last Known Good Configuration Last Known Good is an option on the Windows XP advanced boot menu that you can use when you are having problems starting Windows XP normally. The Last Known Good option reads data from the registry about the last known good boot. When you make a configuration change that leaves the system unbootable, you can use the Last Known Good option to boot the computer. Any changes made since the Last Known Good Configuration, however, are lost.

Layer 2 Tunneling Protocol (L2TP) L2TP is used to create VPN tunnels over a public network. Like PPTP, L2TP provides the functionality needed for VPN communication, but L2TP can also be used over ATM and X.25 networks. L2TP can also use IP Security for data encryption.

MMC *See* Microsoft Management Console (MMC).

Microsoft Management Console (MMC) The Microsoft Management Console is a standard, Explorer-based interface into which you can load various tools known as "snap-ins." The MMC is used extensively in Windows XP and houses such as preconfigured tools as Computer Management. You can also create your own custom MMCs and load various snap-ins that you want to use.

Mini-Setup Mini-Setup is a short setup routine that gathers user-specific information, such as the end user license agreement, username, company, and so forth. Mini-setup is most often used in semi-automated installations, such as RIS.

NetBEUI NetBEUI is a simple, lightweight network protocol that was frequently used in Windows networks. NetBEUI does not support routing, however, and has been widely replaced with TCP/IP, which is the default protocol in Windows 2000/ .NET networks.

Network A network is a collection of computers that are configured to communicate with each other through some means, such as through physical wired connections or even through wireless connections. The purpose of a network is to share resources and manage users and security. A network can contain as few as two computers in a simple home network or can contain thousands of computers and servers in global networks, such as the Internet.

Normal Backup A normal backup, which is also called a full backup, completely backs up all selected files and folders and is often used to back up an entire computer system. A normal backup takes the most time to back up, but it is the easiest backup to use when a restore operation is needed. Because of the amount of storage space required and the time required to run normal backups, many environments use a combination of normal and differential or incremental backups during a given week in order to strike a balance between backup time and restore time. *See also* Incremental Backup and Differential Backup.

NTFS NTFS is the file system of choice for Windows XP. First used in Windows NT and later revised in Windows 2000, NTFS supports advanced features, such as compression and encryption, and offers granular control over system and shared resources through file level permissions.

NTFS Compression Windows XP Professional provides native compression capabilities on NTFS drives. You can compress files, folders, and entire drives using

NTFS compression, but NTFS compression does not work with FAT drives. The purpose of compression is to reduce file and folder sizes so that more data can be stored on a physical disk. Compression is transparent to the user, who opens folders and accesses files as he or she normally would. Compression is not compatible with encryption in Windows XP.

NTFS Permissions Windows XP Professional provides NTFS permissions that can be assigned to users and groups so that you can finely control user access to resources. You can also configure advanced NTFS permissions to individually select special NTFS permissions.

Offline Files Offline Files is a feature that enables users to keep a local copy of a network file on their computer and then synchronize it with the network copy. Offline Files is great in collaborative situations, but it is not compatible with Windows XP's fast-user switching feature. The idea with Offline Files is that a user can make a network file available locally on his or her computer so that the file can be used when the user is offline. When the user is reconnected, his or her locally stored copy of the offline file can be synchronized with the network copy.

Organizational Units (OU) An OU is a container used in the Active Directory to further segment and organize a domain. OUs are often created to hold divisions of users or different kinds of resources, or they may be created on the basis of various other organizational models. An OU can be delegated so that a certain administrator(s) controls and manages it, and Group Policy can be applied to an OU as well. OUs are a highly effective way to manage very large Windows 2000/.NET domains, but they also serve useful functions in smaller domains.

OU *See* Organizational Units.

Paging Like previous versions of Windows, Windows XP supports paging. Paging enables Windows XP to write data that is normally held in RAM to a Paging file on the hard disk when RAM begins to run low. When the data written to the paging file is needed again, it is read back into RAM. The purpose of paging is to allow Windows XP to hold more data in RAM and on the paging file than could be physically held in RAM alone. However, the paging file should never be used as a replacement for physical RAM. You can manually configure the paging file, but Windows XP does a good job of handing the configuration automatically.

Paging File Windows XP uses a paging file, which is a portion of the computer's hard disk that holds data normally held in RAM. The page file is the same thing as "virtual memory." *See also* Paging.

Password Authentication Protocol (PAP) PAP uses plain text passwords, which can be captured in transit. PAP is a very low form of authentication security.

Peer-to-Peer Network A peer-to-peer network, also called a workgroup, contains a collection of computers networked together without any centralized management. Each computer user is responsible for managing resources and access to the network.

Performance Logging Windows XP Performance Monitor provides a logging feature that enables you to log any desired objects/counters into a number of different file formats. You can determine what you want to log and how often the Performance Monitor should sample the data. Then, you can examine the performance issues as they happen over a period of time.

Plug and Play Plug and Play is a standard that enables Windows XP to detect and manage hardware changes on the computer automatically. For example, if a new device is added to the system, Windows XP can automatically install the device and assign the necessary resources, such as IRQ settings, for the resource to function properly. Under most circumstances, no intervention from the user is required.

Point to Point Protocol (PPP) PPP is a serial communication protocol that is typically used to connect dial-up connections to the Internet. PPP is an Internet standard protocol used for information exchange.

Point to Point Tunneling Protocol (PPTP) PPTP is used in VPN connections in which a VPN tunnel is created over a public network, such as the Internet. PPTP supports encryption, but it can only be used on IP networks. *See also* Layer 2 Tunneling Protocol.

Port (Hardware) Generally, a port can be defined as an entry point for a piece of hardware for some kind of communication. For example, a mouse might be connected to a USB port, while TCP/IP communication uses logical ports.

Pre-Execution Environment (PXE) Boot ROM PXE-enabled network adapter cards can boot from the network by contacting a DHCP Server using the BootP protocol. Once a lease for an IP address has occurred, the boot process can continue, as in the case of contacting a RIS Server for installation files.

Print Device A print device refers to the physical device that actually prints words on paper.

Print Driver The print driver is software that enables Windows XP to communicate with the print device so that print commands can be communicated with the device.

Print Queue The print queue refers to a feature on Windows XP computers that allows you to manage documents that are waiting to be printed. With proper permissions, you can pause documents and delete specific or all documents in the queue.

Printer In Microsoft terms, a printer refers to the software that is used to communicate with and manage the print device. You can have multiple printers with different configuration options for a single print device, enabling you to control how the printer is used by different groups on the network.

Protocol A protocol is a standard for behavior. In computing terms, a protocol refers to networking standards that must be adhered to for two computers to communicate with each other. Computers must the use same protocol(s) for communication to work. TCP/IP is the most popular protocol today.

PPP *See* Point to Point Protocol.

Publication Software Using Group Policy, you can publish software to users in a site, domain, or OU via the Group Policy object. Published software is configured under User Configuration, and users can install the software on their computers or not. *See also* Assigned software.

PXE *See* Pre-Execution Environment Boot ROM.

Quota In Windows XP, you configure and assign disk quotas to users. A quota determines how much space a user can access on the computer's hard drive for storage. Once the user reaches the storage limit, you can have warnings automatically sent, or the user can be stopped from storing data until items are deleted. This feature is particularly helpful in managing user disk consumption when Windows XP is used as a file server on a network.

RAID-5 Volume A RAID-5 volume is a fault tolerant solution that combines three or more unallocated areas of disk space on three or more hard drives. A parity bit is used during the write process so that if a single disk fails, the data can be regenerated from the remaining disks using the parity bit. RAID-5 volumes are supported on Windows 2000/.NET Servers, but they are not supported under Windows XP.

Remote Access Remote access refers to the ability to access a network and the network's resources remotely. Windows XP provides the necessary software and protocols so that you can connect to a Remote Access Server on a Windows 2000/.NET network.

Remote Assistance Remote Assistance is a Windows XP Professional feature that enables one XP computer to communicate with another over the Internet. With the user's permission, you can see the user's computer and even configure it remotely. Remote Assistance works via an invitation using Windows Messenger or a MAPI e-mail application and a password.

Remote Desktop Remote Desktop enables a Windows XP computer and another computer with the Remote Desktop client software installed (Windows 9*x*, Me, 2000, and NT) to connect with each other for a remote desktop session. Remote Desktop functions via terminal services and user accounts.

Remote Installation Services (RIS) This is a deployment method for installing Windows XP Professional. Using a Windows 2000 Server, DHCP Server, and the Active Directory, RIS clients can boot from the network and begin automatic installations of Windows XP Professional. RIS clients must support the PXE ROM or their network adapter cards must be on the list of supported network adapters to use an RIS boot disk.

RIPrep.exe (Remote Installation Preparation) This program creates an image from an existing Windows XP Professional installation for an RIS installation. All settings and applications are included in the RIPrep image.

RISetup.exe (Remote Installation Setup) This program sets up the RIS Server once the service has been installed on the Windows 2000 Server from Add/Remove Windows components.

RIS *See* Remote Installation Services.

Roaming User Profile A roaming user profile enables a user to log on to various workstations and still receive the same settings and documents. The profile is stored centrally on a network server and copied to the local computer when the user logs on. *See also* User Profile.

Safe Mode Safe Mode refers collectively to a number of Windows XP startup features that enable you to troubleshoot and repair Windows XP. Safe Mode can be accessed by holding down the F8 key at bootup. Safe Mode includes a number of boot options, such as Safe Mode With Networking, Last Known Good Configuration, Debugging Mode, and several others.

Safe Mode With Command Prompt Safe Mode With Command Prompt is a Safe Mode boot option that starts Windows XP with very few files executed. The GUI interface does not load; only the Command Prompt appears. From the Command Prompt, you can then run utilities and tools as needed.

Safe Mode With Networking Safe Mode With Networking provides a Safe Mode boot, but also loads networking components. This feature is helpful if you need to boot into Safe Mode but still access the network. Under the standard Safe Mode option, networking components are not loaded.

Scripted Installation A scripted installation typically refers to an unattended installation method in which a script is followed. The script answers the prompts that are provided to the user during installation so that no user interaction is necessary. Installation scripts can be easily created with Setup Manager.

Security Group Security groups are used to assign permissions to groups of users. Once security groups are established, they can be granted appropriate permissions to network resources. With the process, you manage user access to resources through groups rather than on an individual basis.

Setup Manager Setup Manager is a Windows XP Professional deployment tool that provides a wizard interface for creating answer files for Unattended installations, Remote Installation Services installs, and System Preparation installs.

Share An item that is shared and available for network access. Commonly shared items are folders, drives, and even Internet connections.

Share Level Security Share level security is available for folders stored on NTFS or FAT drives. Share level security provides you with permission options of Full Control, Change, and Read, as well as Deny.

Shiva Password Authentication (SPAP) SPAP is used in conjunction with a Shiva server and provides a moderate level of authentication security.

Simple Volume A simple volume can be created on a dynamic disk from unallocated space. Simple volumes can be any size and can be formatted with FAT32 or NTFS. A simple volume can only reside on a single hard disk and can be assigned a drive letter or mounted to an empty NTFS folder if desired.

Single Instance Store Remote Installation Service uses a Single Instance–Store feature that prevents the duplication of redundant files. For example, let's say that you have two different RIS images that are used in installations. Instead of redundantly copying hundreds of the same files, RIS stores only files that are different on the second image. This feature conserves storage space when multiple RIS images are used.

Spanned Volume Spanned volumes use two or more unallocated areas of free space on two or more dynamic disks. The unallocated areas are logically combined to create one volume, which is an excellent storage solution, especially when you have several smaller areas of free space on different disks. A spanned volume does not provide any fault tolerance, but enables you actively to use any additional portions of unused disk space for storage purposes. From the user's perspective, the spanned volume functions like any other volume.

Striped Volume A striped volume uses two or more unallocated areas of free space on two or more dynamic disks (up to 32). The areas must be same size. Once created, the volume stripes data across the disks, creating a storage solution with excellent read and write performance. Striped volumes do not provide fault tolerance.

Subnet A subnet is a division of an IP network, designed to segment the network into more manageable pieces and to control traffic. A TCP/IP address always includes a subnet mask.

System Preparation A Windows XP Professional deployment tool (sysprep.exe) that is used to image a Windows XP Professional computer. The image created has no SID, but one is assigned to the new computer once the installation is burned to the hard drive. A third party disk imaging utility is required to deploy System Preparation images.

Sysprep.exe *See* System Preparation.

TCP/IP *See* Transmission Control Protocol/Internet Protocol.

Transmission Control Protocol/Internet Protocol (TCP/IP) TCP/IP is the de facto standard for communication between computers on the Internet and is now the used for most network environments. TCP/IP is a protocol suite that is made up of over 100 different protocols, all providing different kinds of service.

Unattended Installation Unattended installations, using Winnt32.exe, are run with an answer file that answers Setup's prompts. The answer file allows the installation to be completely hands-off, enabling administrators to install hundreds of computers with Windows XP Professional quickly and easily. *See also* Scripted Installation.

Uninterruptible Power Supply (UPS) A UPS is a device that can be attached to Windows XP in order to supply battery power in the case of an unexpected power failure. The UPS device typically provides enough battery power to disconnect network sessions, close applications, and power down the computer safely. Often used on server systems, the UPS option is also supported on Windows XP.

Universal Serial Bus (USB) The Universal Serial Bus is a low-speed hardware interface that enables multiple USB devices to be connected to the same USB root hub. You can connect up to 127 USB devices to a single USB root hub.

UPS *See* Uninterruptible Power Supply.

USB *See* Universal Serial Bus.

User Profile User Profiles enable several different users to access the same computer while keeping their individual settings and documents when logged on. By default, user profiles are stored in \Documents and Settings*username* in Windows XP Professional when a clean install is performed.

Virtual Private Network (VPN) A Virtual Private Network is a secured link established between two computers over a public network, such as the Internet, or even over an Intranet. The VPN connection uses the PPTP or L2TP protocol in order to establish the link. Data transmitted over the link is encapsulated in a PPP packet so that it appears as normal traffic on the public network.

VPN See Virtual Private Network.

Windows Installer Package A Windows Installer Package is a package file (*.msi) that contains all of the necessary files and executables to install some software. Simply double-clicking on the package begins the installation. Windows Installer Packages can be deployed via Group Policy, as well at the site, domain, or OU level.

Windows Internet Name Service (WINS) WINS provides NetBIOS name-to-IP address resolution in Windows 9*x*, Me, and NT clients. Although WINS is still supported in Windows 2000 and XP operating systems, it is provided for backward compatibility, since DNS is the name resolution method used in Windows 2000/.NET networks.

Workgroup A workgroup is a collection of networked computers that are not centrally managed. *See also* Peer-to-Peer Network.

Winnt32.exe Winnt32.exe enables you to install Windows XP Professional using a variety of setup options including the use of unattended installations with an answer file. You can learn more about Winnt32.exe switch options in Chapter 2.

INDEX

A

E

F

G

O

P

Q

R

INTERNATIONAL CONTACT INFORMATION

AUSTRALIA
McGraw-Hill Book Company
Australia Pty. Ltd.
TEL +61-2-9900-1800
FAX +61-2-9878-8881
http://www.mcgraw-hill.com.au
books-it_sydney@mcgraw-hill.com

CANADA
McGraw-Hill Ryerson Ltd.
TEL +905-430-5000
FAX +905-430-5020
http://www.mcgraw-hill.ca

GREECE, MIDDLE EAST, & AFRICA (Excluding South Africa)
McGraw-Hill Hellas
TEL +30-210-6560-990
TEL +30-210-6560-993
TEL +30-210-6560-994
FAX +30-210-6545-525

MEXICO (Also serving Latin America)
McGraw-Hill Interamericana Editores
S.A. de C.V.
TEL +525-1500-5108
FAX +525-117-1589
http://www.mcgraw-hill.com.mx
carlos_ruiz@mcgraw-hill.com

SINGAPORE (Serving Asia)
McGraw-Hill Book Company
TEL +65-6863-1580
FAX +65-6862-3354
http://www.mcgraw-hill.com.sg
mghasia@mcgraw-hill.com

SOUTH AFRICA
McGraw-Hill South Africa
TEL +27-11-622-7512
FAX +27-11-622-9045
robyn_swanepoel@mcgraw-hill.com

SPAIN
McGraw-Hill/
Interamericana de España, S.A.U.
TEL +34-91-180-3000
FAX +34-91-372-8513
http://www.mcgraw-hill.es
professional@mcgraw-hill.es

UNITED KINGDOM, NORTHERN, EASTERN, & CENTRAL EUROPE
McGraw-Hill Education Europe
TEL +44-1-628-502500
FAX +44-1-628-770224
http://www.mcgraw-hill.co.uk
emea_queries@mcgraw-hill.com

ALL OTHER INQUIRIES Contact:
McGraw-Hill/Osborne
TEL +1-510-420-7700
FAX +1-510-420-7703
http://www.osborne.com
omg_international@mcgraw-hill.com

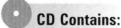

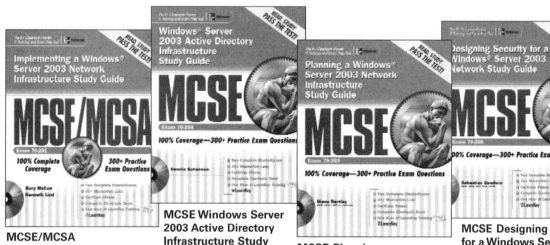

LICENSE AGREEMENT

THIS PRODUCT (THE "PRODUCT") CONTAINS PROPRIETARY SOFTWARE, DATA AND INFORMATION (INCLUDING DOCUMENTATION) OWNED BY THE McGRAW-HILL COMPANIES, INC. ("McGRAW-HILL") AND ITS LICENSORS. YOUR RIGHT TO USE THE PRODUCT IS GOVERNED BY THE TERMS AND CONDITIONS OF THIS AGREEMENT.

LICENSE: Throughout this License Agreement, "you" shall mean either the individual or the entity whose agent opens this package. You are granted a non-exclusive and non-transferable license to use the Product subject to the following terms:

(i) If you have licensed a single user version of the Product, the Product may only be used on a single computer (i.e., a single CPU). If you licensed and paid the fee applicable to a local area network or wide area network version of the Product, you are subject to the terms of the following subparagraph (ii).

(ii) If you have licensed a local area network version, you may use the Product on unlimited workstations located in one single building selected by you that is served by such local area network. If you have licensed a wide area network version, you may use the Product on unlimited workstations located in multiple buildings on the same site selected by you that is served by such wide area network; provided, however, that any building will not be considered located in the same site if it is more than five (5) miles away from any building included in such site. In addition, you may only use a local area or wide area network version of the Product on one single server. If you wish to use the Product on more than one server, you must obtain written authorization from McGraw-Hill and pay additional fees.

(iii) You may make one copy of the Product for back-up purposes only and you must maintain an accurate record as to the location of the back-up at all times.

COPYRIGHT; RESTRICTIONS ON USE AND TRANSFER: All rights (including copyright) in and to the Product are owned by McGraw-Hill and its licensors. You are the owner of the enclosed disc on which the Product is recorded. You may not use, copy, decompile, disassemble, reverse engineer, modify, reproduce, create derivative works, transmit, distribute, sublicense, store in a database or retrieval system of any kind, rent or transfer the Product, or any portion thereof, in any form or by any means (including electronically or otherwise) except as expressly provided for in this License Agreement. You must reproduce the copyright notices, trademark notices, legends and logos of McGraw-Hill and its licensors that appear on the Product on the back-up copy of the Product which you are permitted to make hereunder. All rights in the Product not expressly granted herein are reserved by McGraw-Hill and its licensors.

TERM: This License Agreement is effective until terminated. It will terminate if you fail to comply with any term or condition of this License Agreement. Upon termination, you are obligated to return to McGraw-Hill the Product together with all copies thereof and to purge all copies of the Product included in any and all servers and computer facilities.

DISCLAIMER OF WARRANTY: THE PRODUCT AND THE BACK-UP COPY ARE LICENSED "AS IS." McGRAW-HILL, ITS LICENSORS AND THE AUTHORS MAKE NO WARRANTIES, EXPRESS OR IMPLIED, AS TO THE RESULTS TO BE OBTAINED BY ANY PERSON OR ENTITY FROM USE OF THE PRODUCT, ANY INFORMATION OR DATA INCLUDED THEREIN AND/OR ANY TECHNICAL SUPPORT SERVICES PROVIDED HEREUNDER, IF ANY ("TECHNICAL SUPPORT SERVICES"). McGRAW-HILL, ITS LICENSORS AND THE AUTHORS MAKE NO EXPRESS OR IMPLIED WARRANTIES OF MERCHANTABILITY OR FITNESS FOR A PARTICULAR PURPOSE OR USE WITH RESPECT TO THE PRODUCT. McGRAW-HILL, ITS LICENSORS, AND THE AUTHORS MAKE NO GUARANTEE THAT YOU WILL PASS ANY CERTIFICATION EXAM WHATSOEVER BY USING THIS PRODUCT. NEITHER McGRAW-HILL, ANY OF ITS LICENSORS NOR THE AUTHORS WARRANT THAT THE FUNCTIONS CONTAINED IN THE PRODUCT WILL MEET YOUR REQUIREMENTS OR THAT THE OPERATION OF THE PRODUCT WILL BE UNINTERRUPTED OR ERROR FREE. YOU ASSUME THE ENTIRE RISK WITH RESPECT TO THE QUALITY AND PERFORMANCE OF THE PRODUCT.

LIMITED WARRANTY FOR DISC: To the original licensee only, McGraw-Hill warrants that the enclosed disc on which the Product is recorded is free from defects in materials and workmanship under normal use and service for a period of ninety (90) days from the date of purchase. In the event of a defect in the disc covered by the foregoing warranty, McGraw-Hill will replace the disc.

LIMITATION OF LIABILITY: NEITHER McGRAW-HILL, ITS LICENSORS NOR THE AUTHORS SHALL BE LIABLE FOR ANY INDIRECT, SPECIAL OR CONSEQUENTIAL DAMAGES, SUCH AS BUT NOT LIMITED TO, LOSS OF ANTICIPATED PROFITS OR BENEFITS, RESULTING FROM THE USE OR INABILITY TO USE THE PRODUCT EVEN IF ANY OF THEM HAS BEEN ADVISED OF THE POSSIBILITY OF SUCH DAMAGES. THIS LIMITATION OF LIABILITY SHALL APPLY TO ANY CLAIM OR CAUSE WHATSOEVER WHETHER SUCH CLAIM OR CAUSE ARISES IN CONTRACT, TORT, OR OTHERWISE. Some states do not allow the exclusion or limitation of indirect, special or consequential damages, so the above limitation may not apply to you.

U.S. GOVERNMENT RESTRICTED RIGHTS: Any software included in the Product is provided with restricted rights subject to subparagraphs (c), (1) and (2) of the Commercial Computer Software-Restricted Rights clause at 48 C.F.R. 52.227-19. The terms of this Agreement applicable to the use of the data in the Product are those under which the data are generally made available to the general public by McGraw-Hill. Except as provided herein, no reproduction, use, or disclosure rights are granted with respect to the data included in the Product and no right to modify or create derivative works from any such data is hereby granted.

GENERAL: This License Agreement constitutes the entire agreement between the parties relating to the Product. The terms of any Purchase Order shall have no effect on the terms of this License Agreement. Failure of McGraw-Hill to insist at any time on strict compliance with this License Agreement shall not constitute a waiver of any rights under this License Agreement. This License Agreement shall be construed and governed in accordance with the laws of the State of New York. If any provision of this License Agreement is held to be contrary to law, that provision will be enforced to the maximum extent permissible and the remaining provisions will remain in full force and effect.